FOUR PHILOSOPHIES

Harper & Row, Publishers
New York, Evanston, and London

Third edition

FOUR PHILOSOPHIES
AND THEIR PRACTICE
IN EDUCATION
AND RELIGION

J. Donald Butler

To

L. M. B.   *   J. B. B.   *   P. C. B.   *   M. H. B.

Contents

Part Three: Idealism

Part Four: Realism

Part Five: Pragmatism

Part Six: Existentialism and Language Analysis

Part Seven: Conclusion

Preface

To the extent that communication and understanding are persistent problems, this book should render a service. For its major task is the study of several significant ways of understanding, and its approach to this task takes into full account three different areas of human experience which are too commonly set apart from each other.

Four of the ways of understanding are the four philosophies, which are more systematic than not; they are naturalism, idealism, realism, and pragmatism. Two philosophies, not lending themselves to system, are also considered as sharpening human insight and understanding. The case for the ability of these philosophies to represent on a rather wide scale the rivalries of thought is incidental to the task to which this book is dedicated, and will not be argued at this point. The assumption is, however, that the study of these philosophies with some degree of adequacy will open the way to many of the insights needed for dealing responsibly with the burden of our times.

Our problems would be simpler if points of view, strictly speaking, provided the only basis of division by which we are shut up in groups between which there is little communication. But, unfortunately, this is not the case. Areas of specialization and fields of endeavor are commonly regarded as having their characteristic mentalities. Whether this is actually the case, or is a part of our misunderstanding one of another, would be difficult to determine. But at any rate, those of us who are not scientists regard science in general, and particular sciences as well, as having characteristic philosophies. Those of us who are not educators regard education as having its distinctive philosophy. Those of us who are not exponents of religious faith regard religion as having its own unique philosophy. And to compound misunderstanding all the more, those of us who are not philosophers regard philosophy as having its characteristic philosophy!

In this book philosophies are considered as being systems, or at least clusters, of interrelated assumptions, consciously or unconsciously embraced, which are so basic and general as to be capable of practice in every area of experience and endeavor. Each of the first four philosophies is explained first of all, somewhat purely, as a general and all-inclusive point of view. This is done by sketching its history and outlining its systematic structure. This is then followed in each case by a description of the characteristic practices of the four philosophies, respectively, in the fields of education and religion. The resultant picture of education and religion is not a portrayal of a distinct philosophy for each, but rather both are seen as phases of life in which all four philosophies are practiced. The presentations of existentialism and language analysis are much shorter and not at all systematic. But the impact of each, when and if practiced in education, is explored for each of these philosophies. The resultant picture of philosophy is not a representation of all philosophy as though it were a particular philosophy. Instead, different ways of thinking are seen as being analogous to the melodies which may be played on a single instrument and not as analogous to the instrument itself, which approximates the structure of thought.

It is hoped that this method will make the book a kind of medium of communication itself. In quarters where philosophy is already respected, it is hoped that respect may be borrowed for education and religion, if that is lacking. In circles in which education is respected, it is hoped that understanding may be borrowed for philosophy and religion, if that is lacking. And in groups where religion is exalted, it is hoped that respect may be borrowed for philosophy and education, wherein it is lacking. These may truly be the unwarranted high hopes born of excessive ambition; but they are achievements toward which some of us must work if communication and understanding are to grow and barriers are to decrease at the same time that a shrinking world brings us closer together in less significant ways.

Corresponding to these intentions, a book such as this may fulfill three different functions in the classroom; it may become an aid in the study of philosophy, education, or religion. It has been projected primarily as a text and reference for courses in the philosophy of education. But by varying the selection of chapters to be studied or to receive special emphasis, it can also be made to serve a similar purpose in general courses in philosophy and courses in the philosophy of religion.

Of course, every book becomes dated and is eventually marked by time. Possibly this happens more slowly to books in philosophy than to some others. However, in my use of *Four Philosophies* with students since it first appeared in 1951, and also its revision in 1957, I have accumulated a number of impressions indicating changes and additions which should be made in this book. When the publisher decided that the 1957 revision should be made, thorough restudy of the text and advice of colleagues in the field led me to make the changes appearing in that revision. There was clarification of the comparative approach discussed in the Introduction indicating the limitations of this method. The format of the book remains the same in that edition as well as this one. It is hoped, however, that this will not be interpreted as a rigid structure for philosophizing. A new section was added to each of the four chapters on education, "Education as a Social Institution." This was to correct any impression that the book underscores individualism. Of course, differing philosophies may favor a characteristic social system and will vary by degree, in comparison to other philosophies, in its estimate of the importance of the social over the individual. The chapter "Realism in Education" was almost completely rewritten because of a new source by a realist in Harry S. Broudy's book, *Building a Philosophy of Education* (New York: Prentice-Hall, Inc., 1954). The chapter "Pragmatism in Education" was considerably enlarged, making it more explicit. And the concluding section of the book was materially enlarged by including a chapter on building a philosophy of education, dealing with the form in which it may well be cast. The major change in the final chapter, stating in outline my own philosophy and philosophy of education, was the enlargement on value theory in education.

This present edition is more thorough and includes more distinct changes than the 1957 revision. The Introduction and the Glossary following it include minor changes made necessary by later major changes. Chapter XI, "Strengths and Weaknesses in the Philosophy of Idealism," is almost completely new. This reflects rather marked changes in my own estimate of this philosophy in itself and in its promise for coping with our times. A new section, "Part Six," inserted before the conclusion, is comprised of one chapter each on existentialism and language analysis in relation to education. Existentialism is an unsystematic philosophy which has had great impact on our century in its various strains. Although they have not been made explicit, implicit in existentialism are radical and powerful meanings, which can be inferred and applied to education. Philosophers of education have recently paid more attention to language analysis than earlier philosophies. They have made various attempts to see what its directions may be in education when applied there. As a consequence of the present ascendancy of these two philosophies, presentations of them are included in this book in addition to the older four philosophies which can be treated systematically.

A final and radical revision is that this edition closes with Chapter XXV, "Building a Philosophy of Education." When I addressed myself to the task of revising the outline of my own philosophy and philosophy of education (which would have been Chapter XXVI), I found that my thinking had changed so much that the task would be virtually one of writing a book instead of revising a chapter. The direction of some of these changes is indicated in my criticism of idealism in Chapter XI, my article "Idealism in Education Today" (*School and Society*, Vol. LXXXVII, No. 2145, January 17, 1959, pp. 8–10; reprinted as chapter 48 in *Readings in the Foundations of Education*, Commitment to Teaching, Vol. II, edited by J. C. Stone and Frederick W. Schneider, New York: Thomas Y. Crowell Company, 1965, pp. 328–331; and also as chapter 31 in *Introductory Readings in the Foundations of Education*, edited by Jim Johnson, Harold R. Collins, Victor L. Dupuis, and John H. Johansen, Dubuque, Iowa: William C. Brown Book Company), and in my paper "Preface to a Logic" (*Educational Theory*, Vol. XIV, No. 4, October 1964, pp. 229–254).

Needless to say, more expressions of appreciation relating to this book are due than a preface can include and for most of which a preface is not a sufficiently intimate medium. Consequently, those included here represent only a part of my indebtedness.

I wish to record here my debt to the members of my family for their encouragement and their assumption of additional responsibilities whenever I have been unable to spread my resources far enough to include writing, teaching, administration, and my share of home duties. My profound debt to the late Herman Harrell Horne (1873–1946) is a similar one because of its intimacy. Horne's inspiration and counsel throughout sixteen years of friendship, first when I was a student and later as a beginning teacher, have been benefits which no memorial can repay. He read much of this book while the first edition was in process and made helpful suggestions regarding its improvement. Having been in his time one of America's great idealists, pangs of regret trouble me every time I criticize his thought. But even so, Professor Horne expected penetrating thought and independence from his students, not conformity. So possibly I can be consoled that my criticisms of him and the philosophy of idealism do not break faith with him.

Colleagues and friends in a number of colleges and universities, as well as in my own home institution, mean much to me for their criticism and advice, but even more for their friendship. I still need to record, as I first did in 1951, my appreciation to those who read the manuscript of the first edition, to the end of criticism and advice. They are R. Bruce Raup, W. O. Stanley, E. J. Kircher, and Radoslav A. Tsanoff. Also in this connection, my thanks go to the teachers and their students who have considered the previous editions of this book good enough to be a text or reference for their courses. This, I am sure, is a major basis for the decision of Harper & Row to assign me another "go at it."

Mrs. Gordon Sprain, my diligent secretary and "man Friday," has done all the manuscript work involved in this edition. Her dissatisfaction with anything but the best and her ability to perform it well makes the sense of appreciation all the greater. As I have written before, the endowment of my post at Macalester College by Mr. DeWitt Wallace makes possible my literary efforts to a major extent. Therefore, appreciation is again expressed both to him and the College for this generosity.

This preface cannot end without again acknowledging my gratitude to the University of Pennsylvania Press for permitting me to reprint, as in the second edition, "Building a Philosophy of Education," Chapter XXV. It becomes all the more important now because it stands alone as the conclusion of the book. The chapter was first written as one of the Brumbaugh Lectures at the University of Pennsylvania in 1956.

J. DONALD BUTLER

March, 1967
St. Paul, Minnesota

PART ONE

INTRODUCTION

The Approaches to Philosophy

On first approaching the study of philosophy each student is confronted by the necessity of getting his bearings. For one thing he is in a strange land. At first it seems that philosophy does not have much in common with previous activities. There is a new vocabulary which must be learned before he can understand the philosophers and before he can converse with those who deal with the problems of philosophy.

Nevertheless, there are points of contact at which the relation of philosophy to other phases of experience can be seen. These may be used as approaches by which to effect an orientation to the field. It seems well at the very beginning of this book to aid in this orientation by discussing the following of these approaches briefly: (1) a comparison of philosophy with science, art, religion, and education; (2) an analysis of philosophy which designates its major problems and corresponding fields of inquiry; (3) a reference to the history of philosophy as a stepping stone to an understanding of the spirit and purpose of philosophy; and (4) an overview of different philosophies which are probably the chief types represented in contemporary thought.[1] Inasmuch as there is such manifold variety among philosophies, the explanations offered in this general introduction will not be accurate in every detail. But these inaccuracies will be corrected in the more detailed discussions comprising the body of the book.

A. PHILOSOPHY CONTRASTED WITH OTHER FIELDS

Because many of us are less familiar with philosophy and more familiar with some other fields of human endeavor, contrasting it with these fields presents one method of getting some beginning ideas of the nature of philosophy. More familiar to most people, at least superficially, are science, art, religion and education. If we consider each of these as it is similar to and different from philosophy, certain broad outlines may be suggested which indicate the nature of philosophy.

1. PHILOSOPHY AND SCIENCE

There is one important aspect in which philosophy and science are alike. This is that they are both interested in knowledge. Both of them are fields of inquiry and investigation. Both ask questions and seek to determine answers to these questions. Knowledge is an end toward which both strive.

An important difference between the two lies in the kind of knowledge which they seek. Science seeks knowledge of facts. Apart from the notable

---

[1] Four philosophies are presented systematically in this book. In addition, in Chapters XXIII and XXIV respectively, existentialism and language analysis are discussed. These two philosophies do not lend themselves to systematic treatment.

exceptions of pragmatism, some existentialism and language analysis, philosophy seeks ultimate knowledge; for some philosophies this ultimate knowledge is more fundamental than the facts of science, for others it is constituted by the facts of science. Certainly if it is to keep pace with the times and have any meaning for the contemporary mind, philosophy must take full cognizance of the findings of science.

Facts, it might be said, mark the border line between science and philosophy. Science seeks to determine facts; facts are its end products. By its constantly improving instruments and methods of investigation it seeks to aid mankind by providing it effective knowledge of the facts of life. But philosophy begins its work with these facts. It makes use of them, although leaving particular attempts at their discovery to the various sciences. When therefore a philosopher enters the field of factual investigation, he ceases to be a philosopher and becomes a scientist during his preoccupation with pure facts. It is the significance of facts which interests him as a genuine philosopher. He believes that he can aid mankind by helping to determine the significance of facts, just as scientists serve men generally by discovering facts for them. The field of the philosopher, generally speaking, is a distinct field. Consequently, when the scientist, in addition to establishing facts, proceeds to tell people their meaning for life, he then ceases to be a scientist and is a philosopher as long as he sojourns in the realm of interpretations.

This difference between the two fields can be marked all the more clearly by distinguishing the respective methods of science and philosophy. The methods of science are observation, experimentation, description, and explanation of the immediate relations of facts. The method of philosophy involves interpretation and explanation of the ultimate relations and meanings of facts.

By observation, whether with the bare senses or with highly accurate instruments, the scientist seeks to find the facts as they are. In experimentation he introduces into the observed situation some active element over which he has control, in the attempt to bring out facts which simple observation would not yield. Description is the instrument by which he attempts to record these facts, simply and accurately presenting the details without yielding to personal interests of any sort. His explanations are anchored very tightly to the immediate facts at hand. He may infer causes, but these causes will properly refer only to more immediate relations alone, such as "when A and B are brought together in a certain manner, C is the result which follows."

The philosopher's method, on the other hand, is more inclusive. He takes given facts and, pointing to their relations to the totality of our experience, suggests their meaning for life. He infers from the facts of human experience, the nature of the universe, the meanings and purposes of living. Whereas the method of the scientist is descriptive and observational, his method is interpretative.

One further way in which this difference can be accentuated is by contrasting the differing perspectives of science and philosophy. The outlook of the scientist is necessarily partial and detailed. Science limits its attention to particular situations. It is necessary for it to be fractional in its outlook because its attention is focused, and its concern is to analyze, that the most minute details may be recognized. The outlook of the philosopher is just the opposite. He seeks to be total and comprehensive. He deals with ultimate, final, and all-inclusive meanings. With him, parts are considered eventually in the light of their relation to the ultimate whole, at least to the largest whole which can be conceived.

2. PHILOSOPHY AND ART

As science and philosophy have common ground in seeking truth, so art and philosophy share a common interest in interpreting experience. Neither of them has the primary interest which science has in discovering facts. The chief concern of both is to interpret, appreciate, and enjoy the meaning aspects of facts.

But there are differences in the nature and scope of the interpretation which each attempts. From the standpoint of scope, the interest of the artist is somewhat more limited than that of the philosopher. When the artist interprets, it is the aesthetic qualities of experience with which he deals. He attends to the feeling tones which he finds in his experience. He seeks to catch these and express them so that others may feel what he feels. He is not primarily concerned with the moral aspects of experience. Questions of truth are also secondary. Most important to him are the aesthetic values, and other considerations are shoved to the side for them. The philosopher, on the other hand, is concerned to interpret other phases of experience. While philosophy is concerned with aesthetic experience, it is also concerned with other values, with reality, with knowledge, and with the kind of action which results in the fullest life. Consequently the philosopher extends his interpretative activity into many phases of experience, in addition to the aesthetic.

When we consider the difference in the nature of the interpretation attempted by art and philosophy, we see that the distinction between the two is far more than one of scope, philosophy being broader and more inclusive than art. But as to scope alone, there is no suggestion here that philosophy is superior to art just because it is more inclusive. Were that intimated by philosophers, there would be as much ground for artists to hold that their first love is superior to philosophy because in its narrower field of interpretation it sometimes runs more deeply.

The artist's treatment of beauty is actual, the philosopher's theoretical.

The artist enjoys and appreciates, expresses and creates. The philosopher intellectualizes aesthetic experience. He seeks to analyze the experience of beauty so as to determine what constitutes it. Of course the artist may theorize and the philosopher may be a poet; but the artist's primary endeavor is the actual expression of beauty, and the philosopher's chief task is to parallel the experience of beauty with an intellectual understanding of its nature.

The artist, it would seem, must be free from self-consciousness in his interpretation, in order that it may be true aesthetic value to which he gives expression. If he is highly conscious of his own relation to the situation or experience which he is interpreting, his expression is likely to be hindered or become affected. It is possible that he is most an artist when he is least conscious that he is giving expression to the beautiful. The philosopher is in an opposite situation. His task of interpretation necessitates that he be highly conscious of himself. He is always a factor in his experience and therefore cannot interpret experience without taking himself into account. His interpretative endeavors must be fully self-conscious and deliberate.

3. PHILOSOPHY AND RELIGION

Like science, religion also has common ground with philosophy in being interested in truth. One of its prime concerns, as with both philosophy and science, is gaining knowledge which is dependable and authoritative. But religion is not as purely intellectual as science and philosophy. Ideally, at least, it calls for personal commitment, for practice of a way of life, and the shouldering of social responsibility.

The misconception that philosophy is a kind of religion may be corrected at the outset. Philosophy is not religion, nor does it commonly attempt to take the place of religion. Philosophers may and do oppose religion; but they do not propose philosophy to take its place in kind. William E. Hocking makes this distinction clear when he says that in philosophy we use the third person in speaking of God, but that in religious experience the third person is supplanted by the second person and we must say "Thou."[2]

In order to remain somewhat accurate, it will be necessary to strike a comparison between philosophy, on the one hand, and a more specific religious tradition, on the other. In the western world, religion is largely equivalent to the Hebrew-Christian religious tradition in some one phase of its many expressions. It is this conception of religion with which compari-

[2] *The Meaning of God in Human Experience.* New Haven: Yale University Press, 1912. Pp. 343–344. Also cf. below, pp. 181–182. See also Martin Buber, *I and Thou.* Second Edition. Translated by Ronald Gregor Smith, New York: Charles Scribner's Sons, 1958. This distinction made by Hocking is more especially true for Judaism and Christianity. In Buber and others after him the "Thou" signifies a highly personal relationship, not only between man and God but between man and man as well.

son will be attempted: religion as found in the synagogue of Judaism, in the cathedral of Catholicism, and in the church of Protestantism.

There are at least three essentials which might be described as constituting religion when identified with Judaism, Catholicism, and Protestantism. The first of these is the experience of worship, the feeling of union with God the believer enjoys as he prays privately or worships in the sanctuary. In it is a sense of giving or adoration, and a sense of receiving or being blessed. The second of these essentials is the community of believers, the chosen people, the elect, the saved, the redeemed. It is a company of persons varying, according to the occasion, from a small local gathering to a large assembly in which far-removed geographic areas are represented. It is a company which for the most part is united and agreed in certain essential beliefs. In this company the individual believer feels a warmth and a sense of being at home that he experiences in no other public gathering. The third of these essentials is the constructive program of service and endeavor maintained by the religious group. It may be a movement of reform, an evangelizing program, a charitable service, or a scheme of social reconstruction. While it may take any or all of these forms, it has one unique aim throughout, that of striving eventually to realize in human associations the ideal society of righteousness and peace.

Applying this pattern to the case of philosophy, some interesting observations may be made. The philosopher may be an adherent of religion and participate in all of these essentials of religious experience. But in his philosophizing, strictly and narrowly defined, his worship, compared to the first essential above, is an intellectual love of God (after Spinoza) or a thinking of the thoughts of God after Him (following Kepler). The philosopher's fellowship with others of his own profession, in philosophical societies for example, making comparison with the second essential of religion, is based on the common ground of honest search for truth rather than upon agreement in specific beliefs. And his practical social endeavors, to strike comparison with the third essential, may be in religious uplift or in areas of everyday life other than religion. He may, however, cloister himself completely and prefer abstract thought to practical social effort. So much by way of attempting comparisons between religious experience and the individual experience of the professional philosopher.

But, by and large, how is philosophy related to religion? A number of connections will be suggested.

1. Philosophy examines the bases of belief upon which religion is founded, and it may by virtue of its questioning contribute added intellectual basis for religion. Philosophy, it may be said, specializes in the field of belief. It seeks to examine all beliefs and determine which are those whose foundations are firm and secure. Because of this, it may at times seem to be antagonistic to religious faith. In the cases of many philosophers, this is of

course true. In philosophizing generally, however, this all-inclusive questioning is not necessarily biased; it is the result of the intention to inquire into truth with an attitude of impartiality. It is assumed, of course, that truth is best discovered when the searcher is willing to subject his own predispositions to examination.

2. Since religion, like science, is a realm of experience in which the experiencing subject is related to reality greater than and beyond himself, philosophy can scarcely ignore this area of human experience as one of the sources of data with which its interpretative activity must begin. As shown later in this book, there are at least five distinct philosophies of religion, and four of them hold that religion is an independent and unique realm of experience yielding its own facts.[3] For example, Christians offer witness that they have experience of a historic stream taking form in the early days of the Hebrew people, moving on through their corporate life and the deliverances of their great prophets, culminating in the advent of Christ, and flowing on from Him to each succeeding generation through the written Word and the spiritual fellowship of the Church. This, it is believed, is the purposive working of God in our midst and the revelation to us of His nature, especially in the Person of Jesus Christ. This is a historic stream of fact and religious experience to which philosophy must give adequate consideration.

3. One contribution which philosophy makes to religion is to offer help in understanding the receptacle into which divine truth and life come. For philosophy studies human thought, its categories, and its various patterns of organization; and it is human thought and experience which receive the impact of the Divine; it is not something other than human thought and experience. Just as the philosopher cannot wisely overlook the data yielded by religious experience, similarly the religionist cannot afford to exclude the analytical methods of philosophy and the helps toward integration implicit in the structure of philosophy. For philosophy deals with the structure of human thought and experience, which in turn are the recipients and bearers of the divine inspiration.

4. Philosophy may also do much to refine religious belief. Frequently there is little distinction between folklore on the one hand and essential truth on the other. Many times, also, there are serious inconsistencies in religious thought. This is because the rational implications of beliefs are not followed through logically. Accordingly, the culling of truth from the religious heritage, and the resolving of inconsistencies in religious doctrine, are two of the important refinements of religion to which philosophy can contribute much.

5. Another contribution of philosophy to religion is the help it can offer

[3] Cf. Chapters V, X, XV, XVI, and XXI. Pragmatism is the one exception regarding the facts yielded by religious experience.

in understanding the thought forms of people. Too commonly the gap between those who preach the message of religion and the multitudes who listen to them is the result of misunderstanding. In part it is the old problem of speaking different languages; the vocabulary is common but the meanings are different. To the extent that those who profess and proclaim religion understand the systems of thought which have won and now hold the allegiances of men, they will be able to make their message understood. It is the study of philosophy which will provide this extension of understanding more than anything else.

6. But there is another significant way in which philosophy is related to religion. This is that religion may readily become the appropriate field of practical endeavor in which a given philosophy may find expression. Apparently the philosophy which normally finds its sphere of practice in religion would have to be a theistic one. That is, it must be a philosophy which, having examined belief and inquired of truth, holds that reality is ultimately a Person. In other words, it must be a philosophy which believes in God in the sense indicated by the common usage of the word "God."

Of course, as will be seen, there are contemporary thinkers having religious interests who use the word "God" in a religious setting, but by it they refer in a general way to the object, or concept, collection of values, or composite of forces, as the case may be, which is worshiped. Doing this, they of course apply some other philosophy of religion than that which harmonizes with the essential concept of God which the Hebrew-Christian tradition has held. Question may be raised as to how honestly and how consistently this can be done.

However that may be, the strictly theistic philosopher can use his intellectual beliefs as a harmonious and consistent basis for fulfilling the experiences, associations, and endeavors of a religious life.

4. PHILOSOPHY AND EDUCATION

It is difficult to define education without implying an educational philosophy, an evidence of the intimate relation between philosophy and education. It is interesting to note in this connection that John Dewey defines philosophy simply as a general theory of education.[4] But many other philosophers feel that it is more than this.

If described so generally as to make room for most varieties of educational theory, education would have to be defined somewhat as follows: an activity or endeavor in which the more mature of human society deal with the less mature, in order to achieve a greater maturity in them and contribute thereby to the improvement of human life.

Philosophy is theoretical and speculative; education is practical. Philosophy asks questions, examining factors of reality and experience, many of

[4] *Democracy and Education.* New York: The Macmillan Company, 1916. P. 383.

which are involved in the educative process; whereas the actual process of educating is a matter of actively dealing with these factors, i.e., teaching, organizing programs, administering organizations, building curricula, etc.

There are two chief ways in which philosophy and education are related. (1) Philosophy yields a comprehensive understanding of reality, a world view, which when applied to educational practice lends direction and methodology which are likely to be lacking otherwise. By way of reciprocation, (2) the experience of the educator in nurturing the young places him in touch with phases of reality which are considered in making philosophic judgments. Because of this, those who are actively engaged in educating can advise philosophers about certain matters of fact. That is to say, that while philosophy is a guide to educational practice, education as a field of investigation yields certain data as a basis for philosophic judgments.

As an example of this latter relationship, what is one instance of fact which the science of education yields to the philosopher for further use in the building of a world view? Well, in the practice of education there is intimate association with children, young people, and adults, as students. This close association is an unusual opportunity for observing human nature as it is. A teacher can scarcely avoid the formation of some attitudes as to the nature of man, as he is beheld in the pupil. Is the human individual a mechanism of nature, an organism, a segment of society, or a spirit? The educator may not venture the answers, but he can at least offer the philosopher some solid observations on which to base his conception of man.

Returning to the first-mentioned relation between philosophy and education, what are some of the problems philosophy investigates which have direct equivalents in educational policies? Three chief ones will be mentioned, all of which are considered with some fullness in the chapters on education contained in this book.

1. Most philosophies are concerned with the nature of the self. As has been inquired just above, they ask, Is the self a physical, social, or spiritual unit? Whatever answer is given will go far in determining a person's attitude toward the pupil, in case education is one of his major interests. If the self is a physical unit, then pupils are biological organisms. If it is a social unit, then pupils are little pieces of society. If it is a spiritual unit, then pupils are souls with destinies which outreach both biological and social processes.

2. Philosophy is concerned, among other things, with value; education also must necessarily deal with value, more than most other social institutions. Some of the questions which philosophy asks about value are: What kind of existence do values have? Are there any values which are ultimately real? How does man possess or realize value? Must effort be put forward in the process? Or do values come to us without effort, like an

inheritance? Such questions as these are most relevant to education. If, for example, it is true that effort is involved in the possession of value, this is just another way of saying that experiences which educate are fundamental to any progress in experiencing or realizing value. A way of looking at value philosophically in this instance necessarily looks to educative activities as a means in the important life-task of leaving off the old and entering into the new which is more to be valued than the old. Value thinking in philosophy is also related to education in another important way. Education must have objectives if it is to be effective; otherwise it descends to the level of aimless activity which is the antithesis of educative experience. But how can education have valid objectives unless these are formulated within the context of responsible thinking about value in general? There is too little awareness of this connection between value theory and educational objectives, and much superficial talk about objectives does not go far in perceiving this connection.

3. Having acquired the philosopher's interest to the extent of asking and answering such questions as these, the educator will scarcely stop before determining what his philosophizing implies for the educational process itself. If the pupil is a biological unit only, and the context within which objectives are set is purely naturalistic, then the process of educating will be a purely natural process, in no sense transcending the natural order. But if the pupil is a spiritual being, and the objectives of education are anchored in immortality and an ultimate divine society, then the process by which man is educated must be consistently and carefully refined so that personality is always treated as personality, never as mechanism or near-personality, and so that ceilings are not placed above individuals or societies inhibiting them in reaching out toward the ultimate.

Of course in all of the connections between philosophy and education the certainty of transfer is by no means assured. One educator may enjoy theorizing and be poor in performance of effective practice which grows out of his theory. Another may be at home only in concrete practice, confirmed in the prejudice that theory is unimportant and makes little difference in practice. It is hoped that this book will show up both of these attitudes as inadequate and make the student shun equally the possibilities of becoming a theorist who cannot practice his theory or a practitioner who assumes he can practice without any theory. For there can be no clear and sharp separation between theory and practice. No teacher or administrator however effective in practice can avoid assumptions, conscious or unconscious, as to what it is that he is about. These assumptions, it should be pointed out, are the material of theory, not of practice, and they need both to be examined critically and to be related to other assumptions in the largest context of belief, in order to be adequate as a basis for practice. Furthermore no theory is fully expressed until it is expressed in practice.

Not being an end in itself, theory becomes the evident enjoyment of the dilettante when pursued without responsible reference to practice. It might be said that there can be no practice without theory and no theory without practice, for thought merges into action and action emerges out of thought.

B. THE PROBLEMS OF PHILOSOPHY

Another way of approaching philosophy is by getting an overview of its major problems and corresponding areas of inquiry. This is the systematic approach, for when considered in this way philosophy may reveal itself as having a system and an order of its own.

The three great problems of philosophy are the problems of reality, knowledge, and value. (1) The problem of reality is this: What is the nature of the universe in which we live? Or, in the last analysis, what is real? The branch of philosophy which deals with this great problem is named *metaphysics.* (2) The problem of knowledge is this: How does a man know what is real? That is to say, how do we come by our knowledge and how can we be sure it is true, not error or illusion? The area of philosophy which is devoted to solving this problem is named *epistemology.* (3) The third great problem, the problem of value, is this: What are the important values which are to be desired in living? Are these values rooted in reality? And how can they be realized in our experience? The branch of philosophy dealing with such questions as these is named *axiology.* In addition to these three, but most closely related to *epistemology,* is another branch of philosophy which deals with the exact relating of ideas. This area of philosophy is commonly referred to as the science of *logic.*

Although the foregoing gives a logical overview of the main branches of philosophy, it does not represent the way in which a person is commonly confronted by philosophic problems. This is to suggest that these great problems are related psychologically as well as logically.

If philosophy is "life at the reflective level," as Rupert C. Lodge says,[5] it is likely that most of us come to that level of experience only after such maturing influences as crisis, earnest inquiry, or lofty purpose have had their effect upon us. Plato's plan for his *Republic* was that the philosopher-rulers would come to the study of philosophy at the age of thirty, after mastering many other disciplines. We do not just jump into reflective experience suddenly and by sheer effort. More commonly, we worm our way into an understanding of the problems of life, and often by many circuitous paths.

For most people the problems of value raise the curtain on reflective experience. Ethical questions first disturb many of us from the slumberland

[5] *Philosophy of Education.* Revised edition; New York: Harper & Row, Publishers, 1948. P. 2.

of unconscious acceptance of life. For others it is religious or aesthetic experience, efforts at social reconstruction, or combinations of these which start the awakening. Let us take a case in which problems of moral conduct have aroused the reflective powers and see how this first dawning of the philosophic interest may lead into an eventual facing of all the problems of philosophy.

Here is an individual who is troubled over certain definite questions of conduct. Is this the right way to act, he inquires of himself, or is it wrong? In an attempt to restore his peace of mind quickly, he may hurriedly borrow an answer from custom, convention, or some other external authority; but if thoughtfulness prevails, he will eventually come to recognize the need for some inclusive standard by which to evaluate all matters of conduct. The more general question resulting, if he does follow the path of reflection, will be phrased somewhat as follows: What principle of conduct if followed consistently will bring the greatest moral value into my experience?

But how can such a question be answered? Must I not know what kind of universe I am living in before my answer can have any degree of adequacy? If the law of tooth and claw represents the character of the universe throughout, it will do me little good to live the self-sacrificing life of the Christian saint. Should the universe be an impersonal process throughout, is there much point in my trying to realize personal moral values which would then have no roots in reality? When I think about it in this way my *ethical* question becomes a *metaphysical* one, and I come to recognize that I must know what kind of world this is before I can determine what the moral values are for which to strive.

So now I am confronted with the more formidable task of getting the answer to this still larger question. What is the nature of the universe, essentially? Certain of its aspects make it appear awesome, vast, cold, and impersonal. On the other hand, other aspects make it look warm, beautiful, benevolent, and indicate personality as its truest representation. But how can I know which of these views is true? By what means do I come by my knowledge of the world? And by what method can I test my knowledge of the universe so that I can be sure that what I think I know is dependable and true?

Now behold, my original question has gone through another transition. It first arrested me as a crisis in morality. Then with thought it was transformed into a problem in *metaphysics*. And now it has become a problem of knowledge. Whereas I started out on my train of thought with the question, By what norm can I judge conduct to be good or bad? I now emerge with the *epistemological* question, How do I come by any knowledge at all and how can I be sure that it is dependable?

But there are no more changes. Thought has now brought me to the crux of philosophic experience. Though I may not yet know even the language of philosophy or a single idea expounded by any one of the great philosophers, my queries have brought me notwithstanding to the decisive core of reflective experience, the problem of knowledge.

When I find an answer to this most subtle of questions, I can retrace my steps and find a clear path leading back to my starting point. Having determined, in general at least, what is the character of knowledge and how its validity can be tested, the answers to my two other questions are now indicated.

All of this, of course, does not happen in a day. Though there are moments of sudden revelation and delightful discovery of new insights, it is a process of months and years rather than days and hours.

We have given two parallel summaries of the major problems of philosophy: the former, logical; the latter, experiential. In the more detailed presentation which follows, the order of the first summary will provide the pattern. Metaphysics will be discussed first, then epistemology, next logic, and finally, axiology.

1. METAPHYSICS

Attention, then, is now focused on the problem of reality, the great question with which metaphysics deals. Stated again, it may be phrased as follows: What kind of world is this in which we live? After the wrappings are peeled away, what is the solid core of it which is real and cannot be disputed?

No answers will be attempted at this point, although it may be necessary to indicate what some of them are. The prior concern in this Introduction is analysis. We want to see clearly what the big questions are, and understand what some of the smaller questions are which are included within the scope of each big one.

a. In line with this intention, we can observe that one thing involved in any theory of reality is to understand the character of the physical world. Just what kind of structure is the universe? In the time of the Hebrew prophets it was commonly thought that the earth was surrounded by water and that over the earth the sky was a kind of dome which shut out the water, except for the rain. Mention is made in the prophecies of Isaiah of the "circle of the earth," as though the heavens were stretched out over the earth as a vast curtain, "a tent to dwell in."[6] Indeed, our present conception of the relations and movements of the heavenly bodies is not so old. Only since Copernicus have men grown out of the assumption that the earth is the center of the universe, the sun and the planets revolving about it.

To think in such ways as these about the kind of organization which ties

[6] Isaiah 40:22. R.S.V.

the universe together is to be concerned with *cosmology*. For that term refers to the branch of metaphysics which deals with beliefs as to the organization and orderly arrangement of the various parts of the universe. Of course, there are many things to be taken into consideration in cosmology. Among these there is the nature of time and space, and the factor of causality, both of which will now be considered briefly.

1. "What is time?" a small boy of three asks his father. In answer the parent mumbles some words about watching the second hand of the clock and in that way being able to observe the onward move of time. The answer probably satisfies the child's present need for knowledge. But the father knows that it is a poor answer, one forced upon him by the child's immaturity and the father's own childlikeness in the face of such a difficult question. Some philosophers would approve of this parent's answer because, for them, time, though intangible, is a real passing of events. It is something external and objective to us which we must undergo and endure. It is something which can be measured by physical instruments. And so, according to their way of thinking, our clocks, ticking along or pushing their second hands around the dial at a visible pace, are demonstrating a philosophical truth as to the nature of time as well as telling us the time of day.

But for others, time is something different, as we shall see later.[7] Immanuel Kant regarded it as a kind of form or pattern according to which our minds operate. That is to say, it is not something purely external and independent of us. Instead it is a way in which the human mind must relate itself to the rest of the world, by virtue of the fact that it is an individual mind and not an all-inclusive one, a fraction in the universe and not the whole. Accordingly, to be an individual involves experiencing the universe in a sequence of parts, one at a time, gradually accumulating these experiences so as to develop an ever more mature and complete comprehension of the whole. Necessarily, therefore, our experiences must occur in a sequence; and time is the order in which events succeed one another.

Consideration of the character of space involves a similar pattern. In cosmologies in which time is regarded as external and objective, space is also an external physical reality, as indisputable as rocks and trees. While in cosmologies in which time is regarded as the order according to which individuals must experience events, so too space is regarded as an evidence of man's individuated and finite nature, rather than a physical fact which is purely external and objective. According to the latter, individual experience, by virtue of the fact that it is individuated and therefore fractional, involves the kind of relation to the whole of the universe which we describe in common-sense parlance as being surrounded on all sides by an apparently endless expanse of space.

[7] Cf. pp. 129–130.

2. Causality is an important aspect of the cosmological picture. Most of us are enough the philosopher at some time or another to ask the question, Just how did the world come to be as it is now? This is a common way of stating a phase of the problem of causality, and again the answers are various.

One of the most important answers is the theological one. According to it, God is the First Cause or Creator who has made the physical world. In harmony with this conception, one of the classical arguments for the existence of God has been named the *cosmological argument*. The contention of this argument is that there is such order and design evident in the universe that the only adequate explanation of its cause is that there is a God who created it.

Another answer is proposed in the theory of evolution whenever it is regarded as an ultimate explanation of cause in addition to being a scientific theory describing how things came to be. Evolution regarded in this light offers the explanation that the world in its present form has evolved through long ages of process and change. Starting from inchoate stuff of some sort, the world grew and developed until now it has its infinite variety of forms.

b. Another aspect of metaphysics is the study of man. We do not see the real only in the overall view of the physical universe; we see it also in man, whom we are somewhat egotistically inclined to regard as the most unusual creature in all creation. In fact, it is on this very difference in frame of reference that some of the great issues in philosophy have turned. The early Greek physicists made external Nature their province of study. But when Socrates began to teach, he created a revolution by his insistence that man's own study of himself was the most direct route to reality. "Know thyself" may have been the catch phrase he adopted to underscore what he held to be the true starting point in metaphysical investigations.

Man is an important object of study in metaphysics because he has the unique position of being subject as well as object. For when we philosophize about man we are talking about ourselves. And thinking man is in the singular position of examing his own nature. This becomes significant in view of the possibility that ultimate reality, for which we are looking in metaphysical investigations, is not all on the outside of Nature to be viewed by the naked eye, but instead is behind visible and evident things. If it is possible that reality is hidden from open view in this way, then man's study of himself becomes important; for in looking at himself he can look on the inside as well as the outside. And in his view from within he is supposedly at least one step closer to reality than he is in the observation of Nature from the outside alone.

1. Among the many questions man can ask himself, one which is most significant in metaphysics is this: What am I? Just a body, a physical

organism, a machine? Or am I a soul, a spirit, a mind? Or, perchance, am I both soul and body? Now the answers given to this question, or cluster of related questions, will determine rather completely one's entire metaphysics.

For if I find, as I look at myself from my inside vantage point as subject, that I am purely a physical organism or machine, then I have lost one basis for assuming that somewhere behind the universe there is spiritual reality. If there is spiritual reality beneath or behind the physical world, it is strange I should not get some evidence of it when I look at myself from within.

On the other hand, I may discover a self or soul which, real though it seems to be, cannot be identified simply as body, organism, or psychic process accompanying physical activity. In this case I have a strong basis for looking for further evidences of spiritual reality behind visible Nature analogous to the spiritual self which I find behind my bodily existence. And again, my entire conception of reality will be largely determined by my conclusion that I am a self whose existence is spiritual rather than physical.

2.   There is at least one other consideration concerning man which has a metaphysical connection, the question of his freedom or lack of it. Does man have a *free will?* Or is he so completely a cog in the vast machinery of the cosmos that every act in which he engages is determined for him by forces over which he has no control? In answering this question, a man's observation of his own experience is one of his chief sources of evidence. If a student of the problem concludes that man is free, at least not totally bound by circumstance and fate, this implies significantly that reality has a quality of freedom or novelty, in addition to telling us something important about ourselves. And, contrariwise, the conclusion that man's actions are all predetermined suggests that reality is not only orderly but precise, meticulous, and exact, so relentlessly efficient that there is no place for free choice in it.

3. A third concern about man, which may seem to be predominantly ethical but is metaphysical at least in part, is the moral status of man. Does the moral condition of man affect the kind of existence he has? Or is this question irrelevant, it being assumed that man is a nonmoral species in a nonmoral universe in which morality has nothing to do with existence? There are many however for whom the concern is an exceedingly relevant one, and they offer differing specific answers as to what the moral stature of man is. There are those who say that man is fundamentally good, the child of a reality which is fundamentally good, his evils being the result of mistakes or blocks standing in the way of his natural goodness. Another view is that man is a mixture of good and evil, not purely one or the other. Some of his acts are good and some of them are bad, and so we have a

world in which good and evil are intermixed. There is also the view of man's moral stature according to which he is a morally sick creature who needs to be healed. While he is fundamentally good in intention and always seeks the good in everything he does, there is an ailment in his judgment and sometimes in his will which makes him choose evil when it is really good he assumes his choice will bring. Finally, there are those who, viewing man's moral condition, say that there is more wrong with him morally than a sickness of judgment and will which needs healing. He has gone through a change since his original creation which is so radical as to amount to a fall from original goodness to a sinful state. He is therefore described by the adjective "depraved" and is regarded as being corrupted in his entire nature, unable to make right judgments, good choices, or even to have fully valid knowledge of truth, until he is restored, at least in part, to his original condition.

c. For those of us in whose experience religion has been a primary influence, the most crucial queries of *metaphysics,* if not of all philosophy and thought, are questions as to the existence and nature of God. Of course it is radically decisive to believe or not to believe in the existence of God; for many, not to believe in God is extremely forbidding. It is important however to understand something of the nature of the reality or object we signify when we use the word "God" as well as to believe concerning His existence. Commonly we have placed too much stress on a formal or nominal answer to the question concerning the existence of God and have not been sufficiently concerned about the definition of that ultimate reality we may call God. It is comparatively simple, particularly under propitious circumstances, to say, "Yes, I believe in God." It is quite an other matter, however, to say what we mean by God. For in defining our conception of God, we may easily describe something that might more accurately be called by another name. And also, in denying the existence of God, we may not be disbelieving fundamentally so much as we may be denying the truth of an assumed conception of God which is inadequate and lacks authenticity.

There is a rather wide range of attempted answers to the problem of God. Starting at one end of the gamut and proceeding to the other, they may be suggested. First, there is *atheism,* according to which there is no God, no ultimate reality in or behind the cosmos corresponding to the conception of God held by Judaism and Christianity. There are some atheists who not only do not believe in God but also hold that the idea of God has served definitely detrimental ends in human society. They say that religion has been used as a tool of vested interests to hoodwink the masses, keeping them subdued and in their places, and so maintaining control for the interests already in power. Because of this, it is said, progress has been hindered by religion, not promoted by it.

Then there is *deism,* which holds that God exists but, since His original creative acts millennia ago, He has been scarcely related to or interested in the physical universe. A contrast to this position is *pantheism,* which intimately relates God and Nature, identifying them as one and the same, holding that all is God and God is all. *Polytheism* is another doctrine; according to it deity should be thought of in plural rather than singular terms, there being gods rather than a God. Closely related to this conception is the doctrine of a finite God, according to which there is only one God but there are also other forces outside of Him which limit and hinder Him.

At the opposite end of the progression from atheism, with which we begin, is *theism.* This is the doctrine that God is and that He is the sum and total of all existence, that He is greater than the natural order, and that outside of or beyond Him there is no existence.

d.   A further consideration in metaphysics has to do with number. On the surface, questions of number seem to be so elementary as to make us wonder at their inclusion within the scope of philosophy; but even the most elementary number considerations are not easy, and furthermore they are involved significantly in the most fundamental problems. The most common number questions are the following: How many substances comprise reality? Is reality one? Is it two? Or is it many? These questions will be understood more readily if at first their reference is assumed to be only quantity, not quality.

1.   The belief that reality is one is termed *monism.* And since it is quantity that is emphasized by the term, it is important to note that there can be a variety of monisms. I may believe that reality is physical, or I may believe it is spiritual; but as long as I believe that it is one, I am a monist.

2.   The belief that reality is two in number is termed *dualism.* And again, since quantity is the primary reference of the term, there can be all kinds of dualisms. I may believe that both the physical and the spiritual are real, and if I do, I subscribe to a spirit-matter dualism. I may believe that both good and evil are realities. Those who so believe are upholding a moral (good-evil) dualism. And it should also be pointed out that a person could conceivably believe in both of these dualisms without identifying good with spirit or evil with matter.

3.   To believe in *pluralism* is to believe in many different things as being real. Many honest and sincere thinkers say that they are unable to think of all the many factors and structures of reality as being comprised at bottom of one single substance. Such people are pluralists.

Now there is an important observation to be made on these beliefs about quantity of being. When we speak of reality we usually imply a number of qualifications. The following are three qualifications we expect reality to fulfill: (a) that it is solid and enduring, self-subsistent, not depending on anything else to maintain its existence; (b) that it is bound by no limits of time, and is therefore eternal; and, (c) presumably, that it is also infinite, knowing no limits of space as well as time.

The crisis of the problem of number is more clearly seen when it is viewed with these qualifications of reality in mind. On the one hand, it is questionable whether reality can be dual or plural and still qualify as real. Because of this, most dualisms, being weighted on one side, are unstable. For example, spirit is commonly regarded as more enduring than matter in most spirit-matter dualisms, and good is held to be more powerful than evil in most moral dualisms.

On the other hand, pluralism seems to dilute the meaning of reality per se. The so-called reals, which are regarded as many, are not necessarily qualified by being eternal, infinite, or ultimate; it would be difficult for them to have these attributes and at the same time be many. It may be fair to say that pluralism is as much a denial of monism as it is a constructive solution of the problem of number.

At the same time, it should be observed that monism is not established without difficulty. Infinity, eternity, and ultimateness are all completely exclusive requirements. For any one substance to qualify is to exclude all other possibilities. What one thing is it that deserves this distinction? The whole philosophic career of Spinoza was devoted almost completely to this task of establishing that reality is one. This indicates the greatness of the task involved in establishing monism.

e. The crux of all metaphysical considerations, to which this brings us, is this: What do we mean by existence? This is the great investigation of *ontology,* a major phase of metaphysics. The term ontology contains in its first four letters a form of a Greek verb which means "is" or "to be." We might therefore find some justification for taking liberty with it and coining the world *"isology"* as a synonym for ontology. For the task of ontology is to determine what we mean when we say that something *is.* Exactly what does the infinitive "to be" mean? What is it to exist?

As always, there are several answers. One of the most common is that for something to exist means for it to occupy space and endure through some lapse of time. This makes time and space the basis of existence. However, a question that can be asked in response to this explanation is this: Do time and space exist? And if they do, do they themselves occupy space and endure in time? There are some intangibles, such as truth, goodness, and beauty, which some people would like to think *exist.* Yet they do not fill space, and they seem to be little affected by the passing of time.

So it occurs that there are others who, speaking from a quite different vantage point, say that existing has its basis in mind rather than in time and space. A physical object, they say, has a meaningful place in experience only because it has qualities which make it knowable to mind. If this is more the clue to existing than time and space are, then the way is at least open to the possibility that mind and existence (existing) are identical. In this case, nothingness or nonexistence would be the negative or lack of mind, a metaphysical vacuum, and somethingness or existence would be mind.

Let us now summarize these considerations of metaphysics, with the ontological question at the fore.

As to the number of being, can more than one kind of substance actually qualify as identical with existence itself?

As to the reality of God, if reality must be one and existence is identical with mind, this is tantamount to saying that God exists. But if reality can be more than one, and the space-time order is the basis of existence, then the question about God is no nearer solution.

As to man and the cosmos, if existence is identical with mind, then man and the vast order of which he is a part are both rooted in God and are His creative expressions. But, on the other hand, if space-time is a synonym for existence, questions as to the unity of the cosmos, as well as to the nature and destiny of man, still confront us without any of the possible answers being preferred.

2. EPISTEMOLOGY

The reader is now invited to consider the second great problem of philosophy, the question of knowledge.

A young boy just beginning elementary school was once accosted by an older friend who patronizingly asked him, "Well, what did you learn in school today?" The young child was startled; it was a new and strange question. He didn't really know that he had learned anything that day. Was knowledge something that you could tell when you had acquired it, each day, piece by piece? he thought. The question which was put to him implied a definition of knowledge, whether it was intended or not, and his failure to see any appropriateness in the question implied quite another way of looking at knowledge. It is this rather difficult problem that we would like to study long enough at this point to recognize some of its ramifications.

a. One aspect of knowledge, when considered philosophically, is the possibility or impossibility of getting it. Probably no one seriously doubts that as individuals we have some sort of relation with the world about us, as long as that relation is understood as interaction with, experience of, or information about. But as far as our being able to have indisputable knowledge of the reality constituting the heart and core of existence, there are very serious questions which have been raised.

Starting at the extreme negative, there are three positions which will be mentioned. The first of these is *agnosticism*. The name for this position was coined by Thomas Huxley. Confronted by many friends who were so ready to label themselves as subscribers to this kind of belief or that, Huxley devised a name for himself which did not commit him to any beliefs about reality, unless it was the belief that reality is unknowable. The prefix *a* in the word connotes negation, and the stem of the word represents the idea, "to know," rendering a total meaning of "not being able to know."

A bit less humiliating to our desire for knowledge is the position of the skeptic. *Skepticism,* more exactly defined, is not a negation of knowledge any more than it is an affirmation of the knowing experience. It is simply an attitude of honest doubt as to whether knowledge of anything deserving the name "reality" is possible. There is an element of skepticism in every philosophy, at least in some stage of development of every thinker. It is difficult to see how a full-fledged theory of knowledge can be achieved without at some point seriously questioning the validity of the knowing experience.

It is difficult to name the third position regarding the possibility of knowledge. It may lack a name because it is so much more common than either agnosticism or skepticism and has seldom had to be pointed out by a name. All men take knowledge as a matter of course, most of us never becoming aware that it involves any problems; and most thinkers who consciously face the problem find a way of coming through with some residue which they find valid and to which they can give the name of knowledge. As a result there is this third position, answering agnosticism and skepticism by saying, "Yes, some knowledge is possible." Though a name may be lacking, the position may be described as the *affirmation of knowledge.*

b. A second aspect of the knowing experience is the instrument of knowledge. There are at least five possible instruments of knowledge, two of which are recognized with varying degrees of emphasis in most theories of knowledge. These are sense-perceptual experience, reason, intuition, authority, and revelation.

If a person concludes that sense-perceptual experience is the primary instrument of knowledge, he is embracing a position in epistemology that is known as *empiricism.* In this theory of knowledge reason is subordinated but not excluded. The function of reason for many empiricists is one of co-ordinating the findings of experience. Reason, apart from sensory experience, is regarded as quite helpless to yield any knowledge. Empiricists may or may not recognize some knowledge as certified by authority. Of course, thoroughgoing empiricism will recognize no authority other than scientific method, and that is simply a means of testing experience. However, some people do attempt to make close companions of empiricism in the scientific realm and authority in the realm of religion.

If it is concluded that reason is the instrument of knowledge which is of

reason

first importance, the position embraced is that of *rationalism*. Paralleling an equivalent attitude in empiricism, rationalism does not commonly disdain sense perception as having a place in the knowledge process, but its function is regarded as definitely secondary. While sensory experience provides some of the raw materials of knowledge, the rationalist sees this function as yielding little apart from the work of reason in interpreting, relating, and unifying the results of experience so as to yield meaning and significance. As with empiricism, a thoroughgoing rationalism recognizes no authority beyond reason, but reason is commonly regarded as universal and therefore greater than any individual mind. There are however rationalist who combine reason and authority as instruments of knowledge. For example, while reason sets the form which knowledge takes, Aristotle authenticates the substance of knowledge for some classicists, St. Thomas or the Church certifies the content of knowledge for Catholics, and the Bible provides the material of knowledge for some Protestants.

Another position regarding the instrument of knowledge is termed *intuitionism*. According to it, truth is known by a flash of insight or immediate awareness. Commonly, intuition is regarded as jumping ahead of reason and discerning understandings at which reason later arrives by its own slower means.

Strong reliance on external authority in one's theory of knowledge is known as *authoritarianism*. The authoritarian regards knowledge as being comprised of objective content. He also regards this content as being certified by some agency which is resident within the experience of man. Some of the more commonly accepted certifying agencies for truth are the history of race or nation as constituting a revelation of ultimate reality, and the Church or the Bible as revealing ultimate truth. Authoritarianism, in addition to relying on a human or part-human agency of authority, also apparently finds no gulf between the private experience of the individual and the common experience or history of the human race. According to it, once an item of knowledge becomes a part of the common experience of man, it is a rather simple matter for this knowledge to be transferred into the experience of each individual.

The instrument of religious knowledge known as *revelation* should be mentioned as well. Of course all religious authoritarianism is regarded by its adherents as being based upon revelation; but revelation so linked with authoritarianism is regarded as being largely in the past. However, there is a large body of Protestants who are not authoritarian either in a Roman Catholic or fundamentalist sense. For them revelation is a present instrument of knowledge, comparable to sensation, reason, and intuition. The Bible, the Church, and Christ are the media of revelation, but each is a present event as well as being related to past events.

c. Still another aspect of epistemology has to do with the degree of directness or indirectness there is in the knowing process.

Is there such a thing as direct knowledge? That is, do items or objects of knowledge themselves enter our minds when we come to know them? There are those who give an affirmative answer to these questions. For them, the so-called facts of experience are indisputable intruders into the realm of consciousness, and are just simply known directly as they are.

But there are others who feel that this is an oversimplified description of the knowing experience. Knowledge, it is held, is more complicated than this. The knowing subject and the object known do not ever meet in a direct fusion, in the way two lines do when they intersect each other. Instead, both knowing subject and object of knowledge have respective privacies which are never entirely lost in the kind of meeting involved in knowing or being known. Knowledge is not a direct intrusion into the mind of something foreign to it; it is always a matter of inference, interpretation, or conclusion which the mind constructs in response to the impressions the world makes upon it.

d. As the foregoing consideration strongly implies, the problem of knowledge focuses in the sense-perceptual situation. Of course, concepts, information, intuition, and communication from one mind to another, with language as the medium, are all involved. Possibly communication by mental telepathy may come to be a factor as well. But the real bottleneck in the knowing process, judging by the controversy of philosophers on the subject, is at the level of sensation and perception.

Just what is it that happens when our senses are stimulated? When qualities arise in consciousness and are identified as colors, particular objects, sounds, textures, warmth-cold feelings, etc.? This is the crux of the epistemological problem. And when we recognize that it is largely at the sense-perceptual level that the individual is consciously in contact with the vast remainder of existence which is not himself, we will be ready to agree that sense perception is the great watershed in epistemology, if not in all philosophy.

Are our senses simple gateways to the mind through which knowledge from the external world passes, as light streams through a window? Or are sensations and perceptions patterns of activity by which the individual interacts with the physical and social environment? Or, still again, is sense perception a pattern for the unifying and purposeful effort by which the individual projects himself beyond his own physical limits, thereby developing selfhood and making changes in the world? Questions such as these suggest the markedly divergent epistemologies which result from differing explanations of the individual's sense-perceptual relation with the world.

e. A final consideration in epistemology to be mentioned here is the overall question as to whether the theory of knowledge exerts a preponderance of influence over other philosophic questions. Is epistemology the soul of philosophy, is it just one of the problems of philosophy, or is it unimportant? To answer this question is to anticipate at least five of the six major types of philosophy to be examined in this book. *Idealism* says, "Yes, to solve the problem of knowledge is to imply solutions to all the problems of philosophy. For to determine the character of knowledge is to determine the character of existence itself."

Realism answers with a positive "No." Its mission in the world has been to deny emphatically that knowledge has any causal relation with existence. While epistemology is an important consideration in philosophy, it is just one of the considerations. And to work out a theory of knowledge implies nothing at all for metaphysics. An adequate theory of reality must stand on its own feet and not use a favorable theory of knowledge as a crutch.

Pragmatism, particularly of the *experimentalist* variety, is impatient with all preoccupations in epistemology which follow the traditional patterns. The problem of knowledge, it holds, has been an academic riddle with which cloistered philosophers have amused themselves for too long a time. Centuries have been wasted at this useless sport, to say nothing of years. The problem is never going to be solved, and it is unimportant anyway. Instead of trying to find out how we know, we should get busy at realizing the practical social values that will make this a better world for all men. Who cares about spinning pretty patterns with the subtle threads of epistemology? For *existentialism* epistemology is not a predominant consideration compared to the situation of existing in which a man is at any given time. Epistemology is important in that existence cannot be ignored in any construct which is alleged to be knowledge. For *language analysis* epistemology is important and possibly predominant when narrowed to strictly logical constructs. It is important in confirming statements regarding matters of fact and in validating the logical precision of statements which may pertain only incidentally to matters of fact.

f. To summarize all of this, we will try to sketch the major problems of epistemology which we have discussed. They are these: (1) Is knowledge of ultimate reality possible? The answer is likely to be agnosticism, skepticism, or the affirmation of some knowledge process. (2) What is the instrument of knowledge? In response to this question the answers are given by empiricism, rationalism, intuitionism, authoritarianism, or belief in revelation. (3) How explain the sense-perceptual relation of the individual to the world? The answer is likely to be some form of realism, idealism, pragmatism, or language analysis. In the respective sections in this book on these philosophies, more detailed analyses are made of the epistemologies of each. (4) And finally, is a theory of knowledge significant? The answer is one of the following: for idealism, of utmost importance; for realism, of importance, but no more so than other problems of philosophy; for pragmatism, both useless and detrimental unless closely tied to the active realization of human values; for existentialism, important but not primary; and for language analysis, important in confirming statements about matters of fact.

3. LOGIC

Logic, the third major phase of philosophy, is closely related to epistemology. A person's conclusions about the nature of knowledge will influence his approach to the reasoned control of his experience. Logic is also connected to axiology, another branch of philosophy to be considered in the next section of this chapter. Since there are values which are distinctly logical, logic might also be considered as within the province of axiology. But for the sake of clarity, logic will be kept distinct from both epistemology and axiology in this analysis.

The field of logic may be most easily described by approaching it first as it has been conceived traditionally. Here is a young wife who takes great pride in the small apartment in which she and her husband have temporarily made their home. From time to time she rearranges the furniture to lend variety and interest. But not many new versions in room arrangement are created before she realizes that there are certain limits on the changes she can make. Given a living room of the size, shape, and exposures that hers has, and given just those items of furniture with which the apartment is furnished, the number of possible arrangements is definite. And of these there are some which are not at all acceptable to the tastes of the young couple.

Now logicians have discovered that ideas are like the furniture in this apartment. There is a definite number of combinations of ideas which are possible, and among these there are some which do not make sense. And this leaves a smaller number of arrangements of ideas which are the only "logical" arrangements in which ideas can stand together, make sense, and speak truth. We will try to be more specific without becoming involved in technicalities. There are two kinds of ideas, subject ideas and predicate ideas, which are represented in our speech by nouns and verbs, respectively. Now these two kinds of ideas can be put together in sentences or propositions in a definite number of ways. There are general propositions, like "All men are mortal"; and there are specific propositions, such as "Socrates is a man." Among both general and specific propositions there are those which are affirmative and those which are negative. Both of the examples just stated are affirmative, but the first could be restated as "No man is not mortal" and exemplify the negative.

Since Aristotle, a form known as the *syllogism* has been used for relating one specific proposition to a general proposition and drawing a conclusion. The conclusion is possible only when the subject of the specific statement is included within the class of subjects described by the general proposition. The classical example of the *syllogism,* which also represents its simplest form, is this:

> All men are mortal.
> Socrates is a man.
> Therefore, Socrates is mortal.

But since there are different kinds of ideas and different kinds of propositions, it can be seen that there is room for a variety of relations of ideas and of propositions within the form of the syllogism. Altogether, on the basis of sheer possibility, there are 256 different kinds of arrangement. Of these, 237 are either not logical or else they are virtual repetitions of other arrangements. This leaves 19 syllogistic patterns by which ideas can be correctly related to one another. One simple example of possible arrangements which are not logical are those in which both general and specific propositions are negative. A little thought will make clear that no conclusion can be drawn from two negative propositions. By and large, this is the kind of analysis of thinking which has comprised the science of logic traditionally.

But all of this applies to logic when conceived as dealing only with the conceptual level of experience. Such a treatment fits in very well with a point of view which is strongly rationalistic. But, as we have said, there are philosophies which do not place this much confidence in reason, stressing instead sense perception and experimentation. For these *empirical* philosophies, such a description of logic is not adequate. There is of course a place for a science of the relation of ideas to be used in fitting together into a consistent pattern the data our senses and scientific instruments give us concerning the world. But far more attention is given to the process of getting at our world. For Francis Bacon, for example, logic was a matter of pious observation of the facts of experience. And for John Dewey it is all of this, plus the development and use of a technique for formulating and putting to work the hypotheses which will redirect our experience toward the ends and purposes we wish to bring to pass.

In attempting a systematic treatment of each of the philosophies, a fuller discussion will be made of these extensions or reforms in logic, particularly in connection with realism, pragmatism, and language analysis. At this point, our concern is only to suggest the character of logic, and it has been easier to do this by treating it primarily according to its traditional definition.[8]

---

[8] For other definitions see pp. 170–171, 283, and 388–394.

4. AXIOLOGY

The fourth and last great field of philosophy to be considered is axiology. If we stop to think about it, most of us will recognize that there is a realm of being and a realm of value. While the existence aspect of the things entering into our experience is important, much of our experience is made up of the value and worth which is somehow attached to these things.

That the world *is,* we commonly take for granted; that we know the world as it is, we also commonly assume; but we do most of our living at the level of choosing, desiring, and preferring. "There's no place like home," we say; home *is,* but it is also a *Good Place* to be. Democracy may be difficult to define, but a large number of people have given their lives defending it, so highly has it been valued.

Though it has roots in Plato, Aristotle, St. Thomas, and Spinoza, axiology, the theory of value, is a comparatively young child in the family of philosophy. Ethics, the theory of moral good, is one of the oldest fields in philosophy. And aesthetics, the theory of beauty, has long engaged the serious attention of philosophers. But in recent times many have concluded that there is common ground shared by these fields as well as by all other phases of our living which are concerned with the worth of things. If some fundamental ground can be found for the whole value side of living, it is believed, this will be the key to all of these different value fields. The name axiology has been used, the Greek stem, *axios,* meaning "of like value" or "worth as much as."

There are, of course, different theories of value; and there are different types of value as well. Some of the different theories of value will be examined in this book in their appropriate places, as respective parts of the systematic study of each of the four philosophies. Naturally, the different kinds of value are numerous. Those receiving more direct attention so far from philosophers are the *ethical, aesthetic, religious,* and *social* values. Some others are the economic, political, educational, utilitarian, recreational, and health values.

a. Ethical Value. It is at least possible to consider ethical values as being of two kinds, immediate and ultimate. The moral goods which I seek in my immediate experiences are likely to be determined by the ultimate and eventual good which I conceive to be the end and goal toward which all my life is lived. If I reason that the chief good in life is pleasure, then in the present conduct of each day I will choose those activities which give greatest pleasure and will shun those which do not reward me in this way. If however I regard the ultimate good as the fullest possible realization and perfection of myself, an entirely different attitude in *ethics,* then I will select those present activities which promise to be most rewarding in self-enrichment and my own fullest development.

Of course, I may be skeptical of any essential good in the world, and believe that there is no absolute basis upon which moral judgments can be made. In that case I may feel that the approbation of the social group in which I live is a present value, and so I will see to it that my conduct corresponds to that which is generally accepted by my friends and neighbors. Or I may assume that the acceptable conduct in each situation is that line of activity which satisfies most completely my individual needs and brings the greatest good to the greatest number.

b. Aesthetic Value.   Aesthetic values are a bit harder to discern. People who enjoy them don't do a good job of telling the rest of us what they are; and those of us who don't see them are completely on the outside of the esoteric company which enjoys them. But yet maybe we are enjoying approximations of beauty without knowing it, or suffering from the lack of these values without knowing why.

Here is a family spending a casual evening at home watching television. There has been a series of run-of-the-mill programs, and then one of the leading symphony orchestras is announced. The strains of a much-loved symphony come from the speaker, but the head of the house turns off the machine with the slighting remark, "Who wants to listen to that stuff?" Here is a graduate engineer, able and successful in his own technical field, but because of a strong disposition toward utility his home shows little evidence of aesthetic refinements. Here is another man, a civil servant of the government; his predisposition is toward economic security, and his life is equally devoid of the refinements of art and culture.

But climb six or seven flights of stairs to a little apartment on the mid-Manhattan West Side. Here there is no economic security; there is no great conscience about moral matters; there is little utility such as is provided by modern home conveniences. But, nevertheless, there is value. Exquisite oil paintings are created in this little apartment—at least finished here, if begun on location some other place. These paintings express, for the artist and for the rest of us, some of the things we feel—about "little old New York," for example. To those of us on the outside of the circle, to whom other values are more tangible, it may be of interest that these paintings sometimes, though not always, bring several hundred dollars on the market.

One way in which we value things is by the rather subtle and often unnoticed feeling tones they somehow evoke in us. A beautiful sunset may exalt us or fill us with awe, or we may trace patterns of color in it which simply interest or attract us. Driving across the desert, my car may seem to be rolling along on a treadmill, the landscape staying ever the same and giving me the feeling of awful loneliness. A squalid scene in a neglected section of a large city may fill me with despair and make me want to escape its ugliness. The seemingly endless flow of tones of a symphony may release me and make me feel that I am somehow at home in this world and have a real job to do in it.

These are values which may not have received general attention; but any attempt at full living will probably involve the development of the ability to discern them and aid in the achievement of that creative attitude which will control experience in such a way as to realize as many of the desired aesthetic values as is possible.

c. Religious Value. The values to be shared in religious experience are more easily understood by most of us than aesthetic values, though they may be no more easily experienced. Our living has been more habitually religious than artistic, and therefore we have at least a conceptual basis for thinking of religious values. This is not true of aesthetic experience.

Our religious values are likely to depend on our metaphysics, with the notable exception that religious experience may become a medium of revelation which will affect our metaphysics. Generally we may not see the same values in religious experience if we do not believe in God that we will if we do believe in Him. At this point we can therefore only indicate what may be some of the religious values. Later, in the respective analyses of the four philosophies, we will discuss those religious values which have metaphysical roots in each of them

Some of these values which may be enjoyed by a given believer, his metaphysical beliefs being equivalent, are (1) worship, the enjoyment of worth in the act of adoring God; (2) affirmation, the feeling that the self is confirmed in its higher purposes by being identified publicly with the religious community; (3) fellowship, the feeling of inspiration and buoyancy gotten from the communion of the religious group; (4) assurance, the conviction that behind the phenomenal world is a loving God who even notices the fall of the sparrow; and (5) hope, the feeling of profound optimism that good will conquer evil, that the soul is immortal, and that there is a blessed community which the believer may enter after this life.

d. Social Value. Most of us recognize, at least in theory, that individual man cannot live in isolation but must be related to society. The area of this relationship is the realm in which social values are, or are not, realized. Each of us, even the hermit or the recluse, sustains a certain absolute minimum relationship—we are born of society and because of society we earn a living or live by charity—but not many people get over on to the positive side of value realization in the social realm. We do not discern wisely what is to be gained, nor do we know how to engage in social efforts which are rewarding.

Without assuming a particular theory of social value, it may be said that in being effectively related to society the individual is within the normal context of human life. Being a man, and having all the hungers and capabilities of man, the normal medium in which his living must go on is human society. Even if an individual has an abnormal desire to be rid of society, he cannot be so isolated, apart from death. And if any of us is to stand up to life and make the very best of it, we must embrace fully all of the obligations and opportunities involved in being a friend and neighbor to other individuals; we must also accept those duties involved in being a responsible participant in the common processes of community life, ranging from the local to the global in scope. This is the way to certain rewards, some individual in their return, others commonly possessed by all, which may properly be termed social values.

What are some examples of social value? A few will be mentioned, some of them age-old fixtures of human society, others still beyond our grasp. (1) There is sheer orderliness and dependability in social structure, far to be preferred to the chaos which must have preceded civilization and which now erupts like a volcano, amid the changing fortunes of war, while control is passing from one side to the other. (2) Another is democracy, or the effective participation of individuals in setting the direction of the common actions of society, as preferred to mere obedience to a direction wholly determined by someone else. (3) Then there is the value of a united front and the strength it affords in fighting such common enemies of human welfare as hunger, poverty, crime, disease, and war. (4) And, to mention only one more, there is world peace, that orderliness and dependability of the social structure on a world-wide scale embracing all mankind, which does not break down, forsaking us again to primitive chaos.

5. SUMMARY

Before leaving this discussion of the problems of philosophy, it may be well to name again the four main branches which we have discussed and restate in one concise question the respective problem with which each deals. Fuller summary will not be attempted at this point as the Glossary following this chapter is equivalent to a concise statement of the major problems of philosophy and some of their ramifications.

Accordingly, the four main divisions of philosophy and the respective questions with which they deal are as follows:

1. *Metaphysics:* What is reality?
2. *Epistemology:* How do we come to know anything, and how can the validity of knowledge be judged?

3. *Logic:* What are the valid ways in which ideas can be related?
4. *Axiology:* What are values, and on what basis can their worth be judged?

C. THE HISTORY OF PHILOSOPHY

Two more approaches to philosophy will yet be considered. We have contrasted philosophy with some other kinds of human endeavor. We have attempted a brief analysis of the major problems of philosophy. We will now attempt to show how the study of the history of philosophy may lead the student into an understanding of the subject. And, in the next section of this chapter, there will be a discussion of the comparative study of contemporary philosophic types as a method of entering the field of philosophy.

In taking the historic approach, the student studies the great philosophers and their beliefs, chronological order providing the sequence, or he traces the development of distinctive ideas and movements in human thought as they have arisen in the past. Witness the philosophy shelves in almost any library to see the many books that have been written on the history of philosophy, following these avenues separately or in combination. Three values which can be derived from this approach will be mentioned.

1. If the specific approach is biographical, the human element offers many attractions. Consideration of abstract ideas and beliefs as such may be of little initial interest to many people, while the living drama of the life of a man who struggled with the issues of belief may be very attractive. There is human interest in biography. When a personality begins to live in the mind of the student, there are attractions which lead on into an understanding and appreciation of his thoughts—there are promises of intrinsic rewards for further study. For example, without other attractions leading a student closer, Spinoza might remain a little-known author of difficult writings. But when it is learned that he was excommunicated from the synagogue because of his beliefs, curiosity may lead the student to seek a fuller understanding of those beliefs to which Spinoza held in the face of such great humiliation and pain.

2. The naturalness of this historic method is evident in that an individual man and his belief constitute a very natural unit of study. While the problems of philosophy and the logical structure of philosophic thought have a certain distinctness, it is not possible to dissect a man's thoughts completely and make them fit into exact pigeonholes of systematic arrangement. But when we become acquainted with a flesh-and-blood thinker, he himself is the focus about whom to organize his different beliefs.

3. At the same time, the study of the rise and development of ideas and movements is natural as well. Generally speaking at least, in following this

approach, the student becomes acquainted with the problems of philosophy in the order in which they have arisen, which is quite psychological. There may be much in common between the vantage point of the race at each level of its development and the vantage point of each individual man as he develops; and the historic approach utilizes this common ground. This kind of study is likely to be easier than a sudden jump into contemporary philosophy. In the latter the newcomer is confronted with a number of subtle problems and differing viewpoints between which the distinctions are not clear at first. In the historic method he sees the problems and the viewpoints as they arise and he is provided a natural context within which to understand them. After getting this background, contemporary philosophy becomes more lucid, because present problems and viewpoints are seen as they represent the results of many different movements working in the past until now.

D. THE TYPES OF PHILOSOPHY

The final approach to be considered is the study of the various viewpoints. As has been seen, there are different answers which are given to the variety of questions raised by philosophy. These various answers tend to group themselves in viewpoints that have some characteristic theme which is predominant. By studying these different viewpoints a person may be able to catch the distinctive spirit of each. The more he becomes acquainted with them, the more clearly will he be able to see the different problems which are faced and the distinctive answers attempted in each case.

This approach, like the others, also has its rewards and values. We will first consider two of its values, follow this with a consideration of its limitations, and then briefly describe what we believe to be the outstanding types of philosophy today.

1. VALUES OF THE COMPARATIVE APPROACH

a. The comparative method is an important way of gaining an understanding of contemporary philosophy. Though it may need to be supplemented by a study of the history of philosophy if the student is fully to understand contemporary problems and viewpoints, in itself it comprises an important supplement to the history of philosophy. A comparative knowledge of contemporary schools of thought is the logical completion of a study of historic developments in philosophy. It is a necessary addition if a person is to take his own stand in the midst of the thought of his own day.

b. Another significant virtue of the comparative approach is that it encourages thorough and honest investigation. Too often thoroughness of investigation is inhibited by the dominance of a prevailing point of view. Commonly, the teaching definitely favors the viewpoint of the instructor without there being any acknowledgment that this is the case. Sometimes the prevailing philosophy is openly indoctrinated. The question can well be asked, Is this investigation? Is it not rather a limitation of inquiry which precludes the asking of honest questions and the seeking of honest answers? We can at least inquire whether it is not possible for a teacher to be so free from prejudice as to conduct an honest investigation of the problems of philosophy, fully considering each viewpoint for what it is worth and at the same time openly acknowledging his own loyalty. Although such teaching may not be common, we can at least strive to achieve it in some measure. Surely, if truth is truth it must be capable of withstanding all the investigation that can be directed against it. It may even be that truth can be fully believed and appreciated only to the extent that it is questioned and examined.

If this is right, then the comparative approach becomes a necessary method in teaching and studying philosophy. It is not enough for the student of today to become schooled in a generally accepted viewpoint just because it has become the spirit of the times. If he is to be given the opportunity for considering openly the problems of philosophy and their differing attempted solutions, it means that he must study all of the philosophies. It means also that his own viewpoint shall be assumed in the light of all the possible viewpoints, and that he shall find his own position on the basis of his own preference of that viewpoint to all of the others. This is the way of considered judgment which necessarily involves choice between alternatives, the way of true learning in which the tensions of thought awaken the student to responsible decisions.

2. LIMITATIONS OF THE COMPARATIVE APPROACH

While it is so valued as a method of study that it is adopted as the major approach of this book, the comparative method does have limitations. Some of these are now pointed out in order that more will not be expected of this approach than it is possible for it to yield.

It has already been mentioned that it needs to be supplemented by the history of philosophy; it needs to be supplemented by other methods as well. Chief among these is systematic study in which the composition of a given philosophy is studied quite apart from ways in which it is similar to or different from other philosophies. As is noted at the end of this introductory chapter, this method together with the historical are adopted in this book as important auxiliaries to the comparative method.

Of course, types or schools of thought can be pushed too far. In order to think in terms of major types or philosophic groups it is necessary to generalize. Recurring or much emphasized themes become the basis for characterizing a philosophy and depicting its overall pattern. But this is less accurate, at least in detail, than the study of individual philosophers and does not therefore do full justice to them. In fact, there is little point in arguments as to whether philosopher A fits into this group or that, e.g., is an idealist or a realist. They only make a kind of game of comparative study. While the comparative approach may be used as an instrument of classification, this is not to put it to a very good use, certainly not the best one. Its chief value is that it gives the student a broad perspective in which significant reflective insights can be awakened. Comprising this broad perspective are an understanding of the general outlines of major philosophies and the conflicts between them in which the student will scarcely avoid taking sides.

As to the classification aspect of comparative study, which is distinctly secondary as compared to the acquisition of philosophic insights, it should not be surprising if occasionally we run onto a philosopher who can be correctly placed in more than one of the major systems. In the four history chapters in this book Descartes, Spinoza, Kant, and James are all discussed in two different philosophic contexts. Descartes, Spinoza, and Kant are considered both in the history of idealism and in the history of realism; James is presented in the history of both realism and pragmatism.[9] The reasons are quite clearly given in each of these four instances and cannot be discussed to good effect at this point. But the reader not only is forewarned that such dual classifications do occur but is also advised that this book does not attempt a neat system of classification. What is sought rather is a means by which growing minds can be awakened to decisiveness in the reflective enterprise.

3. THE FOUR PHILOSOPHIES

Conceivably, different schemes of comparison can be followed with profit; therefore no indisputable superiority can be claimed for any.[10] Determination of the pattern to be followed by any given comparative study will hinge first on consideration of the general nature of the pattern

[9] For these discussions of Descartes see pp. 114–116 and pp. 253–255; for Spinoza, pp. 116–119 and pp. 256–257; for Kant, pp. 128–132 and pp. 260–261; and for James, pp. 263–267 and pp. 368–371.

[10] One of the earliest comparative studies in philosophy of education was Herman H. Horne's *Democratic Philosophy of Education* (New York: The Macmillan Company, 1932), in which idealism and pragmatism were compared. The scope of comparison was widened to idealism, realism, and pragmatism by Rupert C. Lodge in his *Philosophy of Education* (First edition; New York: Harper & Row, Publishers, 1937). John S. Brubacher, while following primarily the problem approach in his *Modern Philosophies of Education*, drew the threads of comparison together in the closing chapter of the first edition of this book (New York: McGraw-Hill Book Company, 1939) under the two headings of progressivism and traditionalism or essentialism. But he observed separate pragmatic and naturalistic strains among the

and then on its extent. Regarding the general nature of the pattern, the important issue is this: Shall the pattern be genuinely philosophical? That is, shall it be one which facilitates the pursuance of educational problems to their philosophic roots? In determining the comparative pattern for this book the answer to this question is an affirmative one. It represents the conviction that to philosophize concerning education every problem or issue, when it is considered, must be followed to its deepest roots in reflective understanding and placed in the most inclusive perspective possible. This conviction excludes a classification which limits the context to educational practice or to a supposed level of thought intermediary between practice and philosophy at which educational principles can be discussed apart from their philosophic connections.

The problem of the extent of the classification is more easily answered once the general nature of the classification has been determined. It is impossible and quite absurd to attempt a classification as wide as every shade of philosophical and educational opinion. On the other hand, decidedly different blends of thought cannot be lumped together loosely in order to have a neat classification. The pattern of four philosophies which has been chosen for this book, while by no means perfectly acceptable, avoids the discursiveness of many more or less unrelated types and at the same time does reasonable justice to shadings of difference which are important either as distinguishing between major positions or as demonstrating variations within major positions. And in addition to being an acceptable solution to the problem of extent, the classification in its general nature is distinctly philosophical, making possible and even offering guidance in a thoroughly philosophical treatment of educational concerns.

The four philosophies constituting the pattern for comparative study in this book are *naturalism, idealism, realism,* and *pragmatism.* They are named here in the same order in which they will be taken up later for full discussion, the order in which they have arisen historically.

The meaning of the name *naturalism* is strongly implied in the word itself. It is the viewpoint which regards the world of Nature as the all in all

---

progressives, and similarly, he noted separate idealist and realist strains among the traditionalists. The Forty-First Yearbook of the National Society for the Study of Education (Part I) on philosophy of education (Bloomington, Ill.: Public School Publishing Company, 1942) had among its contributors a pragmatist, a realist, an idealist, a non-Catholic Aristotelian, and a Roman Catholic philosopher. Theodore Brameld in his *Patterns of Educational Philosophy* (New York: Harcourt, Brace & World, 1950) discusses at length four schools of philosophy under the names of progressivism, essentialism, perennialism, and reconstructionism. And the yearbook of the National Society for the Study of Education for 1955 (*Modern Philosophies and Education.* Chicago: University of Chicago Press) has nine chapters representing different points of view which are fairly distinct. Among them are realism, Christian idealism, experimentalism, Marxism, existentialism, logical empiricism, and two others which are a bit difficult to name.

of reality. According to naturalism, the physical universe is all that there is. There is nothing, such as the spiritual, beyond it which is different from the natural. Within man there is nothing, such as a soul, which is different from the natural. Nature is all.

The point of view held by idealists is not as evident in the name as is the case with naturalism. *Idealism* is not the philosophy of the dreamer or visionary who dwells upon utopian ideals for himself or for society. The idealist has moral and social ideals, but philosophers of every other loyalty do too; to the extent that the possession of moral and social ideals is idealism, all philosophies are idealisms. The distinction of philosophical idealism is that it believes reality to be constituted by the same substance as ideas, or minds, or selves. A more exact name, as Hocking suggests,[11] would be "ideaism." Two other names which are near synonyms are "mentalism" and "spiritualism." This position is the antithesis of naturalism. Nature, far less than being the all of reality, is not regarded as real in itself. The idealist insists that all we know about Nature comes to us as thought or idea. Nature, he holds, is dependent upon Universal Mind, or God; it is an expression of Mind. The Mind, which sustains Nature, emerges in man and is his inner essence. Reality, therefore, for the idealist is beheld directly not in the external world but in the inner experience of man. *My idea of it is more real than the thing itself. Nature would not exist if my mind did not perceive.*

While naturalism and idealism have persisted as distinctive philosophies since early in the history of human thought, realism is a more recent viewpoint, arising in early modern times. It is a child of naturalism, but just the same, many realists hold beliefs far different from naturalism. While some realists define reality essentially as naturalists do, there are many realists who are more like idealists in their metaphysics. The single distinguishing characteristic is that realism gives deliberate attention to the problem of knowledge. Early naturalism was preoccupied with metaphysics and largely overlooked the problem of knowledge. At the same time, it is alleged by realism, the idealists twisted the knowledge situation about so as to make it look like a signpost pointing only in one direction, and that was toward an idealist metaphysics. The chief reason, therefore, for the rise of realism was to set us all straight as to the true character of knowledge. Realism accordingly insists that the objects of the external world are real in themselves and are not dependent upon any mind for their existence. The appropriateness of the name is evident in that objects of our experience are regarded as *real* things. They are independent of our minds, and possibly of all mind.

Pragmatism is a still more recent viewpoint. It arose in the latter part of the nineteenth century and is singularly associated with American life and

[11] William E. Hocking, *Types of Philosophy*. New York: Charles Scribner's Sons, 1929. Pp. 248–249.

thought. In its view of reality, the uncertainty and precariousness of our world is stressed. In regard to knowledge, it elevates the use of things above the knowledge of things; utility being of prime importance and capable of realization, whereas knowledge of ultimate truth is impossible and is of little practical value anyway. Strange as it may seem, pragmatism is a child of idealism, even though it is a rebellious offspring. Impatient with the great stress on unity made by idealism, William James revolted by insisting, among other things, that reality is many and that the will of individual man can make a difference in cosmic affairs. John Dewey, unconvinced by either the absolutism or transcendentalism of idealism, revolted by describing reality as a liquid process which is constantly changing and in which there is no abiding Spirit. Dewey's supreme imperative is that man must ever be alert to his changing environment and active in solving the problems it unceasingly presents.

Postscript. As the twentieth century has speedily moved on through world wars, the atomic era, the space age, and many successive upheavals, two philosophies not mentioned here so far have become more and more influential. These are existentialism and language analysis.

Because of this, some consideration of these two philosophies is being included in this book in addition to the four which are presented more fully. Neither existentialism nor language analysis lends itself to systematic treatment. Therefore, they do not comprise major sections of this book as the four philosophies do. A chapter is devoted to each one, however. It is hoped that they will offer some understanding of existentialism and language analysis, respectively, and also indicate the meaning of each for education. These are Chapters XXIII on existentialism and XXIV on language analysis.

So much by way of introduction of the philosophies. Fuller discussion of these chief schools in contemporary philosophic thought is the task to which this book is dedicated.

E. PREVIEW

This Introduction has been an attempt to explore a number of approaches to philosophy, some by way of inviting the reader to come along with us in this study, others suggesting what some of these pathways are. Now, on the threshold of this study, it remains to tie these various approaches together and show how they are to be used in this book.

The major approach to be used, as the title of the book suggests, is the *comparative method*. The succeeding chapters present in some detail the philosophies in the order of their occurrence. The study of each one will comprise a major section of the book.

However, the *historic* (see section C above) and *systematic* (see section

B above) methods are employed in making the overall comparison. In the case of each of the philosophies there is one chapter sketching its history and another giving a systematic synopsis of its major ideas.

As the title also implies, this volume concerns itself with the practice of these philosophies in education and religion. Accordingly, in each of the four major sections devoted to a particular philosophy, there is a chapter presenting the viewpoint as a philosophy of education, and another presenting each as a philosophy of religion. In the case of realism an additional chapter on philosophy of religion is included. This is a discussion of Neo-Scholasticism.

The final chapter in each section is a statement of the strengths and weaknesses of the philosophy discussed. These chapters will, of course, reflect the author's beliefs and will be critical. Attention to the making of one's own philosophy and philosophy of education comprises the concluding part of this book. The final chapter, it is hoped, gives guidance concerning the formal questions involved in building a philosophy of education. In the first two editions of this book, a statement of my own philosophy comprised the concluding chapter, but since my thinking has changed materially (though not radically), this must now wait for another book.

Glossary

naturalist - no set purpose for man.

THE VOCABULARY OF PHILOSOPHY

The vocabulary of philosophy, while different from our everyday forms of speech, is not necessarily difficult. Some helpful explanation of meanings plus a bit of patient study will go a long way toward making the student feel at home among philosophers. In the following treatment of terminology the purpose is twofold: to define terms, and to show, by the outline arrangement, some of the interrelationships between terms and the problems with which they are commonly associated.

I. *Metaphysics.* Theories of the nature of reality.   *What is real.*
   A. *Cosmology.* Theories of the nature of the cosmos and explanations of its origin and development.   *God*
      1. Some considerations in *cosmology* are
         a. *Causality.* The nature of cause and effect relations.
         b. The nature of time.   *Cause & effect -*
         c. The nature of space.
      2. Two distinctive views in *cosmology* are
         a. *Evolutionism.* The universe evolved of itself.
         b. *Creationism.* The universe came to be as the result of the working of a Creative Cause or Personality.
   B. The nature of man as one important aspect of reality.
      1. The problem of the essential nature of the self. There are no particular terms but there are divergent answers which can be identified with general viewpoints.
         a. The self is a soul, a spiritual being. A principle of *idealism* and *spiritual realism.*   *permanent*   *soul - essence - real me*
         b. The self is essentially the same as the body. A principle of *naturalism* and *physical realism.*   *what you see - physical creature*
         c. The self is a social-vocal phenomenon. A principle held especially by *experimentalists.*   *Speaking social phenomenon -*
         d. The self is a sheer fact where it is. It is "thrown" into some situation or place which is the locus of its being. A concept held by some *existentialists.*   *depressing · a thing - self*

idealistic mind - physical self - real self

no purpose → no pre-set purpose   find my own way out   alien   own plans   destiny   existence of self is just a matter of fact.

41

Greek- mind.
soul. spirit -

nature +
Idealism

2. The problem of the relation of body and mind.
    a. *Interactionism.* Mind and body are two different kinds of reality, each of which can affect the other,
    b. *Parallelism.* Mind and body are two different kinds of reality which do not and cannot affect each other. But in some unknown way, every mental event is paralleled by a corresponding physical event.
    c. *Epiphenomenalism.* Mind is merely a function of the brain, an overtone accompanying bodily activity. It is an onlooker at events, never influencing them.
    d. *Double Aspect Theory.* Mind and body are two aspects of a fundamental reality whose nature is unknown.
    e. *Emergence Theory.* Mind is something new which has been produced by Nature in the evolutionary process, neither identical with body, parallel to it, nor wholly dependent upon it.
    f. *Spiritualism.* (A definition common to most *idealists* and *spiritual realists.*) Mind is more fundamental than body. The relation of body and mind is better described as body depending upon mind, as compared to the common-sense description according to which mind depends upon body.
3. The problem of freedom.
    a. *Determinism.* Man is not free. All of his actions are determined, sometimes by forces greater than he is.
    b. *Free Will.* Man has the power of choice and is capable of genuine initiative.
    c. There is a third alternative proposed especially by the *experimentalists*, for which there is no name. Man is neither free nor determined; but he can and does delay some of his responses long enough to reconstruct a total response, not completely automatic but not free, which does give a new direction to subsequent activity.
C. Conceptions of and about God.
    1. *Atheism.* There is no ultimate reality in or behind the cosmos which is Person or Spirit.
    2. *Deism.* God exists quite apart from, and is disinterested in, the physical universe and human beings. But He created both and is Author of all natural and moral laws.
    3. *Pantheism.* All is God and God is all. The cosmos and God are identical.
    4. The conception of God as emerging, for which there is no common name. God is evolving with the cosmos; He is the end toward which it is moving, instead of the beginning from which it came.
    5. *Polytheism.* Spiritual reality is plural rather than a unity. There is more than one God.
    6. *Theism.* Ultimate reality is a personal God who is more than the cosmos but within whom and through whom the cosmos exists.

D. *Teleology.* Considerations as to whether or not there is purpose in the universe.

 1. Philosophies holding that the world is what it is because of chance, accident, or blind mechanism are *nonteleological*.
 2. Philosophies holding that there has been purpose in the universe from its beginning, and/or purpose can be discerned in history, are *teleological* philosophies.
 3. It may be that a special case must be made of the *experimentalists* again on this particular question, as they do not find purpose inherent in the cosmos but by purposeful activity seek to impose purpose upon it.

E. Considerations relating to the constancy, or lack of it, in reality.

 1. *Absolutism.* Fundamental reality is constant, unchanging, fixed, and dependable.
 2. *Relativism.* Reality is a changing thing. So-called realities are always relative to something or other.

F. Problems of quantity. Consideration of the number of ultimate realities, apart from qualitative aspects.

 1. *Monism.* Reality is unified. It is one. It is mind, or matter, or energy, or will—but only one of these.
 2. *Dualism.* Reality is two. Usually these realities are antithetical, as spirit and matter, good and evil. Commonly, the antithesis is weighted, so that one of the two is considered more important and more enduring than the other.
 3. *Pluralism.* Reality is many. Minds, things, materials, energies, laws, processes, etc., all may be considered equally real and to some degree independent of each other.

G. *Ontology.* The meaning of existence as such. To exist, to have being, means what? Study of existence. Theories of existence

 1. Space-time or Nature as identical with existence. To exist means to occupy time and space, to be matter or physical energy (e.g., *naturalism* and *physical realism*).
 2. Spirit or God as identical with existence. To exist means to be Mind or Spirit, or to be dependent upon Mind or Spirit. (Especially true of *idealism*.)
 3. Existence as a category which is not valid. This is held by those, especially the *pragmatists*, who insist that everything is flux or change and there is nothing which fits into the category of existence in any ultimate sense.

II. *Epistemology.* Theories of the nature of knowledge. { metaphysics / Theories of reality }

A. The possibility of knowledge.

 1. *Agnosticism.* The position that conclusive knowledge of ultimate reality is an impossibility.
 2. *Skepticism.* A questioning attitude toward the possibility of having any knowledge.
 3. The affirmation of knowledge. The position that true knowledge of ultimate reality is possible.

4. The affirmation of functional knowledge. The position that knowledge is always fractional, never total, and functions in a present field or situation where it is needed, and that we can appropriate such fractional and functional knowledge (especially true of *experimentalists*).

B. The kinds of knowledge.

1. *A posteriori.* Knowledge which is based upon experience and observation.

2. Experimental knowledge. Not exactly the same as *a posteriori* knowledge because it is not regarded as something finally to be concluded from experience or observation, by induction. Rather, it is something to be put to work in experience as a function which carries experience forward satisfactorily.

3. *A priori.* Knowledge which is self-evident. Principles which, when once understood, are recognized to be true and do not require proof through observation, experience, or experiment.

C. The instrument of knowledge.

1. *Empiricism.* The position that sensation, or sense-perceptual experience, is the medium through which knowledge is gained.

2. *Rationalism.* The position that reason is the chief source of knowledge.

3. *Intuitionism.* A position that knowledge is gained through immediate insight and awareness.

4. *Authoritarianism.* The position that much important knowledge is certified to us by an indisputable authority, such as the Bible, the Church, or the State.

5. *Revelation.* The position that God presently reveals Himself in the Bible and the Church.

III. *Logic.* The science of exact thought. The systematic treatment of the relation of ideas. A study of methods distinguishing valid thinking from thinking which is fallacious.

A. *Induction.* Reasoning from particulars to a general conclusion.

B. *Deduction.* Reasoning from a general principle to particulars included within the scope of that principle.

C. The *Syllogism.* A form in which to cast deductive reasoning. It is comprised of three propositions: the major premise, the minor premise, and the conclusion.

D. Experimental reasoning or problem-solving. A form of reasoning, largely *inductive* but using *deduction* as well, which begins with a problem, observes all the data relating to the problem, formulates hypotheses, and tests them to reach a workable solution of the problem.

E. *Dialectic.* A method of reasoning in which the conflict or contrast of ideas is utilized as a means of detecting the truth. In Hegel's formulation of it there are three stages: *thesis, antithesis,* and *synthesis.*

IV. *Axiology.* The general theory of value. The nature of values, the different kinds of value, specific values worthy of possession.

A. The nature of value.
   1. The interest theory. Values depend upon the interest of the person who enjoys them. Strictly speaking, they do not exist but are supported by the interest of the valuer. According to this theory, what is desired has value.
   2. The existence theory. Values have an existence in their own right which is independent of the valuer and his interest. Values are not qualities or essences without foundation in existence; they are essence plus existence.
   3. The experimentalist theory. That is of value which yields a greater sense of happiness in the present and at the same time opens the way to further goods in future experiences.
   4. The part-whole theory. The key to realizing and enjoying value is the effective relating of parts to wholes.
B. Realms of value.
   1. *Ethics.* The nature of good and evil. The problems of conduct and ultimate objectives.
     a. The worth of living.
       (1) *Optimism.* Existence is good. Life is worth living. Our outlook can be hopeful.
       (2) *Pessimism.* Existence is evil. Life is not worth the struggle; we should escape it by some means.
       (3) *Meliorism.* Conclusions as to the goodness or evil of existence cannot be made final. Human effort may improve the human situation. The final end cannot be assured, but we must face life, not escape it, applying all the effort and resource we can command.
     b. The highest good or *summum bonum.* The end, aim, or objective of living which is above all other ends. In absolutist philosophies it is the ultimate end which by its nature cannot be a means to another end.
       (1) *Hedonism.* The highest good is pleasure. Hedonist philosophies vary in their conceptions of pleasure, ranging from the intense pleasure of the moment to highly refined and enduring pleasure or contentment. *Utilitarianism* is a form of hedonism having society as its frame of reference. According to it, the greatest happiness of the greatest number is the prime objective.
       (2) *Perfectionism.* The highest good is the perfection of the self, or self-realization. Perfectionism may also have its social frame of reference, envisioning an ideal social order as the ultimate objective of society.
     c. The criteria of conduct. From one's conception of the highest good there follow logically certain practical principles for everyday living. Some examples are
       (1) Kant's maxim: act only on those principles which you are willing should become universal moral laws.

   (2) Spencer's principle: action to be right must be conducive
       to self-preservation.
   (3) Dewey's principle: discover the probable consequences of
       what you consider doing, by going through an imaginative
       rehearsal of the possibilities.
   (4) The religious principle: obey the will of God; commit
       yourself completely to the fulfillment of God's purpose
       for yourself and the world.
   d. The motivation of conduct. The kind and scope of the interests
      which guide conduct.
      (1) *Egoism.* The interests of self should be served by an
          individual's actions.
      (2) *Altruism.* The interests of others or of the social group
          should be served by an individual's actions. One realizes
          his own fullest selfhood in seeking the best interests of
          others.
2. *Aesthetics.* The nature of the values which are found in the
   feeling aspects of experience. The conscious search for the principles governing the creation and appreciation of beautiful things.
3. *Religious Values.* The kind, nature, and worth of values to be
   possessed in worship, religious experience, and religious service.
4. *Educational Values.* The kind, nature, and worth of values
   inherent in the educative process.
5. *Social Values.* The kind, nature, and worth of values only realized
   in community and in the individual's relation to society. Some
   more specific kinds of social values are the *political* and the
   economic.
6. *Utilitarian Values.* The kind, nature, and worth of values to be
   realized in harmonious adjustment to or efficient control of the
   forces of the physical environment.

PART TWO

NATURALISM

II

A Brief History of Naturalism

A. *Some Ancient Roots of Naturalism*
   1. LEUCIPPUS AND DEMOCRITUS
   2. EPICURUS
   3. LUCRETIUS

B. *Thomas Hobbes*

C. *Jean Jacques Rousseau*

D. *Herbert Spencer*

E. *Synthesis*

A. SOME ANCIENT ROOTS OF NATURALISM

As far as the history of philosophy in the western world is concerned, naturalism is the oldest philosophy. The earliest figures with whom our histories of philosophy commonly begin were naturalists. Thales, who lived in Miletus, a coastal city of ancient Asia Minor, during the early part of the sixth century B.C., observing water to be such a large constituent of many material and living forms, decided upon it as the one single substance common to all things. The daring of Thales, marking him as a naturalist, is that he found his final substance within Nature. Apparently he did not feel the necessity of going beyond Nature to find ultimate reality. Anaximander and Anaximenes, who lived in the same century, formed, together with Thales, the Milesian school. Both were disposed to explain reality in terms of one substance, and like Thales did not go beyond the realm of Nature to identify this substance. For Anaximenes it was air; but Anaximander's conception had a refinement which anticipated much later times, although it was more general. He contented himself with nothing more particular than an unnamed underlying substance or matter.

But the ancient roots of naturalism have much fuller body in four other men who have been called atomists, only two of whom were contemporaries. Leucippus and Democritus, the earliest of the four, lived in the colony of Abdera on the Thracian coast during the early part of the fifth century B.C., at about the time that Socrates needled the citizens of Athens with his questions. Epicurus (341–270 B.C.), more than a century later, whose career was largely subsequent to Aristotle's, was devoted to the ideas of Democritus. And Lucretius (96–55 B.C.), though not even a Greek and born almost two and one half centuries after Epicurus, was a great admirer of Epicurus. All four are called atomists because they conceived of reality as fundamentally a matter of atoms moving in space. Apparently Leucippus and Democritus were the real creative minds with whom the atomistic view of reality originated. For Epicurus made little significant modification in the original conception; and Lucretius' offering was chiefly literary. His long poem, *De Rerum Natura,* gave beautiful literary expression to this ancient naturalistic world view and preserves for our times its fullest rendering. A closer look at each of these four men will offer a somewhat more detailed picture of naturalism in its ancient form.

1. LEUCIPPUS AND DEMOCRITUS

Leucippus and Democritus explained the world in a common-sense reduction of Nature to two simple things: empty space and atoms. They assumed that there is and can be such a thing as empty space, a vacuum or void containing nothing. This empty space they considered to be the same as nothing, nonexistence, or nonbeing. About the substance filling empty space, giving us all the things making up the world, they reasoned that it must be constituted by small indivisible units piled one upon another. These hypothetical units they called atoms. Common experience gives us numberless instances of objects being broken into parts, and these parts into still smaller parts. Theoretically, at least, division of parts into smaller parts can go on indefinitely. But Leucippus and Democritus argued that there must be some infinitesimal unit which is elemental and cannot be divided further. This, because of its imputed indivisibility, they called an atom, never dreaming of a day of electrons, protons, neutrons, mesons, etc., and a breaking of the atom into parts, revealing each to be a solar system of energy points.

Little was said about empty space, nor could there be; it was a void in which atoms could move. The atoms, however, were considered to be of an infinite variety of sizes, shapes, and weights. Everything in Nature as we now behold it is the result of atoms moving through space. When the atoms come together in clusters, things come into being; when they move apart, objects dissolve and fall into nonexistence. Even mind and soul are made up of atoms, evolving and dissolving in the same manner. But mind and soul are made of fine, smooth atoms which are perfectly round, similar to the atoms of which fire was supposedly composed. Mind and soul, like fire, have great mobility; and their atoms therefore must be very active.

The motion of atoms in space was described by Leucippus and Democritus as sheer motion, not up nor down. The motion might be described as random, in the sense that there is movement in all kinds of different directions. Such random movement resulted in atoms colliding with one another, thence forming clusters and accumulating the mass to constitute such objects as rocks, trees, and planets. But the movement is not random in the sense of being chance movement which is whimsical and uncaused. Leucippus and Democritus insisted that nothing happens by chance; that in the motion of atoms through space and the resultant composition of objects, everything that goes on is the result of corresponding movements which went before and necessarily resulted in these subsequent events.

From this elemental ground, Nature as we now know it has evolved, according to Leucippus and Democritus. Worlds whirled together as the atoms formed large masses in vast swirling motions. Vegetation grew, animals developed, and man arose, his speech and institutions resulting with the same kind of necessity as produced minerals and vegetation.

The practical way of living which these two ancient materialists coupled with their metaphysics of atoms and space was a quiet placid life, as free as possible from the struggles and tensions which commonly mar a man's life when he gets too far away from Nature. Simple habits, simple food, quiet pleasures, balance in work, not overstretching one's self by too much ambition—this is the quiet way of life in harmony with Nature. The aphorisms of Democritus are the typical sayings of a newspaper-columnist philosopher, advising moderation in desires, and promising avoidance of the miseries of excess as a reward.

2. EPICURUS

It was by way of this practical interest in a peaceful life of quiet pleasure that Epicurus was attracted to the metaphysics of Democritus. His poor health may have caused Epicurus to prefer simplicity and contentment as compared to a vigorous life of struggle and achievement. But at any rate, he avoided pain and fear as evils, insofar as he could, and sought peace and enduring enjoyment as the greatest goods. It is unfair to identify Epicurus with a libertine's way of life. He had as little use for intense pleasure as for the struggles of getting ahead in the world. By no means an epicure in his fondness for eating, his stock diet was bread and water. A little cheese was the delicacy added on special feast days. An ascetic in his sex life, he advocated celibacy as the way of greatest quietude. As these habits exemplify, everything was shoved to the side for the uninterrupted enjoyment of the simple rhythms basic in the life of man and Nature. This was to him the little island of contentment where abiding joy was to be found, and launchings out into the waters of pain, pleasure, or struggle were as infrequent and fleeting as could be.

Preservation of this island of the soul's enjoyment was what brought Epicurus to the metaphysics of Democritus. For the view of the world proposed by Democritus banished for him the fear of death, one of the greatest disturbers of man's peace. If the indestructible, of which all Nature is made, is nothing more than atoms moving in space, and if even the soul is made of atoms, very round and smooth ones like those in fire, then the soul need have no fear of the time when it will be dissolved. When death comes and the soul's atoms are dispersed, there no longer will be a soul to suffer the anguish of death. And now, as long as the soul is in existence, its atoms intact, there is no need to fear that which will not be suffered in nonexistence. So, the atom-and-empty-space metaphysics of Democritus was most attractive to Epicurus and reinforced his ethics.

In a brief account such as this, there is little to be said in describing this adopted metaphysics of Epicurus; it is so much the same as in Democritus. Bertrand Russell makes much in his book, *A History of Western Philosophy,* of Epicurus' addition of a kind of free will to the strictly deterministic system of Democritus.[1] In reading such fragments of Epicurus as are available to him, the writer is unable to find such a marked difference on this point. Epicurus does say that some of the atoms "rebound to a considerable distance from each other" and others "merely oscillate in one place when they chance to have got entangled or to be enclosed by a mass of other atoms shaped for entangling."[2] Democritus insisted that all movements of the atoms, random as they are in direction, are the precise consequences of previous causes which could have yielded no other results. But Epicurus suggested that there is something in the distinctive character of individual atoms which determines how much they rebound in collision, and he grants the possibility of chance as operating so as to result in the

[1] New York: Simon and Schuster, 1945. Cf. pp. 246 ff.
[2] Charles M. Bakewell, *Source Book in Ancient Philosophy.* Revised edition; New York: Charles Scribner's Sons, 1939. P. 294.

entangling of atoms. While this is not free will or pure chance, neither is it the perfectly efficient deteminism of Democritus.

Epicurus does go definitely beyond Democritus in considering the knowledge problem. He was at least aware that if objects are made of atoms, and the mind and soul are also made of atoms, some explanation must be found, harmonizing with the atom-space description of reality, making somewhat clear how the impression of an object gets into the mind of the man who beholds it. His solution was that objects give off a kind of film of atoms which is transmitted to the mind through the senses, and there yields a kind of photographic replica of the object. This replica is not a copy pure and simple, for it is constituted by atoms given off by the object itself. It is a valid image of the object, in which the very qualities of the object are retained, having been transmitted to the mind by the particles given off by the object.[3]

3. LUCRETIUS

The exact dates of the life of Titus Lucretius are not known. He probably did not live to be fifty years old, and such a span of life as he had was all contained within the first half of the century before Christ. Tennyson represents him in his poem *Lucretius* as being unhappily married and coming to a tragic end of insanity and death as the result of a love potion given him by his wife. But none of the circumstances depicted in Tennyson's poem are known to be true.

Lucretius must have been a literary genius to have taken the philosophy of Epicurus and dressed it up in such a beautiful poem as *De Rerum Natura*. Significant though he may be as a man of letters, he does not have the distinction of having added to or improved upon the Epicurean system. He wrote his poem to proclaim the doctrine, not to improve upon it. The flavor of his work may be sampled by reproducing a few patches of his poetry bearing upon some of the important phases of ancient naturalism already discussed.

His reverence for Democritus and his overflowing enthusiasm for Epicurus identify him clearly with their tradition. Of the first of his patron saints he speaks in glowing terms when he refers to "the revered judgment of the great Democritus."[4] But when he alludes to the great master, Epicurus, "whose intellect surpassed humanity,"[5] he mounts into flights of praise such as this:

O thou who first from so great a darkness wert able to raise aloft a light so clear, illumining the blessings of life, thee I follow, O glory of the Grecian

[3] *Ibid.*, pp. 290–292. Cf. Letter of Epicurus to Herodotus, from Diogenes Laertius.
[4] Lucretius, *De Rerum Natura*. Translated by W. H. D. Rouse; Cambridge: Harvard University Press, 1928. P. 197. Reprinted by permission of the publishers from Loeb Classical Library.
[5] *Ibid.*, p. 243.

race, and now on the marks thou hast left I plant my own footsteps firm,
not so much desiring to be thy rival, as for love, because I yearn to copy thee.[6]

He boldly argued for the Epicurean ethics of escape from pain when he
says:

> O wretched minds of men! O blinded hearts!
> In how great perils, in what darks of life
> Are spent the human years, however brief!—
> O not to see that nature for herself
> Barks after nothing, save that pain keep off,
> Disjoined from the body, and that mind enjoy
> Delightsome feeling, far from care and fear!
> Therefore we see that our corporeal life
> Needs little, altogether, and only such
> As takes the pain away, and can besides
> Strew underneath some number of delights.[7]

Depicting the atom-space view of reality, he says:

> In these affairs
> We wish thee also well aware of this:
> The atoms, as their own weight bears them down
> Plumb through the void, at scarce determined times,
> In scarce determined places, from their course
> Decline a little—call it, so to speak,
> Mere changed trend. For were it not their wont
> Thuswise to swerve, down would they fall, each one,
> Like drops of rain, through the unbottomed void;
> And then collisions ne'er could be nor blows
> Among the primal elements; and thus
> Nature would never have created aught.[8]

He also includes in his poem the Epicurean explanation of knowledge as
films of objects which get into the mind by way of the senses:

There exist what we call images of things, which like films drawn from the
outermost surface of things, flit about hither and thither through the air; it is
these same that, encountering us in wakeful hours, terrify our minds, as also
in sleep, when we often seem to behold wonderful shapes and images of the
dead, which have often aroused us in horror while we lay languid in sleep . . .

I say, therefore, that semblances and thin shapes of things are thrown off
from their outer surface, which are to be called as it were their films or bark,

---

[6] *Ibid.*, p. 171.

[7] Taken from *Of the Nature of Things* by Lucretius. Translated by W. E. Leonard,
published by E. P. Dutton & Co., Inc., New York. P. 45. Reprinted by permission
of E. P. Dutton & Co., and J. M. Dent & Sons.

[8] *Ibid.*, p. 54.

because the image bears a look and a shape like the body of that from which it is shed to go on its way.[9]

Lucretius, in addition, has much to say about the evolutionary development which followed the hurling together of atoms to form the earth and other planets. This is also in Epicurus but was not singled out for specific discussion earlier. One sample runs as follows:

> In the beginning, earth gave forth, around
> The hills and over all the length of plains,
> The race of grasses and the shining green;
> The flowering meadows sparkled all aglow
> With greening color, and thereafter, lo,
> Unto the divers kinds of trees was given
> An emulous impulse mightily to shoot,
> With a free rein, aloft into the air.
> As feathers and hairs and bristles are begot
> The first on members of the four-foot breeds
> And on the bodies of the strong-y-winged,
> Thus then the new Earth first of all put forth
> Grasses and shrubs, and afterward begat
> The mortal generations, there upsprung—
> Innumerable in modes innumerable—
> After diverging fashions. For from sky
> These breathing-creatures never can have dropped,
> Nor the land-dwellers ever have come up
> Out of sea-pools of salt. How true remains,
> How merited is that adopted name
> Of earth—"The Mother"—since from out the earth
> Are all begotten![10]

B. THOMAS HOBBES (1588–1679)

A full and adequate history of naturalism could by no means make a grand leap from Lucretius in the first century before Christ to Thomas Hobbes in the seventeenth century. It would be obliged to pick its way along many devious paths, searching out the strains of naturalism in a number of little-known men, and after many pages bring the patient reader to the distant point to which attention is now directed after a simple turn of the page or quick movement of the eyes.

The chief justification for this easy transition is, of course, scantiness of space in a larger task which is not purely historical in its purpose. Impor-

[9] *De Rerum Natura*, W. H. D. Rouse translation, p. 251.
[10] Taken from *Of the Nature of Things* by Lucretius. Translated by W. E. Leonard; New York: E. P. Dutton & Co. Pp. 219–220. Reprinted by permission of E. P. Dutton & Co., and J. M. Dent & Sons.

tant as intervening studies might be, it is more significant that in early modern times there was a continuance or resumption of the naturalistic tradition in philosophy. There is not as much unity of pattern in Thomas Hobbes, Jean Jacques Rousseau, and Herbert Spencer as in the ancients, Leucippus, Democritus, Epicurus, and Lucretius; but there is a unity and a common ground, and it is antecedent to some of the world views which are very common today. While now this world view often assumes in one philosopher a realist theory of knowledge, and in another a pragmatic, yet it continues to be an influential world view, which is properly called naturalism. It may also be the metaphysics of an existentialist who is atheistic or a language analyst whose outlook excludes any existence beyond nature.

Francis Bacon (1561–1626), a contemporary of Hobbes who was twenty-seven years his senior, lent greater weight by his influence to a metaphysics of Nature than to a world view rooted in a belief in reality beyond Nature. But as his primary concern was with the methods of knowledge and not with the content or nature of reality, he is more to be identified with the pragmatic tradition in philosophy. Accordingly, the character of his ideas and his impact on man's thought generally are presented in the outline of the history of pragmatism which is the subject of Chapter XVIII;[11] and Thomas Hobbes, Bacon's one-time secretary, whose later greatness Bacon certainly equaled, if he did not surpass it, is now permitted the center of the stage.

As compared to Bacon, who shared the limelight of nobility even as a boy and was surrounded by elders who were convinced that he was an unusual child, Hobbes achieved his greatness against some odds. His father was an ignorant and somewhat indolent vicar who reportedly disappeared from his Westport parish after being embroiled in a slugging match at his church door. Fortunately for young Thomas, his father's brother was a successful and benevolent businessman who saw to it that he was adequately schooled, even paying his way at Oxford. After university he was in the employ of the Cavendish family as a tutor for as long as three generations, during which time he made good use of a well-equipped library to advance his own learning. Evidently he put to equally good effect his association with Bacon as secretary. The most famous result of his work was in the realm of political theory, but he also wrote extensively in philosophy, his politics following quite logically from his general philosophical theory. His complete works, translated into English from the Latin in which he composed them, comprise ten volumes.[12]

Like the ancient naturalists, Hobbes conceived Nature as an affair of

---

[11] Cf. pp. 358–361.

[12] *The English Works of Thomas Hobbes.* Collected and edited by Sir William Molesworth, Bart. London: John Bohn, 1889.

bodies moving in space. He was not, however, an atomist, for he did not agree that any body could be so small that it could not, even so, be divided and made yet smaller.[13] A *body* he defined as a thing which exists in and of itself and has no dependence whatsoever upon our thought about it. Bodies exist outside of us and do not depend on any relation to us.[14] By *space* Hobbes meant a place outside of the mind which can be filled by an object. If you think of a book on your desk as being moved from the place it now occupies to another spot, you can at least imagine a space which was left vacant by the book being moved, a space which could be occupied by another object.[15] There yet remains one other item in Hobbes' description of Nature, namely, *motion;* and motion he defined as "the privation of one place and the acquisition of another."[16] It is that way of behaving seen in Nature by which a body can first occupy one spot, then another, and still another, and so on. Motion is as fundamental as rest; it is not caused by something other than motion; it is its own cause. If a body is in motion, some body which is at rest will have to impede its movement in order for it to come to rest. Contrariwise, when a body is at rest it does not get into motion unless it is pushed by another body endeavoring to get into its place.[17]

Combining these definitions, we have Nature described by Hobbes as an aggregate of things existing outside of our minds, and therefore evidencing the reality of a space beyond us, but also an aggregate of things moving from one place to another in that space which is beyond us. This is the same as the description given by Democritus and Epicurus except that bodies may be both larger and smaller than atoms, and also that Hobbes seems to have been more aware of an observer making this description. Space is defined by him as a kind of beyondness in contrast to the mental processes of the observer.

But there is really another item in Hobbes' description of Nature; this is *time*. Because the movement of bodies in space gives us a "phantasm," a percept, or a mental image, of time. Time is one aspect of the experience we have when we see a body passing out of one space into another. It is the experience of *before* and *after* in motion. Between the *before* and *after* there is some kind of duration which is different from either space or motion.[18]

This attempt to represent the description of Nature offered by Hobbes is

[13] Cf. *ibid.*, Vol. I, p. 446.

[14] This way of defining what a body is constitutes a realistic tendency in Hobbes, because the very character of physical things is set down as being that they are beyond the mind of a knower and do not depend on a mind for existence. This particular theme will be enlarged fully in Part Four of this book.

[15] Cf. Thomas Hobbes, *op. cit.*, Vol. I, pp. 93–94.

[16] *Ibid.*, p. 70.

[17] Cf. *ibid.*, pp. 69–70, 115.

[18] Cf. *ibid.*, pp. 94–95.

a sample of the legitimate subject matter of philosophy as Hobbes defined
it. Philosophy for him was natural philosophy; it is properly concerned, he
held, with the properties of bodies.[19]

As already seen in the regard for the observer and the definition of space
by contrast with the inner mental processes of the observer, Hobbes evidently gave some attention to the knowledge problem. The most elemental
beginnings of knowledge he recognized as the sense impressions, or
"phantasms," as he called them, with which Nature makes its impact upon
us. There is a faculty which bodies have by which they work in us impressions of themselves. This he termed an "accident" or "the manner by
which any body is conceived."[20] Though it may seem to be a philosophical
nicety in these early pages of this book, the pivot question is this: What is
the direction of the movement in this process by which an object works in
us an impression of itself? We have already noted a realist tendency in
Hobbes,[21] and if the movement of knowledge is described by Hobbes as
from the object inward to the knower, this leaning is further confirmed. But
he conciliates instead between movement from the object to the knower
and movement from the knower to the object. He says that our "phantasms" of objects result from an "endeavor outwards in the organ of sense"
together with an "endeavor inwards from the object."[22] Once the impression is made on the sense organ the movement is unquestionably an inward
movement, a typical motion of bodies, one making an impact on another
successively, until the innermost part of the organism is reached.[23]

Our study of Hobbes began with his rather mechanical description of
that phase of Nature which is largely beyond man, though at the same time
it includes him. This is the point at which we find the greatest common
ground between Hobbes and the ancient naturalists. We have turned from
Nature beyond man to man himself, sufficiently at least to recognize a
knowledge problem. Here also we find common ground with Epicurus, who
described knowledge as a movement of atoms from the object inward
toward the mind of the knower. Now we must move even closer to man
and get a picture of Nature as Hobbes saw it in man. Is man free or
determined, and are his actions the result of causes in Nature? What kind
of animal is man, apart from the laws and inhibitions with which the State
surrounds him? How is the State as an institution rooted in the nature of
man? And what of religion and God? To what extent is the nature of God
and religion the legitimate subject matter of philosophy? How does man
come by his knowledge of God? These are further questions with which

[19] Cf. *ibid.*, p. 10.
[20] *Ibid.*, p. 103.
[21] Cf. Footnote 14, p. 57.
[22] Thomas Hobbes, *op. cit.*, p. 391.
[23] Cf. *ibid.*, pp. 66, 103, 390–391.

Hobbes deals, the answers to which will reveal in fuller line the character of his naturalism. They may also cause us to question whether he is rightly termed a naturalist in the light of his treatment of religion.

With regard to the freedom of man, Hobbes held to a rather sane, common-sense view which attempted to combine liberty in individual man with necessity in Nature. Within somewhat roomy limits, individual man was regarded as free; free will, he said, means that a man "finds no stop, in doing what he has the will, desire, or inclination to do."[24] Yet all of men's actions go on within a total framework of cause and effect, so efficient in operation that every act has its first cause in God. "Every act of man's will," he insists, "and every desire, and inclination proceedeth from some cause, and that from another cause, in a continual chain, whose first link is in the hand of God the first of all causes."[25] What may seem to be contradiction in this is explained away in part by citing examples of special types of seeming conflicts which are not contradictions at all. One example is that the captain of a ship will freely dump his cargo overboard if he is beset by a storm which he is fearful his ship will not weather. He is moved by fear but his act is nevertheless free. So Hobbes concludes that "fear and liberty are consistent."[26] Another apparent conflict is exemplified in inanimate Nature. Water runs downhill freely; but at the same time it is necessary for it to run downward. The conclusion of Hobbes: *"Liberty and necessity* are consistent."[27] He generalizes to the effect that Nature, taken all in all, were we able to see its operation from a total vantage point, would manifest "the *necessity* of all men's voluntary actions."[28] ☆

Even when under the dominance of a superior, most men, Hobbes says, think themselves much wiser than the man who is in power.[29] So when it is viewed for what it is apart from the control of political government, we need not expect Hobbes to give us a very flattering view of the human species. The native condition of man, as Hobbes sees him, is "war of everyone against everyone."[30] Individual man is continually in competition with all others, grasping for honor and dignity.[31] His chief joy is in comparing himself with other men and therefore he relishes "nothing but what is eminent."[32] It is best for him to be kept busy, or in an inferior position from which he will struggle for something better, because he is most troublesome when he is most at ease.[33] His hunger for power is such

[24] *Ibid.,* Vol. III, p. 197.
[25] *Ibid.,* p. 198.
[26] *Ibid.,* p. 197.
[27] *Loc. cit.*
[28] *Ibid.,* p. 198.
[29] Cf. *ibid.,* p. 156.
[30] *Ibid.,* p. 117.
[31] Cf. *ibid.,* p. 156.
[32] *Loc. cit.*
[33] Cf. *ibid.,* p. 157.

a restless unquenchable desire that it only eases at death.[34] Political organization is absolutely imperative in order for man to be saved from himself and to have any peace at all. Each individual must surrender his liberty to some form of government if there is to be any armistice at all in this unending warfare of man against man. There are three incentives to peace which appeal to man and which are therefore fundamental in the establishment and maintenance of the State. These are the fear of death, the desire to secure the necessaries of common living, and the hope of obtaining them by effort and industry.[35] If Hobbes correctly observed human nature, the higher animals can well be insulted that modern man has claimed them as ancestors. In this generation of wars, cold and hot, the humorous cartoons are not at all exaggerated which represent the lamentations of apes over the fact that man may be a blood relative—that is, if Hobbes is right.

It is certainly evident that without some kind of government in control, the condition of man is very unstable and his fortunes most uncertain. Reason appeals to every man that he *"ought to endeavor peace, as far as he has any hope of obtaining it."* But prudence also cautions *"when he cannot obtain it, that he may seek and use, all helps, and advantages of war."*[36] Hobbes finds in this fundamental law of reason in man the entering wedge by which orderly government inserts itself into human affairs and gains some degree of control. For from it is derived a principle from which the State has arisen as a social institution. It is this:

that a man be willing, when others are so too, as far forth, as for peace, and defense of himself he shall think it necessary, to lay down his right to all things; and be contended with so much liberty against other men, as he would allow other men against himself.[37]

For the only way to bring men into orderly relation with one another is for them "to confer all their power and strength upon one man, or upon one assembly of men."[38] Such a delegated authority is in a position to enact and execute laws by which some measure at least of order and justice can supplant the natural condition of man in which everyone is at war. But even then, tooth and claw must be the power behind the throne guaranteeing justice, because justice is exacted of men by a terror of punishment which is greater than the benefit they would gain by a breach of the law.[39] In this way "Leviathan," as Hobbes symbolized the commonwealth, is

[34] Cf. *ibid.*, pp. 85–86.
[35] Cf. *ibid.*, p. 116.
[36] *Ibid.*, p. 117.
[37] *Ibid.*, p. 118.
[38] *Ibid.*, p. 157.
[39] Cf. *ibid.*, p. 131.

constituted as "that *mortal god,* to which we owe under the *immortal God,* our peace and defence."[40]

Before leaving Thomas Hobbes, something must be said about his treatment of religion. He is not really equivocal, at one time saying one thing on this subject, and another time something else. But yet it is difficult to place him with regard to religious matters. And this is important; because to the extent that he was a theist, he was not a pure naturalist. First of all, his very definition of philosophy excluded religious considerations; for he went to great length to define philosophy as properly dealing with the properties of bodies. This necessarily limits the scope of philosophical inquiry to the realm of Nature; actually even further, to the realm of matter, bodies moving in space. Later in his first volume, the subject of which is the *Elements of Philosophy,* he tells us that he purposely passes over questions of the "infinite and eternal." His reasons for doing this are contentment with the doctrine taught by the Scriptures, and the miracles which confirm them, reliance upon the custom and reverence for the laws of his country.[41] He also states that questions of infinity and eternity are not possible to a finite inquirer; these are rather to be answered by those who are "lawfully authorized to order the worship of God."[42] In *Leviathan,* however, he argues that men cannot have concepts corresponding to such words as they use to designate the nature of God; the words *spirit* and *incorporeal* are examples.[43]

On the other hand, he urges inquisitiveness about cause and effect as a surer road to knowledge of the existence of God than a fear of the hereafter. For, he contended, if a man inquires into causes, he will be brought successively through a chain of related causes and effects to the point at which he will be forced to recognize God as the "eternal cause of all things."[44] This is evident in what has already been said about the liberty of man being harmonious with a perfectly efficient natural order in which everything proceeds by cause and effect, ultimately from the hand of God.

If Hobbes was sincere in his statements about religion and theology, and it seems likely that he was, we must conclude that he was not a pure naturalist. His philosophy, with the exception of these references to religion, was naturalistic, not only in content but in pattern. He rather simply and somewhat arbitrarily excluded religious matters as not being a legitimate part of the subject matter of philosophy.

[40] *Ibid.,* p. 158.
[41] Cf. *ibid.,* Vol. I, p. 414.
[42] *Ibid.,* p. 412.
[43] Cf. *ibid.,* Vol. III, pp. 96–97.
[44] *Ibid.,* p. 96.

C. JEAN JACQUES ROUSSEAU (1712–1778)

Some justification is required for the inclusion of Rousseau in this brief history of naturalism. As Rousseau took pains to make clear that he was a deist, he can not be classed as a naturalist because of his metaphysics. It is because of two other themes upon which he dwelt that he is sketched here. The first of these is his preference for the quietude of the simple life lived close to Nature, which he held in common with the ancient naturalists. The second is his revolt against society which caused him to glorify Nature and her ways in contradistinction to the ways of society. While his metaphysical beliefs were not naturalistic, his glorification of Nature has had the effect of promoting naturalism, particularly in politics and education.

Only a few months after his birth Rousseau's mother died, and he was left to the care of his father, who was an emotionally unstable watchmaker in Geneva. His formal schooling was comprised by a scant two years of conventional studies and a period of apprenticeship. But his father had books, many not good, although fortunately some of them were history books; and inadvertently the elder Rousseau taught Jean Jacques to read, so early that he could not later remember when it happened. We are told that the two of them sat up all night reading sentimental trash, but fortunately Jean Jacques' interests later turned to history. Becoming a vagabond when a young adolescent, Rousseau wandered through the beautiful Savoy county of France, and in northern Italy, and also spent some years of his life in Paris. At the beginning of his wanderings he exchanged the Calvinistic spirit of Geneva for Catholic influence, was indoctrinated in Turin and converted, but he later strayed from both Calvinism and Catholicism. For a time he became the lover of Madame de Warens, who had been instrumental in sending him to Turin. After being superseded by another lover, and while trying to make good in Paris as a musician, he took up with Thérèse le Vasseur, a stupid and coarse servant girl. Eventually they were married, but reversing the conventional order, children were born beforehand; and to the great amazement of those who have been students of Rousseau, he promptly placed each child, upon its birth, in a foundling institution. He became a student late in life, and it is remarkable that he succeeded in writing such history-making documents as *Émile,* a classic on education; and *The Social Contract,* an influential work in politics.

As is well evidenced by Rousseau's great books, he was capable of quite some intellectual achievement, though not a giant; yet he was predominantly a man of impulse and emotion. His writings did not spring from logic and astute intellectual analysis, as with Voltaire, for example; instead, they were outbursts of emotion, revolts against what is, and proclamations with a reformer's fire of what ought to be. He loved Plato and valued the

Republic as the single greatest work ever written on education. Yet he himself wanted to keep books and ideas away from children until adolescence. He was an impulsive egotist who thought every woman he met had fallen for him; indeed, he was a ladies' man and had many love affairs. But he was not a libertine; when he writes on sex education in *Émile*, he advocates silence until as late an age as possible. He hated the exhibitionism of French women which suggested ideas of sex to youth before their feelings had matured enough to give them an emotional understanding of sex. In contrast, he idolized the innocence of primitive life, in which he held maturation was slower because not stimulated by society, a sort of hothouse forcing by ideas alone. He tried to be a musician, without marked success; but his real genius turned out to be nonfiction writing. His talents were first diverted while on one of his journeys, in 1750, when he saw the announcement of the Academy of Dijon that there would be an essay contest on the subject, "Has the progress of the sciences and arts contributed to corrupt or to purify morals?" So strong was the impact which the announcement of this subject made upon him that he tells us he had to stop by the side of the road and weep for a half hour or more. When he had recovered enough to resume his journey, he says his shirt front was wet with his own tears. His sympathies were with the underdog, the poor, the lowly, the destitute. In all probability his first visit to Paris was one in which he approached the city as a weary foot traveler amazed at the anthills of slums in which masses of humanity were huddled together in poverty and filth. Yet when he wrote his *Émile,* he presented education on the pattern of the private tutor engaged by a wealthy family. With his tongue in his cheek he explains that he chose Émile from a wealthy family because the poor or peasant child, being close to Nature, would get an education anyway. He believed in the goodness of individual man, turning his back upon the doctrine of total depravity which must have made its impression upon him as a child in Geneva. But he was vehement in condemning the evil and corruption of human society. For him, collective man was as bad as individual man, springing from the hand of the Author of Nature, was good. Nature yields us all kinds of goods, but the society of man grasps them and perverts them to evil ends.

Rousseau followed in the tradition of the ancient naturalists in one important particular. This was their desire to remain aloof from the disquieting conflicts, ambitions, and struggles common to human society, and to find comparative quiescence in a simple life lived close to Nature. A good portion of Rousseau's life, particularly the years spent with Madame de Warens, was the existence of a dilettante and a romanticist. Being a part of a genteel household which was maintained by a pension, he was free to commune with Nature, work at his music, and quietly enjoy life generally. The intrigues of Parisian society, the gross artificialities of what was regarded in Paris as civilized and cultured living—these provided a disgusting contrast to a quiet life in the country where one could be close to Nature, even if he were a peasant.

In another important regard, Rousseau was definitely not a naturalist. This was in his religious belief. While he strayed from the Calvinistic and Catholic influences of his early life, never to return, he was by no means a pure naturalist. In a long section in the fourth book of *Émile*, designated "The Creed of a Savoyard Priest," he makes clear that he was a deist. He believed in God, and he believed in God as the Creator of Nature. But he did not think of God as having a present connection with Nature which makes living a warm personal affair of spirit meeting with spirit. Accordingly, he did not provide for direct religious instruction in his education of Émile; he was satisfied to give him a natural religion without carefully formulated creeds and dogmas. This is naturalistic for practical purposes, to the extent that Nature, and not God, is made the context of human living. But it is by no means a pure naturalism, since Rousseau affirmed the existence of God and thought of Nature as His creation.

This brings us to recognition of the original element in Rousseau's naturalism. This is that it was a revolt against the artificiality and corruption of human society. He glorified Nature, not as an eternal and indestructible order of atoms moving in space, as did the ancients. Instead, he exalted Nature as that ever-dependable order which is contrasted with human society in a variety of ways that make it far to be preferred. Nature is dependable; society is fickle. Nature is good; society is evil and crafty. Nature offers us freedom and necessity, if we live close to her; society offers us tyranny and authority. Nature has smooth-flowing rhythms which choose their own time; society is full of hurry and premature actions, prompted by the whims and ambitions of foolish people who do not know Nature.

D. HERBERT SPENCER (1820–1903)

Contrasted with Rousseau, Herbert Spencer was emotionally barren. His writings represent him as a kind of fact-collecting and fact-organizing machine; but his *Autobiography*[45] discloses more warmth of spirit. He was born of strong nonconformist stock, having some ancestors who were ardent followers of John Wesley and others who were adherents of the evangelical movement within the established church. His father, William George Spencer, was a schoolmaster for some time at Derby, the birthplace of Herbert. Nonconformity seems to have been the spirit of the Spencers in matters other than religion. Herbert says of his father, "He was a man

[45] Herbert Spencer, *An Autobiography*. Two volumes; London: Williams and Norgate, 1904.

guided by independent judgment rather than custom";[46] and this was certainly true of himself. He ran away in revolt when his father and mother took him to Hinton for a visit with his uncle and, according to a prearranged plan unknown to him, left him there for schooling. Although he condescended to return after showing up at home again in a few days, his remarkable tenacity was displayed in that when only thirteen years old he undertook and successfully completed a 115-mile journey with little money, almost nothing to eat, and virtually no sleep. He walked practically all the way, hitching only a few short rides. In addition to his tenacity he must have been of superior intelligence, for he was commonly impatient with his schoolmates because of their stupidity; though he could compensate for this if they were agreeable.

His first employment was as a construction engineer on the London and Birmingham Railway. He later turned to journalism, and finally to his own private writing. Beginning at the age of forty, thirty-three years of his life were spent continuously in writing his Synthetic Philosophy, comprised of separate volumes on metaphysics, biology, psychology, sociology, and ethics. This was an unusual accomplishment in itself; but in view of the fact that his health was poor and he could not keep at his work for more than an hour at a time, it was an exceedingly remarkable achievement. His means were modest, not at all adequate to sustain a man of leisure who makes writing an avocation. At one time financial reverses threatened discontinuance of his important work. John Stuart Mill, who was by no means an exponent of Spencer's ideas, offered to underwrite his work. This was declined for reasons of honor chiefly; but Edward L. Youmans, founder and editor of the *Popular Science Monthly* and a Spencer disciple in the United States, secured and invested in this country a large enough fund to guarantee the completion of Spencer's important publications.

The great work on education, *Education: Intellectual, Moral, and Physical*,[47] will be discussed fully in Chapter IV as an example of naturalism in education. At this point, therefore, attention will be limited to a representation of Spencer's naturalism as a general world view.

Although he used the word "force" to describe reality in his Synthetic Philosophy, Spencer held more exactly in his metaphysics that reality is unknowable. He spoke of it as a mystery, the "inscrutable," the "inexplicable," an "insoluble enigma," the "unthinkable." This agnosticism of his was something more than a dogmatic rejection of ultimate truth. By it he tried to describe our human situation with respect to the possibility of securing knowledge of Absolute Being. He did not deny that there is some kind of Being which persists as the foundation of all the phenomena we observe. And he spoke of this Being as Absolute. But he held that when the

---

[46] *Ibid.*, Vol. I, p. 64.
[47] New York: Hurst and Company, n.d.

human mind tries to push out its borders to contain a conception of this Absolute Being, it runs into inescapable conflicts and dilemmas which evidence the inconceivable and unthinkable character of Absolute Being. For example, space and time must be regarded as infinitely divisible. No matter how small a unit of either a person can imagine, it must still be possible that it can be divided further. This Spencer felt was inconceivable. But, on the other hand, it is also inconceivable, he held, to think of space and time as not being capable of infinite division. Similarly, existence without beginning or ending, or a time when space did not exist, Spencer said, are not in harmony with the patterns of human thinking. So the line of philosophizing which he proposed was not in the direction of disclosing the nature of ultimate reality.

What he proposed instead in his Synthetic Philosophy, was to describe all observable reality within one inclusive scheme which embraces all of the sciences. This inclusive scheme he found in the principles of evolution and dissolution.

In getting an understanding of these overall principles of his Synthetic Philosophy, we can start most easily by thinking about the genesis of our own bodies. There was a time, we all know, when each of us was one single cell, a fertilized ovum. We came to be what we are now by a process of growth and development, in which this single cell took in unrelated materials from the physical world, and organized and interrelated them into a multiplicity of cells and structures so as to constitute our bodies with all their maze of organs, parts, and functions. Oversimplified, this process is one by which the homogeneous is made heterogeneous; i.e., the raw stuff of physical being, throughout which there is much sameness in its unorganized form, is organized and particularized into diversified parts among which there is great difference and unlikeness. This is the homogeneous becoming heterogeneous; and the process is summed up in the one word "evolution."

But we all know that though we may now be in the prime of youth or adulthood, sometime this process begins to retrace itself and go into reverse. Health and vigor decline; age creeps up; sickness and disease may have more supremacy. In the natural course of decline, if not by other means, death comes to the physical body. After death, rapid physical disintegration sets in; and in due course all the materials gathered out of the physical world to make the body are lost again in the vast sameness from which they came, "earth to earth, ashes to ashes, dust to dust." This is the process of dissolution, the exact reverse of evolution, the heterogeneous disintegrating and becoming homogeneous again.

Dismal picture that this may be, it does represent quite particularly the way in which the principles of evolution and dissolution are at work in the biological realm. But it also represents, for Spencer, the whole realm of Nature. For millennia this combined process of evolution and dissolution has been going on, and the present state of diversification and organization in which the universe is now, is merely the present state of organization of the raw stuff from which the universe is formed. It will be succeeded by other stages, in an endless and virtually eternal process of growth and disintegration.

Within the context of this discussion it may now be possible to quote Spencer's famous definition of evolution with some hope of his dry aggregation of big words being understood. It is this:

> *Evolution is an integration of matter and concomitant dissipation of motion; during which the matter passes from an indefinite, incoherent homogeneity to a definite, coherent heterogeneity; and during which the retained motion undergoes a parallel transformation.*[48]

This is not only a description of biological processes; in general, the same pattern is the structure of the realms of psychology, sociology, and ethics. Each science describes an area of existence in which rise and development are constituted by organization and integration of heterogeneous and differentiated parts, and decay by the reverse of this process.

Underneath or behind all of this is ultimate homogeneous stuff out of which things evolve and to which they return. It is not far different from the ceaseless falling of atoms through space in which the ancient naturalists rooted their belief. Of course, Spencer tried to be explicit in saying that this Ultimate Being is unknowable. But in building the comprehensive system of his Synthetic Philosophy, he had to say something about its nature. And what he said was that it is force. He was not a materialist, as the ancient naturalists were, who regarded the atoms as constituting an abiding physical substance out of which all things are made. Instead, he was an *energist*, identifying this Ultimate Being as force or energy. This ultimate energy, unlike matter and motion, which are its results, is not perceivable. It is always behind perceived objects and events. Matter, as beheld in material objects, is perceivable. And motion, as seen in the movement of objects, is a fact of experience. Motion is also observable in our movements as we act upon objects. But the foundation of all of these is persistent and continuing force. We know matter by the pressure or resistance of force which material objects exert upon us. Motion also is pressure of force independent of any movement we initiate ourselves. Less observable than either matter or motion, it is nevertheless unmistakably evident as the continuing independent power in the world of Nature. "By the persistence of Force," Spencer says, "we really mean the persistence of some Power which transcends our knowledge and conception."[49]

[48] Herbert Spencer, *First Principles of a New System of Philosophy*. Second edition; New York: Appleton-Century-Crofts, 1896. P. 396.
[49] *Ibid.*, p. 189.

E. SYNTHESIS

By restating as propositions the four ideas which are most common to naturalism as it is represented in this brief history, we may be able to supply some unity to the sketch of the development of naturalism which has been attempted. After each proposition the men who subscribed to it will also be named. The four propositions are the following:

1. Nature is all the reality there is.—Leucippus, Democritus, Epicurus, Lucretius, and Spencer.

2. Reality is comprised of bodies moving in space.—Leucippus, Democritus, Epicurus, Lucretius, and Hobbes.

3. Ultimate reality is force or energy.—Spencer

4. The most acceptable life is possessed by keeping close to the simple and peaceful ways of Nature.—Leucippus, Democritus, Epicurus, Lucretius, and Rousseau.

III

A Systematic Synopsis of the Philosophy of Naturalism

A. The Metaphysics of Naturalism

    1. NAÏVE NATURALISM
        a. Materialism
        b. Energism

    2. CRITICAL NATURALISM
        a. Positivism
        b. Nature as Process
        c. An Elusive Philosophy

B. The Epistemology of Naturalism

    1. NAÏVE NATURALISM
    2. CRITICAL NATURALISM

C. The Logic of Naturalism

D. The Axiology of Naturalism

    1. ETHICAL VALUE
    2. AESTHETIC VALUE
    3. RELIGIOUS VALUE
    4. SOCIAL VALUE

Each of the four philosophies builds upon an attitude which is common and apparently well grounded in the mentality of most people. The common attitude on which naturalism builds is that there is order in Nature and that this order can be depended upon. It is expressed unphilosophically in the common saying, "let Nature take her course."

Because it builds on this common attitude, naturalism has a universal appeal. But the enlargement of an attitude into a philosophy of life means making it a total and all-inclusive mental framework into which all other ideas and principles fit, and to which they are subordinate. This chapter will attempt to outline the total outlook which results when the orderliness and dependability of Nature constitute the all-inclusive theme of a person's thinking.

The pattern of this synopsis will follow the same systematic scheme followed in the survey of the problems of philosophy in the Introduction. First the metaphysics of naturalism will be discussed, next the epistemology, then the logic, and finally the axiology of naturalism.

A. THE METAPHYSICS OF NATURALISM

In his book, *Present Philosophical Tendencies,* Ralph Barton Perry distinguished two kinds of naturalism; he called them naïve and critical naturalism.[1] Although this particular book was written more than sixty years ago, the distinction is still valid and helpful. Leaning upon it, we will attempt to explain what naturalism has said about the nature of reality.

1. NAÏVE NATURALISM

Naïve naturalism includes all attempts to designate some one *substance* as the be-all and end-all of Nature, and therefore of existence itself. Look back into the sketch of the history of naturalism in Chapter II and you will see how this search for some one substance characterizes Thales, Anaximenes, Anaximander, Leucippus, Democritus, Epicurus, Lucretius, and Spencer. In the ancient naturalists this substance was regarded as some kind of inert matter moving in space. Becuase of this they can be accurately named *materialists.* But Spencer's final substance was not solid matter; rather it was energy. Though he was a naïve naturalist, if placed in Perry's classification, he was not a materialist. He is therefore more accurately termed an *energist.* We have then two kinds of naïve naturalism.

a. Materialism. Ever since nuclear physics began to accumulate evidence, and emphatically since the atom bomb, it has been impossible to be a materialist in any strict sense except conceptually. There simply is no one physical substance, no inert matter, which is the least common denomina-

---

[1] New York: Longmans, Green & Co., 1912. Pp. 63–64.

tor of the universe. But matter itself breaks down and has a still smaller and more evasive denominator in energy.

Nevertheless, masses of people still have the mentality of Democritus, Epicurus, and Lucretius. Having little more than emotive responses to atom or hydrogen bombs and only vague understandings of the nuclear physics which bred these terror devices, their world view remains quite unchanged in the atomic age. In visible Nature, assumed to be the world ground, matter is still a kind of rock foundation on which all the structures of human experience stand.

b. Energism. But Herbert Spencer's kind of naïve naturalism is not so much out of keeping with the atomic age. Energy, as the one substance out of which the universe is made, still stands untouched by the exploration of the atom. In fact, the pseudophilosophic explanations current immediately following the first atom bomb explosions were explanations Herbert Spencer might have given before the turn of the twentieth century. "Here at last," the radio commentators then reported, "man has released the final substance out of which the universe is made."

But speculation can at least be made that sometime in the future, maybe far, maybe near, the successor to nuclear physics will make further discoveries which will unseat the energism of Spencer by scientific demonstration, just as materialism has now been unseated. The content of science has always been changing; why should we expect this change to stop with the release of atomic energy?

2. CRITICAL NATURALISM

At least since Auguste Comte, there have been naturalists who were not satisfied with the attempt to explain all things in terms of substance. For them the metaphysics of the naïve naturalists has been oversimple and lacking in refinement. Some other way of defining the naturalistic world view had to be found. One of these was the *positivism* of Auguste Comte.[2] Another has been the attempt to think of Nature in terms of process rather than either substance (naïve naturalism) or structure (positivism). These two kinds of critical naturalism can be made clearer by some further elaboration.

a. Positivism. We speak of the laws of Nature as commonly as we talk about matter or energy. The law of gravity is one of the Ten Command-

[2] Discussion of Auguste Comte is included in the history of pragmatism (Chapter XVIII) rather than in the history of naturalism. This placement is acknowledged as controversial, as well as being indicative of the overlapping between naturalism and pragmatism. Comte is discussed as a forerunner of pragmatism because of his rejection of reality as substance, also a major strain in Dewey, and because of his preoccupation with society in preference to physical Nature, another major theme in Dewey. Cf. pp. 361–365.

ments of Nature for the vast majority of us. Another which has comparable status is the law of cause and effect. We find a certain regularity and dependability in Nature which we have tried to describe by laws such as these. And this regularity and dependability suggest to us a system or structure comprising the natural order, a kind of vast machine whose precision makes possible the prediction of the movements of the stars.

To define Nature in this manner is to devote attention primarily to its form rather than to its substance. Instead of summing it up in terms of the stuff of which it is made, this approach notes the happenings in Nature, the way it acts, and the relations which stand between constituent parts or events. Observing the regularity and dependability of these events and relations, it is concluded that Nature is a system, an interrelated structure.

Of course, the various sciences provide the pathways of knowledge by which Nature is so observed. And because of this, *positivism* is perhaps more commonly defined as complete dependence upon science as the only avenue of knowledge. Shortly, we will discuss both kinds of critical naturalism being presented here as refinements in the world view which blend into realism or pragmatism. Later we will follow this development toward realism and pragmatism as still more pronounced in the realm of knowledge than in conceptions of reality. But at this point we are contented with what is intended to be a simple statement of positivism as a conception of reality. While it is a complete dependence on science as the way of knowledge, what it yields in content is a purely naturalistic world view according to which reality is a system of laws, events, and relationships, and in which substance, either as matter or energy, is not an abiding element.

b. Nature as Process.   A similar definition of Nature, which has even more in common with pragmatism, describes it as a process rather than a system. This form of critical naturalism rejects both the idea of substance and the idea of system. The idea of system is rejected because it leans too heavily on permanence in laws and relationships. Nature is more a process than a structure because, it is held, its laws and relationships are changing as well as its substance. There is a kind of unity in Nature; but it is not the closely knit unity of a machine. Rather it is a *continuity* which runs throughout all things natural.

Herbert W. Schneider, writing his chapter in *Naturalism and the Human Spirit*,[3] exemplifies this kind of critical naturalism in current form. After defining Nature negatively as neither a mechanical unity, on the one hand, nor a conglomeration of existences, on the other, he moves to an affirmative definition. Nature is a motherlike matrix in which all things normal

---

[3] Edited by Yervant H. Krikorian. New York: Columbia University Press, 1944. Pp. 121–134.

transpire and of which they are a part. By normal he does not mean the statistically central tendency discovered by studying a great number of cases. He insists that what is normal can be discovered by other means. "That is natural which works,"[4] he says. While there are many ways of getting out of order, there is only one way of functioning normally. All instances of abnormal functioning are accidents of Nature and are not an essential part of Nature. But all normally functioning mechanisms partake of the continuity of process which is the mother of mothers. This is the matrix in which all things have their beginning and end.

c. An Elusive Philosophy. By this time the reader will have observed that the more naïve the metaphysics of naturalism, the more easily and exactly described it is. As naturalism becomes more critical, it tends to evaporate and distill away into pragmatism or realism. The tendency toward pragmatism in more refined forms of naturalism has been quite evident. Positivism in its lack of interest in substance leans toward contemporary pragmatism. And critical naturalism which defines Nature as process rather than system is a metaphysics which is identical with the Dewey conception of reality.

The realistic tendency in critical naturalism is found only in positivism. The description of reality as a system of events, relations, and laws is quite in harmony with the metaphysics of realisms that are naturalistic. System, as such, reflects more unity than many realists, with their bent toward pluralism and discontinuity, will allow. But concentration of attention on the external events and relations of Nature is in harmony with the spirit of realism.

As the discussion of naturalism now moves into the area of epistemology, its elusive character will become all the more pronounced. In general, it can be said that the more epistemological naturalism becomes, the more it ceases to be a precise naturalism and the more it becomes realism or pragmatism, depending on the particular turn it takes in dealing with the problem of knowledge. Naturalism concerns itself primarily with metaphysics; consequently, its refinement on the epistemological side has yielded contemporary philosophies that are commonly regarded as successors which have completely usurped the place of naturalism as a philosophy.

B. THE EPISTEMOLOGY OF NATURALISM

Just what does naturalism have to say about our knowledge of the world? Naturalism is a distinct philosophy by virtue of its insistence that reality and Nature are identical, and that beyond Nature there is no reality.

---

[4] *Ibid.*, p. 126.

But how does naturalism come by this view of reality? How do naturalists certify their view of reality?

1. NAÏVE NATURALISM

These questions are more easily answered for the earlier naturalists than they are for the modern naturalists who may also be realists or pragmatists, because earlier naturalists were scarcely conscious of the knowledge problem. Somehow they became fascinated by their particular conceptions of the substance of which all existing things were supposedly made, without cross-examining themselves as to how their theory of reality was known to be true.

As has been reported,[5] Epicurus penetrated the surface of this problem a little bit by an ingenious explanation of sense perception, and Lucretius incorporated the theory in his *De Rerum Natura*. This was a kind of photographic reconstruction of sensation, according to which objects yield replicas of themselves in the mind of the beholder. But none of these replicas is precisely analogous to the film of the camera, for, more than being a copy of the object, it is comprised of actual atoms which come from the object itself. These atoms somehow move from the object, through sensory channels, and thence into the mind. Thomas Hobbes, in a much less fantastic treatment,[6] explained sensory knowledge similarly, however, in terms of motion. Objects, he said, just have a tendency to project themselves inward through the senses, and the organs of sensation just have a tendency to endeavor outward toward objects.

To generalize, we may say that naturalists who are more naïve, in that they think of reality as physical substance, whether matter or energy, deal with the knowledge process, to the extent that they deal with it, as an instance of motion. Something in the object moves toward the knowing subject by a physical impulse of some sort, and inward by way of the organs of sensation and nerve pathways, and eventually makes its impact on the knower. In general, this is the way we come by our knowledge of the world about us, according to naïve naturalism.

2. CRITICAL NATURALISM

But modern naturalism is far more critical than this. The ancient Greek physicists who propounded the atomic theory were forerunners of physical science more than philosophy. And although their successors in modern naturalistic philosophy have foresaken their oversimple metaphysics, they make the claim in one way or another that science provides a method which is the only dependable method of knowledge. Some examples of this may be noted before making generalizations about the realist and prag-

[5] Cf. pp. 51–53.
[6] Cf. pp. 55–61.

matist variations on the uses of scientific method as modern forms of naturalistic epistemology.

Francis Bacon,[7] in the late sixteenth and early seventeenth centuries, developed what he regarded as a new organ of knowledge in proposing that deductive method be replaced by inductive method. Men in centuries past had spent too much time, he held, in reorganizing what they thought they already knew. What was needed, instead of this, was direct observation of Nature, in which the observer is face to face with the facts of existence. By seeing Nature as it is, piece by piece, in specific observations, and by accumulating observations one by one, man could build up a knowledge of his world, Bacon held, which would be far more dependable and more useful than knowledge deduced from generalities. He went further, in his *New Atlantis,* to propose this accumulation of inductive knowledge on a wide social scale. Induction was not to be only an individual method of knowledge which each person would use in isolation. It was to be a cooperative social effort in which society would accumulate scientific knowledge by large-scale deliberate plans, different individuals and groups having respective assignments, but each of which would be related to the overall social plan.

Auguste Comte,[8] in the early nineteenth century, became the father of positivism by contending that the scientific attitude is the highest level of intellectual insight. For by investigating reality by means of the exact sciences, he held that laws and relations are disclosed which comprise as accurate a description of existence as is possible. In working out a system of relationships among the sciences, he made mathematics the basis of all, classed astronomy, physics, and chemistry as inorganic sciences, and designated physiology and sociology as organic sciences. He further explained the relations between the sciences as forming a hierarchy; mathematics being the broad base of the pyramid, the inorganic sciences comprising a good portion of the solid superstructure, and sociology being at the very peak of the pyramid. The full range of sociology, according to this system, cannot be appreciated unless one is grounded in the knowledge yielded by the other prerequisite sciences which are foundational to it.

Herbert Spencer,[9] later in the nineteenth century, and two and one half centuries after Bacon, attempted a compendium of knowledge in the volumes of his Synthetic Philosophy. Having a great fondness for factual data, he accumulated great collections of scientific information of many sorts. He was not content, however, with mere mass of accumulation, but organized his data within overarching theories, the largest and most inclusive of which was the theory of evolution. His Synthetic Philosophy was an at-

[7] Cf. pp. 358–361.
[8] Cf. pp. 361–365.
[9] Cf. pp. 64–67.

tempt to put together in one piece the knowledge of all observable reality. In Bacon, Comte, and Spencer, the rise of the modern scientific spirit is represented; and implicit in this is the principle of knowledge that scientific method is the only method of knowledge, although in Bacon the emphasis on science was probably less exclusive of other methods than in Comte and Spencer.

By and large, all three men have one thing in common with realism which modern pragmatism rejects. They all thought of science as yielding items of knowledge which comprise a dependable fund of scientific information. Comte was probably the least naïve about this; he held that the scientific level of insight was superior to the theological and metaphysical because it recognized no substantial abiding element in reality. What science reveals is laws and relations, not substance. Neither Bacon nor Spencer was as leery of substance; Spencer's atomistic theory was actually very close to the theory of Democritus and Epicurus. As Bacon and Spencer accumulated facts by observation, they were collecting real facts, to all intents and purposes. And the accumulation of knowledge which they proposed to build up was to be an abiding fund of knowledge which could be depended upon not to change. Comte was equally confident about the laws and relations revealed by scientific inquiry. These, though not substances, were considered to be abiding structures which could be depended upon to endure.

This confidence in abiding, objective, and external realities which, like the pyramids, stand unaffected by the passing processions, whether of time or inquisitive minds, is the prime confidence of realism. And when the development of naturalism is seen as passing from a naïve materialism and an equally naïve treatment of knowledge as movement of atoms, among ancient thinkers, to a critical metaphysics of laws and relationships, in modern thinkers, and an epistemology which may be summed up as exclusive confidence in science as the revealer of unchanging, objective, external realities—when this development of naturalism is observed, then it becomes explicitly clear that realism is the child of naturalism.

The relation between naturalism and pragmatism is not as intimate, although many modern realists and all contemporary pragmatists may be lumped together as naturalists because they all rely exclusively on science as the one and only method of knowledge. But pragmatists are more critical than realists because they neither accept a metaphysics of substance nor an unchanging structure of laws and relations. Science is the only method of knowledge, not so much because it discloses items of information needed in acting intelligently (although this much is true as long as information is understood as not being truth in any ultimate sense), but because *it is a way of acting intelligently,* also. Science discloses the data of any given situation when applied to it, whether it is individual in a limited sense or vastly social; but science is also a guide to action which opens the way to the resolution of problematic situations, and enables us to exercise control over our circumstances. Here is a theory of knowledge which is far removed from naïve naturalism; although a variation on the major theme, it is still total and implicit confidence in science. The external and unchanging realities of the realist, whether substance or laws and relations, do not provide the frame of reference. Science, as both a means of deriving data and a way of using data for effective action, is itself the frame of reference, the context of all living.

C. THE LOGIC OF NATURALISM

Considered most inclusively, the logic of naturalism, as anticipated by the foregoing discussion of its epistemology, is the logic of science. From Democritus to the pragmatists and naturalistic realists of today, the effect of naturalism, amidst all of its variety, has been to promote science as the method of securing dependable knowledge. The way of knowledge it has preferred to the inward look toward the things of the spirit, or the appeal to authority, has been to direct the senses outward toward Nature.

There are two general observations to be made concerning the logic of naturalism which will help to describe the setting for its more specific discussion. The first is that, most generally considered, formal deductive logic such as was mentioned briefly in the Introduction[10] has a minor place in the methods of logic approved by naturalism. For the preponderance of attention is given to extending the methods of logic beyond formal deductive patterns in order to get at the actualities of Nature.

The second observation is that there is great variation in the methods of logic employed by naturalists. The logic of the earlier and more naïve naturalism is the simple material logic of induction. In modern naturalism, if the epistemology is realistic, greater place is given to deductive logic because of the confidence placed in the independence of relations by realists.[11] If the epistemology is pragmatic, on the other hand, sheer induction is virtually replaced by a more fluid problem-solving technique in which the formulation and testing of hypotheses lessens the necessity for extended induction. Because of this, the realistic refinement of the logic of naturalism will be discussed in the systematic synopsis of realism. And the pragmatic refinement of the logic of naturalism will be discussed as a part of the systematic synopsis of pragmatism.[12]

---

[10] Cf. pp. 27–28.

[11] Logical positivism, an expression of realistic epistemology in a new logic, makes critical use of both induction and deduction and goes beyond them to a language of mathematical and near-mathematical symbols in an attempt at precision and exactness in making meanings explicit.

[12] Cf. pp. 283–285 and 388–394.

This narrows the task of the present discussion to a consideration of simple induction as the logic of naturalism. Of course, the kind of naturalism referred to is more especially the earlier naturalism such as inspired the first steps in the development of scientific method. In its most elementary form, induction is the accumulation of accurate and detailed information by direct relation with Nature. Whereas the formal logic of deduction deals with the *forms* by which propositions are dependably tied together; induction is the collecting of the material on which propositions must be based if they are to be true propositions. Syllogisms may do well in relating propositions correctly; but their value depends almost entirely upon the material truth of their propositions. Does the major premise describe a fact about a class of individuals in Nature? And does the minor premise assert what is fact concerning one individual in that class? On the answers to these questions the whole value of the syllogism rests. How could men ever have come to the conclusion "All men are mortal" without having observed a great number of people and having recognized that their lives were all terminated by death? And to do this is to follow inductive method.

Simple induction involves careful observation of Nature, accurate description of what is observed, and caution in formulating generalizations. The way in which to get acquainted with Nature as it actually is, is to go directly to Nature and see what is there. This means painstaking observation in which there is a rigorous piety ruling out everything but simple recognition of facts. In order to accumulate facts for later use in large masses, or in groups or classes, or for use by others than those making the direct observations, it is necessary to record what is observed, and to do it carefully and accurately, representing the facts only as they are. True enough, one of the chief values of observing and collecting facts is the discovery of generalizations about Nature; but in this stage of induction there must be much caution. It is so easy for wishful thinking or preconceived ideas to influence the handling of the facts. Francis Bacon, the father of inductive method,[13] even advised caution about hypotheses; he regarded them as "anticipations of Nature." Here too, in forming conclusions, as well as in observing the facts and recording them, there must be rigorous natural piety. There must be careful and patient accumulation of the facts until the conclusion almost seems to suggest itself as the only generalization to which the facts could possibly point.

D. THE AXIOLOGY OF NATURALISM

Even a synopsis of the naturalist world view cannot be complete without some consideration of its theory of value. For, as is evident in the sketch of the development of naturalism presented in the preceding chapter, natural-

[13] Cf. pp. 358–361.

ists are concerned with life's values. In fact, modern naturalists of both realist and pragmatist loyalties have given much attention to the study of problems of value.

The present discussion will consider more simply and more generally the naturalistic approach to the character of value and the naturalistic treatment of some important kinds of value. Presentation of the more precise analysis of values made by realists and pragmatists will be reserved for Parts Four and Five of the book respectively. Before taking up the naturalistic approach to ethical, aesthetic, religious, and social values, an attempt will be made to enunciate two general principles in the axiology of naturalism.

The first principle has to do with the general character of values. It is that Nature is the kind of order that just simply possesses values. According to naturalism, the values which people commonly enjoy, as well as others yet to be possessed, are resident in Nature; they do not transcend Nature by being rooted in an order which is above or different from Nature. Stated from a frame of reference other than the natural versus the supernatural source of values, this principle also means that Nature has a qualitative aspect as well as an existence aspect; and when we experience the qualitative elements in Nature, we are experiencing its values. Nature is not just a machine in the sense that it merely functions, and also in the sense that man, being a part of Nature, therefore functions within it as a cog in a machine. Nature is more than a machine in that there are overtones of enjoyment and suffering which go along with this functioning; and these overtones are qualitative, they are values which are enjoyed or endured, as the case may be, concomitantly as the functioning goes on.

The second principle has to do with the way in which the most desirable values are to be realized, according to naturalism. This principle is that the way in which an individual can get the most value out of life is to harmonize his life as closely as possible with Nature. This principle was foremost, it will be recalled, in the thinking of Democritus, Epicurus, and Lucretius. All of these men shared in common the desire to find a life which was as free as possible from pain and suffering. And accordingly they tried to harmonize their lives as closely as possible with the rhythms of Nature, because in this harmony they felt was their greatest peace.

1. ETHICAL VALUE

It is probably fair to say that the ethics of naturalism is hedonistic, as long as this characterization is accompanied by the caution that in the conscious thought at least of many naturalists the highest good is the most highly refined and abiding pleasure.

Pleasure is easily discerned as the highest good in the thought of the ancient naturalists. It is not hard to feel what they must have felt when they desired quietude and freedom from struggle, pain, and fear as the predominant inner possessions continuing uninterrupted through as many of their experiences as possible. Most of us share their desire for this same peace and happiness, although we may not make it such a supreme value that we will sacrifice all other possible values for it. The important thing to note about this highest moral good, first of all, is that it is a thing to be enjoyed; it is something, more on the feeling side of experience, which the person who possesses it undergoes and enjoys as contentment or satisfaction. In contrast with this, there are others, not hedonists, who define the highest good, not in terms of pleasure, although indeed it may be accompanied by pleasure or contentment, but in terms of virtue or sacrificial service, for example. Though pleasure and contentment may accompany the virtue or sacrifice, they are not the basis of choosing either of these values. The virtue or self-sacrifice is so important as the highest good that it is valued even if there is no pleasure or contentment accompanying it, and consciously embraced at times when it is certain that one's lot will be anguish and suffering instead. To a person so framing his conception of moral values, the pleasure ethics of naturalism may seem weak and selfish, because private enjoyment, even though it may be in no way contrary to convention, is placed prior to all other considerations.

While the highest good for naturalists is pleasure, it is important to make clear, in the second place, that many naturalists think of pleasure in the most refined and unoffensive forms when they speak of it as their highest good. George Santayana has written pointedly on this subject in a chapter entitled, "Moral Adequacy of Naturalism." In answer to the common assumption that naturalism necessarily means coarseness in morality, he says: "Why is naturalism supposed to be favourable to the lower sides of human nature? Are not the higher sides just as natural? . . . I think that pure reason in the naturalist may attain, without subterfuge, all the spiritual insights which supernaturalism goes so far out of the way to inspire."[14] Abraham Edel, in his chapter in *Naturalism and the Human Spirit* which deals with naturalistic ethical theory, argues that the act of choosing may be more basic than the reasons which are given for the choice, and that instead of a line of action being chosen because it gives pleasure, the test of a person's being pleased by a given line of action is that he prefers it and continues to choose it. This analysis identifies pleasure so closely with whatever it is that prompts any decision that all choices of value would seem to stem from preferences which are based on pleasure.[15]

[14] George Santayana, *The Genteel Tradition at Bay*. New York: Charles Scribner's Sons, 1931. Pp. 63–64.

[15] Cf. "Naturalism and Ethical Theory," Chapter IV in Yervant H. Krikorian, *op. cit.*, p. 69.

This may raise questions about the evil which is the counterpart of this highest good. How is it conceived by naturalism? Since it is something to be avoided, if not escaped, as we manage our daily life and action, evil would seem to be a quality or kind of experience which is inflicted upon us. Much less is it a quality of events in which we ourselves participate or of which we are causes. Evil is a fact of Nature. There just is evil in the cosmos, in the same way that there simply is good in it. The ways by which we may seek the good, this quiescent freedom from anguish, are considerably more restricted than the ways of living by which evil overtakes us. Otherwise it would not be necessary to give the attention we do to the quest for the good life. There are all kinds of ways in which accidents can happen; but there is virtually only one way, certainly not more than a few ways, of being careful to avoid the accidents of life and possess the unbroken life of peace. And this is rarely possible.

The moral accidents of Nature have commonly been given the name *physical evil*. They are many and well known: earthquake, famine, hurricane, disease, pestilence, etc. Clearly, these are evils of Nature; man has nothing to do with producing them, although he may tolerate conditions which, if corrected, would lessen some of their effects. There are also evils, more clearly moral, which men inflict on one another. War with its inflicted death and destruction is a notable example. Today man has this evil stored up in concentrated form; one atom bomb, or even worse one hydrogen bomb, can telescope years of previous warfare, if not generations, into one instant of time. Such evils, although they are man-made, still appear, because of their massive proportions, to be inflicted evils. It is not so clear that as individuals we participate in producing them. Our chief concern is to avoid them and their effects. Nor is it clear, within the naturalistic perspective, whether individual man is involved in evil in such a way as to make it difficult for him to do good or achieve it. Seeking the good is difficult enough with all of the possible hazards placed in the way by Nature and by human nature in the mass. Does this difficulty need to be compounded further by the acknowledgment that individual man, even when desiring the good, actually inflicts evil on his neighbor? And does the human individual so misconstrue his own intentions that he even involves his own self in evil when he thinks he is intending good? With only great reluctance does naturalism answer either of these questions in the affirmative; the more common answer is "No."

What needs to be noted generally about these various evils, as conceived by naturalism, is that they are qualities and events of the natural order and not the work of some evil force beyond Nature. Evil, though unwanted, is a natural phenomenon.

To summarize, we may say then that for naturalism pleasure is the highest good and therefore the basis of moral judgments; but this pleasure

is very subtle and highly refined for many naturalists. To the extent that a
person is consciously naturalistic in his ethics, he will make his day-by-day
moral choices so as to claim for himself the fullest measure of abiding
pleasure and satisfaction. The evil which it is hoped will be avoided in this
way is purely a product of Nature. It is largely inflicted evil, toward which
the attitude of individual man is rightly passive avoidance. Although men
in the mass certainly inflict large-scale social evils on other men, it is not
necessarily so that individual man unwittingly becomes a cause of evil to
his neighbor and to himself.

2. AESTHETIC VALUE

The chapter on aesthetics in *Naturalism and the Human Spirit* is contributed by Eliseo Vivas and is entitled "A Natural History of the Aesthetic
Transaction." In it a helpful description is given of aesthetic experience,
distinguishing it from other kinds of experience, and a case is made for its
purely natural character. The way to an understanding of naturalism's
approach to aesthetic value may at least be opened by an outline of this
description which also makes explicit some of the ways in which aesthetic
values are conceived as purely natural.

There are two words whose meanings when contrasted may serve to
illustrate the character of aesthetic experience as analyzed by Dr. Vivas.
These are the words "centrifugal" and "centripetal." The first word, "centrifugal," is used to describe any kind of motion which pulls objects away
from the center around which the motion may whirl or radiate. In contrast
with this, the word "centripetal" denotes any kind of motion which draws
objects toward the center around which it radiates. To apply the figure
supplied by these two words, it may be said that most of our experiences
are better characterized as centrifugal because they tend to radiate away
from the momentary center about which they have formed, and they tend
to relate themselves to other experiences. According to Dr. Vivas, they are
referential in character because they refer away from themselves to other
events and connections. The chief distinction of aesthetic experiences, he
argues, is that they are centripetal in character. They focus singly about the
object which is the occasion of the aesthetic transaction, and draw all
significances toward that center. This does not mean that aesthetic experiences are isolated from other experiences and sharply separated from them
by having no connections which relate them. In fact, the richness of
aesthetic experiences will depend to some degree on the ability to draw
meanings from other experiences and focus them upon the object of
aesthetic enjoyment. It is the character of aesthetic happenings that they are
not dissipated by being dispersed throughout a diverse number of connections with other experiences. Instead they draw significances from other
experiences and center them in their object. Any object which so arrests us

as to draw meanings to itself and enwrap us in attention centered upon itself can engage us aesthetically.

For naturalists, as could be surmised, aesthetic experience and the values it yields are both purely natural in character and do not involve any spiritual or supernatural factors. First of all, according to naturalism, the subject who is engaged by aesthetic experience is a child of Nature. While it takes a high degree of development to yield the kind of complex nervous system which can communicate with words and other symbols, and retain meanings long enough to interrelate them in such a way as to yield aesthetic enjoyment of an object, yet that is what Nature has yielded in man. "A pattern of responses of high complexity of co-ordination is possible," Vivas says, "because in the process of evolutionary development a nervous system, highly centralized, came into being."[16] Man, the subject who has aesthetic experiences, is a sentient organism developed by Nature, which is capable of centering his meanings in such a way as to experience aesthetic values. These values, therefore, do not transcend Nature; they are events in the experience of this highly developed organism which is the result alone of evolutionary processes at work in Nature.

There is also a minor sense in which aesthetic values are natural. This is that they are not superior values which only a few select people are capable of enjoying. They are values which touch areas where we all live; they are natural because they are "native in the ordinary experience of all men."[17]

Returning to the major sense in which aesthetic values are regarded as purely natural, two further elaborations may be made. The first is that the essential nature of aesthetic value does not depend upon the relating of a given object of enjoyment to some universal truth or principle. The object does not become a vehicle for expressing something beyond or greater than itself; it is simply the focus of meanings at the time it is beheld. And this is tantamount to saying, in the second place, that the aesthetic experience is not an experience of truth. It may involve the centering of intellectual meanings, and even moral meanings, in the object; but the object does not become the vehicle for expressing any all-embracing truth. Whatever truth is involved, Vivas says, is not of spiritual or supernatural import, but just "the ordinary garden variety of truth, empirical truth, the only truth there is."[18]

3. RELIGIOUS VALUE

As will be made quite clear in Chapter V on naturalism in religion, religious value for naturalists is almost synonymous with value realization as such. The religious life for naturalism is the kind of life which is so lived

16 *Ibid.*, p. 102.
17 *Ibid.*, p. 108.
18 *Ibid.*, p. 118.

in the breach between present actual fact and future possible value as to replace circumstances which destroy value with circumstances which possess and conserve value. It is not possible, therefore, to enumerate or more specifically characterize some values and designate them as the religious values of naturalism. The chief religious value of naturalism is that aspect of Nature which makes it possible to realize values and which sustains values which are worthwhile. Since all other possible values stem from this element in Nature, it is the most worthful object that there is and the greatest value above all others. The most significant life that can be lived is the life which is committed to the achieving of values in one's own life and in the world. So that the prime imperative of a naturalistic religion is that its adherents ally themselves with the value-realizing force in Nature and help to bring into existence values which are not actual in the present.

4. SOCIAL VALUE

One of the ways in which naturalism and pragmatism can be distinguished is that for pragmatism, human society is much more commonly the context in which concepts are forced than is the case in naturalism. For the earlier and more naïve naturalism at least, the more common context is the physical universe. Man and his society, in naturalism, are most commonly secondary to and dependent upon the natural order. Pragmatism has a much more alert social consciousness; and although man and his society are by no means considered independent of physical Nature, yet society is much more in the foreground of thought than is the case with naturalism.

Society is therefore considered less organic in naturalism than in pragmatism, as well as in idealism. It is an aspect or portion of Nature, not so much an organism that has rhythms and patterns which, while not contrary to or above Nature, are yet its own rhythms and patterns. Individual man is therefore considered as Nature's offspring, not a child of society or a segment of society whose very being depends upon the social organism. Although dependent upon Nature, he stands on his own feet, more or less, as far as his relations to society are concerned. There are what might be called certain necessities which make it expedient for him to relate himself somewhat effectively socially; but these are not necessities arising from the operation of society as an organism, so much as they are accidents or exigencies to be avoided by working out some kind of social organization to correct them.

As has been explained earlier,[19] Thomas Hobbes viewed individual man in his native state as at war with himself. He is competitive, he grasps for honor and dignity, he is troublesome, and he is hungry for power. Individual men left to themselves without some kind of control will kill themselves

[19] Cf. pp. 59–60.

in the chaos and anarchy of selfish struggle. The only way that man can be saved from himself sociologically is for individual man to surrender his freedom to some superior social power or organization to which he must give absolute obedience as to a mortal god.

Similarly, Rousseau's naturalism rooted man in Nature rather than society. So much did he regard man as a child of Nature, as over against society, that he proposed in his *Émile*[20] to keep Émile away from society until adolescence. In his *Social Contract*[21] he reveals how the problem of social organization is complicated by the importance of the freedom of man. Individual man, he contended, is not a man unless he is free; if he is in bondage, he is less than a man. Yet unbridled freedom is neither in harmony with his own welfare nor the welfare of society. Evidently some social organization is needed, but one which preserves for man his freedom. This is a rather big order, but one which can be filled rather satisfactorily by democracy. For in democracy, although individual man sacrifices his own individual freedom to obey the will of the State, he preserves his freedom by participating in the decisions which determine what the will of the State is to be.

It would seem that for naturalism social values are synthetic values which result from agreements in which individual men bind themselves together. They are secondary goods, not so much preferred as individual goods, which result indirectly as a consequence of the desire to avoid the greater evils which accompany anarchy. They are not organic values which are determined in part by the very nature of society and which would never be possessed by individual men separately, even if they did not need to be saved from conflict and chaos by some kind of social organization.

Having completed both a brief sketch of the history of naturalism and a systematic synopsis of the philosophy, attention is now invited to two important areas of practice in which naturalism can be seen at work. The two chapters which follow are devoted to the presentation of naturalism, first as a philosophy of education, and then as a philosophy of religion.

[20] See Everyman's Library Edition. Translated by Barbara Foxley; New York: E. P. Dutton & Co., 1938.
[21] See the Gerard Hopkins translation in *Social Contract: Essays by Locke, Hume, and Rousseau.* New York and London: Oxford University Press, 1949. Pp. 169–307.

IV

Naturalism in Education

A. Education as a Social Institution

B. The Pupil

C. The Objectives of Education

D. The Educative Process

There is not a great wealth of literature dealing specifically with naturalism in education, even though naturalism is still commonly practiced in education. This is understandable when it is kept in mind that both realism and pragmatism frequently meet naturalism on common ground. As has already been argued, naturalism is concerned primarily with metaphysics; and when its ramifications are defined, the result, particularly in epistemology, is a deflection into realism or pragmatism. The important symposium on naturalism, already cited a number of times, *Naturalism and the Human Spirit,*[1] epitomizes both of the circumstances here described. Whereas there are chapters in this book on a variety of areas in which naturalism operates—on religion, democracy, ethics, aesthetics, history, sociology, and logic—there is no chapter devoted to education. And the definitions of naturalism are highly divergent. John Dewey, the world's leading pragmatist, contributes the opening chapter, and the book is dedicated to Morris Cohen, a noted realist who has frequently been a critic of Dewey.

[1] Yervant H. Krikorian (editor), *Naturalism and the Human Spirit.* New York: Columbia University Press, 1944.

We are forced by these circumstances to turn back a few years to get a full statement of the naturalistic approach to education. The late Herman Harrell Horne, not long before his death, once remarked to the writer that Herbert Spencer's *Education: Intellectual, Moral, and Physical*[2] is the most recent major work dealing with this subject. In this chapter we will follow the lead given us by Professor Horne and largely base our discussion of naturalism in education on Spencer's famous four essays comprising the book just mentioned.

A. EDUCATION AS A SOCIAL INSTITUTION

It would not be at all surprising if a student were to jump to the inference that naturalism has no rationale for the existence of the school. After all, it has great confidence in Nature and less confidence in human society. This is especially true of the earlier naturalism and is measurably true of modern naturalists who have not taken up the social emphasis given such a boost in our century by John Dewey. In both there is very frequent reference to the guidance which is to be gained for education by following the ways of Nature as evidenced in growth and in the impromptu activities of children. Why have a school at all, if Nature is so important? Maybe it would be better for Nature to take her course in matters of learning, as we permit her to do in prenatal development, in many matters of health, in a good portion of farming, and as some would contend we should do in economics. If naturalism is true, then it may follow that mothers and/or fathers are the natural teachers, and there is no firm basis for adding to institutions, as we have done, making education a specialized function to be fulfilled in a formal agency of society.

But even so this is not the approach naturalists have taken to the formalizing or institutionalizing of education. Herbert Spencer was not unique in finding that the school has a basis for existence in Nature. Learning is a very natural thing, and the fact that the need for it evokes teaching activities from adults is also truly natural. The chief phenomenon on which the need for the school is based is the overlong infancy of man requiring sustained protection and guidance, almost throughout two decades.

In his rate and manner of maturation, man is a greatly retarded creature as compared to other animals. Most of the latter walk within hours of their birth. In a matter of weeks they can fend for themselves. And in a year or two at the most, with very few exceptions, they are completely mature, in most cases already bearing their own young. When they are born they are almost ready-made, not only in completeness of physical equipment but also with mechanisms of behavior all ready to function. But the human

[2] This work first appeared in 1861. The edition to which references are made in this chapter was published by Hurst and Company, New York. No date is given.

infant is a slow individual. He has trouble focusing his eyes. It takes him months to get ready to walk. He learns to talk even more slowly. And he usually is not on his own until well into his adolescent years and commonly even later than this. It is not uncommon that he outgrows his dependence with great difficulty.

But this long infancy of dependence is natural for man; therefore learning is natural for him. Furthermore, while man does not have the ready-made equipment of animals at birth, his lack of this equipment is a strength rather than a weakness, as long as he is sheltered in his early weakness and guided as his slow maturation proceeds to fulfillment. In being without set instinctive patterns of behavior, man has a potential for greater things, and a plasticity in relation to formation of behavior patterns which makes possible breadth and richness of achievements far beyond those of the animals. It is this important dimension of the nature of man which not only makes education possible but requires it as an urgent necessity. And as such, the educational institution is a natural necessity, not an unwarranted creation of man superimposed upon Nature.

B. THE PUPIL

One of the clichés which has been current in education for some time is to the effect that "teachers do not teach subjects, they teach pupils." Whatever this slogan may convey in meaning, it does direct attention to the importance of the pupil, the person being taught, the educand. Though philosophies do not agree as to the importance of the pupil, and certainly not in understanding his essential nature, he is sufficiently central that one task of each of the education chapters in this book is to understand the learner as each of the respective philosophies understands him. The specific task of the second portion of this chapter is to find out what the naturalistic educator thinks of the pupil. What is the picture he gives us of the living raw material with which education works?

The pupil is to the teacher what man is to the philosopher. For man who is interpreted by the philosopher also has various practical engagements, one of which is being a pupil at school in his formative years, maybe a student in institutions of advanced learning during his more mature years, and we hope a learner throughout life. If a philosopher is also a teacher and at the same time is consistent in both thought and practice, he will view man as a pupil in the classroom in the same way he thinks of him when philosophizing. So the doctrine of the pupil is virtually the doctrine of man in the classroom.

It will not do, of course, no matter what our philosophy, to have an armchair conception of the pupil. So as we build this conception we must keep our feet firmly planted in the classroom. For the student of education not yet in service, school visits, practice teaching sessions, courses in educational psychology and sociology, and direct relations with elementary and secondary school students will be valuable preparation for formulating a doctrine of the pupil.

The following statement of the Educational Policies Commission reminds us of the down-to-earth setting in which the pupil is always found, and therefore the kind of setting needed for building a conception of the pupil which ties in with hard facts:

> In classrooms, day by day, thousands of teachers come into contact with children of all sorts and conditions, races and nationalities, religious and ethical backgrounds. From homes of every kind—those broken by disputes of parents, wracked by the uncertainties and distresses of poverty and unemployment, no less than those tranquil in management and supplied by the means of material well-being. From homes poor in spirit, devoid of art, without books, without interest in things above the routine of living and the babble of gossip, thin in culture, perhaps tinged with crime, beset by distempers of mind, no less than from the homes that represent the best in American life.[3]

The naturalist, as Herbert Spencer represents him, first regards the pupil from the physical side. For the child is at the least a little animal, whatever else he may be. He has a body, or, to be more accurate, he is a body, and one of his first requirements therefore is that he be healthy, a vigorous animal, able to stand the wear and tear of living.[4]

Little animal that he is, he is far different from other creatures of the natural world in at least one particular which is significant for education. This is that, compared to other animals, his infancy is a long one. Whereas animals are born with a set of behavior patterns all ready to function, the human baby has to learn everything except his vital bodily processes. Able to walk within a matter of hours after his birth, and fully developed within a year or two, the animal is far superior to the child in the grosser ways of bodily life. At what would seem to be a handicap, the infancy, childhood, and adolescence of the human child are elongated to twenty years, more or less. But this extended immaturity is the occasion for learning many refined ways and entering into richer values, neither of which is possible in the animal world, where learning is limited. This prolonged infancy, which provides the occasion for the much learning needed by men, outlines the function of education in the human race. The human child needs adult guidance and care for a much longer time and to a far greater degree than the animal needs the care of its mother. Not only is the baby dependent upon adults for nourishment; he is just as dependent for his mental nurture. Unable to move about for months after birth, even the development of his

---

[3] Educational Policies Commission, *The Unique Function of Education in American Democracy*. Washington, D.C.: 1937. P. 83.

[4] Cf. Herbert Spencer, *op. cit.*, p. 101.

perceptions is dependent upon the nearness of adults and the objects they supply him.[5]

Dependent though he is upon his guardians for the kind of environment in which he can thrive physically and develop mentally, even so the infant educates himself in great measure. And this is true to a greater degree of all older children. He uses his eyes, ears, hands, and feet—actually his whole body—in an apparently extemporaneous and purposeless activity, but all the while he is building perceptions and establishing relationships. Though his parents must move him about, supply him objects and replace them when they fall, the parents do not create this activity or supply the inner workings of it which are so rich in developmental power. This is the child's own educative activity. This is his contribution to living and learning which is the cornerstone of all of his future education. His spontaneous activity is a natural process of acquiring knowledge on which all afterknowledge is based. Because of this, Spencer held that what the child likes to do is an important index to the kind of activity which is educative for him at a given stage of his development.[6]

As this implies, the child develops throughout his long infancy and childhood according to natural rhythms. And to these rhythms education must be attuned if it is to fulfill its function. Just as the ebb and flow of the ocean's tide follow a rhythm which is its own, so also the growth and development of the child follow unique rhythms, not too commonly observed, but nevertheless present in the child's experience and the sure guide to educative activity. However oblivious of these rhythms parents and teachers may have been in the past, they have not been able to disregard them completely; for wherever there is an effective meeting of adult guidance and childhood response, harmony with the order of natural development is the common ground on which the meeting takes place.[7]

But what relation do the rhythms of natural development have to moral values? Are children naturally so good that their preferences can be trusted as completely as education according to Nature seems to imply? "Not at all," says Herbert Spencer, although enjoyment of activity will abide as an important index to the educative timeliness of the activity for the child. The human child is neither naturally good nor morally depraved; he is a little bit of both. Though "the tendencies of the growing mind are not altogether so diabolical as was supposed,"[8] the child may be innocent regarding evil knowledge, but he certainly is not innocent as far as evil impulses are concerned. He is not born good, nor will he be made good by education. For education has to be administered by adults who are also

---

[5] Cf. *ibid.*, pp. 13–14.
[6] Cf. *ibid.*, pp. 105 and 107.
[7] Cf. *ibid.*, p. 96.
[8] *Ibid.*, pp. 95–96.

human; and even if education as a process could make man good, the adults who must do the educating are not good enough to guarantee an unadulterated success.[9] But this consideration anticipates a fuller description of the educative process as conceived by Spencer, the subject to be discussed after the objectives of education are stated as he has formulated them.

C. THE OBJECTIVES OF EDUCATION

The famous five educational objectives of Herbert Spencer are proposed in the first of his four well-known essays on education, "What Knowledge Is of Most Worth?" They are incidental to his argument that science is the subject matter of paramount importance in the curriculum. For his purpose in stating these objectives was to ask, "What is it that education strives to accomplish?" and then to answer, "It is science which most fully secures these ends." The essay is largely concerned to establish the importance of science, an important service at the time it was written; what little space is given to objectives provides for little more than the mere statement of them.

"Complete living"[10] is the general aim summing up the five specific ones. As this is not a very explicit term, it may be made more understandable by a parallel attempt at generalization in Spencer's third essay, "Moral Education." In this second statement of it he speaks of the "business of life" and elaborates by saying that education should "produce a citizen who, at the same time that he is well conducted, is also able to make his way in the world."[11] These generalizations convey the impression that moral responsibility coupled with practical self-sufficiency are virtues of the educated man. This impression is borne out by the specific objectives which are now to be discussed.

1. *Self-preservation* is the first of the five objectives. In order to live completely, as man has first of all to live, he has to continue his own existence. While instinct is the chief guarantee of this objective, education may also help by acquainting the learner with the laws of health and enabling him to earn a living.

2. *Securing the necessities of life.* It is especially in the realm of developing economic efficiency that education helps in preserving life. Money is not life, but it is a necessity in maintaining life. Education should train directly for success in this important function.

3. *Raising children.* Life must be perpetuated into the future in new generations. But Spencer does not mean mere biological procreation alone.

---

[9] Cf. *ibid.*, pp. 95–96, 173, 220–221.
[10] *Ibid.*, p. 17.
[11] *Ibid.*, p. 178.

The England of his day laid heavy stress on a classical education for boys and a preparation of girls for polite society. This, he felt, was preoccupation with the decorations of life, sadly overlooking simple elementals. Though a bachelor, Spencer held that the most important function that most men and women have to perform is that of being parents. Therefore education should deal unashamedly both with the care of children in the nursery and the discipline of them as growing boys and girls. So much did Spencer believe this that he urged that education be elevated as a subject of study to a position of supreme importance in the curriculum.

4. *Maintenance of social and political relations*. Beyond the home in the far-reaching social structure, man must have some understanding and mastery of social and political processes if living is to be complete. He must be a wise citizen who is equipped for effective social and political action.

5. *Enjoyment of leisure*. Life is not all serious struggle, keeping physically strong, earning a living, being a responsible parent and an earnest citizen. Complete living also includes freedom from struggle some of the time for "gratification of the tastes and feelings."[12]

Though it was important to Spencer, it is not important for our purpose to dwell on the problem as to whether the study of science is the means by which these five objectives of complete living are to be reached. It does flavor their character if we know that Spencer did insist that the knowledge of the various sciences involved was the guarantee of all of them, even to the enjoyment of leisure.

D. THE EDUCATIVE PROCESS

The first time the student considers naturalism as an educational philosophy he might easily guess that if it is desirable for education to follow the order of Nature, as naturalism says, then parents and teachers should not dabble in children's affairs but should leave them to Nature, purely and simply. Nevertheless, naturalism has never made such a proposal; it has held instead that educating is a natural function and that parents and teachers do have a place in it. The chief justification which Spencer offers for education as a deliberate and positive program is to point to man's prolonged infancy and childhood as evidence not only of his need for education but also of the naturalness of its function in his life. The distinctive character of the process as conceived by Spencer can be represented by briefly elaborating eight principles for which he argues in his essays. Some of them are of inclusive significance for the whole educational process; others are specific, dealing with particular phases.

1. *Education must conform to the natural processes of growth and mental development*. This root principle, already touched upon, stems from

[12] *Ibid.*, p. 18.

a concern to understand the nature of the child and follows from naturalism's conception of the pupil. It is the makeup of the learner that determines the character of the learning process, not the designs of teachers or society. For the process must synchronize with the experience of the learner or there simply will be no learning. In order really to get into an understanding of the process itself we must ask, "How?" Just how is education made to follow the order of Nature? What are the guides by which a teacher can know that natural rhythms are setting the pace? The next two principles to be stated answer these questions in part.

2. *Education should be pleasurable;* for children have a good time when they are doing things which the present development of their physical and mental equipment makes them ready to do. This readiness for specific kinds of activity is evidenced by their interests. Consequently, interest in a subject and interest in ways of doing things are guides to parents and teachers, both as to subjects of study and methods of teaching for which children have a natural readiness at any given stage of development.[13]

3. *Education should engage the spontaneous self-activity of the child.* As already noted, the child educates himself in great measure; most of his knowledge is based on what he discovers in his own active relations with things and people. Especially is this the case with our perceptions, developed almost completely by our own unconscious efforts in early childhood but constituting the machinery for a high percentage of our adult experiences. Adults are foolish, therefore, if they do not use this native self-activity as an ally in their teaching. The way to do this, Spencer advised, is to *tell* the learner as little as possible and induce him to *discover* as much as possible.[14]

4. *Acquisition of knowledge is an important part of education.* This was evidently assumed by Spencer in his strong advocacy of science. All of his five objectives called for the study of specific sciences as necessary to their fulfillment. Knowledge of physiology augments instinct in preserving life. As most people earn their living by an occupation in "the production, exchange, or distribution of commodities,"[15] knowledge of mathematics, mechanics, physics, chemistry, and biology is a good guarantee of business success. In order to be good parents and bring up children well, students in school should study physiology and psychology. So that they may become good citizens in later life, they should study sociology. And even for enjoying sculpture, painting, music, drama, and poetry, such knowledges as anatomy, physics, perspective, and psychology are essential prerequisites.

5. But *education is for the body as well as the mind;* and this should not be forgotten. Even if it were possible, there is no point in making a man

---

[13] Cf. *ibid.*, pp. 107–109 and 161.
[14] Cf. *ibid.*, pp. 126–129.
[15] *Ibid.*, p. 41.

mentally fit for life and neglecting his physical fitness. Mind and body must both be cared for and the whole being of the pupil unfolded as a unit. It is with the body that our frequent infatuation with precocity works its greatest havoc, but it is evil in other ways also. We too often want our children to get ahead of the game in building up a bank account of knowledge; and what we sacrifice is of far more value than what we gain. Spencer insisted that the English schools of his time inflicted an excess of mental application on their students and in so doing produced a variety of bad results. What was learned under such hothouse forcing was easily forgotten, he held. The method itself produced a digust for knowledge on the part of the learner. In upholding the ambition for accumulating information, it neglected the organization of knowledge which is more important than the information accumulated. Such a schooling wastes energy, weakens the student, and thereby renders his trained intellect useless in later life, as such artificial forcing is almost certain to entail ill health.[16]

6. There will be correction of these mistakes by a healthy balance of mental and physical activities if *education practices the art of delay,* as it should do. Why hurry, when the real accomplishments of education are achieved by waiting? Hurry ignores and contradicts the natural rhythms of development. Delay is at the same time the unfussed occasion for discerning these rhythms and the opportunity for joining hands with maturation. We mature into much learning at the same time that we acquire it. Maturation should always be encouraged, never retarded by an artificial process which confuses the rhythms of the student, even for himself, while teachers mistakenly assume that they are making haste. All precocity is immature, whether mental or moral; and neither should be encouraged.[17]

7. *Methods of instruction should be inductive.* This follows from Nature's advice that teaching make fullest use of the self-activity of the pupil, telling him as little as possible and encouraging him to discover as much as possible for himself. Spencer lived the life of a fact collector; using several secretaries, he built extensive card-index catalogues of information preparatory to his writing. It was this same "exhaustive observation"[18] which he urged as the essential of effective learning. To *tell* a child this and to *show* him that only make him a recipient of another's observations. If the learning intellect is to be guided to its appropriate food, children must master the art of independent observation and direct acquaintance.

8. *Punishment should be constituted by natural consequences of wrong deeds; should be certain, but tempered with sympathy.* As we should teach in accordance with the rhythms of Nature, so we should also punish as Nature punishes. If we do this, we will be wise in determining the character

[16] Cf. *ibid.,* pp. 283, 291, 300, and 303.
[17] Cf. *ibid.,* pp. 221–222.
[18] *Ibid.,* p. 139.

of the punishment in each case and constant in administering it, yet avoiding anger.

Every time a child puts his finger into the candle flame he gets a burn. Always it happens; always it is a burn. There are no harsh words, no snapping and snarling, just a burn proportionate to the size of the flame and the extent and duration of the contact. But always there is that much. By this means Nature quickly teaches the normal child the dangers of fire, and exemplifies for parents and teachers what is desirable in corrective relations with children.

If, for example, a child is habitually slow in getting dressed and ready to go for a walk with the rest of the family, scolding, harsh words, and ruffled feelings are punishment for everyone else as well as the problem child, and may avail little. Instead, let the rest of the family go for the walk and leave the habitually late child to suffer the natural consequences of being slow, missing the enjoyment for which the other members of the family were ready. When a child begins to expect such consequences as certain to follow if he does not measure up to what is expected of him, he will act so as to enjoy the benefits which follow from appropriate conduct. Furthermore, when punishment of this sort is used, ruffled feelings do not get mixed up with discipline. It is easier for parent or teacher to hold a firm position with the child and yet not lose rapport with him completely. Even the disobedient child should feel that he has not lost all the sympathy of his guardians. But in the common snapping and snarling of parents, the emotional break between parent and child is too sharp and may do more damage than the punishment does good.[19]

Of course there are a few extremely dangerous circumstances in which the child must be saved from the punishment of natural consequences by the arbitrary intervention of adults. The natural consequences of darting across the street in front of busy traffic are too grave, and so the child must learn the danger of traffic by indirect means. Spencer makes exception to his principle of natural punishments for such extreme circumstances and even suggests a sliding scale between arbitrary control in infancy to freedom for facing mutual consequences independently as the individual gains adequate experience. Accordingly, he suggests that there are stages of development in wise discipline which are much the same as the stages to be noted in the history of political rule. At the outset there is autocratic control where it is needed. Later, room is made for the beginnings of constitutionalism in which "the liberty of the subject gains some express recognition." Following this there are successive extensions of liberty as the child evidences readiness for it, and this finally ends in "parental abdication."[20]

[19] Cf. *ibid.*, pp. 184–204.
[20] Cf. *ibid.*, pp. 229–230.

V

Naturalism in Religion

A. The Status of Religion

B. The Nature of God

C. The Power and Goodness of God

D. The Nature of Man

It might seem that a chapter on naturalism as a philosophy of religion could be little more than a formal unit helping to maintain the symmetry of this book. It is understandable that since religion is included as a subject of discussion in presenting the other philosophies, it should also be a part of the presentation of naturalism. But how can naturalism have any place for religion in its scheme of things when there is no recognition of the super-natural in its metaphysics?

The answer to this question is, of course, that naturalism has a different definition of religion. It tries to make of religion, as Dewey has tried to make of intelligence, a naturalized citizen, defining religious experience as purely a phenomenon of Nature. In the nineteenth and twentieth centuries there have been many thinkers within both Judaism and Protestantism who have mediated toward science and have accordingly attempted to redefine their religious ideas so as to make them more harmonious with science. The more extreme results of this mediating tendency have been concep-tions of religion which, although conventional religious terms may be employed, are in close agreement with the conceptions of naturalism or pragmatism. Because of this there is some real pertinence in including studies of naturalistic and pragmatic influences in religious thought in the respective presentations of these philosophies.

The patterns of the five chapters on religion will vary somewhat. The two on naturalism in religion and pragmatism in religion will be shorter than the others and will omit some subjects which do not fit because of the character of a naturalistic treatment of religion.

A. THE STATUS OF RELIGION

If it is correct that the common attitude toward religion is that it has validity and somehow relates us to God, then it is permissible to say that naturalism is inclined to reduce religion to a phenomenon of human experience, the roots and character of which are both purely natural. In great measure, naturalism in religion is a contradiction of the common attitude. It may not imply, however, the overthrow of religion so much as its redefinition in harmony with a purely natural frame of reference. This naturalistic attitude may be understood by attempting to see how naturalists may reply to two characteristic objections to their reduction of religion to purely natural grounds.

Suppose, for example, you say, as many of us do, "But how can we live a good life, shunning gross immoralities, if we do not have the benefit of a Power beyond ourselves to sustain us in doing the right?"

Naturalism answers: "A refined moral life is just as much a work of Nature as is a coarse and vulgar immorality. You are wrong in implying, first of all, that a natural life is an immoral life. And furthermore, your religious experience that a Power from beyond yourself is sustaining you in doing good is a natural phenomenon. Nature is versatile. This experience is no doubt a valid one. You are being sustained in living a good life. For it is in harmony with Nature, when it is inclusively understood, to do good and to avoid evil."

To try another attack, suppose you ask the naturalist this question: "But I have mystical experiences in which the presence of God transforms my whole outlook. And sometimes the chain of circumstance surrounding me works together as if a Will greater than my own were catching me up in its forward surge and giving me a part in a plan and purpose far transcending the deliberate acts of people. How can you explain this?"

Again religion according to naturalism answers: "Here also you see the versatility of Nature. Life is like that. If you are well adjusted to the laws and processes of Nature, you do, in a measure, transcend your own individual limitations and see yourself at times as a part of something much vaster. Religious experiences are comparable to those of the artist when he is lost in an aesthetic enjoyment, giving expression, when he paints or composes, to something, as it were, far greater than himself."

Were you to meet a naturalist and raise these questions with him, leading on into an extended discussion of other similar questions, you would no doubt find that for him the status of religion is that of a phenomenon of Nature, containing within it however many of the same subjective qualities and values which religious people commonly enjoy.

B. THE NATURE OF GOD

Many naturalists do not use the term God. While religion may be a valuable phase of life and the source of genuine inspiration, it is defined as purely natural, an affair of men adjusting themselves to the forces and processes of Nature, thereby achieving a harmonious life. Since this is the nature of religion for naturalists, and since the word God has a historic usage denoting a Supernatural Person, many naturalists do not include God in religion. At the same time, they find in refined religion many of the values that men have found there through the ages. Similarly, they do not, of course, advance rationalistic arguments for the existence of God as some other philosophies do.

But, surprising as it may seem, there are naturalists in religion who do talk about God; and although they do not advance classical arguments for His existence, they regard religious experience as an experience of God and they go on to give some definition of His nature. Notable among such religious naturalists is Henry Nelson Wieman, who in 1927 began an extended professorship in philosophy of religion in the Divinity School of the University of Chicago.

For Wieman, God is the supreme value-producing factor in the world. In order to understand this definition, one must keep in mind the difference between fact and value.[1] Every man is confronted by the world as it actually is at the present moment, the world of fact. Some things about it we like; some things we don't like. That is to say, there are some things we value as good and desirable; while there are some conditions we would like to see changed. This implies the other realm set over against the world of fact, the realm of the possible or potential. That refined use of the imagination, in which we project ourselves into the possible future and envision what could be, is at least a part of our ability to evaluate. But we do not only judge things to be desirable and undesirable. Most of us are not content with what is, either in our own individual circumstances or in the world generally; consequently, we spend much of our lives striving toward

[1] Cf. p. 29.

the realization of what we feel ought to be. And so it is that much of our living is a process of realizing and enjoying values.

Now it is in this phase of experience, readily understood by all of us, where Wieman finds God. God is that structure in the world which makes possible the realization of values, and which both sustains and constitutes value. There is something wholly objective to us in Nature which makes it possible for us to strive for and realize values. This foundation of value and the value-realizing process is not the whole of Nature, however. For there is much in Nature which is not valued as good; and there is also a factor in Nature which moves toward the destruction of value. God is that process within Nature which is a kind of open door to all who would grow in richness of life, and at the same time God is the stable ground in Nature which sustains and constitutes the values by which life is enriched. Because of this, God, the structure of value itself, is the greatest of all values, the most worthful in human experience to which man must adjust if he is to grow in the possession and enjoyment of value.[2]

This is Wieman's description of God. As can be seen, God is defined in impersonal terms and as wholly within the process of Nature. What Wieman has striven for in his philosophy of religion is a scientific approach to the knowledge of God. He claims for his conception the distinction that it is free from the older rationalism and capable of verification by science. It is held to be evident on purely empirical grounds that there is something in the world which makes possible the increase of values. And although this may be a minimum definition of God, it is offered as a beginning which is capable of recognition by the scientific mind.

Two comparisons can be made at this point which may be helpful in understanding the relation between this and other philosophies of religion. Pragmatism has this same stress on value; but instead of giving attention to the foundation of values, the focus is upon the process of realizing spiritual or religious values. Pragmatism does not have time for any supposed metaphysical basis for values, even the kind that Professor Wieman offers. Values are spiritual or religious for pragmatism because of their level of refinement, not because they have roots in any particular kind of reality.[3] Realism as a philosophy of religion is similar to the naturalism of Wieman in taking the empirical approach. The difference is that many realists go quite beyond Wieman's minimum definition. A person can be a realist and

[2] Cf. Henry Nelson Wieman and Bernard Eugene Meland, *American Philosophies of Religion.* New York and Chicago: Willett, Clark and Co., 1936. Pp. 295–299. Also, Henry Nelson Wieman, "God and Value," in D. C. Macintosh (editor), *Religious Realism.* New York: The Macmillan Company, 1931. Also, D. C. Macintosh, *The Problems of Religious Knowledge.* New York: Harper & Row, Publishers, 1940. Pp. 165–173.

[3] Cf., pp. 394–397.

consistently accept Wieman's definition of God. But while they may start with Wieman's definition as a minimum, many realists go beyond him in finding more of the personal and spiritual in the nature of God than Wieman does.[4]

C. THE POWER AND GOODNESS OF GOD

Before turning attention to the nature of man, we may attempt to state what naturalism has to say about the power and goodness of God. We do this because of our predisposition today to know, "Is God unlimited, infinite?" and "Is God perfectly good?" Of recent times the answers of philosophers to the first of these questions has been less assuring, therefore the great concern about them.

Of course, to the many naturalists who are not concerned to use theistic terminology, these questions are beside the point. Nature just is. In it the good and the bad are mixed. While it is vast in its extent and may be infinite, it also may be finite. But within the pattern of definition which Wieman's religious philosophy follows, these questions are more relevant and do have answers.

Is God infinite and all-powerful? Wieman's answer is "No." God is within Nature; He is not all of Nature, nor more than Nature. He is that particular structure in Nature which is sufficiently limited to be described as making possible the realization of value and as the foundation of all value.

But in answer to the other question, "Is God good?" the answer is strongly in the affirmative. Yes, goodness is the distinctive attribute of God. Whereas in Nature and man there are evils which frustrate the realizing of value, a drag which pulls back, or a positive interference, God is the power in Nature making good possible, the very structure sustaining all good. He is therefore the very source of all good, and as such the greatest of all goods, the most worthful, and therefore deserving of worship and complete devotion.

D. THE NATURE OF MAN

One of the perennial concerns of theology has been, and continues to be, the nature of man. The author of the Eighth Psalm gave early expression to this interest, but in the spirit of great wonder that God should condescend to look with favor upon man.

When I consider thy heavens, the work of thy fingers, the moon and the stars, which thou hast ordained;

[4] Cf. pp. 325–330.

What is man, that thou art mindful of him? and the son of man, that thou visitest him?[5]

Two important aspects of this query about man are whether he has a soul and whether he is good or bad. The chapters in this book which deal with philosophy of religion will deal with these two subjects, although necessarily some of the treatments will be scantier than others.

The subject of naturalism and the nature of man is one of these necessarily limited discussions. For naturalists are not as much interested in the soul of man and his moral condition as theology has been. According to naturalism, man is a child of Nature; yet, nevertheless, he is a most significant child. For in the evolutionary processes that have been at work in the universe so far, man is on the very crest of the wave. He has capacities and has achieved heights common to no other child of Nature. True enough, he has selfhood of a sort; but there is such a remarkable gamut of refinement in the achievements in selfhood of different men that it is difficult to say what it is that men possess in common as a self, or, more traditionally, a soul. The self seems to be an organization of experience in each individual which is constantly developing and changing. Such a description is quite far from those which state that man is made in the image of God. The human self is seen by naturalism as an offshoot of Nature, and not as springing from beyond Nature.

When looking at man from the moral standpoint, naturalism tries not to make him either better or worse than he actually is. Child of Nature that he is, he participates in the processes of Nature. He has his drives and he responds to his environment much as any other organism. Both of these are prior in his genesis to the intellectual awakening or degree of self-consciousness which may appear in his adult years to modify and check his primordial nature. Nature has her delicacies and she also has her law of tooth and claw; and man participates in both. There is evil in the world, sometimes in blatant proportions, and man shares in it, excepting, of course, catastrophes of the physical world.

But that man may have an intellectual awakening or develop a degree of self-consciousness is the one hope for his salvation. For when he stops to think about his life, he is standing on the threshold of a level of living which is characterized by a total view. For evil, according to Wieman, is the following of some one pursuit to the exclusion of all others. It is attending to the fraction and neglecting the larger whole which constitutes all of life. If a man contemplates life, he will recognize the difference between value and those ways of living which destroy value. He will also see that although there is rough and tumble in Nature, and mad scramble in the society of man, yet there is a force at work in the world making

[5] Psalm 8:3-4 (A. S. V.).

value possible and sustaining man in the achievement of values. If a man contemplates life to this extent, and acts within a total perspective rather than a fractional one, he is allied with the value-producing factor in the world and is at least on the way toward living the good life.

VI

Strengths and Weaknesses in the Philosophy of Naturalism

A. The Strengths of Naturalism

B. The Weaknesses of Naturalism

This chapter will be paralleled by similar brief chapters at the ends of Parts Three, Four, and Five of this book; also by comparable concluding sections in the two chapters of Part Six devoted respectively to existentialism and language analysis. The purpose of these discussions is to make an estimate of each of these philosophies. This will be done by saying first of all what the strengths of each of the philosophies are, and then by a statement of the points of weakness in each. Having so far completed the presentation of naturalism according to the pattern set down at the outset of the book, attention is now directed to the task of estimating the strengths and weaknesses of this particular philosophy.

A. THE STRENGTHS OF NATURALISM

The chief strength of naturalism as a philosophy is its simplicity. For most of us, at least as we first become reflective, life is such a confusion of a multitude of different influences and factors that we need some simplifying patterns to help us in finding order and design. While it will not be elaborated further, there is also a kind of freedom from presumption in naturalism which in its way is a credit. This may be paralleled by an antithetical presumption, that is the presumption of negating much. Yet the reluctance to affirm much is not without humility and is refreshing in comparison to the pride of knowledge.

To return to the theme of the simplicity of naturalism, it should be said that we are doubtless in as great danger of oversimplifying as we are of being lost in complexity. In the second part of this chapter we shall say something about the oversimplifications of naturalism. But we should pause to recognize the value of simplification and the way in which naturalism contributes a simplifying influence.

Among the sources of confusion and complexity two may be mentioned because they seem to be most obvious. The simplifying influence of naturalism may contribute to the neutralizing of these areas of confusion and may therefore have a measurably beneficial effect.

1. The first source of confusion is ourselves, depending to some extent on the basic dispositions of our own personalities. If we are inclined to be rather definitely introverted, to live a great deal within ourselves, to relate every event and circumstance to the private patterns of our own inner experience, we are likely to find that much confusion results from our inability to keep up with the flow of events. This is because we simply have so much extra work to do in weaving everything together subjectively. We are so much tied up within ourselves that it is with difficulty that we project ourselves outwardly into effective relationships.

When compared to such a complex personal pattern of living, naturalism is exceedingly simple. Living, according to it, is predominantly external. Reality is simply an affair of materials, forces, laws, or processes in motion out in space. And the intricacies of private experience are quite unreal, at least secondary, as compared to these externals of which we are a part. This is not to imply that extroversion is superior to introversion; it does suggest that an exposure to the simplicity of naturalism may help a person out of some of the inner complexities commonly accompanying introversion.

2. The second source of confusion is society, depending to some extent upon whether or not a person's childhood and youth were spent in a rural or urban environment. If an individual grows up in a rural environment, Nature is likely to be much more the context of his life than society. If he grows up in the city, society will be the predominant context, and Nature may seem remote and almost unreal. One child who grew up in New York City had passed a surprising number of birthdays before he realized that the subways and elevateds were not a part of Nature, but actually had to be constructed by men.

Now society can be equally as confusing as the intricacies of private experience. We are born into its patterns; it forms our ways of living and acting before we are conscious of it. And as far as rootage in Nature is concerned, many of the patterns formed by human societies are artificial and unreal. As we have attempted to show, this was one of the discoveries made by Rousseau which became a predominant theme in his writing: society is artificial and its ways need to be corrected by getting back to Nature. There is enough truth in Rousseau's revolt against society to deserve serious consideration for it. Those who have grown up in the city, and others who in addition live out their lives there, are so insulated from the more enduring realities by the artificial patterns of society that they are caught in a complexity of influences which seem at best only half real to them.

In antithesis to this artificiality and its attendant confusion, naturalism is a wholesome simplifying influence. It calls us back to the simple elemental things of Nature which have not been corrupted by human artificialities.

B. THE WEAKNESSES OF NATURALISM

But even though simplicity is the strength of naturalism, it is also its weakness. By and large, naturalism oversimplifies life and existence and does not go deep enough in its attempted explanations. Deeper insights disclose that explanations cannot be as simple as those of naturalism. There are several ways in which this inadequacy of naturalism can be elaborated.

1. In the first place, reality can not be as simply and definitely described as naturalism has proposed to describe it. Reality as atoms falling through space, and all other materialistic descriptions of reality, have been superseded among naturalists by more refined conceptions, as we have tried to show. One of these more refined conceptions, yet a naïve naturalism because it explained reality as one substance, was the energism of Herbert Spencer according to which the ultimate reality is energy or force. But the forsaking of any substance as an explanation, in favor of laws and relations, as in Comte, seems to be a tacit recognition of the need for an even more refined explanation than energy or force. And to go on from the forsaking of laws and relations as constituting a final explanation to the description of Nature as fluid process seems, in addition to being a recognition of a need for still more refined explanations, to be an explanation of Nature approximating the ways of spirit. To speak of the natural as being the normal, as Schneider does,[1] and to go on to say that the normal cannot be defined statistically, but that there is only one way of being normal while there are a multitude of ways of being abnormal, is virtually to speak in the *manner of being* of the spiritual without granting the *existence* of things spiritual.

[1] Cf. p. 72–73.

At any rate, it is evident that Nature is not to be simply and definitely described, as the ancient naturalists and also Herbert Spencer tried to describe it. And in addition it is evident that attempts at its description lead on to successive refinements which approximate spirit, even though the existence of spirit as substance is not granted. Of course, naturalism may be defined as the denial of supernatural reality; but this is a negation, and as such cannot be satisfactory apart from some attempts at affirmation, and these we have contended contain implicitly in them the need for refinement toward more adequate conceptions.

2. In the second place, Nature is not all rhythm and harmony, in relation with which man can find peace and natural benefit. Granted that there is even a majority of areas in which man can only achieve as he works in harmony with Nature, there are still remaining areas in which Nature is not so friendly and man must protect himself from her. We can till the soil fruitfully only as we do it in harmony with the rhythms of sun, soil, and seasons. Our success in nurturing and educating children will correspond in great measure to the extent to which we harmonize our efforts with the nature of personality and the rhythms of growth and maturation. Man can now orbit the earth, probe far distant reaches of space by unmanned craft, and has every promise of soon exploring near neighbors of the earth with his own eyes. All of this has come to pass because we have learned to match our technology to the functioning of the natural order. However, there is another side to Nature not so congenial. Sun, soil, and seasons demand unrelenting toil from the farmer, even in a day of mechanization, which many times amounts to unremitting struggle and by no means unsullied peace and contentment. And sometimes the seasons are fickle, or pestilence comes, and one's efforts are not rewarded with fruitfulness. The same thing can be seen in another area of our civilization uppermost in our minds today. By giving heed to the ways of Nature we have been able to release the energy of the atom, but in its raw form, at least, this energy is unfriendly to us. Knowing well that it could incinerate the race or by some gigantic miscalculation exchange the protective atmosphere of the earth for an interplanetary dead sea foreign to man, the tiny atom makes us quake with fear of unknown disaster, by no means yielding us harmony and contentment alone.

This is not to contend that we can or should ignore the ways of Nature, or resist any exhortation to heed them in simple living. It is to argue that this is not a complete basis for living and that Nature has penalties to exact as well as benefits to offer.

3. The next two weaknesses of naturalism to be pointed out are that it is inadequate both in its epistemology and ontology. Throughout much of the presentation of naturalism as a philosophy it has been observed that naturalism is primarily concerned with metaphysics. It has also been pointed

out that when naturalists address themselves to the problem of knowledge they work out refinements which are either realistic or pragmatic. There is justification therefore in taking naturalism to task for not having a theory of knowledge. This is not just a matter of expecting naturalism to fill out a formal pattern of philosophizing; a criticism prompted by no more than this would not carry much weight. But when naturalists are as concerned as they are to tell us what is ultimately real and what is not, they should also tell us how they have come by this knowledge and therefore how they can certify their conception of reality as true. This would mean giving the kind of attention to theory of knowledge which has been characteristic of realism and pragmatism.

4. But even within the realm of metaphysics, where it specializes, naturalism has not gone deeply enough. This becomes most evident if the question is asked, What is the ontology of naturalism? The ancient naturalists were quite definite in describing being and nonbeing, and readily revealed thereby their lack of depth in ontological matters. Empty space was the same as nonbeing for them; and atoms were the elemental units of being. About later and more refined naturalism such clear-cut statements are not as easily made. But in general it would probably be correct to say that Nature just is, and whatever is, is because it is a part of Nature, and whatever is presumed not to be of Nature, just isn't.

This is not a sufficiently refined handling of the ontological problem. It does not even seem to ask the ontological question fully. If in addition to asking the question, What is it that exists ultimately? a person also asks, What is it that constitutes existing, as such? then the dullness of naturalism's answer to the ontological problem becomes evident. It is Nature, naturalism says, that exists ultimately. But to go on and say that to exist means to be a part of Nature misses the point of the second question. To attempt to say what is meant by the idea of existing, as such, involves going beyond any definition of Nature to a definition of existing. And once this is done, it may well become clear that the idea of Nature is not sufficiently refined to match the insight that is called for by the question, What does it mean to exist?

5. A fifth criticism is that there are some important ways in which man can never be at home in Nature. It is granted without hesitation that there are benefits to be derived by living close to Nature and so avoiding many of the complexities of mental and social involvement. But this plan of life applies for the individual only so long as he continues in his individuality as a part of the space-time world. According to naturalism, his individuality ceases at death and there is no more abiding home than Nature for man to anticipate. This does not do justice, however, to the longings of the human soul. Within the space of this life there may be certain harmony and peace to be found by living close to Nature; but for it to end by the

individual being swallowed up by Nature is inhuman. It must be granted that the particular nature of the deep desires of man do not necessarily offer any clue, to say nothing of a guarantee, of what reality is. For individuality to disappear into nothingness at death may be inhuman from man's standpoint, but were that to be man's eventual end, human longings to the contrary could not make it any different. All this having been acknowledged, it nevertheless remains that Nature cannot provide a home for man. Within her dwelling place, all is not peace and contentment, no matter how carefully we harmonize our lives with her ways.

6. Two final comments will be made concerning naturalism in education and religion. As to naturalism as a philosophy of education, as represented by Herbert Spencer, the chief criticism is that it is not sufficiently complete and comprehensive, although what it does say is said quite well. It is rather earthbound to define the objectives of education, as Spencer did, as those activities for which the study of science can equip us. This becomes evident within the scope of Spencer's own statement, especially when he tries to say in relation to his fifth objective that the study of science can equip us for leisure activities. Geometry, perspective, and mathematics may have some connection with the appreciation of art, for example, but they are a small part of this flight from the earthbound, and it is likely that there are many people who have rather rich aesthetic experiences without benefit of the rites of science. Again, the pupil is not done justice when he is conceived of as a little animal; he is more than this, and any education will be inadequate which does not propose to deal with something more than little animals. The call to design the educative process more in harmony with the rhythms of Nature, to make still another comment, is a call which still needs to be heard today, a hundred years after Spencer's four essays were published. But such a design for education needs to be supplemented by harmonizing it with personal and spiritual rhythms as well.

7. This final comment, a criticism of naturalism as a philosophy of religion, may seem to be prompted more by bias than any of the foregoing attempts to point to weaknesses in the philosophy of naturalism. The comment is that as a philosophy of religion naturalism seems to be largely a matter of words. It would seem wiser and more honest for those naturalists who speak of God as that process in Nature which makes possible the realization of values, to use some other word to denote the value-realizing potentiality of Nature. If this is the most worthful object, deserving the highest loyalty and allegiance man can offer, why can it not be spoken of as such in simple unequivocal words whose meanings are quite clear? It seems to be a linguistic detour, and somewhat confusing, to borrow the conventional terminology of religion and invest it with naturalistic meanings.

PART THREE

IDEALISM

VII

A Brief History of Idealism

Idealism and naturalism have been the two long-standing rivals in philosophy throughout the centuries stretching from ancient to modern times. Although their roots reach back into the past, realism and pragmatism, the other two philosophies, arose in the twentieth century. A sketch of the development of idealism must begin, consequently, like that of naturalism, in antiquity.

In the Western world, idealism began with Socrates and Plato; so our discussion of its history turns first to Plato and his dialogues, from which comes much of what we know about Socrates. From this ancient beginning we shall turn to idealist trends in modern times: first to Descartes, and then successively to Spinoza, Leibniz, Berkeley, Kant, and Hegel. Two final discussions of recent and contemporary idealism in England, Scotland, and America help to bring the sketch up to the present time.

A. PLATO (427?–347 B.C.)

Plato became a disciple of Socrates at the age of twenty, remarkably well equipped in natural endowments to reap the full benefit of Socrates' teaching. He came from a noble family of wealth, was handsome, well developed physically, intelligent, and strong in the love of wisdom. Beginning the search for truth under the tutelage of Socrates, he pursued it throughout his long life of eighty years. After the death of Socrates and Plato's world travels which followed that tragedy, he set himself to the career in philosophy which made him the great master he has long been acclaimed. He launched his Academia in Athens, and there developed and expounded his doctrine as a teacher. As an author he composed his many dialogues, which comprise as many mines of philosophic ores for all modern thinkers, even today.

These writings are the product of a period in which the human mind was becoming conscious of itself and its relation to the universe. They are philosophical discussions couched in drama. In them the narrative develops as Socrates, usually the chief interrogator, plies questions and answers concerning the problem at hand with Parmenides, Protagoras, or whoever else may be engaged in the discussion. The characters in the dialogues portray man the thinker as he investigates as many as possible of the thoughts he might have about the world, himself, and life in general.

The form in which Plato cast his writings suggests a basic disposition which has been common to idealism since his time. Of course drama provides a vehicle which is vivid and full of interest. But it had a greater appropriateness than this in relation to Plato's purpose. Thought is a dialogue; when a man thinks, he becomes all of the characters in a drama set in his own mind. He inquires, he answers his inquiry, he evaluates, he considers first one alternative and then another, he makes up his mind, maybe he finds he must reconsider, he then pursues another direction, and so on. This is the matrix out of which his deliberate beliefs come.

But the individual is not isolated in his thinking function. He is a member of a society of potential thinkers. The dialogue of thought is set in the social mind as well as in the individual mind. A group can have as many different ideas on a subject as there are individuals in the group. If these ideas are brought out into the give-and-take of discussion, a kind of experimentation takes place. As objects and forces can be observed in Nature or investigated in the laboratory, so ideas and beliefs can be tested for validity as they are turned over and over by the group mind and their many ramifications and logical connections are seen.

This is the process that is dramatized so masterfully by Plato. It indicates the primacy for him of mind and reason in the experience of man. He did not center his attention on the forces of Nature, as did the physicists who preceded him. Nor did he attempt a cataloguing of unending observations of heaven and earth, as was later done by Aristotle and others. For him the life of reason was the focus from which all else stems. This is the spirit of idealism, which persists today in no small measure.

One of Plato's central themes is his famous doctrine of ideas. This is a conception of "forms" or universals that are both metaphysically prior *to* and ideals *for* particular things existing in man's world. We should hasten to offer a precaution against the oversimplifications unavoidable in a brief statement such as this. Plato's Dialogues are so numerous and extensive that genuine reserve should hold us back from typing this early "father" of Western philosophy by giving him a label. In particular, the attempt to make his doctrine of ideas a step in the formation of the philosophy of idealism is complicated by the various sources in which it may be found in the Dialogues as well as by the differing stages in Plato's thought that they may represent.[1]

There are ideas, according to Plato, that are so real and enduring that objects of sense are fleeting as compared to them. In fact, physical objects are only imperfect embodiments of ideas, i.e., of the respective ideas they represent. There is the universal idea "bed" of which all particular beds are imperfect expressions. There are also ideas that are not represented in physical forms. These include absolute beauty, goodness, and essence. These are the great realities.

Such absolute existences we come to recognize as true by a process of recollection. That is, we remember the former knowledge of these absolutes that we had in our previous existence before we ourselves were embodied in human form. Physical forms, while they represent to us the ideas basic to physical objects, also remind us of these higher absolute ideas of which we have already had knowledge in another world. It should be noted

[1] Cf. *Phaedo* and *The Republic*, Book X, as sources for this discussion.

for the sake of clarity that these universal ideas are not just convenient classes in Plato's thought into which individual things can be grouped by an inductive progression from particular things to a general class. They are, rather, prior and more fundamental ideas or "forms" from which different particular things are derived, however imperfectly. It is at least understandable that such a glorification of ideas could be termed an "ism," "idealism" being the logical name. If the name "idealism" arose from "ideaism," the *l* was no doubt added for euphony, yielding a more pleasing name and one easier to pronounce.

But it may very well be that there was another root of the philosophy of idealism in Plato that may be even more significant. At least it is free of the ambiguity in the doctrine of ideas that has made it as serviceable to some realists as it is to idealists.[2] This other concept in Plato is *the good*, most notably symbolized in the allegory of the cave.[3] This one good is not only the one "ideal" good to which all men should aspire, but it is also a kind of light by which the mind of man conceives whatever it conceives. Symbolically, it is to the mind of man as the sun is to the physical vision of man; all that man beholds with his eyes he sees not by the power of his own vision but by the *light* that makes vision possible. It is this kind of virtually ultimate importance that "the good" has for man.

Now this theme in Plato is as much as, if not more than, an early thrust in the direction of the formation of the philosophy of idealism as the doctrine of ideas. Which of the two is the more representative of Plato would be very difficult to determine. But fortunately such a judgment is not necessary for our purpose in this historical sketch.

B. RENÉ DESCARTES (1596–1650)

In a more detailed sketch of the history of idealism other ancient thinkers should receive attention, especially Saint Augustine (A.D. 350–430), Bishop of Hippo and a great Christian whose thought was influenced by Plato. But costly as sacrificing greater detail to an overall pattern is, we must pass on to early modern times. Beginning with René Descartes, there was in modern times a consecutive dealing with philosophic problems that constituted a movement toward a distinctive idealist pattern. So our sketch now moves on to this important post-Renaissance figure.

There are two main ideas in Descartes that relate him to the development of idealism. They are that the self is the most immediate reality in the

---

[2] E.g., in the medieval period the word *realism* denoted this same belief in universal ideas in opposition to *nominalism*, the rejection of such ideas that reserved "real-ness" for particular things only, names referring to classes of things and denoting nothing more than convenient groupings. See especially Anselm (1035–1109).

[3] Cf. *The Republic*, Book VII.

experience of each one of us and that the existence of God is evidenced in the experience of each of us by the fact that we have an idea of perfect being. There are other aspects of Descartes' thought that make it necessary to relate him to the history of realism; but in this book only these two ideas, relating him to idealism, will be discussed.

René Descartes was born of parents of means and social position in France. Educated in one of the best Jesuit schools of the time, he was allowed exceptional freedom because of his superior ability. He spent some years in the military service of countries friendly to France, in the midst of which he found sufficient freedom for study to formulate the outlines of his philosophy. After he left military service his inheritance enabled him to devote his life to writing and study. Descartes described one of his solitary episodes in reflection:

> *The setting in of winter arrested me in a locality where, as I found no society to interest me, and was besides fortunately undisturbed by any cares or passions, I remained the whole day in seclusion, with full opportunity to occupy my attention with my own thoughts.*[4]

Although he arbitrarily accepted certain principles as temporary moorings for his daily living while he engaged in his philosophic investigations, Descartes set out with the idea that all-inclusive doubt is the only open road to truth. He brought into question all opinions about which there could be any doubt whatsoever, as well as all lines of reasoning he had hitherto accepted as demonstrations. Further still, he doubted his senses, assuming that until he had more conclusive arguments the world about him was no more real than the illusions of his dreams.

But his line of reasoning brought him to one intuition that he felt could not be doubted. He recognized that in his doubting there was some thinking going on. Someone was doing some thinking, and he himself was the thinker. "It was absolutely necessary that I, who thus thought, should be somewhat." And so he drew the now famous Cartesian inference, "I think, therefore I am."[5] This belief in the reality of the self was to him a self-evident truth that was confirmed by the fact of his doubt.

This is probably the first modern expression of one of the central principles of idealism, namely, the primacy of the self. This principle involves at least two ideas concerning the significance of the self: (1) It is a self-evident reality; i.e., my knowledge of my self is a firsthand immediate experience. Any other object of knowledge is always at least once removed from me by virtue of the very fact that it is not my self which is known. (2) This implies what must be the necessary starting point in thought.

---

[4] *Discourse on Method.* Translated by John Veitch; La Salle, Ill.: The Open Court Publishing Company, 1945. P. 11.
[5] *Ibid.*, p. 35.

Since the self is the only self-evident reality, it is the necessary base of operation in seeking to understand experience. To start from any other point, such as the physical world, is to make a colossal question-begging jump before the reflective study of experience is begun. We must begin with the known, not the unknown, and knowledge of the self is the only immediate knowledge any of us has.

Having accepted the reality of the self as beyond doubt, Descartes extended his glance to discover any necessary connections that would give him conclusive basis for other truths. In so doing he recognized that René Descartes is not a perfect being because he doubts. He felt it was apparent that knowledge is a positive good as compared to doubt, which is negative and therefore imperfect. He then asked himself this question: "Whence did I learn to think of something more perfect than myself?" In answer he argued (1) that since he was imperfect, he could not be the source of the idea of a perfect being. For the less perfect could not be the cause of the more perfect. (2) Again, he argued that it was manifestly impossible for him to receive the idea of a perfect being from nothingness or nonexistence. For nothing cannot be the cause of something. (3) The only remaining alternative for explaining the source of this idea of perfect being, he held, is to believe that such a perfect being exists to cause the idea in him. He had considered nothingness as the cause of the idea, and rejected that as impossible. He had considered imperfect being as the cause. Here both himself and the order of Nature were included as imperfect beings, although at this point in his reasoning he was not sure of the reality of Nature. So only one alternative remained, and it is a possible one; therefore, he argued, it must be the truth. This is that the only cause there can be for an idea of perfect being is a perfect being. Therefore there is a Perfect Being; i.e., God exists. This argument for the existence of God has come to be known as the ontological argument.

Descartes went on to establish the reality of the external world, but examination of this part of his philosophy is excluded here, as it is more closely related to realism than to idealism. At this point in his thinking two principles stand out that are distinctly idealistic and harmonize with the central beliefs that have been held by many idealists. These are that the self is the prime reality and that the existence of God is made necessary by the fact that the self has an idea of a perfect being.

C. BARUCH SPINOZA (1632–1677)

Spinoza is identified with the idealist tradition because of his insistence that there is an unchanging and abiding existence undergirding all things, one of the chief attributes of which is thought.

Baruch Spinoza was a Spanish Jew who lived in Holland. His parents were members of a colony of Sephardic Jews who had taken refuge in Holland after having been driven from Spain by the Inquisition. Apparently Spinoza received a good education from the rabbis and was recognized by them as a student of great promise, one who would undoubtedly become a great rabbi. But Spinoza disappointed them. Searching for broader knowledge, he took up the study of Latin, eventually rounding out a technical training in the language at the school of Van Ende, who had Roman Catholic loyalties. As his critical mind was encouraged by these further intellectual pursuits, he came to hold beliefs that were not in conformity to the orthodoxy of the Jewish colony. Spinoza might have entertained his beliefs unoffensively in private had he not been reported to the authorities of the synagogue. The informer may have been his sister, who wanted to gain his inheritance. But to his credit, he acknowledged his beliefs despite the great personal cost; he later gave his inheritance to his sister. The small Jewish colony in Holland was sensitive to any offense it might bring to the Roman Catholics and Calvinists in whose country they had found asylum. Had it not been for this their case against the mild-mannered Spinoza might not have been pressed. At the age of twenty-four he was excommunicated from the synagogue, and for the remainder of his all-too-short life he had no society he could call his own. Throughout these years he lived a simple life, hardly making ends meet with his polishing of lenses; he gave as much of his time as possible to reflection, writing, and the building of a philosophy that is now honored as most profound.

One of the first things to grasp in trying to understand Spinoza is his doctrine of substance. He believed that there is some enduring substance that exists now, always did exist, and always will exist. This doctrine stands out most clearly as a direct antithesis to the pragmatism of recent times, which has no doctrine of substance, although it is not a unique position in the history of philosophy. Spinoza was not satisfied with the spirit-matter dualism in Descartes, and in his correction of it his conception of substance is important. By substance he does not mean matter, but rather something that is dependably solid and unchanging, as matter appears to be, yet is more enduring than matter.

This substance is one in number. It is impossible that there could be more than one. If it is assumed that there is more than one final substance, such substances cannot be infinite but must be finite. And for a substance to be ultimate, it must also be infinite.

Furthermore, this substance is correctly to be called God. Although to define God as such a substance is not completely in harmony with the commonly accepted Jewish and Christian conceptions of Him, it is not altogether out of harmony with them. Spinoza said, "God is a being absolutely infinite, of whom no attribute that expresses the essence of substance can be denied, and he necessarily exists."[6] The importance of this conception of God in the history of philosophy is that it unites the First Cause of Aristotle and St. Thomas and the Perfect Being of Descartes with the natural world in which they all believed. The result is a belief in one Existence that is both spiritual and, in a sense, physical. It is important to note that spiritual reality was definitely recognized by Spinoza and for him was an important aspect of existence.

God has two significant attributes. Attributes is used to mean characteristics so essential to the nature of God that they could not be different from what they are without God being different. Turn any place in the universe, no matter to how small a part or how isolated a segment, and these two attributes are to be found. They are a part of the very nature of God and are therefore found throughout all existence. These two attributes are *extension* and *thought*. In this chapter we are chiefly concerned with the thought attribute of God in which Spinoza believed.

To say that thought is an attribute of God is to say that He is a thinking being. According to Spinoza, existence is not a blind impersonal or mechanical substance. It is a being that thinks. God knows His own essence and attributes as well as all the multitudinous forms in which He is expressed in Nature. We may say that viewed from the inside—the same vantage point from which God sees Himself—He is mind. Our own human existence is a good analogy. Though we are a body on the outside, extended in space and enduring through time, on the inside we experience ourselves as mental beings. The totality of existence is a vast order built on the same pattern. Though on the outside extended in time and space, on the inside it is mental and spiritual.

Individual man, like the myriads of other objects that make up the universe, is a *mode* or modification of God. In him the thought and extension of God are both present, but they are there in a limited, fractional, specifically individuated object and are therefore modified. But since man is a thinking being and is conscious of his own thought, he is actually a little island of God's essence surrounded by the modes of the time-space order and the modes of his own human form. It is therefore possible for man to have a definite realization of his identity with God. It is not consistent with Spinoza's thought for a given person to maintain his individuality after he dies and so the limitations of these modes are removed. He will no longer be an island of God's essence but will be absorbed again into the totality of God.

This philosophy is probably most correctly termed *pantheism,* for according to it, generally speaking at least, all is God and God is all. Nevertheless, there are idealist principles in it, and the most important of these

[6] *Ethics*, Part I, Proposition XIV.

have been noted. Summarized, they are as follows: There is a substance undergirding the universe that exists eternally and infinitely. This substance is necessarily one in number. This substance is God. Although He is extension, as witnessed by the physical world about us, He is also a thinking being. Man too is a thinking being and, though a small fraction in the universe, is still a part of God.

D. LEIBNIZ (1646–1716)

Gottfried Wilhelm von Leibniz came by his philosophical pursuits honestly, for his father was professor of moral philosophy in the University of Leipzig. Although his father died when he was only six years old, the evidence indicates that the family was left in good circumstances economically, and the father's library kept intact. After the age of ten this unusual boy was allowed to make himself at home among his father's books, and with their help he prepared himself for the university. At the age of fourteen he entered the University of Leipzig to study law and philosophy. When he had reached his twentieth year, he had completed all the requirements for the degree of doctor of law, but because of his youth the degree was not granted. Although the University at Altdorf did confer the degree and in addition offer him a professorship, he entered the legal profession and filled high posts in government, which later took him to both Paris and London. Scholars as different as Bertrand Russell, the great British philosopher, and Karl Barth, the distinguished Swiss theologian, speak of Leibniz in levels of praise reserved for only a few men; at the same time, neither of them agrees with him except in minor matters.[7]

The ideas of Leibniz are recorded for the most part in shorter writings, such as letters to friends, summaries written in answer to questions about his philosophy, and articles for journals. His letters to Arnauld were not published until the nineteenth century, some two hundred years after his death, and other writings were unpublished as late as 1901 and 1903. He apparently declined to publish those writings during his lifetime for two reasons. He knew that some of them would not be received well by his contemporaries. In others he stated his own discovery of errors in Aristotle's logic, and because of his great respect for Aristotle it was difficult for him to believe the truth of his own discoveries.

Because his writings fall into two groups, those he was willing to have published and those he withheld, Bertrand Russell contends that there are two philosophies in Leibniz. The one that is more generally known Russell considers "optimistic, orthodox, fantastic, and shallow"; the other he calls

---

[7] Cf. Bertrand Russell, *A History of Western Philosophy*. New York: Simon and Schuster, 1945. P. 581; and Karl Barth, *Protestant Thought from Rousseau to Ritschl*. New York: Harper & Row, Publishers, 1952. Pp. 54–57.

"profound, coherent, largely Spinozistic, and amazingly logical." The latter of these two philosophies, assuming Russell's characterization is correct, is not a source for the philosophy of idealism so much as for modern logical positivism and language analysis. It will therefore be considered here more incidentally than the former.[8]

Leibniz paralleled Spinoza, whom he visited on one occasion, as a successor to Descartes. Both men attempted a kind of improvement on Descartes' dualism between the spiritualism of self and God on the one hand and the mechanism of a machine-like universe on the other. As has already been indicated, Spinoza tried to do this by conceiving God as both thought and extension. Leibniz attempted the improvement by trying to show that the created order is a vital living realm of being. Whereas Descartes held to a dualism and Spinoza to a monism, Leibniz was a pluralist. He apparently resolved the dualism of Descartes by a pluralism, rather than by a monism as Spinoza did, in order to explain the individuation found in a world made up of myriads of particular and distinct entities.

Perhaps the most characteristic aspect of the philosophy of Leibniz is his concept of *monadism,* the doctrine for which he is most commonly known and by which he tried to give a clear picture of the world as it really is. Leibniz used the term monad to describe the simple, indivisible units or entities that make up the cosmos. Monads have a number of characteristics, some of which will be mentioned. Each monad is different from all others. Monads are subject to continual change. Their change, however, is caused from within, as no cause from without can affect the interior of a monad. There are different kinds of monads.

1. There are simple monads, which have only the most general perceptions and desires. They are the elemental entities that constitute all material things, inorganic as well as organic. Their inner psychical state is similar to the inner experience a person has when he is in a deep, dreamless sleep. To think of the physical world as made up of such living units is *panpsychism,* the theory that Nature is physical or mental. It is tantamount to saying that the universe is made up of myriads of little organisms that are physical rather than mental. This conception seems fantastic, especially when we remember that Leibniz lived most of his life in the seventeenth century. But when we stop to compare, we can see that it may not be far removed from some conceptions of twentieth-century physics. Matter comprised not of space-filling substance but of points of electrical energy that do not themselves occupy space is not far different from a world comprised of Leibnizian monads, except that energy points are commonly assumed to be in some sense physical.

2. There are more complex monads, for which Leibniz reserved the

8 Cf. Bertrand Russell, *op. cit.,* pp. 581, 590–596.

name "soul." These have a greater awareness than simple monads do and enjoy sharper perceptions. They are also capable of remembering, so there is a certain consecutiveness in their experience. The soul of an animal is this kind of monad. Though the body of the animal, as those of higher organisms, may be made up of a great many simple monads, the psyche of the animal is the more complex kind of monad Leibniz called a soul.

3. There is a still higher and more complex type of monad to which Leibniz gave the name "spirit." A spirit has all the powers of souls and simple monads but has in addition the power of reason. Spirits are able to relate the items of their experience rationally and so obtain knowledge—knowledge of necessary truths, of self, and of God. Although most of us live the greater portion of our lives on the "soul" level of mere perception and continuity of events, men are capable of the higher "spirit" level of experience. It is reason that distinguishes men from animals. Our bodies, like theirs, are made up of almost countless simple monads, but our inner psychological essence is a monad of this highest sort, best denoted by the name "spirit."

God is a monad of the last type, but He is unique in being without limits and in having a total and all-inclusive perspective. The first of these two distinguishing marks is a familiar one, but the second needs to be explained in the context of Leibniz' thought. God is unique in being free from limitations because man and the almost infinite number of other monads all have limitations. Being without windows, as Leibniz said, they certainly do not have doors! The contrast between God and the monads in terms of perspective is a bit more difficult to describe. Each monad, according to Leibniz, mirrors some measure of perspective of other monads. This reflection of others varies in acuteness and approximation of perfection among the levels of monads. Nevertheless, each of them, including man, has its own perspective, however imperfect, in relation to the entire cosmos. God has no imperfection in this perspective; He sees the whole of the created order not only in its entirety but also perfectly, knowing every entity or particular monad comprising it.

Leibniz' concept of pre-established harmony has been generally known, but especially as a part of his solution to the mind-body problem. It does, however, relate to the entire cosmos comprised of monads, in the context of which the pre-established harmony of the mind and body of man can better be seen. Pre-established harmony is a kind of counterbalance for Leibniz' pluralism of monads, each having its determination from within itself rather than from force applied from without. Despite the myriad of entities comprising this pluralistic cosmos (not strictly a *universe*), chaos does not occur because in the original creation God established a harmony among the many monads. This harmony is a kind of internal timing or direction within each monad, matched precisely by that of every other.

Here the often used analogy from Leibniz of the two (or, more accurately, many) clocks is pertinent. None of the clocks ever needs to be reset, which would be *occasionalism,* a concept wholly repugnant to Leibniz, because in the beginning they were set in perfect harmony and they never gain or lose time. Incidental to this conception or implicit in it are two other important concepts. One of them is that the original creation was, as it were, once and for all time. For example, when a child is conceived and born, a new act of creation does not take place but rather an existing lower level monad is elevated to the level of "spirit." The other concept is that the pre-established harmony among the monads excludes all possible events not in accordance with this harmony; therefore, Leibniz created his often used word *"compossibility,"* possibility that is possible only together with other pre-established conditions. It is in part in relation to this concept that Leibniz spoke of our world as the best of all possible worlds, a well-known theme of his that has been both praised and ridiculed. While God could and did conceive of many possible created orders, the cosmos He did create was the best of all the possible ones.

It is in this setting of pre-established harmony and compossibility as well as monadism that the solution of the mind-body problem, for which Leibniz is famous, can best be seen. Remember that the monads cannot be affected by external causes. They are completely independent and in a sense completely free. Whatever movement or change goes on within a given monad must be due to inner causes and cannot be brought about by influences impinging from without, i.e., exerted by other monads.

When the relation of body and mind is considered in this context, it is clear that the activities of a spirit could scarcely be brought about by its physical body; nor could the monads comprising the body be affected by the spirit. Yet we all must recognize the high degree of unity there is in body-mind relationships. Leibniz' solution of this difficulty is that of "pre-established harmony,"[9] particularly expressed in the parallelism of body and mind.

In this connection the analogy of the *two* clocks (rather than many) makes the mind-body relation quite clear. The respective clocks of body and mind are so perfectly designed by the watchmaker to keep the same time that throughout the life of the clocks their every movement exactly corresponds. Neither is affected by the other; they both work as though the other did not exist, so far as any casual connections between them are concerned. Yet their activities correspond exactly in every detail. The mind in no way influences the events of bodily life; nor does the body affect the mind's activities. But God created the two with such perfect correspondence

---

[9] Cf. *The Monadology,* propositions 1 through 30. See George Martin Duncan, *The Philosophical Works of Leibniz.* New Haven: Tuttle, Morehouse, and Taylor, 1890. Pp. 218–222.

to each other that bodily activities always match mental activities, and vice versa. There is pre-established harmony between body and mind and therefore a remarkable unity of experience in our day-by-day activities.[10]

Leibniz' treatment of the problem of knowledge seems to be incidental to his monadology, which, of course, is his metaphysics. He says that there are three grades of notions: (1) There are *sensible* notions that are equivalent to specific sensations—the pain of the pinprick or the greenness of the grass, for example. (2) There are notions that are *sensible* but in addition are *intelligible*. In these *common sense* operates as well as specific sense organs. Apparently Leibniz refers to the power of perception when he speaks of common sense in this connection. These higher notions are gained by the kind of relating of specific sensations that takes place in perception. (3) The third and highest grade of notions are those that are *intelligible* only. They are ours by virtue of our power of understanding or reason. The two higher types of notions are both intelligible and distinct, but the lowest grade of notion is confused, although clear enough for such notions to be recognized.[11]

There are two great principles that are guides in discerning truth: the principle of contradiction and the principle of sufficient reason. (1) If a given proposition represented to be true involves a contradiction, it cannot be true. Truth is the antithesis of contradiction. (2) A supposed fact cannot be judged to be fact and therefore real and truly existent unless there is sufficient reason "why it is so and not otherwise." We may observe, for example, that the square of the number 4 equals $1 + 3 + 5 + 7$ (the sum of the first four odd numbers), and similarly that the square of 5 equals the sum of the first odd numbers; but we cannot assume that this relation of squares to an equal sum of odd numbers, beginning with the number 1, will always exist whatever number we choose unless we can figure out a sufficient reason why it should be so. It should be noted, however, that by sufficient reason Leibniz did not mean only a sufficient cause. The sufficient reason may well be a past event producing a present result; but it may also be, among other possibilities, a purpose to be fulfilled in the future that requires a present event.

It is on the ground of sufficient reason that Leibniz establishes his belief in God, thus tying his theory of knowledge to his metaphysics. The present set of facts that comprise the world as it now is must have had efficient causes[12] in previously existing facts. These in turn must have been caused

---

[10] Cf. *A New System of Nature.* See George Martin Duncan, *op. cit.*, pp. 71–93, especially pp. 91–93.

[11] Cf. *On the Supersensible Element in Knowledge, and on the Immaterial in Nature.* See George Martin Duncan, *op cit.*, pp. 149–158.

[12] As first used by Aristole in contrast to material, formal, and final causes. It may be exemplified by the energy and work of the craftsman as he gives "materials" a "form" which fulfills an "end."

by others farther back in the chain, and so on. Leibniz holds that there must be a sufficient or final reason outside of this infinite series of efficient causes. This final reason must be found in a necessary substance in which all the details of these successive changes are implicit. This necessary substance is God.[13]

To summarize, what is it that is idealistic in the philosophy of Leibniz? His monadology is idealistic in that the monads are conceived as points of mental force and not physical. His treatments of human selves as spirits and God as a spirit without limits are both important items in the metaphysics of idealism. His epistemology leans toward idealism, particularly in his treatment of the different levels of notions and his principle of contradiction. All of these are more fully worked out in Berkeley, Kant, and Hegel.

E. GEORGE BERKELEY (1685–1753)

Little is known of the early life of Bishop George Berkeley. He was born in Kilkenny, Ireland, probably the only child of his father's first wife, no doubt an Irish woman. There were other children, apparently by a later marriage. He entered Kilkenny School at eleven and received a very good education. There are indications that he was a precocious student. On one occasion, intrigued by a hanging he had witnessed, he and a fellow student contrived an experiment by which they hoped to find out what it felt like to be hanged. The experiment was almost too successful, but Berkeley's friend rescued him just in time from the dormitory-room hangman's noose. At fifteen he entered Trinity College, Dublin, where he later became an instructor, and then entered the ministry of the Episcopal Church in Ireland.

He was quite a traveler, journeying in England, on the Continent, and even to America, before settling down in 1734 as Bishop of Cloyne (Ireland), his most important position. As a younger man he had been well received by such men of letters as Addison and Steele. His trip to America was really a tragedy; he went there to establish a college in Bermuda and to make his home in the New World. But either Berkeley was visionary or his friends in England failed him, for the grant for the projected college never materialized. After a two-year sojourn in Providence, Rhode Island, brokenhearted, he took his young wife, a bride when she set sail with him from England, and an infant son born in America and returned to his homeland. After almost twenty years as Bishop of Cloyne he retired to Oxford for the few months before his death.

Berkeley wrote a number of major treatises in philosophy. The most

[13] Cf. *The Monadology*, propositions 36–39, p. 223.

Idealist

important is *The Principles of Human Knowledge*,[14] which presents forcefully the revolutionary character of his idealism. The present exposition of his point of view is based on this work.

One step in understanding Berkeley is to recognize one or two of the philosophic ideas that were popular in the early eighteenth century. The discoveries in physics made by Sir Isaac Newton had received lofty acclaim and had given rise to a commonly accepted world view. According to this popular philosophy, the real character of the universe was material bodies moving in space and controlled by rudimentary mathematical laws, such as the law of gravity. Berkeley revolted against the commonly accepted implication that matter is the substratum of the universe. He insisted that no one has ever experienced matter firsthand and that it is a conception of the mind, a theory rather than a fact. Therefore, he thought it was foolish to assume that this conception represented an actual reality. After all, he argued, man has no more direct experience of matter than he has of God, in fact not so much.

But we must try to get a glimpse of some of the detail in Berkeley's point of view and so catch more of its total import. Berkeley found the key to the problems of philosophy in solving the problem of knowledge. Correctly understand the character of knowledge, he thought, and you will have taken the major step in understanding the character of reality. To be more specific, the falsehood into which most men seem to fall is the assumption that *things* can exist without some *mind* to know or perceive their existence. This was the mistake of the materialists. They thought the so-called external physical world was an independently existing world. This led them into the greater error of assuming that matter is the self-subsistent substance that exists by its own strength and is the material of which the universe is made.

Berkeley felt it was strange that people should assume that houses, mountains, rivers, trees, etc., exist by themselves even when there is no mind at hand to perceive them. To say that a thing *exists*, he contended, is to say that a sensible object (an object that stimulates our senses) is perceived by some mind. The proverbial question about the tree falling in the forest is pertinent at this point in Berkeley's argument. Does the falling tree, in the heart of the forest where there is no man, make a noise? The answer is no, according to Berkeley, if for the time being we rule out any consideration of God's presence in the heart of the forest. In order for a falling tree to make a noise, there must be a mind there to interpret as noise the concussion of the tree against other trees and the ground. There is no existence without perception. *Berkeley*

[14] George Sampson (editor), *The Works of George Berkeley*. London: G. Bell & Sons, 1897. Pp. 153–252.

To be is to be perceived. Reality is what the mind tells us it is.

The things we actually see when we see an object are "so many sensa-tions, notions, ideas, or impressions on the sense."[15] Nor are these images inside of the skull, separated from the object "out there." The object and the sensations are the same and cannot be separated from each other. We might say that the objective world is to the mind of man as written music is to the musician. The raw material that makes music, whatever it is, must be refracted through the soul of the musician before it comes out as music. So it is with the world we experience every day: it is what it is because it is refracted through a perceiving mind. It does not exist as a world of objects and meanings without a mind to perceive it.

But what is the raw stuff of the world before it is refracted through the perceiving mind? Could it not be Newtonian "matter," somehow support-ing the potentialities that in perception become length, breadth, thickness, color, sound, pain, pressure, etc.? This was the position John Locke took and is roughly the position held by some modern realists. No, Berkeley would not listen to such an explanation of the character of reality. He held that it is not possible if his theory of knowledge is correct. How can something physical affect something mental? And what can be similar to an idea except an idea? If my perceiving mind gets ideas from the world surrounding me, then that world has to be a world of ideas. It cannot be a world of matter.

It is important to note at this point that Berkeley *did* assume that there must be something "out there" that is the substratum of ideas. We should not misinterpret him by saying that the world is a creation of the human mind and that any of us can fashion any kind of world we want for ourselves. According to this misinterpretation, all we would need to do would be to think the kind of world we desire, and, presto, we would have it. This is far from what Berkeley intended and may be recognized as similar to the psychology of escape. What Berkeley did affirm is his belief that the existence of the world as we experience it is dependent upon perceiving minds. But an important companion proposition is that the human mind is not the creator of its perceptions. We are on the receiv-ing end of our experience, not the creating or producing end, where the texture of the objective world is determined.

It is what is "out there" that produces our perceptions; and the "what" behind the objective world is Spirit. It is not matter; it is Spirit. This is the metaphysics Berkeley felt necessarily followed from his theory of knowl-edge. There is only one substance that is the substratum of both the mental and the objective world: this substance is Spirit, or God. By Spirit Berkeley meant a simple, undivided, active being whose two principal activities are creating and perceiving. Perceiving is the understanding aspect of spirit,

[15] *Ibid.*, p. 181.

and creating is the willing or volitional aspect. This metaphysical theory is that reality is what we experience it to be within ourselves, i.e., mentality. Since the world about us is a meaningful world of ideas, it must be the creative expression of an Infinite Mind, or God.

Though it is not too important, we may now return to our tree-in-the-forest question, with Berkeley's conception of God as the context. Does the falling tree make a noise when no human mind is at hand to perceive it? Yes, it does in the sense that there is an Infinite Mind everywhere in whose perception the qualities of experience exist. Of course the Infinite Mind creates these qualities, but He also perceives them.

One further detail of Berkeley's epistemology should be mentioned. He held that our knowledge of self and of God is an indirect or inferred knowledge. We only know directly those objects that can be perceived. The self cannot be an object of sensation, nor can God. Therefore, knowledge of our own existence and of the existence of God is inferred and not received directly.

Before leaving Berkeley, it is appropriate to note that he has been frequently criticized for his subjectivism and to assess the accuracy of this allegation. The chief basis, if not the only one, that makes this criticism legitimate is that Berkeley preferred enjoying the world to becoming involved in endeavors that led to progress and the improvement of man's lot. He compared the world to a book, and in using this figure commented that when we read a book, we read it to enjoy its meaning, not to parse all its sentences. According to his way of thinking, we should lay greater stress on the leisurely appreciation of the world than on the scientific analysis of its character. Had all philosophers thought like Berkeley on this subject, science might not have achieved its present advanced state. Nevertheless, recognizing this somewhat weak basis for the accusation is no reason to regard Berkeley as the symbol of subjectivism. We should remember that he did not deny the actuality of the external world, however much he may have winced at the parsing of its sentences by science, and that he was almost radically empirical in insisting that our ideas all come from the external world in some way and are particular, not general or abstract. Such a reminder reflects a very objective Berkeley, whose thinking was tied inseparably to the world beyond him.

The idealist elements in Berkeley scarcely need to be pointed out in summary. He was an idealist through and through; as some would mistakenly say, idealist in the most revolutionary, extremist, subjectivistic expression of the point of view. His two prime doctrines are: (1) The world, as we experience it, depends on our perceiving consciousness for its existence in the form in which we know it. "To be is to be perceived." (2) This being the character of knowledge, the necessary substratum of the objective world is revealed to be Spirit, Infinite Mind, God.

F. IMMANUEL KANT (1724–1804)

Immanuel Kant is one of the greatest philosophers of all time. There are few who do not honor him as a thinker of the greatest magnitude. Versatile and many sided though he was, in this historical sketch only those portions of his philosophy that are clearly related to idealism will be discussed. They are his precise analysis of the knowledge process and the metaphysical principles he held, such as the reality of the self and its freedom, the moral law and the imperative to fulfill it, immortality, and God.

Kant was born in Königsberg and lived there except for short periods of tutoring when he was a young man. His parents were humble Germans. Kant conjectured that his paternal grandfather emigrated from Scotland. These lowly forebears were members of the Pietist sect and brought up their children in the spirit and teachings of this devout group. Their son Immanuel retained throughout his life a profound respect for the high pietism of his home, but because of revulsion at his later encounters with lower forms of religious practice, he chose not to be identified with any forms of worship during his adult life.[16] Kant attended the University of Königsberg for six years, putting himself through by coaching well-to-do students. Whereas the strong tendency among his fellows was to prepare for one of the professions, Kant chose to focus his attention on learning as such. After an interlude of some years, during which he won recognition by his tutoring, he returned to Königsberg as an instructor in the University. Here he worked laboriously for fifteen years before he received the deserved recognition of full professorship. He taught a variety of subjects, and at the rate of sixteen to twenty-eight hours weekly. It has been conjectured that this is one reason for his late arrival as a productive scholar. His first major work, the *Critique of Pure Reason,* was published in 1781 when he was fifty-seven. But the delay was well counterbalanced by the period of productivity that followed. In the next ten years or so he turned out a number of important works, including the *Critique of Practical Reason,* the *Critique of Judgment, Fundamental Principles of the Metaphysic of Morals,* and *Religion Within the Limits of Reason Alone.*

A friend of Kant's returned to him the manuscript of the *Critique of Pure Reason* when only partly read, saying that he was sure he would lose his reason if he read it through to the end! The student, therefore, need not be surprised if patience is required to understand Kant. Because of the great comprehensiveness and caliber of his thought, it often seems that there is no end to the detailed excursions on which he takes his reader.

His purpose in this great work was to make a thorough examination of

---

[16] Cf. Theodore M. Greene in his introduction to Kant's *Religion Within the Limits of Reason Alone.* New York: Harper & Row, Publishers, 1960. Pp. xxvii–xxix.

reason, leaving no aspect of it untouched. In attempting to do this he has shown that conscious reason is the unifying center for all of our experience. We realize this only after engaging in an analysis such as Kant's because we unconsciously assume that the world about us has a unity of its own. According to Kant deeper insight reveals that it is our own conscious experience that gives our world its unity.

Let us think of my own individual private experience. The world is represented to me by means of my various senses. At this moment I have a multitude of sensations, now that I have stopped to give attention to them. They include the brightness of the sunlight coming through the window, the whiteness of the snow outside, the brownness of the table on which I write, the feeling of hardness that my pencil has, the sound of voices in another part of the house, the slight coolness of the atmosphere in my room, and a dull pain in the finger I injured the other day. These are just a few of them. (1) Each one of them is an infinitesimal representation of an almost microscopic part of the world about us. (2) I am passive in experiencing these sensations rather than active. They are simply impressed on my organism in some way, and now that I have stopped to think about them I am conscious that they are there. (3) Furthermore, they are unrelated at the sensory level. It is simply that the sun is bright, the snow is white, my finger hurts a little, etc. They are a chaos of representations. (4) And finally, it is to be noted that they are *re*presentations, not presentations; i.e., they are copies (after a fashion) of what is "out there" in the physical world. This is not to say that there is brightness, whiteness, hardness, and pain "out there." These are the sensory experiences that are represented to me in consciousness. But there is something out there that causes these sensations, and that something is separate and distinct from the sensations I have.

It is at higher levels than sensation that my experience of the world takes on unity. One of these is the level of perception. Notice that when I tried a few moments ago to describe some of my sensations, I could not describe them as they are on the purely sensory level. I talked about the brightness of the sunlight *coming through the window,* the whiteness of the snow *outside,* the brownness of the table *on which I write,* the feeling of hardness *my pencil has,* the sound of voices *in another part of the house,* and my finger, *which was hurt the other day.* There is already a certain unity in these sensations, once I have sufficiently recognized them to describe them. Consciousness is actively relating these sensations (in fact I had already related them without being conscious of doing it). All of them are placed in time and space. It is the whiteness of the snow *outside,* the hardness of *the pencil,* etc. My reason is so constructed that it has two predispositions for perceiving the qualities of sensation. These predispositions are space and time.

Some psychologists have held that there are "favored forms" in perception. For example, we tend to see things as circular, they say, that at best only approach the form of a circle as we actually sense them. For Kant, we might say that space and time are the two favored forms of perception. We relate all of our sensations by locating them in space and time. Because of these we see objects that are units in themselves as external to us and as related to other objects in an orderly way. By this Kant apparently meant to say that there are not specific segments of space and time in the world outside that separate objects and events and that our sensations copy for us. Instead, our minds relate the fragments of the world coming to us through sensation by locating them in time and space. Whatever the external world is in its ultimate character, it is amenable to the temporal and spatial forms apparently habitual to reason, but it is not made up of given segments of space and time.

Although the categories of space and time bring unity into experience at the perceptual level, they do not explain the total unity of experience we enjoy. The relating of fragmentary sensations by locating them in space and time is only a partial approach to unity. It is reason (the word is used here to refer specifically to the power of relating ideas logically) that fits perceived objects into their respective classes and thus supplements perception in giving us the perfectly integrated experience we all normally possess. Kant spoke of this aspect of mind as the *understanding;* the classes in which we group objects according to similarities and differences are *conceptions.*

The understanding being what it is, there is a definite number of kinds of conceptions possible. Kant claimed to have examined all of the possibilities and discovered that reason being what it is there are just twelve kinds of conceptions. These he calls *categories.* Within the twelve categories of the understanding there are four groups of three categories. In other words, the categories are grouped according to whether they are concerned with conceptions of *quantity, quality, relation,* or *modality.* As an example of the further breakdown in Kant's table of categories, the three categories of *quantity* are *unity, plurality,* and *totality.* We shall go no further into the Kantian deep waters. We now have an outline of Kant's theory of knowledge, even though it is an inadequate sketch. The point to be made by way of generalization is that in the experience of knowledge and the mind's relation to its world, the direction of movement is from the mind toward the world, not from the world to the mind, with the slight exception of the level at which unrelated *sensa* are received. The understanding, with its categories, has an organizing machinery by which it approaches the world and relates things logically. By the perceptual categories of space and time the reason approaches its world and brings order to chaotic sensations, unifying them in distinct and definite objects. These perceived objects are the raw material with which the understanding works. For example, a cluster of sensations perceived as a given tree is related in reason to a class of objects denoted as trees. The process of perception is in turn dependent on conception; there has to be a logical classifying of objects in order for them to be recognized (cognized) for what they are. It is only at the most elementary sensory level that reason is passive and receptive. In sensation the external world impresses itself upon us, and this is a passive process from the knower's standpoint.

An important question to ask at this point is this: What is it "out there" in the external world that gives us these sense impressions? Kant's answer was that there is of course something "out there" that produces these qualities in our experience. This something he calls the *thing-in-itself.* He said further that the thing-in-itself cannot be known. It defies our knowledge. If it once entered into reason, it would then be a representation and no longer what it is in itself. Therefore, it must always be unknown. Some post-Kantian idealists have said that the thing-in-itself is Universal Reason, or God. But Kant at this point gives us an agnostic answer, although in his *Critique of Practical Reason* and the *Metaphysics of Morals* he bases belief in God on moral grounds.

There is a subtle knowledge of the existence of the self that is a part of rational experience as it has been described by Kant. The self cannot be isolated as an object and become the center of consciousness directly. But as we are in relation to the world, we see the activities of the self—these rational, relating, ordering, unifying activities. The unity of our experience is an identical element running through all experiences. In being conscious of this identity we have a knowledge of self from within as a subject in relation to the objective world.

In his *Metaphysic of Morals* and *Critique of Practical Reason* Kant expounded other principles quite common among idealists. As some of them are discussed more fully in the next chapter to exemplify the ethical values of idealism, they will be only briefly mentioned in concluding this discussion.

1. He believed that there are universal moral laws. An individual, he held, cannot morally engage in some act if he sees that such an act cannot be universally practiced by all men. An individual murder, for example, may appear to be justified by itself, but when generalized so that it becomes a universal practice, it would result in race suicide.

2. He believed that man has a feeling of obligation to act in obedience to these moral laws. This sense of duty is not in any way the result of experience. It is rooted in reason just as the categories of perception and conception are. It is therefore called a *categorical imperative.*

3. He believed in freedom. According to Kant, it is possible for an individual to act purely out of desire or intention to do good, i.e., to fulfill

the moral law that reason, free from any dependence upon experience, ordains as the guide to conduct. To be honest because honesty proves to be the best policy is not being moral. Honesty under such conditions is motivated not by its own value, but by the extrinsic return it brings. To be honest when I know that there will be no compensation for it, or without any anticipation of the compensations that may result, is to act morally. This is giving expression to the *good will* that is really the only unqualified good in man's world.

4. He believed in the immortality of the soul. This doctrine is a direct outgrowth of his conception of man's obligation to the moral law. The ultimate good for man is the perfect harmony of his will with the moral law. But this is "a perfection of which no rational being of the sensible world is capable at any moment of his existence."[17] An infinite progress is therefore necessary in order for this perfect holiness to be achieved, and this means that the soul of man must be immortal.

5. Finally, Kant believed in the existence of God. He felt that the categorical imperative and the lack of moral guarantees in the natural world make the existence of God necessary. We find that we have in us an obligation to moral law that is directed toward the end of achieving moral perfection. It is necessary that there be a Supreme Intelligence as the cause of this moral obligation in us. Again, the moral law requires obedience of us, but in the natural world there is no guarantee that contentment shall accompany obedience. It is necessary, therefore, that a higher order than the natural world be assumed, a society of moral selves and a Supreme Being, in order for blessedness to be guaranteed to those obeying the moral law.

Although the doctrines of Kant just listed are accepted by many idealists, it is probably more important to keep in mind his more difficult theory of knowledge as a distinctive contribution to the development of idealism. There are antecedents of modern realism in Kant's theory of knowledge also; but this careful analysis of the knowing process was the springboard from which modern idealism got much of its momentum. To say that the self contributes both quality and unity to the objective world, as Kant did, is to reaffirm much of Berkeley's epistemology, but with more penetrating analysis. This was the important contribution of Kant to the development of the philosophy of idealism.

G. HEGEL (1770–1831)

A more extended and inclusive history of idealism would give more detailed attention to developments preceding and following the career of

17 *Critique of Practical Reason*, in Theodore Meyer Greene (editor), *Kant Selections*. New York: Charles Scribner's Sons, 1929. P. 358.

Hegel, supposed by many to have been the culmination of the idealist movement. Probably the most important figure linking Kant and Hegel was Johann Gottlieb Fichte (1762–1814).

Fichte was a disciple of Kant. On one occasion, now historically important, he visited Kant at Königsberg. Not making any impression upon the great master, he stayed in the city long enough to write an article on some phases of the Kantian philosophy not then worked out by Kant. Fichte's idol was so impressed by the treatise that he had it published. Almost overnight the once unimpressive aspirant became a philosopher of repute. His eventual position of most strategic influence was the chair of philosophy at Berlin, later occupied by Hegel.

Fichte was profoundly interested in the ethical side of life. He thought of reality as a morally purposeful Will and regarded the phenomenal world as designed to develop the will of man and bring his character into being. Kant was wrong, said Fichte, in speaking of a thing-in-itself and regarding it as unknowable. Reality is an "Ego-in-itself"; this is the phrase Kant might better have used. There is a Universal Ego on the other side of the phenomenal world, just as for you and me there is a finite ego on our own subjective side of experience. To each one of us the world surrounding us is a notself that gives us resistance and so brings out of us effortful accomplishment, by which we achieve our fullest selfhood.

In his book *The Spirit of Modern Philosophy*[18] Josiah Royce, one of Hegel's most effective expositors in this country, takes this great idealist to task because he never had a crisis in his life. Royce seems to feel that Hegel was either too tough-minded or else took life too much as it came. The student trying to break into an understanding of his philosophy will not find it hard to agree that Hegel lacked warmth. Regardless of other impressions, because of the vast comprehensiveness of Hegel's doctrine, the student can scarcely miss recognizing his greatness.

The parents of Georg Wilhelm Friedrich Hegel lived in Stuttgart and were moderately well-to-do people. Their son attended the University of Tübingen, there to be a fellow student of Frederick William Joseph Schelling (1775–1854), who rose to fame before Hegel did. Schelling's help played at least a small part in Hegel's rise to success at Jena; but when he became established there as a professor in 1805, he broke with Schelling and criticized his philosophy. After the battle of Jena in 1806, a decisive defeat for Prussia, Hegel lost his professorship and was not re-established in the academic world until 1816, when he became a professor at Heidelberg. During the intervening years he kept persistently at the task of building his philsophy, maintaining himself by working as a newspaper editor and later as headmaster of a boys' school. After two years at Heidelberg he was called to Berlin to fill the chair made famous by Fichte. There he

[18] Boston: Houghton Mifflin Company, 1892.

Dialectic

Before he perceives God — Hierarchy of mental process

remained until his death in 1831. During his Berlin period he was the undisputed leading philosopher in Germany, too much the fair-haired boy of the government, however. People of other countries came to Berlin to study with him, including a significant number from America.

Hegel had a great weakness for paradoxes. A story is told that on one occasion during his student days he went out with a group of fellow students to study the stars. The night turned out to be cloudy, entirely unsuited to stargazing. But, boys being boys, they found other things to engage their interest and didn't return to the university until the small hours of the morning. They were appropriately reprimanded by an official of the institution and admonished with some such words as these: "From now on, do your stargazing in the daytime." Just the kind of contradiction that delighted the embryonic young philosopher. On another occasion, when he was visiting in the country, a large bowl of cherries was placed before him one morning at breakfast. The young lover of paradox did not enjoy eating the cherries half so much as he enjoyed musing on his reaction to this bowl of plenty. How often in town, where fruit was scarce, had he longed for an abundance of cherries. But now that the abudnance was at hand and he could eat his fill, he was not nearly so hungry for them. These apparently unimportant incidents in his life may suggest an important clue to his difficult philosophy.

Whoever attempts to write an exposition of Hegel, particularly a short, sketchy one, faces a paradox in his own method to begin with. If he thinks he understands Hegel and is therefore determined to be conscientiously accurate in his exposition, he is quite certain not to succeed in making himself understood. If, on the other hand, he is out to make his exposition clear and understandable, he is likely not to be accurate and true to Hegel in everything he says about him. Is there any way out of this dilemma? The reader will have to be the judge.

Unless he has an unusual imagination, it would seem that the student of anatomy must make a major adjustment when he does his first vivisections. If his previous knowledge has been entirely based on textbook, lecture, chart, and diagram, he now has some remarkably new factors with which to deal. Anatomical parts are now handled and seen as related to one another in three dimensions, often while many vital functions are still going on.

The philosophy of Hegel may be compared to many other philosophies in much this same way. It is a philosophy of multiple dimensions, whereas most others are stated in straight-line arguments in which one point can usually be seen to follow another quite directly. There are few clear-cut statements in Hegel like Berkeley's "to be is to be perceived." Instead, words are used to draw many circles of different sizes and relationships, crisscrossing each other at every angle, which, after patient study and

Evil is the reason we understand good. compare,

thought, the student can eventually visualize as being fitted together to make a perfectly symmetrical sphere.

One aspect of this is seen in a motif running through Hegel's philosophy to the effect that parts must always be viewed in relation to the whole, never in isolation. Thornton Wilder, in his play *Our Town*, exemplifies this motif vividly, though in funmaking criticism of Hegelian influence in this country just before the turn of the century. In the story it is reported that Miss Jane Crofut has received a letter from the minister in the town where she used to live before moving to Grover's Corners. The envelope in which the letter was mailed bore the following address:

Jane Crofut; the Crofut Farm; Grover's Corners; Sutton County; New Hampshire; United States of America; Continent of North America; Western Hemisphere; The Earth; the Solar System; The Universe; The Mind of God.[19]

It is in much the same way that each item of experience is viewed by Hegel. Each individual is related to the totality of the cosmos and cannot be understood correctly apart from this totality.

Would you find the value of any single fact in experience? You will never grasp it by trying to deal with the fact in isolation. You must relate it to the whole. It is only in this setting of total relationship that the true significance can be found. Similarly, would you discover yourself? Would you become the real self it is in you to become? Then you must relate yourself to the totality of the cosmos and all existence. Just as the address on Jane Crofut's letter wittily symbolizes, you will find the full meaning of your own life only by relating it to the totality of all things, which for Hegel is The Absolute Idea.

Hegel's attitude toward Kant ties in closely with this emphasis on totality. He felt that Kant gave a reasonably dependable account of sense perception and the mind's power to unify its experience. Though he didn't entirely agree with his analysis of the categories of the mind, Hegel felt that metaphysics would never be the same after Kant had subjected knowledge to such a meticulous examination. No longer could philosophers take for granted their habits of thought; this was the great service rendered to philosophy by Kant. But, according to Hegel, Kant was entirely too subjective. He treated mind as a fact of a person's inner makeup but could not see mind "out there" in the world objective to man and independent of finite mind. To do this was to break existence apart into a dualism not justified by the facts and which of course runs counter to any attempt at conceiving reality as a unified totality. Kant recognized the "that" of existence when he spoke of the thing-in-itself, but he was in error in not attempting to tell

[19] Thornton Wilder, *Our Town*, in Burns Mantle (editor), *The Best Plays of 1937–38*. New York: Dodd, Mead & Company, 1938. P. 75.

us something about the "what" of existence as a part of his critical philosophy. Now a "being" assumed to have no knowable qualities (as is the case with Kant's thing-in-itself) is not far different from a "nothing," which of course has no real being. In fact, for Hegel the two are virtually the same thing. Therefore, Kant's thing-in-itself is an abstraction. The real being that is "out there" in any instance of knowing is comprised of the very qualities it has in relation to the absolute whole. It is the "what" of perception just as much as it is the "that" referred to as the thing-in-itself by Kant. It is not an unknowable thing-in-itself; it is a being possessing knowable qualities.

To enlarge on this in accordance with what seems to be the broad outline of Hegel's philosophy, it is probably correct to say that reality in its ultimate, final, and absolute essence is Mind or Spirit objectified in and for Itself. This reality is not just the substratum of the physical world; it is the final goal or objective toward which all creation moves. The natural world, a world of phenomena and finite beings, is a process of becoming. It is a sort of cosmic funnel through which temporary and transient beings move from sheer being or nothingness, at the entrance of the funnel, to Absolute Being, at the other and much narrower opening. Mind is something to be achieved by creation at the same time that it is the self-subsistent Absolute Idea that is the substructure of the phenomenal world. The natural order is very significant in Hegel's system, however; Nature is necessary to Mind as a means of objectifying and realizing itself.

Hegel is not correctly characterized as a pantheist. For him the natural order is a finite and temporal aspect of the Absolute Mind, which is infinite and permanent. Though it is necessary as a means of objectifying Mind, it has its foundation in Mind. Mind is greater than Nature, not Nature greater than or equal to Mind, as in pantheism.

The method of thought followed by Hegel should now be in evidence. His youthful interest in paradox emerged in his thinking as a philosophical pattern. "Stargazing in the daytime" and "a ravenous appetite for cherries when there are none, but little craving when there is a plenty" became in his maturity a formalized logic commonly referred to as "dialectic." There are three stages in this method that together comprise a triad, they are: thesis, antithesis, and synthesis. The all-inclusive triad in Hegel's philosophy, described just above, is (1) thesis, the Idea; (2) antithesis, Nature; and (3) synthesis, Mind or Spirit. The thesis and antithesis, as their names indicate, are contradictory or in some way opposed to each other. The synthesis combines into a unity the positive and affirmative elements of both. Another triad already mentioned may be formalized as follows: (1) thesis, being; (2) antithesis, nothing; and (3) synthesis, becoming.

Enough has been said to imply that this system of conflicts and paradoxes is, for Hegel, rooted in the very character of existence. There is unity through contrast woven into the very texture of the cosmos. Dialectic is also the pattern by which thought moves. The limitations of our own finite minds are revealed to us by the contradictions into which our thoughts lead us. When we find a contradiction in our thinking, it is an indication that there is some higher unity to be found by synthesizing the affirmative elements in the contradiciton. Still another aspect of this multidimensional philosophy in which dialectic functions is history. The history of the human race is a story of successive contradictions and conflicts that have been resolved only by successive syntheses that cause new triads to arise in the social process. Progress is made through the long ages by the eternal pendulum swing of thesis and antithesis in human affairs.

The realm of morals is also amenable to this dialectical movement. The age-old problem of the human race that has given most trouble is that of the origin and nature of evil. Is evil a positive principle that stands on its own feet? How can this be if there is unity in the cosmos and somehow an ultimate good? A self-subsistent evil can hardly be harmonized with a good God. One way Hegel states this triad in ethics is to set innocent intention against evil in thesis-antithesis arrangement and then find the synthesis in conscience. Innocence has an affirmative aspect: there is some positive value to be desired in the innocence of the small child. But in order for innocence to achieve a full possession of itself, it must be exposed to evil and thereby the consequences of its intentions. It is out of the conflict between intention and responsible recognition of consequences that innocence may emerge in a fully realized and self-possessed conscience. Evil does not, therefore, have independent existence, but it is a necessary aspect of the full realization of good.

One final glimpse of Hegel's philosophy may be gotten by comparing it to other systems of philosophy as Hegel viewed the comparison. Hegel does not think of his position as an out-and-out contradiction of every other philosophy not harmonizing with it, but he is nonetheless confirmed in his convictions. He regards his philosophy as the grand synthesis in which all other philosophies are to be found in their place and tied together with the supplementing conceptions that they themselves have omitted. Viewed in the light of Hegelian idealism, the history of philosophy is the story not of distinctly different points of view but of the growing up and maturing of man's thought. To study any contemporary cross section of philosophic opinion, points of view must be arranged in some kind of ascending scale, each representing a stage in the progress of Mind toward its ultimate realization. Absolute idealism is the ultimate inclusion of the truth of all points of view in one grand, overall, all-inclusive world view. Or compare different levels of refinement among people; you will find much the same growth of Mind in evidence. The mind of the market place, for example, with its rather crude perceptions and dull insights, represents a lower level in the development of Mind than do those of the philosopher-kings of Plato's *Republic,* who were to gain their right to rule by virtue of achieving their great love of wisdom.

How can we now summarize a philosophy such as Hegel's, an exposition of which is at best a summary skecth itself? Like Berkeley, Hegel is an idealist through and through, but in a different way. The phenomenal world with all of its manifold interrelationships is a manifestation of Infinite Mind realizing itself in finite and temporal processes. At bottom, the so-called physical world is Idea; this is the foundation it rests upon. At top, the far-off end toward which it moves is Mind, Spirit, the Infinite Idea, fully realized in and for itself. Viewed from man's finite vantage point, every aspect of this temporal world is a part of the groaning of creation as it moves toward the Absolute End. Thought, history, wars, social institutions, politics, ethics, religion, and art—all of these and many others are phases of this eternal activity of Absolute Mind.[20]

Postscript. In about 1820 a young man who styled himself a competitor of the great Hegel came to the fore in Berlin. So sure was he that he was a greater philosopher that he scheduled a series of lectures at the same hour as a popular course offered by Hegel. The sequel was sad and disappointing. Almost no one turned up to hear the newcomer, and the series petered out for lack of an audience.

This young man was Arthur Schopenhauer (1788–1860). He has since become famous as one of the world's greatest pessimists, sharing the honors with Gautama Buddha. But he deserves all the recognition he has received. For one thing, he wrote philosophy so that it could be understood. For another, he formulated a theory of aesthetics that is as inspiring as his pessimism is despairing. And even his pessimism may evoke something more positive in those who study it. It is much easier to detour his dismal view of life by trying to psychoanalyze him than it is to take his blows on the chin and meet them with more appropriate counterthrusts.

We note him in passing because he was one of the great idealists who, like Fichte, should certainly be included in any adequate history of idealism. His theory of knowledge bore similarities to that of Berkeley. "The World," he said, "is my idea." But his metaphysics was unique. The ultimate reality behind the phenomenal world was for him a universal Will. He elevated music to the highest place among the arts because it does what no art that uses objects of the phenomenal world as models can do. It gives expression to the surge of the infinite Will that is underneath all phenomena and is pulsating in the human breast, the very substructure of the

---

[20] Cf. William Wallace, *The Logic of Hegel.* Oxford: Clarendon Press, 1874.

cosmos. His great masterpiece was *The World as Will and Idea*,[21] a title eloquently suggestive of the spirit and character of his philosophy.

H. RECENT AND CONTEMPORARY IDEALISM IN ENGLAND AND SCOTLAND

Following the period of Kant and Hegel, in whom idealism reached a full expression, there was a surge of idealist influence in countries other than Germany. In France, Henri Bergson (1859–1941) became the exponent of a kind of idealism closest to that of Schopenhauer among those mentioned in the foregoing sketch, but because of its intuitionism and not its pessimism. In Italy, Benedetto Croce (1866–1952) and Giovanni Gentile (1875–1944), both idealists, achieved renown as philosophers and had some part in affairs of state. Differing somewhat in their approaches to politics, Gentile was for two years Minister of Education in Mussolini's government and Croce was ardent in opposing it. The influence of idealism should also be connected, at least indirectly, with the dialectical materialism of Ludwig Feuerbach (1804–1872), Karl Marx (1818–1883), and Friedrich Engels (1820–1895), which in the twentieth century produced the socialist revolution in Russia. Not because the official philosophy of the U.S.S.R. is idealism should a connection be made, but because it was developed as a counterthrust to idealism. The dialectical materialists embraced the dialectic of Hegel but rejected his idealism; they accepted the form of Hegelian thought but substituted a materialistic metaphysics for Hegel's idealistic metaphysics. Hence the name dialectical materialism, although the position is sometimes referred to as the Hegelianism of the left.

Because of his influence in more recent times, Edmund Husserl (1859–1938) is included here as still another Continental philosopher related to the idealist stream of thought. He was professor of philosophy at Freiburg and Martin Heidegger (1889–) of existentialist fame, was his distinguished student and successor. Husserl is known as an exponent of phenomenology, which would at first appear to set him over against idealism as an opponent. Yet his preoccupation with phenomena was not directed to particular objects or facts of the empirical world. He was interested rather in all phenomena possible to any physical order which is relative to consciousness, as all orders must be with which mind can have a knowledge relationship. Husserl had some similarity to idealism, whether or not he would have been pleased with this characterization, because his phenomenology was a *transcendental phenomenology* centered upon con-

[21] Fourth edition. Translated by R. B. Haldane; London: Routledge & Kegan Paul, 1896.

ceiving the kinds of phenomena possible to Nature and prior to the orderly arrangements constructed by mathematics and the various sciences. It was not, therefore, a phenomenalism limited by descriptive accounts of objects and events actually occurring in the natural order.

To extend attention beyond the Continent, it can be said that the influence of idealism in Britain and America has been pronounced. And for English-speaking students the tracing of this influence is most important. In England, the earliest evidence of attraction to the philosophy of idealism was the poetry of Samuel Taylor Coleridge (1772–1834). That Coleridge studied Kant, Fichte, Schelling, and Hegel is definitely known. But although his writings were collected by Joseph Henry Green (1791–1863), a surgeon and intimate friend, and published under the title, *Spiritual Philosophy, Founded on the Teaching of the Late S. T. Coleridge* (1865), his idealism seemed not to have had much effect on British thought generally. Following Coleridge, Thomas Carlyle (1795–1881) appropriated the spiritual values of German thought and, though less a philosopher than Coleridge, gave them a more convincing statement.

Here and there, a professor was to be found who rejected the more prevalent English *empiricism* and favored an idealist position in his teaching. But it was not until after the middle of the nineteenth century, when Benjamin Jowett (1817–1893) inspired a great revival of interest in Greek philosophy, that German idealism really took root and began to flourish. Jowett is most famous for his translations of Plato; but the Greek philosophy in which his work brought revived interest had such close parallels with German thought that study of the latter followed as a natural consequence.

In 1865 there appeared an English work on idealism which was of such caliber and depth as to set in motion in Britain an idealist intellectual movement. The book was *The Secret Hegel* (two volumes) by James Hutchison Stirling (1820–1909). This countered the inertia of British empiricism, and there followed a torrent of idealist interest, study, and writing. In 1876 the journal *Mind* was established. While it was not a publication dedicated to idealism alone, it did provide a medium of expression for the new movement. Many treatises on subjects in idealism appeared subsequently, and scholars emerged into prominence whose names are now symbols of the idealist movement. Some of the more important men will be mentioned.

John Caird (1820–1898), vice-chancellor and principal of Glasgow University, was builder of an idealist philosophy of religion. Edward Caird (1835–1908), his younger but more illustrious brother, was successor to Jowett as master of Balliol College, Oxford. The younger Caird's major service was the interpretation of Kant and Hegel to the English mind, writing major works on the philosophies of both men. Thomas Hill Green

(1836–1882) was professor of moral philosophy at Oxford. According to Rudolf Metz in his book, *A Hundred Years of British Philosophy,* Green built successfully on the foundation laid by Stirling in developing idealist thought in England, more than any other man. Andrew Martin Fairbairn (1838–1912), principal of Mansfield College, Oxford, studied in Germany as a young man and like John Caird was builder of a Hegelian philosophy of religion. Francis Herbert Bradley (1846–1924), fellow of Merton College, Oxford, was a philosopher of the first magnitude and author of many works. Probably his most famous book is *Appearance and Reality* (1893). Bernard Bosanquet (1848–1923) held several university posts before 1908, but after that time, having private means, he spent most of his time in independent writing and lecturing. The two British names probably most heard in recent discussions of idealism are those of Bradley and Bosanquet.[22]

I. RECENT AND CONTEMPORARY IDEALISM IN AMERICA

At the beginning of the nineteenth century, America had little interest in things German. Few Americans were able to speak German; furthermore German dictionaries and grammars were scarcely to be found anywhere. To our great-great-grandparents living at that time it would have been hard to believe that German thought and culture were to have such an effect as they proved to have before the turn of the century.

This influence from Germany first began to trickle in through the writings of Coleridge and Carlyle. In these, the early English assimilation of German idealism was made available beyond the barrier of language. Coleridge's *Aids to Reflection,* edited by President James Marsh of the University of Vermont and published in 1829, did much to encourage the rise of New England transcendentalism.

Ralph Waldo Emerson (1803–1882) did much the same thing for idealism in America that Coleridge and Carlyle did in Great Britain. He was not however as directly influenced by German idealists as these men, nor was he as deliberate in the desire to give expression to the new wisdom of idealism. He was less a philosopher in the systematic sense and at the same time more original. Emerson voiced the spirit of transcendentalism found in his own soul, maybe in some ways nourished there by German philosophers (he did study in Göttingen in 1824), but for the most part an independent shoot growing and flourishing by itself. Like Coleridge and Carlyle, his literature prepared the ground in which a vigorous philosophical idealism later took root.

[22] Cf. Rudolf Metz, *A Hundred Years of British Philosophy.* Translated by J. W. Harvey, T. E. Jessop, and Henry Stuart. Edited by J. H. Muirhead. New York: The Macmillan Company, 1938. Pp. 237–446.

The other factors bringing German influence to America were the exodus to Germany of Americans in search of advanced study and the importing of German scholars to American universities. Some of these imported professors may be mentioned. Frederick A. Rauch (1806–1841) was president of Marshall College in Pennsylvania from 1836 until his death. Carl Follen (1796–1840) was the first teacher of the German language in Harvard. Francis Lieber (1800–1872) was first a professor at South Carolina College and later became professor of history and political science in Columbia College, New York. And Louis Agassiz (1807–1873) became professor of natural history in Harvard in 1848.

The names of a few famous Americans who studied in Germany will reflect the other side of this reciprocal movement. They are Edward Everett, later the president of Harvard; George Ticknor, the first professor of modern languages in Harvard; George Bancroft, eminent historian; Henry Wadsworth Longfellow; Horace Mann, leader in the mid-nineteenth-century educational revival; Henry Barnard, teammate of Mann in the revival of American education and first United States Commissioner of Education; Henry P. Tappan, president of the University of Michigan; and G. Stanley Hall, pioneer psychologist and president of Clark University. It is estimated that by 1850 fully one hundred Americans had been enrolled in the German universities of Göttingen, Berlin, Halle, and Leipzig.

This suggests the channeling of German influence in America. Philosophical idealism, of course, was only one of the currents which flowed through these channels. The first really deliberate step in setting in motion the American idealist movement was taken in St. Louis, Missouri, for there in 1866 the St. Louis Philosophical Society was formed and in 1867 the *Journal of Speculative Philosophy* was launched. William T. Harris was the leader of the St. Louis venture but of almost equal importance was Henry C. Brokmeyer's contagious interest in Hegel. Born in Germany, Brokmeyer (1828–1906) came to the United States when he was seventeen. He attended Georgetown College and Brown University, but apparently was far from being a scholar. It is not quite clear just how he came by his taste for Hegel, but he was an ardent disciple and had the enthusiasm to win others to his first love.

William T. Harris (1835–1909) went from Connecticut to St. Louis in 1857 as a teacher of shorthand. Within eleven years he was the city's superintendent of schools and a national figure in education. He became acquainted with Brokmeyer shortly after his arrival and was attracted to Hegelianism through his influence. The formation of the Kant Club followed some years later. This was a small group within the St. Louis Philosophical Society devoted to the study of Hegel. But the most important result relating to the spread of Hegelian influence was the *Journal of Speculative Philosophy*. In its pages Hegel was made to "speak English" over a period of twenty-six years of publication (1867–1893). Harris was an educator as well as a philosopher, and was consequently involved in heavy administrative responsibilities throughout most of his career. In 1880 he resigned his position in St. Louis to become the directing genius of the famous Concord School of Philosophy, significant as an attempt at merging the New England transcendentalism and Hegelian idealism. But this New England venture did not pan out as well as Harris had reason to expect and in 1887 he became United States Commissioner of Education, the post in which he remained until his death. Inspiration of many in the St. Louis group, founder and editor of the first philosophical journal in this country, one of the most important national leaders in education, and popular lecturer, William T. Harris, it can justly be said, was the fountainhead of the American idealist movement.

As though children constituting a new generation, there were later exponents of idealism in America, each having a university post as his center of influence. These may be loosely termed the successors to the St. Louis "school" in the spread of American idealism. George H. Howison (1834–1916) was a member of the St. Louis Philosophical Society in his younger days while teaching mathematics at Washington University. After studying in Germany and holding positions in several universities, he became professor of philosophy in the University of California, the strategic situation with which his name is most commonly associated. Among his famous students are two outstanding realists, E. B. McGilvary and A. O. Lovejoy. W. P. Montague, another realist, was an associate of his for a time.

Borden Parker Bowne (1847–1910), after studying in Germany and following a brief career in journalism, became a professor at Boston University. There for years he made a valuable contribution by his teaching and writing. Many students of religion and ministers of the Methodist Church came under his influence. His most famous student was Edgar Sheffield Brightman, Bowne's successor in the Boston University chair.

Josiah Royce (1855–1916) was probably the greatest single exponent of idealism in America, although never identified with the St. Louis group. Reared in the Far West, he did advanced study in Germany and at Johns Hopkins in this country. Discovered by William James while he was studying at Johns Hopkins, Royce was brought by him to Harvard and eventually became a professor there, to remain for the rest of his life. Among his outstanding student-disciples were William E. Hocking of Harvard, the late Mary Whiton Calkins of Wellesley, and the late Herman H. Horne of New York University.

James Edwin Creighton (1861–1924) grew up in Nova Scotia. There he studied at Dalhousie College with J. G. Schurman. A year after Schurman was invited to Cornell, Creighton followed in order to continue his studies with him. After further work in Germany he became an instructor at

Cornell, cofounder with Schurman of the *Philosophical Review,* professor of logic and metaphysics, and eventually dean of the Graduate School of Cornell for eleven years just before his death.

As the following chapter will be a brief analysis of idealism as given expression by recent and contemporary idealists, nothing is said at this point to reflect the individuality of the points of view of the American idealists just mentioned. It is to be noted, however, that they are by no means of one mind. All can rightly be regarded as figures in the idealist succession in America; but all are distinctly original thinkers, not mere mouthpieces for Hegelian ideas.[23]

J. SYNTHESIS

Having outlined the history of idealism, it now remains to draw a few threads together that may indicate the distinctive and common ground on which most idealists unite. If synthesis is restricted to the more central beliefs commonly reiterated throughout the development of idealism, three sets of propositions can be drawn up that will help to suggest the idealist position at a glance. They have to do with three chief subjects: God, the self, and knowledge. The synthesis is as follows:

On God

1. Ultimate reality is of the same substance as ideas.—Plato and Hegel
2. Behind the phenomenal world is an infinite Spirit that is both substructure and creator of the cosmos.—Leibniz and Berkeley
3. One of the two attributes of God is thought.—Spinoza
4. The existence of God is made necessary by certain factors in selfhood.
   a. The fact that I have an idea of perfect being necessitates that perfect being exists.—Descartes
   b. The fact that I can perceive qualities in the objective world necessitates a God to create these qualities.—Berkeley
   c. The fact that there is a category of imperatives in the self necessitates God as the one who guarantees contentment as the accompaniment of moral obedience.—Kant

On the Self

1. The self is the prime reality in the experience of a person.—Descartes, Berkeley, and Kant

[23] Cf. Walter G. Muelder and Laurence Sears, *The Development of American Philosophy.* Boston: Houghton Mifflin Company, 1940. Pp. 217–310 and 485–528. Also Harvey Gates Townsend, *Philosophical Ideas in the United States.* New York: American Book Company, 1934. Chapters VI and VIII.

2. Human selves are like God in that they are spirits, unlike Him in that they are finite.—Leibniz
3. Man as a thinking being is a part of God.—Spinoza
4. The human self has freedom of will.—Leibniz and Kant

On Knowledge

1. By examining his own ideas and testing their consistency, man can achieve truth.—Plato, Leibniz, and Hegel
2. The self reads meaning and unity into the objective world.—Berkeley and Kant
3. Value and meaning are obtained by relating parts and wholes.—Hegel

VIII

A Systematic Synopsis of the Philosophy of Idealism

A. The Metaphysics of Idealism
1. THE REALITY OF THE SELF
2. THE NATURE OF THE SELF
3. A SURROUNDING WORLD WHICH IS SPIRITUAL
4. THE ONE AND THE MANY
5. THE PROBLEM OF EVIL
6. FREEDOM
7. SUMMARY

B. The Epistemology of Idealism
1. FOUNDATIONS OF IDEALIST EPISTEMOLOGY IN BERKELEY AND KANT
2. IDEALISM AND CRITICAL REALISM COMPARED
3. SOME KNOWLEDGE BY DIRECT EXPERIENCE
4. THE FACT OF SELFHOOD MAKES NECESSARY THAT THE WORLD BE A SELF
5. SYSTEM AS A TOUCHSTONE OF TRUTH
6. SUMMARY

C. The Logic of Idealism

D. The Axiology of Idealism
1. ETHICAL VALUE
2. AESTHETIC VALUE
3. RELIGIOUS VALUE
4. SOCIAL VALUE

A. THE METAPHYSICS OF IDEALISM

In beginning the synopsis of the philosophy of naturalism in Chapter III, it was asserted that each of the four philosophies builds upon an attitude which is common to most people; hence its appeal. The common attitude on which naturalism builds was stated to be the confidence that there is orderliness in Nature and that Nature can be depended upon. The equally common attitude on which idealism builds is the rather unconscious disposition most of us have to feel that in some way we ourselves are real existent beings, not transitory illusions, not dreams nor fancies. Just how much the unconscious influence of our classical and Christian traditions is responsible would be hard to determine; but most men, of the street, the farm, the market place, or where you will, have the idea that they have a soul which is different from their bodies and somehow more enduring and permanent. Although it may not be this particular phrasing of it for all idealists, it is this motif common in human life which is refined and brought into full bloom intellectually by idealism.

While belief in the reality of the self is well woven into the thought structure of most of us, we have difficulty enlarging this belief into a comprehensive spiritualistic philosophy of life, as idealists do, because our living has its locus so completely in our bodies. When we use the personal pronoun, likely as not we are referring more to the body than any spiritual entity within or behind it. "How do you feel?" we say when inquiring about a person's bodily health. When we speak of the mind, unless we are more exact in our terms than most people, we are probably referring to the brain. Sometimes we speak of "using our brains" or "using our heads" when we really mean "using our minds." The word "soul" for most of us is strictly a part of the vocabulary of religion. It is a sort of vague something which resides inside our bodies somewhere and somehow. More theory than fact for most of us, we may come to doubt its reality and make it the subject of jokes, because we've never been able actually to locate it and only the preacher talks about it as though he were serious. Yet we will rise up in arms to fight for our belief in our own reality and worth, or if in the majority, laugh out of court anyone who would cast any doubt in our minds about the reality of our own existence.

To analyze and build out of this hazy belief an all-inclusive philosophy of life is the job which idealists have set themselves. As we shall attempt to show, there are many difficulties in the position and many varieties of opinion on details. But by and large idealists hold that mind or spirit as each man experiences it in himself is fundamentally real and that the totality of the universe is somehow mind or spirit in its essence.

1. THE REALITY OF THE SELF

René Descartes[1] no doubt stated the belief in the reality of the self as clearly as any when he said, "I think, therefore I am." Doubt may become one of the most direct routes to the discovery of the self. For in doubting everything, as Descartes did, even to the point of questioning if the world about us is any more real than our dreams, we can scarcely fail to observe before long that there is someone who is doubting. Doubt is thought, and thought involves a thinker. Of course many have disagreed with Descartes' belief that in his doubt he discovered the self-evident fact of his own reality. David Hume, one of the chief objectors, found only mental states in his introspection, not a thinker. But idealists have concurred in the principle of Descartes' discovery although they have differed in detailed elaborations of it.

That the self is, if it is, is a significant item in the content of reality. Of course it is important to know what it is; but *that* it is, is also decisive. While the immediacy of the self is more relevant to epistemology, it is also of concern in metaphysics. If all knowledge is possessed by a knower, if every beginning in philosophizing must be made with myself—because I am the one who wants to know, and the one who will know if and when I do get dependable knowledge—this of course tells me something about the knowledge process; but at the same time it is a decisive item in the content of truth to know that I am. For idealists this affirmation is true for every knower; he himself, whoever he may be, is the piece of reality from which all knowing must move outward. Nor is this emphasis upon the immediacy of the self subjective because, it is contended, it also has the objective reference that for every person the fact of his own selfhood is true.

2. THE NATURE OF THE SELF

What the self is in essence must also be added to the knowledge that it is, for its existence to have decisive significance. If the self is identical with the body and only that, or if it is a unit of society and only that, then the fact that it is has no ultimate meaning. But if the self, in addition to its identification with the body and its inseparability from society, is a soul, then the way is open to a thoroughly spiritual and supernatural view of all reality. For, as Wilbur Urban has said, to deny the self as a spiritual reality is to reduce man to the level of the biological order. But to affirm the reality of the self is to think of man as a child of a higher order rather than an offspring of the biological process alone. "We are trying to decide," he continues, "whether we are really merely high-grade simians or whether we are sons of God—in more philosophical terms, whether our intelligence,

[1] Cf. pp. 114–116.

reason, and all that these terms connote, are really merely biological adaptations or have also a transcendental meaning and *status*."[2]

Charles M. Bakewell tells us that the soul is not "that curious metaphysical hybrid, a disembodied spirit, external to the body, and stepping into the body and out again as a man might step in and out of a boat." Instead, he says, "the soul is the life of the body, but it is more than this, for it is also transcendent of bodily limitations; and the body is the expression in the physical order of the nature of the soul."[3] He goes on to say that the body is under the control of the nervous system, nervous tissue having "the peculiar property of being, under limitations, sensitive and directly and immediately responsive to the desire and volition of the knower, to the creativity that is the soul."[4] This he declares is an ultimate fact.

To say that the self is spiritual is not to say however that it is a simple homogeneous unity. Nor do we easily put our fingers on it, as it were, and say "there I am." The self is a unity, yet it is a multiplicity. In an undifferentiated simple potentiality, it is a unity at birth. When fully realized in that ultimate day which is far off, it will be a differentiated unity. It will have many and various facets, dimensions, and expressions, but they will not be in conflict with each other. The self will have itself in hand and will be a unity above and beyond its multiple expressions, having sloughed off the unworthy selves which at times it has been.

But in this life we are all living in an interval. Since earliest infancy we no longer have had the simple undifferentiated unity of potentiality not made actual. Nor do we achieve, except very imperfectly, the differentiated unity of a self fully made actual in terms of the ultimate values for which it is intended and by which it must be judged. Most of us, even in what we call mature life, are still playing roles after the manner of the adolescent. We don't know who we are or who we want to be; so we are sometimes this and sometimes that, depending on the group we are in or the hidden ends we are seeking, not uncommonly hidden even from our own consciousness. We are insincere, we are at odds with ourselves, and it is often very hard to find the trace of unity in us.

A part of the secret of our difficulty is that we are being objects too much of the time and too seldom do we give the subject a chance, which we really are and are intended to become. We have not learned the art of

[2] Wilbur M. Urban, "Metaphysics and Value," in George P. Adams and William P. Montague, *Contemporary American Philosophy*. New York: The Macmillan Company, 1930. Vol. II, p. 371.

[3] Charles M. Bakewell, "Continuity of the Idealist Tradition," in Clifford Barrett, *Contemporary Idealism in America*. New York: The Macmillan Company, 1932. P. 36.

[4] *Loc. cit.*

We interpret world as —

" Conscious demand of rational reasonable self."

losing the object self—the ego-image by which we are fascinated or held in servitude—to find the subject self.

A measure of this kind of recognition of the complexity of selfhood is essential to our own self-understanding and acceptance. It is also of exceedingly great significance in education, as should become clear later.[5] How can we teach unless we develop some real facility for discerning the real selves behind the object selves students present to us? And how can we do this unless we are so mercilessly sincere and frank with ourselves that the subject in us will have a chance to be the teacher? How much of our teaching and learning, so called, involves object selves meeting object selves could not be determined. But if this is an approximately true account of the nature of the self, then it follows that there can be no genuinely educative transaction in the classroom unless subject is meeting subject with a minimum in interference from object selves, playing roles and posturing for effect and, without recognizing it, seducing both teacher and pupil, as well as the educative process.

3. A SURROUNDING WORLD WHICH IS SPIRITUAL

The counterpart of the idealist's belief in the reality of the self is his belief that the world about him, the notself, as Fichte might say, is spiritual, made of the same stuff as the self.

Now this belief is established with more difficulty than the belief in the reality of the self. But detailed attention to the how of both of these beliefs must wait until a later section of this chapter when idealist epistemology will be discussed. It is one thing to sketch the belief that the self is real; it is another thing to understand how idealists come to know that the self is real. The same is equally true for the belief in the world as a spiritual order. How do they know this is true? These more difficult problems are a part of the epistemology of idealism. Reference is now made to them with two purposes in mind. (1) It is to be noted that only half the story is told when the idealist metaphysics is outlined. The how of these beliefs is equally significant. (2) And it should be indicated that the jump the idealist makes from the self to the surrounding world—by which he concludes that the world is spiritual—is the crux of the idealist epistemology. We cannot deal directly with the how of this leap at this point, although it will be indicated. The chief concern now is to get some understanding of the way in which the idealist looks at his surrounding world. In order to do this, we shall examine a number of recent idealists to observe their respective ways of depicting the world.

Employing the same starting point used above as an entree to the belief in the reality of the self, the "I think" of Descartes, Bernard Bosanquet (1848–1923) finds a clue as to the texture of existence generally. He

[5] Cf. pp. 191–196.

contends that Descartes does not tell the whole story when he says "I think." To approximate more closely the inclusive truth, he should say, "It thinks in me." Bosanquet apparently means that to think of the individual self as an isolated thinker is not to do justice to reality. The individual self is only one individual unit in the whole of reality—one individuated part of the whole. Therefore, what goes on in the self is not only an evidence of the nature of the individual self. It is fully as representative of the nature of the whole world of which the self is a part. If the focus of attention is arbitrarily limited to the individual, it is quite right to say, as Descartes did, "I think." But when totality is the frame of reference, this statement is both inadequate and deceptive. We should rather describe this inner experience as "it thinks in me." That is to say, reality is a thinking being of which I as an individual am an integral part.[6]

Wilbur Urban lays great stress upon the intelligibility of the world. The fact that the world is capable of interpretation seems to imply much to him about its character. And it is at this point that many idealists will insist that idealism is synonymous with philosophy. For, they contend, it is the spirit and purpose of philosophy to interpret the meanings of the world. If the world is not amenable to interpretation, then there can be no philosophy. But if the world is capable of being interpreted, as it seems to be, not only is there philosophy, but there is necessarily a philosophy such as idealism as the true philosophy. For if the world is capable of interpretation, it means that it is tuned to the same key as mind, and therefore is spiritual rather than material or mechanical. "The world, therefore," as Urban says, "is viewed as a 'logical' or spiritual totality—not mechanical in structure, but organic in the sense that the part expresses within itself something of the meaning of the whole."[7] Though Professor Urban regards his position as something beyond both idealism and realism, he does make this argument from philosophical intelligibility one of the cornerstones in his thinking. "The existence of objective meanings and values in the world," he says, "implies some kind of 'mental life' as the core of reality. . . . We cannot detach meanings and values from mind without becoming unintelligible."[8]

G. Watts Cunningham lays stress upon system as a clue to the character of reality. System and intelligibility are closely related. For, as Urban says, "meaning is inseparable from the notion of system."[9] Recalling Berkeley's "to be is to be perceived," Cunningham says that for a thing to exist does

[6] Cf. Bernard Bosanquet, "Life and Philosophy," in J. H. Muirhead (editor), *Contemporary British Philosophy*, Series Two. New York: The Macmillan Company, n.d. P. 61.

[7] Wilbur M. Urban, "The Philosophy of Spirit: Idealism and the Philosophy of Value," in Clifford Barrett, *op. cit.*, p. 105.

[8] *Ibid.*, pp. 105–106.

[9] *Ibid.*, p. 105.

not necessitate that it be the psychological object of thought, but it does make necessary that it be the logical object of thought. " 'To be' is not necessarily 'to be perceived,' but it is necessarily 'to be implicated,' " he says.[10] Accordingly, an object does not have to be psychologically present to a thinker in order to exist, as Berkeley held. But an object must be a logical part of a system in order to have being. According, therefore, to this view of the world, reality is a logically related system.

John Elof Boodin finds that there is "nothing inert in nature. Sensitiveness," he says, "characterizes nature at all levels of orgniazation of energy."[11] He speaks of two realms, the realm of matter and the realm of spirit. Apparently he grants the possibility of some kind of material or mechanical order existing; but the realm of spirit is definitely more inclusive and may possibly encompass the realm of matter. Professor Boodin puts it as follows:

> The realm of matter and the realm of spirit are the two great realms, and it is the realm of spirit which overlaps. Here we have the great contrast. Matter spends its energy in radiation, spirit grows rich by expression. The more it spends the more it has. If it spends nothing it dies. Therefore, it is more blessed to give than to receive. Matter is the realm of routine as contrasted with the free creativeness of spirit.[12]

J. A. Leighton regards personality as the key to reality. The richest individuality clearly evidenced in the world he finds in the spiritual personality. This richest individuality is then the sample which gives us some clue to the meaning of the whole. "Since," he says, "the meanings and values of existence reside in individuality, everything in the universe must in the end be subservient to the fulfillment and perduration of personality-in-community . . . the cosmos must have Meaning and must honor Value."[13] Professor Leighton's statement, while descriptive, at least implies a big problem in idealist metaphysics to be discussed shortly. This is the problem whether the spiritual whole which idealists find reality to be is solid unity or a multiplicity of individual personalities.

Mary Whiton Calkins (1863–1930), one of the really great women of American philosophy, has stated the idealist metaphysics in a warm and personal way. No doubt the kernel of her idealism can best be presented by listing a few propositions as she has stated them herself in her *Credo* published in *Contemporary American Philosophy*. They are as follows:

[10] G. Watts Cunningham, "A Search for System," in George P. Adams and William P. Montague, *op. cit.*, Vol. I, p. 272.

[11] John Elof Boodin, "Nature and Reason," in George P. Adams and William P. Montague, *op. cit.*, Vol. I, p. 157.

[12] *Ibid.*, p. 163.

[13] J. A. Leighton, "The Principle of Individuality and Value," in Clifford Barrett, *op. cit.*, p. 167.

1. The Universe contains distinctively mental realities; it may or may not also contain non-mental entities, but in any case irreducible mental realities exist.[14]

2. Mental realities are ultimately personal . . . the mental phenomena which I directly observe are not percepts, thoughts, emotions, and volitions in unending succession, but rather perceiving, thinking, feeling, and willing self or selves.[15]

3. The universe is through and through mental in character . . . all that is real is ultimately mental, and accordingly personal, in nature.[16]

4. The universe literally is one all-including (and accordingly complete) self of which all the lesser selves are genuine and identical parts, or members.[17]

5. By Asolute Self *as absolute* I understand, in the first place . . . all-including self: no shred of reality, however base, can be outside of it.[18]

6. The Absolute Person *as self* I describe as a conscious being; and by "conscious" I must mean essentially what I mean when I describe myself as conscious. In other words I must hold that the Absolute Self genuinely perceives, thinks, feels, and wills.[19]

In this statement there is what Wilbur Urban calls the idealist minimum, belief in some kind of mental reality (proposition 1). There is the attributing of a personal quality to this mental reality (proposition 2). There is the universalizing of mental reality so that it is regarded as the all-inclusive essence of the world (proposition 3). There is the further step of defining this universal mental essence as a Self (propositions 4, 5, and 6). And there is an attempt at synthesizing the beliefs in the selfhood of God and the selfhood of human individuals by saying that the latter are lesser selves and genuine members of the total self (proposition 4). This last is the problem already mentioned and now to be discussed in the section immediately following.

We have now added another important phase to this synopsis of idealist metaphysics. In sections 1 and 2 above, the idealist belief in the self as a spiritual reality was presented. We have now attempted to show that the idealist matches this belief in the self with the belief that the entire universe is through and through mental and spiritual in character. At the very least it is mental stuff of some sort. And it may be a Mind or Self, warmly personal in nature. This is a second major principle in the metaphysics of idealism. Now to go further in trying to understand this important part of idealism we must face the question of the unity versus the multiplicity of

[14] Mary Whiton Calkins, "The Philosophical *Credo* of an Absolutistic Personalist," in George P. Adams and William P. Montague, *op. cit.*, Vol. I, p. 200.

[15] *Ibid.*, p. 201.

[16] *Ibid.*, p. 203.

[17] *Ibid.*, p. 209.

[18] *Ibid.*, p. 212.

[19] *Loc. cit.*

this ultimate mental reality, Mind, or Person. The answer to this problem will be decisive in determining whether reality is an abstract mental stuff, a Self, or a multitude of selves.

4. THE ONE AND THE MANY

This extremely difficult problem of idealism is essentially one of deciding between monism and pluralism. As shown already, idealists generally agree that ultimate reality is spiritual, but there are some ramifications which are difficult to work out in uniting belief in Ultimate Self with belief in the reality of individual selves.

Is there just one substance and only one, i.e., Universal Spirit or God? Or are there many separate and distinct individual selves, i.e., the spirits of all the individual men which ever did and ever shall have existence in this world? This is the issue. If an idealist takes his stand in an affirmative answer to the first of these questions, saying that Universal Mind is unimpeachably the supreme reality, he would seem to disregard the reality of individual finite minds, rob them of uniqueness, and do away with immortality as a continued personal existence after death. But if he answers the second question affirmatively, saying that individual selves are unimpeachably real, he would seem either to make God a sort of collection of individual selves not having much unity, or else a finite God who, while having somewhat more power than others, is yet just one among many individuals. Is there no way out of this dilemma?

We will look at the monistic side of this issue first, then the pluralistic. Finally, we will try to determine if there is some nearly adequate synthesis which idealists have worked out in answer to this problem.

Bernard Bosanquet represents very well those idealists who, adhering rather closely to Hegel's metaphysics, place greater stress on the unity of reality than on its multiplicity.

1. One line of reasoning followed by Bosanquet in concluding that individual selves are parts of the total Universal Mind is the argument that the part can never be equivalent to the whole. It is impossible, he says, for a finite human mind to comprehend completely all of reality. For to do so would be to become identified with the totality of all that is, and to achieve an understanding which is incompatible with the kind of particular existence which human minds have. Therefore, whatever else it is, the human self is certainly a part of the whole, a fraction and not the totality.

2. Considering the nature of spirit, Bosanquet finds a solid basis for believing in unity also. He recognizes that nothing can be more actual than the gradations of spirit as seen in the various forms and levels of life in the world. But even so, he observed that throughout all of these gradations spirit is the same stuff. He seems to grant the possibility of a quantitative pluralism, but not a pluralism of quality. Permeating all the various levels

of individual existence is one essence, namely, Spirit. This, Bosanquet contends, implies a fundamental unity. There is a single Spirit running throughout all the individuated forms making up the world.

3. From still another point of approach Bosanquet finds that the whole, by its very nature, must be greater than the sum of its parts. He says that there is quality in the whole of reality which does not reside in any of the parts. There is meaning in the totality of Spirit which cannot be found in the imperfect individual souls of men and which does not manifest itself in their understanding of reality. "Where grades of life and vision are represented as correlative to grades of mind," he says, "there is an obvious basis and presumption for the idea that in an ultimate sense the whole means more than it appears either in the imperfect souls or to them."[20]

J. A. Leighton objects violently to this passion for unity when it is so strong as to deny individuality and selfhood. 1. "Idealism," he says, "commits suicide on the alter of abstraction, if the finite individual is regarded as merely a *part* of an Absolute Experience or Absolute Self."[21] "A self is real," he contends, "and realizes and conserves value not as a mere *part* but as a *self-active, intrinsically valuable member* of a world, within which it is a world."[22] He readily agrees that the self grows by continuous self-transcendence, constantly reaching beyond itself and including larger areas within its experience. But self-transcendence, he insists, is not self-negation nor self-obliteration. This is the falsehood into which he believes idealists like Bosanquet fall. They are so concerned to preserve the unity of the total spiritual reality that they obliterate individuality and make it of little account. Leighton rejects the position that finite selves are "mere parts" of an all-inclusive Mind. He gives three reasons as his refutation:

(1) I cannot conceive *how* this could be so in terms of experience. (2) It conflicts with the conception of individuality as implying the free *membership* of self-active beings in a community. (3) It undermines the entire notion of value. If value is real only in and for selves, it disappears if selves disappear.[23]

2. Over against the highly unified conception of ultimate mind which Bosanquet holds he describes the universe as a spiritual community. He tells us that the term universe "means only the actual community of the diversity of an immense multiplicity of finite individuals." There is sufficient freedom and openness in the cosmos to make elbowroom for individuality and selfhood. "The members of the world do hang together; but in a loose-jointed way, which permits some free play among them. There is a

---

[20] Bernard Bosanquet, *op. cit.*, pp. 70–71.
[21] J. A. Leighton, *op. cit.*, p. 147.
[22] *Loc. cit.*
[23] *Ibid.*, p. 150.

cosmos only in the sense that its members are in intercommunication."[24]

3. To conceive God according to the pattern described by Bosanquet would make Him a terrible monster, Leighton holds. He would have to "swallow and digest all finite experience, good, bad, and indifferent, sane and insane, true and false."[25] If individuality and value have a real status in the universe, the supreme Reality must possess Selfhood and Personality. "If the supreme Reality is self-conscious, self-active, thinking and willing, it is personal. If it has not these powers in full actuality, it is not only not personal, it is even *subpersonal.*"[26] But since the necessary perfection of God, so conceived, must exclude all evil from His being, then God must be finite and limited. Leighton says, "I conceive of Him as the perfection of personality; therefore finite in that He does not include all that is."[27]

Alfred Hoernle's summary of the types of idealism is now in order. All of them except *critical idealism* will be seen to grow out of this problem of the one and the many. And the discussion of Kant's contribution to idealist thought contained in Chapter VII[28] provides a basis for understanding this kind of idealism as well. The four types according to Hoernle are:

a. *Spiritual Pluralism*, which interprets Reality as a Society of Spirits.
b. *Spiritual Monism*, which interprets Reality as the manifestation, or objectification, of a single Spiritual Energy.
c. *Critical (Kantian) Idealism*, which avoids offering a theory of Reality but makes clear that every form of experience, because of the universal and necessary principles of "Reason" in it, has a contribution to make to the theory of Reality.
d. *Absolute Idealism*, which attempts a synthetic, or synoptic, interpretation of Reality in the light of its various "appearances."[29]

Mary Whiton Calkins has attempted a synthesis of this conflict between the one and the many. She has called herself an absolutistic personalist. In Hoernle's summary of types she would most likely be identified with the absolute idealists.

She quotes the following poem from the pen of Edward Sandford Martin by way of suggesting illustratively what her synthesis is:

> Within my earthly temple there's a crowd.
> There's one of us that's humble; one that's proud.
> There's one that's broken-hearted for his sins,
> And one who, unrepentant, sits and grins.

[24] *Ibid.*, p. 158.
[25] *Ibid.*, p. 147.
[26] *Ibid.*, p. 149.
[27] *Ibid.*, p. 165.
[28] Cf. pp. 128–132.
[29] R. F. Alfred Hoernle, *Idealism as a Philosophy*. New York: Doubleday & Company, 1927. P. 306.

> There's one who loves his neighbor as himself,
> And one who cares for naught but fame and pelf.
> From much corroding care would I be free
> If once I could determine which is Me.[30]

Now in the case of finite self, she tells us that "no one of these conflicting selves but the articulating whole of which they are parts constitutes the human *me*."[31] And, similarly, to apply the illustration to God, the Universal Self, none of the particular selves is the real essential Self of God, only the integrating whole, of which they are all parts. So, "all the human selves may be and are parts of the One Self."[32]

There are several important ideas woven into this synthesis. First, that the whole-part relation is the most basic of all relationships. More will be said about this in discussing idealist axiology later in this chapter. About this basic relation Miss Calkins comments as follows:

> The ultimately real relations are those of whole and part, of including and being included. The beings of the universe are, from this point of view, all of them parts of some including entity, and are thus related to each other indirectly.[33]

Second, there is the idea that this relation makes necessary the existence of some being which is an all-including whole. Reason must eventually bring us to some all-inclusive whole which is an ultimate unity. On this root idea she has this to say:

> However many the wholes or including entities, each must constitute a part of an ultimately all-including being, the Absolute. For any lesser including entities must themselves be related, seeing that they are (to say the least) alike and different; and thus, by the very argument just outlined, they must be parts of an all-including and self-related being.[34]

The third and last of these basic ideas is that "to be individual is to be unique, to stand in a class by oneself, to be irreplacable by anything else, however similar."[35]

All of these ideas she weaves together into the one overall conception of an Ultimate Self who is a unified self because of and in addition to the individuated selves within Him, and of human selves which, though indeed parts of the Absolute Person, are unique parts, "individuated by absolute will and inviolably distinct from every other embodiment of absolute purpose."[36]

---

[30] Edward Sandford Martin, "Mixed," in *A Little Brother of the Rich and Other Verses.* New York: Charles Scribner's Sons, 1899. P. 49.

[31] Mary Whiton Calkins, *op. cit.,* Vol. I, p. 216.

[32] *Loc. cit.*

[33] *Ibid.,* pp. 210–211.

[34] *Ibid.,* p. 211.

[35] *Ibid.,* p. 216.

[36] *Loc. cit.*

5. THE PROBLEM OF EVIL

Another knotty problem for idealism, closely related to the one-and-many problem, is the why and what of evil. Of course, this question, having to do with ethical value, is also properly a consideration within the province of idealist axiology. But it does have a certain metaphysical side which cannot be passed over at this point in our discussion. How can the many be a part of the One, for example, if they partake of evil and the One is perfectly good?

So often in the literature of idealism the theory of evil is suggested more by what is not said than by positive statements that it seems wise to deal with it here in a direct, if sketchy, manner. Conservative religion speaks of a personal devil. The New Testament frequently mentions "the evil" or "the evil one." Common discussion of human affairs often alludes to the forces of evil in the world. Our question is, Do any of these conceptions have an equivalent in real existence, according to idealism? Is evil a real thing having substance and standing on its own feet? The characteristic answer of idealists to this problem has already been hinted in the discussion of Hegel in Chapter VII.[37] It may be stated in this way: Evil is not self-subsistent; it is the necessary possibility in a world where individuals have the freedom to realize the good. Only perfection is ultimately real. God, Universal Mind, is wholly good. Some idealists dissent from this view, and for them we shall let J. A. Leighton speak. William E. Hocking has a rather explicit metaphysics of good and evil which will be discussed as representing the majority opinion.

Using the human parent as an analogy, J. A. Leighton grants that there is a certain limited scope within which it is understandable that God voluntarily limits Himself in order to permit individual persons to exercise initiative and become self-determining. But this is inadequate as an all-inclusive explanation of the fact of evil in the world. Such a theory of evil is so much verbiage when offered as a total explanation, according to Leighton. He insists that there are too many "brute contingencies" in the world "that seem to ruin human lives" for such a conception of evil to satisfy. After all the causes of evil emanating from man are fully considered for what they are worth, there is still a residue of evil left which is unaccounted for. Earthquake, flood, hurricane, and pestilence are a few of these evils not caused by man. Leighton therefore finds it necessary to think of God as both finite and perfect, evil having some kind of status outside of Him.[38]

Turning to Hocking's treatment of evil, the following assertions may be made.

[37] Cf. pp. 136–137.
[38] Cf. J. A. Leighton, *op. cit.*, p. 165.

1. Ultimate Self is one and is good. Optimism, for Hocking, requires such a union of monism and moral perfection as attributes of God. This is a "belief in an individual Reality not-ourselves which makes for rightness, and which actually accomplishes rightness when left to its own working."[39]

2. At the same time, evil is an actuality in the present world of human affairs. The word "actual" is used here to denote that which has become act and fact in the flesh-and-blood world of human relationships. In this world evil is an actual fact. Individual men are not altogether affirmative and positive in their moral achievements. They are commonly not their brother's keepers. They treat one another as means to ends in making money, and in satisfying their passions of anger and lust. They make wars. They are lethargic in allowing disease, poverty, and ignorance to thrive insidiously and uncontrolled.

3. But this actual evil seen from one vantage point is the seamy side of good. Put in terms of the individual, Hocking says, his faults are "the seamy sides of his virtues, having their reality and their ultimate relief in the heightened life of those same positive qualities—his wrath as part of his *spirit,* his hesitation as a phase of his self-consciousness—to be relieved by more self-consciousness, his shiftlessness an incident of his ideality—to be remedied by a more vigorous ideality, not mere battle against shiftlessness."[40] Accordingly, wars, poverty, ignorance, and disease—to select some of the bolder patterns of evil in the world—are all negatives, the absence of adequate motives for good. War is the absence of the positive purpose and controls which constitute peace. Poverty is the result of the inadequate valuation of man which does not elevate him above impersonal economic rewards. Ignorance is the absence of positive truth and the lethargic lack of desire to possess it. Disease is the accompaniment of both ignorance of and disregard for the conditions of health.

4. In other words, sin, which we may define as committed evil, is a missing of the mark, the same as in one of the New Testament conceptions. The all-kinds-of-misses at target practice provide a good figure for the infinity of moral misses which take place in the flesh-and-blood world of human experience. Of course, missing the mark is to be expected in a world where new individuals are constantly being born and are given the latitude in which to grow to maturity. But missing the mark is just an aspect of the opportunity to find one's self and become a real person in the ultimate spiritual community of selves. It is not a fundamental and binding mechanism of ultimate reality in which human nature is irrevocably in-

[39] William E. Hocking, *The Meaning of God in Human Experience.* New Haven: Yale University Press, 1928. P. 177.
[40] *Ibid.,* p. 178.

volved. It is a transient aspect of the temporal world, not a permanent characteristic of Ultimate Mind. It is a part of the immaturity of man's world, a negative which is absent in the positive perfection of God.

5. This is as much as to say that there is no efficient cause for evil. It is not to be explained by attributing its existence to certain antecedents which are adequate to bring it about in the same way as an Aristotelian efficient cause might do it, for example.[41] As Radoslav A. Tsanoff says, "Evil is not a discrete quality of particular things or experience; it is relative and has no status in isolation."[42] And as Saint Augustine has said, "How then can a good thing cause an evil will? How, I say, is good the cause of evil? When the will, turning from the better of two alternatives, chooses the worse, it becomes evil; not because that is evil to which it turns, but because the turning itself is vicious."[43]

6. From the standpoint of the development of the individual, when an evil is past it is nonexistent. Since there is nothing solid in events themselves, a past sin when forgotten and dropped from consciousness has no status in reality. The only reality is the Ultimate Mind in whom there is no evil. Evil events, when past, are therefore nonexistent. Several statements of Hocking tie together to draw the outline of this attitude toward past sin. "Any experience dropped by us is dropped absolutely," he says. "Even though the One may attend to what we let go, our letting go is one of the absolute facts; a stitch dropped by ourselves is dropped by the World, irrevocably dropped."[44] "There is no monism on the level of events," Hocking tells us. "History falls by quantities into the abyss, and this is the unstinted opportunity for our sifting—even yet all too unradical. The only hope of finding the Real to be one and good is such sifting-right, in the circumstance that the universe is not utterly organic, and that we are not compelled to absorb into our structure all the false scaffolding we have raised."[45]

7. A corollary of this principle of dropping evils from our personalities as immaturities sloughed off is that there is the significant possibility that an individual who does not aspire to the good can be sloughed off into the abyss of nonexistence together with forgotten events. That is to say that in living I face an eternal issue: either I renounce evil and aspire to the good which is ultimate, or else I fall short of the good by willfulness or indolence and thereby relinquish my existence as an individual. For, as Hocking says,

---

[41] Cf. pp. 249–250.

[42] Radoslav A. Tsanoff, "The Theory of Moral Value," in Clifford Barrett, *op. cit.*, p. 220.

[43] F. R. M. Hitchcock, *St. Augustine's Treatise on the City of God*. New York: The Macmillan Company, 1922. Pp. 80–81.

[44] William E. Hocking, *op. cit.*, p. 180.

[45] *Ibid.*, pp. 180–181.

there is leisure in the working out of the ultimate goal and "the creator has been generous with time, with the material of existence, the cloth of history, and most of it is wasted. It looks at times as if he had been equally prodigal of men."[46] And as Boodin sees this crisis of individual souls, "the structure of value is eternal, but our participation in it lies in our own control. To choose freely to realize, in our individual lives, the beauty of spirit is the great affirmation; to refuse to do so is the great negation.[47]

8. Finally, what about the evils in the world for which man is clearly not responsible? How can these be tied into this scheme which defines evil as negativity, the seamy side of good? Well, as Fichte would say, these apparent evils in the very texture of the natural world are prods for awakening the human spirit and spurring it to active achievement. Man's relation to Nature could not be altogether soothing and comfortable, or the human spirit would be allowed to sleep on and never awaken to achieve consciousness or conscience. Disease is the negative in the world urging man to a self-achieved realization and evaluation of health as a positive good. Floods are a negative spurring man to the control of water power, saving life and resource, harnessing Nature's waters for controlled farming, and her electricity for abundant production and comfortable living. Lest it be argued that these are human values rather than permanent spiritual values, it should be pointed out that these positive benefits are the temporal aspects of permanent spiritual values. Health of body is essential to vigor of mind and spirit, while an agriculture and industry producing the world's goods in abundance are essential to that liberation of the human spirit which means freedom in all the higher realms of intellect, feeling, and constructive action.

As A. M. Fairbairn says, even death itself, which may properly be viewed as the great evil from the human standpoint, awakens us to value life and make the most of the precious opportunities it affords while they are here.[48]

So much for a number of the aspects of the idealist treatment of evil. These several items will suggest how idealists regard evil as negative and ultimately nonexistent, while at the same time recognizing its actuality and destructive bad effects in the world in which we live.

6. FREEDOM

Belief in freedom is common among idealists, as has been evident in the foregoing discussion. Of course, this does not mean that idealists think that

---

[46] *Ibid.*, p. 181.
[47] John Elof Boodin, *op. cit.*, Vol. I, p. 166.
[48] Cf. A. M. Fairbairn, *The Philosophy of the Christian Religion.* New York: The Macmillan Company, 1902. Pp. 141–146.

we have freedom as individuals to do whatever we please, without limits. There are boundaries to my freedom as an individual which stand simply because, as an individual, I am a part and not the whole of reality. I might like to revert to the fairyland days of childhood, step on a magic carpet and be whisked to the other side of the world in no time.But in actuality I have to wait on the slower methods of reason and science. I am not the whole, I am a part, and I have to conform to the ways of the cosmos rather than expect the universe to yield to the whims of one little individual. Anyway, there would be no cosmos, no order, if individuals had the power of action with which to realize their whims and fancies. In such a world everything would be chaos and conflict.

But within a more limited sphere, the orbit in which the individual self moves, there is freedom of choice and freedom of action. In fact the essential genius of the self is initiative, an outward urge which makes its impact on the stuff of the external world and thereby discovers itself at the same time that it expresses itself to other minds. Josiah Royce setting the example, "self-determination" might be a more exact term to use than "freedom." We are free to determine our own selfhood, according to idealism; and this is something quite different from extreme determinism, according to which the individual is only a cog in the machinery of the universe, subject to circumstances and to a fate over which he has no control at all.

The significance of this power of self-determination confronts us most decisively in the most crucial moral issue of individual existence. Do I choose to realize my selfhood by becoming devoted to and by striving to achieve the perfection of the Absolute Self? Or do I prefer indolence, mediocrity, or willful resistance in hindering the achievement of divine ends by humankind? The first alternative is the affirmation of individual selfhood. The second is the negation of both selfhood and individual existence. The fact of initiative and self-determination is seen most clearly in such a significant and sharply divided issue.

7. SUMMARY

By way of brief summation, a general outline of the idealist metaphysics may be described in the following propositions:

1. The self is the prime reality of individual experience.
2. Ultimate reality is a self.
3. Ultimate reality may be one self, a community of selves, or a Universal Self within whom are many individual selves.
4. Evil is not a real existent value; it is the negation of value.
5. The individual self has all the freedom essential to self-determination.

B. THE EPISTEMOLOGY OF IDEALISM

The epistemology of idealism has been heralded as the heart and center of this philosophy; and there are two reasons for believing this to be the case.

1. First of all, it is to be observed that the theory of knowledge is basic in any philosophy. I may spin the finest webs out of beliefs about reality. Indeed, the foregoing sketch of the world as the idealist sees it may impress the reader as just one of these finely spun yarns. But unless I have some pretty solid reasons for believing my ideas of the world are true, they are no better than so much illusion or fancy. I may surround myself with a set of ideas which will make the world a fool's paradise. It may be fun living in such an imagined world,—while it lasts. But if it is untrue it will eventually be broken on the rock of reality, and the awakening will be a shock. Even before the rude collapse of such an imagined world takes place, there is still the lack of adjustment between the person who believes in it and the rest of the world, which in itself is of greater value than all the fool's paradises we can build out of fanciful ideas.

2. But idealism adds to this a further reason for the prime significance of knowledge. The argument is something like this: "Understand the nature of knowledge and you will have the key to the nature of reality." To suit the liking of idealists, people generally are all too naïve in accepting so-called truth as true. The preacher expounds a certain religious content from the pulpit and the congregation supposedly accepts it as true content. The teacher of science expounds to his students the latest discoveries in his field, the students usually accepting them as the true content of that science. The newspaper parades certain ideas before the people in the hope that the people will accept this propaganda as the true content in politics.

But *content* has a way of changing as time goes on. Religious doctrines develop and grow so that the content of pulpit utterances can be seen to change, even when the identity of the preacher remains the same. Scientific knowledge is constantly developing, so that the content of science taught in the classroom changes noticeably, almost from year to year. And newspapers change hands, also political influences rise and fall, so that a given press may expound one doctrine during one period, and the direct opposite in another. How enviable is the position of the listener, the learner, and the reader! If not too gullible, they can read and listen to the ideas of the indoctrinators with amusement. And they can laugh when the spokesman or editor makes an about-face in what he says, offering some lame excuse for the change. How do we expounders of ideas live down the embarrassment which attends the conflict in the variety of truths we allege to be true?

Idealism may be said to embrace a modified skepticism. Idealists are not satisfied to give and take in truths as though they were neat packages which can be bartered and exchanged as so much merchandise. They cannot accept an alleged truth without also approving the process by which it has been discovered. In fact, the process of discovery is the certificate of the idea. For the ultimate content is revealed by the nature of knowledge to be the minds which give and take in ideas. And any content less than this, which parades itself as ultimate truth, is a parody. But all of this needs to be enlarged with some measure of detail, in order to show how the idealist believes that knowledge by its very nature reveals the character of reality.

1. Foundations of Idealist Epistemology in Berkeley and Kant

The ideas of Berkeley and Kant, already discussed in sketching the history of idealism, are important in getting at the theory of knowledge. George Berkeley[49] insisted that the character of the world as we experience it so much depends upon mind that there is no such thing as existing without someone perceiving it. The meaningful world of objects, colors, sounds, etc., which we all enjoy is just that world because it is refracted through our perceiving minds. It is like music after being refracted through the soul and instrument of the musician. Now the grand leap from this experience of the individual mind to belief in God is made in this way: Since the world is a world of quality and meaning, as I experience it, there must be Ultimate Mind who puts meaning into it. How can I get meaning and quality out of the world unless some One invests it with those very meanings and qualities? This is the essence of Berkeley's argument.

Immanuel Kant, as Hoernle tells us,[50] was a critical idealist. He gave us an analysis of the knowledge process without making any leap beyond the phenomenal world to formulate a belief about reality. As he did not find the character of reality implied in the character of knowing, he as much favors critical realism[51] as idealism. In his analysis of knowledge[52] he found (1) pure sensation to be a chaotic process in which all kinds of sensory stimulations are passively received by the mind. (2) The chaos of sensation is resolved into orderliness by the two categories of perception, space and time, which group sensory qualities into objects and events. (3) Further unity of a conceptual and ideational sort is achieved by such rational categories of the mind as the need for linking causes and effects, for example.

---

[49] Cf. pp. 124–127.
[50] Cf. p. 156.
[51] Cf. pp. 271–273.
[52] Cf. pp. 128–129.

Now in the process of the mind's knowledge relation with the phenomenal world a certain identity can be observed running through all experiences which we have of the world. This identity is the self of the individual knower. But as for finding a self or mind behind the phenomenal world, Kant does not grant any possibility of this in his analysis of knowledge, although he insists upon it in his ethics. It was the idealists who followed him that made this leap beyond his critical idealism. Fichte spoke of the Ego-in-itself; and Hegel insisted that since to exist means to be in relation, there can be no thing-in-itself. He held instead that reality is identical with the qualities revealed in our knowledge.

2. IDEALISM AND CRITICAL REALISM COMPARED

At this point the reader can make some clarifying comparisons by associating the idealist theory of knowledge with that of critical realism.[53] The two epistemologies are almost identical in their analysis of the act of knowing. They differ in their inferences about that which is behind the phenomenal world. Critical realism holds that the qualities of experience are separate and distinct from existence as such. A number of realists have followed Santayana in the theory that there is a realm of essences which is separate from the realm of being or existence. But idealists hold that there is no need for theorizing about a realm of essences, as the qualities of our experience are identical with being. The reality behind the phenomenal world which we behold in perception is a being which is replete with all of the qualities, meanings, and values which experience yields us. This being is Mind, and it gets itself across to us through Nature as its medium.

3. SOME KNOWLEDGE BY DIRECT EXPERIENCE

It now remains for us to get some more of the detail of the idealist treatment of knowledge as it appears in some recent and contemporary idealism.

Mary Whiton Calkins tells us that by *direct observation* she has knowledge of the self and its limitations. "Because I encounter mental reality," she says, "directly experience it, realize it as somehow significantly different from what I observe as bodily process or physical reality, I assert its existence."[54] She further elaborates this direct discovery of herself as follows:

In recognition, for example, I am conscious of myself as persisting, as the same self who earlier preceived this same object; in rebellious volition I individualize myself, set myself up against other selves, realize myself as unique. In feeling and perceiving I am conscious of myself as passively related to

[53] Cf. pp. 271–273.
[54] Mary Whiton Calkins, *op. cit.*, Vol. I, p. 201.

my environment, whereas in willing and in affirming I am aware of myself
as in active creative relation with surrounding objects.[55]

Regarding direct knowledge of the limits of the self, she says:

In . . . direct experience of myself . . . I am aware of myself as, at many
points, involuntarily limited, thwarted, and hampered. But this direct awareness of myself as involuntarily limited involves and includes the direct consciousness of something-which-is-in-some-sense-outside-me.[56]

Through direct observation she claims to have found two indisputable
realities: (1) the fact of the self and (2) the fact that the self is limited by
something beyond it. These two self-evident facts of experience she holds
are contradictory unless there is some similarity of substance between the
self and the notself. For her the only solution to the contradiction is in
believing that the notself is also a self. These two "seemingly contradictory" assertions, she says, "are reconcilable only if this some-what-other is
conceived as a greater self of which I constitute an identical part. In fully
knowing myself I therefore know the nature of that including self which is,
from one point of view, other than I, because greater, but which, since I am
actual part of it, also is a greater myself."[57]

Not all idealists would agree with Miss Calkins that there is outright
direct experience of the self, although the difference is likely one of definition. When Descartes said, "I think, therefore I am," did he mean to
convey that he directly observed the self or that he directly observd some
thinking going on and found it necessary to infer that there was a self who
was doing the thinking? Berkeley frankly acknowledged that our knowledge of the self is a notion—something not observed directly, but a necessary inference from our experience. J. E. Creighton says, "The consciousness of the self is . . . no original datum, but something progressively
communicated to the individual through his contact with nature, and especially through social contact with his fellow-men."[58]

It may be that the self can be observed directly in introspection. But if
so, it is not found in prolonged periods of intense self-examination so much
as in those short flashes of self-knowledge which come as accompaniments
or by-products of the activities in which we engage. We see ourselves
enjoying a game of golf or carried away by a symphony; keeping a house
which is warm, inviting, and restful; cringing in fear under shellfire or a
bombing raid; yearning for a better world and striving to find our place in

[55] *Ibid.*, p. 202.
[56] *Ibid.*, p. 208.
[57] *Ibid.*, p. 209.
[58] J. E. Creighton, "The Social Nature of Thinking," in D. S. Robinson, *An
Anthology of Recent Philosophy*. New York: Thomas Y. Crowell Company, 1929.
P. 146.

it; hating the forces that produce calamitous outbreaks of evil in the world; relaxing, becoming passive, and renewing our strength for new effortful struggles. It is in the flashes of self-observation almost unnoticed in these activities and others still more commonplace that we most clearly see the self.

4. THE FACT OF SELFHOOD MAKES NECESSARY THAT THE WORLD BE A SELF

With the reality of the self assumed as the most immediate and self-evident fact any of us can experience, many idealists find that the nature of the rest of existence is strongly implied. Josiah Royce tells us to watch closely whenever a man tries to proclaim his view about the world. He may insist that the real world must have any number of possible characteristics; but no matter which he upholds, it is important to note that it is always *his* ideal which is attributed to the world. If he insists, for example, that the world must be regarded as independent of our minds because that is the only wholesome view, then he "announces an explicitly idealistic theory, since he defines the nature of reality in terms of his ideal of wholesomeness."[59]

Royce goes on to tell us that our views of the world are always "conceptual constructs" because we interpret the universe as the "expression of the more or less conscious demands of the rational self."[60] But this is not as subjective a process as it might seem, for the principle of contradiction is always the ultimate warrant for such an interpretation. "If I assert that there is no truth, I assert that it is true that there is no truth, and consequently contradict myself."[61] And so the demands of logical coherence guarantee that there is truth. Many of my interpretations of the world, though they are *my* interpretations, can be checked for validity in this way.

Wilbur Urban's argument for intelligibility is another instance of selfhood providing us a strong suggestion as to the nature of reality. The world of self, he holds, is a world of intelligence; in it there are qualities, meanings, and values. It is suicidal, therefore, he holds, to divorce these values "from the only metaphysic that makes their validity intelligible."[62] The values we find in experience must be rooted in existence or the world becomes utterly unintelligible.

J. E. Boodin finds that science must be supplemented by the primitive knowledge yielded by selfhood in order to "give us back the unique reality

[59] Josiah Royce, *Lectures on Modern Idealism.* New Haven: Yale University Press, 1919. Pp. 236–237.

[60] *Ibid.,* p. 243.

[61] *Loc. cit.*

[62] Wilbur M. Urban, "Metaphysics and Value," *op. cit.,* Vol. II, p. 374.

of individual activity."[63] He tells us that it is "in our moral, aesthetic, and religious experience that we grasp the individual significance of things and selves and the spirit of the whole."[64]

And finally, Miss Calkins, in one of her convincing arguments, holds that the very character of selfhood makes necessary eventually in the progression of our thought the recognition of a Self which is all-inclusive. For, as has already been noted in reference to her philosophy, it is only an all-including Self that can reconcile the two contradictory but self-evident facts of self and a somewhat-in-a-sense-beyond-self.[65]

5. SYSTEM AS A TOUCHSTONE OF TRUTH

There is another principle which is relied upon by idealists as a test of truth. It is the logical principle of coherence. According to it, truth is orderly and systematic, a web of closely intertwined relationships. In this particular aspect of the idealist theory of knowledge, stress is not placed so much upon Berkeley's "to be is to be perceived" as on the Hegelian principle stated by G. Watts Cunningham as "to be is to be implicated." The first is psychological; the second is logical. Recall that Hegel said of Kant's thing-in-itself that there is no such entity. For, he said in effect, thinghood involves just such relationships as our perceptions reveal to us as the qualities of objects. And without these relationships there is no object, no entity at all. It is these very relationships which constitute the real thing itself.

Now if this principle is true, then full awareness of relationships is essential in getting at truth. It will get us nowhere to pare away the qualities of an object one by one, assuming that eventually we will get at the thing itself. Nor will it benefit to try to deal with some object, problem, or part of experience in isolation from the rest of existence. Every object, every problem, every part of experience, is what it is just because of its relation to the whole. True knowledge of them can only be gotten, therefore, by seeing them in their relations to the whole. Because of this, synopsis is a long suit of idealism, since it provides a way of preserving an approximately total perspective while viewing some part in greater detail.

And to go one step further, showing the completeness with which this principle is applied, individual mind, so it is held by many idealists, *depends upon relatedness for its very existence.* Just as there can be no object in isolation from totality, so also there can be no mind without relation to the whole. Three propositions will indicate this particular aspect of mind:

[63] John Elof Boodin, *op. cit.*, Vol. I, p. 164.
[64] *Loc. cit.*
[65] Cf. Mary Whiton Calkins, *op. cit.*, Vol. I, p. 209.

1. Mind reveals itself in the experience of the individual as having definite structure (e.g., the Kantian categories of perception and conception).
2. Nature is revealed by the mind of the individual as having definite structure.
3. But individual mind has no reality apart from its relation to the order of Nature.

As J. E. Creighton has said, "What we call nature is not a miscellaneous assemblage of facts which are mechanically impressed upon us. It reveals itself to us rather as a continuous set of problems and answers, as that which affords at once the necessary stimulus and the verification of our thinking."[66] The interplay of the individual mind with Nature he finds to be much like the interplay between minds in social relationships.

In a similar way, individual mind sustains much the same relationship to society as it does to the natural order. Just as the individual mind must be in relation to the natural order to have definiteness and solidity, so also it must be related to other thinking minds. Creighton tells us that, as individual minds, our problems are set for us largely by what other minds have thought and are thinking; that in solving a problem there is always reference to the ideas and suggestions of others; and that in the verification of our solutions there is always reference to the experience of others. "It appears certain," he says, "that without the stimulus afforded by the direct contact with other minds, the individual would not come to a consciousness of himself. We come to know ourselves through learning to know others: our fellow is the medium in which we see the nature and meaning of our own mind reflected."[67]

6. SUMMARY

The idealist epistemology may be summarized, in part at least, in the following propositions:

1. Idealism and critical realism are alike in their treatment of perception, except that idealism holds that the qualities we perceive in the world are rooted in existence.
2. Some idealists hold that we have direct experience of the self, that it is a self-evident fact; others find the existence of the self to be a necessary inference.
3. Selfhood being what it is, and the surrounding world being so well tuned to the experience of self, it is believed by idealists that reality is a Self.
4. Since nothing can be conceived to exist without being in relation to other things, many idealists believe Reality to be a logically unified total system, a Universal Mind.

[66] J. E. Creighton, *op. cit.*, p. 145.
[67] *Ibid.*, p. 146.

C. THE LOGIC OF IDEALISM

Formal logic, already outlined briefly in the Introduction,[68] is heavily stressed by idealism. Since mind is the prime reality, and since the interpretation of our perceptions and the unifying of our ideas are the methods of knowledge, it is important to master the science of formal logic. It is a tool by which our thinking can be examined and rendered coherent. Therefore it is of primary significance.

But whence the material of logic? Surely there have to be some solid and accurate ideas with which to begin, or formal logic can yield us nothing of value. Harmonious with the emphasis upon relatedness just discussed, idealist logic does include induction as well as deduction. For induction is a means of relation to Nature and society which yields the material with which formal logic must work to be fruitful. Accordingly, J. E. Creighton in his famous *Introductory Logic* tells us that the material of logic comes from our social experience. There are a great number of generally accepted truths, he holds, which have been verified by a great number of individuals, "a perament body of knowledge which no one thinks of calling in question."[69] These are the materials of logic. Such truths come from two main sources. Some of them comprise the everyday knowledge of men, and the others have been yielded as accurate knowledge by the various sciences.

Creighton regards inductive and deductive logic as really being similar, although the former takes particular objects as its starting point and the latter begins with general concepts or judgments. The two methods are similar in the significant fact that both seek to discover the common bonds linking objects, events, and such. They both try to discover the logical relations by which things and groups of things are tied together. In typical idealist fashion, Creighton underlies his treatment of logic with the distinctive belief that "the various pieces of our knowledge are never independent of one another, but form an organic whole, like the members of a living organism, that certain facts follow, as we say, from certain other facts."[70]

We may be able to illustrate this. Many textbooks on logic use the circle as a symbol of the classes of objects described by a given proposition. For the premise, "All men are mortal," for example, two circles, one within the other, are used to describe the inclusion of all men within a still more general class of mortal beings.

For the premise, "Socrates is a man," a small circle may be used to represent the individual, Socrates. An X or simply a dot would be sufficient for the diagram in this case, but too often there are minor premises

[68] Cf. pp. 27–28.
[69] J. E. Creighton, *An Introductory Logic*. New York: The Macmillan Company, 1919. P. 15.
[70] *Ibid.*, p. 383.

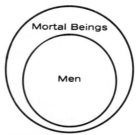

which refer to a smaller class rather than to a single individual, so it is better to keep to the circle as the symbol. Now in making our thinking graphic, it is important to get Socrates in the place exactly described by the statement, namely within the circle which describes men as a class.

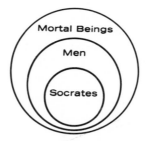

It may be boringly simple to make the observation that had Socrates been described as a mortal being, he would have to be placed in the larger circle in the diagram, but outside the circle representing men, and there would then be no clear indication as to his relation to men. In other words, an alleged syllogism having as major premise the proposition, "All men are mortal beings," and as the minor premise the proposition, "Socrates is a mortal being," could have no valid conclusion as to whether or not Socrates is a man. This use of diagrams may seem quite unnecessary with such a simple example; but when the student of logic is confronted by subtly involved statements such as,

> None but the express train does not stop at this station.
> The last train did not stop,
>
> . . . . ,

then the use of diagrams is more than welcome.

In addition to making the reasoning clear, the circles reveal that there is common ground which is identical in certain judgments and by which they can be seen to be logically related. In some cases the circles illustrating propositions overlap, rather than one being contained within the other. In other cases the circles are completely exclusive of each other, representing instances in which no conclusions can be drawn. While so far in this

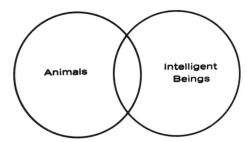

discussion only deductive reasoning has been illustrated by the diagrams, Creighton holds that induction seeks to discover just these same relations, which the circles illustrate, although it begins with particulars rather than with universal premises.

In a certain fraternity house a siege of several typhoid cases occurred among the men. Now there were several fraternity houses and three dormitories in this college community, but no other typhoid cases. In trying to locate the source of infection the investigators were perplexed to learn that X fraternity took milk from the same dairy as served the other houses and the dormitories. This house also patronized the same grocers. But when it was revealed that fresh vegetables were purchased at a farm a few miles in the country which none of the other houses had patronized, the investigators felt they had a possible clue as to the source of the typhoid. This problem in induction may be diagramed in circles.

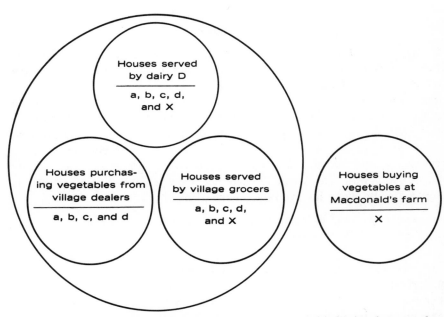

The above (*left*) are possible but not likely sources of infection because the agents are common to all the houses. The above (*right*) is the one isolated case of house X being served by an agent not common to the other houses, therefore a likely source of the infection.

It can be seen by such instances of induction as this that there is a discovery of identical elements and differences, indicating classes and groups, much the same as in deductive reasoning.

Of course, idealist logicians such as Creighton and Bosanquet, being more objective and speculative in their approach, are more greatly preoccupied with such phases of logic as those just described which function at the conceptual level of experience. Whereas idealists who sit at the feet of Berkeley and Leibniz as much as they listen to the teachings of Hegel will be as much interested in the logic of percepts as in the logic of concepts. Accordingly they regard science, inductive method, and the individual's own sensory contact with the world as being important sources for the material of logic, the content of thought. Doubtless they will agree quite fully with the realist and pragmatist in their insistence that formal logic be extended so as to take perceptual values into full account.[71] Miss Calkins, J. A. Leighton, and E. S. Brightman are representatives of this latter emphasis in idealism.

However, most idealists will agree that there is one important way in which formal logic can be used to check the validity of some of the material of logic, in addition, to checking the form of logic. Following Plato and Hegel especially, in the beliefs that truth must be consistent and that the demand for unity which most of us feel is deeply rooted in the very texture of existence, they hold that certain general concepts or judgments can be tested by the principle of contradiction, although they cannot be checked by scientific method.

Look at some examples to see what they mean. Let us examine the often-repeated adage, "All rules have exceptions." The most direct way of checking its validity by formal logic is to use the minor premise, "This is a rule," as the next step in our examination. In this premise the word "this" refers, of course, to the major premise, "All rules have exceptions," as a particular rule falling within the general class of rules which it describes. The result is the following syllogism with the conclusion not yet formulated:

> All rules have exceptions.
> This is a rule.

Now, what conclusion can be drawn? Apparently it follows logically that "This rule has exceptions." Now compare, if you will, the conclusion with the major premise. The premise states that all rules have exceptions. But the conclusion is to the effect that this very rule has exceptions. And that is tantamount to saying that there are some rules which do not have exceptions.

It can be seen that such reasoning blows both hot and cold. The application of formal logic to the content of the original premise reveals that it is

---

[71] Cf. pp. 283–285 and 388–394.

contradictory. It would seem for this reason that the statement cannot be completely true. In this way the validity of the material has been checked by the formal process of deduction.

A similar instance can be cited which is much more vital to philosophizing. It is the principle some daring souls have ventured to uphold in contending that "There is no truth." Not following through on all the steps, let us try to check this by building a syllogism which examines its content. The result will be either of the two following series:

1. There is no truth.
   This is a truth.
   Therefore, it has no existence or validity.

2. There is no truth.
   This is not a truth.
   (No conclusion is possible, but to state the minor premise is to deny the validity of the major premise.)

Whichever of the alternative minor premises is used, the result is a contradiction. Apparently a man cannot assert that there is no truth without attempting to state a truth, the possibility of which he denies in his statement.

A number of other instances could be added, but these two will indicate how logical form can be used in some cases to check the validity of the material which supposedly logical propositions contain. This, of course, is dialectical method. To some philosophers it is little more than black magic or sleight of hand. But many idealists swear by it as a method of thinking which is rooted in the very structure of mind and reality. Must the truths we believe support and reinforce one another? Must our thinking be consistent? Many idealist say, "Yes."

If the idealists are right in this insistence upon unity and coherence, and if the above picture of overlapping, telescoping, and interlacing circles is an accurate diagrammatic representation of truth, then we see the often-mentioned whole-part relation emerging in idealist logic. We have already become acquainted with this principle in idealist metaphysics,[72] and we shall see it again in the axiology of idealism.

From the idealist point of view the growth and development of knowledge, whether in the individual mind or in the experience of the race, is a matter of extending vision so that individuals and classes are seen in their larger and more complete relationships. To the mind of limited development and to the less mature, experience is a matter of wholes which are accepted quite unconsciously, without any insight into or appreciation of the complex interrelationships which constitute them as wholes. The more

[72] Cf. pp. 154–157, especially the reference to Mary Whiton Calkins on pp. 156–157.

knowledge is developed, the more analysis and synthesis take place, and wholes are seen with deeper insight as being constituted of interrelated parts. Before the birth and development of insight in me, they were undifferentiated wholes to which I responded with comparative mental blindness. Now, though I will always have more complex ramifications and relations to explore, they are differentiated wholes. I have broken them down into their constituent parts, at least mentally, and have put them back together again. Therefore they are more fully appreciated.

D. THE AXIOLOGY OF IDEALISM

A general theory of value which is a natural expression of the idealist philosophy may be outlined by making explicit the following three propositions:

1. The values human beings desire and enjoy fundamentally are rooted in existence. They are real existents.
2. The values of human life are what they are largely because there are individual persons to possess and enjoy them.
3. One important way in which individual persons can realize value is by actively relating parts and wholes.

These three statements about value are not necessarily consistent, forming a coherent axiology; but they can be made consistent and be tied together to comprise a theory of value. We will enlarge on each of them and attempt to show how they can be made to fit together. The result will be an idealist axiology, but not the only value theory possible to idealism.

1. In introducing the reader to the field of axiology *per se* in the Introduction,[73] it was asserted that there is a realm of being and a realm of value. The intention of this statement was to point out that an object may be known to exist in the temporal world without its having any value for us. Home is a fact for many people. But "no place like home" is not a real value experience for everyone who has a home. The intention was not to suggest that being is one thing and value is entirely another affair, for this distinction is one of the critical issues in axiology. And it is to this very issue that the proposition first stated above is directed. Many idealists insist that values are not like the morning mists, here today and gone tomorrow. They are rooted in existence. They are part and parcel of reality. We enjoy values, not only because our emotions and sentiments are appropriately aroused so that we have certain desirable feelings, but *because the things we value are realities which have existence* themselves and are rooted in the very structure of the cosmos.

Wilbur Urban, one of the guiding spirits who have pioneered the way in

[73] Cf. p. 29.

axiology, has been most outspoken in his insistence that value and exist-ence are not and cannot be divorced. He states his position emphatically when he says:

I hold that there can be no existence without value and no value without existence. Reality is neither mental or material, but a realm in which thought and thing, fact and value, are inseparable.[74]

2. The second proposition is to the effect that values are largely what they are because of the individual persons who possess and enjoy them in their experience. This could be a diametrical contradiction of the first proposition. J. A. Leighton is one of the exponents of this theory, and he has already been identified as an ardent champion of individuality. As was shown in discussing the problem of the one and the many,[75] Leighton is suspicious of any metaphysics which so exalts *one unified world ground* as to endanger the reality and uniqueness of individuals. Similarly, in axiology he does not favor any theory which makes values *per se* real in the abstract because of what he regards as the tendency of such a theory to detract from the uniqueness of the individual person's value experiences. One of his statements of this attitude toward value is as follows:

Values are real only in and for selves that feel them. There are really no such entities or subsistents as *Truth* or *Beauty* or *Goodness* and the like. There are concrete truths, things felt to be beautiful, satisfying goods for themselves. *Individuality is both the locus and the measure of value.*[76]

But if a synthesis between spiritual monism and spiritual pluralism is possible in idealist metaphysics, as Miss Calkins holds, for example,[77] then it is also possible in axiology to think of values as being rooted in existence (Urban) and at the same time believe that the principles of individuality and value are closely identified (Leighton). There is a close parallel for this in the knowledge theory of Berkeley. He insisted that objects do not exist for us as individuals unless we perceive them. But he also insisted upon the existence of God in whose perception all objects exist whether perceived by man or not. If Berkeley's epistemology is valid, then an idealist axiology can be built, closely paralleling it, which will synthesize the first two propositions stated above. It could be framed something like this: "Value exists only for the individual person when he works out those adjustments which realize value for him, and when he has the emotional experience which is the enjoyment of value. However, God exists, and in Him all value resides, in Him is that perfection in which all possible positive values are fully realized and enjoyed."

[74] Wilbur M. Urban, "Metaphysics and Value," *op. cit.*, Vol. II, p. 375.
[75] Cf. p. 155.
[76] J. A. Leighton, *op. cit.*, p. 138.
[77] Cf. pp. 156–157.

3. The third proposition states a principle, typically idealist, to be supplied in the effort to realize the fullest value and make the most of life. If, as Miss Calkins says, "the ultimately real relations are those of whole and part, of including and being included,"[78] then the individual can enlarge his experience, sharing values already existent in the Universal Self, by the deliberate effort to see all phases of life in harmonious relation to totality. As shown above,[79] logical values result from correctly recognizing whole-part relations. Aesthetic values are possessed when a work of art is understood and appreciated as a differentiated whole, its constituent parts analyzed and synthesized. Social values are realized when an individual recognizes his place as no more than a part in the total society and is willing to grant to all other individuals their due privileges. Religious values arise as the individual practices his relation to God, the total Person, in worship, fellowship, and service. But further instances will not be itemized here, as there will follow a more detailed discussion of four significant kinds of value: the ethical, the aesthetic, the religious, and the social.

1. ETHICAL VALUE

Clifford Barrett says of Immanuel Kant that he "developed the most important expression of perfectionism yet given in the modern world."[80] Since an idealist's ethics is likely to be some form of perfectionism, we will let Kant's statement of it in his *Metaphysic of Morals* represent for us the idealist treatment of ethical values.

According to Kant, there are at least two moral values which are themselves rooted in existence. These are (1) persons and (2) the moral imperative, both of which will bear some discussion.

1. Individual men are persons. By their very nature they are more than individual things or individual organisms. They are minds, personalities, souls. As such they have potentialities far higher in quality and ultimate worth than are found in any other forms of individual existence. Therefore they are *ends,* and never can be *means*. Relations between individual men must always be such as are harmonious with the fact that persons are *ends*. It will not do for me to treat a man or a class of men as slaves, as cogs in an industrial or war machine, in order that I may make money or advance an empire. They are *ends* in themselves and deserve more than to be slaves to other persons or means to some impersonal objectives.

2. In every man there is an imperative to do good which is innate, as much a part of his nature as sensation, perception, and thought. Just as mind is so formed as to relate sensations in space and time, it is also

[78] Mary Whiton Calkins, *op. cit.*, Vol. I, pp. 210–211.
[79] Cf. pp. 170–175.
[80] Clifford Barrett, *Philosophy*. New York: The Macmillan Company, 1935. P. 330.

formed so as to see duty as the guide to conduct. Certain categories are basic in the make-up of mind; categories of knowledge have already been described in part.[81] The category of duty is just as basic as these categories of knowing, woven into the very texture of individual selfhood. Furthermore, reason reveals that there are certain moral laws which are universally binding; for if all men were to disregard them, social order would give way to confusion and chaos.

Now in addition to these two values which are evident in present individual and social experience, there are at least four other values which are anticipated by them and are to be realized ideally by men. They are (1) obedience to universal moral laws, (2) the good will, (3) the society of ends, and (4) immortality.

1. Universal moral laws are ethical values which become essential in human relations because individual men are persons. Men being persons, I as an individual can only act in those ways which I am willing should become the practice for all men. I cannot will that stealing should become a universal practice, as that would destroy all privacy in the possession of property. I cannot plead an exception in my own individual case without recognizing by my exception that universal respect for property is the necessary moral law. So it is with all important questions of conduct, such as the evils condemned in the Ten Commandments. Adultery, killing, and dishonesty are all contrary to respect for individuals as persons.

2. The good will is a value which follows both from the necessity of moral laws and from the fact of the categorical imperative. Since I have the experience of oughtness and since reason enables me to recognize necessary moral laws, it is possible for me to act with no other motivation than the desire to fulfill the moral law. Not just to be honest because it is the best policy, not just to refrain from murder to protect my own skin and avoid family feuds, not just to sell goodness in order to get goodness in return, with interest, but *to do right because I know it is right and necessary*, giving no attention to the selfish returns which may or may not result from my good deed—this is the good will, a positive moral value which I can realize, the only unqualified good possible in human experience.

3. The society of ends about which Kant speaks is a blessed community, a society of good persons similar to the Kingdom of God proclaimed in the New Testament. This society of ends is a value which follows both from the fact that individuals are persons and from the necessity of universal moral laws. Both anticipate an ideal society; both are purposefully orientated toward a utopian community of moral souls. If individuals are persons and if all individuals control their conduct in harmony with complete respect for persons, human society will become just such an ideal society of ends. Moral laws are what they are because individuals are persons, and so

[81] Cf. pp. 128–132.

become the laws of such a kingdom of ends. Therefore, the blessed community of selves is anticipated and longed for by the human race, and men are bound to strive for its realization.

4. The corollary of the society of ends is that individual immortality is also a value. The anticipated ideal society is the social aspect of the individual value we speak of as immortality or eternal life. Since, as individuals, we are persons, we have in us the beginnings of an immortal existence. Since reason reveals to us necessary moral laws, and our own natures impel us toward the fulfilling of these laws, we see immortality implied as our destiny. And since the fulfillment of the moral law is such a big job—too big for the span of human existence—immortality is implied as necessary to existence as a person.

Finally, one practical word should be written as to how we may realize these moral values. One forthright admonition which sums it up in a rather arid rule is "Obey the moral law." This rule of life means at least two things, and these constituent rules have more flesh and blood, and are pulsating with greater warmth. They are (1) "So live as to treat all people as persons," and (2) "Live as though you yourself are a member of an ideal society of ends." As one of Kant's gems advises us:

Act so that in your own person as well as in the person of every other you are treating mankind also as an end, never merely as a means.[82]

2. AESTHETIC VALUE

Arthur Schopenhauer has been to aesthetics what Kant has been to ethics, a great creator in the idealist tradition. So we will use his treatment of the aesthetic experience contained in the third book of *The World as Will and Idea* by way of helping to make vivid some of the aesthetic values of idealists.

Art for Schopenhauer was "the flower of life."[83] And for him this statement was not a burst of sentiment. It was a characterization based on a thorough analysis of the values which he enjoyed in art. At an opposite pole from J. A. Leighton,[84] he found individuality to be the problem of life instead of its great value. For Schopenhauer the chief trouble with the world is that it is broken up into individuals, i.e., *individuated*. To be an individual human being meant to him desire, struggle, striving, attendant pain, temporary satisfaction, followed no doubt by satiation and boredom, then a return to struggle and striving again. If, he thought, an individual

[82] Immanuel Kant, *The Fundamental Principles of the Metaphysics of Ethics.* Translated by Otto Manthey-Zorn, New York: Appleton-Century-Crofts, 1938. P. 47.
[83] Arthur Schopenhauer, *The World as Will and Idea.* Fourth edition. Translated by R. B. Haldane and J. Kemp; London: Routledge & Kegan Paul, 1896. Vol. I, p. 345.
[84] Cf. pp. 155–156.

could only shatter the shape of things which marks him off as an individual, he could be released from this squirrel cage of individuality, constantly rotating from desire to temporary satisfactions, to boredom, and back again. Now, art is the flower of life because it is a level of human experience to which individuals can rise and in which there can be a temporary release from individuality.

Look first at the visual arts, painting and sculpturing in their various kinds. When we have an experience of enjoying beauty, whether in the contemplation of a work or in the creation of it, there are two important values we possess. They are (1) knowledge of the object, and (2) existence for a moment as a will-less subject (not an individual) receiving impressions of the Ideas which are behind the phenomenal world.

1. By knowledge of the object, Schopenhauer does not mean knowledge of the particular object but of the Idea (Platonic Idea)[85] which the particular object represents. An amateur draws a charcoal sketch of his dog, attempting to preserve in some visual form the beauty of the dog's build, the toughness of his muscles, the spunk and clownishness of his personality. Is this a true art experience, according to Schopenhauer's aesthetics? No, it is probably not, because the interest is attached to the individual dog. The amateur would only achieve true aesthetic value when his love for his dog was transcended by an interest in the Idea "dog" and he tried to catch in his sketch, not the traits of his own pet alone, but the revealing traits of doghood as such.

2. The other value to be possessed in the enjoyment of visual art is the losing of individuality and the achievement of such complete objectivity that we are virtually unconscious and almost completely will-less subjects of knowledge. Experiencing this value is for me to feel that I am no longer an individual, but a sort of mental screen upon which the eternal Ideas behind Nature are projected, art being the projecting mechanism. When my friend's painting, "Old Fashioned Bouquet," makes me an enjoying subject in whom quaint flowers beautifully arranged become an object of pleasure in which I am momentarily lost, I then enjoy this other value in visual art.

But to turn from visual art to music, Schopenhauer finds even richer aesthetic value in this medium. In music there is no equivalent to the first value described in visual art, namely knowledge of the object, for music is not concerned with objects or Ideas. It is concerned with Will, the essence which is behind the Ideas just as the Ideas are behind Nature. There is, however, a value equivalent to the loss of individuality as a will-less subject of knowledge. This is the release from the snare of individuality which comes in being identified with the Ultimate Will and becoming the will-less subject who feels the surge of that Will.

Music is the highest of the arts, for it is independent of the forms of

[85] Cf. pp. 113–114.

Nature. Music is transfigured Nature and could exist to an extent without the natural order. The flow of tones in a Brahms symphony, for example, expresses what is behind Nature, much as Nature expresses it, but without using any of the forms of Nature. Nature is an expression of the Will and of Ideas, but it is the kind of expression which necessarily employs the principle of individuation. Music is an expression of will which is free both of the Ideas and the principle of individual forms. So it comes as close as anything can approach the objectification of the whole Will. It is more thing signified than it is the sign. It is the *"copy of the Will itself."*[86] Seen in this light, the world described as embodied music is virtually as accurate a characterization as when it is described as embodied Will. So when a person loses his individuality in the enjoyment of a tonal flow, the subtly beautiful creation of a master, he becomes closely identified with the essence of things, and with the whole undivided essence, as closely as is possible, while he still remains a creature of the natural order.

3. RELIGIOUS VALUE

William E. Hocking has distinguished himself among contemporary idealists by the attention he has given to religion and religious experience. From his book, *The Meaning of God in Human Experience,* there can be gleaned a number of direct suggestions as to what the religious values may be for an idealist.

By and large he finds that axiology and religion are intimately related. The relation is that a person's religious convictions, if he has them, will determine significantly what the values of life shall be for him. Stated more specifically, Hocking holds that religion is as much a matter of ideas as it is of feelings, and that the root ideas in religion are bound to constitute a criterion by which the rest of life is judged. Of course, most central of the ideas in religion is the idea of God. We must have a God-idea, Hocking insists; we can't blindly accept the consolations, comforts, and inspirations of religion on a feeling basis alone. There must be some metaphysical thinking in order to have these feelings. This God-idea is the most used of all ideas, not as object of thought, but as function in our thinking. And it will be the chief determinant of the value level of a person's consciousness. So, for the religious person at least, the conception of God is likely to be the hub of all value experience, and from it all values will stem.

Turning now to some of the specifically religious values, there are two which are supreme. Six others may be mentioned which are important, but they are derived from the two central ones.

1. One of these two central values is the experience of God in the self-consciousness. In worship or prayer and in the practical functioning of the religious consciousness, God is thought of at least in the second person; He

[86] Arthur Schopenhauer, *op. cit.*, p. 333.

is Thou. This value stands out when contrasted with philosophical and theological thinking about God. In these, reference is made to Him in the third person, as an object of thought but not necessarily present in consciousness. But in worship the Him becomes Thou. And in coöperative effort where it is believed that God is Companion, Colaborer, or Partner, the pronoun We may more accurately describe the religious consciousness of the believer. Then he is united with God in companionship and common effort.

2. The second of these two great religious values is the experience of love for God. This, Hocking says, is a simple impulse which is "in the ground of the soul," almost instinctive. It is more basic than the love of life and is the ground out of which the love of life springs. Though it encompasses such desires as the longing for spiritual self-preservation, for ultimate judgment of life, for perpetual renewal of the worth of life, and for immortality, it is essentially a simple urge toward God. To the mystic who experiences this value, it is virtual sacrilege to try to find justification for the experience. For him the ecstasy of this moment of adoration is its own justification.

3. One of the less fundamental values is the transformation of the self which sometimes takes place in worship, and in which the whole-part relation is significant. In worship the believer finds his true self by consciously relating himself to the Whole Self in a face-to-face meeting. The experience of the finite self being what it is, we all easily get lost in a peculiar kind of error, an error which involves a mistake in the very kind of self we allow to have expression in us. "We begin to get in our own way," Hocking says, "and so to defeat our own work. We can find no radical remedy except in getting rid of that self: and no radical way of abandoning that self except by reverting to the whole."[87] But in worship and prayer, directly facing God, we rediscover the true selfhood we are sincerely trying to realize. We do this by orientating ourselves again to God. We leave behind the erroneous self, and the true self which it is in us to become again has the upper hand. We are renewed, redirected, and in a measure transformed.

4. To mention another of these secondary religious values, Hocking finds that religious experience has value on an epistemological score. For it is possible to have some new knowledge of truth divulged to us in a worship experience. That is to say that insights are sharpened and understandings are sometimes given birth in us which reason and experience have not revealed to us so far.

5. Another value arising in religious experience is an enlargement of the capacity of creativity. Whereas many aspects of living are readily encrusted

[87] William E. Hocking, *op. cit.*, p. 411.

in routine, Hocking finds in the religious motive "a weariness of the old, the habitual, the established."[88] If religious experience does have this motive, then worship may include the value of "preparing the soul for the reception of novelty."[89] In alliance with the Absolute is the grand opportunity of the individual to be set free in genuine creativity. For, with attention turned away from blind routines, and with the individual grounded in his relation to the Absolute, a relation which according to Hocking is the foundation of true reflection, the rarely opened door of creativity is set ajar and blind routine can be transcended by a genuinely creative imagination.

6. There is also in religion the experience of vicarious success. A person may feel that he has failed in the realizing of some good. He may even doubt if he or his generation shall ever succeed in achieving divinely intended ends at all. But in the religious consciousness comes the consolation that though I may be imperfect, there is One who is perfect with whom I am allied; though our generation may fail miserably in translating the divine intention for human society into flesh and blood, yet the goodness of God is supreme, and the City of God shall surely be built in spite of present failures. Such are the vicarious successes with which religion may console us.

7. Coupled with this value is its complement, which Hocking terms "prophetic consciousness." Though there is penitence in worship and compensation in vicarious success, there is also something more virile as far as actual accomplishments are concerned. In the fully awakened religious consciousness there are occasions when a course of action may be seen as the divinely intended good to be performed, and in full affirmation the self may perform the act knowing it shall stand forever fulfilled and eternally significant. One of the last fruits of religion, it is only after long arduous labor that such a literal, prophetic, and responsible faith is produced in us.

8. Finally, a very general value of religion is that if it is based on reality, it will enhance all other human attachments. Hocking insists that religion which does not enrich human relationships is not based on a God-idea which is rooted in reality. Religion to be legitimate must contribute to human values and not detract from them.

To summarize, the religious values as Hocking discerns them are consciousness of God, love for God, transformation of the self, some knowledge of truth, the development of creativity, enjoyment of vicarious success, deliberate actualizing of divine goodness, and the general enhancement of all human relations.

[88] *Ibid.*, p. 364.
[89] *Ibid.*, p. 365.

4. SOCIAL VALUE

One criticism which has been leveled against idealism is that it has not fostered a sense of social responsibility in those whom it has influenced. Rather commonly regarded as being preoccupied with things "abstract" and "spiritual," it is frequently waived aside as an "ivory tower" philosophy. There may be some justification for this criticism since there have been two developments away from idealism, both having a strong social emphasis. As has been noted, idealism in America has been referred to as Hegelianism of the right, whereas dialectical materialism, the philosophy of Russian communism, has been called Hegelianism of the left. This is because Marx and Engels were influenced by the dialectical method of Hegel, but reacted against his metaphysics by substituting for it a radical materialism. The result has been a philosophy which has been ardent in its attention to social theory. The other instance is that the pragmatist philosophy of John Dewey also actually arose out of idealistic influence. Dewey came of age philosophically under Hegelian tutelage, but he reacted against idealism eventually, although still holding on to some of the dialectical method. What all the influences were which caused this revolt cannot easily be determined; but it is clear that social theory is a dominant concern of Dewey and those who have followed him.

Although it may be true that idealism in America during the late nineteenth and early twentieth centuries was not as positive in social theory as it should have been, it should be noted that this failure is not essential to the character of idealism. Because there are certain principles central in idealism which have necessary social bearings and others which offer great promise, if applied, for the positive realization of social value. Before enlarging upon this, a pertinent remark should be made anticipating the next chapter, which deals with the educational practice of idealism. It is that, whatever the more general social failures of idealism may have been, the philosophy has been nevertheless a positive influence in American education and in former times framed its educational objectives in social as well as individual terms.

The idealist conception of society, in the first place, gives the philosophy an essentially social bent. For, according to it, society is not an aggregation or collection of individuals; it is an organism in which individuals participate. Individual selfhood is not something which can grow in isolation; it is given birth through the social process and comes into actual self-realization only in relation with society as its medium of nurture and development. This is not to say that individuals are subordinate to society, although Gentile, who was Minister of Education in the Fascist regime in Italy for a short time, did make the individual completely subordinte to the State and national culture. For many idealists, if not for the great majority, the individual realizes his selfhood only within society, at the same time that individual and society are both ends. The individual progresses from more to more in his own self-realization, society providing the necessary matrix for this process. And at the same time, society progresses from more to more in a process of realizing the ultimately good society.

This strongly suggests that the overall principle of social value is the part-whole relation. Guided by it, social theory will be comprised of a broad framework in which there is an appropriate and acceptable place for every individual, group, institution, and segment, of whatever kind, in no way detracting from the welfare of the whole. This is reminiscent of the principle of justice enunciated in Plato's *Republic,* another intimation of the essentially social character of the philosophy of idealism.

It may make this theory of value more concrete if we go on and state three principles of social organization which stem from it, and which can be put to work practically at the local community level where the vast majority of us live. These are the principles of representation, coördination, and planning.

1. The principle of representation is that every part of a society or a community should have opportunity to participate in the deliberations as well as in the activities of the whole. Attempts at practice of this principle can be seen in large-scale proportions in democratic governments and in the United Nations; however, its implications may be more difficult to see at the local community level. In most communities there is a variety of different kinds of segments which make up the whole. There are racial or nationality groups; different economic levels; different occupational groups, such as the professions, business interests, agricultural interests, and the trades; different religious faiths; different political loyalties; and so on. A community cannot realize its fullest value, according to this principle of representation, without providing a genuine opportunity, by means of some concrete organization and structure, for all of these different parts of the whole to find their place in both deliberations and activities of the community. It is essential that they be represented in the deliberations because it is at the level of deliberation that decisions and plans are made. And people do not participate fully when they only have part in the activities but have nothing to say in determining what those activities shall be.

2. The principle of coördination is that in the deliberations of a community organized representatively direct attention should be given to the relating of individuals, groups, and services so that each segment of the community will have some consciousness of the function fulfilled by every other; that there will be no duplication or competition between services; and that no area of real community need will be neglected. This principle provides one of the central themes for the deliberative life of the community, another being the theme of planning, to be mentioned momentarily.

One of the chief reasons for representative organization, other than its own intrinsic value, is that it provides the means by which interrelationships can be established, welding all the parts more completely into a functioning whole.

3. Finally, the principle of planning is that communities need not remain devoid of deliberation, blindly allowing social processes to go on as they will, but that communities can muster powers of deliberation, formulate some objectives, and guide social processes at least partially in the direction of fulfilling these objectives. When there is representative community organization providing a medium of coördination of groups and activities, a community is at least partially in a position to become self-conscious about its reasons for existence, its own particular genius, its particular problems and needs, and the goals the fulfillment of which are relevant in the light of this community self-understanding.

The three foregoing principles have been stated with the local community level as the frame of reference because in doing so they could be made most concrete. It should be remarked again, however, that they are involved at all levels of social experience in realizing social value according to the idealist approach, ranging from the local community to the most inclusive society possible on earth which presents the pressing task of building a world community among the nations.

A sketch of the history of idealism and a systematic synopsis of the philosophy have now been presented in broad outline. The two chapters which follow in this section devoted to idealism will present studies of this philosophy as it operates in two important areas of practice, namely, in education and religion.

IX

Idealism in Education

A. Education As A Social Institution

B. The Pupil
1. THE PUPIL IS A SELF
2. THE PUPIL IS IN THE PROCESS OF BECOMING

C. The Objectives of Education
1. OBJECTIVES FOR THE INDIVIDUAL
2. OBJECTIVES FOR SOCIETY
3. SYNTHESIS

D. The Educative Process
1. THE TEACHER
2. IMITATION
3. INTEREST, EFFORT, AND DISCIPLINE
4. SELF-ACTIVITY
5. THE CURRICULUM
6. METHOD
7. SUMMARY

Unlike naturalism and realism, there is an abundance of literature on the meaning of idealism in educational practice. For in the same manner as pragmatism, its rebellious offspring, idealism has shown great interest in education and has decidedly influenced educational thought and practice. As has been noted,[1] William T. Harris, one of the most influential figures to date in American education, was an idealist. And in the generation or two succeeding him there have been idealists of note who have unblushingly embraced education as the field of practice in which their ideas could be put to work with great effect.

Probably no man in recent American education has been as much an exponent of the idealist philosophic tradition as the late Herman Harrell Horne (1874–1946), who, throughout a thirty-three-year professorship at New York University, worked with distinction in the history and philosophy of education. The late Michael Demiashkevitch, formerly at George Peabody College for Teachers, has written on idealism in education with real effect. B. B. Bogoslovsky has given eloquent expression to some phases of idealism in his narrative portrayal, *The Ideal School.*[2] William E. Hocking, though occupied for the most part with general philosophy, has given us some telling thoughts on education. The late Rupert C. Lodge (1888–1961), professor of logic and history of philosophy in the University of Manitoba and an avid student of Plato, has written two excellent books on the philosophy of education; one is his general text, *Philosophy of Education,* and the other a study of Plato's educational theory.[3] Though he speaks of his own philosophy as balanced philosophy, he presents his comparative studies of educational philosophy as an idealist would. And abroad, Giovanni Gentile, Mussolini's first Minister of Public Instruction, worked out his Educational Reform in Italy on idealist principles, as opposed to the previously more prevalent positivism and naturalism.[4]

Drawing on the fund of literature sent to the presses by such men as these, we shall try to deal with the salient characteristics of a typically idealist education. First we shall discuss the basis for the existence of education as an institution, according to idealism. The next step will be to describe the pupil as he is seen through idealist eyes. Then we shall state the objectives of education as idealists conceive them. And finally we shall discuss somewhat specifically a half-dozen factors among those comprising the educational process when under idealist direction.

[1] Cf. pp. 142–143.

[2] New York: The Macmillan Company, 1936.

[3] Rupert C. Lodge, *Philosophy of Education.* First edition, 1937; revised edition, 1947; New York: Harper & Row, Publishers. Also, *Plato's Theory of Education.* New York: Harcourt, Brace & World, 1947.

[4] Cf. Merritt Moore Thompson, *The Educational Philosophy of Giovanni Gentile.* Los Angeles: University of Southern California Press, 1934. Pp. 21–35.

A. EDUCATION AS A SOCIAL INSTITUTION

If idealism has a rationale for the existence of the school, it must be one that is fundamentally opposed to that of naturalism. Education must exist as an institution of human society because of spiritual necessity and not because of natural necessity alone. The idealist movement of the nineteenth century, particularly, exalted human culture and human institutions as being expressions of spiritual reality. Education is an institution made necessary by man's need for culture but in a way somewhat different from the realist assumption concerning this necessity.

Man can only be made a man by a cultural birth. As Comenius, who was a realist rather than an idealist, contended, if man is to become a man, education must form him. He is formed as scarcely more than an animal by his biological birth, although he has full potentiality for humanity and what might even be called a kind of divinity. But left to himself, he will be formed by whatever culture happens to surround him. If the culture is that of wolves, as in some few notable instances has been the case, he will behave more like a wolf than a man. If the culture is the parochialism of an isolated hamlet or an ethnic settlement in a large city, he will be formed accordingly. These will measure the limits of his cultural birth.

One reason for the existence of the school is so that in a fuller and more representative sense, embracing as far as possible the breadth of humanity's contemporary life and the backward reach of its history, individual children may be given cultural birth as men. In this formation it is hoped that the fullest possible range and depth of humanness will make the formation exceedingly rich.

Thus far idealism and realism are generally in agreement concerning the rationale of the school. But many idealists have injected a significant additional element. It is that God somehow speaks through the culture of man. The contention is that as the school inducts the child into the richness of meaning implicit in being human, it also provides him with bases for inferences concerning the nature of the Ultimate and Divine. This is explicitly stated by Horne, as will be noted later in this chapter in his definition of education. If this contention is true, then education is a human necessity in order for man to be made truly man; in some measure also it is divinely intended, because of its cultural function as a means of general revelation through which a person may come to see the ultimate context of his life to be that of Spirit, not human culture alone, much less the natural order alone.

Another basis for the necessary existence of the educational institution is in the social nature of man. This may not have been exploited as much by idealists as it could have been. But Horne has on occasion made it explicitly clear that man is a *socius* at the same time that he is an individual. This theme has also been heavily underscored by pragmatism, but in another metaphysical setting. The middle decades of the twentieth century have seen a renewed, if not new, emphasis on the social self. Depth psychologies have lent weight to this direction and the concept is embraced in both spiritual realist and idealist world views. The point is that if individual man is a *socius*, an objective projection of society in an individuated form, then education is necessarily a social process and not altogether individualistic. If to be a man, or to be a self, is to be a *socius*, then a man must have a social setting in which to become a man. This would seem to be an adequate requirement in itself that education be formalized as an institutional affair. If ramified somewhat, this principle might also require negation of private tutoring as the total means of education for anyone. It might also mean the recognition of the common school as possessing unique social values not to be found in any privately or parochially sponsored schools. But these possible implications would require further study. The point stressed here for idealism is that the social dimension generic to individual man requires that his education be social.

There are three other institutional aspects of education, possibly minor ones, that deserve at least mention. Some idealists have held that the school is an agency of society. All that has been said so far would confirm this very generally. But if by being an agency of society it is meant that the school is under the control of society and will expect the complete conformity of each individual to the culture, serious question must be raised. The truly social and communicative character of the school is seriously threatened whenever this narrower understanding of agency is presupposed. Society needs the school. And the social self needs the school. But neither the needs of society nor the needs of the social self will be met within this narrow concept of agency. By itself it is inadequate and self-defeating as a rationale for the institution of education.

Occasionally the intellectual role of the school is played up by an idealist as the basis of its existence in a way that gives the school prerogatives it does not have and reflects unfavorably on other institutions. Is it fair, for example, to say that the school is the mind of society?[5] If the school is the mind of society, what are the nonintellectual functions of law, medicine, politics, the Church, business, and others that make them so indispensable? It may be that a definition of the intellectual role of the school can be formulated in which it is acting as a "mind," but in a particular way, not exclusively. This definition relates to the question just discussed of whether

[5] Theodore M. Greene, "A Liberal Christian Idealist Philosophy of Education," in Nelson B. Henry (editor), *Modern Philosophies of Education*. Chicago: University of Chicago Press, 1955. Pp. 115–117.

the school is the agent of society. The school should be uniquely a thinking institution in the sense that it will give leadership and guidance in thinking. It will encourage thinking and "mind functions" in other institutions and not discourage such. But this means it cannot be an agent that follows the leadership of society; instead it must stand at the edge of the future and urge society ahead into new forms. In short, it must lead.

This brings us to the third and final of these characterizations of the role of the school. This is that the school is uniquely, although not exclusively, a value-realizing institution. Of course every institution that has any reason for being has some connection with a transition or a transfer in values. But of all human institutions, none stands balanced so delicately between the present and the future as the school that is doing its job. Human life is constantly flowing in. The surrounding environment is unworthy in great measure and calling for change for the better throughout. And the march of time makes movement into the future ever the order of the day. Where, such circumstances prevailing, should transition in values, if not transformation, be more the point of vision, concern, and effort than in the schools?

B. THE PUPIL

We must now define the pupil as he is seen when idealism is the guiding philosophy of education. For the idealist the approach to the pupil is in itself important. It is not enough to observe the phenomenal side of his existence; he must look beyond the perceptible self of each pupil and recognize the outline of a more basic being. Giovanni Gentile stated this requirement:

> *The teacher must not stop at the classification of the pupil or at the external observation of his face or behavior. He must enter into the very mind of the child where his life is gathered and centered. . . . (He) must not read into the child any spontaneous and independent impulses of his own.*[6]

1. THE PUPIL IS A SELF

The more discerning approach for which Gentile called is a clue to the central principle in the idealist treatment of the pupil. This is that the pupil is a self, a spiritual being. It can easily be seen that this follows from the idealist metaphysics already outlined.[7] As we have attempted to show, the idealist system stems largely from the belief that the central core of individual experience is a spiritual being. This has a direct significance when this way of thinking is taken into the classroom. The idealist teacher, ardently believing in the self as a spiritual reality, cannot look at pupils as

[6] As quoted in Merritt Moore Thompson, *op. cit.*, pp. 70–71.
[7] Cf. pp. 148–150.

mere bodies without spirits. Beneath all the appearances by means of which he perceives the pupil, he beholds a deeper and more real individual who is a spirit. The pupil is a personality whose foundation is not a body alone but a deep underlying spiritual reality.

Some more specific statements by two educators generally recognized as idealists and by a third who advocates some significant changes in progressive education, will help to make this picture more definite.

Gentile had this to say in describing the pupil as a spiritual self:

> *If personality be the pattern of integration, then the I is the active and living core which directs and gives form to the pattern, unity to the diversity of experience, and which focuses all the elements into separate acts only as a process of abstraction for practical purposes.*[8]

Herman Harrell Horne offers a concrete picture of the pupil that at the same time has much in common with Gentile. Not wanting to be misunderstood as a theorist who overlooks flesh-and-blood children when philosophizing about the pupil, he said:

> *Education must yield the theory that the mind is an isolated entity caught in this mundane sphere and detained in the body as its prison-house, in the favor of the theory that mind and body together constitute one organic unity.*[9]

Of course, Professor Horne was writing at a time (1904) when idealism was much in the saddle and the tendency toward the kind of abstraction he wished to modify was much greater than it is now. In another statement in his *Philosophy of Education* he explained more fully the nature of the "organic unity" he says the pupil is.

> *Consciousness, as we know it in our present mode of existence, manifests itself only as the correlate of a nervous system. . . . It is also the basis for any conception of the fundamental place of the body in any general plan of education. The body is the home of the mind, in the forceful New Testament phrase, "the temple of the Holy Ghost."*[10]

Not wanting this conception to be misconstrued as exclusively individualistic, in a later section of his book he goes on to include the social aspect of the pupil's life. Of this he said:

> *The individual is a whole and he is also a part of a larger whole. It is the nature of an individual to be both himself and a* socius. *Individuality is not a narrowly circumscribed sphere, but is a large circle inclusive of one's fellows. The individual really finds his own unity in the service he can render to many selves.*[11]

[8] Merritt Moore Thompson, *op. cit.*, p. 48.
[9] Herman Harrell Horne, *The Philosophy of Education.* Revised edition; New York: The Macmillan Company, 1930. P. 37.
[10] *Ibid.*, p. 64.
[11] *Ibid.*, pp. 142–143.

In a much more recent statement Horne summed up his conception of the pupil:

> *Our philosophy dares to suggest that the learner is a finite person, growing, when properly educated, into the image of an infinite person, that his real origin is deity, that his nature is freedom, and that his destiny is immortality.*[12]

B. B. Bogoslovsky in his book, *The Ideal School,* has advanced some supplements to an experimentalist philosophy of education that deserve attention. Among them is an idealist treatment of the selfhood of the pupil. In order for the personality to be full-fledged, it must be "conscious of itself as something larger and more comprehensive than any single attitude."[13] Another characteristic of personality is unity or oneness; there can be no serious "separatistic" tendencies this side of the abnormal.[14] And a third characteristic is uniqueness or individuality: "There are few things more nauseating," said Bogoslovsky, "than a society of standardized minds, even if they are standardized on a rather high level."[15] Personality so understood is of supreme value, and respecting the personality of the pupil as the supreme value is a disposition that should underlie all education. This, Bogoslovsky said, makes it imperative that three related values should always be actual in the educative process. These are sincerity, integrity, and the avoidance of oppression.[16]

That he makes the self distinctly superior in education is clearly seen when he discusses the issue of environment versus the initiative of the individual. He readily grants that environment does influence the individual, but he also insists that the individual determines his environment just as much as he is determined by it, if not more. "It is the individual personality which actually picks up stimuli that affect it, selects them, and in this way creates and determines its environment . . . more liberally and in its social aspects *the creation of the environment by personality* has the priority."[17] This suggests that the self of the pupil is something deeper than the physical, that it is superior to it and able to produce changes in physical surroundings.

2. The Pupil Is in the Process of Becoming

But there is another aspect of the pupil that is important for most idealists. To say that the pupil is a spiritual being is to express what

[12] Herman Harrell Horne, "An Idealistic Philosophy of Education," in the *Forty-First Yearbook of the National Society for the Study of Education,* Part I, "Philosophies of Education." Bloomington, Ill.: Public School Publishing Company, 1942. P. 155.

[13] B. B. Bogoslovsky, *The Ideal School.* New York: The Macmillan Company, 1936. P. 362.

[14] Cf. *ibid.,* p. 383.

[15] *Ibid.,* p. 386.

[16] Cf. *ibid.,* p. 387.

[17] *Ibid.,* p. 454.

idealists believe to be an important insight, going deeper into the essential nature of the pupil than many other philosophies do. But there is a companion insight that is also of great importance, and this has to do with the moral situation within which every pupil must be viewed.

As we have discovered,[18] idealism does not gloss completely over the fact of evil in the world. While it grants to evil no ultimate existence, it recognizes its bitter actuality in this present order. This is not only to bow to undeniable fact, but also to recognize that the possibility of doing evil is necessary in an order in which men are created free and given the opportunity to realize the ultimate goodness of God.

This moral situation of the whole human race is an important part of the learning situation as viewed by idealism. The idealist teacher who knows his foundations does not fuss over his pupils with sentimentality just because he believes they have souls. He can scarcely shut his eyes to evil, which commonly makes the world outside the classroom a rather dismal place; nor can he deal in the classroom or with the pupil as if both teacher and pupil were disengaged from that kind of world. To state that pupils are souls may be to state an important description of them. But implicit in it are some complicated considerations, such as what is potential in the student, what is actual in him, and what is the nature of the process of becoming by which transition is made from the potential to the actual. To analyze these aspects of the pupil's nature is to be confronted by the problem of immortality and the issue of morality.

In regard to the first, immortality, idealists are not agreed. Those placing great stress upon the absolute unity of the Ultimate Spirit hold that at death the limitations that mark out the individualities of people in this life are erased, and the finite spirit, separated for a time from the Universal Spirit, is lost again in that infinity of being from which it came. But differing from them are many idealists who regard individuality as a prime value not in opposition to the unity of God. In the manner of Miss Calkins, whose solution of this problem has been described,[19] they believe in another world in which fully realized individual selves live in a blessed community within God.

The hiatus between the present existence of the pupil and such an immortal ultimate existence is something more than the difference between time and eternity, this world and the next. It is a moral separation. The few years of life on this planet, in which the still shorter period of schooling is most formative, constitute an opportunity for making actual in self what at birth or immaturity is only potential. It is a time for the decisive realization of ultimate values. And the way in which the pupil embraces this decisive

[18] Cf. pp. 158–161.
[19] Cf. pp. 156–157.

opportunity may determine his destiny, both in this world and in the world to come.

Horne finds that both the pupil and the educative process are understandable only when seen as rooted and grounded in Ultimate Mind, which is both self-active and actually realized. And it is in the process of becoming, through which self-realization is achieved, that he sees the pupil's true mission in life, "Education," he said:

> . . . *finds itself unable to understand how the development of unrealized mind which it secures can occur without implying that, underneath its whole process and giving power at every point, is the one realized mind.*[20]

> *The sufficient source of that self-activity which education finds in man is reached thus only in an absolute self-active whole. The ultimate reality, which education implies to be mental and actual, it also implies to be self-active. . . . The self-activity of man, conditioning his education, is the clearest expression in the limits of time of the immanent and transcendent self-activity of reality. It is as though in man realizing his destiny through self-activity, the Absolute beheld himself reflected. The Absolute is; the finite becomes.*[21]

Concretely, then, are pupils good or bad, according to idealism? As compared to Rousseau's contention that man is good as he springs from the hands of Nature, what do idealists say? Their answer is that at birth the pupil is neither good nor bad; he is potential and can become either good or bad, depending upon his environment, surrounding influences—education, of course, included—and his own will. But since realization of ultimate values is such a stupendous life task, it is much easier, and may be more likely, for him to shrink back into evils than to push onward in realizing the good. "Bad characters," said Horne, ". . . are not born they are made."[22] But he grants that the bad are made with greater ease than the good. He finds an inborn basis for conscience in children and stresses the great importance of education as a process which feeds conscience, nurturing it in one direction or the other.

> *The sense of natural justice, unless perverted, seems to be very strong in children. There is a natural basis too for conscience in the sense that something is right, that there is a right. What is held to be right is a matter of education and training and life-associations. Conscience grows by what it feeds on.*[23]

But this does not mean blindness to the actual behavior of people. As Horne said in one of his last writings:

[20] Herman Harrell Horne, *The Philosophy of Education*, p. 264.
[21] *Ibid.*, p. 268.
[22] Herman Harrell Horne, *This New Education*. New York: Abingdon Press, 1931. P. 178.
[23] *Ibid.*, p. 180.

The idealistic conception of the learner in no wise minimizes the fact that our pupils, like ourselves, are often ignorant, negligent, unaesthetic, wilful, perverse, enslaved by bad habits, and far removed from their proper estate. Such conditions, however, only accentuate the necessity and importance of education. They do not mean man is uneducable. They only mean he is not yet educated, indeed, never will be completely educated—that is what his immortality portends.[24]

C. THE OBJECTIVES OF EDUCATION

Since idealism as a philosophy of education stems from the belief in the reality of the self, it might at first seem to follow that its educational objectives should be purely individualistic. This is by no means altogether true. Although some opponents of idealism find it too individualistic, and while an inadequate social concern on the part of idealism may have been one factor contributing to the rise of the pragmatic educational philosophy, idealism fully practiced in education necessitates a courageous shouldering of social responsibilities. For the objectives for which idealism would strive have, of their own necessity, a social as well as an individual frame of reference. We shall adopt, therefore, in this treatment of objectives, two main vantage points: first the individual, and then the social. At the close there will be some inclusive considerations, tying the two together.

1. OBJECTIVES FOR THE INDIVIDUAL

Gentile, the Italian idealist, speaks of self-realization as the ultimate aim of education, by which he means a process of spiritual becoming.[25] This developmental process is a kind of rhythmic flow in the experience of the individual between his present active subject self as one pole of the rhythm and some past phase of the self that is less mature, or an object self, as the other pole. In this surge of spirit, the present active self is continually achieving new insights, assimilating its various fractional selves into the whole self as a unity, eventually coming to a full understanding of its own essential nature. Such an expanded and fully realized self, eventually achieved, is the ultimate value in education as well as in life itself because it reflects the ultimately real Spirit of which the individual self is a part.

Bogoslovsky, as a part of the policy of the ideal school he visualizes in his book, describes the educational objective for the individual in two ways. In terms of knowledge it is a total outlook, and in terms of the self it is the achievement of a superior life. Objecting to the segregation of subjects common to the conventional school because it encourages a premature specialization, he designs his ideal school to prepare "*thorough, com-*

[24] Herman Harrell Horne, "An Idealistic Philosophy of Education," in the *Forty-First Yearbook of the National Society for the Study of Education*, pp. 155–156.
[25] Cf. Merritt Moore Thompson, *op. cit.*, p. 49.

petent specialists in universals."[26] No second- or third-rate specialists are to be tolerated as outgoing students. What the school wants as its products are people who are at home in the world as a whole. The superior selfhood desired for each pupil includes the possession of the richest values of all sorts, such as being happy; readiness to endure suffering with dignity, even gleaning value from it; helping others to live this superior life; and, throughout, sensing the significance of a life so lived. "Our aim," he said:

> *... is to help students to live rich and significant lives, to build harmonious and colorful personalities, to enjoy to the utmost the glory of being happy, to face suffering when it comes with dignity and profit, and finally to help other people to live this superior life.*[27]

Horne said that truth, beauty, and goodness are the spiritual ideals of the race, and therefore the supreme task of education is the adjustment of the child to "these essential realities that the history of the race has disclosed."[28] He argued that the mind of the race is the individual mind written large. In both, the three ultimate modes of consciousness are knowing, feeling, and willing. These three modes in the racial mind present the individual with a spiritual environment of three modes: the intellectual, the aesthetic, and the moral. Education is one of the important adjusting agencies that mediate between the individual mind and the spiritual environment surrounding him. In fulfilling this task it must bring the individual to seek the truth and avoid error, to feel beauty and transcend ugliness, to achieve good and conquer evil.

In one of his last statements of aims, Horne phrased the educational objective of the individual in terms of a hierarchy of values, arranged according to the extent to which each value contributes to the realization of man's absolute goal. As is evident in the following, this is a more integrated statement visualizing a perfectly integrated person as the objective to be realized by education in each individual:

> *We might put good health at the bottom of the hierarchy, and yet esteem it highly as a basic value for all the others, enhancing the richness of each and all of them. At the top of the scale would come worship as bringing man into conscious relation to the infinite spirit of the universe. Next to worship would come character in the individual and justice in society as indicating the will of man toward the eternal right. Next would come the production and enjoyment of the beautiful as revealing the infinite perfection. Next would come knowledge as the thinking of the thoughts embodied in the structure of the universe. And then the skill requisite to one's economic independence, which is related both to personal character and to social justice, and which should bring man into sympathy and harmony with the creative spirit of the*

[26] B. B. Bogoslovsky, *op. cit.*, p. 132.
[27] *Ibid.*, p. 131.
[28] Herman Harrell Horne, *The Philosophy of Education.* Revised edition, p. 102.

universe . . . these values are all interrelated. The body and the mind and
the different functions of the mind all constitute one unity. The ideal suggests
the integrated individual in an integrated society growing in the image of the
integrated universe. The individual and society are not yet integrated because
the finite and the temporal express only inadequately the infinite and eternal.[29]

2. OBJECTIVES FOR SOCIETY

One of the chief problems involved in formulating the social objectives
of education within a democracy is the relation between education and
class distinctions. Should education try to level up or down, or is there
some other way that a common education can serve the purposes of all
groups in a democratic society?

Regarding Dewey's insistence that culture and social efficiency are
identical when both are given broad meanings,[30] Horne agreed that some
leveling up of vocation and a corresponding leveling down of culture are
commendable. But he held that as the two are not completely identical,
there are limits to the feasibility of this plan. "Not all culture can or should
be set to work," he said, "and . . . not every vocation can carry all the
culture a human being requires."[31] On this same question, Bogoslovsky
thought that leveling was not the solution but rather differentiation. A
discerning education, he said, will serve as an agency of differentiation,
opening to everyone "opportunities in proportion to his ability to use
them."[32] This tallies closely with the further solution Horne suggested to
supplement the new education's attempt to enrich the lives of those in
vocations and to increase the social efficiency of the cultured. "Democracy," he said, "is a spiritual unity in a social variety."[33] All classes, races,
and levels are not to be welded into one piece. They are to be united in
spirit and in the effort to pursue common ends, while preserving their
distinctive qualities (not class distinctions) which lend the richness and
variety to the whole. "Brotherhood," Bogoslovsky said, "is the soul and
essence of real democracy."[34] It should therefore be the social objective of
education, at least in a democracy:

In the spirit of brotherhood one approaches his fellow men, not claiming
his rights or declaring their social status, but as a person to person in terms
of human understanding, affection, and love.[35]

[29] Herman Harrell Horne, "An Idealistic Philosophy of Education," in the *Forty-First Yearbook of the National Society for the Study of Education*, p. 186.
[30] John Dewey, *Democracy and Education*. New York: The Macmillan Company, 1916. Cf. Chapter IX, "Natural Development and Social Efficiency."
[31] Herman Harrell Horne, *This New Education*, p. 93.
[32] B. B. Bogoslovsky, *op. cit.*, p. 519.
[33] Herman Harrell Horne, *This New Education*, p. 118.
[34] B. B. Bogoslovsky, *op. cit.*, p. 520.
[35] *Loc. cit.*

Michael Demiashkevitch, writing about social progress as a purpose of education in his book, *An Introduction to Philosophy of Education,* finds two complementary forces at work in society, making sound progress possible. There is the "mobility-aspect," which is seen in the clamor for social changes; and there is the "equilibrium-aspect," represented by the social institutions that conserve the past as an inheritance by which the present generation can profit. Demiashkevitch proposed that the school, in educating for social progress, has the twofold task of giving both of these aspects expression. But he weighed the balance of emphasis on the side of the equilibrium-aspect. He felt that the mobility-aspect gets adequate expression without any aid from the schools. The danger is that each new generation will not be sufficienlty in touch with the equilibrium-aspect of social progress; the school can help society keep its balance by placing its emphasis here. Of course, some idealists would not agree with this particular judgment.[36]

William E. Hocking offers some pertinent thoughts on education in his book, *Human Nature and Its Remaking,* in which the social objectives of education are implied. He too speaks of two complementing functions of education, and they correspond closely to the equilibrium and mobility aspects cited by Demiashkevitch, although he fits them together with a different emphasis. He calls these functions communication of the type and provision for growth beyond the type.

1. By communication of the type he means giving to the young the accumulated heritage of the race so that each new generation can benefit by the nurturing experience the race has had and not be reduced to the necessity of starting all over again from the beginning. This is a definite antithesis to the progressive principle of holding tradition at bay and not abusing the minds of the young with knowledge before some function is discovered for it in present experience. Hocking holds that anything less than communication of the racial fund is an inadequate education, for the lack of it results in a vacuum, which handicaps the new generation, giving the young inadequate cultural food for healthy nourishment and growth.

2. But, as may already be evident, the kind of education advocated by Hocking is not a matter of pure conformity to the cultural and social heritage, cutting the new generation to fit the human culture into which it is born. Communication of the type is necessary in order to bring the new generation to the starting point of its mission in the world. Complementary to this task of education is the additional one of giving the new crop of men the raw materials with which to build beyond the present. The communication of the type is a springboard from which a new plunge beyond the type

[36] Cf. Michael Demiashkevitch, *An Introduction to Philosophy of Education.* New York: American Book Company, 1935. Pp. 339–342.

is to be made. "We may at least conduct our youth," Hocking said, "to the farthest point in our own horizon. . . . 'For each man,' we may say to them, 'there is a region of consciousness more nearly just and free than others, looking out toward absolute truth.' "[37]

3. SYNTHESIS

Placing particular emphasis on synthesis in conceiving the objects of education, Horne wrote in his book, *The Psychological Principles of Education*, that the educational ideal must embrace all the various historical ideals, including each as a part in the whole, where truth is found. Concerned for the individual, it must include "culture, knowledge, and development"[38] as aims; devoted to society, "it must aim at efficiency, character, and citizenship,"[39] for "individual aims are also secondarily social, and the social aims are also secondarily individual."[40]

Horne's definition of education has become a famous one and will serve well as a concluding statement of idealist objectives in education. It is:

Education is the eternal process of superior adjustment of the physically and mentally developed, free, conscious, human being to God, as manifested in the intellectual, emotional, and volitional environment of man.[41]

Summing up as it does a detailed step-by-step analysis of the biological, physiological, sociological, and philosophical aspects of education, the definition has as its context a full understanding of man and the total environment in which he is confronted by spiritual reality. The core of the definition, concerned with the ultimate objective of education, is contained in this abbreviated statement of it: *Education is the eternal process of superior adjustment of a free, conscious, human being to God.*

D. THE EDUCATIVE PROCESS

One overall characterization of idealist-inspired education is that it is ideal-centered. It is not wholly child-centered, subject-matter-centered, nor society-centered; it is ideal-centered. What, exactly, does this mean? Does the idealist build his program of education using as his guiding pattern some romantic vision of what he would like the child to be and some

[37] William E. Hocking, *Human Nature and Its Remaking*. New Haven: Yale University Press, 1918. P. 278.
[38] Herman Harrell Horne, *The Psychological Principles of Education*. New York: The Macmillan Company, 1908. P. 37.
[39] *Loc. cit.*
[40] *Ibid.*, p. 38.
[41] Herman Harrell Horne, *The Philosophy of Education*. Revised edition, p. 285.

utopian picture of a perfect society? Although some critics feel that this is not only what idealism does but also is its great weakness, we do not have a fair picture of what is at least intended by the idealist educator if we simply wave him aside as a visionary.

In trying to understand the idealist philosophy of education it is important to remember that the exponent of this philosophy is primarily a metaphysical idealist and secondarily a moral and social idealist. The ultimately real, he says, is Spirit; and this ultimately real Spirit is absolutely good. Individual children of men as actually found in the classroom may be far from the goodness of God in moral achievement; and present society may fall far short in resembling the coming City of God. But since ultimate reality is *ultimate,* and since present man and his society are transitory, education must be conformed to the ultimate, which is God, rather than to present man and present society, which are uncertain and changing.

This is what is meant by ideal-centered education. Are they centered in ideals because they are wishful, man-made objectives? No. They are centered in ideals because the Ideal, now poorly realized in man and society, is the ultimately real foundation of all things. Such an ideal is the only sure foundation. All other alleged bases of education are temporary.[42] Bogoslovsky made one of his characters reduce this to apt pedagogical phrasing:

> [With] your . . . implication that a reaction by an "average normal kid" . . . must be taken as the criterion for evaluation of educational activities . . . we should disagree fundamentally. We here do not believe there is such a beatific, perfect, and permanent state of normalcy to which everything else is subordinated. On the contrary, in education as in everything else the very essence of progress is a deviation from normalcy, overgrowing it, so that an average normal person of today would become subnormal tomorrow, and a level that is supernormal now will be considered just normal in the future.[43]

Proceeding to describe somewhat concretely what an ideal-centered education becomes in practice, we will discuss several factors as they operate in the idealist-inspired education: first of all the teacher, because of his prime importance; then imitation and interest, effort, and discipline because they are the chief psychological media through which the teacher-pupil communication goes on; next, the self-activity of the pupil, which is the heart of education, according to idealism, the main stream of genuine learning. Turning to the materials to be used, the curriculum will be discussed as it is defined by idealism. Following these considerations, and becoming still more concrete, some specific teaching methods will be discussed, explaining why and how the idealist likes to use them.

[42] Cf. Herman Harrell Horne, *This New Education*, p. 82; and B. B. Bogoslovsky, *op. cit.*, p. 213.
[43] B. B. Bogoslovsky, *op. cit.*, p. 440.

1. THE TEACHER

To a great extent the teacher is central in the idealist pattern of education. This is not, of course, because the teacher is all and the students are nothing; that is bad pedagogy from the standpoint of idealism, if not from that of every other philosophy. It is because the teacher is more the key to the educative process than any other element comprising it. He is in the singular position of determining what the student's opportunities for learning and growing shall be. To a large extent he sets the character of the environment in which the learning takes place. He personally confronts the pupil as the single most important influence in his learning experience. He organizes the subject matter and is largely the mouthpiece through which it comes to the learner. He conceives objectives or accommodates them to immediate learning experiences when they are handed down to him by superiors.

The importance lent to the role of the teacher by idealist educators becomes evident even after a cursory reading of some of their dissertations. The writings of the idealists contain the following varied functions, which the teacher should fulfill.

1. *The teacher is the personification of reality for the child.* For as reality itself is the only teacher, ultimately, so "it is only empirically that one man can be called the teacher of another."[44] For the immature, the teacher is the universe made personal.

2. *The teacher should be a specialist in the knowledge of pupils.* "As it is impossible to teach a subject without thorough knowledge of it, it is equally impossible to teach a student without thorough knowledge of him."[45]

3. *The teacher should be an excellent technician.* While idealism is not alone in upholding the standard of professional excellence for the teacher, it does place great stress upon this achievement. For if the teacher is to be all that is required of him, if he is to set the whole tone of the learning process, then he must be professional in every sense of the word, fully the master of professional techniques.[46]

4. *The teacher should be the kind of person who commands the respect of the pupil by virtue of what he himself is.* The good teacher does not openly demand respect; his bearing is such as wins it.[47]

[44] Merritt Moore Thompson, *op. cit.*, p. 72.

[45] B. B. Bogoslovsky, *op. cit.*, p. 421. In fact, Bogoslovsky goes on to say that it is too much to expect every teacher to possess full knowledge of each student. And he proposes, at least for his ideal school, that there be special teachers whose only job is knowing pupils and advising teachers of subjects about the individual pupils they have in their classes.

[46] Cf. Educational Policies Commission, *The Education of Free Men in American Democracy.* Washington, D.C.: Educational Policies Commission, 1941. P. 63.

[47] Cf. *loc. cit.*

5. *The teacher should be a personal friend of the individual student.* To be a good teacher is to be a good friend.[48]

6. *The teacher should be a person who awakens in the pupil the desire to learn.* Teaching is not making pupils learn by the sheer force of coercive measures. True teaching makes "learning so attractive and compelling in interest that pupils . . . want to learn."[49] The role of the teacher includes evoking the enthusiasm of pupils, and even enlisting their affection.[50] The teacher is a life-sharer who "enters into and takes upon himself the lives of his pupils that they may become one with him. . . . Teaching at bottom is the art of stimulating the growth of the soul; no less conception of it is quite true or worthy."[51]

7. *The teacher should be a master of the art of living.* This ought to be one result of greater maturity and wider experience, equipping him to interpret life to his pupils.[52] As one who possesses some mastery of the art of living, the genuine teacher can lead the pupil in a spiritual process in which his own creative activity provides the pupil with an example that awakens initiative.[53]

8. *The teacher should be a co-worker with God in perfecting man.* At times he becomes the very father or mother of the pupil's soul.[54] All of his instruction and guidance should be so designed as to develop his pupils.[55] His is the task of perfecting mind, the highest form of existence in the cosmos.[56]

9. *The teacher should be one who capably communicates his subject.* The good teacher is in a peculiarly significant position of mediation. He knows both his students and the subject matter he teaches, and he therefore becomes "the medium of communication between the pupil's mind and the subject-matter."[57] Because of this it is measurably true that he is the "priest of man's spiritual heritage."[58]

10. *The teacher must be one who appreciates the subject he teaches.* As children more commonly imitate those practices they see others enjoying, so also they learn more readily those things presented to them as having real value.[59]

11. *The teacher who really teaches is always learning at the same time*

[48] Herman Harrell Horne, *This New Education*, p. 75.
[49] Herman Harrell Horne, *The Philosophy of Education*. Revised edition, p. 274.
[50] Cf. Educational Policies Commission, *op. cit.*, p. 63.
[51] Herman Harrell Horne, *The Psychological Principles of Education*, p. 33.
[52] Cf. *ibid.*, p. 39.
[53] Cf. Merritt Moore Thompson, *op. cit.*, p. 70.
[54] Cf. Herman Harrell Horne, *This New Education*, p. 75.
[55] Cf. Herman Harrell Horne, *The Psychological Principles of Education*, p. 39.
[56] Cf. *ibid.*, p. 40.
[57] *Ibid.*, p. 39.
[58] Herman Harrell Horne, *This New Education*, p. 75.
[59] Cf. William E. Hocking, *op. cit.*, p. 262.

that he teaches. It is not likely that effective work is done when the teacher merely repeats what he knows, leaning heavily on past learning. He must actively give himself in each new teaching situation, learning as he teaches, gaining new insights himself, creatively reorganizing his own understanding of his subject, all the time he is inducting the learner into his own special field.[60]

12. *The teacher is an apostle of progress* if he fulfils his entire role. For teaching properly conceived is not an unrelated fractional matter of instructing or training or conditioning a few individuals in some obscure classroom. It is the important job of helping to give birth to the new generation spiritually and is definitely related to the purposes toward whose realization history moves.[61]

13. *The teacher should also be a maker of democracies.* If he captures the spirit of genuine teaching, his classes will practice democracy as well as extol it. And his students will have at least their classroom experiences as demonstrations of what living democractically can mean. Depending upon how much such experiences capture the devotion of students, they may become a democratizing influence in other groups.[62]

14. An appropriate final characterization of the ideal teacher is that *he ought to be a study in self-elimination.* The good teacher must of necessity be a vigorous person who inspires, arouses, and awakens students by what he is and the way he conducts himself. But he must also be acutely sensitive to the developing selfhood of his pupils, always ready to give latitude for expression and growth. His profession is not one of glorifying himself but one of losing himself in helping his pupils to give birth to what it is in them to become. There is always the rhythm between subject- and object-selves in the private experience of the teacher, as well as in the experience of the pupil. And the discerning teacher will find that his most effective teaching personality is the one in which his active subject-self is uppermost and the personality that displays his object-self is lost unself-consciously in the job of wooing his students to a higher life.[63]

2. IMITATION

It is scarcely a step from the teacher as initiating influence in the school life of the child to the subtle process of imitation, one of the psychological means by which that influence is assimilated by the pupil. The two are so continuous that sharply defined distinctions are more logical than actual.

A gay young New Yorker having his fling in Paris once acted the part of a Russian nobleman to favor a friend who was trying to impress another

---

[60] Cf. Merritt Moore Thompson, *op. cit.*, p. 52.
[61] Cf. Herman Harrell Horne, *This New Education*, p. 75.
[62] *Loc. cit.*
[63] Cf. William E. Hocking, *op. cit.*, pp. 277–278.

American of great wealth, grasping for easy money being at the bottom of the deal for both parties. The unanticipated complication was that the wealthy American had a most attractive daughter, with whom the New Yorker fell deeply in love. After living a lie in her presence longer than he could endure, he eventually unburdened his soul to his ladylove and revealed his identity as a fellow American. To his great humiliation, the confession was met with this reply: "You needn't have told me; I knew you were from Princeton all the time."

Regardless of philosophic position, we are confronted by the fact that social relations do yield similarities in the thoughts and actions of people. Members of the same family share patterns of appearance, speech, and action even when the children are adopted. Communities have individualities that mark their members. Many a school has its characteristic spirit, which leaves its stamp on its graduates. Such observations present little difficulty of verification. It is not in acceptance or rejection of such facts but because of the variety of ways in which they are interpreted that differing educational philosophies have different doctrines of imitation.

Idealism says that common habits of life arise because youngsters naturally imitate their elders and by this process grow to maturity, sometimes attaining levels of achievement above those they imitate. Since imitation is natural, they hold that the educator is forced to cope with it in some way; and since it may produce much-desired results, his best strategy is to give direction to it by employing it in the work of the schools.

Gentile, for example, reproves adults for being amused by the young child when he so evidently copies someone else. It is possible that actually he does no more copying at his level than we do at ours. The father writes a letter, so the little child scribbles on a piece of paper. On the surface this may appear to be copying; but implicitly it is the originality and creative capacity of the child emerging in its earliest observable forms.[64] That this is so Horne witnesses by another observation. He asks us to recall what a great many things there are that the child could imitate that never evoke any response from him at all. All youngsters let far more slip by them unnoticed than they single out for imitation. There is an unconscious rejecting taking place as continually as there is a conscious accepting. And these rejections of the child, unconscious as they are, "declare his individuality and strengthen it."[65] Hocking implies that imitating is all a part of society's process of bringing a new will into existence in the individual. That this should be most demonstrated in similarities of action is not surprising, for "bringing a will into existence inevitably tends . . . to reproduce the type."[66]

[64] Cf. Merritt Moore Thompson, *op. cit.*, p. 76.
[65] Herman Harrell Horne, *The Philosophy of Education*. Revised edition, p. 179.
[66] William E. Hocking, *op. cit.*, p. 264.

One profitable use of imitation is to set before the students some models of work of distinct excellence and to direct them in deliberately following their patterns. This is a method particularly adaptable in art, music, literature, and composition. A mother, herself an accomplished musician, taught her son the violin by having him follow closely some recorded interpretations by great masters. This device enabled her to develop the boy's unusual talent far beyond her own level of musicianship. Let it be quite clear, however, that the idealist educator is not aiming at an apelike mimicry; he feels rather that close study of excellent works of art will awaken the creative powers of the learner. As Demiashkevitch stated this theme, "True originality seems to be best achieved after careful study and imitation of masters in a particular field—by surpassing the great masters."[67]

But the general attitude in idealist educational philosophy is that the most effective use of imitation is in focusing it upon great personalities. Two selections from Horne present well this idealist principle:

It is in the realm of personality and its influence that the principle of imitation has its highest educational service.[68]

The child through imitating others, becomes aware of his own capactiy for a wide variety of acts that he otherwise would have believed were beyond his powers.[69]

Since it is more fundamental to become an excellent person than it is to create a work of excellence, closely connected as these two achievements may be, the child should be much exposed to men of inspiring greatness. Bogoslovsky tells us we should make much use in the schools of "the treasury of great achievements in living left to us by those geniuses and artists who have created beautiful lives. Probably there is nothing more important than a life beautifully lived."[70]

Making this recommendation specific in the plan for the ideal school of which he wrote, Dr. Bogoslovsky pointed to school assemblies as offering a wonderful opportunity for the study of great men. As human nature especially in its mob formation "is much more prone to destructive and ugly forms of expression than to constructive and fine forms,"[71] assemblies should give students "common experiencing of something significant."[72] When students are trained for such common experiencing in small groups, when assemblies are carefully planned in total setting—architecture of assembly rooms, lighting, temperature, seats, and general atmosphere—

[67] Michael Demiashkevitch, *op. cit.,* p. 196.
[68] Herman Harrell Horne, *The Philosophy of Education.* Revised edition, p. 184.
[69] *Ibid.,* p. 180.
[70] B. B. Bogoslovsky, *op. cit.,* p. 137.
[71] *Ibid.,* p. 136.
[72] *Loc. cit.*

and when the program is carefully worked out from prelude music and manner of the entrance of students to the final emptying of the room, then in large groups they can study significantly the lives of great men. Four phases of inspiring personalities to which attention should be directed are:

> . . . *the actual everyday social and mental environment in which the "hero" lives, his main characteristics and typical attitudes, the content and method of his achievement, and finally the growth and use of his contribution in the course of time and especially its significance for us.*[73]

But there will be much of the less deliberate kind of imitation whether we like it or not. And because of this the more mature people constantly associating with growing children in and out of school are factors of decisive importance. Hocking tells us that children adopt the beliefs of those "whom they instinctively recognize as happy, and no others."[74] Viewed from one side, he holds this to be a protection of the child from an unworthy society. For if youngsters find "no hero in the flesh from among the supporters of the existing order,"[75] there is no danger that they will be dominated by that order.

Horne sees both morality and religion involved in the imitative process. Children are going to imitate somebody, he says, and "if there is no worthy model to offset the suggestion of the unworthy, the imitation is also inevitably of the unworthy."[76] It is therefore imperative for teachers themselves to be the best living models who can stand before their classes. Echoing Saint Paul, Horne urges that "the highest duty and privilege of the teacher is to be in whatsoever things are true, honest, just, pure, lovely, and of good report what he is willing for his pupils to become."[77] Actually, he explains, this is the crux of the whole problem of teaching morality and religion in the schools. Whereas the character of the public school does not permit the direct teaching of religion, and whereas the nature of both morality and religion defy their complete transmission by pure instruction alone, the personality of the teacher can convey both.

> *The quandary of the school as to how to cultivate morality and religion without being able (in the nature of things, and not simply because of legal enactments against religious instruction) to teach them is solved through the provision of teachers with personalities worthy of imitation by the pupils.*[78]

His further treatment of the religious phase of the principle of imitation reveals Horne's acceptance and understanding of the Christian doctrine of

---

[73] *Ibid.*, p. 137.
[74] William E. Hocking, *op. cit.*, p. 263.
[75] *Loc. cit.*
[76] Herman Harrell Horne, *The Philosophy of Education.* Revised editon, p. 181.
[77] *Ibid.*, pp. 185–186.
[78] *Ibid.*, p. 185.

the Incarnation. Human personality, he implies, reveals by its imitative bent the need for an incarnation of the Ideal Person.

The Ideal Person, as conceived definitely, by any mind, is the unity of all the perfect characteristics that one knows. This person may have been concreted once in human history, as in Jesus, in which case the process of imitation, and so religious growth, can go on far easier than when the ideal remains impersonal.[79]

3. INTEREST, EFFORT, AND DISCIPLINE

Interest, effort, and discipline are intimately connected devices of education about which a current issue turns. Should the teacher lean heavily upon interest, he is likely to be labeled as "soft"; if effort and discipline are his weapons, he is "hard." These are the labels, but the matter is not so simple. A deliberate use of interest, effort, and discipline involves careful consideration of the functions and limitations of each.

For the sake of clarity, definitions are in order. By *interest* we refer to such a totally positive attraction of the student to the job at hand that he need exercise no conscious or voluntary exertion, much less require urging from the teacher. By *effort* we mean the conscious and voluntary exertion of the student by which he brings himself to do a job not engaging sufficient interest spontaneously. And by *discipline* we mean some extraneous action by the teacher to carry the pupil through to the completion of the task in hand. This may vary from subtle prodding to the use of physical punishment.

First of all, an enlargement upon the meaning of interest should be made in which some typical idealist blends are preserved. Horne defines interest as "a pleasurable activity of the self"[80] involving three elements. There must be a person to possess the interest, there must be an object to which interest may cling, and there must be an engaging quality of attractiveness about the object.[81] Effective use of interest, Horne insists, involves recognition of the law of apperception. There are many things that students at almost any level already know and many things in which they are already interested. Effective use of interest involves making connection, therefore, with the knowledge and interests already in the minds of the students. "Their expression will interest where the teacher's impression will fail."[82] Gentile tells us that since interest is the feel of the subject-self passing over into the objective-self, it is both attractive and fatiguing. It is attractive because this rhythm of the self is creative activity; but it is also fatiguing because such creative activity involves an ascent to a higher plane.[83] Hock-

[79] *Ibid.*, p. 182.
[80] *Ibid.*, p. 189.
[81] Cf. *loc. cit.*
[82] *Ibid.*, p. 196.
[83] Cf. Merritt Moore Thompson, *op. cit.*, p. 54.

ing explains that interest is based on the establishing of mental momentum.
But he significantly points out that since momentum is gained only when
there is difficulty, activities must confront the student with some difficulty
in order to be interesting.[84]

But attractive as interest may be, it is not a sufficiently broad base to
provide all the education needed. Doing a thing because one loves it, Horne
said, is "too ideal to be always practical, and at times too individualistic to
be socially desirable."[85] The enjoyment motive is not adequate even for
individual conduct, said Bogoslovsky. For one thing, there are frequently
jobs to be done "now" that will not wait for us to be moved by the spirit of
enjoyment. And when attention is turned to group motivation, he believes,
it is all the clearer that enjoyment is inadequate as a motive. It can scarcely
regulate the behavior of all the participants in a group project adequately
to develop the project successfully.[86] Horne explains that there are really
two kinds of interest: immediate and remote. It is immediate interest that
is productive of spontaneous activity and thus leads to involuntary effort.
Remote interests, not being so directly connected with present satisfactions, lead to voluntary effort. Horne's argument is that since life requires
both immediate and remote interests of us, education, in order to adjust to
life, should also require both of students.[87] Running beneath all this is an
undercurrent that should not be overlooked: interest calls out effort. The
two cannot be sharply separated as though there were an interest education
and an effort education. Interest evokes effort, and interesting activity is
carried forward because the interest arouses enough effort to move the task
on its way to completion.

Conversely, Horne believes that effort may give birth to interest. The
teacher or parent may urge the child to a task that to him is not attractive,
yet later the child may discover that he is genuinely interested and needs to
exert no conscious effort in order to keep going. In scattered instances the
study of a musical instrument is a case in point. The beginning is often set
almost totally in effort, maybe distasteful, maybe forced on the subject by a
fond parent. But there are cases in which a transition occurs, and the
unwilling musician becomes a budding artist who enjoys his music genuinely enough to produce under his own power all the effort it requires of
him.[88]

At the least, effort is a supplement to interest. Like a faithful friend, it is
always standing by, a resource on which to call when interest fails. To be
practical, we must recognize that after the teacher uses all his genius for

[84] Cf. William E. Hocking, *op. cit.*, p. 271.
[85] Herman Harrell Horne, *This New Education*, p. 85.
[86] Cf. B. B. Bogoslovsky, *op. cit.*, p. 500.
[87] Cf. Herman Harrell Horne, *This New Education*, p. 87.
[88] Cf. Herman Harrell Horne, *The Democratic Philosophy of Education*. New
York: The Macmillan Company, 1932. P. 174.

attraction, there still will be need for effort and, as Horne says, "the school will still be a training-ground for voluntary attention to unattractive tasks."[89]

At the best, effort is not just a substitute for interest, but a metal rib in character, which lends strength and enables it to stand in its own right. To quote Horne again: "Effort . . . is the will to do one's duty when one doesn't want to. It is listening to the still small voice of conscience instead of the whirlwinds of passion."[90]

Gentile found sheer discipline, which is separated from the constructive movement of the teaching process, undesirable. He regarded discipline as an intimate part of the personality and directive activity of the teacher. Inherent in genuine teaching there is discipline, the teacher himself being the primary element of discipline. But discipline for its own sake, unattached to teaching, is foreign.[91] It is not out of harmony with such insistence that discipline be attached to teaching that Horne spoke of free discipline as an end product rather than a point of departure. To come to disciplined achievement through freedom, he said, is the slow and painful way of the race. Education has by-passed this long and costly route by beginning with discipline and moving toward freedom. Accordingly, in the formation of the disposition to do the right, some coercion is needed. "Authority begins by being external; it is sufficient if it ends, through habit-formation and self-control, in becoming internal."[92]

4. SELF-ACTIVITY

Where is it that education actually takes place? When a pupil really learns something, gains some new insight, or takes an actual step forward in a refining and maturing growth, where is it in the whole subtle process that change goes on? Idealists say that it is within the self of the pupil. To the casual observer watching the overt behavior of pupils, this is not much different from the pragmatist doctrine that the learning is in the response of the learner. That is to say that it is what students do in reaction to what is done to them that constitutes the core of education.

Idealists will accept this dictum as long as its scope is not limited to a description of a behavioral process alone. Students, it is held, are more than responding organisms or social units that have a strong bent toward interaction. They are souls who are capable of a genuine initiative, and their responses are the struggles of that initiative germinating and growing into full bloom. Consequently, the locus of the acts of development that

[89] Herman Harrell Horne, *The Philosophy of Education*. Revised edition, p. 204.
[90] *Ibid.*, p. 199.
[91] Cf. Merritt Moore Thompson, *op. cit.*, pp. 91–92.
[92] Herman Harrell Horne, *This New Education*, p. 89.

constitute education is a private sanctuary inhabited only by the student himself. No teacher or parent can enter it; he can only surround it with the most promising influences and the most inviting situations. It is the action of the child in response to what the teacher does that constitutes the actual education, and the subtle roots of this action no outsider can touch. Consequently, for idealism all education is self-education.

Horne, especially, elaborated this principle. "The educational process," he said, "is not so much the stimulus shaping the individual, as the individual responding to the stimulus."[93] In quite another setting he said, "All educative experiences are personal in character. It is a person who has the experience, even when the experience is of things."[94] This root principle of all knowledge, feeling, and will is that "the mind is the source of its own reactions on the world."[95] Because of this, growth can come only through self-activity. It is only by this process that the mental self of the pupil can be developed. And this means self-direction, "the mind's ability to frame and follow self-appointed goals."[96] Abbreviating a somewhat fuller statement, this is made quite emphatic in the following:

The development of mind is from within out, not from without in. . . . The teacher may lead the pupil to the fonts of learning, but he cannot make him drink. Teaching is not so much the cause of learning . . . as it is the occasion or condition of learning. The cause of learning is the pupil himself and his effort. . . . The ultimate responsibility for winning an education rests with the will of the pupil.[97]

Making his approach by considering attention and inattention, Gentile tells us that "spiritual act does not presume attention; it is attention." He thought of inattention as either one of two things: "a divergent attention, namely, one directed toward an undesirable object, or it is spirit which is failing to ascend to the highest levels that mark the continued development of the spirit."[98]

Demiashkevitch both upholds the principle of self-activity and offers caution as to its meaning. He insists that "it is clearly the duty of the school to promote the wholesome curiosity and imagination of children."[99] But he draws back on the reins when he reminds us that initiative and originality do not mean "jumping forth blindfolded."[100] Instead they mean the taking of steps forward in the light of the achievements and

[93] Herman Harrell Horne, *The Philosophy of Education.* Revised edition, p. 275.
[94] Herman Harrell Horne, *This New Education,* p. 96.
[95] Herman Harrell Horne, *The Philosophy of Education.* Revised edition, p. 170.
[96] *Ibid.,* p. 171.
[97] *Ibid.,* pp. 273–274.
[98] Merritt Moore Thompson, *op. cit.,* p. 50.
[99] Michael Demiashkevitch, *op. cit.,* p. 286.
[100] *Ibid.,* p. 194.

mistakes of others, improving upon the work of others wherever possible.[101]

Self-activity leading to self-development, according to idealists, is not an abstract process having little relation to bodily or temporal factors. To develop the self certainly includes development of the body and fully embraces physical education.[102] But, of course, development of the body is limited to developing and strengthening what is given the individual by birth. Education cannot add to the nerve cells of the brain, but it can fully develop capacities for which potentiality exists in the individual.[103] Furthermore, self-development takes time. It is a series of transitions from the potential to the actual that goes on through successive stages of growth. This means that time is a most important condition of education.[104]

Self-activity is by no means the equivalent of overt activity, according to idealism. That children want to be active is one expression of their disposition toward growth and development. But there is nothing predetermined about the nature of the occupation in this affinity for activity.[105] Demiashkevitch thinks it is important for teachers to realize that there are some children "who do not like manual work and whose desire for activity finds expression in what may be called purely mental occupations."[106] And Bogoslovsky gave a good example of this very thing in his treatment of art education. He feels that the appreciation of art, though it may appear to be passive, is as much an activity as the creation of works of art. Both should be included in the learning experience of the student.[107]

This, the core of idealist education, is of course freedom of will in another guise and cannot be separated from character education. For idealism it is probably true that all education deserving the name is character education, for it gets at the springs of action and tries to guide action in the right way. Horne found that belief in freedom of will is one of the prime essentials of good character. For to regard one's self as simply a "creature of circumstance" is likely to form a bad character. "One must struggle to be good; to be bad one has only to quit."[108] Demiashkevitch, also defining character in terms of will, said that it is "the will actively to promote good and oppose evil, and to do this with a constancy that may be described as certainty."[109] Making quite specific the meaning of freedom, Horne said it

[101] Cf. *ibid.*, pp. 194–195.
[102] Cf. Herman Harrell Horne, *The Philosophy of Education.* Revised edition, p. 95.
[103] Cf. *ibid.*, pp. 41–42.
[104] Cf. *ibid.*, p. 207.
[105] Cf. Michael Demiashkevitch, *op. cit.*, p. 173.
[106] *Ibid.*, pp. 215–216.
[107] Cf. B. B. Bogoslovsky, *op. cit.*, p. 161
[108] Herman Harrell Horne, *This New Education*, p. 179.
[109] Michael Demiashkevitch, *op. cit.*, p. 279.

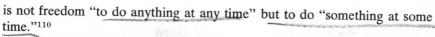

is not freedom "to do anything at any time" but to do "something at some time."[110]

Hocking distinguished between will and free will, urging that a will must be developed in the individual before he can exercise a free will. The child not only lacks the materials to choose from, but still more than this, "he does not know what he wants. The first task of education is to *bring his will into existence*. . . . The whole meaning of education," Hocking says, "is wrapped up in this process of evoking the will: and apart from it nothing in education can be either understood or placed."[111]

When the child reaches adolescence, this growth of will takes on an urgent form, which Hocking describes as "readiness to assume responsibility." Two common expressions of this sense of responsibility are the building of one's own philosophy of life and the desire to make one's way in the world. Thinking of the first of these, Hocking interprets the youth's predicament as follows: "He appreciates for the first time that he has his own life to lead; he finds himself morally alone; he can no longer endure to see things through the eyes of others."[112] In regard to the second, Hocking insists that the only right environment for the "readiness to assume responsibility" is the actual responsibility it craves. Give the boy or girl a real job, he admonishes, and let him have the experience of filling a responsible place in the world: "The boy who passes his adolescence without knowing the feeling of doing a day's work for a day's wages is risking not only a warp in his instinctive make-up, but a shallowing of all further work in school and college."[113]

5. THE CURRICULUM

Except for consideration of the teacher, factors in the learning process so far discussed in this section will impress some readers as abstract. Imitation, interest, effort, discipline, and the self-activity of the pupil—it is hard to put your finger on any of these. Isn't there *something*, some will say, that is to be learned in school? Is learning all a matter of functions and processes? Isn't there some substance in the affair, somewhere? What about the materials of education, the traditional three R's, and the multiplication of school subjects that have taken their place? There must be *something* to be studied and to be learned. Can we look to idealism to give us a learning process with solid substance at its core, or must we await realism for that?

Hocking, for one, insists that education must offer something positive.

---

[110] Herman Harrell Horne, *The Philosophy of Education*. Revised edition, p. 277.
[111] William E. Hocking, *op. cit.*, p. 258.
[112] *Ibid.*, p. 274.
[113] *Loc. cit.*

The first right of children, he says, is not that "they be left free to choose their way of life,"[114] but that they be given something positive. Children have the right to benefit by the best the race has to offer. Not to give the children the content of racial experience to date is like asking them to make bricks without either straw or clay. The peril of each new generation is not that it will be unduly dominated by the society from which it springs. The real danger is that, through neglect or an inadequate education, it will never be "searchingly exposed to what is noble, generous, and faith provoking."[115] This, Hocking feels, is one of the chief defects of recent education.[116]

According to Horne, the way to get a solid foundation for curriculum construction is to conceive clearly "the ideal character of man and the characteristics of an ideal society."[117] Then, "select those experiences, activities, life-situations, and studies that, according to one's best judgment, best contribute to those ideal ends."[118] Horne acknowledges that there will be conflicting views about these ideal ends. But this conflict need not give way to chaos; it can be made the basis for constructive thought in educational philosophy. More specifically, every curriculum to be adequate must include schoolroom equivalents of the three aspects of racial achievement, namely, intellect, emotion, and will. By this Horne means "there must be some science, some art, and some volition"[119] in every student's program of study.

As implied by this, the curriculum cannot be limited to the content of instruction. It includes content, of course, but it also must include "occupations, productions, achievements, exercise, and activity."[120] The books studied by pupils do not themselves constitute the objective reality with which the individual student is to be confronted. "They are but temporary earthen vessels in which the treasures of natural and human truth are kept."[121] Certainly there must be a course of study including all the conventional branches of both liberal and vocational education. But it must be remembered that all the various subjects are only to be used "as means to the great end of living completely through understanding life. Information will become knowledge, books will become tools, and the best ideas will become ideals."[122]

[114] *Ibid.*, p. 260.
[115] *Loc. cit.*
[116] Cf. *ibid.*, pp. 259–261.
[117] Herman Harrell Horne, *This New Education*, p. 90.
[118] *Loc. cit.*
[119] Herman Harrell Horne, *The Philosophy of Education*. Revised edition, p. 146.
[120] Herman Harrell Horne, *The Psychological Principles of Education*, p. 32.
[121] Herman Harrell Horne, *The Philosophy of Education*. Revised edition, pp. 145–146.
[122] Herman Harrell Horne, *This New Education*, p. 120.

Bogoslovsky proposes a novel arrangement of the curriculum in his *Ideal School*. Not liking the sharply segregated subjects of study in the conventional school, he proposes four general areas of study and development, all interrelated. Even the structure housing the school is to be designed to give a distinctive place to each of these four phases. Viewed from the air the building will be a perfectly symmetrical cross, each arm of which will house one of these four main departments. The first, the *universe* division, is to be an enlarged science department in which students study the "inanimate forces of nature, the origin of our solar system, the developing of life, all background of the human drama."[123] The second section is the *civilization* division, offering an inclusive study of the social sciences. "By civilization," Bogoslovsky explained, "we mean all the activities, achievements, and institutions of humanity, which control our environment so as to provide the necessities of life, security, and comfort—all that we do to get rid of dangers, fears, and privations. Food, clothing, shelter, technology, communication, and government are all within this field."[124] In the *culture* division, which is the third, "philosophy, art, literature, religion, interpretation and evaluation of environment"[125] are to be included. The fourth section, named the *personality* division, offers study of "the physical, physiological, emotional, and intellectual factors that together make up human beings . . . different types of personalities and . . . the most interesting individuals who have actually existed or have been created by art."[126] These four divisions are to be closely tied together by the *personality building* section housed where the four arms of the cross converge. In this central division is "the final summing up, coordination, or integration of everything that is done in the other sections in terms of helping students systematically and persistently, to build continuously better and better personalities."[127]

Without drawing such a blueprint, Demiashkevitch claimed that the public secondary school should give an enriching and stimulating general cultural education.[128] In making his brief for the informational side of school learning, he outlines three objectives to be fulfilled by it: (1) The student should acquire enough general information to know how and when to search for reliable information on problems he will have to face. (2) He should come to possess "sufficient knowledge of the fundamental truths, moral, social, and scientific, ignorance of which would make him dangerous to himself and others." And (3) the mind of the pupil should be

---

[123] B. B. Bogoslovsky, *op. cit.*, p. 133.
[124] *Loc. cit.*
[125] *Loc. cit.*
[126] *Ibid.*, p. 134.
[127] *Ibid.*, p. 135.
[128] Cf. Michael Demiashkevitch, *op. cit.*, p. 409.

imbued with "standards of lucid, profound, fruitful, and careful reasoning," inculcating in him "the habit of hard and accurate thinking."[129]

Of course, to take this position regarding the curriculum makes it necessary for idealists to face pointedly the issue between learning by direct experience and learning by secondhand or vicarious experience. And, confronted by this issue, most idealists are quite definite in insisting that all education cannot be by direct experience, as is the assumption underlying the experimental tendency in recent education. Remarking on the watchword "education is life," Horne objects that education cannot be all of life. Though it is true that we are educated by all of our experiences, some of these experiences we should be better without. "The function of the school is necessarily limited to exemplifying certain phases of life at the best possible."[130] "Not everything has to be learned by acquaintance, however desirable this might be; most things have to be learned by description."[131] The question of timing is also involved. To learn by experience as a consistent policy means that knowledge is not introduced until the learner discovers a need for each item of knowledge in experience. But idealists hold that this is both dangerous and costly in many phases of life. One thing that the old generation can do for the new is to give it the benefit of past experience and so enable the young to be prepared for many critical experiences before they occur. As Horne explained, "It is all very well to have need before knowledge in mild cases, but in cases of serious need it is good to have the knowledge ready."[132]

Demiashkevitch acknowledged that direct experiences impress us more than experiences indirectly gained and leave deeper traces in memory. But he held that their power of impressing us has nothing to do with their value for future reference. It is the content of the experience that counts then, and much knowledge and information that will be of great value in future critical situations can be obtained indirectly, even if it is less vivid.[133] Nor is such secondhand experience stultifying to the student, at least not if it is really understood. For understanding involves a kind of recreating for ourselves, or reorganizing of what is learned. And this is a stimulating process, not one that inhibits the student.[134] Turning to a social aspect of the issue between direct and indirect experience, Demiashkevitch held that the democratic form of government is based largely on vicarious experience, since the voter has to be guided by "recorded worthwhile direct experience of others."[135] He says that therefore the schools of a democ-

---

[129] Cf. *ibid.*, pp. 279–280.
[130] Herman Harrell Horne, *This New Education*, p. 86.
[131] *Ibid.*, p. 88.
[132] *Ibid.*, p. 84.
[133] Cf. Michael Demiashkevitch, *op. cit.*, p. 169.
[134] Cf. *ibid.*, p. 192.
[135] *Ibid.*, p. 170.

racy should send out into society students who have appropriated through secondhand sources much of the existing wealth of human experience. And this of course means that there must be much book learning in the schools.[136]

6. METHOD

The final aspect of idealist education now to be considered is a practical one, namely, teaching methods. What method or methods will the idealist teacher use? Could you spot an idealist by catching him doing things in certain characteristic ways in the classroom?

First of all, idealists are likely to insist that they are creators and determiners of method, not devotees of some one method. Contrasting themselves to the experimental tendency in recent times and the wide adoption of the project method, they may say something like this:

"Yes, we believe in experimentation, activity, and the project. But we insist that doing is just one among many methods, not *the* method. There are various methods from which we can select those that best serve our purposes at the time."

Still speaking in general terms, we can say that the idealist prefers that an informal dialectic be in process in the classroom most of the time. Instead of students being confronted constantly by specific directions in which a definite path of action or thought is laid out for them, he prefers that there always be alternatives of thought, at least, if not alternatives of action. Since it is the self-activity of the pupil in which genuine education and development take place, he wants the student to be confronted by decision and selection as much of the time as is practicable. Certainly he doesn't want the pupil's will crippled by having all his decisions and selections made for him.

1. Because of this, questioning and discussion are probably the prime methods for many idealists, at least when the subject under study involves thinking and readily lends itself to this treatment. In leading discussion the teacher can do many things by careful use of thought-provoking questions. He can lend significance and meaning to the content being studied. He can confront the student with alternatives evoking his judgments. The teacher can open to him alternatives of thought that might not otherwise occur to him. And he can represent to the student something of the breadth of ideas and opinions he will face when he goes out into the world on his own. Parenthetically, it should be remarked that the idealist teacher uses questions not so much to find out what the student knows as to cultivate the student's judgment.

In addition to the teacher's ability to create dialectical situations by means of question and discussion, the students themselves, by virtue of

[136] Cf. *ibid.*, pp. 170–171.

their various backgrounds and unique individualities, will create their own dialectic, usually without knowing or intending it. The skillful teacher is the one who will make the most of these resources of the students, letting the conflicts of their own thinking have free course, using these resources fully and never substituting his own questions or ideas for them. These latter are reserves of initiation to be used when, for one reason or another, the thoughts of the students do not strike fire.[137]

Care should be taken, however, that discussion does not degenerate to the level where it is little more than an ill-prepared pooling of ignorance or a clearing house for empty words. Horne readily acknowledges that discussion can be wasteful unless in the hands of a skillful leader. "Successful use of it," he says, "not only requires a good leader, but presupposes experience, study, observation, and knowledge on the part of those participating."[138]

2. Lecture is another method idealists may use, but here again there are precautions in its use. There is a legitimate place for good expository presentations by the teacher in which accurate representations of objective information are made or in which precepts, beliefs, or interpretations are wisely offered as counsel.[139] The dangers to be avoided are that the lecture may become a phonographic recitation of facts or ideas, on the one hand, or an autocratic institution, on the other, allowing no place for student questioning, response, or judgment.[140]

Another legitimate use of the lecture, according to idealists, which of course comes as an accompaniment, is as a creative work of art inspiring students and evoking their response much as a painting, poem, or symphony might do it. Bishop Grundtvig's influence in the Danish Folk High Schools, which brought glorification of the lecture into those schools, is an instance of this kind of practice. Often students were requested not to take notes, so that there would be no artificial device separating student and lecturer, the spoken word being given free course as medium of communication and response.

3. A third important method of idealism is, of course, the project, in which students, singly or in groups, pursue a constructive task themselves. Observation and experimentation there will be, at least in the physical and biological sciences, starting with problems and religiously following the steps of scientific method. Excursions and projects beyond the walls of the school will occasionally supplement book learning by face-to-face relation with real community and social situations. There will be essays to be written, notebooks to be assembled, all kinds of reference leads to follow in

[137] Cf. Herman Harrell Horne, *This New Education*, pp. 122–123.
[138] *Ibid.*, p. 83.
[139] Cf. *ibid.*, p. 83.
[140] Cf. *ibid.*, p. 74.

libraries, creative writing, sketching and painting, sculpturing, and number-less other engaging occupations to be used whenever they grow out of the unit of study at hand.

While idealists are definite in their insistence that all learning is not doing, especially if doing is regarded as overt activity, they still embrace doing without too much hesitation as a real and legitimate part of the educative process.[141] On this score Horne at one time estimated that his own thoughts on education were about 50 percent in agreement with what was then known as progressive practice.[142]

7. SUMMARY

Having described some of the detail in the idealist educational process, we shall try to sum up and tie the parts together in one unified picture.

1. The teacher is the creator of the educational environment of the child and the chief source of his inspiration.
2. One important and valuable means by which student response is given birth is imitative activity, especially when given direction by worthy models of creative work and a noble teacher personality.
3. Another valuable steppingstone to student response is interest. Prefer-ably, interest should permeate the greatest majority of school activities. Sometimes, of course, it will need to be supplemented by the student's own effortful application. And on occasion this latter may need rein-forcing by the pressure of external discipline.
4. Throughout all teacher activities the result sought is the active response of the learner. It is only when the self of the pupil becomes attached to activities by its own initiative that real growth and development of self get started.
5. As to curriculum, there must be much objective content and much book learning if there is to be solidity in education and students are to have a rugged mental diet. But lest education be no more than impartation of knowledge, the curriculum must go beyond books and subject matter to include direct experiential relation with actualities.
6. Teaching methods should be used that create a slight feeling of sus-pense for the student—suspense to be resolved only by his own decision or active effort. Questioning and discussion lend themselves admirably to this purpose, but there is also much place for solid instruction, as in lecturing, and for pupil activity, as in projects employing con-structive and creative work.

[141] Cf. *ibid.*, pp. 82–83.
[142] Cf. *ibid.*, pp. 121–122.

X

Idealism in Religion

As has been evident in the foregoing chapters in this section on idealism, this philosophy is sympathetic to religion. Furthermore, it can be said that on occasion it has joined hands with religion to the extent of providing the structure for intellectualizing religious faith and experience. In Saint Augustine, in the fourth and fifth centuries, there was a significant blending of Platonic and Christian thought which was of signal influence in Christendom until Saint Thomas Aquinas assumed the position of intellectual leadership in the thirteenth century. Again, in the nineteenth century, Hegel projected his idealism into the realm of religion in his famous philosophy of religion; and this in turn inspired succeeding works, some of which remain influential to the present time, although realism took over as the more predominant influence in religious thought, following the first decade of the twentieth century. Two of the notable philosophies of religion which were inspired by Hegelian influence were written by John Caird and Andrew Martin Fairbairn.

Drawing chiefly on more contemporary sources of idealist religious thought, this chapter aims to be a sample of the manner in which idealists transpose religious faith and experience into intellectual terms. Though somewhat fuller because of the affinity of idealism and religion, the chapter follows the same pattern as the other philosophy-of-religion chapters in this book.

A. THE STATUS OF RELIGION

The distinct flavor of the idealist attitude in religion may be tasted most readily by looking first at idealism's insistence on the rational element as basic in religion. For it is held that although religion may well have non-rational roots, it cannot be irrational in its best and truest forms. There must be a context of ideas somewhere in religious experience or consciousness if it is to avoid vagueness or superstition. This structure of ideas is also necessary in order for religion to communicate with the rest of life. William E. Hocking's book, *The Meaning of God in Human Experience*, is one of the great books on the philosophy of religion in the idealist tradition, more recent than the works of Caird and Fairbairn. In it Hocking carefully examines the roots of religion in feeling and then concludes that these are not adequate. He finds that thinking is also essential in religious experience, although it may be more submerged. We cannot worship God without having some ideas about Him, he says. We must have a God-idea; and this God-idea, he declares, is not so much the object of our thinking as it is the tool by which we think.

Turn now to the complement of this insistence by idealism that religion must be rational. Do idealists mean to say that our ideas of the religious object are the same as that object itself, i.e., our idea of God the same as God? In contending for reason, do they hold that religion has arisen out of the conscious reason and is therefore secondary to thought? Neither of these seems to be the case. There is rather general recognition that the springs of religion, both past and present, are deeper than man's conscious reasonings or intentions. People have sought to relate themselves to the supersensible, rituals have grown up, and the institution of religion established, all in response to deep-rooted needs compared to which conscious reason and intention appear quite secondary. The idealist is quite in agreement with the realist in recognizing religion as distinct, *sui generis*, not to be resolved into something else, or reduced to some least common denominator in the experience of man. However, reason we also have; and

[1] New Haven: Yale University Press, 1912.

ideas we will have whether or not we intend them. At the same time, idealists do not hold that these ideas are identical with their objects. Specifically, for religion, the idea of God is not the same as God Himself. Room is left remaining between the finite mind of man and the Infinite Object beyond, so that the system of ideas is always being adjusted to meet the demands of a consciousness confronted by that which it can never fully comprehend.

But although idealism does not make reason prior to religion, it is inclined to find value in the refinement of religion by reason. Popular religion, whether ancient, primitive, or offshoot of modern culture, is crude and out of joint with the totality of experience. One of its chief lacks is rationality. Of course, there is the real danger that something may be lost if the introduction of reason is harsh and unsympathetic. But properly employed, the recognition of some measure of responsibility for intellectual consistency in religion will bring with it refinements that will transform the sporadic into something solid, strong, and full of value which is widely relevant for the very culture out of whose needs it has grown.

B. OUR EXPERIENCE OF GOD

In the first two major sections of Chapter VIII more was said about our experience of God, as the idealist understands it, than can be stated here. For in considering the metaphysics of idealism and especially its epistemology, we were dealing with that outside edge of experience where the idealist finds himself confronted by the fact of God.

In perception, first of all, we are confronted in consciousness by a world rich in quality and value. Yet analysis never reveals the source of that quality outside of consciousness unless it is an all-embracing Mind beyond us. As I look out my study window and behold the mat of green made by my neighbor's trees, I enjoy a beautiful color quality of greenness; it is outside of my window and it belongs to the trees. But light wave lengths as such do not have greenness; neither does chlorophyl. The greenness is a quality of consciousness, not a quality of something inert, yet it comes from beyond; it is not my own creation.

Multiply this by the millions of sensory qualities in our experience of the world and you have a glimpse of one frontier of human experience. Conscious experience is shot through and through with quality and value which is made of the stuff of consciousness, yet comes from beyond us. Perception is an enigma unless the beyond is Mind creating these qualities.

Look at our relation with the world at another level where conscious reason enters. In addition to perceptual responses to the world, we make rational responses. We find meanings as well as qualities. The cloud means rain, a job means money, and money means food and shelter, if not comfort and pleasure. We are always making rational connections such as this between our private experience and the world. The striking fact, all the more striking that it is accepted as routine by all of us, is that there is correspondence between the world and our meanings. Reason can work it out abstractly that two plus two equals four. But the world responds accordingly; and whenever twos and twos are brought together, there always are fours.

Stated generally, this is to say that the world is intelligible. Intelligence in the human mind makes demands upon the world, and the world responds in the language of intellignce. Now, how can this be, the idealist asks, unless there is also Intelligence beyond? Human mind is not out of joint with the world which is its environment. Actually, there is a remarkable degree of synchronization between reason and the world. How can this be, unless the world itself is grounded in Reason?

Turn to still another dimension of our experience, one which strikes closer home, touching the very heart of individual personal experience. My own selfhood seems indisputably immediate; I can scarcely deny my own existence. Yet, of as great value to me as my own self are the persons whom I love, whose companionship makes my life largely what it is. Without them I would scarcely care to live, certainly not without some companions who could take their places were they lost to me. Yet, can I be as sure of their existence as I can be of my own, which is apparently indisputable? All my knowledge of them comes from beyond the range of my own consciousness, just as my knowledge of the world does. If I cannot be sure of their existence as well as my own, they are indeed lost to me, and furthermore all other possible companions who might take their places are also lost. Everyone shrinks back from solipsism. Could anyone be convinced that he alone existed and all else, as well as everyone else, are uncertain representations of consciousness—could anyone be convinced of this, he would shrink from it as a horrible existence. Yet to face such stark subjectivity is to face another fringe of our experience where the fact of God is seen. My own existence, so dear to me yet of no value in isolation, as well as the existence of my loved companions, both arise out of the same ground, a World Self out of which all other selves are given birth. I had existence before I became conscious of myself as existing. I arose out of community, and I became conscious of myself as distinct, by my relation to others and to other things. The cart is before the horse when, like a solipsist, I question all existence but my own. My companions, and all other persons, are grounded in this same community of relationship, existing first and becoming conscious of existence as a consequence. This all-inclusive community or World Self is the warrant, not only of the reality of friends with whom I commune, but also of my own reality. This is a part of what Hocking means when he says that the God-idea is not the object of thought but the tool with which we think. We cannot think of ourselves and our associates in terms equivalent to what we experience ourselves and others to be without the context of a world ground which is Spirit.

We have just reviewed three of the frontiers of human experience where idealists feel that we are confronted by the fact of God. These are frontiers where perceptual quality points to the Creator of that quality; where intelligent responses to our intelligence reflect Cosmic Intelligence; where the fact of selves in communion calls for a World Self as the ground for that spiritual fellowship. All of these frontiers are more experiential than rational; and the attempt here has been to present them as descriptions of experience and not as arguments.

Of course, the rational element is here. Idealism holds that it is present of necessity; that while reality and our experience of it are prior to the dawning of reason in us, yet reason cannot be divorced from our experience of reality. Reason has a normal function to fulfill as companion to the experiential. When we stand on these frontiers of human experience, it is legitimate for reason to speak and say what our views from these frontiers mean. And what reason says is that God is the answer. Where do the qualities of experience come from? God. How is it that the musical scores of reason and Nature harmonize enough to make melody? God. How can I be sure of myself and those whom I love as being real? God is; this is the answer.

C. THE ARGUMENT FOR THE EXISTENCE OF GOD

We go on then to sketch the idealist's intellectualization of his experience of God. Our attempt will be to put into fuller argument form what it is that the idealist says as he stands at the frontiers of human experience, such as are described above, and beholds God. Of course, the idealist does not give as high a place to argument as the Neo-Scholastic. He will scarcely use the word "demonstrate" in connection with his arguments. They do not demonstrate in the same way as a laboratory experiment or geometric theorem may do. His arguments instead make intellectually consistent what is found in experience. And while this is not "proof," it is something of equal value with proof; it brings experience into harmony with one's own experience of selfhood, a test just as telling as proof; for after all the self has arisen out of the world and its nature must therefore be somewhat of a guide to the nature of existence.

The famous ontological argument for the existence of God is the characteristic argument. It has its roots in Saint Anslem (1033–1109) and Descartes, but is enriched by fuller overtones in modern idealism than it possessed in either of these early thinkers. We will first look at these earlier statements of it, and then consider its present use by idealists.

Anselm's ontological argument was an attempt, in typically scholastic fashion, to construct a single argument which would convince almost any kind of man once he was confronted by it. It was to be to the Gospel what the short TV announcement is to advertising, a simple cogent inducement, thrust into the mind of the hearer and touching a soft spot of responsiveness. If we are fair in breaking Anselm's argument into stages, his contention was as follows: (1) "Even the fool" can understand that the human mind can conceive something so great that beyond it nothing greater can be conceived. (2) And this greatest of all, beyond which no greater can be conceived, cannot exist in the mind alone, but must exist in reality as well. For if it were in the mind alone, a still greater could be conceived, i.e., the greatest, existing in reality as well as in the mind. (3) To be still more insistent, Anselm said that it is impossible to conceive of such a greatest as not existing. For, he held, if we try to conceive of that beyond which nothing greater can be conceived, yet as not existing in reality, we actually are not conceiving the greater beyond which there is none. We can still go beyond it and conceive the greatest *as existing,* and this is greater than the so-called greatest not existing except in the mind of man. (4) Anselm held that such a greatest, existing both in the mind of man and in reality beyond man, must therefore exist.[2]

The ontological argument as phrased by Descartes has already been presented,[3] but we will review it briefly and compare it with Anselm's argument. The starting point for Descartes' argument was the reality of the self. In relation to its context, his theistic argument was the second step in a thought movement which, after doubting everything, first found the reality of the self to be self-evident, then moved from this conviction to the reality of God, and thence to belief in the reality of the external world. Having faced the reality of his own existence as indisputable, the specific argument is launched as Descartes fastens his attention on the fact of his own imperfection. That he exists is a fact; but that he is imperfect is also a fact, for whereas knowledge is superior to doubt, he doubts and does not possess knowledge. Now, since there is one who exists and is at the same time obviously imperfect, yet conceives of an existence which is perfect, there must be some other existence beside himself which is perfect. The form of this phrasing, it can be seen, is the same as in Anselm, but there is a slightly different content. Whereas Anselm talks about "that than which

---

[2] Cf. the argument as quoted from the *Proslogion* by Seymour G. Martin, Gordon H. Clark, Francis P. Clarke, and Chester T. Ruddick in *A History of Philosophy.* New York: Appleton-Century-Crofts, 1941. Pp. 271–272.

[3] Cf. pp. 115–116.

nothing greater can be conceived," Descartes speaks of "perfect Being." Descartes is sure of his own being, but since he is equally sure that his being is imperfect and incomplete, he is convinced that there is other being besides himself which is complete and perfect. He asks what could possibly be the cause in him of this idea of perfect Being. In answering his question, he holds that imperfect being could hardly be the cause, because it is as repugnant to think of a lesser causing a greater as it is to think of nothing causing something. And Descartes himself, who possesses the idea, is an imperfect being. Therefore, he holds that perfect Being must exist beyond his own mind, and must be the the cause of the idea of perfect Being in his mind. And this is to acknowledge that God exists and is the "perfect being upon whom I [am] dependent, and from whom I [have] received all that I [possess]."[4]

Such are the historic roots of the argument. Now, let us see it in its present use by modern idealists. John Laird, although not an idealist and not one who subscribes to the argument, has correctly characterized it in his book, *Mind and Deity*,[5] as not the ontological argument but the "Grand Ontological Assertion."[6] William E. Hocking, who leans heavily on this argument in his book, *The Meaning of God in Human Experience*, is careful to point out that when he speaks of the idea of God, he is not speaking of an imagined or fanciful idea, such as a centaur or a moon made of green cheese, the kind of thing the mind could conjure up while roaming at will without hindrance. The God-idea, instead, is the leap of the mind when confronted with the actualities of empirical experience. The idea of which he speaks is not the child of reverie, but is given birth when the self is in actual face-to-face adjustment to and relation with the world beyond self. The God-idea of which he speaks is the idea which arises when man is standing at the frontiers of experience, some of which have been described. When he experiences perceptual quality and is confronted by the need for an adequate source from which that quality comes to him; when he experiences the world responding to his intelligent thrusts at it, by seeing it act in ways which the language of intelligence can interpret; and when he enjoys his own existence, communing with his companions as existing, and is thereby confronted by the necessity for a spiritual world ground out of which all persons could arise—when in these and other ways man is actually and actively in relation with the world—then it is that the God-idea is the mind's answer. The modern form of the ontological argument is that when, in such face-to-face relation with reality beyond self,

---

[4] Cf. *Discourse on Method*. Translated by John Veitch; La Salle, Ill.: The Open Court Publishing Company, 1945. Part IV, pp. 34–43.

[5] London: George Allen and Unwin, 1941.

[6] Cf. *ibid.*, Chapter I.

this idea arises as the answer—as natural a response to that which is beyond as color quality is a response to light waves—then it is reasonable to conclude that it is that-which-is-beyond which gives birth to the idea in me, just as the beyond gives birth to color quality in me when the world plays on my perceptual apparatus. This God-idea is not a purely subjective work of imagination. It is the child of actual relation with that which is outside of me. It is therefore reasonable to say that God is speaking through that actual relation and giving birth to the idea in my mind. This is not to imply that the idea does justice to the nature of God as He is in reality; but it is to hold that the idea corresponds to the fact of God's existence and to His nature as being Spirit.

D. THE NATURE OF GOD

And now, to carry the exposition on into a new phase, what has just been said is the clue to the least common denominator in all idealist definitions of the nature of God, that ultimate reality is Spirit. The so-called physical world is not self-sufficient; it is a derived order of existence, having its foundation in Spirit. The substratum of all existent things is the one underlying synonym of existing *per se,* namely Spirit.

But when we try to be more specific in our definitions than this least common denominator is, we are in the midst of great difficulties. Because, as has been noted, there are several kinds of idealism and quite some variation in their delineations of the character of ultimate reality. The most critical point seems to be the problem of the one and the many, an outline of which we have already presented.[7] The alternatives of this problem, as they bear upon conceptions of the nature of God, are these:

1. Is God such a homogeneous unity that none besides Him can have any eternal existence? If an affirmative answer to this question is the true one, then personal immortality could scarcely be the hope of individual men.

2. Or, instead, is the antithesis of this correct? Is God a composite of a multitude of selves? If an affirmative answer to this question represents the truth, then while immortality would be man's destiny, God would scarcely have the unity and integrity possessed by human persons.

3. In order to meet the demands of those religious experiences in which man as a person finds himself in relation with One who at the least has the characteristics of personality, idealism has to find some sound middle ground between these two antithetical poles. There is need to conceive of ultimate reality as Spirit which is unified, but not to the exclusion of finite individual personal unities. There is need also to conceive of Spirit as

[7] Cf. pp. 154–157.

having room for multiplicity within its unity, yet not to the extreme at which unity gives way to multiplicity and there is no tension or homogeneity binding all into one.

Now the fact is, as was noted in discussing the one and the many, there are idealists who follow each of these alternatives. There are those who think of ultimate reality as Spirit which is general and diffused in form. Although the ultimately real is considered to be Spirit, not matter or anything purely naturalistic, it is not personal. Spirit is a sort of rarefied existence which is beyond the struggles and pains and joys of man. While each man has a certain individuality within the span of this present life, that individuality will someday be lost again in the all of the Spirit from which it was once differentiated by birth. Bernard Bosanquet and F. H. Bradley in England, and Benedetto Croce in Italy, are exponents of such an idea of God. This is a conception which harmonizes with the spirit of Eastern mysticism, and is a basis for understanding the common yearning of Buddha and Schopenhauer, to be liberated from the individual existence of this life and absorbed again into the unindividuated Whole.

To turn again to the second of the three alternatives, there are idealists who cling to the extreme opposite conception of God. Being much more enamored by the individuality of man, these idealists insist that, whatever God is, He is not such a completely unindividuated whole that no real existence is granted to the human personality. It seems that American philosophers have been more inclined to this stress upon individuality. This is actually the point at which William James staged his revolt against Hegelianism. Refusing to think of the universe as a "block universe" in which there is no room for freedom or individuality, he launched a kind of pragmatism not far different from this pluralistic extreme of idealism. J. A. Leighton's voice has already been echoed as an apostle of individuality,[8] and some of the members of the personalist school are on this side of center, especially in their assertions that God is finite, limited by His own individuality and by His granting of individuality to human persons.[9]

But it would seem that those who attempt to find a middle way, in preference to either of these extremes, are more in harmony with one significant disposition of idealism, namely, synthesis. For those who follow this third alternative think of God as a personal unity within whom there is a multiplicity and variety which does not subtract anything from His unity. The synthesis of Mary Whiton Calkins was presented briefly in the course of the synopsis of idealism.[10] We will now consider the conceptions of

[8] Cf. pp. 155–156.

[9] Cf. for example Gerald F. Ensley, "The Personality of God," in Edgar Sheffield Brightman (editor), *Personalism in Theology*. Boston: Boston University Press, 1943. See also Edgar Sheffield Brightman, *The Problem of God*. New York: The Abingdon Press, 1930.

[10] Cf. pp. 156–157.

William E. Hocking and A. M. Fairbairn. The former exemplifies recent idealism in America, and the latter was a British exponent of idealism in religion who wrote his greatest work, *The Philosophy of the Christian Religion*,[11] shortly after the turn of the present century. In both of these men there is a blending of idealistic thought with the Christian doctrine of the Trinity, which in the case of Fairbairn is especially positive.

In reading Hocking on the nature of God, most of the overtones are found which are called for as the synthesis of the triad presented by the idea of the one versus the idea of the many. But, like the lost chord, they are illusive and are not easily caught simultaneously in one unified conception. God is the Absolute, and there is about Him a certain aloneness which sets Him apart, aloof from human familiarities. At the same time, our thought of Him is not to be rarefied in conceptions which present Him as "some thinner and weaker sort of world-unity easier to imagine and believe in than a personal world-unity."[12] God is personal without having any of the "case-hardened" characteristics and limitations which the concept "personal" has for us because of its use to denote human individuals. But He is also near to us and throbbing with vitality in the real experiences of this life: "Other Mind, an individual Subject, wholly active."[13] The pledge of the unity of human nature, it is only by holding to Him as our primary attachment that the balance of our individuality is held steady. Probably it is the very nature of God, and man's relation to Him, which make it so difficult to conceive Him. He is externally related to me, and as such He seems personal; but I am also related to Him from within, and as the Whole of which I am a part, He seems impersonal.[14] There is a significant footnote appended to Hocking's Hibbert Lectures, *Living Religions and a World Faith*,[15] which strongly suggests dependence upon the doctrine of the Trinity for enlightenment at this point. In it Hocking states that this Christian doctrine may offer help in solving still existing tangles regarding monotheism, polytheism, and pantheism. The following paragraph, with which he concludes, highlights both the difficulties of conception and the relevance of the trinitarian doctrine as an answer to the need for synthesis.

. . . while the doctrine of the Trinity remains a mystery over which subtleties may be endlessly poured out as intellectual libations, in its total tangible effect it is an admonition that pure monotheism is not enough, whereas tri-theism is too much and too many; the true idea of God lies between them; it must at least contain a procession out of the infinite reserve into the life of the universe and men, and without abandoning its absolute selfhood. This doctrine

[11] London: Macmillan & Co., 1902.
[12] William E. Hocking, *op. cit.*, p. 334.
[13] *Ibid.*, p. 332.
[14] Cf. *ibid.*, Chapter XXIII.
[15] London: George Allen & Unwin, 1940.

is much more valuable as a mystery to be jealously guarded from solution than in any possible philosophical translation. For as a mystery, it stands simply for the indispensable parameters of any tenable idea of God.[16]

Rough outline that it is, this summary of the idealist conception of God is now to be concluded by a paraphrase of Fairbairn's exposition of the doctrine of the Trinity. For in philosophy he felt the need for synthesis between rigid monism on the one hand and disunified pluralism on the other. And in the Christian religion he found a historic revelation of God which satisfies this very demand. The basis of the paraphrase that follows will be found in his two greatest works, *The Philosophy of the Christian Religion* and *The Place of Christ in Modern Theology.*[17]

Because Jesus Christ was what He was, Fairbairn says, we cannot correctly think of God from the standpoint of external relations alone. We must think of Him as known in His inner relations. He is not just the deity conceived over against the universe; He is Godhead conceived according to His own nature. In addition to being an object of natural knowledge, He is the subject of supernatural revelation. In addition to being known by the reason as a sufficient cause of the natural order, He is known by revelation as having an inner nature which is personal.

This inner knowledge of the personal nature of God is revealed in the consciousness of Christ, which was essentially a filial consciousness. He knew Himself as the Son, and God as the Father. The two together were conceived in Jesus' mind as forming a unity over against man. This unity was so real that for man to see the Son was for him to see the Father. Yet there was distinction within the unity. The relation was necessary rather than voluntary. It was a relation which had been for all eternity; the Fatherhood was no older than the Sonship. The nature of this relationship was love. In order for it to exist, there had to be a subject bestowing love and an object rejoicing in receiving that love. And being a relationship of love, it was a social relation. Again, it was a rational relationship; and that means that God is an active intelligence from which the eternal Logos that forever abides within Him forever goes out from Him in expressed reason. What is true of Christ as the Ideal Son in this relationship is also true of humanity, which He embodies. Humanity is the son of God in the mind and heart of the Godhead, and existed as such from the time that it was conceived.

The moral nature of God is made vivid by the revelation of the Godhead which we have in Christ. Since God is Father and Son, personal and moral relations must be the very essence of His being. A God who would not be without a Son is a God who would not be without moral qualities in exercise. This conception of the Godhead also supplies the necessary con-

[16] *Ibid.*, p. 237.
[17] New York: Charles Scribner's Sons, 1893.

nection between eternity and creation. It is no longer a question of whether or not the creation is eternal, and if not what it was that caused the Creator to create when He did. God is now understood as Father of perfect moral goodness, whose nature is love. It was this love which supplied the motive of creation. Love is the desire to give; and the creation was the satisfaction of the desire to form objects upon whom this love could be bestowed. It was the way to the realization of the perfect happiness which He had willed. Such an understanding of the Godhead also provides a synthesized view of providence. God is not placed by it at one extreme where he is understood as completely transcendent, making Nature a deistic universe. Nor is He placed at the other extreme of complete immanence, making of the universe a pantheistic order. He is the synthesis of transcendence and immanence.

The constant initiative of God, always necessary to all the good which man enjoys, is made immediate to us by the Holy Spirit. God is immanent in Nature in power; He is immanent in man in Spirit. Physical existence is the form of the Divine energy; religion is the mode of the Divine presence. Without this immanence, the incarnation would be an isolated case of intervention; with it, it becomes the constant experience of man. God, in the salvation of man, has expressed Himself in three essential causes: the Father who gives, the Son who is given, and the Holy Spirit who renews and reveals. The Father is the source, the Son the medium, and the Spirit the distributor of grace. And all three are made efficient because they are united as one. The Son enables us to understand the being and action of the Godhead from within the Godhead; the Spirit enables us to conceive its being and action which is without. The Spirit is the immanent presence of the Godhead in us in personal form. All good in us is His creation, all truth His revelation. We are void of the Divine, except as we allow Him to fill our being. He is, as it were, the energy of the Godhead in constant incarnation, and this He accomplishes by such a revelation of truth as communicates life and determines conduct. And in addition to this, He organizes life by creating and renewing the Church. He inhabits the societies constituted by the souls He creates, as well as the individual souls themselves.

E. THE POWER AND GOODNESS OF GOD

The next step is to consider briefly the extent of God's power and goodness. These two are related in the thought of today because there are thinkers, among them idealists, who cannot harmonize omnipotence with the fact of evil in the cosmos. The crisis is seen in this light: If God is all-powerful, He evidently is not all good; or if He is perfect goodness, then He must be limited in His power, and is therefore finite.

The specific question in this section is, What is the idealist position in regard to this problem? We will give two answers. One, representing most idealists, is to the effect that God is both all-powerful and perfectly good. The other is the answer of E. S. Brightman, according to which God is good but finite, hemmed in by a number of limitations.

It is not necessary to deal at length with the majority idealist position here, as a somewhat full statement was made in presenting the metaphysics of idealism.[18] Absolute idealism equates God with ultimate being. There is nothing, according to idealism, which *is* finally and ultimately, but God or that which He undergirds with His own being. Now, in contrast, much that exists in the world of human experience will not endure; it is purely temporal. Much that we see (including persons) is either in the process of becoming, i.e., achieving an enduring existence, or else it is in the process of decay, falling away into nothingness. Both of these processes are so intertwined in the affairs of life as to make the present world exceedingly complex and, in one particular sense, very delicate. Both the wheat and the tares are growing in the same field, and no one can lash out with the sickle with any assurance of separating the two. So different are these two kinds of existence, however, that the same word hardly suffices for both meanings. It is quite one thing to exist within and by virtue of the temporary structure of time and space. It is very much a different matter to exist ultimately and finally.

The latter type of existence is God's existence; the former is that to which He gives limited duration. Out of it may come some selves sufficiently like Him that He may give them eternal existence, starting with their creation in the world. But there will be much waste; much will slough off into the abyss of nonbeing and death. Now, if this approximates a true picture of one aspect of the nature of God, then it is true that he is both all-powerful and perfectly good. Always existing, without beginning and without end, giving a kind of existence to all else, He is of course the source of all being and all power. He is also perfectly good in Himself; for evil is limited to the sphere of approximate existence, a necessary factor in the process of becoming and decay. Truly enough, He has permitted evil temporary existence as the crisis necessary to the making of selves, but neither is He evil in any part, nor did He intend evil, nor did He give evil any foundation sustaining its existence.

A different picture of God is painted for us by E. S. Brightman, however, somewhat disturbing as compared to the calm which may attend acceptance of the more common view that God is both omnipotent and devoid of all evil. Although the personalists, with whom Brightman is more particularly associated, are inclined to stress the individuality of men more than the unity of God, Brightman seems to be in close agreement with such philosophers as Hocking and Calkins in his solution of the problem of the

[18] Cf. pp. 158–161.

one and the many, according to which there is room for multiplicity of beings within the unity of God. Yet he removed himself from them to quite a distance when he defined God as a finite God within whose very nature there are limitations. Of course, it is quite commonly acknowledged that God voluntarily limited Himself when he granted free existence to human persons. But Brightman makes clear that he is speaking of limitations additional to this one when he speaks of the difficulties against which God struggles. We will mention some of these limitations.

1. There is in God what Brightman calls "an eternal Given element" which is not a product of the will of God. A possible analogy might be the relation of heredity and will in our own makeup. At birth, at least, we are what we are by virtue of the biological forces that have produced us. By individual initiative we may do a great deal with this original endowment; but one thing is sure, and that is that we cannot change it, making it different in kind from what it is. Our wills have no causal relation to it. Original endowment at birth is analogous to what Brightman calls the Given in God. It is something about Him which is what it is and is not the result of His own will. This is one of His limitations. The presence in the world of evils uncaused by human wills, such as "earthquakes, cyclones, and disease germs,"[19] Brightman attributes to this aspect of God's nature which is not willed by Him.

2. Another of God's limitations is seen by Brightman in His capacity for growth. While God is eternal, Brightman insists that He is also temporal and that time must enter His very being. This is to present us with the conception of God as One who is actually developing and growing. Brightman tells us that His perfection and the perfection of the world "consist in their perfectibility."[20]

3. Another hindrance is a limitation of knowledge, i.e., God is not omniscient. Chiefly, the kind of knowledge God does not have is specific knowledge of what a free man will do at a given time. He may know fully the nature of every individual man; but to the extent that men are free, He cannot know what choice a given man will make in a particular circumstance. This limitation is both imposed by the freedom of man and related to the temporal character that Brightman insists is a part of the nature of God.

4. The final limitation to be made explicit is evident in the dialectical character of the world. Brightman, epitomizing idealism, finds all reality to be full of "opposition and contrast," everything having its opposite and every thesis its antithesis. This is not an aspect of the phenomenal world alone, he holds, but is rooted in the very nature of God. God too has His oppositions and tensions, Brightman says, struggling and gaining victory

[19] E. S. Brightman, *The Problem of God*, p. 125.
[20] *Ibid.*, p. 130.

over opposition only after paying a great price. This tension and struggle is seen in the Cross of Christ, in which we behold God as saving only "through the shedding of blood."[21]

F. THE NATURE OF MAN

Enough has been said already to present the idealist insistence that individual man is a self, a spiritual unity which is more than a physical organism or unit in the social process. The chief task remaining, therefore, for a short discussion of the nature of man in connection with idealism as a philosophy of religion, is to make more explicit the idealist approach to the moral condition of man.

However they may deal with the past history of man or his innate predisposition to good or evil, idealists are not romantically blind to the fact that in actuality men are guilty of all kinds of evils, great and small. Left to themselves without some higher guidance men are pretty sure to produce and involve themselves in all kinds of moral difficulties. While man is intended for goodness and godliness, he more easily gives himself to activities which fall far short of these high ends, if they are not outright contradictions of them. It is apparent that he needs to be allied to a sustaining power not in himself alone in order for him to fulfill his true purpose.

Like the part of a whole, man does not find true equilibrium in stable goodness unless he is somehow in relation to God and His purpose in the world. There are at least two aspects of the need for this relation. The first is that the goodness God intends for man is of such a high character that he cannot realize it apart from His help. And the second is that there is something in the essential character of godliness and the life of the Spirit which makes necessary that man's realization of it can only come when he loses himself in the love of God. The Incarnation is God coming to man and establishing with him a relation which he cannot build by himself, and which makes it possible for him to enter into the higher eternal selfhood for which he is intended, a selfhood which is negated if he is separated from communion with God.

It is evident within the psychological realm that the truest and highest self of each of us is only liberated into full creativeness of activity when we completely lose ourselves unself-consciously in some activity which is beyond ourselves. Idealism says that on the ontological level this same liberation may take place in an even deeper sense. We only find ourselves truly living in a dimension which is eternal, and not purely temporal and human, when we are lost in the purpose of God and in identification with Him. Jesus taught this in such sayings as "whosoever shall lose his life for my

[21] *Ibid.*, p. 135.

sake shall find it,"[22] and "seek ye first the Kingdom of God and His righteousness, and all these things shall be added unto you."[23]

The moral condition of man may be described for idealism as potential. Man is neither already good nor evil in his essential makeup. He is a potential self and he becomes good or evil according as his potentiality is wrought out in actualities. Historically, man has been blithely persistent in actualizing evil rather than good, although there has been much good in the world in spite of this weakness. Where evil has become actual rather than good, man has failed to arise to his high calling of communion with God. His prime need has always been for an awakening of consciousness which would reveal to him that he "lives and moves and has his being" in God and to act in harmony with this consciousness.

[22] Matthew 16:24.
[23] Matthew 6:33.

XI

Strengths and Weaknesses in the Philosophy of Idealism

A. *The Strengths of Idealism*

B. *The Weaknesses of Idealism*

Now that an exposition of the philosophy of idealism has been completed and its practice in education and religion explored, attention is turned in conclusion of this section to consideration of its strengths and weaknesses.

The writer should acknowledge before this discussion is presented that in some measure at least he can speak from within the idealist tradition. Shortly after he was attracted to the pursuit of philosophic interests, he came under the influence and teaching of Professor Herman Harrell Horne, who, throughout a rather long career, was an influential spokesman for idealism as a philosophy of education. Since Horne desired independence of judgment in his pupils more than agreement with his own point of view, the writer never felt any pressure to agree with or to accept Horne's idealism. Nevertheless, the inner pressures of inspiration and increasing insight were compelling, and much was acquired for which the author will always feel indebted to Professor Horne. As a consequence, the writer still agrees with some of the central themes in the philosophy of idealism but at the same time he is convinced that as the years have passed he has come to be able to see this philosophy with increasing objectivity. Because of this he may be able to expose some of its weaknesses as well as estimate its enduring powers.

A. THE STRENGTHS OF IDEALISM

There are four comments about idealism in general that relate to the spirit of the philosophy and lend it strength, if not the power to persist through changing historical perspectives.

1. Idealism justifiably makes the reality of the self the focal point of philosophizing. The fact that the basic intuition regarding the reality of the self is so strong in every one of us makes it necessary that any philosophy do justice to this intuition in order to be at all adequate. No other philosophy, except existentialism, has a central intuition as immediate to selfhood and to our existence as persons. In this particular aspect at least, idealism is more adequate than other philosophies because its point of departure and primary focus are an intuition that is more basic and primary in the naïve experience of each one of us than is the case with the intuitions central to other philosophies.

2. Idealism is also correct in insisting upon the centrality of the self in gaining and organizing knowledge. While this contention discards all conceptions of knowledge that make it impersonally objective, it should not also be interpreted as necessarily subjective. To argue, as idealism does, that whenever there is knowledge it is someone's knowledge does not imply that knowledge is dreamed up inside the so-called subjective world of the alleged knower without any reference to objective happenings or events. It is rather to hold that whatever it is that we derive from the objective world, which we may call knowledge, or less ambitiously, information, has to be derived by a person and organized by him. Events and happenings do not yield anything like knowledge unless they strike fire somehow with consciousness of some kind. Knowledge does not relate to happenings, events, or objects alone. Also, knowledge does not relate alone to persons isolated from external events or objects. Knowledge only happens when a being who has a capacity for knowing crosses paths with entities external to him about which he does something, such as characterizing or organizing them. Transposed from the concept of knowledge to that of learning, this line of argument leads also to the insistence that the act of learning and whatever may result from it are personal and in no sense purely mechanical or objective.

3. Accordingly, idealism is right in stressing the human and personal elements in life and education. While the present argument may bypass a meta-theory of value, which continually brings all particular values and value systems into question, there is no intention of ignoring the importance of this more basic consideration. Within the limits of the present

discussion, however, we may not presume too much if we say that the humanizing and personalizing elements in idealism are preferable to anti-thetical values and other value schemes. The former may also be closer approximations of reality. At the same time that the rapid advance and sophistication of science has enhanced many human values, the increase of science threatens to mechanize us and subvert man to something less than his true humanity. This threat would still persist even if we could be assured that nuclear destruction of the race will be averted by the common fear all nations have of nuclear warfare. Idealism can live with science, value it, and join in its advancement, but at the same time it can also insist, as it does, on the superiority of the human and personal over scientific achievement.

4. The final strength of idealism to be mentioned here is that it is a comprehensive philosophy. It deals with both metaphysics and episte-mology as equally important considerations. There are consistency and interrelationship of principles necessary in both of these fields. This same consistency also follows through with some adequacy in matters of logic and in various realms of value. The comprehensive system of thought that has resulted has been practiced to good effect in such important areas as education and religion. This comprehensiveness is a quality that measures up well with other philosophies and is superior to most.

B. THE WEAKNESSES OF IDEALISM

At the same time that it has evident strengths idealism also has its weaknesses. In the last two or three decades, in point of fact, we have witnessed events as well as changes in thought which have set these weaknesses in clearer perspective. There is now more doubt than ever before whether idealism as a philosophy can stand up to the changes of history unscathed.

1. One weakness of idealism, which may be unavoidable, is the great difficulty with which it is correctly understood. This difficulty is made evident by the abundance of misconceptions concerning it.

One of the most common is that idealism is primarily concerned with ideals, or more extremely, that it is a visionary utopianism. This idea identifies it wtih a general social or moral idealism, which is common to all philosophies that have any desired values or objectives whatsoever. Few if any can be excepted from this. It is with too great ease also that idealism is romanticized or mysticized, even by some of its alleged adherents. Another mistaken identification is the occasional equating of the philosophy of idealism with some of the occult groups that luxuriate in a vague spiritual-ism, separated from and out of joint with empirical and social processes. This mistaken identity misses completely a certain hardheadedness in idealism, which is a part of its insistence on relatedness, specifically relation to empirical process and to social experience.

Such problems in comprehension raise serious questions as to whether idealism can become a popular philosophy at all, so great is the hazard of distortion and corruption. But the problems cannot all be laid at the door of the philosophy; they also have sources in our generation. A larger section of our generation than some would like to admit will have no "nonsense" about the alleged meaning of life. And those who comprise this segment are not all adolescents or denizens of the coffee house. Many allegedly "settled" adults share this same impatience but hide it much of the time under the cloak of conformity. We are a generation in revolution, and what is more, we may before too long have our more outspoken progeny. How can idealism go over with such a generation any better than pragmatism, realism, existentialism, or language analysis? We have had our fill of nicely systematized ideologies and neat value systems calling us to sign the pledge of loyalty. It is not true that we would rather be "safe" than dead. We will not settle for phony truths. We want the real, whatever it may be, the ring of authenticity, by whatever name it may be called.

Other misinterpretations of idealism, adding to its difficulties, are to be found at a more knowledgeable level. One is the version of idealism that makes it a subjectivism according to which nothing exists except in the mind of the individual. Bishop Berkeley is as much to blame for this misconception as anyone in the history of idealism; but even when someone tags Berkeley with this misconception, he makes it evident thereby that he has failed to read all of Berkeley.[1] Another misconception is that idealism teaches that the conceptions a given mind or the social mind forms concerning reality are identical with reality. This again is a kind of subjectivism and is also an identification of specific ideas with reality. Idealism not infrequently comes close to this idolatry, if it is not actually guilty of it. But to hew a straight line, idealism should never make this false identification. Whereas our approximations of the nature of reality must always take the form of ideas, the specific ideas we have are not themselves the full comprehension of reality nor equivalents of it. Room must always be left for improvement, development, correction, and complete abandonment. There may be a vast disparity between our ideas and the reality they seek to approximate.

We return then to the difficulty in understanding the philosophy of idealism and a possible intimation there may be in it. At its best, we may say with some propriety that within its comprehensive system there is such an interlacing of refined insights that the student can easily miss a number of them or mistake one of them for the whole philosophy. This may be unavoidable; it is certainly so to the extent that difficulty of comprehension

[1] Cf. pp. 124–127.

must accompany truth. If difficulty is an accompaniment of truth, then ease of understanding, while it may be an argument for popular appeal, is not necessarily an argument for the truth of a philosophy. Peace based on understanding may come to us only after struggle and difficulty, if not great agony.

2. To the extent that metaphysics and ontology are deemed important, it may properly be said that the critical idealism of Immanuel Kant and those who may be his successors is weak metaphysically and ontologically. While Kant achieved greatly in his analysis of human knowing, possibly more than any other thinker in the whole range of man's history, he bequeathed to succeeding generations a metaphysical riddle. What is the thing-in-itself? Can it ever be known at all?

It should be said that this has been a most intriguing enigma, which has set at least two great movements of thought on their way. The magnificent philosophical system of Hegel was constructed in some great part as a solution of Kant's problem. American pragmatism, in the first instance at least, was set on its way when Charles Sanders Peirce arose to the challenge of Kant's epistemological dead end.

But some are convinced that Hegel's magnificent system was just that —a magnificent system, not the truth. Still others are unconvinced by the utilitarian answer of pragmatism to Kant's problem. William James inadvertently betrayed this point of dissatisfaction, and incidentally did pragmatism a disservice at the same time, by talking about the "cash value of an idea." And this was in a culture that was already on its way to becoming one whose dominant themes are commercial success and finesse in public relations.

So critical idealism, as presented to the world by Kant with great honesty and without flourish, poses for us to this day a significant critical question, which remains unanswered. This strain in idealism leaves many of us at sea, without any sure conviction about whether there is any enduring being at all, or what its nature is if there is one.

This may not, however, prove to be a weakness in the Kantian form of idealism when viewed from a longer historical perspective. It may instead be a reminder to man of his perennial situation as far as knowledge of reality is concerned. If so, any diligent generation will take Kant on again and try to cope with him better than Hegel or Peirce did. After all, it may even be possible that Hegel's idealism and the pragmatism of Peirce, James, and Dewey never fully asked Kant's question, to say nothing of answering it.

3. It is well, as has already been noted in pointing to one of the strengths of this philosophy, for idealism to be as comprehensive and inclusive as it is. But comprehensiveness must be genuine and not purely schematic.

It was probably significant in the development of philosophy for it to reach the point, most particularly in Hegel, at which it intended to deal with all aspects of life and existence. This is a laudable effort, although possibly unattainable. Its danger is one of settling for less than actual inclusiveness and freezing into a schematic arrangement that is allegedly the equivalent of comprehensiveness but is not actually equal to it. It may be, for example, that the major concerns of philosophy are metaphysics, epistemology, logic, and axiology, together with the respective clusters of problems subsumed under each. But this schematic structure is not of necessity the measure of genuine comprehensiveness. And what is important to observe at this point is that idealism is tempted to assume that this is the case, if it does not occasionally do so.

Not infrequently idealists have identified idealism and philosophy. On such occasions they have made a double assertion by implication. The first is that a person is not philosophizing unless he deals with all the questions to which idealism addresses itself. The other assertion implicit in the affirmation is that at the top of the spiral of philosophic pursuit and achievement, the philosopher will necessarily become an idealist if he follows onward and upward to the end.

An obverse form of this false identification of philosophizing, with an accepted schematic structure, has been used as a defense against alleged intruders into the philosophic domain. The *enfant terrible* of philosophy today is existentialism, especially in its more popular forms as expressed in the drama, the novel, and the visual arts. It is alleged on occasion that existentialism is not a philosophy because it does not conform to the schema of the philosophic craft and is, therefore, too fractional and unsystematic to qualify. But why? May not new patterns be as legitimate as old patterns? Is it not even conceivable that they may prove to approach the philosophic task in a better way than older and more accepted forms?

4. Idealism has already been applauded in this chapter for its emphasis upon the centrality of selfhood. But now it is necessary to qualify this appraisal, because such an emphasis has to be both subtle and refined in order to have validity. Unless this is the case, it may be a weakness rather than a strength.

Selfhood can be conceived on at least two levels, if not on many levels, or in a series of progressions from the lower to the higher, as it were. Selfhood at all levels cannot validly be considered central to a philosophy, although it is the self, however defined, that must do the philosophizing at whatever level it may take place. The criticism being ventured here can be made more easily and more clearly if we speak of only two levels of selfhood, although a series of levels may be a more adequate description.

There is the level of selfhood that is most easily exemplified by the self at birth. Can it be said that the self at birth is properly central in a philosophy, except as an object of respect and hope? It is an object of respect because it is a human life and an object of hope because of what it may become. But this is far different from asserting that the self at this level is a reality, already actual, and as such is an unequaled clue to the nature of reality.

The other level of selfhood, in this oversimplified reference to what may actually be a series of levels, is that one at which, by some miracle, the self has acquired a kind of existence different from the first level. The existence the self has at this second level is different from the temporal and transient existence that biological procreation can produce. It is an existence that in some way transcends temporal and transient things, from which it gains an enduring power, among other things, that the temporal and transient do not have.

It is only of this kind of self, however a person may come by it, that the idealist emphasis upon the centrality of selfhood is completely valid. As has been said, it is the self that must do the philosophizing at whatever level it may exist, if there is to be any philosophizing for it—a virtual truism. But it is only the self of the second level that can in any sense comprise an index to the nature of reality. And this distinction is not at all clear in the philosophy of idealism.

5. There is some indication in our time that the view of man held by idealism needs to be revised, possibly rather radically. To approach this in terms of some of the events of our recent past, there is real point in the observation that man, as he has shown himself to date, is not the man he was defined to be by the idealism of the nineteenth and early twentieth centuries. We now live in a nuclear age in which, because of the fear of what man may do with his new playthings, we find ourselves continually on the brink of nonexistence. How real the likelihood of racial self-destruction is we do not know. We are not too interested in finding out, and we hope that its very possibility will be its own deterrent.

About two decades ago the world was shocked by the terrible destruction of human life at Hiroshima and Nagasaki. At the same time, we were forced to realize that the nuclear age had dawned. Moving backward again from the cataclysm of World War II to World War I, the prelude then played out is remembered by many as the perpetration of war, by man upon man, in proportions not before known and virtually involving the whole world, or at least bringing it to a kind of standstill until the issue was temporarily settled. The historic context out of which the philosophy of idealism arose antedated all of this.

At the most superficial level of description, the man we now see is not the man for whom idealists had expressed such hope in the march toward ever new vistas of progress envisioned for him onward and upward. Compared to the idealist hope for man, the man we have known from 1914 through 1945, and on into the nuclear and space ages, is a monster.

Of course, the question is wide open as to how historic events can legitimately serve to change philosophic concepts. Is philosophy above history? Do its concepts hold regardless of what history unfolds? Or does history provide grist for the philosophic mill in much the same way that science does? Do its data need to be as seriously considered? These questions are too large to be explored here, so anything we now venture should presume as little as possible upon the answers to them.

It would seem, at least superficially, that the idealist view of man is now dated and is somehow irrelevant in our present historic setting. At any rate, the present generation, rightly or wrongly, calls it into question. Is man as good and does he hold out as much promise as the idealists have claimed? Does his potentiality for good have any more likelihood of becoming actual than his potentiality for evil? Most important, is there any such guarantee in view of the fact that those who guide him in education, religion, and government are also men? Is there even the possibility that man's potentiality for evil is more likely to be expressed in what he actually does than is his alleged potentiality for good?

Whether the would-be successors of the older idealists like it or not, these are the kind of questions this generation is asking about man. And they will need to be answered to the satisfaction of this generation if idealism is to persist as anything other than a philosophic relic.

6. Finally, bringing to a close this appraisal, two related questions that are quite specific should be raised as possibly pointing to still another real weakness in idealism, especially, as a philosophy of education.

They are: (1) Should the objectives of education be stated in moral terms? and, coordinate with this, (2) Is all education of necessity character education? These questions will be posed without raising the more basic question concerning the category of objectives as such. It has been a part of the pattern of educational philosophy almost throughout the history of education to formulate objectives that education is supposed to achieve. While the question needs discussion as to whether this is a valid category, such a discussion would apply to all philosophies, not only to idealism; consequently, its relevance is more general. We will content ourselves here, therefore, with discussion of only the two specific questions already raised, as they may help in examining the worth of idealism as a philosophy of education.

If objectives are going to be conceived at the intended high level of self-realization at which idealism points them, is it enough for them to be phrased only in moral terms? Does not idealism really intend some trans-empirical meaning as it formulates its objectives for education, and not something to be achieved only within the transitory world of man? If the answer to this question is "Yes," as seems to be clear, then it would appear that objectives are more religious or theological than they are moral. Self-realization or even self-perfection, within the spirit of idealism, are derivative from some kind of connection with or belief in a Universal Self. How then are objectives characterized as moral except in a derivative sense? Are they not by implication religious? And should this deeper intimation not be made explicit in idealism's formulations of objectives? Occasionally explicitness on this point comes to the surface, as for example in Horne's definition of education.[2] But for the most part, there is satisfaction, often even in Horne's writings, with stating objectives in ethical terms.

To the extent that the argument just stated is valid, then it would also follow that all education is not character education in the last analysis. Rather, the frequent assertion by idealism to this effect only deals with a by-product and not the ultimate end. It should rather be said that instead of all education, in the end, being character education, it is religious education. Or, stated more precisely, all education, within idealist intentions, deals in the end with matters of faith, not only with morals. Education is, therefore, character education in a derived sense. Since it deals with the whether or not of ultimate faith, it necessarily becomes engaged with the kind of living which is fidelity to that faith. But it is submitted here that such a concern at bottom is a concern with faith and, therefore, only in a derived sense a concern for character.

[2] Cf. p. 200.

PART FOUR

REALISM

XII

A Brief History of Realism

A. Aristotle

B. Saint Thomas Aquinas

C. John Amos Comenius

D. René Descartes

E. Baruch Spinoza

F. John Locke

G. Immanuel Kant

H. Johann Friedrich Herbart

I. William James

J. The Neorealists

K. The Critical Realists

L. Synthesis

Realism as a distinctive philosophy is of recent origin. The ancestry for particular strains is probably as old as that of any other philosophy, yet modern realism as a deliberate school of thought arose in the twentieth century.

There are many brands, so it is somewhat presumptuous to attempt an exposition of the point of view. But it is probably safe to say that all forms of realism have one thing in common which is the distinctive emphasis of all. This is a revolt against the theory of knowledge of idealism and the metaphysics which the idealist theory implies. As has already been shown, idealists hold that the qualities of experience depend upon a knower for their existence and do not subsist in themselves. In order to avoid complete and irrational subjectivism while holding this theory of knowledge, it is necessary for them to believe in God as the Universal Knower in whose mind all of the qualities of human experience exist whether a human knower beholds them or not.

Since the turn of the century, realists have been out to refute this line of reasoning and to construct their own epistemology to supplant it. In the minds of many of them, this mission has now been pretty well accomplished and idealism accordingly squelched. Realists insist that the qualities of our experience are real independent facts of the external world. They are unchanged by entering the ken of the knower, and do not depend on any mind, finite or infinite, for their existence. The qualities of experience stand on their own feet. The world about us is a real world, not a world of phantasy.

However, realists do not agree when they go on from this point to build a metaphysical system. Some of them believe in God even though they do not reason their way to that belief via the route of idealism. The existence of God is not made necessary for them by the nature of human knowledge. Other realists do not believe in God. They think of reality in a purely naturalistic sense. Still others suspend judgment as to the existence of God, while accepting the world described by science as the real world.

In attempting to sketch the development of realism historically, it is hardly possible to point a finger at successive figures in the history of philosophy and say, "These are realists." Instead we must study those ideas of some of the great philosophers which evidence realist leanings. In more recent times we can find philosophers who quite fully exemplify the realist viewpoint. And in contemporary philosophy we can be quite specific, describing different kinds of realism and naming exponents of the different schools of thought.

A. ARISTOTLE (384–322 B.C.)

The realist spirit can be found in the history of philosophy as early as Aristotle, if not in the early physicists who preceded Plato, and in one particular, also, in Plato. Democritus and Leucippus have already been discussed in sketching the history of naturalism. They were interested in metaphysics rather than epistmeology and have therefore been regarded as naturalists rather than realists. In the case of Plato, to the extent that he regarded the Universal Ideas as independent of infinite mind, in this particular he too could be considered as one who prepared the way for the philosophy of realism. But with this possible exception, Plato was the father of the philosophy of idealism, and we have been content to identify him only with that tradition.

Although Aristotle was a student of Plato for twenty years and was greatly influenced by him, there is much in his philosophy which is a reaction to Plato's thinking. Plato was given to dealing with universals; Aristotle was interested in particulars. Plato was absorbed in ideas; Aristotle was fascinated by things. Plato envisioned ideal ends; Aristotle kept his nose to the grindstone of present actualities. Whereas Plato recognized various sciences of his day as they fitted into the total scheme of knowledge, Aristotle ardently advanced the cause of science by spelling out the detail of a number of sciences with surprising fullness for his day.

Accordingly, in his *Physics* Aristotle states that Nature is the starting point for philosophizing and needs not to have its own existence proven. "It is clear to everyone," he writes, "that there are many things of the kind we have just indicated [animals, plants, earth, air, fire, and water], and he who would try to demonstrate the more apparent by the less apparent shows that he cannot distinguish what is and what is not evident."[1]

Accepting Nature as a self-evident reality in this way, he attempted analytical descriptions of different aspects of the natural order and so made valuable contributions to the development of the sciences. Instead of involving himself in the whether-or-not of the natural world he tried to find an adequate explanation of the causes which brought it into existence. These two themes are only instances of the many interests which motivated Aristotle in making his remarkably extensive and voluminous studies, and which indicate the realist disposition of this remarkable man.

In attempting to define what he means by the term soul, for example, he finds it necessary to consider the different levels of life. There is the lowest level at which is found only the nutritive faculty, the power of receiving nourishment. This is the level of plant life. In animal life, exclusive of man,

---

[1] *The Works of Aristotle.* Translated into English under the editorship of W. D. Ross. Oxford: Clarendon Press, 1930. Vol. II, *Physica.* Book II, Section 1, 193a.

there is the nutritive faculty as in plants, but in addition there are others. There is the faculty of perception, and this makes possible the desiring faculty. In the case of some animals there is the power of locomotion. And in still others there is the faculty of thinking. It is within this last group that man is classified; he is a thinking animal and his true function is to live rationally. This is one of the more famous instances in Aristotle's writing which exemplify his disposition toward analytical description.

Another noted passage in which the yen for analysis, but of the explanatory type, is evident is a section in the *Physics* in which four different kinds of causes are discussed. These both explain how things come into existence and provide lines of investigation to be followed in studying into the nature of a thing.

There is the *material cause,* "that which composes a thing," such as the bronze of the statue. There is the *formal cause,* "the form or the model of things," such as the figure which modeled for the artist as he molded the cast for the statue. There is the *efficient cause,* "the source from which movement or rest comes," such as the artist whose effortful activity produced the statue. And there is the *final cause,* "the end and goal of a thing," such as the conception of the statue in the mind of the artist, the David which Michelangelo saw in the rough block of marble. Or to use another figure, health is the final cause of the "constitutional" walk the professor takes each day.[2]

Aristotle does not go on in this much paraphrased section of his *Physics* to connect his analysis of causation with a consideration of a final cause or causes behind the universe, explaining how it came to be. But elsewhere he speaks of the first cause as the Prime Mover who is himself unmoved. He holds that there must be a first cause, as an endless chain of causes does not make sense. An infinite regression in causation explains no more than the myth of the world on the shoulders of Atlas. God is defined therefore as the first efficient cause underlying all existence, but He himself is unmoved by another cause which might be presumed as being prior to Him.[3]

B. SAINT THOMAS AQUINAS (1225?–1274 A.D.)

Like Aristotle, Saint Thomas Aquinas is not so much an exponent of the philosophy of realism as he is one of the great thinkers in history who shared the realist spirit. A most significant figure both in the history of philosophy and the history of theology, he was of such caliber in the

[2] *Ibid.,* Book II, Section 3, 194b–195b.
[3] Cf. *The Works of Aristotle.* Translated into English under the editorship of W. D. Ross. Oxford: Clarendon Press, 1908. Vol. VIII, *Metaphysica.* Book XII, Chapters VI and VII, 1071b–1073a.

development of Catholic thought that he supplanted Saint Augustine, who for centuries before his time had been the great authority in Catholic theology. Today his thought is regarded virtually as the criterion of truth by many contemporary leaders in the Catholic Church.

The religious aspects of his philosophy are not peculiarly realistic, but other parts of his elaborate system not only have much in common with realism but in addition are embraced by modern realists, particularly those who are concerned to build a philosophy of religion which is consistent with their realism. In order to deal to some extent with the complicated relations found in contemporary thinking between physical realism, religion, and the philosophy of Saint Thomas, two chapters are included in this section, the one, "Realism in Religion," and the other, "Neo-Scholasticism."

Probably the most distinctly realist strain in the philosophy of Saint Thomas is his belief in the reality of matter. In Chapter XVI of his *Summa Contra Gentiles* he struggles with the relation between God and material substance out of which the world is apparently made—and in his day there was no physics which denied the existence of matter. If God is spirit, is matter something separate and distinct from Him, "preadjacent matter," as Saint Thomas would say? Did matter coexist eternally with God before the creation of the universe? And was the process of creation, therefore, one in which God acted upon matter so as to mold the universe out of it? This sounds plausible to our common-sense judgment; but God is presumed to be infinite, having no limits at all. And if matter coexisted with Him before the beginning of the world, then God does have limits. That portion of existence which was matter then was not God, and in the present order the same distinction would seem to hold.

The answer of Saint Thomas to this problem is that God is both infinite and eternal, without limit, and without beginning or ending. Therefore, matter did not coexist with Him in the eternities before the universe was made. God created matter, yes; He made it out of nothing. And this primary matter, created by God, is the primary substance out of which the different kinds of things and different individual objects comprising the world were made. Matter is not an uncaused essence or existence. God is the first cause, the unmoved mover, as Aristotle held, and matter depends upon Him for existence. The act of creation was an action of giving concrete form to objects, primary matter being both created itself and sustaining a potential relation to individual objects, the formed objects being actual as compared to the potentiality of primary matter.

It may be said that matter had a practical reality, at least for Saint Thomas, which amounted to a kind of independence in relation to mind. He said, in one place, "Primary matter is in some way, for it is being in potentiality."[4] God created both primary matter and concretely formed objects and living beings; but apparently no temporal separation was made by Saint Thomas between these two stages of creation. Primary matter is being in potentiality and has no status as independent being apart from God, on the one hand, and from individually formed objects, on the other. But once formed in specifically individuated objects, matter seems to be something quite separate and distinct in character from God. For all the practical purposes of the limited day-by-day experience of man, it is an external physical substance which is different from the mind and soul of man in quality as it is different from God.

It makes little difference that the new physics has intervened in recent times to redefine the physical world for us, and that atomic explosions have demonstrated that we can no longer think of physical substance as something solid and inert; for Saint Thomas defined primary matter as being in potentiality. A person can still believe in nonpersonal physical energy or force, which for all practical purposes is just as real and unyielding as what was formerly believed to be matter. Most modern realists appear to agree with Saint Thomas in his recognition of the reality of matter, as long as it is defined as physical energy or as being in potentiality. Many of them would be content to think of this nonmental physical force as uncaused, and would not therefore go along with Saint Thomas in regarding it as depending upon God. But many realists who are interested in religion embrace this additional part of the argument of Saint Thomas as well.

C. JOHN AMOS COMENIUS (1592–1670)

John Amos Comenius was more theologian and educator than philosopher, but he believed in a realism that was refreshingly simple. Though he may not have contributed to the development of the philosophy of realism, his ideas will be enlightening to the student trying to understand this point of view.

Comenius was a bishop in the Moravian Church. His life was spotted with disappointments and sorrows. His parents died while he was a child. He was still a young man when the Thirty Years' War broke out, and soon thereafter he lost his wife and child. Like other Moravian pastors he was forced to wander about in Moravia and Bohemia evading the persecution of the Jesuits. When he was one of the older students in a Latin class, as a boy, the need for classes in the school separating different age levels was early impressed upon him. He became a writer of textbooks, and particu-

[4] *The Summa Contra Gentiles.* Literally translated by the English Dominican Fathers from the latest Leonine Edition. London: Burns & Oates, 1923. Vol. II, Chapter XVI, p. 25.

larly stressed the connecting of words with objects of sense in teaching languages. One of his great ideals was to bring together in a compendium all of the scientific knowledge of the day, so that scientists would not be working in isolation without knowledge of what had already been done in their respective fields. As the universities had not yet recognized the importance of the sciences, he also wanted to establish an institution, worldwide in its respresentativeness, which would be given wholly to the advancement of the sciences. During a sojourn in England there was some promise that Comenius would get the opportunity to realize this dream, but preoccupation of the British government with war and prior political claims brought diappointment to this hope. Comenius then went to Sweden, where he was sponsored in educational rather than scientific writing.

The interesting conception of mind which Comenius held is distinctly realistic, although his religious beliefs did not harmonize with it. The mind of man, he said, is "like a spherical mirror suspended in a room," which "reflects images of all things that are around it."[5] This is a vivid figure for describing the character of the mind. If a person has not experienced it, he can easily imagine a crystal ball suspended in a room as a sort of chandelier. He can see how every object in the room would somewhere produce its image on the ball. Each person coming into the room would have his likeness reflected on the ball-like mirror from his very first appearance in the doorway. It is easy to draw the analogies from this figure. The spherical mirror is the mind of man. The room is the external world. Everything in that world somehow reflects its image upon man's mind.

It is to be noted that the figure attributes to the mind a passive character. It is the external world which projects its images upon the mirror. The mind, if we hold true to this figure, does not reach out and in some active way embrace its world. Nor does the mind in any way give character to its world by reading meanings into it. Mind is the passive recipient; the world, though not exactly active, is the impression agent. There are a number of subtle elements in the knowing process as it is understood by modern realists which are not apparently taken into consideration by Comenius. But his conception of mind is the same as theirs, although not as fully refined.

D. RENÉ DESCARTES (1596–1650)

The two phases of the philosophy of René Descartes which were incorporated in the outline of the history of idealism were his insistence upon

---

[5] John Amos Comenius, *The Great Didactic*. Translated and edited by M. W. Keatinge. London: A. & C. Black, 1907. Part II, p. 41.

the self-evident reality of the self and his particular version of the ontological argument for the existence of God.[6] But, whereas Descartes was idealistic in these two parts of his thought, he was at the same time realistic in his belief in the reality of the physical world. It therefore becomes necessary to consider this phase of his philosophy in sketching the history of realism.

The fact that one and the same man may be considered as contributing to more than one philosophic tradition is no doubt confusing to the student of philosophy. But it is important to remember that types of philosophy are not as distinct and well defined as the viewpoints of given philosophers. Philosophic types are sufficiently distinct to warrant the comparative approach in studying philosophy; further, the comparative approach will help the student to gain a somewhat impartial overview of the problems and viewpoints of philosophy. But we must not overwork the patterns of types and comparative study in order to achieve a neat scheme of organization, and do it at the expense of an accurate and dependable knowledge of the field. Some philosophers have embraced aspects of divergent points of view, contradictions notwithstanding. In some instances there are shades of meaning in distinct points of view which come so close together that they would almost seem to fuse into agreement. Of course, viewpoints do not need to be decisively distinct in every particular. It will eventually become evident to the reader, if such an observation has not been made already, that there are points on which philosophies agree as well as points on which they differ. Viewpoint A and B may unite in opposing philosophy C on the solution of problem x; whereas philosophies B and C may join forces in refuting viewpoint A on the answer to problem y.

As has already been observed, Descartes believed that doubt is essential in achieving any conclusive knowledge of truth. Accordingly, he is at first somewhat disturbing to the unphilosophic soul who naïvely accepts the physical world as being as real as it appears to be to his senses. "I am desirous that they should know," Descartes says, "that all the other propositions [i.e., other than the existence of God and of the soul], of the truth of which they deem themselves perhaps more assured, as that we have a body, and that there exist stars and an earth, and such like, are less certain."[7] For, he argues, we are no more sure that there are external objects which correspond to our impressions of these things than that there are such external objects corresponding to the images we behold in our dreams.

It is clear that there is a dualism suggested in Descartes' treatment of the knowing process. There are the mental images or representations which our

[6] Cf. pp. 114–116.
[7] *Discourse on Method*. Translated by John Veitch; La Salle, Ill.: The Open Court Publishing Company, 1945. Pp. 40–41.

senses give to us of the world beyond the self. Over against these stands the external world about which at least two questions can be asked. (1) Is the outside world real? Can we believe and accept as true what our senses tell us about the world? (2) Is the external world just as our senses picture it to us, or do our senses help give it its qualities although there is something real out there upon which our senses work?

The second of these questions may be a refinement in the understanding of the knowing process which Descartes did not achieve, although there is indication that he answered this question by accepting the same dualism which is held by critical realists today. This is that the mental images of the external world given to us by sense perception are numerically distinct from the real external world out there which is represented to us by these images.[8]

At any rate, the first of these questions is clearly raised by Descartes. Is there any real world out there, or are my senses deceived? In giving his answer, he returns to his belief in God as a perfect being. Now a perfect being is of course perfectly good and would not stoop to deception. The external world appears to be real, just as my senses give me experience of it. Either God is deceiving me or else the physical world is real. Since God is a perfect being, the answer to this question is assured. God will not deceive, therefore the physical world is a real world.

So far Descartes' position could be idealistic, except for the apparent conception of the physical world which he holds. Though its reality is guaranteed to him by the goodness of God, it is yet a physical, extended, material world of a very mechanical sort. In spite of the fact that he revolted against Scholasticism, Descartes appears to be close to Saint Thomas in this conception. Although God is necessary in order to establish the reality of the physical world, and although this belief is logically prior to the belief in the universe, God and Nature still seem to be quite separate and distinct. This is another dualism in Descartes, but it is metaphysical instead of epistemological, as the one referred to above. God is spirit, but the world is an extended mechanical order, if not a material one. Descartes' persisting interests in mathematics and the sciences would seem to justify this interpretation of him. In fact some students of the history of philosophy feel that the spiritual side of his metaphysics was not held with complete sincerity, but was an accommodation, in part at least to the doctrines of the Church, in order that he would be permitted to carry on his scientific investigations unmolested by the Church.[9] This judgment of Descartes is neither justifiable nor fair. At the same time, there is a genuinely realist leaning in his thought, although idealist elements are unmistakably present.

[8] Cf. pp. 271–273.
[9] Cf. Frederick Albert Lange, *History of Materialism.* Boston: James R. Osgood and Company, 1877. Vol. I, pp. 243–248.

E. BARUCH SPINOZA (1632–1677)

Some parts of the philosophy of Spinoza have already been presented in
the chapter on the history of idealism;[10] but the fact that there are many
modern nonidealist philosophers who love Spinoza is evidence that other
than idealist plants have taken root and flourished in the fertile soil of his
thought. More specifically, his doctrines that extension is an attribute of
God, and that the will is not free, affiliate him with the realist tradition.

absolutism

His doctrine of substance, previously discussed, is virtually as much
realist as idealist; for realists insist as much as idealists upon an unchanging and abiding reality. It has been shown that Spinoza was a monist; he
insisted that there is only one substance. All realists would not go along
with him on this. They are not sure that the universe is *one* in the last
analysis. Some of them feel that it may be many, in actuality a *pluraliverse*.
Nor would all realists agree with Spinoza in speaking of God and substance
as identical. Many of them would readily accept extension as an essential
attribute of existence, but would reject thought. This suggests the most
distinctly realist element in Spinoza.

God or substance has extension as one of its two attributes. Whereas the
final substance is a thinking thing, it is always an extended thing. There is
no thought without extension in time and space, according to Spinoza. It is
at this point that those of us who have been nurtured in the Hebrew or
Christian traditions are brought up short by Spinoza. For according to him,
God is not a disembodied spirit who can exist apart from the physical
world. He is not however, identical with the physical world, nor is He dependent upon it. Instead, He is the only existing substance, and upon Him
the physical world stands. The relation is even closer than this; the extendedness of the physical world is a part of the very essence of God. It
is just as much His nature to be extended as it is His nature to think.

Many realists are not so sure that existence is a thinker. But they are
sure that extension is fundamental in the nature of things and that this
external extendedness of the universe should be the frame of reference for
all of our attempts to understand our experience. Certainly the frame of
reference should not be mind, whether mind of man or mind of God.

Some realists find in Spinoza's two attributes of substance an answer to
their dualism between mind and matter. How can the external world, which
is apparently physical, enter into my mind, which is apparently mental? In
addition, how is my mind related to my body? Psychology shows how
completely dependent the mind is upon the brain and central nervous
system, and yet mind seems to be so different in quality from these. But
when I think of existence as a psychophysical monism, one substance

[10] Cf. pp. 116–119.

which has both mental and physical aspects, then I can see both how external objects can take on meanings in mind and how mind and body can be different and yet closely identified as aspects of the same substance.

There is another characteristically realist element in Spinoza, although it may be secondary; it is his attitude toward will. He holds that will is not a part of the essence of God. It is a mode of thought, and thought in turn is an essential attribute of God. Therefore thinking is more basic than willing. Willing is not a general characteristic of existence, but rather it is a specific form in which thought is expressed (a mode rather than an attribute), and thought is a general characteristic of God (an attribute). Consequently, there is no freedom of will in God or man. Will is a disposition to act which is the result of some cause other than itself, the second cause brought about by a third cause, and so on to infinity. This means for the individual human mind that there is no general faculty of volition. There are only specific tendencies to act in specific situations as a result of a chain of causes which gives rise to the idea of acting in a given way in a given specific situation. The philosopher's name for this particular attitude about will is *determinism.*

To summarize, then, the realist elements in Spinoza's thought are these: There is a substance which exists eternally and infinitely. This substance is extended in time and space, and there is no thought apart from it. There is no freedom or chance in the universe; everything comes to pass as a result of effects and causes following upon each other with an unbroken dependability and efficiency.

F. JOHN LOCKE (1632–1704)

John Locke was an Englishman of Puritan ancestry. Though his mother died when he was a small child, his father, a lawyer and member of the Parliamentary army which opposed Charles I, saw to it that he was well cared for. His father apparently knew the art of being a companion to his son, and this is reflected in Locke's educational principles. Aided by scholarships, he was educated at Westminster School and Christ Church College, Oxford. Locke was a versatile man of many interests and gifts. As physician, confidential secretary, and educator, he was closely identified with the house of Shaftesbury for three generations. This also placed him in line for a number of important public posts. Never too strong physically, poor health at one time enforced a sojourn in Europe, and the stay was extended as an exile when Charles II came to power. This absence from England was really a fortunate occurrence when considered in the light of Locke's contribution to knowledge. For during this time he brought together the notes he had been making for years and wrote the works for which he is now famous. The student of education will be interested to study Locke's educational principles as stated chiefly in his *Some Thoughts Concerning Education*.[11] Attention is focused here upon his general philosophy as contained in his *Essay Concerning Human Understanding*.[12]

Locke was at great pains to show that there are no innate ideas in our minds. Contrary to a belief current at the time, he held that we are neither born with ready-made ideas nor are such ideas dormant in us and recognized by us when we mature sufficiently to use reason. Mind, instead of being already formed at birth, is an unformed something to which experience gives definiteness. At birth it may be compared to a blank sheet of paper upon which the world then proceeds to write its impressions. All knowledge comes from experience and is either impressed upon us by sensation or arrived at by logical demonstration. Experience is the source of all knowledge; and sensation and reason are the two avenues through which this knowledge comes to us.

There are three different kinds of qualities or perceptions which come to the mind by way of sensation.

1. *Primary qualities* are characteristics which are essential to the very nature of objects. In order for a physical object to be what it is, it must occupy space, i.e., have length, breadth, and thickness. It must also have solidity and be capable of motion. A candle, for example, has all of these qualities and continues to have them even after it is burned. Though the wax is no longer in the same shape it was before the wick was lighted, it still fills space, still has weight, and is still capable of being moved. These characteristics, essential to the nature of any physical object, are termed primary qualities by Locke. He names them specifically as "solidity, extension, figure, and mobility."[13]

2. *Secondary qualities* are not so easily defined as they are exemplified or contrasted with primary qualities. They are not essential characteristics of physical objects. An object may or may not have them and yet have all the general characteristics of objects as such. Colors are good examples of secondary qualities; so also are sounds, tastes, smells, and some tactile sensations such as hardness, softness, temperature, texture, and pain.

3. A third kind of qualities to be noted are the *tertiary* ones. These are the powers somehow resident in objects enabling them to make changes in other objects. Locke's example is the power of fire to produce a new color or consistency in wax or clay.

So much for the classification of the qualities of experience by Locke. With this as a background, the important phase in his thought contributing to the development of realism is now to be caught. All of these qualities are produced in our minds in the same way, but they are not all resident in the

[11] London: Cambridge University Press, 1934.
[12] Second edition; La Salle, Ill.: The Open Court Publishing Company, 1912.
[13] *Ibid.*, p. 53.

external world just as we experience them in our minds. This latter point needs full explanation; but before passing on to it, just a statement about the way in which the physical world produces ideas in us. It is largely by a process of motion, according to Locke. There is some kind of motion caused by the object which stimulates the appropriate senses, sends impulses along the nerve pathways, eventually reaches the brain, and produces the mental result we experience.

Now to resume the consideration of how our experience of the qualities compares with what is "out there" in the external world. Locke tells us that there is a marked difference between primary and secondary qualities at this point.

1. *Primary qualities,* as we experience them in the mind, correspond directly to the characteristics of the external objects which give them rise in our minds. When for example I look at a candle and see height, thickness, and shape, and when I hold it in my hands and feel solidity, I am getting impressions of real height, thickness, shape, and solidity which are out there in the candle. There is a direct correspondence between the images which I have in my mind and the primary characteristics which the candle out there in the external world has, whether I experience them or not.

2. But this is not the case with the *secondary qualities.* They are not "out there" in the same form in which I experience them. In the object, secondary qualities are powers of some kind which are supported by the primary qualities and able to stimulate the experience of the respective secondary qualities in my mind. But they do not exist "out there" just as I see, hear, or feel them, etc. In other words, there is no direct correspondence between the secondary qualities I enjoy in my mind and the object from which they come. To return to the figure of the candle, I see it as a red candle; it seems to me to have a soft texture; when lighted, its flame is a yellowish-orange. But none of these images are "out there." Instead there is only some power present there which is able to produce them. My mind participates in creating these qualities. It is not out of harmony with Locke to assume that there is some chemical element present in the wax which so refracts light as to transmit a certain wave length to my eyes. This wave length stimulates the optic nerve with a specific kind of impulse which is carried to the brain. But it does not become redness until somehow translated into mental terms in my mind. This is true for all of the secondary qualities.

This treatment of primary and secondary qualities by Locke is a potential springboard for either idealism or critical realism, depending upon the kind of jump which is made. As has already been shown,[14] Berkeley made the idealist jump, virtually saying to Locke, "If your secondary qualities have no direct correspondents out there in the external world, then your

[14] Cf. pp. 124–127.

primary qualities don't have any either." This is what Berkeley preferred to believe, and he built his idealism on that treatment of the process of perception.

The modern critical realist makes a different kind of jump. He says to Locke, "You are not right about the secondary qualities. There is something out there which corresponds both to primary and secondary qualities; but you are absolutely right in distinguishing between the image in the mind and the external object which produces the image. There is always a dualism between the experience of the knower and the external world which produces that experience."

This is the story of Locke's contribution to realism. There are two more items to be mentioned, but these are not distinctly realistic. One of these is that Locke held that the existence of matter is no more demonstrable than the existence of spirit. He seems to have held a spirit-matter dualism. One is as likely to exist as the other, he says, and apparently he is at no great pain to weight the balance in favor of either one.

He does, however, hold that the existence of God can be demonstrated logically.[15] One of the statements of this demonstration is as follows: By intuition I know that I exist. I also know by intuition that nothing can not produce something. Something has always existed; for if this were not true, I who now exist would either have been produced by nothing or else by something which in turn arose out of nothing. And this has already been acknowledged to be impossible. This something which always existed must be most powerful since it would have to be the source of all power. It also must be a knowing something, or how could it produce knowing things, such as man. Therefore there must be a God who is an eternal, all-powerful, and all-knowing Being.

To sum up, the realist principles in Locke's philosophy are as follows: There are no innate ideas in the mind. All of our knowledge comes to us by way of experience. The mind is for the most part passive in experiencing the natural world. *Primary qualities* exist in the external world just as we experience them. Although *secondary qualities* are different in our experience from what they are in their potential forms in the object, they are yet caused in us by the external world. The external world makes its impressions upon our minds by somehow setting impulses in motion which reach our minds through the gateway of the senses.

G. IMMANUEL KANT (1724–1804)

The philosophy of Immanuel Kant has been discussed as a part of the development of modern idealism.[16] But there are at least two points at

---

[15] Cf. John Locke, *Essay Concerning Understanding*, pp. 315–330.
[16] Cf. pp. 128–132.

dualism in theory of knowledge knowledge does not affect its object

which Kant is allied with modern realism as well. These are the dualism in his theory of knowledge, which is comparable to a similar dualism in critical realism, and the implication in his idea of the *thing-in-itself* that knowledge does not affect its object fundamentally. These two similarities to realism will be discussed in order.

As has been indicated, Kant believed that our sensory experiences and perceptions are *representations of* the external world and not direct presentations of it. For him our private experience of the world is our *private* experience, and the images which we have of the world are separate and distinct from what is "out there" in the world. Now, although this representative theory of knowledge may be idealistic, it is not necessarily so. It is also embraced by the critical realists.

The other of these points of common ground with realism is the doctrine of the thing-in-itself. While Kant is rather disconcerting to most idealists in holding that the thing-in-itself is unknowable, he is somewhat encouraging to the person who favors belief in realism. Although the realist would not favor Kant's agnosticism, he finds an opening in this doctrine for his realist metaphysics. Remember that realism has arisen chiefly as a revolt against the insistence of idealists that since our knowing process is much as Kant described it to be, then the universe must be a rational, knowable being, a Universal Mind. But Kant, who probably worked out the detail of the idealist epistemology more fully than any other single man, did not himself go on to hold the idealist metaphysics. He did believe in God, as has been shown, but on moral grounds and not as a logical result of his theory of knowledge.

The very fact that Kant stopped short of idealism by not assuming that the character of human knowledge reveals the character of the thing known reveals in him a temper which is close to that of modern realists. It is this very assumption about reality which they refuse to make. Our minds do not affect the objects we experience, they say, nor do those objects in any way depend upon mind for their existence. They are either *represented* in our consciousness as Kant said (critical realism), in which case there is a real world out there which corresponds directly to the world which is in my consciousness; or they are *presented* to my consciousness (neorealism), in which case my consciousness in some way embraces the object of knowledge itself, and I experience it just as it is and just as it was before it entered my experience. In either case, of course, there is no unknown thing-in-itself. Things just enter into consciousness and are known.

H. JOHANN FRIEDRICH HERBART (1776–1841)

Johann Friedrich Herbart was more educator than philosopher, although he was Kant's successor in the chair of philosophy at Königsberg. As he exerted a great influence upon American education in the late nineteenth and early twentieth centuries, the student of education will be concerned to place him in the philosophic tradition with which he has most in common.

Herbart's father was a lawyer of some standing in Oldenburg, Germany. His mother was the daughter of an Oldenburg physician and a remarkable woman who more than made up for the lack of attention which her husband gave to the rearing of their son. The victim of an accident in his infancy—a fall into a tub of almost boiling water—Herbart was a delicate child and was for that reason tutored by his mother for several years. He was well equipped when at the age of thirteen he entered the Gymnasium at Oldenburg. He finished his secondary-school course at the age of eighteen and passed on to the University of Jena, where he became a student of the idealist, Fichte.[17] He was greatly stimulated by Fichte but believed him to be in error in many of his ideas. It is probable that from this time he became conscious of his leaning toward realism. After Jena, chiefly through the good graces of his mother, who followed his studies closely and augmented his social life at the university, he became tutor to the three children of the governor of Interlaken, Switzerland. As the children were eight, ten, and fourteen years of age, and of different temperaments, and as Herbart was an eager young man of brilliant analytical powers, this experience was most conducive to the building of a theory of education. After two years as tutor he studied in Bremen and in Göttingen, where he obtained his doctor's degree. In 1809 he received the call to the renowned chair of philosophy in Königsberg.

Although Herbart was an admirer of Kant, he was not an exponent of Kantian philosophy. He was one of the first to attempt a formulation of psychology as a science, but in his psychology there is enough metaphysics to reflect his predisposition toward the philosophy of realism, as already noted. Distinguishing the soul from the mind, he defines it as a perfectly simple, indivisible essence without parts of any kind. It has no innate talents nor is it a *tabula rasa* on which impressions are made by the world. It is neither concepts, feelings, nor desires, nor does it have forms of perception and thought.

The mind is a sort of manifold of self-preserving ideas or concepts (self-preserving for the soul) which the soul builds up as a result of its contact with the physical world. These concepts are apparently *representations* in the Kantian sense. They are impressions made upon us by the physical world and are copies in consciousness of the objects of the physical world which result from the soul's contact with them. In his formulation of his psychology, Herbart goes to great lengths trying to work out the ways in which these *representations* unite with one another in clusters to form

17 Cf. p. 133.

apperceptive masses, the strength of these masses being roughly proportionate to the size of each. It is the strength of the different clusters of representations, together with the power of momentary impressions, at the very time they are being made, which determine which apperceptive masses will rise into consciousness and which will fall below the threshold of consciousness into the unconscious, or remain there, failing to have sufficient strength to rise above the threshold. According to Herbart's way of thinking, there is an unconscious battle of concepts going on in the mind all the time, the result of which is the determination of what actually comes into consciousness and what does not.

The important point related to our line of thought is that the mind is defined in terms of its content. According to Herbart, mind is not an active agent which produces changes in the world surrounding it. It is rather the sum total of impressions which results from the soul's relation to the world. It is not difficult to see how such a conception would favor a formulation of educational principles in which the assimilation of subject matter by the student is the primary practical objective.

As is the case with the soul, so also with matter; it is unknowable and cannot be defined. At the same time it is a reality of the external world, not something to be reasoned away. It is something which actually exists and produces the phenomena which we experience as making up the space-time world. There is an implication in Herbart that soul and matter are different aspects of a third common substance. "The difference between soul and matter," he says, "is not a difference in the nature of the simple essences, but it is a difference in the manner of our apprehending them."[18] But he does not clearly resolve this possible dualism, as, for example, was attempted by Spinoza as his chief philosophic task.

I. WILLIAM JAMES (1842–1910)

Later on, in the fifth major part of this book, William James is placed in the pragmatist tradition in America. If we were arbitrarily limited by some rule of thumb to the identification of a philosopher with one tradition only, it would be pragmatism with which James would still be associated. But we are not so limited, and it also happens that James has a direct connection with the birth of realistic thought in America. This connection, made more explicit, is that he came to hold that consciousness is a function and not a substantial entity; that when objects are experienced in consciousness, they are directly *presented* in consciousness, not *re*presented; and that the universe is many, not one.

Almost sixty years after his death, William James is still one of the most

[18] Johann Friedrich Herbart, *A Text-Book in Psychology*. Translated by Margaret K. Smith; New York: Appleton-Century-Crofts, 1894. P. 121.

popular philosophers that America has produced. He was born into privileges which few Americans of his generation knew. His father, Henry James, Sr., was heir to one twelfth of what is estimated to have been a three-million-dollar fortune. Restless by nature, influenced by the teachings of Swedenborg, interested in writing, and fortunately having money at hand to secure the realization of most of his wishes, he made his family a virtual band of troupers. Native New Yorkers (William was born in New York City), they moved to Europe at least three times, once when William was scarcely more than an infant, again when he was thirteen, and a third time when he was seventeen and became enrolled at the "Academy" in Geneva. New York City, Newport, London, Paris, Boulogne, and Geneva are among the cities where the James family at some time made its home. The best schools were selected for the children in the course of these travels, and if one didn't suit, change was made to another quickly.

William seems to have succeeded fairly well in conserving the greatest value from these unusual privileges, while at the same time overcoming the instability encouraged by so many changes. He was unimpressed by his early formal schooling. His first yen toward a profession was an interest in art. While in Paris he studied painting seriously, and his father brought him back to Newport in order for him to study with William Hunt. But at the age of nineteen James gave up art for science, no doubt a fortunate decision for the world, and entered Harvard to study with Louis Agassiz. For several years, studying both in Europe and America, he was immersed in biology, medicine, psychology, and philosophy. Nor was his involvement in these fields one of the objective student only. He had a problem of understanding himself, conquering his own neuroses, and achieving a wholesome psychological integration and adjustment. Much of his own personal problem seemed to converge in the whether-or-not of freedom of the will, a facet of his thinking to be followed more fully later. But by 1873, when James was thirty-one, he was completing his first year as instructor at Harvard, inspiring his students, and opening a long and notable classroom career, first teaching physiology, then psychology, and finally philosophy.

William James has the unique distinction, as has already been observed, of having fathered the two movements in American philosophy which, until the outbreak of the Second World War at least, were the two most popular philosophies in America, namely, realism and pragmatism. In 1904 James published an article in the *Journal of Philosophy* which was the opening gun in the campaign of modern realism. The striking title of the article was "Does Consciousness Exist?" suggesting the revolt James was making against idealism and much speculative philosophy which had gone before him.

He held in this paper that the old dualism of "thoughts" and "things," spirit and matter, inner consciousness and outer world, is at fault in assuming consciousness to have reality. Instead, he held, consciousness is a nonentity; it has no existence of its own. It is a function of experience and not a substance. Consciousness, James says, is merely "a witness of happenings in time."[19]

Knowing is a simple relation with *presented* objects in experience. The book which you are now holding in your hands and reading, for example, is not *re*presented to your mind. There are not two books, one with a history in time—author, publisher, bookstore, etc.—and the other a mental image in your consciousness. It robs experience of life and vitality to look at it in this way, however logical it may be. There is just one book. The one that has a history in time is the very book which is in your private experience, and vice versa.

Our mistake has been in assuming that the world revolves about self and that therefore all experiences are private experiences of the self. This is as erroneous as the pre-Copernican assumption that the sun revolved about the earth. Experience itself is the axis about which all experiencing revolves. It is therefore fallacious to assume that my experiences are my own private possession. They are public, they are functions of an all-embracing experience (not an experience of an all-embracing Person, as in idealism, however); and since my organism is in relation in these experiences, my consciousness witnesses them.

To carry the thought further, experience is not a substance. It is not made up through and through of some general stuff so that all experiences have some common essence. "There are as many stuffs as there are 'natures' in the things experienced," James says.[20] "Experiences is only a collective name for all of these sensible natures, and save for time and space (and, if you like, for 'being') there appears no universal element of which all things are made."[21]

James is a pluralist. There are all kinds of qualities, substances, or essences which exist in time and space. There is not one common substance. Experience is a kind of relation which takes place between these substances and the objects which they comprise. Physical organisms can enter into the kind of relation constituting experience and so can "have" experiences. To be conscious of these experience relations is just to be aware that they are going on. As far as having consciousness of consciousness itself, there is no such thing, according to James. He states that when

---

[19] William James, *Essays in Radical Empiricism*. New York: Longmans, Green & Co., 1912. P. 5.

[20] *Ibid.*, p. 26.

[21] *Ibid.*, p. 27.

he tries to be conscious of his consciousness, about all that he finds is that he is breathing. Put somewhat grotesquely, he substitutes "I breathe" for Descartes' "I think" and therefore is unable to infer an "I am."

J. THE NEOREALISTS

By 1910 the realist temperament had become sufficiently pronounced in America that a group was formed by six professors of philosophy for the purpose of making their realism more explicit, and expounding it and defending it. Although the ramifications of the point of view emerging among them may not have been clearly worked out at the time, they felt that there was a position, sharing more of the scientific spirit, which was far to be preferred to idealism, which up to their time had been predominant in America.

These six charter members of the neorealist movement were Ralph Barton Perry and Edwin B. Holt of Harvard; Walter T. Marvin and Edward Gleason Spaulding of Princeton; and, Walter B. Pitkin and William Pepperell Montague of Columbia.[22] In 1912 these men published cooperatively their essays, which comprised a manifesto entitled *The New Realism*.[23]

There were other realists of note who did not join this group but who were nevertheless strong exponents of the point of view. And of course there have been many lesser lights who have been subscribers to neorealism since the movement was first publicly launched.

As an exposition of realism is attempted in the following chapter, enlargement of the positions taken by these men will not be made here. Their central concerns were to refute the idealist principle that knowledge produces changes in the object known, and to insist that the knowing experience is a simple relation of knower and object in which the object is directly *presented* to consciousness.

K. THE CRITICAL REALISTS

The disapproving responses which were evoked by *The New Realism* did not all come from those who subscribed to points of view other than realism. One result of the reaction among other realists was the formation of another group in 1916 and the eventual publishing in 1920 of another

---

[22] Cf. William Pepperell Montague, "The Story of American Realism," as reprinted in Walter G. Muelder and Laurence Sears, *The Development of American Philosophy*. Boston: Houghton Mifflin Company, 1940. P. 421.

[23] Edwin B. Holt, *et al.*, *The New Realism*. New York: The Macmillan Company, 1912.

manifesto, the *Essays in Critical Realism*.[24] The members of the critical-realist group were Durant Drake of Vassar, Arthur O. Lovejoy of Johns Hopkins, James Bissett Pratt of Williams, George Santayana, who was then already retired from Harvard, Roy Wood Sellars of Michigan, Arthur K. Rogers of Yale, and C. A. Strong of Columbia.[25] As was the case among the neorealists, also, there were many variations and differences among the critical realists. Montague describes this situation by saying that "the members combined agreement in epistemology with disagreement in metaphysics."[26]

The central purpose among them was to correct the epistemology of the neorealists, which seemed to them to lack refinement much in the same way as the naïve realism of earlier philosophers. They rejected the neorealist position that objects are directly *presented* to consciousness. Their correction was that objects are not presented; they are *represented*. The object which I experience in consciousness is numerically distinct from the physical existent "out there" which causes the object which I experience in consciousness. For one thing, it was believed by these men that knowledge must be *representative* in order to explain the errors of perception, for example. The position is none the less realistic for its rejection of the *presentative* theory of knowledge of neorealism. The physical existents "out there" in the physical world, which produce in consciousness the objects of our experience, though not in consciousness are yet real in themselves. They stand on their own feet; they depend on no mind for their existence, nor are they changed in any way by entering into knowledge.

L. SYNTHESIS

With this sketch of the development of realism before us in retrospect, it may be appropriate to consider whether a composite of propositions might be drawn together from it which would suggest in outline just what the realist position is. If synthesis is limited only to those propositions which are quite surely realistic and on which realists are likely to agree regardless of their differences, it appears that two sets of statements can be made: one on the physical world, the other on mind.

On the Physical World

1. Nature is a primary self-evident reality, a starting point in philosophizing.—Aristotle

[24] Durant Drake (editor), *Essays in Critical Realism*. New York: The Macmillian Company, 1920.
[25] Cf. William Pepperell Montague, *op. cit.*, p. 426.
[26] *Loc. Cit.*

2. The physical world is real, at least for the duration of the temporal order.—Saint Thomas and Descartes

3. There is no thought without extension.—Spinoza

4. The primary qualities of experience exist in the physical world.—Locke

5. There is something which produces my sensations and perceptions, the thing-in-itself, which cannot be known to be mental in character.—Kant

On the Character of Mind

1. Mind is like a mirror receiving images from the physical world.—Comenius

2. The mind of a child at birth is similar to a blank sheet of paper upon which the world proceeds to write its impressions.—Locke

3. Mind is a manifold of ideas or concepts.—Herbart

4. Consciousness is not a substance, it is an awareness of experience, and experience is a medium in which objects and organisms are related.—James

XIII

A Systematic Synopsis of the Philosophy of Realism

A. The Epistemology of Realism
>   1. EPISTEMOLOGICAL MONISM
>   2. EPISTEMOLOGICAL DUALISM

B. The Metaphysics of Realism
>   1. PLURALISM
>   2. DETERMINISM
>   3. MIND
>   4. THE WORLD
>   5. GOD

C. The Logic of Realism

D. The Axiology of Realism
>   1. ETHICAL VALUE
>   2. AESTHETIC VALUE
>   3. RELIGIOUS VALUE
>   4. SOCIAL VALUE

For the great majority of people the world is unquestionably real, just as it is experienced. If queried as to its reality, they hasten to respond with an indignant "Of course it's real!" All of us in our more naïve moments of unconscious activity and enjoyment assume this same attitude of accepting the world at face value. Even the idealists in their "unofficial moments" are guilty of such naïveté, so the realists say.

This is the common-sense point of view which is refined intellectually by realism. Naturalism builds upon the confidence most people have in the orderliness and dependability of Nature. Idealism is a comprehensive philosophy which has resulted from intellectualizing the common belief in the reality of mind and self. Correspondingly, realism is the refinement of our common acceptance of the world as being just what it appears to be. According to it, things are essentially what they seem to be, and, furthermore, in our knowledge they are just the same as they were before entering our consciousness, remaining unchanged by our experiencing them.

But there is more in realism than at first catches the eye. Clear and simple as this basic tenet seems to be, it is not as easily worked out intellectually as might be expected. There are ramifications of the realist pattern to be understood, as well as some differences among realists.

A. THE EPISTEMOLOGY OF REALISM

The character of this philosophy is such that it is advisable to consider the epistemology of realism before the metaphysics. For theory of knowledge is the most completely distinctive element in realism, and at the same time the area in which realists find enough common ground for major agreement. Yet, as was strongly hinted in the history of realism, there are two major positions in epistemology dividing the loyalties of realists, depending upon their belief as to whether objects are *presented* in consciousness or *represented*. Accordingly, this synopsis begins with a fuller outline of these two positions in epistemology than has been possible up to this point.

1. EPISTEMOLOGICAL MONISM

The neorealists describe the knowing process as closely identifying the knower with the object known. They say that the objects of the external world are *presented* in consciousness, not *represented*. They mean to say that when I perceive an object, it is the same identical object in the world "out there" which is in my consciousness. There is not some "go-between" which mediates between me and the object, such as a mental image of the object which is in my consciousness but not "out there" in the object.

Your relation with some familiar article may be used to illustrate this simple presentation of objects. Think of your favorite tennis racket, for example. You always liked, let us say, the grain of the wood of which it is made and enjoyed the luster of its polish. The designs made by the reds and greens in the woven gut have a certain eye appeal. But the "feel" of the racket is its main asset. You selected it because it seemed to have just the right weight and the proper balance as you would swing it in making imaginary serves and fast returns. On the court your racket has lived up to your judgment of it in the sport shop. When it connects with the ball, there is a high-pitched *ping*, and in addition there is that "feel" of enjoyment in your muscles which makes it seem that this racket is almost a part of you.

Now for the realists who are epistemological monists, this racket which you experience through a number of sensory channels is no "phony" mental image. It is a real wood and gut racket (whatever that may be). The same strong racket that slams the ball on a kill is the identical one which is in your consciousness and of which you enjoy the feel, and like the grain of the wood and luster of the polish. True enough, the racket is made up of physical materials. And equally true consciousness seems not at all to be physical. But there is some way in which the physical material, which makes up the racket, and your consciousness can converge upon or intersect one another in a game of tennis. And when that happens it is the real physical racket which is in your consciousness and not some bogus copy of it.

In fact, this point of convergence or intersection of your experience and the racket may be significant in understanding what neorealists mean by mind. Mind, according to them, is a relation between your organism and an object, such as the tennis racket, which is made up of all the sensory and perceptual experiences you get in hitting a tennis ball. When it is defined in this way, it is evident that mind is not all within the skull or even underneath the skin, as we have commonly thought. Mind is as much "out there" in the orbit of the racket as it is "in here" inside the body. If this is the case with mind, then it is understandable that the qualities of the object are the same qualities which are in consciousness. It is the very design of the grain, glisten of polish, weight, balance, and *ping* of the strings possessed by the racket which are also in your consciousness. The object characterized by these and other qualities is one solitary object, not two, one of them in the space-time world and the other in your consciousness. This is what is meant by epistemological monism and the *presentative* theory of knowledge held by neorealists.

reality

2. EPISTEMOLOGICAL DUALISM

But many realists, particularly the critical realists, are dualists in epistemology rather than monists, the more to add to the distraction of the student of philosophy. To put it crudely, these realists disagree with most that the neorealist or his disciple has to say about knowledge. Objects are not presented; they are *represented*. There is a "withinness" to mind not adequately recognized by neorealists. And the qualities an object has in mind are different from whatever it is in the object which gives us those qualities. But return, if you will, to our former example, the tennis racket, for explanation of this principle.

Contradicting the explanation given by the neorealist, the critical realist will tell you that your consciousness and the physical racket never converge upon or intersect one another. True enough, you have an experience of your tennis racket which has all the ring of reality about it, and it is a completely valid experience. But it is naïve to assume that the qualities which the racket has in your consciousness are also present in the racket itself. To be more accurate and more discerning, so they say, there is something underlying the phenomenon you call "tennis racket" which gives you the qualities you experience. The "feel" of the racket, its weight, its balance, the grain design in the wood, its luster, the *ping* of the strings, and such, are all qualities which are not possible without a minded organism which can be conscious of the feel of muscles in motion, visual brightness and design, auditory pitch and timbre, etc. In other words, there are two objects which have a valid claim to the title "my tennis racket." It is hard to say just what the one of these objects is which is the cause of the tennis racket I experience when I take it in hand and start to play. It is some peculiar arrangement of physical forces which is able to give me just these qualities. But the tennis racket in consciousness is well known to me, having all the qualities so far described and many others, were I to stop and enumerate them. This does not detract at all from the externality of the object. It is out there in time and space. My consciousness has not created it; it has made its own peculiar impressions upon me. But it is important to distinguish the object in consciousness from the combination of physical forces which produced that object in consciousness.

Hazarding repetition, more should be said about the qualities of conscious experience. It is evident from the discussion so far that the critical realist regards these qualities as separate and distinct from the external physical forces producing them in consciousness. They are certainly numerically distinct, and are probably also qualitatively distinct. That is to say that the physical patterns which produce qualities in our consciousness have a different identity from those qualities, and are probably quite different in their makeup from the counterparts which they produce in our consciousness. A probable example is the comparison of a given wave length of light and the quality of redness it gives us when refracted through our eyes, optic nerves, and brain. There are two different patterns, the wave length and the color; and these two different patterns are truly different.

A good many critical realists have accepted Santayana's doctrine of essences as a way of explaining the qualities of conscious experience which is harmonious with realism. According to this theory, there is a realm in which qualities *subsist* as well as a purely physical space-time realm in which objects and forces *exist*. This realm is the realm of *essences*, the qualities being called essences. According to this doctrine, the qualities of the consciously experienced tennis racket (returning to our figure) are neither dependent upon the external physical forces comprising the substratum of the object nor on the consciousness of the minded organism. They are independent essences which subsist in themselves; and when, for example, you take your tennis racket in hand, to juggle it or to start to play the game, these essences give content to your conscious experience so that the racket has a "feel," a weight, a balance, the strings a *ping*, etc.

It is at least evident that realists who are dualists in epistemology identify mind more closely with the organism than the neorealists do. Mind, for them, is not so much "out there" in the relation of organism and object as it is within the body. It is part and parcel with the brain and central nervous system. But fuller discussion of mind is more appropriate as a part of the section on the metaphysics of realism, which follows.

B. THE METAPHYSICS OF REALISM

There is great variety in the metaphysical beliefs of realists. There is so much variety, in fact, that realists could never be grouped together if they did not have certain common ground in epistemology. Though the whole gamut of beliefs from naturalism to some kind of theism is found among them, it may be possible to draw an outline of metaphysics in which a pattern can be discerned that is necessarily realistic, although there will be actually many variations on the pattern. Such an outline may be drawn by trying to answer such questions as the following: (1) How do realists believe generally about the number of final substances making up the cosmos? (2) How do they believe about freedom and necessity in the conduct of man? (3) What is their conception of mind? (4) What kind of description do they give us of the universe? And (5) do they believe in God?

1. PLURALISM

The tendency of most realists seems to be one of veering away from unity rather than one of finding unity in the universe. A number of realists are unashamed pluralists. Many are dualists. And a few are monists. Generally, they seem to inherit William James' reaction away from a "block universe." A pluralistic or at least a nonunified cosmos seems to them to give more elbowroom and liberates the human spirit from the feeling of cosmic stuffiness that may accompany monism.

For the pluralists it is not easy to say just what the many different substances or entities might be. Realists such as Morris R. Cohen and Bertrand Russell hold that the cosmos is made up of a number of entities having various relations to one another and various qualities. Dualisms are more easily defined, because the very recognition of a dualism suggests the character of the forces which are competing with each other in the world. Among realists there are dualisms of mind and matter or physical mechanism, and of good or God and evil. Durant Drake provides an example of monism in his belief that mind is not something separate and distinct from physical existence.

We might name a number of substances or processes in all of which a given realist might believe as existing ultimately and comprising the cosmos. He might accept physical or electrical energy as basic in the nature of things. He might also recognize mind as something which exists by itself and does not depend upon physical force. He might believe in certain laws or principles as ultimates in the universe, such as the law of gravity or the moral laws of the Ten Commandments. He might believe in God as a finite spirit working in this cosmos to bring greater good out of it. And he might also regard evil as a positively real, if unwanted, force in the world, working against God and the realization of individual and social goods. Such a hypothetical pluralism is definitely a straw man, but it is a real possibility within the pattern of realism, and is actually quite common at popular levels of thought.

2. DETERMINISM

In dealing with the problem of freedom versus necessity in individual living, realists are more commonly on the side of necessity than on that of freedom. Most realists hold to some form of determinism as a necessary alternative to the anything-can-happen kind of world which many of them feel is implied by the idea of free will.

As a rule, realists are strong in their respect for the orderliness, accuracy, and objectivity of science. Many of them hold that philosophy has no peculiar insights of its own and that its job is to generalize upon the findings of science. And it appears that the older physical sciences are relied upon with greater confidence than the newer biological and social sciences. Accordingly, there is a common tendency among realists to think of the world as a mechanism such as the physical sciences have commonly described.

Though the world is a pluralism, the operation of causes and effects is essential to its orderliness. The multiple forces interrelated in the universe can only have such effects on one another as are appropriate to the causative influences they exert. Therefore no single event just happens by chance; it is the only event which could have taken place, the forces immediately surrounding the event being what they were. Now the human individual is a part of this world of cause and effect, living within and not outside of it. Therefore, he can scarcely be regarded as possessing some sportive independence of the law of cause and effect, such as freedom of will.

However, the matter is not as coldly mechanical as this for many realists. Durant Drake, for example, is strong in opposing that form of belief in free will which regards causes for our actions as being at least partially absent, but he does assert that choosing and willing are facts of our experience. He recognizes our volitional impulses as causes of subsequent events. At the same time he recognizes limits which circumscribe the will, and holds that in any case the impulses to action are grounded in such causal influences as inherited disposition, past life, and environment. According to Samuel Alexander, although mind and consciousness are not independent of body and the space-time world, the conscious state immediately preceding a given act does participate as a cause in producing that act. States in consciousness are always accompanied by neural or bodily events, so an event in consciousness is never more than a cooperating cause in bringing about some act in the space-time world; but it is a cause.

J. B. Pratt is apparently an exception rather than an example of the common realist attitude toward will. He is clearly a realist in his epistemology, and he speaks of his own philosophy as personal realism; but in dealing with freedom and necessity, he places heaviest stress upon the self as the vital factor in conduct. In relation to action, the self is for him the central causal factor, interjecting itself into the observable world by the acts that it performs. Such a conception of the self and its freedom of action seems to be much closer to the idealist attitude toward freedom of the will than to the determinism more common among realists.

3. MIND

No doubt most realists accept William James' dictum, "no psychosis without neurosis." For according to them mental life is always rooted and grounded in bodily existence. Without embracing this position before examining it, we can recognize evidences in our experience tending to support this attitude toward mind. Many accidents suffered by the body also have their effect on the mind; also in periods of physical illness, mental energy may be somewhat depleted. When my body is laid low for a few days by influenza, my mind is not exactly equal to solving a difficult problem. Sometimes, as an antidote for drowsiness, I may drink some cold water, or take a brisk walk in the fresh air, in order to arouse myself and get sufficiently awake mentally to do the job before me. One teacher paces the floor in his office before class, smoking a cigar, to get himself toned up for his teaching job; others pick up a cup of coffee at the lunch counter on their way to class. Each one of us can draw a great many such examples from our own experience which evidence the intimacy of the relationship between mind and body.

Some realists, more than intimately relating mind and body, make mind itself a kind of relation which effectively joins the organism with the environment. Accordingly, mind is defined not as something different from the organism; it is conceived as one of the ways in which an organism acts, as a function, just as respiration and metabolism are functions. It is that particular kind of activity which may be described as interacting with or responding to the environment. There are a number of different ways in which objects or entities can be related to one another in the space-time world, and mind is one of these relationships. Objects, for example may be related numerically. Object x may be one of a group of three, x, y, and z. Objects may also be related in space; object x may be to the left of object y and to the right of z. And they may be related in time; x may come before y and follow z. In much the same way, if one of the objects is the kind of highly developed organism that has a complex nervous system, there can be a mind relation, which is really no different in quality, some realists say, from a number, time, or a space relation. Organism A can react to object x, or to x, y, and z, simultaneously, and may even have what we commonly call a consciousness of the objects to which it responds. In such a case, the relation is just one of the many kinds of relations possible in the space-time world, and what we call consciousness is simply an awareness of what is going on, which neither adds to nor detracts from the actual relation itself.

Bertrand Russell explains this view of mind by comparing it to the commonly recognized fact that objects or entities can coexist in the same instant of time. He points out that every event is related to a number of other events in such a way as to be "compresent" with them. They occur at the same instant or at such closely succeeding points in time as to be temporally connected with one another. Now mind, he says, is one example of such a set of compresent events. "The contents of one man's mind at one time—i.e., all his sensations, images, memories, thoughts, etc., which can coexist temporally" is a case of compresence.[1]

Other realists think of mind less in terms of the external relations of an organism and more in terms of the inner experience of the creature. For them, mind may be defined as the inside of the brain. In all the activity of a highly developed animal, there are highly complex neural processes going on. Psychology has revealed many of these processes, and has for example

---

[1] Bertrand Russell, "Logical Atomism," in J. H. Muirhead, *Contemporary British Philosophy*. First Series. London: George Allen and Unwin, 1924. P. 380.

identified certain areas of the human brain with different mental activities whose corresponding physical functions seem to take place in these respective areas. But however well the psychologist may refine his methods of study, he is likely never to be able to see these mental activities from the point of view of the subject who is experiencing them, except as he observes them in his own mind. This is the inside of the brain which some realists call mind. It is that aspect of behavior which only the experiencing subject beholds. "This mental life of an organism," Durant Drake says, "is the very substance of what, if it could be perceived from without, would be called its cerebral processes."[2] Roy Wood Sellars asks, "What prevents us, then, from holding that, in our consciousness, we are literally on the inside of the functioning brain-mind? As we discriminate in consciousness, so does our brain-mind discriminate and differently respond to situations."[3]

Still another conception of mind held by some realists, seeming to place it on a level definitely above pure physical activity, has it that mind is a distinctly new quality which has emerged in the evolutionary process. At any rate, mind and consciousness are taken pretty much at face value, it not being felt that they can be adequately explained by using physical terms and activities to do the job. Mind, as we see it in man, is a new quality, it is held, representing a level of existence clearly above or at least distinct from physical existents and relations. Mental activity probably does depend upon physical foundations, but there is quality at the mental level not present in the physical activity which corresponds to it. Subtract the conscious experience of the subject from a given piece of behavior, and it cannot be said that the behavior would be exactly the same as it was before the conscious experience was divorced from it.

There are at least two aspects of conscious mind which are made significant in this conception: the ability to unify experience and the function of enjoying or undergoing activities. Though his approach is different, drawing from experiments in psychology, Samuel Alexander shows how it is conscious mind which unifies our experience of our world, in much the same way that Kant made the very same point.[4] J. B. Pratt insists that if self is an evident fact of our experience, we must recognize it as such and not try to explain it away in the name of achieving a neat philosophic scheme. "If, therefore," he says, "a sound epistemology shows that such things as recognition and thought are meaningless unless there be a unifying subject or self, the only conclusion that can be drawn is that such a self

[2] Durant Drake, "The Philosophy of a Meliorist," in George P. Adams and William P. Montague, *Contemporary American Philosophy*. New York: The Macmillan Company, 1930. Vol. I, p. 287.

[3] Roy Wood Sellars, "Realism, Naturalism, and Humanism," in George P. Adams and William P. Montague, *op. cit.*, Vol. II, p. 279.

[4] Cf. Samuel Alexander, *Space, Time, and Deity*. London: Macmillan & Co., 1920. Vol. II, Chapter I.

does actually be."[5] In addition, according to Alexander, the experiencing subject shares quality in his experiences which is not at all to be found in the external relations or behavior in which the body is engaged. This is a matter of enjoying, or undergoing, it may be suffering, getting the "feel" of what is going on, and probably evaluating, at least implicitly, the desirability or lack of desirability attributed to the experience.

To summarize, three differing, but not completely different, conceptions of mind have been sketched by way of helping to suggest the realist pattern in metaphysics. The first is the more external view of mind as a relation of organisms and objects in the space-time world. The second is the description of mind as the subject's inside experience of behavior. And the third, which is probably more the exception than the example, is that mind and consciousness are unique as compared to physical things, almost spiritual in essence if not actually so.

4. The World

A certain orderliness in the universe is rather generally recognized. If we know where to look for the Big Dipper, we always find it in its regular place. The Greeks coined a word in their language for this apparent orderliness of the world. They called it *kosmos* to distinguish it from things which are in disorder or chaos. And this name came eventually to be synonymous for the totality of the universe.

Realists are for the most part agreed that the universe is a cosmos of a kind, orderly to the extent that order is possible within a plurality; but there is little else that they hold in common in their descriptions of the cosmos. There are as many and as wide variations in their beliefs about it as has already been seen in their descriptions of the number of ultimate substances, freedom, and mind. Some of these varying cosmologies will now be suggested, considering first the definitely physical and naturalistic descriptions and proceeding to those which are psychical or spiritual.

It is common for realists to describe the world in much the same way as naturalists. For many of them the world views of Democritus and Lucretius, among the ancients, and Herbert Spencer of the last century, are quite acceptable after being corrected in their detail so as to conform to the findings of present-day physics. No need is felt by them for some higher-than-natural factors in describing and explaining the total order of things. E. B. McGilvary, for example, sees little reason why the common-sense world of space and time doesn't tell us pretty much the story about the order of things. And, in a similar way, A. O. Lovejoy regards the space-time order governed by the laws of physics as the real order of things, "a

[5] J. B. Pratt, *Personal Realism.* New York: The Macmillan Company, 1937. P. 289.

matter
essences

single, public, spatial, or spatio-temporal order, in which the laws of physics hold good."[6]

Another cosmology which is naturalistic is Santayana's; but it has an aesthetic turn which distinguishes it and which also relates it closely to his critical realist epistemology. The qualities which represent the world to us in perception, according to critical realism, he calls essences. As already pointed out, these essences are neither dependent for their immediate existence upon the perceiving mind (idealism) nor on the external world (neorealism); instead, they subsist in themselves and comprise a realm of their own. The realm of essences is additional to the realm of existence or being, which physics describes for us, although ultimately dependent upon it. So there are at least two phases of the cosmos: the sphere of "the familiar pictures painted by the senses" [essences], and the realm of matter which "may be called gravity or an electric charge or a tension in an ether . . ." which will "continue to rejoice in its ancient ways, or to adopt new ones" [being].[7]

A. K. Rogers, also one of the critical realists, holds a naturalistic view of the cosmos but sketches in the social process in such a way as to indicate that Nature is not interested in the objectives for which man struggles. He sees the world as a community of persons activated by a number of concrete motives. He also sees it as a physical order comprising the stage for man's struggle to realize his purposes; but Nature is nothing more than a stage for the human drama, being little concerned whether it turns out well or ill in the end. "In any case it is a thoroughly real and substantial sort of world, which to all appearances would not be very much put out were the human race to vanish altogether."[8]

For Roy Wood Sellars the term naturalism best describes his conception of the cosmos. According to him, the world is completely self-sufficient, and whatever place mind has in it is not primary. But he does not compare Nature to a mechanism; rather he says it has ways more like those of an organism. The following principles represent this kind of world pretty well, as long as it is remembered that it is held that throughout Nature there is this vital element of change and development:

(1) the self-sufficiency of nature as against popular supernaturalism or the sublimated sort called transcendentalism; (2) the basic significance for our world of space, time, and causality; (3) the denial of concentrated control in

[6] A. O. Lovejoy, "A Temporalistic Realism," in George P. Adams and William P. Montague, *op. cit.*, Vol. II, p. 103.

[7] George Santayana, "Brief History of My Opinions," in George P. Adams and William P. Montague, *op. cit.*, pp. 254–255.

[8] A. K. Rogers, "Empiricism," in George P. Adams and William P. Montague, *op. cit.*, p. 228.

the universe and in this sense the acceptance of pluralism; and (4) the rejection of the primacy of mind.[9]

Recognition of a psychical or spiritual element is to be observed in the cosmologies of some other realists. C. A. Strong takes the position that physics, in abandoning the concept of matter, has made it all the more possible to believe that the substantial element comprising the substratum of all existence is something psychical in character. He further identifies this substance as feeling or emotion:

Since physics has abandoned the conception of matter as ultimate and substituted for it that of energy, without professing to explain what energy is in itself, and since the progress of my own thought has led me . . . to conceive feelings as not even necessarily coincident with the data of introspection, it seems to me that physics and my philosophy have been approaching the truth from opposite sides.[10]

On the outside, Strong holds, Nature is as physics describes it, energy; on the inside it is feeling or emotion.

J. B. Pratt, consistent with other tendencies toward the spiritual already noted in his philosophy, agrees with Sellars that the cosmos is much like a living organism. But the cosmic organism is a minded organism, he says, which is capable of conscious purposes, expressing these purposes in the universe much as human minds express their purposes in the actions of their bodies.

The causation that runs through it (the universe) is not the Newtonian push-and-pull, but something much more like the organic causation that one finds in living organisms.[11]

The facts of Emergent Evolution, therefore, seem to point toward the conclusion that the development of at least one part of the universe has been largely directed by conscious purpose.[12]

The second of these statements constitutes for Professor Pratt an "over-belief" or ultimate guess; but he holds that it is more probable than any other hypothesis that has been offered so far.

Much the same picture of the world is presented by Montague. There is a "mind-stuff" on the inside of the universe, he says, which is to the physical world what our minds are to our bodies. *"As our physical brains are to the conscious minds that throb within them, so is any material structure or particle to the 'mind-stuff' that must constitute its real and*

---

[9] Roy Wood Sellars, *op. cit.*, p. 274.

[10] C. A. Strong, "Nature and Mind," in George P. Adams and William P. Montague, *op. cit.*, p. 323.

[11] J. B. Pratt, *op. cit.*, pp. 360–361.

[12] *Ibid.*, p. 365.

inner nature."[13] By itself, Montague says, this hypothesis cannot make a very strong argument for acceptance. But when it is held by a physicist such as Eddington, and based on his own religious experience as well as inferences drawn from his science, then it takes on a richer significance.

5. GOD

Of the several different answers to the problem of God, it is likely that every one is upheld by some member in the family of realism. Since fuller discussion of this subject is offered in Chapter XV, at this point the realist attitude toward belief in God will only be considered briefly by way of indicating the realist pattern in metaphysics.

Of course, there are realists who are atheistic. Those who define mind in terms of matter or physical process, and who think of the cosmos in a thoroughly naturalistic sense, of course have no place for God in their metaphysics.

Those realists who define mind as the inside of nerve and brain activities, and regard the cosmos as having a similar parallel of inner and outer events, have an evident basis for a pantheistic conception of God. If the thing-in-itself on the inside of Nature is a Mind or Spirit, and the phenomenal world is the outside manifestation of this Spirit, the cosmos takes on a certain awe for the believer in this doctrine which may evoke worship.

William James introduced a novel idea in his polytheism or doctrine of a limited God, which has been taken up by some who have followed the realist tradition. James of course revolted against the "block universe" of absolute idealism, which seemed to him to leave no room for initiative. At the same time he found real values in religious experience, of which his book, *The Varieties of Religious Experience,*[14] gives ample evidence. So he wanted to think of God as a force for good in the cosmos who is Himself struggling with forces, the control of which is not already guaranteed, "a God down in the dirt." Evil is undeniably real and is one of these forces with which God struggles; but there may be others. The spice of living is in man's realization that by putting the weight of his life on the side of God he may be able to help God in determining the final outcome. Neither Pratt nor Montague, in whose philosophies the religious element is strong, feel that a polytheistic philosophy of religion or the doctrine of a finite God, such as this, will endure and command serious attention for long. But these ideas have had certain appeal recently and do fit in readily with the pluralistic tendencies of many realists.

Samuel Alexander has developed a unique doctrine, according to which

---

[13] William P. Montague, *The Ways of Things.* Englewood Cliffs, N.J.: Prentice-Hall, 1940. P. 293.
[14] New York: Longmans, Green & Co., 1916.

God is emerging by evolutionary process out of the space-time order. He believes that there are different levels of existence in the cosmos, each new level emerging out of the cosmos as previously developed to that point and representing a new and novel achievement. As has already been shown, Alexander believes in mind, as possessed by man, as being the last of these distinct and new levels of evolution. There are further levels of achievement to come, each as distinctive as the last, God being the totality of the cosmos plus all of the achievements toward which the evolutionary process is moving. Within Nature there is a yearning toward greater things, an urge toward fuller development, which together with the fulfillment of these goals constitutes God. To many scientific minds, who have felt it necessary to give up traditional conceptions of God, this conception seems to conserve the values of traditional theology, at the same time being in harmony with the findings of science.

Both J. B. Pratt and William P. Montague hold conceptions of God which are close to the traditional doctrines of Judaism and Christianity. Pratt calls his philosophy of religion Spiritual Pantheism; but by it he appears to connote more than pantheism. He intimately identifies God with Nature, as in pantheism; but he also thinks of God as a consciously purposing life.

> The purposiveness of this common life, manifested in all things, leads me to believe that it is a conscious life; and that the relation between it and the physical world is that intimate and unique relation which we find between our own conscious lives and our bodies.[15]

> God would thus be no invisible ruler to whom the cold processes of reason might point, but the warm and living whole, which we see with our eyes whenever we open them, and in which we live and move and have our being. The heavens declare the glory of God, for they *are* His glory. The firmament does not show His handiwork, but is itself, seen in the true light, very God of very God.[16]

Montague's definition of God is similar, although in it he sketches in the light and shadow of God's relation to evil. He rejects the idea of a God made finite by a force of evil in the world which is beyond His control and completely foreign to His nature. He feels that evil is within God as far as the geography of its existence is concerned; but it is different from God and therefore not of God. The implication is that God, while being the totality of all existence, is self-limited by the freedom which He allows to the individuals making up the cosmos, at least at the human level if not at other levels. This makes evil possible within God and yet are not essential to the nature of God or His purpose. The following is one representative statement of Montague's theism:

[15] J. B. Pratt, *op. cit.*, p. 375.
[16] *Ibid.*, p. 378.

The God that I believe to be most probable is infinite and eternal like the universe which is His body, all-perfect in Himself and in His will to good, but limited in power by that totality of possible and actual beings which is within Himself yet not Himself, and which in what we may call evolution is undergoing the endless leavening and perfecting that such an infinite chaos would require.[17]

C. THE LOGIC OF REALISM

In the general discussion of logic in the Introduction,[18] an outline of formal logic was sketched and it was indicated that there are some ways in which modern philosophers have felt that formal logic must be extended in order to be adequate as a science of knowledge. Most realists would insist upon these extensions.

However, there is also a high evaluation placed upon formal logic by them. Realism attaches great importance to relations which stand between entities, units, or parts making up the world of Nature and mind. There are spatial relations, temporal relations, numerical relations, and others. *There are also logical relations.* Now any science which deals with relations is important because it may give us a fuller understanding of them and help us in making our own adjustment to the world more effective. Since formal logic is one of these sciences, it is of great importance and value. It can give us an analytical knowledge of the ways in which ideas can be related effectively, and it can enable us to avoid falsehood and error in our thinking.

But in modern times the sciences which have inquired into the nature of the physical world have contributed vast content to our knowledge. They have not been so much concerned with formal logic as with material logic; they have not drawn their conclusions from premises rationally established, as is done by the use of the syllogism. In a scientific age, for example, it seems foolish to conclude that the planets move in circles because they are heavenly bodies, heavenly bodies being perfect and circles becomingly perfect orbits. Actually, science has shown that the orbits of planets are ellipses rather than circles.

Students of science make observations after tedious study of datum upon datum provided by the naked senses or scientific instruments augmenting the senses. Consequently science provides an important supplement to the formal logic of the syllogism. The science of drawing conclusions after identifying particulars with a given class about which something is known is valuable as long as the general statement comprising the major premise is true. But if it is not based on fact, all the rules of the syllogism are of no avail to bring truth out of the reasoning which follows from it. It is science

[17] William P. Montague, *op. cit.*, p. 123.
[18] Cf. pp. 27–28.

that can give us major premises which are actually based on fact, because it investigates the facts of the natural world.

But in addition to yielding important information to comprise the content of thinking, science has developed a technique which is an important supplement to the method of formal logic. As the syllogism has been the form in which thinking has been cast by way of examining its validity, scientific method has virtually become the form in which investigation is cast in order to guarantee its validity, and also in order to yield actual results in knowledge and the control of experience which probably would not be achieved without this method. The steps of the scientific method may be stated as follows. It may be of interest to compare them to the steps of the syllogism. They are:

1. Define the problem to be solved.
2. Observe all the factors relating to the problem.
3. Formulate a hypothesis or hypotheses which may meet all of these conditions and so solve the problem.
4. Test the hypotheses by putting them to work in controlled situations in which the problem factor is the only variable one.

It can be seen that for realism there is a logic of investigation as well as a logic of reasoning. The one functions largely at the level of sense perception; the other more especially at the conceptual level. Both are important in any effective adjustment to the real world and in any adequate control of our experience.

Montague suggests still other "ways of knowing" which have their contribution to make to the material of logic. (1) The accepting of authoritative statements of other people, he says, "must always remain the great and primary source of our information about other men's thoughts and about the past."[19] (2) Intuition, of the mystical sort, may also be a source of truth for us, but we should always be careful to put such knowledge to the test of nonintuitive methods before accepting it. (3) Particularly in the realm of practical or ethical matters, the pragmatic test, "how effective it is in practice," may be a valid source of truth. (4) And even skepticism also has its value in truth-seeking; it may not yield any positive truth for us but it can save us from cockiness and smugness, and help us to be tolerant and open-minded.[20]

Bertrand Russell, who came to philosophy by way of mathematics, has always held that particular science in high repute as an instrument of truth, as is the case with many other realists. He feels that traditional logic needs to be supplemented by the science of mathematics because of the inaccuracy and vagueness both of words and grammar. He thinks that if logical

[19] William P. Montague, *op. cit.*, p. 41.
[20] Cf. *ibid.*, pp. 40–51.

relations are to be stated accurately, they must be represented by mathematical symbols and equations; words are too bunglesome. *Principii Mathematica*,[21] in the writing of which Russell and Whitehead collaborated, is a large work which is written in mathematical equations entirely. The disadvantage of such a refinement in logic as it represents is that it makes illiterates of most of us; but that it may have the merit of greater accuracy than the logic of words is one of its likely virtues.

D. THE AXIOLOGY OF REALISM

Among realists there are at least two general theories of value: (1) that values are simple indefinable elements which are experienced for what they are when we experience them, and (2) that values are dependent upon the attitudes of the sentient beings experiencing them.

According to the first of these theories, those qualities of our experience which we prefer or desire, and to which we attach worth, have something about them which makes them preferable or desirable. For example, here is a young woman who takes a fancy to browns. She dresses in browns as much as she can; and she even buys brown-tinted stationery and uses brown ink. Now of course, it may be explained that because of her olive skin and dark complexion, browns "go well" with her coloring. But what do we mean by "going well" and how do we further explain that she is the one who is so strongly attracted to the color? Many people's tastes are for clothes and colors that, while looking well on someone else they have seen wearing them, do not look at all well on themselves. According to this first theory, the answer is that there is just something about browns that uniquely suits them not only to this young woman's coloring but also to her temperament.

But according to the second theory, the key to the evaluation is to be found in the interest which the young woman has in browns. There is a certain color quality of brownness which we frequently experience; but unless we have some special interest in it or disposition to be attracted by it, it has no special aesthetic value for us. It is because the young woman in question is especially disposed toward browns that they have the value for her that they do. And other people like to see her in browns because they have an interest in the harmony between brown and her coloring. There could be an interest in other harmonies or in contrasts which would favor other colors, and these would provide just as strong a basis for placing such a high value on them.

Professor G. E. Moore, a pioneer in modern British realism, is an exponent of the first of the theories of value we have stated; and Ralph

[21] Alfred North Whitehead and Bertrand Russell, *Principii Mathematica*. Cambridge, England: At the University Press, 1925–1927.

Barton Perry, author of a major work in axiology,[22] is an exponent of the interest theory. Superficially, at least, it is not difficult to recognize that the two theories could be united in a synthesis. This is done by George Santayana; for him values are simple indefinables, but our experience of them depends upon our interest in them.

Let us now consider some of the values possible to realists in the fields of ethics, aesthetics, religion, and social affairs.

1. ETHICAL VALUE

Montague may exemplify a realist approach to moral value, as long as it is remembered that his metaphysics grants the reality of the spiritual, whereas many realists are naturalistic in their metaphysical beliefs. Montague finds the ethics of John Stuart Mill to be quite acceptable; for him, the moral good can be defined from the vantage point of society as "the greatest happiness of the greatest number." Such a definition of the highest good, he believes, increases the power of moral imperatives, if anything; certainly it does not carry less weight than the imperative which might be stated as "you ought to do right because it is right." When there is a greater and more inclusive good to be realized for me as an individual as well a for society as a whole, the call to achieve that good is just as compelling as any Kantian categorical imperative.

But there is a question as to whether the good is to be defined in terms of happiness or virtue, or both. Montague finds fault with hedonism because in defining good as pleasure it overlooks the genuine value there is in virtue. He finds that both happiness and virtue are irreducible goods, and therefore that any theory of moral value must take full account of both of them.

On the side of happiness this much can be said: In the practice of morality, many of us have become so conditioned by foregoing the pleasures of the present in order to realize a greater good in the future that we have fallen too commonly into the ethical fallacy of assuming that there is value in the sheer repression of the desires of the moment. Such repression in itself is not a value; rather it is the greater good to be realized by it which is the value. It is frankly to be acknowledged that there is good in sensuous enjoyment; the point in repressing momentary desires is in making sure that the setting for the present enjoyment in question is in harmony with the greatest happiness both of myself and the society of which I am a part.

But this is not the whole story, because virtue is also a genuine value. For one thing, there is benefit in examining moral issues critically and thereby achieving a higher and fuller perspective than we could possibly enjoy by blindly satisfying our momentary urges as they arise. Also, if we believe

[22] *General Theory of Value.* **New York: Longmans, Green & Co., 1926.**

that the self is not a thing of the moment but that there is a future self (we hope a more fully developed self), we will recognize that we have obligations to that self, much as to the other selves of society, not to lessen its happiness by grasping present enjoyments. In other words, because there are *"permanent possibilities* of happiness they should take precedence over any transitory *actual* happiness which would corrupt them."[23]

But Montague feels that there is a way of harmonizing these two goods. Man, he says, has both a spiritual nature and sensory desires. Although the spiritual nature cannot be defined in terms of sensory desires, the converse is possible. Sensory desires are the momentarily *actual* expressions of spiritual nature; but they are only fractional as compared to the *permanent potentialities* of spiritual nature. So the dicta of conscience are not alien to our sensory nature; they are reminders of the greater magnitude of the self which is yet to be achieved. "Spirit is to be thought of as the *permanent potentiality* of desire; and sensory satisfaction as the temporary actualization of spiritual need. The one is to the other as the sphere is to the circle."[24]

2. AESTHETIC VALUE

There is a close relation between the refinement of perception and the ability to enjoy aesthetic values. Consider, for example, two people putting together a jigsaw puzzle. The one has crude perceptions; his clue to matching the pieces is the patterns made by the mechanic who cut the picture into the several hundred parts comprising the puzzle. First of all, he starts looking for pieces with straight edges because he can be pretty sure that they form the border. His companion, in contrast however, has more highly refined perceptions of color and visual pattern. He pays less attention to the shapes of the pieces of the puzzle; instead, he notices likenesses in colors and patterns in the picture which continue from one piece of the puzzle to another. While one of these kinds of visual perception may not be superior to the other, the person who has mastery of the greater variety of visual perceptions will no doubt have the greater proficiency in putting the puzzle together.

It is believed by some that much the same relation exists between the development of visual perceptions and the ability to appreciate the visual arts. Tests in art appreciation have been constructed which are based on this principle. Some allowance will no doubt have to be made for the person who just seems to enjoy a work of beauty without ever having given deliberate attention to the refinements of perception. Possibly such a person's perceptions have been developed unconsciously by peculiarly favorable influences, whereas most of us have to give effortful attention to such

---

[23] William P. Montague, *op. cit.,* p. 154.
[24] *Ibid.,* p. 598.

refinement. But nevertheless there does seem to be some connection between the two.

Apparently this would be Sellars' approach to the enjoyment of aesthetic value. He refuses to accept the kind of factualism according to which people regard their own tastes as final just as they actually are, saying, for example: "That's just the way I am, I just like this, and I just don't like that." The man who spurns good symphony music does it not because his tastes are different, but because he has failed to consider all that constitutes a symphony. He does not recognize the more subtle harmonies. He does not get the "feel" of such a rich and continuing flow of tones. He has not stopped to think of the painful struggles, or releases into raptures of joy, which may have been in the heart of the composer for years before being given expression in this music. Nor does he think of the many different instruments and the many different musicians making up the orchestra, nor of the many years they have devoted to music. Probably he has not observed the difference in quality between the brasses, the strings, the woodwinds, and the drums. Nor does he stop to think that there is a conductor directing the music who, in addition to being a master in his own right, is throwing himself heart and soul into the job of bringing out of the symphony just what he believes the composer wrote into it. Sellars believes that when people stop to consider such things as these in relation to any work of art, they cannot rationalize inferior tastes with a factualism that holds that our tastes are "just what they are, and that's that." The appreciation of beauty in the world is a good to be achieved only after our insights have been sufficiently refined to behold the subtle ways of beauty.[25]

Montague regards aesthetic value as the enjoyment resulting in experience when cognition and feeling blend. By cognition he apparently means all that has just been said about perception as related to the enjoyment of beauty. But he does not find the experience of beauty in the perception itself. It is when our recognition of the more subtle qualities of experience is accompanied by feelings somehow attached to those qualities that we enjoy aesthetic values.

By way of determining the worth of our tastes he suggests the following criterion: "The judgment that is based on the more inclusive experience is superior to one based on only a fragment of that experience."[26] Such a norm may be able to explain away the factualism in axiology which Sellars is concerned to refute. According to it, people who by circumstance or immaturity have been confined to a limited and fractional experience also have tastes that are less refined.

[25] Cf. Roy Wood Sellars, *The Philosophy of Physical Realism.* New York: The Macmillan Company, 1932. Pp. 451–452.
[26] William P. Montague, *op. cit.,* p. 128.

Montague also makes an appeal for an enlargement of art, which in itself may be a reflection of the realist temperament. He feels that beauty has been too narrowly conceived; value, he says, may be more properly termed the object of aesthetic appreciation and expression, because there are other kinds of aesthetic value in addition to beauty. Pleasure and joy are not the only emotions to be objectified in art. Broadly speaking, the objectification of any emotion is art. "Pain, sorrow, terror, horror, anger, cruelty, and even loathing and disgust, if they are adequately externalized or objectified, become things of aesthetic value."[27] Possibly Professor Montague would agree that most of the arts have now recognized this broader field of expression to be their province.

3. RELIGIOUS VALUE

One aspect of the relation of axiology and metaphysics can be seen by looking again at what has been said about realism and belief in God,[28] and then considering what religious values are possible to realist in the light of this. For those who do not believe in God, experience will not be rooted in a Divine Being whom we can worship, reverence, and in whom we can place our trust. Faith and hope will not have validity as religious attitudes because they will have no real object. Of course, if it is true that such values have no root in reality, it is well to know the truth, even so. But there are also realists who believe in God; and for them many traditional religious values are rooted in reality and therefore are valid.

First of all, we may look at some of the approximate religious values claimed by realists who are not theists. Santayana, as one example, finds consummate beauty in the liturgy of the Roman Catholic Church, although he does not find truth in the dogma of the Church. And Christopher Garnett holds that a person who does not believe in God may possess holiness as one of his values—a holiness which if he believed in God would be fused with divinity. By it Garnett means "seeing the values of human living steadily and as a whole," the root value from which ethical goodness, aesthetic beauty, and speculative wisdom are derived. It is especially to be discerned in the lives of great geniuses of human history who have been creators in morals, art, religion, and science. "The deepest expressions of holiness are found in the lives of the great religious teachers of mankind, Christ, the Buddha, Moses, Lao-tze, Confucius, and others."[29] There are other approximations of religious values which are possible to realists not believing in God. A person may follow Auguste Comte and believe in the Great Being which human society may constitute for him. There are many

[27] *Ibid.*, p. 138.

[28] Cf. pp. 281–283.

[29] Christopher Garnett, Jr., *The Quest for Wisdom.* New York: Appleton-Century-Crofts, 1942. P. 273.

people who have striven with a devotion quite as intent as religious devotion to bring about a society of man which will be free of the imperfections and injustices of our present world.

Close to this kind of devotion, but having more in common with religion as understood and practiced traditionally, is the religion of Samuel Alexander. God being the whole of the present universe plus its urge toward Deity, as he believes, there is basis for worship of a God who is real in the actual world of the present but who is also to be greater in the future. This metaphysics makes divinity possible as a value presently realized in a measure, but to be even more fully realized in the future. Holiness as defined by Garnett is a possible value for those who follow Alexander's line of thought.

Montague, as we have seen, believes in God as having both infinity and perfection as attributes; therefore divinity—man's experience of a relation to a Being greater than himself—is a bona fide value. As already explained, Montague finds evil present in the cosmos and therefore within God, but not of the essence of God. Explaining the actuality of evil in this way, he is free to see both the totality of existence and moral perfection united in God; and assuming such a metaphysics as a basis, divinity is a legitimate value in human experience.[30]

4. Social Value

It may be that there is more in common in the approaches made to social philosophy by naturalism and realism than would be expected, inasmuch as there are realists who are not naturalistic in their metaphysical beliefs. Two attitudes common to both may be mentioned. In the synopsis of the philosophy of naturalism, it was observed that for naturalists the physical universe is much more commonly the context of life and thought than is society.[31] This is also the case for most realists. Even in the case of the spiritual realist, for whom spiritual values are primary, the physical cosmos seems, even so, to loom up as the primary foundation of living, in preference to either the private personal experience of the individual (as in idealism) or social experience (as in idealism or pragmatism). The other attitude toward things social which many realists hold in common with naturalism is the emphasis on the individual as the basic unit of organization, in preference to conceiving society as an organism which has a unity and solidity of its own. The real world is such that it is broken up into individuals; and as far as human life is concerned, individual men are fundamental units. They are not fundamental necessarily because they are selves who are to be respected as such; even though for nonnaturalistic realists they may be all of this. But individuals are fundamental because

---

[30] Cf. William P. Montague, op. cit., Chapter VI.
[31] Cf. pp. 84–85.

there is no other unit which is so concretely and distinctly cut off as a unit. At the least, for the realist, whether he is a naturalist or a supernaturalist, the individual is an organism, a real body, about which there are no guesses, nothing hypothetical or theoretical. And if also a soul, as with spiritual realists, yet the body is very much the locus of all of the individual's acts, if not all of his thinking, feeling, and willing.

To the extent that it is correct to say realism is similar to naturalism in these ways, the approach to social value of realism proceeds from the assumption that however important social values are, the foundations of their existence are the physical universe and individual man. For the social process depends upon these two fundamentals and does not have its own basis for existence in itself.

As to social phenomena themselves, realists are likely to be quite "realistic" in making allowance for things as they actually are. This is one point at which realism as a technical philosophy may blend into what is popularly understood as being realistic. Accordingly, there is not as much disposition on the part of realists to judge actual social conditions by the ideal as in idealism. It is not strange to realists, for example, that individual men commonly need to be prompted to desired action by incentives, and more specifically that mercenary gain will move them to action where the vision of an ideal will not. Since individual men are distinct individual units, since they are physical organisms at least, and since they have to live by bread and either sink or swim in the economic stream in proportion to their own enterprise, what else should we expect? It is only "natural" that money is as powerful as it is in moving men to action. It follows then that if any social group, local or more inclusive, is to organize itself so that positive social benefits are to be enjoyed by the group as a whole, it must hold out real incentives to individual men and not depend only on the power of an ideal to sell itself.

The method of realizing social values will not rely heavily, therefore, on the personal power and inspiration of great leaders, nor will its central theme be the relating of parts and wholes, as in idealism. It will be reliance upon effective mechanisms of relationship and organization. Discover those incentives which will evoke from individual people the kind of activities which are desired of them, and build community organization, at any level, which makes use of these incentives, and the result will be the desired social relationships. Social value will result when it is determined what the desired social values are, when real incentives are recognized which will make people act in the direction of these values, and when mechanics of social organization are used which are real—real because they are based on real incentives. This is a formula of social value which is true to the pattern of realism, although there are no doubt many and wide variations on the pattern.

A sketch of the history of the philosophy of realism and a systematic synopsis of the point of view having now been completed, the next step in the pattern of treatment follows. Accordingly, the next two chapters look to the practice of realism in education and religion. A third is appended, dealing with Neo-Scholasticism, and indicating what the significant variation on the pattern of realistic philosophy is to which many Roman Catholic thinkers subscribe.

XIV

Realism in Education

A. *Education as a Social Institution*

B. *The Pupil*

C. *The Objectives of Education*

D. *The Educative Process*

What kind of program of education results when the philosophy of realism determines the educational policies? This is the question now before us as we turn our attention to this important area of human endeavor and look at it with the eyes of a realist. Before discussing realistic practice in education in some detail, we should notice that not all educational practice which corresponds with realism is the conscious expression of a realist philosophy of education. Some educators are conscious of their realism and are deliberate exponents of it. Many others, however, follow realist practices without having considered the philosophic implications which may be implicit in their professional activities. Possibly the present analysis may be of help to this second group by providing them a basis for comparing their professional practice with their more inclusive beliefs about life and reality. However that may be, as far as this analysis is concerned, we shall include in the discussion such educational policy as follows from the tenets of realism, whether the exponents of given policies evidence awareness of affiliation with realism or not.

The cause of realism as a philosophy of education has been greatly advanced in recent years by the scholarship of the present generation of realist educational philosophers. Two decades ago, students who sought to discover the explicit meaning of realism in education had to turn to the writings of nonrealist educational philosophers. But this is not now the case. Professor Harry Broudy's book, *Building a Philosophy of Education*,[1] published in 1954, is a full and complete philosophy of education written by a committed realist. It is certainly the first major work in realist educational philosophy since Herbart's *Science of Education* (1806). Since it is a more comprehensive work than any of Herbart's, it may not be an exaggeration to declare it the chief writing on realism in education since the *Great Didactic* of Comenius (1632).

A. EDUCATION AS A SOCIAL INSTITUTION

In accordance with the pattern which has been followed so far in this book, the first concern in analyzing realism as a philosophy of education is to see in what way the rationale of the school is conceived by realists. What is the reason for existence of the school? Why need education be formalized as a social institution? And what are the distinctively realist answers to these questions?

John Amos Comenius[2] in his *Great Didactic* describes the unique function of the school in a manner which will symbolize modern realism even though he wrote in the seventeenth century, long before the school became a universal institution. He said that man is not made a man only by his biological birth. If he is to be made a man, human culture must give direction and form to his basic potentialities. This necessity of the school for the making of man was made vivid for Comenius by reports which had come to him of children who had been reared from infancy by animals. As has become common knowledge in our own century because of other more recent observations, we know that children reared by animals take on patterns of living which are like those of animals even though they have human potentialities. They walk on their hands as well as their feet; they gnaw and tear food with their mouths; they snarl and howl like the particular animals with which they had lived, and do not use words until they are taught them by other men. The recognition of this by Comenius caused him to consider the education of men by men just as essential to man's birth, as a human creature, as is procreation. He therefore defined education as formation and went so far as to call the school "a true forging place of men."[3]

[1] Englewood Cliffs, N.J.: Prentice-Hall.

[2] Cf. pp. 252–253.

[3] John Amos Comenius, *The Great Didactic*. Translated and edited by M. W. Keatinge; London: A. & C. Black, 1907. Part II, p. 228.

John Wild has stated virtually this same conception of the school in the mid-twentieth century although in somewhat more refined form. He asserts that human group life as well as much that is distinctly human is not inherited by the new generation but is learned and preserved only by education. The tendencies we inherit by birth, he says, are indeterminate, and flexible. They lend themselves therefore to further determination and direction. This task of determination and direction of man's inherited tendencies is in large measure the task of the school. Furthermore, it is an urgent necessity of human society if disaster is to be avoided. Accordingly, education is both a basic need and a basic right of man. It is the essential duty of any society to make sure that all children born within it are properly educated. Among all the basic rights, the right to be educated is "the most precious and the most in need of adequate realization."[4]

Harry Broudy conceives the school as having essentially this same function, but in his book, *Building a Philosophy of Education*,[5] he deals most explicitly with the relation between education and government, pointing out the area in which education is dependent upon government and the areas in which it is autonomous. He insists that regardless of the type of government a society may have, it will necessarily bring formal education under its jurisdiction because it is a social institution which is affected by, at the same time that it has an effect upon, all other institutions. There is, however, a division of labor in society, one of the reasons social institutions come into existence. Each social institution has some unique role to play, a duty that no other institution can discharge. In this orbit of its unique role each institution has a degree of autonomy. Specifically for education, if certain conditions are fulfilled by it, it has the prerogative to speak with authority concerning its own unique affairs and should not seek guidance from government or from any other institution in these matters. The function of the profession of education in matters uniquely educational is that of guide, not of the guided. The conditions which must be fulfilled in order for educators to have such authority are these: Education must possess a body of tested knowledge and its practitioners must base their art on this knowledge. These conditions being supplied, education as a profession can claim to be the final arbiter as to what is to be taught (curriculum), as to how the teaching should be done (method), as to the organization of the school system (administration), and as to the qualifications of those who shall be permitted to teach at any level of instruction. This argument advanced by Broudy concerning the authority of education is based on a distinctively realistic assumption about knowledge, i.e., that

---

[4] Cf. John Wild, "Education and Human Society: A Realistic View," in Nelson B. Henry (editor), *Modern Philosophies and Education.* Chicago: University of Chicago Press, 1955. Pp. 37–41.

[5] Harry Broudy, *op. cit.*

the science of education is a body of knowledge which belongs to a profession and is no more the possession of all of the people than is the science of medicine.[6]

Catholic realists, while not as explicit about the reason for existence of the school, are concerned to make clear that human authority cannot be the sole controlling power of the schools. Jacques Maritain upholds the right of the body politic to promote among its citizens through education a common creed as it were on which "national communion and civil peace can depend," but he makes clear that this common creed is both human and temporal, essentially practical; it is not a consensus concerning ultimate values and meanings.[7]

John D. Redden and Francis A. Ryan insist that the state is only one of the societies which have something to say concerning education. The Church is another of these societies and it therefore denies the State total control of education. The school's chief purpose is "to further, through instruction, discipline, and pupil activity, the development of . . . physical, social, mental, and moral training." The home cannot delegate these functions completely to the school, nor can the Church abdicate its role in determining the character of these processes.[8]

B. THE PUPIL

The second concern in this analysis of realist educational philosophy is the human material to be educated. Apart from scientific description of him, and possibly in addition to it, what is the nature of the pupil? What is his essential makeup and what does it imply that education should do for him?

There are two doctrines in the philosophy of realism as presented in Chapter XIII which have implications for the realist teacher's understanding of his pupils. These are the doctrines of mind and of determinism. If mind, as some realists hold, is a kind of relation between objects, at least one of which happens to have a highly developed nervous system, then the pupil is to be defined as an organism with a highly developed brain. He is superior to other objects in the space-time world by virtue of the fact that he is able to relate objects to one another in the little segment of space-time of which he can be conscious. Apparently inanimate objects do not do this and animals do not do it as effectively as children. The teacher by whom

---

[6] Cf. *ibid.*, pp. 97–101.

[7] Cf. Jacques Maritain, "Thomist Views on Education," in Nelson B. Henry, *op. cit.*, pp. 72–77.

[8] Cf. John D. Redden and Francis A. Ryan, *A Catholic Philosophy of Education.* Milwaukee: The Bruce Publishing Company, 1942. Pp. 116–119.

this conception of mind is preferred will look at his students as organisms engaged in the age-old task of effecting appropriate relationships in the space-time world.

A realist educator may, however, define mind as the inside of the brain and attribute a certain degree of privacy to individual minds.[9] He may go further in approximating a spiritual conception of the pupil and still be consistent with some realist philosophers.[10] He may define mind as a unique thing, distinct at least in quality from bodily existence, which unifies experience, enjoys (or suffers, as the case may be) the things it undergoes, and consciously projects purposes into the world. With such a conception of mind as a part of his educational philosophy the teacher will regard his pupils as selves who can enter into the meanings of their experiences, conceive purposes, and in a measure realize these purposes in their activities.

There is yet the problem of the initiative of the pupil. Is he free, capable of developing a control over his environment? Or is he so much the product of heredity and environment that his actions are already determined for him? And what difference does the answers to these questions make in the teacher's attitude toward the pupil?

If a teacher accepts the rather complete determinism of some realists,[11] he will not consistently deal with his pupils as though they are free. One of the chief tasks of education, as such a teacher will view his job, is to help pupils to recognize the irresistible necessity of the physical forces making up the world. To help in achieving such a recognition, and adjusting one's living so as to go with the stream of these cosmic forces, will be the important thing instead of struggling futilely and punily against them. The attaining of such a resigned peace will be one of the chief values of life.

If, however, a teacher accepts the modified determinism of Durant Drake[12] or what would seem to be the self-determinism of J. B. Pratt,[13] his conception of the pupil is quite different. In the first case, he will want his charges to recognize the causative forces at work in the world, over which they have no control, but he will also wish to develop the initiative of the individual boy and girl so that they will achieve the ability to control their experience to the extent that such control is possible. In the latter case, even greater stress will be placed upon the development of the purposing power and volitional activity of pupils. For this will be regarded as the genius of personal life, and it will be the chief task of education to develop this genius.

[9] Cf. pp. 276–277.
[10] Cf. pp. 277–278.
[11] Cf. pp. 274–275.
[12] Cf. p. 275.
[13] Cf. p. 275.

Since the appearance of Professor Broudy's book, *Building a Philosophy of Education*, we need no longer depend on inferences such as these from realist philosophy to the nature of the human material with which education deals, or what at best was the casual thinking of realist philosophers concerning the pupil. Instead, in Dr. Broudy's chapter on "The Structure and Dynamics of Personality," there is a very adequate and significant statement by a realist educator on which we will draw for the major portion of this section. Broudy describes the pupil by elaborating four principles which, according to him, comprise the essence of the human self. These are the appetitive principle, the principle of self-determination, the principle of self-realization, and the principle of self-integration.

The appetitive principle, mentioned first, has to do with the physiological base of personality. Our appetites disclose the need of our tissues to maintain and reproduce themselves. Physiological life, and therefore the life of personality, can not go on unless these necessary tissue needs are supplied. In order for us to do anything about our tissue needs, except on an animal level, we must be aware of them; and in being aware of them, we realize that pleasure and pain are central. Furthermore, our tissues retain afterimages of pleasures and pains beyond the moment of their immediate occurrence. Since we relate these feelings to the events with which they occur we become conditioned by them and there is a kind of "knitting together" of what were formerly separate elements leading us to avoid the painful and seek the pleasurable. Because of this, in part at least, our desires become attached not only to tissue needs but also to the "signs and symbols of their satisfaction."[14]

It turns out then, even when we begin at the physiological level, that all desires are not necessary desires; their objects are not always the direct and urgent satisfaction of bodily needs. Many of them have their roots instead in the meanings accompanying tissue needs and their satisfaction. Because of this, a large majority of our desires are borrowed from the culture in which we live and have the "labels 'desirable' and 'undesirable' "[15] fastened upon them by the culture. They do not therefore automatically organize themselves into a life which is good, because desire by itself does not enable us to distinguish between real needs and "felt" needs.

This is educationally important. If teaching always begins with the problems of the learner, or felt needs, it may miss completely the *real* needs of the learner. For the object to which the feeling of need may be attached is not necessarily the real need with which the learner must cope. Learning must be guided by other aspects of personality in order to be related to the real and the good.

Some of this further light is shed by the principle of self-determination.

[14] Harry Broudy, *op. cit.*, p. 58.
[15] *Ibid.*, p. 59.

Another fact of our experience somewhat comparable to tissue needs, is the resistance which the self meets in people, objects, and events. Were it not for this resistance, it is doubtful if any self would ever be distinguished from its environment. By way of finding ourselves we soon discover that there are "powers that we cannot budge by the power of our command."[16] While one discovery I make is that "there is an I which has desires and satisfactions and pains,"[17] another is that there are "I's who behave in a similar way, and there are Its who behave still differently from the I's."[18]

The self has continuity, formal structure, antecedents in the past, and a yearning toward the future. Our experience has some continuity throughout changing events and places; and in order to explain this we must recognize that the self is a common factor in all of these experiences, even though there are gaps in consciousness such as when we are asleep or under anesthesia. The self has form as well as continuity. While "it is not a hard bit of something,"[19] it does have a pattern of activity rather commonly denoted by the term "human nature." Any actual individual self at a given point in its history is the result of its total history to that point. But this historical reference of the self has a prospect in the future as well as a retrospect in the past. For the self is a "straining toward the future"[20] in addition to being a result of its past. Furthermore it is aware of this living toward the future—so much so that it can be said also that the self is its "envisioned possibilities."[21]

To view these characteristics of the self makes clear how central to selfhood freedom of the will is. Resistance at the physiological level might well be called frustration of desire; but resistance at the psychological level is seen more clearly to be frustration of the will. Freedom of the will is not the ability to do anything which is desired; it is rather freedom "to carry out our thought-out decisions."[22] This is the first right of man and a man cannot sacrifice it without ceasing to be a man. Our loss of self-determination is not always by stealth, by having someone else take it away from us. We lose it frequently by default—by lack of diligence or by escape when we fall away into the lethargy of habit, conformity, or indulgence. Freedom is fashioned, therefore, not by desire alone but by "desires as weighed and chosen by a thinking Self."[23] As for determinism, rationality requires that we recognize the validity and dependability of cause-and-effect relations; but we do not need to hold to determinism with the meaning that "all of

---

[16] *Ibid.*, p. 63.
[17] *Loc. cit.*
[18] *Ibid.*, pp. 63–64.
[19] *Ibid.*, p. 65.
[20] *Ibid.*, p. 66.
[21] *Loc. cit.*
[22] *Ibid.*, p. 68.
[23] *Ibid.*, p. 69.

our experience is the result of physical forces."[24] Our power to symbolize is one element of our experience that does not bear out the truth of this kind of determinism.

By far the greater proportion of our human activity takes place in terms of meanings and not in terms of events. Further, meanings can be manipulated and combined, while events cannot be. Also, "events act on each other, but events do not mean each other."[25] How meanings and events get together in consciousness is the problem of epistemology; but the fact is that they do get together and this is "of crucial importance to the structure of human personality."[26] This meeting of events and meanings in consciousness is one of the important conditions of human freedom. For our freedom is more precisely the "possibility of varying our responses to forces that we do *not* control."[27] It is more accurately denoted as "reflective freedom" as compared to "natural freedom." In part the great importance of education can be seen in that our freedom is reflective, because such freedom needs knowledge. In order to be reflectively free we need knowledge from the various disciplines which will show us the ways meanings can be handled. While such knowledge should not be permitted to close the door to further experimentation, it will eliminate for us a good bit of wasted motion in covering ground which the race has surveyed before us, sometimes with a great amount of care.

The third principle of selfhood, self-realization, supplements freedom as such with value concerns. Freedom does not carry built-in guarantees that it will be turned to good ends. In order to be freedom it "must be free to make us miserable."[28] The *how* of choosing, as well as the *what* which is chosen, is a necessary ingredient of the good life. If we are sad today in our modern cultures and civilizations, sometimes having nostalgia for the innocence and simplicity of primitive life, it is because we have paid in some great measure for our cultural achievements. We have lost our innocence and paid the price of "toil, suffering, and even neurosis,"[29] for literature, art, science, and philosophy. But once having tasted the flavor and value of these, we cannot forget them.

"The power to become a Self"[30] is among the generic powers of value realization which we inherit in varying degrees as individuals. The potentiality for selfhood in a particular degree is one of the givens with which each of us must begin. The content for this self-realization, while its form comes from our human nature, must come from the culture. It is the

[24] *Ibid.*, p. 71.
[25] *Loc. cit.*
[26] *Ibid.*, p. 73.
[27] *Ibid.*, p. 72.
[28] *Ibid.*, p. 78.
[29] *Ibid.*, p. 79.
[30] *Ibid.*, p. 80.

educational provisions of a culture which must bring the potentiality for selfhood and its content together. If the gap between the two remains wide, it is because "the educational arrangements of a culture are inadequate to close it."[31]

Self-realization should not be regarded as the striving of perfectionism, which has a far-off goal of transcendent perfection as its objective. Instead, its goal is a present functioning of "self-perfecting" continuing through each moment of our living, as long as there is "systematic use of our thinking."[32] Nor is self-realization an individualistic concern. The duty of self-realization is social as well as individual. It carries with it the imperative that there must be realization for all human selves.

The fourth and final principle which depicts the nature of the pupil is the principle of self-integration. It is the principle in selfhood which keeps self-determination and self-realization from going off in all directions. There is something exclusive about values; to realize some of them eliminates the possiblity of realizing others. Furthermore, effort is involved, in most cases sustained effort, which means that the self must be applied wholly and with commitment. When there is wholeness of self there is a criterion for determining which desire is compatible with the self, among all the possibilities. When there is no wholeness, such a judgment cannot be made.

Of course, strictly speaking, it is not correct to speak of integrating the self, because the self is by its very nature a unifying principle. It is a central function of the self to unify. Integration is "the unifying of many selves with one personality."[33] There is a tendency in Nature for entities to cluster together; the same is true of our experience. Similarities and differences are factors in this clustering. Irritation frequently results, because sometimes items of experience do not easily match any cluster or grouping. These items may get lost, overcome as it were by clusters which submerge them; on the other hand, such strange items are sometimes sufficiently unique and disturbing to transform the cluster in which they are lodged. These groupings of items in experience can, of course, become so disconnected from each other as to break the unity of the self and comprise virtually separate selves. Such nearly autonomous constellations are common in normal personal life, while the more extreme development of this phenomenon is the abnormal multiple personality.

The final consideration here is the source of patterns of integration to which the self can turn for help. The social order is one of these. In dependence upon society one of the normal supplements of the self can be found; but there is also a great danger in this. Whereas integration may be achieved by borrowing patterns of order from society, as in conformity, yet

[31] *Ibid.*, p. 81.
[32] *Ibid.*, p. 85.
[33] *Ibid.*, p. 87.

this may amount to complete violation of self-determinaton, since the integration which comes to pass is not achieved *by* the self.

Another possible source of order is long-range purpose. In attachment to purposes, self-determination is in full flower, but of course there are great hazards, hazards which may be implicit and necessary to human life. "Great purposes are neither inborn or very common,"[34] and they always must be questioned. Are they worthy of our devotion? And are my particular abilities suited for such a devotion? Regarding both of these questions, there is ample evidence in our experience that we can easily make mistaken judgments.

Catholic realism may be able to accept in modified form much of Broudy's conception of the self. While being as much concerned to include in its view of man his appetites and his rationality, it is also positively supernatural in its understanding of man and finds the effects of his original sin to be a perennial problem.[35]

Professors John D. Redden and Francis A. Ryan in their book, *A Catholic Philosophy of Education*,[36] assert that, while the child is intended to be socially useful and to enjoy temporal happiness, what is more significant is that he has a supernatural destiny. They quote from Pius XI to make it clear from indisputable authority that the learner is

. . . man whole and entire, soul united to body in unity of nature, . . . fallen from his original estate, but redeemed by Christ and restored to the supernatural condition of adopted son of God, though without the preternatural privileges of bodily immortality or perfect control of appetite.[37]

Temporally, man has a dual nature; i.e., he is both body and soul. But he "is not body alone, nor soul alone, but body and soul united in substantial union."[38] There is an important implication for child development and education in this unity within duality. That is that since

. . . all constituent capacities of the child must blend into an integrated totality to form one individual, one character, one personality, who responds as a unit from free choice, they cannot and do not develop separately but simultaneously.[39]

Original sin must be fully considered in accordance with the teaching of the Roman Catholic Church if any conception of the pupil is to be true and adequate. What must be recognized is that "original sin deprived man of

---

[34] *Ibid.*, p. 90.
[35] For a fuller statement see Chapter XVI, "Neo-Scholasticism," Section D, "The Nature of Man."
[36] *Op. cit.*
[37] As quoted by John D. Redden and Francis A. Ryan, *op. cit.*, p. 144, from Pius XI, *The Christian Education of Youth*. New York: The American Press, 1936.
[38] John D. Redden and Francis A. Ryan, *op. cit.*, p. 144.
[39] *Loc. cit.*

preternatural privileges, bodily immortality and perfect control of his desires."[40] This is not the same as saying, as some Protestant traditions have taught, that man is totally depraved and essentially sinful in all of his acts. Man has been redeemed from his original sin, and it is its effects which persist in man, not original sin itself. These effects are marks of deprivation still left upon man. Consequently, he is "less able to attain truth," is "less able to seek good," and is "more inclined to evil." In baptism man's soul can be "cleansed of original sin itself" but these defects remain. They can be corrected only by "the enlightening of the intellect and the strengthening of the will through discipline and training."[41]

Before bringing to an end this section on the nature of the pupil, and in the two remaining parts of this chapter as well, attention will be given to some conceptions implicit in education in Soviet Russia. It is important to see as clearly as possible the continuity between social theories and educational philosophies. In cases where affinities can be recognized between a political system and a particular philosophy of education, these should be pointed out. The student has become acquainted by now with the remarkable differences among realists at the same time that there is common ground among them, particularly in stressing the objectivity of knowledge. There is naturalistic realism, there is spiritual realism, and there is Roman Catholic realism. While it would be inappropriate to use the term "communistic realism" to designate it, there is nevertheless in the philosophy of communism the same stress on objectivity of knowledge found among realists with other political and religious loyalties.

Educational theory in Soviet Russia views the individual child in terms of the collective life of which he is a part. The official philosophy of Soviet Russia is dialectical materialism,[42] and the educational policies which have been deliberately formulated by educational leaders in Russia follow logically from the doctrines of dialectical materialism. The intention is to educate children within an intellectual environment which is purely naturalistic, by interpreting every area of thought and experience by means of scientific explanations. The individual students who are the recipients of this education are necessarily viewed within this same naturalistic setting. They are not therefore partakers of a spiritual order; they are segments of a materialistic process. But the collective life of communism is more in the foreground of this conception of the pupil than this bold general statement of it makes evident. In the first place, it might be somewhat out of harmony with the pattern of communistic thought to try to define the nature of the pupil in individual terms, as we are doing. For in the outlook of communism the community is primary, virtually taking the place of the

[40] *Ibid.*, p. 145.
[41] *Loc. cit.*
[42] Cf. pp. 139, 184.

individual. It is contended, however, that this emphasis does not destroy individuality, because while the community is the primary concern, it still must be built of individuals, and a high type of society can only be achieved when the individuals comprising it are highly developed.[43] The primary importance of the community has a significant place in the psychology of childhood, for example. It is held by Soviet educators that the nature of the child is such that he needs to be complemented by collective life. Because the child lacks knowledge and experience, he needs the help of society in order to act wisely. He needs the help of society in making decisions and forming judgments, except in the simplest and most elementary matters. Because of his immaturity and lack of development, he needs the ordered patterns of society as a setting in which to grow and mature, in order that he shall experience the security which is one of his prime psychological needs.[44] Furthermore, the nature of education when set within a communistic society makes it necessary that the collective emphasis be very strong, as compared with attention to the individual, if the objectives of a communistic society are to be realized by its education. This balance between individual and collective emphases is described as follows by B. P. Yesipov and N. K. Goncharov:

> To educate a member of our Soviet society means to educate a person who understands the interests of this society and who has no personal interests opposed to the collective interests. With us there are no contradictions between individuality and society. But while we are desirous of cultivating in pupils the spirit of collectivism, we pay due attention to the personal tendencies, needs, and interests of each child. The education of the individual pupil proceeds through the collective, and the collective grows and becomes stronger through the education of each of its members.[45]

C. THE OBJECTIVES OF EDUCATION

Some angles of a realist approach to the formulation of the objectives of education have already been implied in the systematic synopsis of realism. Axiology parallels the study of education's objectives; for our theory of value, and our decision as to what the values of life are specifically, will determine to a great extent the objectives we set for ourselves in education. Consequently, ethics, aesthetics, philosophy of religion, and beliefs as to

[43] Cf. Beatrice King, *Changing Man: The Education System of the U.S.S.R.* London: Victor Gollancz, 1936. Pp. 27–28.

[44] Cf. Beatrice King, *Russia Goes to School*. London: Published for The New Education Book Club by William Heinemann, Ltd., 1948. Pp. 32–33.

[45] *I Want to Be Like Stalin*. Translated by George S. Counts and Nucia P. Lodge from the Russian text on pedagogy by B. P. Yesipov and N. K. Goncharov. New York: The John Day Company, 1947. Pp. 37–38.

what the economic, political, social, utilitarian, and other values are will point the way to objectives in education.

If a student of education embraces a theory of ethics like that of Montague, briefly outlined in Chapter XIII,[46] he will probably want to control his practice of education in such a way as to bring his students to the enjoyment of the values this theory secures. He will want to bring out in them the ability to enjoy fully the pleasures of life when circumstances make such present enjoyments appropriate. But he will also want to give them the self-control by which to repress their desires and forego present pleasures when their own greatest self-realization and the welfare of others dictate that present pleasure should be sacrificed to a future which is fuller.

Similarly, in regard to aesthetic values, should a teacher feel that they are only to be possessed to the extent that perceptions are refined and experience is enlarged,[47] then he will try to open the way to possession of such values for those whom he teaches, by leading them in activities which will sharpen perception and broaden experience.

In the same manner, the teacher's theory of religious values will affect his objectives for the religious experience of his pupils, though they may never be made explicit in the classroom. If he does not believe in God but nevertheless feels that a totality of perspective is a desirable quality in human experience, he will not be content if his pupils fail to realize this value. If he feels that this totality of perspective ought to take the form of devotion to society and the building of a better world, he will scarcely avoid inspiring this in the children by unconscious tuition, should he refrain from direct inculcation of this belief. But should he believe in God, in the way in which Montague does, for example, he will no doubt cling to divinity as one of the supreme values of life. Accordingly, he will desire for his pupils that they come to feel that at the heart of reality is divinity in which they are rooted and grounded, One whom they can trust implicitly and toward whom worship is the normal and appropriate expression.

The same logic will hold for all the other values to which a given educator may cling; they will somehow find their place in his objectives as a professional man. If freedom from want is a bona fide economic value for every man, and if constructive participation in communal life is a genuine social value, to cite only two other types of value, then these will become educational objectives, somewhere tied into the envisioned end toward which educational activity is directed.

Again, however, in this section we turn to Professor Broudy for our chief example of educational objectives as formulated by an avowed realist educator. Chapter 2 of his book, *Building a Philosophy of Education,* is

[46] Cf. pp. 286–287.
[47] Cf. pp. 287–289.

concerned entirely with aims in education. In approaching the formulation of aims, Dr. Broudy recognizes that there are different levels at which aims are held in the school, and because of this he questions whether there can be common aims for education. Aims are the possession of the person who consciously holds them for himself. Consequently, the pupil may have his aims, the teacher his, the parents theirs, the administrators theirs, the members of the school board theirs, newspaper editors theirs, political leaders theirs, and so on. Need there be any wonder that we have confusion of educational aims when they are considered only at the level of that which is desired by each one who plays a role in the school or in relation to it?

Discussion of aims can be somewhat more fruitful when it is guided by some effort to transcend the particularity of these various roles and possibly to find in them a common object desired by all. One of the most important educational reforms of our times has embraced such an effort to get beyond the discrepancies between the various roles in the educational enterprise. This has been the concern of those who generally might be called progressive educators to underscore the importance of the "felt needs" of the learner. If learning must begin, as they have insisted, with the "felt needs" of those who are to learn, then we have a fundamental focus for educational aims which is more basic than the objectives each of us holds from the vantage point of his own particular role in education. But it has already been made clear by Broudy's conception of the pupil that in his judgment a dependable clue to educational objectives is not to be found here. "Felt needs" and real needs, he insists, are not necessarily identical, and it is therefore possible to miss the point of education entirely if we make "felt needs" our guide. Of course such experienced desires may be made a means to the discovery and fulfillment of real needs; but this is something quite different.

Broudy proposes instead the possibility that an objective fundamental to the desires of all may be found in the good life. This is to assume that every choice which a man makes intends the good life, however mistakenly, "for no one knowingly chooses evil."[48] The really big question of course is "whether we can discern any general features of life which we can say will make life good for any man."[49] The concept of the good life is social as well as individual; the good society can not be defined without reference to the good individual, and vice versa. There is, however, a kind of priority of concern for the good individual in education because teachers work directly with the individual and only indirectly with society. If the good life can be made the general objective for education then the task of the school is to "transcribe the good life, the good individual, and the good society

---

[48] Harry Broudy, *op. cit.*, p. 33.
[49] *Loc. cit.*

into learnings that presumably will contribute to their production."[50] The good life as the general aim for education must be carefully defined so that objective norms for the good life balance the subjective preferences which influence choices. It by no means refers to what "some person or persons happen to like at a given moment";[51] it is rather determined by the structure of human personality. For "human nature has a structure that is everywhere the same, and . . . this structure demands for its own preservation the form of action characteristic of the 'good' life."[52] Dr. Broudy's analysis of this structure we have already seen, as it comprises his definition of the nature of the pupil.[53] Central to personality, in addition to the appetitive principle common to all animal life, are the forms of *self-determination, self-realization,* and *self-integration.* These forms qualify the nature of the good life for mankind; and the good life as an educational aim for man needs to be measured by these three forms. It remains, however, to look at the subjective and objective aspects of the good life as Dr. Broudy sees them and to understand the way in which he unifies them, giving us the three forms just mentioned for determining what the good life is.

The subjective estimate of life is of course the estimate a person has of his own life. Does he regard it as good or bad? The grounds, or at least some of the important grounds, on which such a judgment is made are the presence or absence in his life of pain, anxiety, self-respect, and a tension toward the future to which interest is attached.

As to pain, no one desires it "for its own sake, and unless the suffering is a means to something less painful, it is about as near to a pure evil as can be imagined."[54] As to anxiety, a chronic domination of our lives by it certainly is not consonant with the good life. While occasional physical danger may lend excitement to life, the most disturbing perils we face are less tangible threats to selfhood. "The dangers of losing prestige, security, and love, although not so violent as the dangers of war, are even more potent in their destruction of confidence."[55] Some of the roughness of these threats is shielded from the person who is made happy by the presence of those who love him for what he is. Most of us at least suspect that we are "somewhat short on merit and therefore crave the earthly grace that an unselfish and unquestioning love supplies.[56] In addition to freedom from pain and anxiety, a person needs to feel "that he counts for something and deserves to. . . . He needs the conviction that his presence makes a

---

[50] *Ibid.,* p. 34.
[51] *Ibid.,* p. 50.
[52] *Ibid.,* p. 51.
[53] Cf. pp. 298–302.
[54] Harry Broudy, *op. cit.,* p. 37.
[55] *Loc. cit.*
[56] *Loc. cit.*

difference in the world; he needs to be needed."[57] Unfortunately many look for outward confirmation of this self-respect in "recognition, titles, better jobs with bigger desks, and prizes in competition of all kinds."[58] Finally, for a life to be judged good by the person who is living it, it must contain an element of excitement and be interesting. This means that it must strain toward the future in an absorbing way so that there will be the sense of having "a stake in future events."[59]

The objective estimate of the good life does not always agree with this subjective estimate. The educator as he looks at the pupil and his future will correct the pupil's subjective judgments by a perspective which is more objective. As to pain, first of all, the teacher will make it an aim "to help the pupil avoid unnecessary hardship and pain as far as learnings can accomplish this. He knows that knowledge, skill, and ingenuity both in the individual and in social arrangements can mitigate physical ills and hardships."[60] Yet at the same time he knows that pain, suffering, and hardship are not always avoidable and because of this the good life must be measured by another yardstick, namely, *"the attitude of the individual toward these evils."*[61] Accordingly, there will need to be courage for dangers, temperance to season pleasure and pain, liberality in giving and receiving, and justice in apportioning pleasure and pain among our fellows. Because of this added measure which the objective estimate of the good life gives, "the educator makes character development coordinate with knowledge an aim for the individual—knowledge to avoid and mitigate evils and character to secure the best possible balance among pleasures and pains over the long pull of a lifetime."[62]

Anxiety and its attendant emotional discomfort and insecurity are more complex. Much of it is hidden consciously or unconsciously from those on the outside who make the objective estimate. The educator of course recognizes that "some fear and anxiety can be alleviated by knowledge and skill."[63] But we have not learned from mental hygiene that many "emotional maladjustments . . . have their origin in what psychologists call childhood or infant conditioning."[64] How much can education do to compensate for or eliminate these causes? The surest answer to this kind of problem is to educate for its avoidance in the next generation. This would mean educating for parenthood and teaching young parents how to avoid

[57] *Ibid.*, p. 38.
[58] *Loc. cit.*
[59] *Loc. cit.*
[60] *Ibid.*, p. 41.
[61] *Loc. cit.*
[62] *Ibid.*, p. 42.
[63] *Ibid.*, p. 44.
[64] *Loc. cit.*

the kind of conditioning which will later result in such emotional difficulties. But is this properly the task of formal education?

Regarding self-esteem, the objective judgment does not give it the importance which the subjective judgment of the self does, realizing its need for respect; instead the objective judgment estimates the merit of a person in terms of the service he renders. Of course such an estimate necessarily involves the concept of difference of capacities among individuals. Whatever his level of ability, if a man measures up to it and produces accordingly, he is deserving of respect from those who look upon his life objectively.

It is in every case better that a man fulfill his possibilities for the good life than that he should fail to do so, and in this respect heroes and peasants both get "A" for effort. But if he who might have been a fine scientist is content to fulfill his life as a simple peasant, our judgment will not be lenient. Undeveloped potentiality is a spectacle that men view with regret and often with impatient anger.[65]

Finally, regarding tension toward the future as a quality of the good life, the objective estimate insists that this tension be of a certain kind. It is not enough that there be tension toward the future to which interest can be attached. "The tension to qualify as good must issue from striving after a goal that somehow contributes to the common good."[66] It is imperative that the interesting quality of life come from "commitment to great goals that develop the individual's powers for the common good."[67] Implicit in this judgment is an assumption concerning the nature of man, which is this:

. . . that his most important dimension is that of the future and not the present, i.e., the important dimension of his life is "what might and what ought to be" rather than what is and what must be.[68]

Returning now to the forms of selfhood, *self-determination, self-realization,* and *self-integration,* a union between the subjective and objective estimates of the good life can be found. In these forms are found the normal functions which the self should fulfill, and in fulfilling them the self will be in constructive relationship with society, from which the objective estimate comes. In the highest sense, pleasure and pain will be evidences of the fulfillment of these functions. "Pleasure . . . is a sign that some function is being carried out well; pain is a sign of the contrary state."[69] Of course

[65] *Ibid.,* pp. 44–45.
[66] *Ibid.,* p. 45.
[67] *Ibid.,* p. 46.
[68] *Loc. cit.*
[69] *Ibid.,* p. 48.

when pleasure is such a sign it is not just any kind of pleasure. It is a pleasure which is attendant upon fulfillment of the functions which distinguish man from other forms of organic life. And these are self-determination, self-realization, and self-integration.

Therefore, the virtuous man becomes the yardstick for the good life, and it is a yardstick that does justice to both the individual subjective estimate and the social objective one. It represents the search for happiness and pleasure, but it is an enlightened reflective search. It stands as a corrective to individual caprice and to social rigidity.[70]

As can be recognized by consulting the famous encyclical of Pius XI on Christian education, Roman Catholic educational thought is explicitly theological in its definition of the good life. It flows from cooperation on the part of education with the grace of God. Its objective norm is the example and teaching of Christ. And in essence it is supernatural.

Catholic thought holds that the immediate objective of education is "to cooperate with divine grace,"[71] and that it should do this as a means of "forming the true and perfect Christian."[72] This of course is education for the child who has been baptized by the Church and thereby is regenerated. It is further conceived in Catholic doctrine concerning education that this "forming of the true and perfect Christian"[73] which education is to accomplish is really the formation of Christ Himself in the child.

The "true and finished character," which is intended as the final end of such an education, is a supernatural man who is made so by a supernatural grace with which education works as an agent. He is "the supernatural man who thinks, judges, and acts constantly in accordance with right reason illumined by the supernatural light of the example and teaching of Christ.[74]

Official Soviet educational thought has formulated its objectives of education with collective life as its chief referent. There is much less emphasis on the individual than in the realism of Broudy or in Catholic realism. And the "objective estimate" of the good life, as in Broudy, is made so extensive and dominant that there is scarcely a place for the "subjective estimate."

Three important objectives of Soviet education which harmonize closely with the communist blueprint for society are an appropriate attitude to-

---

[70] *Loc. cit.*

[71] As quoted by William J. McGucken in "The Philosophy of Catholic Education," in Nelson B. Henry (editor), *Philosophies of Education.* The Forty-First Yearbook of the National Society for the Study of Education, Part I. Bloomington, Ill.: Public School Publishing Company, 1942. P. 265.

[72] *Loc. cit.*

[73] *Loc. cit.*

[74] *Loc. cit.*

ward labor, Soviet patriotism, and an appropriate state of discipline in the individual.

1. The communistic attitude toward labor, which is to be instilled in every boy and girl, was characterized by Stalin as the recognition that labor "is a matter of *honor*, a matter of *glory*, a matter of *valor* and *heroism*."[75]

2. Soviet patriotism, which is to be nurtured in every individual, involves both party loyalty and the recognition that the cause of communism is harmonious with the cause of the toiling masses of all the other nations of the world. In terms of loyalty, patriotism means "devotion to the Communist Party and supreme readiness to serve the cause of Lenin and Stalin."[76] In terms of sympathy with labor throughout the world, it means "the understanding that the interests of our people and the interests of the toiling masses of the entire world are indivisible."[77]

3. But the possession of these two attitudes is not considered sufficient for the products of the Soviet educational program; there must be a strong state of personal discipline undergirding them. In their much-used work on pedagogy, Yesipov and Goncharov say, "To rear Soviet patriots means, at the same time, to rear people who clearly understand the purposes of our construction, people of indomitable *will*, people of purpose."[78] More specifically this state of discipline means:

. . . to study and work honestly, conscientiously, and with maximum efficiency, to exhibit concern for ever greater success for himself and his comrades, to be polite and considerate in his relations with his fellows, to show respect for his elders, to help those in need, to take care of public property, and to encourage others to do likewise.[79]

This state of discipline is characterized more explicitly still in the following six qualities which Yesipov and Goncharov say comprise it.

In the first place it is *conscious*, that is, it is founded on an inner conviction of the necessity of following definite rules and regulations in conduct which in turn are based on an understanding of their meaning and significance. In the second place, descipline is *self-initiated*, that is, it is not a discipline of simple obedience, but rather a discipline which is linked with the desire to fulfill in the best possible manner a given assignment, order, or commission. More than this, it is linked with a readiness always to do one's duty, not waiting for an order or a reminder, but displaying initiative. In the third place, discipline is *firm*, that is, it is unquestioned obedience and submission to the leader, the teacher, or the organizer. Without this there is no discipline;

[75] As quoted in B. P. Yesipov and N. K. Goncharov, *op. cit.*, p. 34.
[76] *Ibid.*, p. 36.
[77] *Loc. cit.*
[78] *Ibid.*, p. 39.
[79] *Ibid.*, pp. 94–95.

submission to the will of the leader is a necessary and essential mark of discipline. In the fourth place, discipline is *organizational*, that is, it is a discipline which prompts and habituates the pupil to the precise organization of individual and collective work, to organization in games and life. In the fifth place, discipline is *comradely*, that is, it is founded on mutual respect of the members of the collective. In the sixth place, discipline is *resolute*, that is, it surmounts difficulties, prompts the completion of every task, subjects conduct to high purposes, and conquers motives of low degree.[80]

D. THE EDUCATIVE PROCESS

With Broudy's philosophy of education as our primary example we now turn to the educative process. This will be of one piece, we should reasonably expect, with conceptions of the school as a social institution, the nature of the pupil, and the objectives of education, heretofore considered in this chapter within the reference frame of realist educational philosophy. What kind of activities are to be carried on within the school, according to realism, in order to attain the kind of objectives realist educators set for the schools? Put another way, what is the process, as realism sees it, which bridges the gap between the uneducated pupil and the more or less finished product which is desired?

Harry Broudy is far from being a naïve realist for whom the knowledge experience is a simple collision between knower and object. His epistemology is very similar to that of the critical realists which has been discussed in Chapter XIII under the heading "Epistemological Dualism."[81] There is therefore in Broudy's thought no purely mechanical treatment of the educative process, according to which it is a simple transmission of information, conditioning of the pupil so as to conform him to his environment, and use of discipline in reinforcing both of these processes. As would be expected from this discerning student of both philosophy and education, the educative process is described with subtlety and insight.

As far as curriculum is concerned, both the traditional subject matter and the problem-centered concept are rejected as inadequate. But while the conception of curriculum which Broudy builds includes more than either, it does combine subject-matter and problem approaches.

The traditional curriculum of the schools with its heavy emphasis on subject matter has lofty objectives, but too commonly these objectives are lost in the sweat of the classroom. What is ideally desired by the subject-matter curriculum is mastery of information plus the acquisition of certain habits deemed to be valuable. Examples of these are observing accurately, thinking clearly and logically, sticking to unpleasant tasks unflinchingly,

[80] *Ibid.*, p. 95.
[81] Cf. pp. 271–273.

promptness, neatness, and industry.[82] But too often when learning gets under way these fine ideals are forgotten and the only one which determines the process is mastery of information. And unfortunately this commonly degenerates to the level of mere "memorization of the factual content of the subject."[83]

The problem-centered curriculum also has a laudable objective in its intention to deal with the problems of the pupil and to use these as a means by which to lead him into knowledge. But problems which can qualify to do this are not as plentiful as they are assumed to be and the gaining of knowledge by means of problems has such a narrow focus that it is more akin to "raiding" than to studying. To begin with, in order for a problem to provide the focus for a unit of study which is adequate, it must fulfill two qualifications. It must be, of course, a real problem for the students involved. And it must require thought, in many cases even systematic thought. But many problems which are immediate and real to students are not those which necessarily involve systematic study of some area of knowledge. And those problems which do make necessary a resort to the encyclopedia and the library will require more of the student than looking up relevant information. More than this is involved, and the more systematic the study needed, the greater the demand for something more than relevant information. Such needed knowledge may also involve the mastery of terminology and specialized concepts which are a kind of shorthand. In addition it may require a network of hypotheses and generalizations as an apperceptive mass for the particular knowledge which is relevant to the problem at hand. And further, a specialized method of investigation may be called for which in some sense is peculiar to the given field of knowledge in which the problem-motivated student is making his sortie.[84]

In preference to either of these familiar approaches, Dr. Broudy proposes that the curriculum is the means of forming desirable habits. But he hastens to caution us that habit as the clue to curriculum is very broadly inclusive in definition and not a simple mechanism to be forced upon the learner by conditioning. Habits are not confined, as the layman might surmise, to "semi-automatic, thoughtless actions."[85] They are rather dynamic in nature, they vary considerably in flexibility, and they are a unity of content and form.[86]

. . . The objectives of the curriculum are habits or tendencies to acquire, use, and enjoy truth. . . . It is suggested that the way to form these habits is by mastery of organized subject matter. Once we realize what it means to

---

[82] Cf. Harry Broudy, *op. cit.*, p. 148.
[83] *Ibid.*, p. 156.
[84] Cf. *ibid.*, pp. 152–156.
[85] *Ibid.*, p. 160.
[86] Cf. *ibid.*, pp. 160–161.

master such subject matter, we shall be disabused of the notion that it is *merely* the memorization of facts.[87]

Among the various habits which are capable of giving form to the curriculum, Broudy mentions the following: symbolic habits, habits of study, research skills such as library skills, observation, and experimentation, habits of using knowledge such as experimental method, analytical or critical thinking, the deliberative skills of group discussion, application of principles, evaluation, and finally habits of enjoyment. All of these serve in some way to give form to the curriculum and are therefore important; but because of their generality of application and use, symbolic habits and habits of study are of primary importance. Symbolic habits of course involve the effective use of words, and consequently the mastery of reading skills is foundational. Habits of study are a variation on reading skill and require special attention. While we do teach to read more effectively than ever before, we do not so commonly teach the special variety of reading skill which involves careful analysis and study, and which is qualitatively different.

As habits give form to the curriculum, it is almost redundant to observe that the content of the various areas of knowledge fills in this form with substance. Now of course the range of human knowledge as represented in the various arts and sciences is so great that any curriculum must be selective. The content of a given curriculum must therefore be chosen according to such norms as: What is most generally applicable? and What is most urgently needed by the students? It is important to keep in mind at the same time that this content has to have form; and it is essential that the content selected be "incorporated into the habits of using knowledge rather than haphazardly sprinkled" in memory.[88] More specifically, Dr. Broudy proposes for the elementary and secondary schools that there be courses in the natural sciences, in social studies, and in an area he describes as being concerned with "living with the self." But he also proposes that each of these areas have problems courses paralleling the content courses which would be designed to give the student experience in using the particular kind of knowledge of each area. In the natural sciences, there would be courses in chemistry, physics, and biology, together with a problems course in the art of using the knowledge of these particular sciences. The social studies would not be broken into more particular areas, so there would be one unified approach to the social sciences paralleled by a problems course providing experience in becoming effective and responsible in relation to the social order. In the "self-sciences" courses Dr. Broudy includes psychology but he also adds the arts, poetry, literature, biography, philosophy,

[87] *Ibid.*, p. 181.
[88] *Ibid.*, p. 185.

and possibly religion. These courses would be paralleled in his proposed curriculum by a problems course in value experience, providing opportunity for building habits of making value judgments and achieving value.

There would be other blocks of courses not taken by all students, as would be the case with those described so far. That is, there would be various special subject-matter and vocational areas. Also, and for all students, there would be a guidance program which would be in addition to both content and problems courses. This guidance program, however, would not be primarily therapeutic. While the schools have legitimate responsibilities for guidance of youth, they do not primarily have the role of psychiatric diagnosis and treatment. Instead, within a more general educational context, this guidance program should provide "the opportunity for the individual to practice the habits of enlightened self-analysis and the use of knowledge in value decisions."[89]

Coordinate with curriculum, another dimension of the educative process is method. By what means does Dr. Broudy propose to order content, given form by habits, so that it is an effectual learning experience for the student? We need not discuss specific methods here, according to conventional forms, although Broudy does bring his theory of method to bear upon the specifics of Socratic method, disputation, memorization, lecture, activity method, and audio-visuals. What is more important and is most germane to a complete philosophy of education is a general theory of method; and this particular realist does not fail us at this point.

The point of departure for method is motivation. That teaching must gear into interests is almost a truism today. While Broudy agrees with this practical necessity confronting the teacher, he points to its deeper significance. Interests, he says, are expressions of deeper and more fundamental urges. And these he identifies as the principles which are the very essence of the human self. This connects theory of method necessarily with the nature of the learner, as it certainly should be connected. It will be recalled that these basic principles of the self are self-determination, self-realization, and self-integration. As long as method helps the student to apprehend knowledge as relevant to these fundamental urges of his being, there will be no danger of indifference and lack of interest.[90]

At some point in the movement of learning and supported by sound motivation, there will be the launching-out by the learner in trial or act. Broudy means to emphasize, by calling attention to this, that learning is active and the student must be actively engaged. But he does not want to be interpreted as making all activity an affair of the large muscles. Progressive education and problem-centered learning have fallen prey unjustly to

---

[89] *Ibid.*, p. 203.
[90] Cf. *ibid.*, pp. 215–216.

this misinterpretation. What Broudy is concerned to emphasize at this point is that "the mind is active—reaching out to its object." And more commonly than not the learner is highly active when he appears to be passive.[91]

Another point, or really an event, in the movement of learning is the experience of insight. This is the real turning point in every instance of learning; it is the "really crucial step." The emergence of insight in the learning experience is crucial because it can make the difference, for example, between trial and error and an effective pattern of action, transforming the former into the latter. Trial-and-error learning is a "slow staggering progress"[92] because in it there is no perception of the connection of particular acts with particular results. But when the learner comes to see the connection between the stimulus at hand and the particular response to it which brings success, trial and error is no longer necessary; instead he can move directly to the effective pattern of action.

The great significance of insight is not lessened by the fact that the action pattern may need to be practiced to be effective; and in this, trial and error is of course involved, although it may also be that an insight is so intimately a part of mastery and control of action that it will be experienced only in action, and when it is achieved practice is already largely in the past. Insight does not of course preclude the necessity for some trial and error. Very often trial and error precedes it. But there are instances also in which the learner leaps directly to the efficient response without any antecedents in action; if there is any trial and error on these occasions, it occurs in the imagination. Whenever and in whatever manner it comes, insight is the pivot of the learning experience. *"Regardless of what is to be learned,"* Broudy says, *"the learning moment is the one in which the organism achieves the organization."*[93] And upon this teaching should be intently focused, for "it is the business of instruction to help the learner to become aware of the pattern that constitutes the right response."[94]

The essence of teaching method, then, is in matching *possible learning* tasks with the levels of abstraction of which the pupil is capable. As is well known, people vary in the levels of abstraction of which they are capable. There is also some advance in this capacity as a person grows from infancy to adulthood, although it is certainly not an evenly gradual development, and there is much variety in the way individuals grow in powers of abstraction, as in all other capacities. Experience constantly confronts children and adults alike with concrete objects, events, and movements. Our sensations and perceptions are continually engaged by the world; but our powers

[91] Cf. *ibid.*, pp. 216–217.
[92] *Ibid.*, p. 218.
[93] *Ibid.*, p. 219.
[94] *Ibid.*, p. 220.

of conception are not called into play to an equal degree, depending in some great measure upon our capacity for insight.

It is this disparity between experience of the concrete and experience of the abstract with which the guidance of learning must always be concerned. The burden of teaching must always be an answer to the question: What learning task will engage the abstractive powers of the student and direct them to the subject matter it is intended he shall learn? There are always therefore two parallel elements in method. "One is the adaptation of the material of instruction; the other is the procedure used to bring about the apprehension of this material."[95] Every teaching situation accordingly demands that the learner do something and it also requires that the teacher "arrange matters" so that the learning demand placed on the student is a reasonable one, geared to his readiness and therefore designed to elicit insight and so fulfill the learning task with the greatest economy of time, effort, and value for the student.

The Roman Catholic conception of method is distinct in comparison to Broudy's realistic treatment of method, at least to the extent that it supplies the ingredient of the authority vested in the teacher. Redden and Ryan assert that this is essential in authentic Catholic thought. The meaning of the term "teacher" is "one who has authority over others for the purpose of instructing them in knowledge, skills, attitudes, and ideals consonant with their true nature, ultimate end, and highest good."[96] This authority of the teacher is derived from God, they say, quoting from the Epistle to the Romans to the effect that every person should be subject to the governing authorities, whose authority in turn comes from God.[97] In a similar vein, distinctly religious means for making changes in persons are added to the more commonly accepted educational means. Redden and Ryan specify these as "prayer, the sacraments, and grace. They are intrinsically efficacious in that they cause human beings to make desirable changes in their own lives."[98]

The curriculum, therefore, according to Roman Catholic thought, should contain authentic religious elements if it is to accomplish the true purpose for which curricula are intended. Accordingly, Redden and Ryan say that the essentials of the curriculum are as follows:

The doctrines of holy Church; the system, order, and beauty found in nature, art, and moral conduct; the intellectual, social, vocational problems of one's fellow man, and of the civilization in which one lives; the interdependence between the individual and society; and the necessity for purposeful cooperation with others in the family, the state, and the world.[99]

[95] *Ibid.*, pp. 225–226.
[96] John D. Redden and Francis A. Ryan, *op. cit.*, p. 339.
[97] Cf. Romans 13:1.
[98] John D. Redden and Francis A. Ryan, *op. cit.*, p. 346.
[99] *Ibid.*, p. 375.

That the curriculum should be so constituted is a necessity, in the light of the ends to which it must lead. But it is also incidentally disclosed to be the right kind of curriculum as called for by our western culture, so they argue, inasmuch as our heritage has been so completely shaped by religious influences.

Much of the present social heritage in western civilization was accumulated under religious sponsorship, and owes its sanction to religion. The influence of religious materials is seen in a true philosophy of life. Government, and the democratic philosophy of life, properly so called, are founded basically on true Christian principles which are observable in every aspect of life.[100]

Education in Soviet Russia has also placed great confidence in the content of the curriculum as a molding force by which the culture shapes the new generation. But while the connection as such between civilization and the heritage to be taught are the same for both, civilization and heritage in Soviet Russia are associated in a way which is far removed from the connection made between the civilization and religious heritage of the West in Roman Catholic thought. The connection is stressed by both Catholic and communist, but the purpose in making the identification is radically different in each. A purely verbal impartation of content within the walls of the classroom has not been considered adequate by communist leaders for the development of the kind of productive efficiency essential to a communistic society. It must not only be supplemented by actual training and experience in the respective trades and technical areas, but in addition the two must be closely interrelated. While training and experience are essential to instruction, instruction is essential also to training and experience.

One of the more general areas in which there is this kind of reliance on instruction is in polytechnical fields. Marx defined polytechnical instruction as education which "inculcates the general principles of all the process of production and at the same time gives the child or youth practical training in the use of the simplest tools of all industries."[101] The program of the Communist party calls for "free and compulsory general and polytechnical instruction (providing acquaintance in theory and practice with the main branches of production) for all children of both sexes" as its goal.[102] A. Pinkevich reports that Lenin defined polytechnical instruction as including:

(a) a groundwork of knowledge of electricity; (b) its application in the mechanical industry; (c) its application in the chemical industry; (d) basic knowledge about the plan of electrification of the R.S.F.S.R.; (e) an acquaint-

[100] *Ibid.*, p. 381.
[101] As quoted from a resolution written by Marx for the First Congress of the First International, 1866, by A. Pinkevich in *Science and Education in the U.S.S.R.* London: Victor Gollancz, 1935. P. 28.
[102] As quoted by Pinkevich, *op. cit.*, p. 28.

ance with the Soviet economy and the work of electric power stations and industrial plants; and (f) a knowledge of the principles of agronomics.[103]

There is also reliance upon instruction in inculcating a materialistic world view in Russian children. Where as there are reports that communist leaders faced the necessity, after the revolution got under way in Russia, of accommodating their attitude toward religion to the indigenous religious loyalties of the people, the explicit intention has been to teach children in the schools a materialistic world view. Professor Pinkevich in his *Science and Education in the U.S.S.R.,* published in 1935, describes this intention as follows:

> Soviet education aims at creating human beings grounded in a scientific materialistic outlook, people who endeavor to make life happy in this world rather than in some world to come. Hence it is an anti-religious education. The Soviet school is not a mere secular school as this is understood in America and France, it is conducted on distinctly materialistic, i.e., anti-religious lines.[104]

That education in Soviet Russia is realistic in its use of molding and adjusting devices, in addition to its emphasis on knowledge, is well exemplified by the "Rules for School Children" adopted by the Soviet People's Commissars of the R.S.F.S.R. on August 2, 1943. There are twenty of these rules, and a pupil is subject to punishment or even expulsion from school if he disobeys them, depending upon the extent of his disregard of them. They are as follows:

1. To strive with tenacity and perserverence to master knowledge, in order to become an educated and cultured citizen and to serve most fully the Soviet Motherland.
2. To be diligent in study and punctual in attendance, never being late to classes.
3. To obey without question the orders of school director and teachers.
4. To bring to school all necessary books and writing materials, to have everything ready before the arrival of the teacher.
5. To appear at school washed, combed, and neatly dressed.
6. To keep his desk in the classroom clean and orderly.
7. To enter the classroom and take his seat immediately after the ringing of the bell, to enter or leave the classroom during the lesson period only with the permission of the teacher.
8. To sit erect during the lesson period, not leaning on the elbows or slouching in the seat; to attend closely to the explanations of the teacher and the response of the pupils, not talking or engaging in mischief.
9. To rise as the teacher or the director enters or leaves the classroom.

[103] As quoted by Pinkevich, *op. cit.,* p. 30.
[104] *Ibid.,* p. 34.

10. To rise and stand erect while reciting; to sit down only on permission of the teacher; to raise the hand when desiring to answer or ask a question.
11. To make accurate notes of the teacher's assignment for the next lesson, to show these notes to the parents, and to do all homework without assistance.
12. To be respectful to the school director and the teachers, to greet them on the street with a polite bow, boys removing their hats.
13. To be polite to his elders, to conduct himself modestly and properly in school, on the street, and in public places.
14. To abstain from using bad language, from smoking and gambling.
15. To take good care of school property, to guard well his own possessions and those of his comrades.
16. To be courteous and considerate toward little children, toward the aged, the weak, and the sick, to give them the seat on the trolley or the right of way on the street, to help them in every way.
17. To obey his parents and assist in the care of little brothers and sisters.
18. To maintain cleanliness in the home by keeping his own clothes, shoes, and bed in order.
19. To carry always his pupil's card, guarding it carefully, not passing it to other children, but presenting it on request of the director or the teacher of the school.
20. To prize the honor of his school and his class as his very own.[105]

Reference has already been made to the intention of Soviet education that the pupil shall achieve a disciplined personal life. It should now be said that Soviet education also leans upon discipline as an external pressure bringing the pupil into line. This does not mean that educators in Russia overlook the important supplement to external disciplinary measures constituted by the inner promptings of the pupil; but there is forthright use of discipline as an external pressure. The "Rules for School Children," for example, are backed up by penalties for disobedience. And, more generally, Yesipov and Goncharov acknowledged that

. . . in developing discipline in pupils we may apply at times threats of punishments themselves, if regulations are violated. Also we may assume that the pupil will refrain from such violations because of fear of displeasing adults in positions of authority, fear of disapproval on the part of the collective, fear of the reproaches of his own conscience, and fear of the unpleasant experience of shame.[106]

---

[105] As reproduced in the Appendix of B. P. Yesipov and N. K. Goncharov, *op. cit.*, pp. 149–150.
[106] B. P. Yesipov and N. K. Goncharov, *op. cit.*, p. 96.

XV

Realism in Religion

A. *The Status of Religion*

B. *Our Experience of God*

C. *The Nature of God*

D. *The Power and Goodness of God*

E. *The Nature of Man*

Realism compares well with idealism in its potentiality as an intellectual structure for religious faith. For it is not limited to naturalistic redefinitions of terms when it projects itself into the realm of religion, as is the case with naturalism and pragmatism. In part, this is the case because realism is primarily an epistemology; but it is the case more especially because it is characteristic of realism to argue that the method of knowledge as such does not reveal anything concerning the character of reality. Naturalism, on the other hand, is bound to its metaphysics as its chief constituent; and pragmatism, though also primarily an epistemology, is bound by a metaphysics necessarily implied in its theory of knowledge. While there are realists who are naturalists, there are also realists who are supernaturalists.

In its influence in religious thought, realism has, at the least, not been without success in its opposition to idealism. For to the strongly realistic bent occasionally outcropping in traditional religious thought and practice realism has added its positive insistence that a scientific epistemology is appropriate in the religious realm and does not necessarily prejudice those who use such a method of knowledge in favor of a naturalistic metaphysics. At any rate, it would seem that since World War I realism has been more popular as a religious philosophy than idealism.

A. THE STATUS OF RELIGION

The typical realist attitude toward religion is one of taking it as a fact, studying it as it is, and building up theories about it only as the "real" facts permit. Religion is not regarded as being dependent upon ideas about reality; rather it is independent, having its own distinct roots. For example, A. C. Garnett, in his book, *A Realistic Philosophy of Religion*,[1] says the fact that religion has survived many great changes in belief indicates that it is independent of specific ideas.

Realism approaches religion as an independent object of experience to be studied as it is found in experience without first superimposing preconceived ideas upon it. It opposes rationalism in religion; broadly defined, empiricism is preferred as a more dependable method of study and one which is fairer to religion. After all, religion has a history, religion is objectified as an institution in society, and people have religious experiences which are quite as distinct as other kinds of experience. Why then should religion be based on thought experiences alone, or made secondary to them? Is it not as much an "object" of study as chemical elements, health, or economic and social forces?

Religion is not a realm of application or practice only, where ideas derived from metaphysical pursuits are put to work. It is a legitimate realm of discovery as well. Its predicament in this regard is comparable to that of education. For years, the philosophers, psychologists, and sociologists were content that the educators should serve them by putting into practice some of the results of their pure sciences. But the educators have since emancipated themselves by repeated declarations that the science of education is not a field of application alone, but rather its own legitimate field of experimentation and discovery. In a similar way, some realists hold that religion stands on its own feet and is an object of study as well as a unique realm of discovery.

B. OUR EXPERIENCE OF GOD

The experience of God, then, is prior to ideas concerning His nature. By experience of God is meant a direct face-to-face meeting with something in

[1] Cf. p. 9. Chicago and New York: Willett, Clark and Co., 1942.

the world beyond self which is greater than self and worthy as a religious object. Such a direct experiential relation is more basic than religious ideas because it objectifies religious experience and makes it from the beginning an outward connection with the beyond-the-self; whereas preoccupation with religious ideas complicates religious experience in a network of relations between one's own concepts, rarely letting him get outside of himself. This approach is not only considered the only right one by the realist but is also offered as a great help to those who have experienced difficulty in believing in God because of forbidding elements presented by more distinctly theological conceptions. If a person begins with the simple objective experience of that beyond-the-self whose working is independent of his own initiative, he has the most elemental knowledge of the existence of God and will find it easier to go on in attaining an intellectual understanding of the nature of God.

The late Douglas Clyde Macintosh has been one of the great contenders for this disposition in religion, breaking ground in a realistic analysis of religious knowledge. The book, *Religious Realism*,[2] which he edited and to which several kindred minds contributed, is a manifesto on realism in religion. Its status is comparable to that of *The New Realism* (1912) and *Essays in Critical Realism* (1920), both manifestoes in the development of the general philosophy of realism.[3] *The Problem of Religious Knowledge*[4] by Macintosh is an important book in the same strain and still more recent than the one he edited.

For the starting point in understanding what is referred to above as direct experience of God, we must turn back to what we have already said about the epistemology of realism in Chapter XIII.[5] There realism was presented as breaking apart into two main schools, according as the process of knowledge was analyzed: the neorealists saying that the knower is in direct contact with the object known, and the critical realist saying that the object in the mind of the knower is not the same as the object in the outside world which it represents. The new realists say that objects are directly *presented* to mind; the critical realists say that objects are *represented* in mind.

Macintosh has built a theory of religious knowledge which combines elements of these two treatments into a synthesis. With the new realists he agrees in part by saying that some qualities are directly presented to mind; and therefore mind has some direct relations with its objects. With the critical realists he agrees also in part that some of the qualities we experience are made up of the fabric of our experience and are not directly a part

[2] New York: The Macmillan Company, 1931.
[3] Cf. pp. 266–267.
[4] New York: Harper & Row, Publishers, 1940.
[5] Cf. pp. 270–273.

of the object itself. Now, when in our experiential relations with the world we are confronted by that-which-is-beyond-us (and much of our experience is of this sort, because the stimuli which call our senses into action originate from outside of us), we have a complex relationship in which some things we experience are direct *presentations* from beyond and other elements are *representations* given birth by consciousness itself. But, and this is the keystone of the synthesis, there is enough overlapping between the *presentations* and the *representations* to leave a common ground in which knower and object impinge on each other directly, and the knowledge relation in this common area is both immediate and direct.

It is at the perceptual level where we have our most elemental experience of God, and this is a direct empirical experience. No sense object or group of them, no value or composite of them, is given the name "God" in this analysis. God, at the least, is that independent reality beyond consciousness whose dependable working is evident in my contact with the world. And my experience of this independent reality is as direct and immediate as any sensory experience is. The accompanying diagram illus-

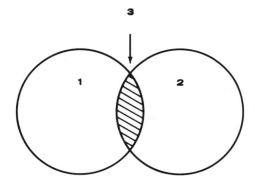

1. This circle represents the realm of individual consciousness.
2. This circle represents the realm of independent reality.
3. The shaded area represents the overlapping of the two, the common ground of direct relationship between the two.

trates this. As the two overlapping circles suggest, independent reality is greater than all of its presentations in experience. Not all of the qualities I experience in my own consciousness, at the same time, are the presentations of independent reality; some of them are legitimate creations of my own consciousness. Consequently, there is a certain disparity between consciousness and independent reality, and between these disparate parts there is no equivalence in knowledge. However, individual consciousness and independent reality do overlap or coincide sufficiently that there is an ample area in which the relation between consciousness and independent reality is direct and immediate.

It may not be inappropriate to suggest that the newer Protestant thought which has emerged since the revival of theology in the twentieth century is more in harmony with this pattern of knowing than with idealism. Existentialism has also been very influential in this thought. Whereas the new theology is a theology rather than a philosophy, and while Emil Brunner, who has been one of its exponents, insists that philosophy of religion must always remain of secondary or tertiary importance for Protestant theology, there is yet a certain similarity of pattern coinciding with realism.[6]

Dealing first with the three similarities, it is to be observed that the new theology takes science and scientific method very seriously. The inclination is to accept the findings of science, in the various realms of human knowledge, as authoritative truth. Especially in the scientific study of the Scriptures, the results of critical scholarship are likely to be accepted as the last word about the dates, authorship, authenticity, form, etc., of the various documents comprising the Bible. A second observation as to similarity with realism is that for the new theology reality is primary and the knowing consciousness is secondary. What we do to reality in the knowing process, if not a figment of the imagination, is of little import. It is what reality does to us which is significant. Accordingly, the third similarity is that for this new theology the primary function of the believer in knowing God is *receptivity*. Active projection of the self outward to bring form to the raw materials of religious experience should not have the center of the stage; the primary motif is rather passive willingness to receive impression, to be written upon.

The fourth item relating to the new theology's treatment of knowledge, already characterized as radically supernatural, is that the way of knowledge is not purely a perceptual meeting of knower and object, but rather revelation of God in Jesus Christ. The description of knowledge given by Macintosh is more radically empirical than is the case with the knowledge theory of the new theology, even though it is more empirical than rational. The only knowledge of God we can have, according to this school in Protestant thought, is what God gives to us by breaking through both the natural order and the patterns and systems of human knowledge in Jesus Christ and so showing us Himself as He is.

C. THE NATURE OF GOD

Enough of the realist's approach has now been described so that the reader can understand that realists are not particularly interested in arguments for the existence of God. Religious realism starts with an objective minimum of which we have direct experience in the world beyond the self; and there is little feeling of urgency to argue for the existence of that of which we have direct experience. We turn then to consideration of the

[6] Cf. Emil Brunner, *The Philosophy of Religion*. Translated by A. J. D. Farrer and Bertram Lee Wolf; London: Ivor Nicholson and Watson, 1937. Chapter I, "The Meaning of Philosophy of Religion for Protestantism."

nature of God as realists understand it. And since this is to turn from
method to content, we are confronted by the same diversity of belief discovered in Chapter XIII when we considered the metaphysics of realism.
For it bears saying again that realists are united only in epistemology; in
metaphysics they practically run the gamut of possibilities.

By way of sampling this range, as far as it is indicated in definitions of
the nature of God, we will begin where we left off in Chapter V when we
presented Henry Nelson Wieman's definition of God as the impersonal
structure, basis, and constitution of value in the world.[7] Such a definition is
realistic as well as naturalistic; as will be seen later, Macintosh does not
wholly disagree with this conception. It is more naturalistic than realistic,
however, because in it the knowledge process is not a primary frame of
reference and it defines God as being completely within the realm of Nature. While there are important differences in the content of the beliefs held
by the two men, Macintosh is clearly and confessedly realistic because of
his great concern to build a method of religious knowledge which is antithetical to idealism.

Macintosh finds Wieman's conception of God to be a satisfactory point
of beginning, but goes on from it to approximate a definition of God as
person. True to his realistic character, he is emphatic in insisting that the
religious object is an existent object not depending on man's consciousness
for its existence. This is the extension into religious experience of the naïve
realist principle in perception that the physical world exists independently
of the mind which perceives it. Just as the physical world is independent of
the knower, so also is the religious object independent of the person experiencing it in religious experience.[8] This independently existing religious
object may be thought of at the minimum as "the divine-value-producing
factor in the universe." That is to say that there is a "minimum reality or
power" which can be depended upon to promote the production of divine
values whenever man makes "a certain right specifically religious adjustment" to this reality.[9] But if religion at its practical best is value, it is
necessary that religion must have roots in value already realized. In order
for God to be worthy of worship or, as Wieman says, the most worthful,
He must be the true ideal already actual. That is, value cannot just emerge
in the world without having some adequate source in value already realized. At the same time, in order for man's sense of moral obligation to have
any meaning, there must be a realm in which ideal value is not yet fully
realized. These two conditions, Macintosh says, are satisfied by a conception of God as one *"whose will is perfectly good but whose good will is not*

---

[7] Cf. pp. 98–100.
[8] Cf. D. C. Macintosh, *The Problem of Religious Knowledge*, p. 349.
[9] Cf. *ibid.*, p. 378.

yet fully realized in man and in the world."[10] This definition starts on a common ground with the naturalistic conception of Wieman, but goes on, guided by necessity, to an understanding of God which is not naturalistic, at the same time holding consistently to a realist epistemology.

A. C. Garnett finds his clue to the meaning of God in the altruistic will. True also to the realistic treatment of knowledge, he insists, like Macintosh, that the religious object exists independently of him who beholds it. The prophets of religion, he says, have not created an ideal and then proclaimed it. What they did was to see that "the true nature of the purposive process that works within the individual is not merely a will to his own good, but rather a disinterested will that seeks, in and through him, to produce the good wherever it may be possible."[11] Instead of being capable of description as the value-producing factor in the world, God is known to us primarily, Garnett says, as "the altruistic will that seeks, in and through each individual, the good of all."[12] Now, the important question is, "Is this altruistic will the will of a Person?" Garnett answers by saying that it depends on how we define personality. If we mean by personality an "isolated center of consciousness,"[13] then God is not personal. For to give Him this attribute would reduce Him to a level at which His relation with men would be merely social, like the relation of the father to members of his family. Nor does such a conception do justice to the omnipresence of God. The disinterested will must be thought of as rooted in "neutral substance present in each organism"[14] if it is to be a truly disinterested will having no favorites or vested interests. On the other hand, if personality is defined as "an organization of will,"[15] then God is personal. For He is known to us, not only as will, but as a disinterested altruistic will which seeks the good of all through each, a personality including all other personalities.

William Pepperell Montague, who has already been placed as one of the original new realists,[16] has contributed a chapter in Macintosh's *Religious Realism* in which he proposes a realist understanding of the Trinity. He frankly acknowledges the need, in beginning his meditation, for going beyond the world to explain the world, in this way ruling out a purely naturalistic metaphysics as inadequate. Viewing the physical world, as it is described by present-day science, as made up of an array of points of energy in rapid motion, he asks how it is probable that a world of such homogene-

[10] *Ibid.*, p. 406.
[11] A. C. Garnett, *op. cit.*, p. 124.
[12] *Ibid.*, p. 146.
[13] *Ibid.*, p. 245.
[14] *Ibid.*, p. 287.
[15] *Ibid.*, p. 288.
[16] Cf. p. 266.

ous entities could come into existence unless they sprang from a common source. The probability, he concludes, is small; and therefore he holds that a common world ground is necessary. It is when he proceeds to consider the nature of this world ground that he proposes a trinitarian conception. The first phase of the world ground, which he likens to God the Father, is a phase of sheer being, at which level the common ground of all being is "expressing itself in the production of . . . being in maximum abundance."[17] The second phase, likened to God the Son, is a level or aspect of the world ground in which the total of all essences is integrated in an organic personal unity and whose motion is toward incarnation in existence. While Montague says there is nothing impossible or absurd about the "Soul of the World" writing Himself into history as Jesus of Nazareth, at the same time he holds to a more diffused conception of the incarnation, as the tendency of this integrated sum of the essences to exist in the world. The third phase of this world ground, likened to God the Holy Ghost, is an unending purposeful activity by which human persons are brought more and more into harmony with one another and with the personality of the totality.

Reference should also be made at this point to what the new Protestant thought says about the nature of God, paralleling the comparable reference made in the preceding section to the epistemology of the new theology. In Emil Brunner's book, *Revelation and Reason,* there is a short exposition entitled "The God of Revelation,"[18] in which God as revealed in Christ is described as wholly different from God as discovered by speculation, as self-revealing Subject, as Person, as Lord and therefore Creator, as Wholly Other in contrast to man and his world, as Love, as completely to be identified in the thought of man with His kingdom, and as Trinity. Brief elaboration will be made of each of these characterizations.

1. The God of revelation is different from the God of speculation. This characterization is prompted by the desire to keep the distinction clear between idea and reality. What theistic philosophers do, it is contended, and especially those who "prove" the existence of God by arguments, is to construct an idea of God and make that idea the equivalent of God. The movement of revelation is quite the reverse of this movement of speculation; for in revelation, God, who is really and actually God, discloses Himself, and the recipient of revelation is thereby related, at least somewhat, to God as He actually is, and not to an idea about Him.

2. The God of revelation is the absolute and unconditioned Subject. This characterization is closely related to the distinction just made; an idea

---

[17] William P. Montague, "The Trinity: A Speculation," in D. C. Macintosh. *Religious Realism*, p. 499.

[18] Emil Brunner, *Revelation and Reason.* Philadelphia: The Westminster Press, 1946. Pp. 42–49.

of God is always an object, something frozen, dead, not quite real, because it is an idea; but God in self-revealing activity is not an object. He is an active subject, right at the time actively relating Himself and disclosing Himself to the recipient of revelation.

3. The God of revelation is Person. Self-disclosure or self-communication is the essence of personality. A person can only be known by self-communication; partly because of the privacy of personality, and partly because of the very essence of a person is only expressed when the person projects himself as active subject in the act of disclosing himself. To say that God is Person is not to take a prized kind of existence familiar to us within human experience and conjecture, "God is like this." For the phenomenon of personality has gained recognition by man only because of the Biblical revelation; we have come through the centuries to recognize the uniqueness and self-identity of human personalities as a result of the influence of the Bible's presentation of a self-communicating God.

4. The God of revelation is Lord and therefore Creator. This characterization is intended to give singular emphasis to the sovereignty of God. When the creatorship of God is given priority over the lordship of God, the tendency is to think of God as little more than a first cause. But when the sovereignty of God is given priority, then creatorship takes on its true significance; creation is actually the bringing into being out of nothingness. In the Bible, the recipients of revelation thought in just this pattern: they were first impressed by the lordship of God and because of this recognized Him as Creator, as the One apart from whom there could be no independent existence.

5. The God of revelation is Wholly Other. This characterization points to the Absolute transcendence of God. He is to be contrasted with man and his world as entirely separate and distinct in nature, wholly other. And because of this He is incomprehensible and unfathomable, never to be fully understood by man. While in revelation He discloses Himself to man so that man is directly confronted by Him, yet one of the most inclusive intellectual generalizations prompted in man by this confrontation is that God is unfathomable; revealed, yes, but also revealed as a mystery never to be fully known.

6. The God of revelation is Love. This characterization is a direct antithesis to the absolute transcendence of God, for it is a contradiction of wholly otherness, or holiness, for one to be spent in self-sacrificial giving of one's self to that compared to which it is wholly other. This, Brunner says, is "the central mystery of the Biblical revelation," that God should be willing "to give Himself wholly and entirely to His creature, to the final limit of the death on the Cross."[19] The self-communication and the self-surrender constitute the direct revelation; i.e., the love of God is both the

[19] *Ibid.*, p. 46.

source and the content of the revelation; for God "wills to reveal Himself *because* He loves" and at the same time "He wills to reveal *that* He loves."[20] Furthermore, because of the unreserved human response called out by this total self-giving of God, is the love of God fulfilled and therefore identified with His holiness, in this way relieving the antithesis of love and holiness. "Only because God gives Himself so unconditionally can the creature love Him unconditionally; only because he thus places the creature in communion with Himself can His will in the creature be fully realized."[21]

7. The God of revelation is to be completely identified with His kingdom, in the thinking of man. This characterization in its negative aspect is a correction of speculation and abstraction in religious knowledge; in its positive aspect it is an affirmation that God is always in relation to man, never aloof and disinterested. God is not to be thought of apart from His rule or kingdom, the divine order not yet conformed to by human affairs, but nevertheless ultimate and permanent as compared to human society. The God of the Bible is always in relation to men; and the God-man is the goal from all eternity, "the basis of the creation of the world as well as of its redemption."[22] This lends a kind of social empiricism to religious knowledge, according to which God is never so much to be found in speculative or mystical withdrawal from the world, as in the welter of human processes.

8. The God of revelation is Father, Son, and Spirit. This characterization of God as three persons in one is closely connected to the relatedness of God just mentioned; for to be always related to man and forever identified with a divine rule involve both incarnation and unity of the many in one by spiritual bonds. God is what He is in Himself; He is revealed to be what He is in His incarnate Son; He lifts man to the level of truly personal existence in the fellowship of the Holy Spirit, a fellowship of love in which each lives for the other.

In His very being God is One who loves. He loves before the world exists. He loves His Son from all eternity. In Him He loves the creature before He creates him. He creates him because He loves him and He reveals His love to him, which He has from all eternity, as He Himself from all eternity is Love.[23]

D. THE POWER AND GOODNESS OF GOD

William P. Montague, who has already distinguished himself as one of the realist characters in this book, is outspoken on the problem of God's

[20] *Loc. cit.*
[21] *Loc. cit.*
[22] *Ibid.,* p. 47.
[23] *Loc. cit.*

power and goodness. He jars us a bit with his blunt phrasing of the question in an essay in his book, *The Ways of Things*. This is how he puts it:

If God were all good, He would wish to abolish evil; and if He were all-powerful He would be able to abolish evil. Therefore, since He doesn't abolish evil, it must be either because He won't or because He can't.[24]

Since Montague has dealt with the problem so forthrightly and since he speaks for some realists, we will allow a statement of his solution of the problem to exemplify a realist way of handling the problem. But it must be remembered that realists do not unite in metaphysics at all, and that some realists may hold quite different beliefs concerning the power and goodness of God. For example, because realism generally has an attitude of reluctance toward unity, a central principle in idealist metaphysics, there is no necessity that evil be regarded as the result of God's self-limitation, as Montague regards it. In fact even Montague finds some attraction in the God-and-the-devil dualism, but rejects it as a polytheism.

Montague's chosen answer to the problem comes out of a dialectical struggle. On the one side in this struggle is pantheism, a conception placing God beyond good and evil. This, he says, makes God devoid of the ethical virtues which would "endear him to us."[25] And on the other side is conventional theism, which "oscillates between sheer inconsistency on the one side and something very like Pantheism with its nonmoral God on the other."[26] In trying to find the middle ground of synthesis in the midst of this dialectic, he emerges with a conception of God as good but finite, "a will to good" that is "everywhere pressed in by death, destruction, wasteful conflict, and confusion."[27] However, since the finiteness is purely the result of the freedom which men enjoy, and virtually a self-limitation by God, he actually approaches a conception not far different from what he calls "orthodox theism." Unlike Brightman,[28] he does not speak of any limitations essential to the nature of God which make Him finite. The limitations all come from the beings to whom He has given existence and out of whose freedom He intends to bring greater good.[29]

E. THE NATURE OF MAN

The variety in realist metaphysics, which is broad enough to include most every shade of doctrine between materialism on the one hand and

[24] William P. Montague, *The Ways of Things*. Englewood Cliffs, N.J.: Prentice-Hall, 1940. P. 113. The entire passage is italicized in the original, but the italics have not been carried over in the quotation.
[25] *Ibid.*, p. 115.
[26] *Loc. cit.*
[27] *Ibid.*, p. 122.
[28] Cf. pp. 232–234.
[29] Cf. pp. 282–283.

supernaturalism on the other, also applies in conceptions of man. As to the physical versus the spiritual constitution of man, there are many realists for whom the self is little more than a behaving organism which is under the necessity of efficient adjustment to the physical world. There are also realists who define reality as spiritual and in harmony with this metaphysics approximate a conception of the self which is similar to that of idealism. For them individual man has a self which is more than his body and which may be independent of it, a self which may develop into an ever larger self, eventually achieving immortality. Since these variations in realistic conceptions of selfhood have been represented in the discussion of realism as an educational philosophy,[30] additional elaboration will not be made here. But some attention must be given to the moral condition of man as it may be understood by realists.

Realism observes man as it finds him in actuality, and describes him as he reveals himself by his behavior. Inasmuch as realists do not commonly make much of consistency or unity as a metaphysical principle, they need have no hesitation in calling a spade a spade as they look at the condition of man. Evil may be a brute fact in the structure of the cosmos, as it well appears to be when our attention is focused on the affairs of man. Intellectually this is not disconcerting to the realist mentality, because the tendency is to think of the cosmos as a plurality of existences instead of making of it one unified whole. Correspondingly, depravity may be a brute fact in the essential constitution of man. Like naturalists, realists may acknowledge that the world is just what it appears to be, a complex of good and evil interwoven. And man, being so much a child of the natural order, may also have as much evil in his nature as good, if not more. Any attempts, therefore, to better the condition of man are visionary unless they are rooted in this kind of grim recognition of man as he actually is, seeing him in the rough, a creature of tooth and claw, as well as giving countenance to his more attractive potentialities.

The newer Protestant thought shares some of this grimness as it views natural man; it holds out no hope for him apart from what God can do for him when he yields to God His rightful place in his life. But before the moral condition of man is depicted, one reference must be made to the essential constitution of man as the new theology sees it. Individual man is clearly a person; he is not just an organism; he is made in the image of God. Since revelation is a personal encounter, "the fact that God reveals Himself through His Word presupposes that man is a being who has been created for this kind of communication," a person capable of person-to-person intercourse and more especially "communication through speech."[31]

[30] Cf. pp. 298–304.
[31] Emil Brunner, op. cit., p. 48.

The moral condition of man is that he is a sinner. He is a sinner who is not without responsibility for his sin; for there is implicit in him an "original revelation" from which he has turned away, and the turning away is the essence of his sinning. This "original revelation" was "instituted by the Creator"; its perversions have taken the form of self-imposed world views or mythologies.[32] The essence of man's sin is in turning away from God, because in turning away he has put himself before God. All natural men who have not responded to this original revelation by giving God His rightful place as supreme are in this condition; they have set themselves up in God's place as the captains of their own souls. Man's only salvation is in "allowing himself to be determined by the Word of God," and thus in coming to love God who has loved him first.[33]

[32] *Ibid.*, pp. 52–53.
[33] *Ibid.*, p. 54.

XVI

Neo-Scholasticism

A. The Status of Religion

B. The Argument for the Existence of God

C. The Nature of God

D. The Nature of Man

A young Jewish professor of philosophy in a nonsectarian college which was given birth by a Protestant denomination once characterized his own philosophy of religion by saying, "I am suffering from Thomistic poisoning." Both his affiliations and his remark suggest the importance of another line of religious thought, to be outlined in this chapter, which sometimes gets the name "realism" and actually has much in common with the realist pattern in philosophy. This is Neo-Scholasticism, a modern restatement of the philosophy of Saint Thomas Aquinas which has won its disciples today both within and without the Roman Catholic Church. One phase of its current attractiveness is the rather large province it gives to science, all the while accompanied by the insistence that modern science has made no discoveries which affect materially the central ideas in Saint Thomas. One example of this has already been noted in the discussion of Saint Thomas in sketching the history of realism; it is his conception of primary matter.[1] Since Saint Thomas defined primary matter as "being in potentiality," his

---

[1] Cf. pp. 251–252.

conception of matter is unaffected by nuclear physics, for example, which has now demonstrated the nonexistence of inert matter. Saint Thomas never asserted that inert matter had an independent existence as a kind of raw stuff out of which everything was made; therefore there is no conflict between his conception of matter and the conceptions of it resulting from the newer physics.

A. THE STATUS OF RELIGION

According to modern followers of Saint Thomas Aquinas, religion is the all-inclusive context of human life, the truths of which we possess by means of reason and revelation. There are two kinds of theology, both having their legitimate place in instructing us in religious knowledge, although one of them is superior to the other. The lesser of the two is *natural theology,* which includes philosophy as a discipline but also amounts to rather heavy reliance on the philosophy of Aristotle. The greater of the two is *supernatural theology*, comprised of the teachings of the Roman Catholic Church, which are accepted as revealed truth. Each of these will bear some elaboration.

First, religion is the all-inclusive context of human life. There is agreement between the Neo-Scholastic, idealist, and realist that religion is an independent and unique phase of life having its own independent roots. That is, there is agreement on the part of Neo-Scholastics, as far as the statement goes. They do not embrace it fully, however, because religion can scarcely be termed a phase of life. It is the totality of life on which all other aspects are based and in comparison with which they are secondary matters. Consider government, for example. The State, though a legitimate institution bringing order and control into human society, should not have final authority over the lives and destinies of men. Such authority as the State has is a borrowed power. Whereas expediency now makes it necessary for the Church to accommodate itself to a variety of types of government, and while the Church is able to place a certain stamp of approval upon different kinds of states, yet it alone is the bona fide institution where authority over the lives of men ultimately resides. True religion plays no second fiddle; it is the queen of man's affairs, the source from which these affairs deserve their legitimate existence.

The all-important reason for this, to speak of *supernatural theology* first, is that the Roman Catholic Church is the oracle of revealed truth. The only institution stemming directly from Christ and the Apostles, it is thereby qualified to speak the truth of God to men. It is the authenticated possessor of divine revelation, the teacher of *supernatural theology*.

This does not mean, however, that there is no legitimate place for knowledge derived from other sources. For, as indicated in the opening paragraph of this section, there is another recognized realm of knowledge known as *natural theology*. Great thinkers have contributed much to man's knowledge and they deserve serious study. Aristotle, the great logician and organizer of knowledge, by whom Saint Thomas was greatly influenced, is a notable case. Also, as we should give heed to great thinkers, neither should we disregard thought itself; for reason is a true vehicle of knowledge. Humanly speaking, truth must be approached rationally, and by demonstration proven to be true. Although man would certainly be lost without the Church and *supernatural theology,* especially as far as the essence of truth is concerned, by reason he can demonstate the validity of truths which are confirmed authoritatively by *supernatural theology.* For example, the truth of the existence of God can be demonstrated by rational arguments which are fully convincing to reason. At the same time, *supernatural theology* complements arguments for the existence of God, first, by confirming the truth of the argument from a source beyond man; and second, by revealing the nature of God, a kind of truth which is quite beyond rational demonstration. A good example of the Neo-Scholastic's conception of this relation between *natural* and *supernatural theology* is provided by K. F. Reinhardt in a sentence he has written toward the close of his "demonstration of God's existence" in his book, *A Realistic Philosophy.*[2] It is this: "thus, while we do not claim to have contributed to the comprehension of God's essence, we have tried to demonstrate the *necessity* of His *existence.*"

B. THE ARGUMENT FOR THE EXISTENCE OF GOD

Unlike idealism and modern realism, Neo-Scholasticism does not make the experience of God prior to a rational understanding of that experience. Our experience of God comes to us through the sacraments of the Roman Catholic Church and the priesthood which administers them. The only approach to the knowledge of God apart from the ministrations of the Church is the rational approach of logical argument. In the realm of *natural theology,* reason is more basic than direct experience. We cannot know God directly by intuition or by sense observation; but we can apply logical reasoning to the data of experience and arrive by this pathway at knowledge of the existence of God. So, to hew to the Neo-Scholastic line, we do not talk about our experience of God first of all and then about how we know Him; we first consider arguments for the existence of God.

Observe a Neo-Scholastic launching out into rational demonstration of the existence of God and you will see a realist at work. People are commonly misled by the pronounced emphasis on spiritual reality in Thomism.

[2] Milwaukee: The Bruce Publishing Company, 1944. P. 89.

Because of this Thomists are sometimes called idealists.[3] But this is a mistake, as it ignores the Thomistic epistemology, which has far more in common with realism than with idealism. We have already seen that realists run the gamut in metaphysics while agreeing pretty well in epistemology. Why then call Neo-Scholastics idealists, when it is only their metaphysics which has some similarity to idealism? Spiritual realism has as much in common with idealism as Thomism has. The more accurate classification is that Neo-Scholasticism constitutes another variety of religious realism in its metaphysics; its epistemology is as hardheaded as that of any other kind of realism.

The point of departure is the physical world, taken as much for granted by the Catholic philosopher as it is by any naturalist. Here in the external physical world we see existence which is unyieldingly independent of us, says the Neo-Scholastic. It is actual, present, impersonal existence. Now, if we analyze a little bit, we realize that the physical world is made up of all kinds of things. There are many different kinds of objects and entities. There is a whole array of qualities which give different objects their respective natures; i.e., each kind of object is distinct, according to the unique combination of qualities it possesses. Also, things change and decay; some objects, such as animals and men, are born, grow, reach their prime, then decline, die, and decay. And in addition, inanimate entities change their form, also going through a cycle of generation and dissolution. Viewed overall, the physical world is a panorama both of greatly divergent objects and objects in many different stages of existence. In all this cosmic panorama the Neo-Scholastic finds one aspect common to all the vast variety of things and their stages. This common aspect is that they all *exist*. While there are differences in essence which make concrete things uniquely individual, in all the variety of essence there is commonness of *existence*.

True enough, relations of cause and effect produce many of the changes evident in the world by which one form or stage of existence becomes another. But, and this is important, sheer cause-and-effect relations between different existing things are not an adequate basis for existence as such. If this were the case, there would not only be an infinite regression of causes, one thing being caused by another, and it in turn by another, and the next by still another, and so on *ad infinitum;* but there would be some point in the regression of causes at which existence itself would have to be caused. And this is an impossibility. How can something be caused by nothing? How can something which *is* be the result of something (?) which *is not?* So, says the Neo-Scholastic, all existing things which make themselves evident in the phenomenal world are rooted and grounded in a

---

[3] Cf. the editor's introduction to Pierre J. Marique, *The Philosophy of Christian Education.* New York: Prentice-Hall, 1939.

common substratum of existence, in that which is because it is. In Aristotelian terms, there is an ultimate *efficient cause* for all the different varieties and stages of being which constitute the physical universe; and this ultimate cause is the *Unmoved Mover,* that existence which is the common foundation of all existing things.

Roughly, this is a sketch of the trend of the Neo-Scholastic argument considered adequate to demonstrate the *existence* or *thatness* of God. There is one further step in the argument, however, which adds to sheer *existence* sufficient *essence* or *whatness* to identify Divine Intelligence with ultimate *existence.* The path on which this added step is taken is the famous argument from design. Briefly, it is said that there is pattern and purpose in the world which is only to be understood as the result of intelligent intention; therefore ultimate existence, the Unmoved Mover, the finally efficient cause, must be *Intelligence.* Now there are characteristic Aristotelian overtones in a fuller appreciation of this argument. The design beheld in the world is not a simple structural design; it has many dimensions. In the welter of existences making up the world, each has its own distinctive end or purpose, its own *entelechy.* Now such fulfillment of ends would hardly happen by chance, at least not with as much consistency throughout the gamut of existences as it actually does. Combine this aspect of the world with the observation already made that there must be a common substratum of existence as such, and we have Ultimate Being which is Intelligent, and which purposefully gives being to all the constituent entities comprising the cosmos. This makes a great deal of sense; whereas anything short of it does little justice either to the fact of existence or to the fact of fulfilled purposes, both confronting us on every side in the world surrounding us but independent of us.

C. THE NATURE OF GOD

Intellectual formulations concerning the nature of God are quite different from the argument just outlined demonstrating His existence. For while argument regarding the existence of God deals with the *thatness* of God; formulations relating to His nature try to penetrate to His *whatness* and answer the question, What is God like? The former task is better suited to the intellect than the latter; because while the existence of God confronts us in the actualities of the phenomenal world, there is no such immediacy about the nature of God. He escapes our attempts at definition chiefly because the machinery of definition is designed for the creature world of concrete individuals, not for the Creator, Who is beyond everything He has created.

More specifically, to attempt to define God is to try to fit Him into some class or genus, whereas He is beyond all encirclement by classification. Definition, to be strictly appropriate, needs to give up attempts at positive statement and instead proceed negatively, saying what God is not. Even so, when this is done, thought will continue to draw logical circles of classification; but the circles drawn, instead of including God, will exclude Him and so indicate His nature in part by a negative logic of exclusion.

To be strictly appropriate, we just said, this would be the kind of definition that should be followed. Actually, however, scholastic philosophy does make positive statements of definition. The practical necessity of this will be recognized; at the same time it will be noted that there is a sense of the inadequacy of the statements. Of course the negative element is sometimes present even when the form of the proposition is not negative. That is to say that while the proposition may affirm, it will also convey this comparison: God is not different specifically, He is different totally, and must be grasped in terms of His complete diversity from us, rather than on the basis of specific contrasts or differences. This in itself is one of the affirmations of Neo-Scholasticism about God.

As has been explained before, it is in regard to the nature of God that revelation is most pertinent. There is a historic revelation of which the Church is the mediator; and this disclosure of the Triune God for the salvation of man is the great supplment of intellectual formulation, and also the great source of content for that formulation. Attention is most closely focused here upon the content of revelation, the nature of God as represented in the teachings of the Church; the manner of the revelation is reflected only incidentally. For this statement we lean most heavily on Cardinal Mercier, who, together with colleagues in the Higher Institute of Philosophy at Louvain, compiled the two-volume work entitled *A Manual of Modern Scholastic Philosophy*.[4] First the exposition will be outlined by listing ten propositions regarding the nature of God; then each proposition will be taken up, one at a time, in the order listed, enlarging upon it by way of trying to make its meaning more explicit. The ten propositions are:

1. God is not extended.
2. However, God is immanent in His creation.
3. God is absolutely subsistent.
4. In Him, existence and essence are identical.
5. God is pure actuality; there is no potentiality in Him.
6. God is perfect, actually.
7. The goodness of God and the being of God are identical.
8. God is infinite in perfection; His goodness is unlimited.
9. The eternity of God transcends all time limitations and measures.

[4] Authorized translation and eighth edition by T. L. Parker and S. A. Parker. London: Routledge & Kegan Paul, 1916–1917.

10. God is *one*, of necessity, not two, nor many; all other individuals are excluded from being what He is by virtue of what He is.

1. *God is not extended.* Comparison with Spinoza will be helpful in understanding this proposition.[5] Spinoza described God as having two attributes: the one, thought, the other, extension. Never, he contended, does thought exist without extension into the time-space world. Now, the position of Neo-Scholasticism is a contradiction of the extended aspect which Spinoza attributed to God. Thomism only partially agrees with Spinoza that God is thought; He is thought plus other attributes, but certainly He is not extended, nor any part of Him, into the phenomenal world. He is in no sense identical with Nature; He is beyond Nature, the foundation of Nature, the Creator by whose hand Nature has been formed.

2. *However, God is immanent in His creation.* This is a correction of an unwarranted implication that some might draw from the first proposition, to the effect that God is wholly transcendent and has little to do with this world of time and space. But Neo-Scholastics insist that God is present in His creation and cite Saint Thomas to authenticate this position. Cardinal Mercier quotes the *Summa Theologica* on this question to the following effect:

God is in all things by His *Power*, inasmuch as all things are subject to His Power; He is in all things by His *Presence*, as all things are bare and open to His eyes; He is in all things by His *Essence*, inasmuch as He is the cause of existence to all things.[6]

3. *God is absolutely subsistent.* The demonstration of the existence of God, in addition to demonstrating the fact of God's reality, does call attention to one important aspect of His nature. It identifies Him as Being, as such, the very opposite of nonbeing. He is the only one who exists absolutely; He depends on none other for His existence, and all others derive their existence from Him. This is a very important distinction between God and created beings.

4. *In Him existence and essence are identical.* There are at least two ways of getting at the significance of this proposition; one by comparison with critical realism, such as that of Santayana, and the other by considering the difference between the potential and the actual. The second of these approaches will be reserved for the discussion of proposition 5, which is a complement of this one. Santayana makes a complete distinction between existence and essence. The essences or qualities which we experience, as for example in music or art, constitute one realm. The brute force of the physical world, completely independent of our subjective interests, is another realm. These two have little to do with each other.[7] By contrast, Neo-

[5] Cf. pp. 117–118 and 256–257.
[6] Cardinal Mercier, *op. cit.*, Vol. II, p. 80.
[7] Cf. p. 165 and 279.

Scholasticism finds these two realms to be unified in God. He is existence and He is also fully actualized essence. In Him essence exists, and in Him also existence is actual value, not potential value yet to be realized.

5. *God is pure actuality; there is no potentiality in Him.* In human nature there is a clear difference between what is actual and what is yet potential. Human society, for example, is now actually in a state of delicate balance, having emerged from a total war, had the aggravation of brush-fire wars, established a world peace organization of real stature, but having not yet made the agreements between nations and groups which would be the structure of a peaceful world. At the time of writing, this is one of the aspects of society as it actually is. But within this actuality are evident potentialities for possible actualities in the future. There is dangerous potentiality for more war and destruction; and there is some potentiality for peace. Only further developments will determine which of these potentialities will become actual. But such is not the case with God; He is not a composite of potential and actual, as man and his world is. There is not that in His nature which is only implicit or about to be. He has no potentialities which are not realized. He is pure actuality; all that He is, is fully consummated reality.

6. *God is perfect, actually.* This proposition, it can be seen, follows logically from what has just been said. If God had potentialities which are not yet actualized, then He would not be perfect. For there would yet be something for Him to become, which now He is not. And this is not perfection, because it lacks something. Perfection, in order to be perfection, must be actually wrought out. And God being perfect, His perfection is actual.

7. *The goodness of God and the being of God are identical.* The truth of this proposition is implied in several of the foregoing statements; it needs now to be made explicit. What it affirms is that the existence of God and the moral quality of His character are necessarily one and the same reality. They are inseparable except in logical analysis, when at one time we talk of the being aspect of God, and at another of the ethical aspect of His nature. Being and goodness are necessarily united in Him. For, while evil is a negation of being, God is Absolute Being. Therefore, for Him to be is to be perfect; and for Him to be perfect is for Him *to be,* absolutely and actually.

8. *God is infinite in perfection; His goodness is unlimited.* One reason we have difficulty in thinking of God as infinite is that we are finite. On the face of it, this is a truism, unless we recognize that our word "infinite" gets its meaning by contrast with our word "finite." We are limited, drawn about by a circumference on every side which cuts us off as individuated, finite creatures. When we think of God in terms of dimensions we must somehow transcend our own limitations, but in addition we must also leap

beyond the very structure of limitation as such. We cannot just think of the largest possible dimension, then stretch that to something larger, and so on. What we have to do is to try to conceive the very opposite of our experience of limitation, the contradiction of it, and then apotheosize that, i.e., say "God is like that." Now, applying this to the goodness of God, we get the picture of Him as One whose goodness knows no circumference whatsoever. No encirclement of any kind surrounds Him.

9. As with all space limitations, so also with all limits of time, *the eternity of God transcends all time limitations or measures*. As we have to espouse the negation of space limitations as representing the infinity of God to us, so we need to understand the eternity of God in terms of the negation of time limits and measures. For Him there is no time, but, as Augustine says, "Thy To-day, is Eternity."[8] We cannot think of God so much in terms of endless time as we need to think of Him as having such vast comprehension that everything for Him is within one ever-present now. So much are we humans the creatures of time, enduring through succeeding moments, days, and years, that with difficulty we transport ourselves in thought to a vantage point from which we can imagine all events telescoped into the timeless present of one vast all-inclusive Consciousness.

10. *God is one, of necessity, not two nor many; all other individuals are excluded from being what He is by virtue of what He is*. This final proposition deals with the singular uniqueness of God. The mere impact of the cumulative character of the foregoing statements stirs one's consciousness with the idea that this One about whom we speak is One like whom there is no other. And to go further, analyzing the relation of single propositions to this generalization is to see more reason for its being held true. For example, if *God is absolutely subsistent,* as proposition 3 states, can there be any other thing which is self-subsistent? God being that very root and ground of all being as such, there can be no other who shares this fundamental existence. Cardinal Mercier, however, fixes on the infinity of God to clinch this point, saying that there cannot be two *infinite beings*. Consider the possibility. If, hypothetically, there were two infinite beings, one of two alternatives would have to characterize their relation to each other. Either (1) one would be dependent on the other, or (2) they would be completely independent of each other. Now if (1) one is dependent on the other, then the one which is dependent is not infinite. And if (2) it is assumed possible that there is another infinite being besides God, which is completely independent of Him, then God is not infinite. For in that case there would be some being which is in addition to His own, and limits Him to the extent that it exists. Both of these suppositions are evident impossibilities; and it becomes evident that, being infinite, God is of necessity *One,* not two, nor many.

[8] As quoted from the *Confessions* by Mercier, *op. cit.,* Vol. II, p. 87.

D. THE NATURE OF MAN

Neo-Scholasticism could not be represented even sketchily without making its conception of man at least somewhat explicit. In doing this something should be said as to the essential character of man, that is to say of what he is constituted; also his nature as a moral being and his moral condition need to be described. In doing the latter it is necessary to make three things specific; these are the natural and normal end he has as his goal in life by virtue of his being a man, and the power this end has over his actions; his possession of freedom of will; and the privations of his will which result in sinful acts.

First of all, the essential character of man is that he is a rational animal in which body and soul are united as one. He may be classified as an animal because there is a material principle basic in his makeup; he has a body, and this body, in addition to having the nutritive functions of vegetation, has the locomotive powers and appetites of animals. But man is more than an animal; he is a rational animal. He is capable of reasoning, whereas animals are not. This means that man knows abstract ideas and perceives "universal necessary relations obtaining between objects thus abstractly conceived";[9] and animals show no signs of having such knowledge.

The body is the material principle in man and the soul is the rational-spiritual principle in man; but in man these two are united in one. The material or corporeal side of man "is alive, grows, experiences sensations and forms desires, feels pain and pleasure." The spiritual acts of which the soul of man is capable are intellectual abstraction, self-reflection, voluntary movement toward the good, and the initiation of free, rational volitions. However, these two principles are not separate and distinct; but rather *"the corporeal, sentient subject and the rational soul do by their union form one single substance, one nature, one person."* This union is effected by *"the rational soul being the substantial form of this single substance."*[10] This substratum of every vital act, the soul, is a spiritual being; and this means that it is "capable of existing and acting without depending intrinsically upon an organ, or, in more general terms, upon matter." However, "it is possible for a spiritual being to depend *extrinsically*, or *indirectly*, upon matter. And this is the case with the rational soul which depends on the sense-organs inasmuch as these have to furnish it with a material object for its operations."[11]

In turning attention to the moral nature of man, it is necessary to consider his ultimate end before taking up the freedom of the will and the

[9] Cardinal Mercier, *op. cit.*, Vol. I, p. 281.
[10] *Ibid.*, p. 302.
[11] *Ibid.*, p. 295.

privations of the will which result in sinful acts. According to Neo-Scholasticism, man, so constituted as a rational being in whom soul and body are united as one, has a natural end which matches this his essential character. This natural end is what it is in him to become, comparable to an Aristotelian final cause.[12] The final end of a house, for example, is a place of abode; that is what it is made for. It may be put to other purposes, but this is the end to which it is perfectly matched both by intention and the way it is constituted. Man has a similar end for which he is intended and constituted, and this end or goal necessarily governs his actions to an inclusive extent because it is the unconscious substratum of his being, a given in his makeup, apart from any conscious willing or intending on his part. The essence of this ultimate end of man is moral goodness, perfection, godliness, a state comprised of acts of "contemplative knowledge of God."[13] Accordingly, it is given in man that he should seek this ultimate good; this is so almost to the extent that man cannot choose to do otherwise, for it is intended in him and he is constituted for that good as his normal and natural end. Consequently, with only notable exceptions, every man is seeking to reach this ultimate goal of goodness in all that he does. It may be, as will be explained later, that he is often mistaken in assuming that certain actions are in harmony with this ultimate good; but his intentions are nevertheless good in choosing them, because he assumes that they are steps in the direction of this good.[14]

For the Neo-Scholastic, man possesses liberty of action; he is free in his choices. This, it is held, is a necessary aspect of a moral order. Man is not determined in his actions by inner laws or by external forces; he chooses freely in determining what a multitude of specific actions shall be. Of course emotion and appetite participate in decisions between alternative pathways, as well as reason; but the rational side of man's nature is capable of having the upper hand to the extent that an individual is not predisposed toward a given action by appetite, beyond the potentiality of reason to intervene and redirect his intentions. Freedom of will for the most part is a phenomenon of choosing means and not choosing ends. This means that the multitudinous choices which a man makes in his lifetime are choices of specific acts as means to the fulfillment of his ultimate end. These operations of free will are not most commonly and most normally choices of ends, i.e., deliberate choosing of evil against good, as such, or vice versa. Man is however capable of such choices, although they are not representative of the great body of his decisions and actions. And in this is seen one of the weaknesses of free will by the Neo-Scholastic. This particular use of free will to choose between ends rather than means is an imper-

[12] Cf. p. 250.
[13] Cardinal Mercier, *op. cit.*, Vol. II, p. 219.
[14] Cf. *ibid.*, pp. 214–223.

fection of free will; it is putting the function of willing to a use for which it is not intended. The normal and natural function of free will "is based on a spontaneous, necessary inclination of the faculty towards the good in general";[15] it is only operating in its legitimate province when man is inclining in the direction of his natural end, ultimate goodness. Man is only free, therefore, when his choices are prompted by this given inclination of his being.

The sins of man, according to Neo-Scholasticism, result from privations of the will. This is true both at the level of choice between means and at the level of choice between ends. The evident fact that man actually commits an infinite number and variety of evil acts which are out of harmony with the ultimate good which is his natural end is explained by defects of the will which make possible these deviations from the good. The sinfulness of man is similar to physical disease or deformity. If a person's sense of sight is impaired, his vision deviates from a true representation of what he sees, in accordance with the kind of defect his eyes have. The indistinctness of objects and the faulty perception are comparable to sin; the defects in the eyes which cause this faulty vision are comparable to the privations of will which are the cause of sin. Similarly, if an animal is crippled, it limps when it walks. The limping is analogous to sin in the moral realm; the deformity of the leg is analogous to the defects of the will. As already indicated, free will operates most commonly and most normally at the level of choice between means. It is therefore at this level that sin most commonly occurs. The privations are mistakes in selecting the kinds of actions which are in harmony with the natural good, basic to the constitution of man as man. These privations and their resultant sins are therefore not as serious and are more easily remedied than privations of will which operate at the level of choosing ends. They are mistakes of detail, as it were, and not defects in intention regarding the total life pattern. The privation of the will which is mortal is that will can be misused in the deliberate choice of evil in preference to good; this privation is mortal because it is a defect in the total pattern of life and not a mistake in detail. If a person persists throughout his life in this perversion of will, choosing evil as an end rather than good, and never repenting of it, he is beyond redemption, and his necessary plight is eternal punishment.[16]

---

[15] *Ibid.*, Vol. I, p. 272.

[16] Cf. *ibid.*, Vol. I, pp. 274, 293; Vol. II, pp. 239, 246. See also R. Garrigou-LaGrange, *God: His Existence and His Nature*. Translated from the fifth French edition by Dom Bede Rose; St. Louis, Mo.: B. Herder Book Co., 1941. Vol. II, p. 381.

XVII

Strengths and Weaknesses in the Philosophy of Realism

A. The Strengths of Realism

B. The Weaknesses of Realism

The final task in this study of the philosophy of realism is one of making an estimate of some of the strengths and weaknesses in this point of view. Wherein is its value, and at what points does it fall short? These are the questions now confronting us.

A. THE STRENGTHS OF REALISM

The chief strength of the philosophy of realism is to be found in its cardinal principle that whatever is real is independent of any knower who may come to have knowledge of it. While the substance of this contention is that the strength of realism is to be found in this principle, it is not the same as saying that this cardinal principle of realism is acceptable in its entirety. The core of the principle in which this real value is to be found can be indicated by restating it in a more limited form, such as "whatever is real is independent of every finite individual who may come to know it." This affirms the independence of reality as compared to the individual knower and his ideas about it. But it does not affirm, as many realists do,

346

that reality is independent of any mind whatsoever, whether finite or infinite.

This much of realism, exclusive of its more general doctrine that Mind is not basic to reality and being, is a wholesome correction of the more subjective tendencies sometimes found among idealists. However much the individual mind needs to participate in the knowing transaction in order to yield the composite of percepts and concepts constituting knowledge, reality still remains independent of all of this; and the individual does not make reality, he only discovers it. Since he is an individual, he cannot possess knowledge of it without participating in perceptual and conceptual transactions which are creative; but the creativity is limited to his own experience of or knowledge of, and does not affect ultimate being itself.

Realism accordingly demands of us that we recognize the importance of relation to that which is beyond ourselves. However fascinating our own mental processes may be to us, and however much we may enjoy living within ourselves, where do they get us if these mental processes and subjective states are not dealing with the actualities of the objective world beyond ourselves? It is absolutely necessary that we be in touch with facts, and the philosophy of realism impresses upon us the urgency of this in its insistence that reality is independent of us. There follow from this influence of realism all of the values for mental health which were mentioned in giving an estimate of some of the strengths of the philosophy of naturalism.[1] To the extent that a person is inclined to get lost in his own private experience, realism's insistence on being related to the world as it is can help to bring simplicity and clarity to take the place of the complexity and confusion accompanying excessive preoccupation with one's own subjective orbit.

This is the chief ground of the strength of realism as a philosophy of religion. Whereas its extreme variety in metaphysics virtually amounts to as many philosophies of religion as there are variations in metaphysics, the more naturalistic ones quite inadequate, and those open to the spiritual and supernatural more acceptable; yet, throughout, there is this common insistence that the real is independent of our knowledge processes. Therefore all realistic philosophies of religion hold in common the requirement that a distinctively religious adjustment involves being related to that which is beyond ourselves, at the least. The consequent good effect in religious experience is to favor emphasis upon the objective in preference to dwelling upon the subjective.

B. THE WEAKNESSES OF REALISM

1. Apart from the fact that idealism had been in the saddle in American philosophy for some time, it is hard to understand the violence of the

[1] Cf. pp. 104–105.

realist revolt against the idealist principle that the character of knowledge as such reveals something about the character of reality. The principle with which the philosophy of realism has proposed to supplant this idealist principle is that the character of knowledge as such reveals nothing about the nature of reality; although specific items of knowledge may disclose specific characteristics of reality. But even on the basis of a realistic theory of knowledge, how can knowledge fail to reveal something by its general character? Admittedly, does it not reveal, for example, that reality is independent of the knower, and that, to some extent at least, reality is knowable? Are not these two general characteristics of reality implicit in the realist theory of knowledge?

Once it is admitted that the individual has the kind of knowledge relation with the world beyond him which is something less than a complete mismatching and complete disjointedness—i.e., there is sufficient synchronization of external stimuli and sense perceptions that the relation makes a little sense—once this is admitted, then the knowability or interpretability of the world is affirmed, at least partially. And this approximates the cardinal knowledge principle of idealism, that reality is capable of interpretation. Not that it has all been interpreted or ever will be, or that it is perfectly understood, or ever will be fully comprehended; but that the individual has a cognitive relation with that which is beyond him, which, being less than complete disparity of man and reality, indicates that reality is capable of some interpretation. Therefore it is not completely different in character from the mind or spirit of man who interprets it.

2. Another weakness of the philosophy of realism is its tendency to embrace pluralism in preference to a more unified view of reality. It is easy to understand the hesitancy to embrace a quickly won unity before having tasted quite fully the complexity of life and existence. But it is quite another thing to be enslaved by this complexity and variety after having tasted of it, and to give up hope of ever finding any unity in the cosmos. Of what profit is reflection, if it yields no more integration and interrelationship than this? If mature thought can yield no more unity of understanding, it is little better than the kind of common-sense antithesis to reflection which takes life to be just one thing after another, and no more.

3. Another weakness common to some realists, particularly Santayana and those who follow him in holding his doctrine of essences, is the separation of value and being into two distinct realms. This, it might be said, is a qualitative aspect of the favoritism of realism for discontinuity as compared to unity and interrelatedness, for pluralism in preference to monism. If values are abiding, they must have some rootage in existence. And if existence is anything more than a sheerly neutral persistence or endurance, then it has value woven into its very texture. In fact, the value-being dualism, like all others, is a weighted dualism, the contention being that the

essences or qualities which sentient beings undergo or endure are little more than an accompaniment of existence, a sentient parallel to the blind processes of Nature which will fall into nothingness when sentient beings cease to be. This is arid sophistication, man using the assumptions of realism to read himself out of existence. Yet he has to describe the existence in which supposedly he does not participate; he has to imagine the arid persistence of blind energy without qualities of any kind which will continue on when he, who has to do the imagining, and all other sentient creatures, will have ceased to exist. How can he be sure that his thought has any descriptive or predictive value unless the existence he tries to describe has some kind of qualitative correspondence to the qualities of his own thought and experience?

Whatever this may be philosophically, on the psychological side this view splits life into two: the existence side and the value or essence side. And some adherents of this kind of realism have cloistered themselves quite exclusively on the value side, enjoying the essences, as aesthetes, but communicating little with the world and having little to do with the ongoing struggles of individuals and of the whole society of man. As compared to this, there is a much more sane approach in recognizing interrelationship between value and existence, value being rooted in existence and existence being filled full of value.

4. As to the realist approach to education, at least three criticisms are in order: its conception of the pupil is not adequate, it makes too much of the transmission of content, and it lays too much stress on formation of the pupil. Each of these will be taken up in order.

Strictly speaking, of course, there is no single realist conception of the pupil; instead there are several realistic conceptions of the pupil. This happens, when realism is put to work in education, as a result of the great variety of metaphysical beliefs held by realists. The more nearly naturalistic the conception of the pupil is, the less adequate it is. For pupils are something more than physical organisms having highly developed nervous systems. Conversely, the more nearly the pupil conception of a realist educational philosophy approaches the recognition that pupils are selves rooted in an existence which is more fundamental than their bodies, the more adequate it becomes. But even in a close approximation of this view of the pupil there may be lacking a sufficient unity of body and mind. For even in spiritual realism and Neo-Scholasticism there is enough of the general tendency of realism to regard the physical as independent that a genuine unity of body and mind is scarcely achieved.

5. In taking up the second criticism of realism as an educational philosophy, that it places too much confidence in the transmission of content, it may be well to look first of all at the more general character of this prime confidence of realism. Realists insist that reality is independent of mind;

that it is unchanged by any transactions in which it is in relation with mind. Reality therefore has characteristics which can be described; there need be no cogitation about these characteristics, they are just what they are. Therefore the descriptions of science are accurate descriptions; and if a person wants to learn what the world is like, science can tell him. Similarly, the cultural and religious heritages are definite; either of them can be accurately described. To come to know them is to be informed about the specifics by a descriptive presentation of them. Such is the confidence of realism in content or subject matter. Education must be full of this sort of thing in order to accomplish anything. But when the realist goes on to make explicit just what this dependable content of teaching is, he seems to get into difficulty. What he at first assumes to be the dependable descriptive content of science seems on closer scrutiny to be very fluid in character, much more like the changing content pragmatists insist that science is, as compared to what realists would lead us to believe it is. So also with the cultural and religious heritages; they seem not to be so much a changeless fund of knowledge as a flowing stream of which we ourselves are a part and out of which we have come.

To go on from this point to affirm what true content is, is to make a big affirmation, too large for the present task of criticism and not primarily germane to it. But this much will be said: The true content is to be found, not in the substance of science or culture, as in realism, nor in a flowing stream of change, as in pragmatism, but in the One who is behind and beneath these, who is the Changeless One, but who is also the Living One, therefore having all the freedom and vitality of an ever-flowing stream of change.

6. As much need not be said regarding the third and last criticism of realism as a philosophy of education; this is that realism places too much stress upon the formation of the pupil. There is of course formation of the pupil by the culture and more specifically by the home and school. And much of this formation is in its place, particularly at the level at which it goes on quite unconsciously. But for education as a self-conscious institution of society to devote itself deliberately to the function of formation is for it to fail to arise to full recognition of individual selfhood, not only for its own sake but also for its potentiality for renewing and remaking society. Where selves are concerned, and they are primarily concerned in education, the only adequate formation, and in the long run the only effective formation, is formation from within. And that more closely approximates inspiration and self-realization. When education centers its efforts primarily in formation it fails to reach the level at which it deals with selves as selves.

PART FIVE

PRAGMATISM

XVIII

A Brief History of Pragmatism

A. Some Ancient Roots of Pragmatism
1. HERACLITUS
2. THE SOPHISTS

B. Francis Bacon

C. Auguste Comte

D. The Pragmatist Tradition in America

1. CHARLES SANDERS PEIRCE
2. WILLIAM JAMES
3. JOHN DEWEY

E. Synthesis

A. SOME ANCIENT ROOTS OF PRAGMATISM

Pragmatism is admittedly a modern philosophy—even more distinctly, a modern American philosophy. It was born in recent times and is a child of America, more than any other contemporary system of ideas. Yet it did not spring from nowhere; it has roots in the past and some of them are ancient. Two of the earliest appearances of beliefs found in the pragmatism of today occurred in the teachings of Heraclitus and the Sophists; so in trying to understand the background of pragmatism we first turn to these early Greek philosophies.

1. HERACLITUS

The life span of Heraclitus is not exactly known. Windelband places his birth between 540 and 530 B.C. and says that his death could scarcely have occurred before 470 B.C.[1] He was the child of a most eminent family of Ephesus. What we know of his ideas comes to us by way of a few fragments of his own writing and references to him by others, particularly Plato and Aristotle, who wrote when his ideas were still current. While not fully representing the philosophy of Heraclitus, even as expressed in the fragments, the stress he places upon the fact of change in the world is one of his most distinguishing marks. And since this is the strain of thought modern pragmatism holds in common with him, we will limit our efforts to outlining some phases of his doctrine of change.

There is a kind of poetic dualism to which he gave expression in a variety of ways. On every hand he beheld opposites: the soul and water, water and earth, day and night, winter and summer, war and peace, satiety and hunger, fire and air, the living and the dead, the waking and the sleeping, the young and the old, the cold and the warm, the moist and the dry.[2] But these opposites did not appear to him as ultimately separate forces, entities, or states opposing one another. Instead they constituted for him appearances which pass into one another, changing and becoming their opposites. Earth becoming water, water becoming soul, day becoming night, and night becoming day, the young becoming old, and so on, infinitely. So that the apparent forms which are in evidence in the world about us were not abiding realities for Heraclitus; they were stages in the process of eternal change pervading all things.

The real, then, for him, was the constant flux and movement by which perceptible things change and become something different. This is made poetically vivid in three of his sayings:

All things flow; nothing abides.
One cannot step twice into the same river.
Into the same rivers we step and do not step; we are and we are not.[3]

Thinghood and substantiality are not adequate categories for understanding this ever-flowing reality. Heraclitus came closest to using these

[1] Cf. W. Windelband, *History of Ancient Philosophy*. Translated by Herbert Ernest Cushman; New York: Charles Scribner's Sons, 1899. P. 58.
[2] Cf. *The Fragments* as compiled by Charles M. Bakewell in his *Source Book in Ancient Philosophy*. Revised edition; New York: Charles Scribner's Sons, 1939. Pp. 28–35.
[3] *Ibid.*, p. 33.

categories when he described reality as fire. "All things are exchanged for fire," he said, "and fire for all things, just as wares are exchanged for gold and gold for wares."[4] Another saying gives a pantheistic turn to the nature of this eternal flux, by the use of the term God to denote it.

God is day and night, winter and summer, war and peace, satiety and hunger. But he assumes various forms, just as fire when it is mingled with different kinds of incense is named according to the savor of each.[5]

Matching these thoughts with modern experimentalism, one or two observations can be made. First, there are no pantheistic elements in pragmatism, as in Heraclitus. Second, the kinds of opposites described by this ancient citizen of Ephesus are somewhat unsubtle and crude as compared to John Dewey's labor and leisure, the intellectual and the practical, the physical and the social, the individual and the world.[6] The latter dualisms represent conflicts in society. But their resolutions are imperative, as Dewey sees it, and are to be brought about by means of social change and the educative process. In the third place, and this is the most important observation, the concept of change is fundamental both in Heraclitus and modern pragmatism. In both philosophies reality is not described as a substance which has some kind of solidity or dependability; instead, it is a constant flux, like the ever-changing waters of a river.

2. THE SOPHISTS

Also from Plato and Aristotle we learn of certain itinerant teachers about whom there must have been much talk in the fifth century B.C. They were known as Sophists and were apparently quite a rage among Athenian youth. In Plato's *Protagoras,* which among other things is a vivid portrait of Protagoras, the great Sophist, young Hippocrates is agog with excitement as he comes to Socrates with the news that Protagoras is in town. And he wants Socrates to arrange an introduction for him so that he can study with the great teacher. The history of philosophy generally has not shared this admiration of young Athenians for the Sophists. The word Sophist has been more often a stigma than a compliment. Windelband blames Plato and Socrates for this disposition of students of philosophy toward these traveling teachers. He says they depicted the Sophists in a bad light and the unfavorable impression they gave of them was not fully justified.[7]

Protagoras and Gorgias, chief among the Sophists, and their disciples,

[4] *Loc. cit.*

[5] *Ibid.,* p. 32.

[6] Cf. John Dewey, *Democracy and Education.* New York: The Macmillan Company, 1916.

[7] Cf. W. Windelband, *op. cit.,* pp. 111–112.

were popularizers of philosophy. They tried to bridge the gap between the school and the market place by their teaching and extend the circle of those enjoying the benefits of knowledge and virtue. While this was an honorable intention which was doubtless successful in many instances, it gave way to corruption. The Sophists taught for a fee, and this was of course bad manners in a society where the avocations of a free man, such as music and philosophy, were never undertaken for pay. Practice of such a policy robbed philosophy of its lofty pedestal of respect and made it a mere trade pursued for the sake of money. This would not have been too bad, had a balance been kept between professional service and financial return. But apparently this was not the case. The impression in the dialogues is that fees were a prominent interest of the Sophists and that they prospered fairly well as they barnstormed from one town to another.

This insincerity took another form which was even more serious, if more subtle. Protagoras, Gorgias, and the lesser lights gambled heavily on the facile use of words. In the dialogue, *Gorgias,* Socrates more than once calls Polus to account for substituting praise for definition, thereby confusing his hearers. At ridiculing the opponent, confusing the discussion, and at other similar means of sliding out of tight places the Sophists were clever artists. The citizen of a modern democracy can scarcely escape the guess that they must be the inspiration of many of our politicians.

But this insincerity was the companion in practice of the belief which was more fundamental in the thinking of the Sophists and which most closely compares with contemporary pragmatism. Torn between the total change of Heraclitus, on the one hand, and the total unchange of Parmenides, on the other, the sneaking suspicion that nothing could be certainly known to be true grew on them until it became their key conviction. They were not only skeptics, questioning the possibility of knowledge; they were agnostics, confirmed believers in the impossibility of knowledge.

Three propositions held by Gorgias show how complete was this distrust. The first proposition was "nothing exists." The second, "if anything did exist we could never know it." And the third asserted, "if perchance a man should come to know it, it would remain a secret, he would be unable to describe it to his fellow-men."[8]

Protagoras agreed with Heraclitus that all things change. And he therefore defined knowledge as sense perception.[9] One phase of eternal flux, he held, is comprised of the stimulations arising from the world about us which impinge upon man, chiefly by means of his sense organs, and evoke from him a response. There is a sort of synthesis in this two-sided process in which stimulus and response coöperate. This synthesis is the experience of sense perception which is the result of both stimulus and response. For

[8] "A Saying of Gorgias" in Charles M. Bakewell, *op. cit.*, p. 67.
[9] Cf. *Theaetetus.*

example, something in an apple stimulates our visual senses, we respond, and the resulting experience is the perception, "the apple is red." The accompanying diagram may help to make this conception clear. Neither

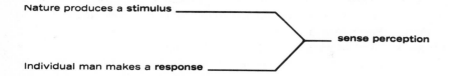

Nature produces a **stimulus**

sense perception

Individual man makes a **response**

stimulus, response, nor the resultant sense perception can be considered a representation of reality. All are but phases in the constant flux which is everywhere. However, each sense perception is the nearest approach to genuine knowledge that man can have. And therefore the saying for which Protagoras is famous, "man is the measure of all things,"[10] which in this setting can be correctly understood to mean, "individual man is the measure of all things." That is to say, whatever perceptions I have at a given time, those perceptions are true for me.

But our chief interest is to note how much of the philosophy of the Sophists is preserved or revived in pragmatism. First of all, as to the agnostic strain, it can be said that the Dewey variety of pragmatism is equally distrustful of knowledge. Although John L. Childs asserts that experimentalism avoids "wholesale skepticism" by not asking for "wholesale knowledge,"[11] the fact still remains that the philosophy seeks to provide no basis for certainty in knowledge. Protagoras' definition of knowledge as sense perception provides a point of departure for another important parallel between pragmatism and this ancient philosophy. Dewey joins Protagoras in accepting the Heraclitean principle of change. More subtle than Protagoras and, incidentally, more sincere, he does not dignify sense perception as knowledge. But, defining all thinking as experimentation, he regards hypotheses tested by experiment as being the nearest approach to knowledge which is available to man. For the sense perception of Protagoras he therefore substitutes tested hypotheses. This gives a greater range to knowledge so called than does the definition of Protagoras. For experimentation is something beyond and outside of the private perceptions of an individual. It goes on in the world outside the individual and is necessarily a social process in which more than one person participates. Dewey therefore does not support the contention of Protagoras that individual man is the measure of all things. Rather, the social mind, by virtue of its ability to experiment, is the measure of all things.

[10] "Two Sayings of Protagoras" in Charles M. Bakewell, *op. cit.*, p. 67.
[11] Cf. John L. Childs, *Education and the Philosophy of Experimentalism.* New York: Appleton-Century-Crofts, 1931. P. 102.

B. FRANCIS BACON (1561–1626)

Forgetting, for the time being, these ancient roots of pragmatic thought, we turn to a more recent century which yielded a man who is acknowledged by John Dewey to have anticipated the outlook of pragmatism.[12]

Francis Bacon was a child of the English court in the days of Queen Elizabeth I and Mary Queen of Scots. Both his mother and father were people of social and political position, so it is no wonder that he became a career politician. Spedding says that before the age of sixteen he evidenced no unusual abilities.[13] But his later achievements set him apart as a near genius. For one thing, he combined a life of scholarship with a vigorous and successful life of statecraft, which culminated in achieving the position of Lord Chancellor. His active public life was accomplishment enough in itself, especially considering the intrigues of the Elizabethan court. But to add to this the composition of his *Essays, Novum Organum, Advancement of Learning,* and *The New Atlantis,* and even to be suspected by some to be the real author of Shakespeare's plays, is to evidence an exuberance of ability and intellectual penetration which few men have ever displayed. Of course the Bacon of politics must have supplied subject matter for the Bacon of letters. But the single work, *Novum Organum,* was so penetrating and revolutionary that the scope of both its purview and influence was necessarily to be measured in centuries rather than decades. To have written this treatise alone would have distinguished him.

The explicit aim of *Novum Organum* was to work a revolution in human knowledge. Bacon regarded the beliefs of men as too much the prefabrication of their minds, having little relation to actual reality, if any at all. Even science, from antiquity to his time, he found to be a perpetuation of accepted ideas instead of a method of research and investigation by which new knowledge is gained.[14] Aristotle came in for his share of blame under Bacon's pen for causing human knowledge to have become so egocentric.[15] For Aristotle was the formulator of deductive reasoning and creator of the syllogism; and these devices of abstract reasoning entangled men in their own minds, at the same time turning their eyes away from the world of Nature, the study of which really should have been the major concern of science.

Man, whether viewed as a single individual or as the whole society of men, was observed by Bacon to be much like the spider, building a web out

---

[12] Cf. John Dewey, *Reconstruction in Philosophy.* London: University of London Press, 1921. Pp. 37–38.

[13] Cf. James Spedding, *The Life and Times of Francis Bacon.* Boston: Houghton, Osgood and Co., 1878. Vol. I, p. 1.

[14] Cf. *Novum Organum,* Book I, Aphorism VIII.

[15] Cf. *ibid.,* Book I, Aphorism LXIII.

of the juices of his own body. Around himself man had clustered an extensive array of ideas and beliefs, really very imposing, but actually false and of no value. False, because it was a homocentric web spun out of the mind and had none of the real solid substance of external Nature in it.

If a new and effective system of knowledge were to become the possession of the human race, Bacon insisted that men were under the necessity, first of all, of banishing from their minds the idols which were engaging them in false worship, and then, being so cleansed from the vast accumulation of falsehoods, get down to simple observation and experimental study of Nature.[16] Among the bad knowledge habits of man, Bacon singled out four, pointing his finger at them as idols of the mind to be destroyed.

1. Man as a species has the habit of imposing his own nature on whatever comes into the range of his senses, much the same as curved mirrors impose their contours on the objects which they reflect. This is the idol of the tribe.[17]

2. The second habit of knowledge is the individualized form of the first. Just as the race at large imposes its character upon its knowledge of the surrounding world, so man as an individual molds his view of the world to fit his own mental patterns. As an analogy of this, it may be pointed out that whereas all mirrors impose contours as such on reflected objects, a particular mirror imposes its particular contour. For example, your mind may be comparable to a convex mirror, and mine to a concave. While both of us modify our knowledge of Nature by our mental contours (the idol of the tribe), each of us as an individual possesses a unique pattern: your knowledge tending to enlarge the real thing because the mirror of your mind is convex, mine tending to be smaller than its object because my mental pattern is concave. This habit of knowledge is called the idol of the den.[18]

3. A third habit of the mind arises from the necessity of using language in communication. The very character of words is inexactness, making much room for vagueness, inaccuracy, and confusion of meaning. Because of this the tasks of getting accurate knowledge, and particularly of transmitting it, are fraught with great difficulty. Too often in an attempted meeting of minds, even when we use the same words, in actual meanings we are speaking different languages. This difficulty of the human mind is called the idol of the market place.[19]

4. The other thought habit into which the human species falls is that of adopting systems of dogma and allowing them to become so important as to preclude new thought or investigation. To Bacon, systems of dogma

[16] Cf. *ibid.,* Book I, Aphorisms XXXIX and XL.
[17] Cf. *ibid.,* Book I, Aphorism XLI.
[18] Cf. *ibid.,* Book I, Aphorism XLII.
[19] Cf. *ibid.,* Book I, Aphorism XLIII.

were like dramas. They are staged before the people by way of the various means of communication, much as plays engage the theater audience. They are most effective in captivating men, and as long as people are under their spell the forthright discovery of truth is pushed backstage, scarcely being acknowledged as a possibility at all. This habit of the human mind, true to the figure, Bacon called the idol of the theater.[20]

The task to which this approach opened the way for Bacon was, first, to replace Aristotle's deductive logic with an inductive logic which always makes its beginnings in observation of things as they are (Book I), and secondly, to show, by a series of rather tedious examples, the kind of knowledge to be derived in this way as well as to suggest further lines of investigation for which these might prepare the way.

In another work, *New Atlantis,* he deals with another aspect of science which was anticipatory of pragmatism. This is the use of science as a guide to the management of society, and its maintenance as a common possession of society. In *New Atlantis,* the narrator, together with a company lost at sea, visits a strange nation located in the then unknown South Pacific. Such order and decency as was found there has not yet been practiced by any society. To mention only a few achievements, there was careful observance of all laws of sanitation, unusual fruits and vegetables were produced by scientific cultivation, government was most harmonious and orderly, and the family was both a stable and healthy institution. Relations with other nations were kept under control largely by secrecy. Emissaries were sent out into other parts of the world every three years. These were men who spied out the knowledge of other countries and brought it home to their own people. In this way an up-to-date knowledge of other nations and their achievements was maintained, with other nations not deriving a corresponding benefit from the people of Atlantis. This information, together with the knowledge yielded by a great company of researchers, was pooled in common records, and the scientific work of the nation was carried forward as one united and coördinated plan. In this imaginative narrative, Bacon was enough ahead of his own century to project the possibility of such completely fantastic inventions as airplanes and submarines.

As is suggested in the foregoing discussion, there are two ideas in Bacon of which much is made by modern pragmatism. They are inductive method and science as a social pursuit.

While inductive method is by no means identical with pragmatism, it occupies an important place in that school of thought. Granting little if any place to deductive thought, and doubting the validity of all generalizations, pragmatism seizes upon particulars as having value as particulars which is lost when they are lumped together in generalizations. Each new situation is taken as unique and therefore to be faced freshly, without superimposing

[20] Cf. *ibid.,* Book I, Aphorism XLIV.

Father of induction - Bacon

generalizations upon it which may have applied in former situations but whose applicability in the present needs yet to be determined. To such a frame of mind, Bacon's polemic against deduction is most welcome, as well as his case for a new method which breaks beyond the barriers of the mind to observe the external world. Dewey heartily embraces this aspect of Bacon by saying:

> . . . his acute sense that science means invasion of the unknown, rather than repetition in logical form of the already known, makes him . . . the father of induction. Endless and persistent uncovering of facts and principles not known—such is the true spirit of induction.[21]

An editorial in *The New York Times*,[22] a few days after the atomic bomb had first come to light, made a strong plea for more of the kind of coordinated scientific effort which had produced the bomb. "Prima donna" research, it was held, will take years to solve such problems as cancer, whereas, if the atomic bomb project is any guide, coordinated and unified scientific studies promise much earlier victories in this field. At the same time that this argument is reminiscent of *New Atlantis,* it is also a doctrine many pragmatists have been expounding for years. Science, they hold, is not an individualistic preoccupation with researches whose practical value is dubious. It is rather a social pursuit in which the group is to be unitedly engaged in a common purpose. Not only should problems of national defense and physical health be tackled by such coordinate efforts, but the problems of society should be attacked by these same procedures. The deplorable lag between social and moral advancement on the one hand and technological advances on the other has been upon us for decades because we have not extended science, making it a social pursuit dealing with social problems as well as those more commonly regarded as scientific problems. And so at this point again Dewey embraces Bacon. Of him he says:

> When William James called Pragmatism a New Name for an Old Way of Thinking, I do not know that he was thinking expressly of Francis Bacon, but so far as concerns the spirit and atmosphere of the pursuit of knowledge, Bacon may be taken as the prophet of a pragmatic conception of knowledge.[23]

C. AUGUSTE COMTE (1798–1857)

Still another evident root of pragmatism in the old world is the positive philosophy of the Frenchman, Auguste Comte. Comte was born at Montpellier, where his father was receiver-general for taxes. With the exception

---

[21] John Dewey, *op. cit.,* p. 34.
[22] Cf. "The Lesson of the Bomb," Sunday, August 19, 1945, p. B8.
[23] John Dewey, *op. cit.,* p. 38.

of some time spent in school at Montpellier, he was educated in the École Polytechnique in Paris, distinguishing himself as a brilliant but rebellious student. For a number of years he earned his income by examining the boys applying for admission to the institution.

Such striking peculiarities were the companions of his intellectual brilliance that a case history of this Frenchman would make him anything but an attractive person. To cite some instances, in one of his writings he deliberately offended the men who elected him every year to his position as examiner for the École Polytechnique. They responded to this attack as he might have expected, and when his income was cut off, he appealed to John Stuart Mill, also, incidentally, the benefactor of Herbert Spencer. Mill induced three of Comte's fellow countrymen to help finance his work for a year. At the end of this time, two of them withdrew their support, not feeling that Comte had turned out work adequate to justify the gifts. Instead of being grateful for the favor he had received, Comte returned evil for good and became indignant. His only marriage resulted in a separation which cost him added financial burden. Sometime after this estrangement occurred, a short friendship with Madame Clotilde de Vaux established a lifelong attachment. When eventually Madame de Vaux was overtaken by death, Comte responded to this finality with a refusal to allow death to terminate such a beautiful companionship. For years Comte visited her tomb each week and made a practice of recalling her memory three times every day.

But his powers of mind are as much beyond question as these odd ways were eccentric. It is reported,[24] for example, that Comte had an unusual and tedious method of composition. He visualized mentally everything he wrote, having sentence structure and sequence carefully worked out. Then, resorting to paper, he reproduced in writing the section of composition already in form in his imagination. Just to examine the more than eight hundred pages of his *Positive Philosophy*[25] and to read a few of the meticulous paragraphs is to marvel at this method of writing.

As has already been explained, the positivism which Comte created has become a rather common attitude today. It is a kind of naturalism which regards laws and relations as fundamental rather than physical or spiritual substance of any kind.[26] This becomes much clearer if the student understands Comte's three stages of progress. He held that men pass through three levels of intellectual insight as their thinking develops and becomes more refined. These stages in the order of progression are the theological, the metaphysical, and the positive. In the theological stage, man believes in

[24] Cf. John Morley, "Auguste Comte," in *Encyclopaedia Britannica*, fourteenth edition.
[25] Translated by Harriet Martineau; New York: Calvin Blanchard, 1855.
[26] Cf. pp. 71–72.

supernatural powers as the foundation of existence. In the metaphysical, the next higher stage, he believes in some substances or powers as the root of existence, but does not think of these as supernatural. In the third and most refined phase of development he recognizes the laws revealed by the exact sciences as constituting the final and ultimate structure of things. This level of intellectual insight, proposed by Comte as the highest and most refined, it should be observed, is both antisupernatural and antimetaphysical. Not only is reality nonspiritual; it is also nonsubstantial. All the existence there is, is laws or relations such as are revealed by science.

It follows, of course, that Comte was deeply enmeshed in the sciences. Once a teacher of the subject, he regarded mathematics as the basis of all the sciences. The whole range of scientific discipline he broke down into six distinct sciences: inorganic science, astronomy, physics, chemistry, physiology, and sociology. The first four of these he grouped together as dealing with inorganic phenomena and the last two as dealing with the organic. The order in which they are listed indicates a relation of dependence between the sciences. For example, sociology, the last named and in many ways the most significant science for Comte, cannot be fully understood unless the student knows physiology. Knowledge of physiology depends on knowledge of chemistry, chemistry depends on physics, and so on backward in the regression.

To center attention on sociology, to which *Positive Philosophy* gives most space, it can be shown, Comte says, that the three stages of progress briefly described above have all served valuable purposes in bringing man to maturity in his ability to cope with society. The theological philosophy first held by man filled an important function in bringing progress; for at this early level of thought man could not have comprehended laws as such, and would have floundered hopelessly had he not been able to grasp at the belief in supernatural power as a source of help. This belief was also valuable as a basis of social organization because it brought the necessity of the clergy, a professional class dealing with this phase of man's life. In this way, speculation as a pursuit was broken off from day-by-day practical engagements as the specific occupation of a special class, and a way was thereby opened to intellectual progress that otherwise would not have been.

The metaphysical stage is not as well defined as the theological, Comte says, because its function was less definite. In fact, it was a transition between the theological and the positive, and as such provided no far-reaching beliefs nor did it determine any social structures. It was a period whose coming and going were both gradual. In a measure it coexisted with the other two stages some of the time. The attempt in the metaphysical stage to provide substantial substitutes for the belief in the supernatural cushioned the shock of the conflict between the theological and the positive, and provided an intellectual medium in which positive philosophy gradually gained the ascendance and theological philosophy gradually declined.

The positive stage in sociology brought a recognition that there are laws which govern social and political relations just as there are laws of physiology, chemistry, physics, and astronomy. Consequently, according to Comte, the summit of intellectual insight is the realization that man can cope with society by discovering these laws and working in harmony with them.

There are at least two streams in the positive philosophy of Comte which have flowed into twentieth-century American pragmatism. They are the positivistic treatment of metaphysics and an intense interest in social relations.

As has been indicated, there are some points at which the distinction between pragmatism and naturalism may be almost purely academic.[27] If by the term naturalism we refer to the more naïve metaphysics which regards some nonspiritual substance as the foundation of all existence, as early materialism did, then the distinction is very easily made. For pragmatism, such as that of Dewey, believes in no enduring substance of any kind. But the distinction is made with a little more difficulty, if by naturalism is meant a positivistic view of the universe in which all is laws and relations, no substance, as in Comte. Such a metaphysics is similar to pragmatism in that it rejects substance as the essence of reality but different from pragmatism (and incidentally much closer to realism) in that it regards laws and relations as constant and unchanging. A naturalism which holds neither substance nor laws and relations to be unchanging, but defines Nature as process, is identical in its metaphysics with pragmatism. But to return attention to the second of these three comparisons of naturalism and pragmatism, it is pragmatism's rejection of substance which makes it similar to the positivism of Comte and which qualifies it as being on the highest level of Comte's scheme of three stages.

The other common ground between pragmatism and the positive philosophy is a positive social interest. In recent pragmatism, following the pattern of Comte, the social sciences get much attention. Ideas are seen as always arising in social contexts and as necessarily having social significance if they have any value. All life, and therefore all education, must flow out into social change in order to be intelligent and purposeful.

Two differences may be mentioned in taking leave of Comte which set the philosophy of Dewey quite apart from it. One thread running throughout the positive philosophy is the assumption that there is law and order in the universe. This, on the face of it at least, makes the universe more static than it is assumed to be by Dewey. Comte is also definite in his belief in progress; his three stages, which are fundamental throughout his thought,

[27] Cf. p. 73.

suggest that man has made progress and that there will be progress in the future. Dewey is less clear on this point. He believes that there certainly has been progress on the technological side of life, and that there can be progress in the social and moral realms if we apply science as effectively in these areas as we have in technical fields. But progress is not guaranteed. The only thing man can do is face his situation directly and be intelligent and purposeful in striving for progress. At the same time, actual success cannot be certainly predicted.

D. THE PRAGMATIST TRADITION IN AMERICA

The names of three Americans are commonly associated with the rise of pragmatism in this country, where it has become one of the most influential philosophies, and because of which the American mentality is frequently characterized as pragmatic by citizens of other lands. These three names are those of Charles Sanders Peirce, William James, and John Dewey. Peirce was the originator of the single root idea from which pragmatism has grown. James popularized the idea and lent it some shades of meaning never intended by Peirce. And Dewey wrought out the full-fledged philosophy, making it more radically experimental than both Pierce and James intended it to be, and building out of it an inclusive world view with its own peculiar implications for every phase of life. The connection of each of these men with the rise of pragmatism in America will now be discussed more fully.

1. CHARLES SANDERS PEIRCE (1839–1914)

Charles Sanders Peirce is a little-known philosopher, even in America. This happens to be the case because Peirce was unable to get more than one of his books published and was not successful in claiming a professorship by which the teaching of his ideas could have won him acceptance. Even had he secured such an opportunity, he might have been so out of joint with his clientele, both because of his personal traits and the ideas he held, that acceptance would likely have escaped him anyway. But in spite of these circumstances, the appraisal which may be made of Peirce as the years pass is likely to be a more favorable one. In the face of all of his adversities, he was a prolific scholar; to date eight volumes of his collected papers have been published.[28] And one of his admirers, James Fiebleman, who estimates Peirce as "one of the greatest philosophers America has thus far produced,"[29] has set out to show that Peirce was a

---

[28] Charles Hartshorne and Paul Weiss, *Collected Papers of Charles Sanders Peirce.* Cambridge: Harvard University Press, 1931–1935.
[29] James Fiebleman, *An Introduction to Peirce's Philosophy.* New York: Harper & Row, Publishers, 1946. P. xvii.

systematic philosopher who carved out a distinctive point of view, a consistent and coherent structure, although Peirce himself did not take pains to present his thoughts in systematic form.

He was born into the home of a Harvard professor of mathematics, a creative thinker and teacher who injected a generous seasoning of philosophy into his teaching. Under his father's guidance, Charles Peirce studied Kant's *Critique of Pure Reason* for two hours a day throughout more than three years, and came to the point at which he almost knew this classic by heart.[30] This was followed by the study of a number of other philosophers, among whom was the medieval scholastic, Duns Scotus, who, next to Kant, probably influenced Peirce most. He studied at Harvard as an undergraduate without distinction and went on into graduate work in chemistry to acquit himself with distinction. Apart from his continuous writing and occasional lecturing or teaching, his single and most steady position was with the United States Coast and Geodetic Survey, with which he was connected for about thirty years. His single longest association with an academic institution was his five years of lecturing on logic at Johns Hopkins between 1879 and 1884.

Although Peirce is commonly considered as being in the ancestral line of American pragmatism, his connection with the philosophy of pragmatism is really only at one point. This is that early in his career he formulated a criterion for determining the meanings of ideas and coined the term pragmatism as a name for this doctrine in epistemology. William James, his friend and clubmate, took up both the criterion and the name, and enlarged the original idea far beyond Peirce's intention, to make of it a rather complete philosophy, quite different from and out of harmony with the system which Peirce sought to build throughout his long career of writing. Except for this early idea, taken over by James and extended to have a still more radical meaning by John Dewey, Charles Sanders Peirce was a realist, not a pragmatist, much more to be compared to Bertrand Russell or A. N. Whitehead than to either James or Dewey. But this early idea which Peirce called pragmatism will have to be made more explicit in order for his connection with the philosophy of pragmatism to be made plain.

Between 1872 and 1874 there was a little philosophical circle in Cambridge which took the name, the Metaphysical Club. Both Peirce and James were members of this group and apparently its leading lights, for the club held its meetings sometimes in the study of Peirce and sometimes in the study of James. One can easily imagine the kind of discussions which took place in this little circle throughout the two or more years of its frequent meetings. While Peirce had conceived the idea of his pragmatism as early as 1871, it was more fully defined and the name coined in the course of

[30] *Ibid.*, p. 11.

some of these discussions. It later got into print in the form of two articles entitled "The Fixation of Belief" and "How to Make Our Ideas Clear."[31]

It has already been noted that Peirce had been a student of Kant from his early youth. He was meticulously familiar with the *Critique of Pure Reason* and fully cognizant of the fact that Kant's patient analysis of the knowledge process did not yield any sure content regarding the nature of the thing-in-itself.[32] Now Peirce, as revealed by the further unfolding of his philosophy, was the antithesis of a subjectivist. One point at which he can be easily seen to part company with what has come to be known as pragmatism and joined hands with the realists is that he wanted to be completely objective. Mathematics, careful scientific investigations and tabulations, and logic were his close friends. And none of these did he regard as psychological descriptions of the way the mind works; such is a subjective interpretation of them which he consistently opposed. They are all descriptions of the way Nature acts; mathematics, exact science, and logic are all descriptions of objective patterns in Nature. At the time of these early discussions in the Metaphysical Club, this insistence on being objective may not have been fully defined in his own mind; but being in his makeup in implicit form at least, it is not hard to imagine his positive dissatisfaction with Kant, however much he respected him as a great thinker. It was not at all acceptable to him to stop, as Kant did, at the end of his meticulous analysis of knowledge without yielding anything as to the nature of reality in itself. So Peirce sought to make up for this deficiency in Kant, and bridge the gap, in part at least, between the subjective processes of the mind and the objective realities of the world.

His early formulation of pragmatism was his attempt to do this. What he said was something like this: "To determine the meaning of any idea, put it into practice in the objective world of actualities and whatever its consequences prove to be, these constitute the meaning of the idea." Now this is much more than one popular version of pragmatism which says, "If ideas work, they are true." Pierce's criterion of ideas was not only, or maybe not so much, a test of the truth of ideas as a means of determining what the content or essence of an idea is. Kant left him with no content or essence, only an elaborate analysis of the knowing process, the end product being that the essence of a thing can never get into knowledge, because by the very process of getting into knowledge it is no longer the essence of the thing-in-itself but something translated into knowledge terms. Now according to Peirce's criterion, this lack of essence is supplied; for the essence of an idea is considered to be identical with the consequences which result when it is put into action. By putting an idea into action it is placed in

---

[31] *Popular Science Monthly*, November 1877 and January 1878.
[32] Cf. pp. 129–131 and 260–261.

consequential relation with the actualities of the objective order of things, and therefore the eventualities which follow in action from this consequential relation display what the essence of the idea is.

2. WILLIAM JAMES (1842–1910)[33]

Unlike Peirce, William James was and continues to be a very popular philosopher; he was a winsome person who had a delightful public presence and a dynamic teacher who thrilled and inspired his students. He was therefore in a position to give currency to Peirce's pragmatic idea which Peirce himself could not possibly have gotten for it. While it may be true, at least from Peirce's standpoint, that he overplayed his hand and encouraged the growth of a pragmatic way of life which became far more inclusive in meaning and application than Peirce's original idea, yet his success in this role was pronounced. One glimpse of James as propagandist for pragmatism can be gotten from his Lowell Lectures, delivered in December, 1906, and January, 1907, and published under the general title, *Pragmatism.*

This is the principle of Peirce, the principle of pragmatism. It lay entirely unnoticed by any one for twenty years, until I, in an address before Professor Howison's philosophical union at the University of California, brought it forward again and made a special application of it to religion. By that date (1898) the times seemed ripe for its reception. The word "pragmatism" spread, and at present it fairly spots the pages of the philosophic journals. On all hands we find the "pragmatic movement" spoken of, sometimes with respect, sometimes with contumely, seldom with clear understanding. It is evident that the term applies itself conveniently to a number of tendencies that hitherto have lacked a collective name, and that it has "come to stay."[34]

James was further qualified to be an apostle of pragmatism by the vitality of his own conviction; for in the very depths of his own personal life he had applied the pragmatic principle to such good effect that it had meant the difference between insanity and mental health; at least this was his own judgment, he fully believed it had meant the difference to him "between death and life."[35] So, whereas he applied Peirce's original principle more inclusively and probably more vitally at the level of experience where all of us have to live, philosopher or not, he did it from the very depths of his soul, not only sincerely, but passionately, as the approach to life which had resolved the great crisis of his own experience, a near-religious crisis.

Somewhat before the days of the little Metaphysical Club to which he

[33] Cf. pp. 263–266.
[34] New York: Longmans, Green & Co., 1907. P. 47.
[35] As quoted by Horace M. Kallen in his introduction to *The Philosophy of William James Drawn from His Own Works.* New York: The Modern Library, n.d. P. 29.

and Peirce belonged (1872–1874) and maybe coinciding in part with that period, James was passing through deep waters. His physical constitution seems not to have been too rugged to begin with, and added to this the weight of his philosophical doubts proved to be almost too much. There came a time when he dreaded his own existence and had visions of himself falling into a type of insanity which had left a deep impression on him during his study of medicine. At times suicide had seemed to him to be a wise change for the better. During these few years while he was a near invalid, as he acknowledged later in his autobiographical chapter on "The Sick Soul," his condition was such that, as he put it, "If I had not clung to scripture-texts like 'The eternal God is my refuge,' etc., 'Come unto me, all ye that labor and are heavy laden,' etc., 'I am the resurrection and the life,' etc., I think I should have grown really insane."[36] Now an important part of the change in direction which began his return to recovered mental health was his decision to believe in the freedom of his own will. In his condition, this belief was not just an intellectual assent. That part of it was a small part. An indication of the fact or thatness of his freedom could be supplied by the recognition that in suicide he could, by his own initiative, do something about his own life. The far more important thing was that his acceptance of his own freedom of will meant putting that idea to work and discovering its essence and meaning after the fact, instead of reading it in abstractly beforehand. It was a kind of venture of faith in which the meaning of freedom was to be found in the results which flowed from acting on the idea that one is free. And the consequences which followed from this turning point amounted to the kind of change in his personality which meant coming into his own mentally, growing out of his fears, and sloughing off the morbidness which had enchained him. By the winter of 1873 he had begun his teaching and was having a great beginning success with his fifty-seven students. One day, so his father has written, he came home and after walking the floor with great animation for a few moments, burst out with this exclamation: "Bless my soul, what a difference between me as I am now and as I was last spring at this time! Then so hypochondriacal and now with my mind so cleared up and restored to sanity. It's the difference between death and life."[37]

This change is of profound interest from the standpoint of mental hygiene; but it has another significance for us in this discussion. This change, which was so important for his own mental well-being, was the consequence of putting the idea of free will to work. It was the essence of free will, it was what free will meant: health, well-being, the finding of one's place, the ability to do one's work effectively and well, and, in addition,

[36] William James, *The Varieties of Religious Experience*. New York: Longmans, Green & Co., 1916. P. 161.
[37] As quoted by Horace M. Kallen, *op. cit.*, p. 29.

one's enjoyment of all this. Because these were the consequences of acting on belief in freedom, they constituted for him the essence of being free.

The pragmatist principle as William James defined it may also be discussed here in the light of its bearing on religious belief; this will help to show the more inclusive character of the principle as James elaborated it, and at the same time offer a sample of his world view. His treatment of belief in God can be approached from the context of his belief in free will. Freedom of will appeals to us, he says, only as a relief, i.e., a relief from a world of past and present in which things are not what could be desired. If the past were perfect and the present completely satisfactory in the values they provide, what reason would there be for wanting to be free? To want to be free to make things inferior to what they have been and now are makes little sense. We want to be free because things have not been in the past, and right now are not what we want them to be. Free will is the hope to make them better, a hope which displays its essence only as freedom is put to work and higher values are realized.

Now religious belief is related to this same growing edge of our experience. Belief in God becomes meaningful only as it is projected into the thicket of experience where it can make a difference in life and events, and display its essence by means of whatever the consequences are. Belief in God is not significant, contrariwise, when it is made synonymous with the assumption that redemption has already been accomplished, that the universe is perfect as it is, and that all things have been finished and completed. "Pragmatism shifts the emphasis," James says, "and looks forward into facts themselves. The really vital question for us all is, What is this world going to be? What is life eventually to make of itself?"[38] The heart of theology is stated simply in Browning's *Pippa Passes,* "God's in his heaven, All's right with the world," and for that no rational definitions are needed.

James asserts that experience shows the hypothesis of God "certainly does work"[39] and therefore is true. He cites his own book, *The Varieties of Religious Experience,* as a witness that his kind of pragmatism cannot be charged with being atheistic. "I firmly disbelieve," he says, ". . . that our human experience is the highest form of experience extant in the universe. I believe rather that we stand in much the same relation to the whole of the universe as our canine and feline pets do to the whole of human life."[40] As the figure implies, the higher spiritual order to which man sustains this inferior relation is a multiplicity instead of a single Universal Person, a spiritual pluralism rather than a monism. This multiplicity leaves room for improvement, an opening in which the positive endeavor of

[38] William James, *Pragmatism,* p. 122.
[39] *Ibid.,* p. 290.
[40] *Ibid.,* pp. 290–300.

man can effectively come to grip with realities which are yet indeterminate and unfinished, and in so doing to help in the realization of the ultimate good.

As will become quite clear in the following chapter, this pragmatism which James expounded is somewhat different from the twentieth-century experimentalism which John Dewey has fathered. It was not naturalistic in its metaphysics, and it regarded truth, once it was verified by the pragmatic principle, as having a degree of permanence; whereas Dewey's version of pragmatism is naturalistic and scarcely invests truth with any degree of permanence. Yet James broke ground for Dewey and helped set the stage for a philosophy which may still be the most influential one in America today.

3. JOHN DEWEY (1859–1952)

So great has been the acclaim of John Dewey that on the occasion of his ninetieth birthday, in October, 1949, he was honored by a host of men and women who raised the sum of $90,000 as a birthday gift, $1000 for each year of his life, which he forthwith invested in benevolent causes close to his heart. He was also invited back to his old home in Burlington, Vermont, where he was born in 1859, the son of the proprietor of a village store, and was given the rare welcome accorded only to a widely renowned native son.

Dewey received his early education in the public schools of Burlington, following which he entered the University of Vermont, where in the course of his undergraduate work he became acquainted with Professor H. A. P. Torrey, an exponent of a brand of realism common at the time which had been imported from Scotland. Following graduation in 1879 he taught for two years in a high school in Oil City, Pennsylvania, and one year in a country school in Charlotte, Vermont. Then, after this three-year intermission in his studies, he returned to his alma mater for a year of private study in philosophy with Professor Torrey. The next year, 1882, he went to Johns Hopkins University to do graduate work, and by 1884 had completed his requirements for the Ph.D. degree, presenting *The Psychology of Kant* as his dissertation.

At Johns Hopkins he came under three different influences which were all additional to the Scottish realism of Torrey. These influences constituted the matrix in which the formative development of Dewey as a budding philosopher went on. The chief of these was George Sylvester Morris (1840–1889) who was an ardent disciple of Hegel and in close sympathy with the English idealists, John and Edward Caird, and Thomas Hill Green.[41] The next strongest influence was that of G. Stanley Hall and his experimental approach to the study of psychology. The third influence

[41] Cf. pp. 140–141.

*List
 Influences on
 Dewey*

available at Johns Hopkins, which strikingly did not apparently touch Dewey much at the time, was Charles Sanders Peirce, who, it will be recalled, was lecturing there on logic.[42] Dewey seems to have dismissed Peirce as a formal logician, and at that time his own interests were quite antithetical to formal logic. Under the guidance of Morris he carried on his studies and loyally shared his idealist sympathies. At the same time he studied with Hall, though not extensively, and acquired at least the beginnings of a positive interest in psychology which was to prove of great importance in the formulation of the viewpoint for which Dewey has become famous. Apparently both Morris and Hall were on trial at Johns Hopkins at that very time; both were being given the opportunity to display their wares and show what they could do in their divergent ways while the university officials decided which direction Hopkins should take. Should it be the historical-philosophical emphasis, or should it be the experimental-scientific? By 1884 the question was answered; G. Stanley Hall and the experimental-scientific approach won out. And accordingly, Professor Morris left Johns Hopkins for the University of Michigan. Though it may be surprising to those who know John Dewey only as the twentieth-century exponent of experimentalism, he went with Morris to Michigan and there began his teaching career, as an instructor.[43]

This development witnesses the strength of Dewey's allegiance to idealism; while he had learned from Hall, he had followed Morris and he had come to near maturity as a philosopher agreeing with the main outlines of the idealism of Morris. Some of the overtones of this loyalty should be written in here. Sympathy with Morris meant disagreement with British empiricism, a disposition which apparently stayed with Dewey after he forsook idealism. It meant a somewhat reluctant respect for Kant, with Hegel being elevated above Kant as supplying in metaphysics that which Kant could not supply, the doctrine of Universal Mind. It meant a profound interest in ethics, and a recognition that ethics and theology are necessarily related. It meant a prime interest in each individual as a metaphysical ego, and the conception of the chief end of each man as the realization of the personality which it is in him to become.

By 1894, when Dewey became head of the Department of Psychology, Philosophy, and Education at the University of Chicago, he had forsaken, however, the metaphysics of idealism and was on his way to developing an empirical version of idealism in which the nonmechanical patterns of that point of view still persisted, but in which also there was no metaphysics of a Universal Mind, embracing all in a unity of being. But there is some

[42] Cf. pp. 365–368.
[43] Cf. Morton G. White, *The Origins of Dewey's Instrumentalism.* New York: Columbia University Press, 1943.

detail to be written into the picture to depict somewhat the changes which had taken place during the 1884–1894 decade. On the personal- and professional-record side there were some events of interest. After being in the University of Michigan for two years as an instructor (1886) he was made an assistant professor and in the same year he married Alice Chipman, a recent graduate of Michigan. This, the first Mrs. Dewey, was his companion in life for forty-one years until the time of her death in 1927; she was the mother of their six children, and the foster mother of a boy they adopted in Italy. During the academic year 1888–1889 Dewey taught at the University of Minnesota, but after this one year he returned to the University of Michigan to stay until he assumed the post at the University of Chicago in 1894 which has already been mentioned.

The other changes which had taken place are not as easy to catalogue. Morton G. White, who has examined rather carefully the stages by which Dewey's thought was formed,[44] concludes that the changeover from idealism was quite definite by 1892. The single greatest step in this transition was the forsaking of theism and the exclusion from his outlook of the doctrine of a Universal Self, which he had shared with his old mentor, Professor Morris. White says that by 1892 he had come to regard the Universal Self as superfluous.[45] And quite parallel to this, as far as the individual self is concerned, he came to feel that individual selfhood could be described in a thoroughly behavioristic fashion.[46] He dropped the conception of the self as a spiritual ego or soul, and no longer regarded the individual will as an efficient cause which produces changes in the events of the world. Instead, he began to think of the individual as a concrete social phenomenon whose acts are part of a social stream of interactivity and not individually caused by free will.[47] Another aspect of his turning away from the idealist metaphysics of Universal Mind was the inclination to think no more of social institutions as a manifestation of Absolute Mind, and to replace this metaphysical doctrine with a strong emphasis on the cultural environment as having pervasive influence in forming the ideas, beliefs, and intellectual attitudes of individuals.[48] Another aspect of this change was that Dewey ceased to think of intelligence and the world as unified by the metaphysical substratum of Mind and came to emphasize the social function of intelligence instead. In his changed outlook intelligence became something to be put to work in organic social endeavor to the end that changes for the better might be wrought in the world. He eventually came to hope for the time when science would be applied to all of the world's

[44] Cf. *ibid.*, p. 106.
[45] Cf. *ibid.*, p. 47.
[46] Cf. *loc. cit.*
[47] Cf. *ibid.*, p. 106.
[48] Cf. *ibid.*, p. 58.

problems, the social and moral as well as the technological, for in science he saw the method by which intelligence could become effective in the world.[49]

This may serve as a sketch of the changed Dewey who in 1894 assumed an important chair in the University of Chicago. In this post his success was notable; and to distinguish himself even more than his work in technical philosophy and psychology would have done he started his Laboratory School where some of his ideas were put to work in an experimental attempt at revamping education, a move which was no small factor in the rise of the progressive-education movement in America. All was not smoothness, however, and in 1905 he left the University of Chicago for Columbia University, where he was a distinguished professor of philosophy until his retirement twenty-five years later in 1930. In addition to his teaching and writing, he was courageously active in many social causes envisioning the betterment of the condition of the common man, he lectured widely, and he rendered distinguished service to education in several countries other than his own. Dewey was one of the most productive writers that the nineteenth and twentieth centuries produced; a study of his bibliography alone needs to be an extensive work.[50] It is likely that _Democracy and Education_[51] will stand as his single greatest book. Some of the reasons for this estimate may be given. It is the first full statement of his own peculiar kind of pragmatism in mature formulation. It is significant also, and a distinct new departure in philosophy in this regard, because of its close identification of philosophy and education, equating philosophy with a general theory of education. The book has been in publication for over forty years; and regardless of a student's agreement or disagreement with its argument, there is a kind of prophetic foresight in the book which has given it an enduring relevance even after the beginning of the so-called atomic era, though it was written and published before the United States had entered World War I.

As the remaining chapters in this section devoted to pragmatism deal primarily with the thought of Dewey and those who have followed him, nothing further will be attempted at this point by way of making his philosophy any more explicit.

E. SYNTHESIS

There are at least five propositions that can be extracted from this survey of the development of pragmatism which will suggest some signifi-

[49] Cf. *ibid.*, pp. 102–103.

[50] See M. H. Thomas, *A Bibliography of John Dewey, 1882–1939.* New York: Columbia University Press, 1939.

[51] New York: The Macmillan Company, 1916.

cant attitudes of contemporary pragmatism. They are gleaned from all of the sources which have been discussed; but only those have been included which are generally in agreement with the philosophy of Dewey. They will prepare the way somewhat for the more detailed exposition of the Dewey variety of pragmatism which is to follow in the next chapter. The propositions and those who have subscribed to them are as follows:

1. All things flow; nothing remains the same.—Heraclitus and Dewey.

2. It is impossible to gain knowledge of ultimate reality.—The Sophists and Dewey.

3. Hypotheses tested by experience constitute the nearest approach to knowledge which we have.—The Sophists (a modification of their treatment of sense perception) and Dewey.

4. Science should become a social pursuit by being applied cooperatively to the study of all of the problems of man.—Bacon, Comte, and Dewey.

5. In order to determine the meaning of an idea, it must be put into practice; the consequences which follow constitute the meaning of the idea.—Peirce, James, and Dewey.

XIX

A Systematic Synopsis of the Philosophy of Pragmatism

A. The Epistemology of Pragmatism
1. PRAGMATISM COMPARED TO RATIONALISM
2. PRAGMATISM COMPARED TO EMPIRICISM
   a. The Pragmatic Treatment of Sense Perceptions
   b. Pragmatic Knowledge Not An Accumulation of Facts
   c. Experimental Method

B. The Metaphysics of Pragmatism

C. The Logic of Pragmatism
1. THE PATTERN OF LOGIC
2. SOME CHARACTERIZATIONS OF PRAGMATIC LOGIC

D. The Axiology of Pragmatism
1. ETHICAL VALUE
2. AESTHETIC VALUE
3. RELIGIOUS VALUE
4. SOCIAL VALUE

Each of the other systematic chapters in this book, which have preceded this one, was introduced by designating the intuition which the philosophy then under discussion has elaborated into an inclusive system of thought. It may be helpful to make the same kind of beginning in making a synopsis of this fourth philosophy. Pragmatism builds on the intuition that experience is the proving ground in which the worth of things is made plain. While its twentieth-century exponents hail it as a new philosophy, they do not regard the reliance on experience for which it stands as a new thing. Respect for experience and its power to show the worth of things is almost as old as the human race itself. What pragmatism has done has been to translate this confidence in experience into the language of the schools, to intellectualize it and make it at home in the ranks of the learned. For millennia it has been native to the field and the market place; in recent decades it has been flourishing in classroom and laboratory, and on the printed page. While the prime intuition of the more naïve naturalism has been confidence in Nature and her orderly working, and idealism has taken its stand by the reality of the self, and realism has built upon the conviction that reality is independent of mind, in distinction from all of these pragmatism has said, "Experience is the real test of all things."

In examining the other three philosophies we have seen that the development of a system has always been more involved than the simple intuition from which it stems. This is also the case with pragmatism; and our present task, therefore, is to represent in outline the system of thought for which confidence in experience has been the primary base.

A. THE EPISTEMOLOGY OF PRAGMATISM

There is a sense in which pragmatism, like realism, is an epistemological philosophy, concerned primarily with the method of knowledge and only incidentally interested in metaphysics. As will be seen later, this statement is not strictly true. Pragmatism does have a theory of reality, and it is greatly devoted to the study of values. In fact, its concern for epistemology, far from being an academic interest in the riddle of knowledge, is basically a concern to make things work and so to realize present value. But as a working generalization with which to begin an explanation of pragmatism, it is approximately correct to say that pragmatism is primarily a theory of knowledge. Because of this, we study pragmatism first of all by looking at its epistemology, and allowing this to be the gateway to an understanding of its metaphysics, logic, and theory of value.

It should be made clear at the outset that the pragmatist treatment of knowledge does not fit the traditional pattern of philosophy. We must therefore forsake labels such as *rational* or *empirical,* and *inductive* or *deductive,* certainly in the beginning. The most likely approach is to contrast pragmatic knowledge theory with these traditional forms of analysis, especially with *rationalism* and *empiricism*. In fact, Dewey gives us the cue for this approach in Chapter IV of his book, *Reconstruction in Philosophy*,[1] entitled "Changed Conceptions of Experience and Reason."

The reader may wish to look back in this text to the general introductory discussion on the instrument of knowledge in the Introduction[2] and the terms under this same heading in the Glossary.[3] As in these discussions, it is to be noted that *rationalism* is the position in epistemology according to which reason is the chief instrument of knowledge, whereas *empiricism* holds that sense perception is the medium through which knowledge comes to us. These two positions are antithetical; and in relation to them the pragmatic treatment of knowledge lies somewhere between their extremes, including in addition some overtones which are in neither.

1. PRAGMATISM COMPARED TO RATIONALISM

Certainly, pragmatism is not rationalistic. It does not begin with universal truths or principles and then deduce specific items of knowledge from these. By contrast, pragmatism is leery of all generalizations, whether a priori or a posteriori. It regards experience as radically specific and particular. Particular things are so markedly individual that no universals can do justice to them. Something is lost in generalizations which renders them both inadequate and oversimple. They are not true in themselves, and they do not correspond sufficiently with the individuated character of facts to be of much value.

Yet there is a rational element in the pragmatic treatment of knowledge which saves it, as we shall see, from getting lost in the forest of infinite particulars. Sheer facts themselves do not constitute knowledge for the pragmatist. Like rationalism, it is the pattern of successful organization of facts which is central in knowledge, and not unorganized brute facts. Just what this pattern of organization is, it is difficult to make meaningful at this point. According to what has already been said, it is evidently not a universal truth or principle. Neither is it an inductive generalization formulated after a great number of individuals have been studied. Instead, *the pattern for organizing facts, which constitutes the core of knowledge, is a hypothesis which works successfully.* Such a pattern of organization is more acceptable than a priori generalizations because it is suggested by the particulars in each unit of experience where hypotheses are needed. It is better than an inductive generalization because it is intimately related to a few particulars constituting a unit of experience, and not so general as to spread thin over a multitude of cases. And it is better than both because it

[1] London: University of London Press, 1921.
[2] Cf. pp. 25–26.
[3] Cf. p. 44.

is not just an item of knowledge, but a way of acting which brings a needed result.

2. PRAGMATISM COMPARED TO EMPIRICISM

On the other hand, to contrast pragmatic knowledge with empirical knowledge, it must be said that pragmatism is not empirical in the traditional sense. There are two ways in which this contrast needs to be made clear. First of all, pragmatism does not think of the senses as gateways for knowledge and of sense perception as a passive affair of receiving impressions from the outside world. In the second place, as partially explained already, pragmatism does not regard any compilation of facts as constituting knowledge, even when those facts are yielded either by sensation or by such refined sensation as scientific observation. Of what value is a whole catalogue of data, if the data are not put to work to yield desirable ends?

Pragmatism is empirical in that its frame of reference is always sense-perceptual experience, not predisposed principles of reason. But it is not empirical in a way which assumes that sensation yields ready-made facts, like neorealism,[4] or that there is any virtue in an accumulation of a fund of scientific knowledge derived from observation. In this regard just mentioned, pragmatism is actually more radically empirical than traditional empiricism, especially the kind which has been so common in British philosophy. The pragmatist sticks so close to sense perception as his frame of reference that there is no willingness to accept knowledge verified in the past at face value, even if the verification is scientific. The present unit of experience, individual or social, as the case may be, is the thing; and accumulated data of the past must pass the test of present experience no matter how honorable their former verification.

In order to explain more fully, it is necessary to go back now and enlarge on the two ways in which pragmatism is not empirical; then we will look at its insistence upon the method of science as its one important identification with empiricism.

a. The Pragmatic Treatment of Sense Perception. Pragmatism is not purely empirical in its understanding of sense perception. Pure empiricism treats sense perception as realism does; accordingly, sensation is a passive process of receiving impressions or stimulations from the world beyond the self. This pragmatism does not grant; sense perception, it holds, is neither passive nor purely receptive. In sensory relations with the world, we are actively engaged in a give-and-take with the world; we are doing things to the world and/or objects at the same time that they are doing things to us, impressing us or stimulating us. It is not true to the character of experience to think of the senses as merely gateways, the eye gate, the ear gate, and so

[4] Cf. pp. 270–271.

on, when sensation is an avenue of active relation with the world. When an infant is confronted by an object, he does not first behold it and undergo an impression; he acts upon or with it, reaches for it, shakes it, or bites it.

To be more analytical and try to explain how we experience qualities and values, it may be fair to say that pragmatism is closer to idealism in its epistemology than to realism. For pragmatism, there is no simple intersection of knower and object, from which direct knowledge results. It is only as we are engaged in active experience with things that qualities come to light in such a way that we "know" them. This is not a purely subjective affair, however. We ourselves are in experience when this happens and the objects are also in experience; and it is because of experience and by means of experience that there is any meeting at all. Experience is a kind of ocean in which selves and objects are afloat, and which provides the medium for all meetings of selves and objects. As the figure implies, experience is neither private nor subjective; it is public and objective. I do not possess experience privately; it engages me; I am possessed by it.

One further explanation is needed. This is that experience is not primarily an affair of knowing; it is first of all a process of acting, doing, living. Such "knowledge" as we have is only incidental to doing and acting. And as such it is not knowledge of an unchangeable sort, which is always true; but it is limited, approximate knowledge, always relative to the present unit of experience. Because of this added overtone in pragmatism's analysis of knowledge, it can be seen that the precise word for describing knowledge for pragmatism is not the adjective, *experiential,* which might be acceptable to many idealists, but rather the descriptive, *experimental.* Because what is known is always known on the way to achieving a satisfactory outworking of a given unit of experience. What is known is a hypothesis working satisfactorily; the resolving course of action in an experiment, not just an item of knowledge but an item of value in addition being made actual in experience.

What has just now been said leads on naturally to a description of the knowing process as it has been formalized by John Dewey. But before entering upon this final phase of the discussion, we must first show the contrast between pragmatism and that kind of empiricism which lays stress upon the accumulation of facts.

b. Pragmatic Knowledge Not an Accumulation of Facts. We have already noted how Francis Bacon in the sixteenth and seventeenth centuries made a rather successful revolt against deductive logic.[5] In place of deduction and the syllogism, he urged men to banish the idols of the mind and study Nature directly by observation. His sharp antithesis to rationalism

[5] Cf. pp. 358–361.

was induction, the observing of facts as they are, accumulating such facts by the multitude, and so gaining a basis for conclusions which are harmonious with Nature as it is. Looked at within the mentality of pragmatism, this revolt was justified in its violence, but it was not well founded on its positive side because of its mistaken conception of what it is that constitutes knowledge. For it glorified direct observation and accumulation of fact at the expense of failing to achieve patterns of organization which give direction, purpose, and meaning to the use of facts. Herbert Spencer was guilty of the same failure, in spite of the fact that he has been accused of organizing more knowledge than he took in.[6] He was a receiver and cataloguer of facts. While he was a rather adept creator of theories for organizing his facts, he was not the active experimenter in practical affairs who made his data flow toward putting hypotheses to work.

While having an eye for facts, pragmatism rejects fact accumulation, the acquisition of a storehouse of knowledge, as a vice rather than a virtue. The content of scientific observation is not unimportant; it is a necessity and its value becomes distinctly evident when this content provides hypotheses for experimental action. But more important than observation and the content it yields is the *method* of science. This method includes observation-getting, but contains in addition a way of doing things which has direction and keeps thought moving with experience.

c. Experimental Method. Now we are ready for the method itself. Pragmatic method is proposed by its supporters as nothing more than a conscious formulation of what goes on all the time in our experience, and has gone on in human experience for centuries. Only we had to wait for the slow struggle into existence of science in recent centuries, to become sufficiently aware of the genius of experience, to be able in turn to determine what effective method is.

When experience flows smoothly and effectively in a satisfactory direction this is what happens: (1) Always there is movement; never does life stand still. Sometimes this movement is smooth and easygoing; often the flow runs into an obstacle which demands that something new or different be done. (2) These occasions are constituted by tensions or problems in experience which, though they may be unpleasant, are the times of great importance when a new direction is determined, affecting all the subsequent flow of experience. (3) When an individual or a group is confronted by such an obstacle, the first thing done, if it acts effectively and with direction—which means with intelligence—is to observe all the facts which comprise this particular unit of experience, marked out by the particular

[6] Cf. Will Durant, *The Story of Philosophy.* New revised edition; New York: Doubleday & Company, 1938. P. 391.

obstacle which is faced. This, it can easily be seen, is not an orgy of collecting facts or making observations; it is getting into hand all the pertinent elements which relate to the immediate experience, and which vitally concern us because we ourselves are involved and our fortunes are at stake. Necessarily the collecting of data will have an end because experience is temporarily dammed up and waiting for the cue to flow again, but in the right direction. (4) This cue is suggested by the observation of data. As the situation is studied, the data tend to fall into a pattern, or maybe alternative patterns. Whatever patterns of action are suggested by the analysis of the situation become hypotheses on which to act. Now this is not a matter of pure trial-and-error activity. There could be blind trial and error without any study of data, even without any consciousness of a problem. There is more insight in pragmatic method than this. The patterns are meaningful, purposive ways in which the different aspects of the problem situation can be woven together to get—it is hoped—a satisfactory result. There is trial and error to the extent that there is more than one hypothesis, and when several are put to test before the solution is found. (5) The testing of hypotheses is the next and final step. It yields a satisfactory completion of the unit of experience when a hypothesis works in such a way as to satisfy the demands of the present unit of experience and to make experience flow smoothly again in a manner which holds out greatest promise for succeeding experiences.

This is the pragmatic method of knowledge. It yields two things: (1) knowledge, to the limited extent of a sense of the particular way of acting which is acceptable in a particular unit of experience, and (2) value, to the extent that there is action in addition to judgment or conclusion, and something is done which yields changes and brings needed results.

B. THE METAPHYSICS OF PRAGMATISM

How formulate the metaphysics implied by a methodology such as this? The assignment is not an easy one. As can be seen, pragmatism is heavily weighted in epistemology, so heavily, in fact, that it has been accused of having no metaphysics. Of course, Dewey did say in *Creative Intelligence,* published in 1917, that "the chief characteristic of the pragmatic notion of reality is precisely that no theory of Reality in general . . . is possible or needed."[7] However, in his Paul Carus Lectures, *Experience and Nature,*[8] published in 1925, he included a chapter entitled "Existence as Precarious and as Stable" which, as the title suggests, does say something about existence. In a review of *Experience and Nature,* at the time of its appearance, George Santayana regarded it as a metaphysics and characterized the gen-

---

[7] New York: Holt, Rinehart and Winston, 1917. P. 55.
[8] La Salle, Ill.: The Open Court Publishing Company, 1925.

eral viewpoint presented as *"the dominance of the foreground."*[9] In 1927 a book entitled *The Metaphysics of Pragmatism* appeared which was written by Sidney Hook.[10] Dewey wrote the preface to this volume and appears thereby to have given consent that the assertion implied in the title of Professor Hook's book, that pragmatism has a metaphysics, is not completely fictitious. In 1931 Professor John L. Childs' book, *Education and the Philosophy of Experimentalism,*[11] was published. In Chapter III, entitled "Has Experimentalism a Metaphysic?" Dr. Childs, who is one of the most loyal exponents of pragmatism today, assumes that there are several general assumptions in experimentalism concerning existence, and he tries to make some of them explicit.

It is not without some precedent, therefore, that this synopsis of pragmatism includes this section on metaphysics. Following the lead of Professor Childs more particularly, an attempt will be made as simply as possible to say how the world is pictured when looked at through the eyes of a pragmatist. Before launching this attempt the reader may be reminded that the world view now to be outlined is a refined naturalism. In the synopsis of naturalism[12] it was explained that as naturalism becomes more refined it may become either realistic or pragmatic, depending on the turn it takes. If the refinement results in a lack of confidence in substance as such, as in positivism, and in a preoccupation with Nature as process rather than substance or law, the resultant metaphysics is the same as that which is now to be outlined more fully.

This outline of the metaphysics of pragmatism will be first given in brief in a series of ten propositions. These will be followed by an explanatory statement enlarging upon each of the propositions. In each of these ten assertions, the word *world* will be used to refer generally to the process or order within which man lives; the term *world* as used in these statements might be regarded as roughly synonymous with the words *cosmos, Nature,* and *reality.* The equivalence cannot be exact because pragmatism does not dwell upon orderliness as implied in the word *cosmos,* nor upon an independently subsistent reality as implied in the words *Nature* and *reality.*

The ten propositions are as follows:

1. The world is all foreground.
2. The world is "characterized throughout by process and change."[13]
3. The world is precarious.
4. The world is incomplete and indeterminate.
5. The world is pluralistic.

[9] Printed as an essay in *Obiter Scripta.* New York: Charles Scribner's Sons, 1936. See p. 223.
[10] La Salle, Ill.: The Open Court Publishing Company, 1927.
[11] New York: Appleton-Century-Crofts, 1931.
[12] Cf. pp. 70–73.
[13] John L. Childs, *op. cit.,* p. 45.

6. The world has ends within its own process.
7. The world is not, nor does it include, a transempirical reality.
8. Man is continuous with the world.
9. Man is not an active cause in the world.
10. The world does not guarantee progress.

An explanation of each of these assertions will now be offered in the order in which they are listed.

1. *The world is all foreground.* While this characterization of pragmatism made by Santayana implies the criticism that pragmatism misses the importance of background in its view of reality, it may have explanatory value as well in pointing to the strong tendency of pragmatism to center all attention in the particular unit of activity in which individual or group is engaged at any given time.

In every instance of giving attention to something, we know that there are two aspects in the area coming into the range of attention. There is the figure, the object central in attention upon which all active effort is focused. Then there is the ground, the background or situation of which the object or figure is a part. The latter enters attention as a kind of generalized unit or field in which the figure is central. If any analogy can be drawn for philosophy from this phenomenon of attention, it is that metaphysics is the ground and that specific activities in which we engage, day by day, are the successive figures. But pragmatism has rejected this traditional way of looking at things. General background, it holds, is not prior to the specific activities in which experience engages us.

Pragmatists are not concerned with the discovery of some all-embracing reality which is the background for every experience and for all human activity. Their closest approach to such a general background is to insist that the recognition that there is no such all-inclusive reality is the general background within which individuals and societies must live if they are to be effective. This accounts in part at least for the fact that pragmatism lays more stress on society and the social sciences than it does on Nature and the physical sciences. Society is the ongoing human stream in which significant events take place; compared to this, Nature, conceived as an unchanging order in the background, is an abstraction.

2. *The world is "characterized throughout by process and change."* The world is like an ongoing stream. For pragmatism we may say that everything that confronts us in our experience—the universe, the cosmos, everything that has the appearance of objective reality—is, like a river, an ever-flowing stream of change and movement.

Of course, we all recognize that life is full of change and movement. We ourselves grow and develop to maturity, and in later years fail and decline. Events come and go, one set of circumstances is replaced by another, and in turn by another, and so on in a long succession. Fortunes change, so that those who are now prosperous are not always so. None of us can rest on our oars and expect life to wait for us. It keeps moving; and we must keep on our toes to keep up with it.

But pragmatism means more than this when it tells us that the world is an ongoing stream. By this statement we are to understand that there is nothing which is static or permanent; there is nothing which is outside the flowing river of life's changes. Everything is in flux and movement. While it is recognized that there are varying rates of change, yet all is change. The things which change more slowly, and seem sometimes to be permanent, are regarded as structure. The things which change more rapidly constitute process. But, though at different rates, both structure and process change, and all things flow onward.

3. *The world is precarious.* In a world in which all things change there can be no complete security; for change means unpredictability and hazard. Uncertainty and precariousness, pragmatism holds, must be accepted therefore as inevitable; and in all of our attempts to cope with circumstance we must always be ready to meet unexpected happenings which may as easily be unfriendly to us as friendly.

4. *The world is incomplete and indeterminate.* A world which is all movement and change is far different from a closed universe in which every part functions with the precision of a machine. The machinelike universe is a completed structure; there is nothing to be added to it. It is also so efficient that there is no room for chance of freedom in its operation. The universe of pragmatism is quite unlike this. It is unfinished, possibly still growing, and so within it there is much room for additions and improvements to be made by the inventive powers of man. There is also room for chance, for contingent events which could not possibly be predicted. The pragmatist does not regard man as having freedom of choice, but he does find room in the flow of events for man to engage in experimental activities in such a way as to change the direction in which events flow.

5. *The world is pluralistic.* Again, a world which is all movement and flux is not a unified world in which all things are closely knit together in a total unity. Much less is it a world in which all things could ultimately be reduced to one substance. The flowing world in which pragmatists believe is a world of many different things, a world of multiplicities, strictly speaking, a multiverse rather than a universe.

6. *The world has ends within its own process.* By this characterization of the world the philosophy of pragmatism attempts to explain the place of objectives or values in life. As will be shown later, pragmatists have applied themselves seriously to the study of value. They are most alert to the distinction between what is and what "ought" to be; although for them the idea of oughtness is not so applicable to values as is the idea of unrealized possibilities implicit in present circumstances. The idea of oughtness con-

veys the impression that there is a moral imperative attached to the realization of values. And this in turn may suggest ultimately real values which comprise a moral norm to which human experience ought to conform and by which man is ultimately measured. It is in antithesis to this, in part at least, that the world is conceived as having its own ends within the texture of its own processes. Objectives and values are not ultimate; they are terminals in experience which are more or less transitory. Some of them are quite clearly means to other ends, toward which experience directly flows onward, once they are realized. Others are values to be possessed for what they are at the time, as ends in themselves, but from which we pass on to other things, although these ends do not become means to other objectives.

7. *The world is not, nor does it include, a transempirical reality.* This proposition explicitly declares the nontheistic, nonmystical, nonspiritual character of existence as conceived by contemporary pragmatism. As seen vividly in William James, pragmatism leans heavily upon the dynamic and active character of experience; it is a moving thing and can never be shut up to the static and unchanging. James, however, did not find the existence of a spiritual world to be antithetical to a dynamic and changing world. But Dewey, since his early departure from idealism, and those who have followed him, have felt it necessary to root a dynamic experience in a changing and precarious world in which there are no unchanging substances and no unchanging relations. In fact, ever-changing experience and this ever-changing order are virtually identified as one and the same thing. While there are many people who see no conflict between a human experience which is dynamic and an ultimate reality which is Person or Spirit, contemporary pragmatism, or experimentalism as it is sometimes called, asserts itself to be completely naturalistic or atheistic, at the same time that it preserves much of the freedom and abides by many of the patterns common to the nonmaterialistic and nonmechanistic world view of idealism.

8. *Man is continuous with the world.* For one thing this proposition is intended as a refutation of the traditional dualism between the inner rational experience of man, on the one hand, and Nature, on the other. Dewey has insisted that the problem of knowledge, which he alleges has claimed far more of the attention of philosophers than it deserves, is greatly simplified if the place of man in Nature is correctly recognized for what it is. This is to imply that we have a knowledge problem chiefly because we assume that man as a knowing creature is separate from Nature. This assumption, pragmatists insist, is mistaken. Man is not separate from Nature; he is a part of Nature and continuous with it.

One of the chief evidences cited by Dewey as demonstrating the continuity of man and Nature is the theory of evolution.[14] Accepting this

[14] Cf. John Dewey, *Democracy and Education.* New York: The Macmillan Company, 1916. Pp. 392–395.

theory as a valid explanation of the way in which new species have come into existence, he extends it so that it yields the further conclusion that man is an integral part of Nature. Much less than being a creation given birth from a source higher than Nature, and even less than a new kind of creature emerging in Nature, man is described as completely and totally a child of Nature, born both within and of Nature. Reason in man is a disclosure of a characteristic of Nature, not of a higher order in which man uniquely participates, as compared to the remainder of the natural order; reason is a phase of Nature instead of being a sample of a higher and more inclusive Logos upon which Nature depends. Consequently, there is such close correspondence between the events of man's reason and the events of the world as to constitute continuity. Our thoughts are not of one substance, and the events of Nature of another; and therefore there is nothing remarkable about reason in man deriving meaning from events in Nature. They are both of the same piece; and therefore meaning and event, sign and thing signified, move along together in the same stream.

9. *Man is not an active cause in the world.* This characterization of one aspect of man and his relation to the world concerns the efficiency of the activity of man in influencing events which take place in the world. It indicates the middle-of-the-road position which pragmatism has attempted to take in the age-old argument between exponents of free will and determinism. Despite the stress laid by William James on free will, contemporary pragmatism does not take its stand on the free will side of the argument. Nor does it accept a complete determinism which leaves no room for man to influence the direction which the events of the world take. Man is not regarded as an active cause in the world, an initiator of movement which sets events beyond himself into motion and brings something to pass which otherwise would not have taken place in Nature if his initiative had not injected itself into events as a cause. But man is nevertheless capable of the kind of interaction with the world which changes the direction of events at certain crucial points.

This capability of man can be exemplified by a reference to the psychological phenomenon of a delayed response. Pragmatism argues that all of man's action is by no means adequately described by the simple and efficient stimulus-response bond. Man is not just a machine which responds automatically, each time an appropriate action in accordance with the stimulus received. Though much action does go on at this level of automatic response, there is in addition an important level of action at which responses are delayed long enough for them to be the result of a sufficient comprehension of the situation for the action to be a somewhat total response, instead of an automatic response which is partial at best and therefore inadequate to the situation. In the course of building this delayed response, an important reconstructing or redirecting activity goes on in the experience of man which affects the course of events flowing from the response. This reconstructing or redirecting is not a cause of the events which follow from it; it is a kind of handling of causes or forces, of which man is a part, which helps determine their future direction without effecting any essential change in them.

10. *The world does not guarantee progress.* This characterization of the world makes explicit for us one of its ethical aspects. Specifically, it proposes to say how much basis for hope there is in the world. While the proposition is stated negatively, and is to the effect that the world does not guarantee progress, it does not thereby put the pragmatists on the side of pessimism. Similar to the position taken in relation to free will and determinism, the position here taken is a kind of middle ground between optimism and pessimism. It is more correctly characterized as meliorism.[15] According to it, the world does not offer positive guarantees on which man can securely base his hope. At the same time, the world is not so constructed as to predetermine the future in ways which are unfriendly to the interests of man. The world is indeterminate with regard to values, and in relation to this indeterminacy man's redirecting power can be applied in such ways as to determine the future. There is as much likelihood that man's redirection of the events of the world can work in the direction of his own future benefit as it can work to his own detriment. But one thing is certain: man must face the world, he must engage actively in the events of the world, if there is to be any redirecting done, and if anything determinate is to be brought out of the world's indeterminacy. Nothing of value will come to pass if man escapes from the world's events and allows them to take their own course. This stand amounts to a kind of moral imperative in pragmatism; but of course it is not regarded as having absolute status. It is that man must face life courageously and bring out of it what he can. The end is not guaranteed; but the only way a desirable end can be brought about is for man to face life and make the most of it by his own diligent effort.

C. THE LOGIC OF PRAGMATISM

In first calling attention to the field of logic in the Introduction, the statement was made that there are many today who are not satisfied with traditional logic and are therefore insisting that logic must be reformed by extending it radically into the sense-perceptual level of experience.[16] Under the leadership of John Dewey, pragmatism has clamored most loudly for this reform. Dissatisfied with any mere tacking of new material on to the old cloth of traditional logic, Dewey has outlined the radical

[15] Cf. p. 45.
[16] Cf. p. 26.

reform which he feels must take place in logic for it to cope with our times.[17]

Unlike Immanuel Kant, who in the nineteenth century exalted the logic of Aristotle as being so complete that virtually nothing could be added to it, Dewey has insisted that Aristotle's logic is so completely out of joint with the twentieth century that scarcely any effectiveness can be expected to result from its use. He argues that the very adequacy of Aristotle's logic for the Greek world of his day presages its inadequacy for our day.[18] This inadequacy hinges rather largely upon the two differing conceptions of Nature held in Aristotle's time and ours. In Greek science, Nature was regarded as a "bounded and closed" system,[19] the kind of conception which gave rise to naturalism as a philosophy in Democritus, Epicurus, and Lucretius.[20] But the conception of Nature which twentieth-century science gives us is more like a universe with its lid off, of which William James often spoke. It is an open system in which change and movement are constantly going on; not just the change or movement of atoms falling in space, as in Democritus, but a more radical movement reflected by the content of modern natural science as "changes formulated in correspondence *with one another*."[21]

Greek science and logic dealt with facts and the generalizations which could be made about them, whether approached inductively or deductively; accordingly, the Greeks regarded the relations of facts as quite incidental. Even the kind of relation involved in acquiring facts was pigeonholed as a matter of learning and not therefore a concern of logic. Modern science has almost completely reversed this order; relations constitute its primary and central concern, not brute facts apart from relations. Dewey characterizes this radical difference by remarking that "it is not too much to say that what Greek science and logic rejected are now the head cornerstone of science—although not yet of the theory of logical forms."[22] By this last he means to observe that while there is a radical difference between modern science and Greek science, the reforms have not yet taken place in logic which yield a comparable difference between modern logic and the logic of Aristotle.

Although Aristotle's logic is completely inadequate to be teamed up with present-day science and culture, it was nevertheless remarkable in the context of its own science and culture. And from its particular genius in this regard we can take a cue as to what the function of the new logic must be;

[17] John Dewey, *Logic, The Theory of Inquiry*. New York: Holt, Rinehart and Winston, 1938.
[18] Cf. *ibid.*, p. 65.
[19] *Ibid.*, p. 93.
[20] Cf. pp. 49–55.
[21] John Dewey, *Logic, The Theory of Inquiry*, p. 93.
[22] *Ibid.*, p. 91.

for the logic of our day must do for the science and culture of our time
what the logic of Aristotle did for the science and culture of his. This was
that Aristotle's logic "included in a single unified scheme the contents of
both the common sense and the science of his day."[23] It is a comparable
function which must be fulfilled by logic for the present generation; it must
provide a form or medium of communication between the science of our
time and the common-sense habits and activities in which people of all
walks of life engage, regardless of level of education or understanding.
More specifically, the demand on the new logic is that it be "a unified
theory of inquiry through which the authentic pattern of experimental and
operational inquiry in science shall become available for regulation of the
habitual methods by which inquiries in the field of common sense are
carried on."[24]

1. THE PATTERN OF LOGIC

The most important thing to say about this new logic in a short discussion, such as is comprised by these few paragraphs, is to outline its pattern;
and in this, we necessarily establish a connection right away with the
discussion of the epistemology of pragmatism which opened this chapter.
This connection is that the pattern of logic which pragmatism proposes as
the new logic adequate for the science and culture of our time is the pattern
of experimental method. In experimental method there is a form of inquiry
which can mediate between the technical science of the research laboratory
and the everyday common-sense inquiry of home, field, and market place.
The pattern outlined above was comprised of five steps: activity, problem,
observation of data, formulation of hypotheses, and testing of hypotheses.[25] While the general pattern outlined in Dewey's *Logic* is essentially
the same, the stages are described somewhat differently and therefore need
further discussion at this point.

a. *"The Indeterminate Situation."* Inquiry is evoked by a field or unit of
experience which is problematic; a situation which raises questions in our
minds or causes us to doubt. Dewey mentions a number of adjectives which
characterize these indeterminate situations in which inquiry begins. "They
are disturbed, troubled, ambiguous, confused, full of conflicting tendencies,
obscure, etc."[26] As will be brought out later, they are not so completely
indeterminate as to cause panic. Rather they center about a few uncertain
factors, other elements of the situation remaining stable for the time being
and allowing us to focus attention upon the elements which make the
situation indeterminate.

---

[23] *Ibid.*, pp. 95–96.
[24] *Ibid.*, p. 98.
[25] Cf. pp. 381–382.
[26] John Dewey, *Logic, The Theory of Inquiry*, p. 105.

b. *"Institution of a Problem."* The indeterminate situations with which inquiry begins are not at first primarily cognitive in character; i.e., they are not primarily concerned with knowledge. They are more intimately a part of living and acting than purely intellectual; they are vital situations, and therefore the knowledge aspect of them is only one phase. Because of this, a step has been taken in the direction of effective inquiry when an indeterminate situation becomes a problematic situation in the mind of the person confronted by it. For then the knowledge aspect of the situation has come into focus sufficiently for a definition to be attempted regarding what it is in the situation that makes it indeterminate. This is what is meant by the institution of a problem. Formulation of the problem is important, for without it the situation remains undefined and whatever is attempted toward a solution is brute trial and error or mere "busy work."[27] On the other hand, proportionate to the extent to which the problem has been well formulated, a pattern is already taking shape to guide the successive stages of inquiry effectively.

c. *"The Determination of a Problem-Solution."* This stage of inquiry carries the definition of the problematic aspect of the situation further, approaching the formulation or discovery of solutions. One of the first things to be noted in defining the problem presented by an indeterminate situation is that the situation is not indeterminate throughout, but that the indeterminate elements tend to take form in a pattern while the other elements provide a comparatively stable background not problematic in itself. To proceed this far is to be on the way in observing the data relative to the problematic factors. And to focus on the pattern into which the problematic factors tend to fall is virtually to be throwing out feelers in the direction of possible solutions. This is one point at which the instrumental character of ideas, so stoutly upheld by pragmatism, comes sharply to focus. For the ideas of possible solutions to the problem situation are not regarded as abstract mental things which are lifted out of the mind and applied to the situation. Neither are they regarded as mental replicas of the objective or "existential" facts of the situation. They are indigenous ideational-existent emergents which are given birth, right in the situation itself.

d. *"Reasoning."* Of course all of life's situations are filled full of meanings, and meanings commonly have symbols by which they are communicated from one person to another. These symbols also serve a single individual in a solitary way, by providing a means by which he can effectively transfer meanings from one situation to another. Now, in coming to the solution of a problematic situation, possible solutions will often come to mind from similar or comparable situations, of which the present situation has reminded us. But these possible solutions can never be applied blindly

[27] Cf. *ibid.*, p. 108.

in the present situation as though ready-made for it. They must be modified and adapted to meet the peculiar factors comprising the present situation. Even if they do happen to fit without any modification, an understanding of the relation of solution and problem will not result if the solution is applied blindly.

e. *"The Operational Character of Facts-Meanings."* The word "operational" may be defined as referring to activities which are rather clearly overt, not inner, not purely mental or emotional. The operational realm is the realm of practice, an area in which observable behavior is going on and producing effects which are objectively evident. In the pattern of logic which Dewey has proposed, both facts and meanings are regarded as operational. It is not uncommon for facts to be considered as nonoperational as well as operational. For it is assumed by some that facts may be observed, as in the older empiricism, as static and fixed, therefore not within the process of some operation which is going on at the time. But Dewey treats facts as operational because in any effective observation of them in a movement from problem to solution, they are observed not for what they are in themselves, but for their significance in relation to this movement toward solution. In themselves facts are somewhat neutral in meaning; and, contrary to the assumption of the older empiricism, when they take on meaning they do it within the frame of reference of a problem-solution movement.

Similarly, meanings are also operational. And this may appear to be as difficult to uphold as the contention that facts are operational. For while facts may seem to be finished and complete in themselves, and therefore at least have the appearance of not being in motion all of the time, meanings, on the other hand, do not have existence. They are only the possibilities of a situation and have no objective existence until they are put into operation long enough for their consequences to be produced in action. But Dewey's argument is that the operational movement progressing from problem to solution is the frame of reference for meanings as well as for facts. Meanings are tied to operation by virtue of the circumstance that it is in operation that they have their effect; they lend direction to further observation; they are projected ways of acting upon existing conditions.

The significance of these two assertions for the overall pattern of inquiry is that it is only as we recognize that both facts and meanings are operational, are tied integrally to the problem-solution movement of experience, that solutions are possible at all.

f. *"Common Sense and Scientific Inquiry."* The genius of this pattern of logic for our time is that it supplies what has been lacking since science has advanced by such great strides beyond the logic of Aristotle. This is a common pattern within which both scientific and common-sense activities can be unified. The legitimate difference between science and common sense is a difference of subject matter; it is not legitimate that there should be such a discrepancy between the two that common sense cannot benefit by the refinements of science. The reform in logic proposed by Dewey is offered as an outline of the way in which this great gulf can be bridged. For the problems with which science deals are not suspended in mid-air, having nothing at all to do with life at the common-sense level; they have their rootage in the soil of common sense. And similarly, the solutions of problems, to which scientific inquiry leads, reflect back into common-sense experience.[28] A much-needed unification can be brought about between the two, therefore, if the pattern of science can be made available to men of all stations in life, and their common-sense activities be given direction by this same fruitful pattern of inquiry.

2. SOME CHARACTERIZATIONS OF PRAGMATIC LOGIC

Now that the pattern of thought is outlined, there are several characterizations of the pattern as a whole which might help make it clearer and also suggest its revolutionary character. Four of these characterizations will be presented by way of concluding this discussions of pragmatic logic.

a. In this pattern of thought, logic is regarded as autonomous. This characterization can be elaborated by comparing the pragmatic pattern in logic to induction and deduction. Both induction and deduction, it may be said, superimpose a pattern upon any given situation in which thinking is involved. If deduction is followed, the pattern of the syllogism is brought in from the outside, as it were, and applied to the present situation in which a problem of thought is to be worked out. Similarly, if induction is followed, the pattern of extended observation of particulars and building conclusions which apply to all of these particulars is imported into the situation and applied somewhat arbitrarily. Pragmatists argue that each indeterminate situation is more unique than to permit this wholesale importing of patterns from outside the situation. The contention is that the patterns of thought must arise from within the situation because they cannot be peculiarly effective in that situation if they are ready-made forms which are imposed from the outside.

b. This pattern of logic is closely related to the biological realm. This is to say that the indeterminate situations in which thought goes on are vital situations intimately tied up with the onward flow of the life processes of organisms. Consequently there is more than a coincidental connection between the pattern of inquiry and the strugglings of animal existence. In indeterminate situations and in the problem-solution movement characterizing them, thought and life constitute one continuous process. They are

[28] Cf. *ibid.*, p. 66.

not distinct levels of existence; and they do not have different patterns of organization. This is the logical aspect of the metaphysical principle already stated according to which man and Nature are continuous.

c. The pattern of logic is closely related to the culture. This is a companion to the characterization just given. For pragmatists, logic is as closely tied with the culture as with the processes of animal existence. Indeterminate situations have their sociological context as well as their biological. Individual men do not act and think in isolation from the society of which they are a part. Of necessity they do their inquiring within a context of meanings which are supplied by the social group. Consequently, language, as a system of symbols for meanings, together with "arts, institutions, traditions, and customary beliefs,"[29] as media of communication, are all contributors to each indeterminate situation in which thought goes on.

d. Indeterminate situations may be either individual or social, immediately circumscribed by time, or broadly inclusive. This last characterization of the pragmatic pattern of logic is a necessary addition to the one just stated. It may be easier to outline the pattern of logic in individual terms and in relation to a strictly immediate and present situation. But this does not do justice to it; for individual thought is never isolated from society and culture in any important sense, and although there are limitedly immediate situations which are faced both individually and socially, in point of time, there are also situations which stretch out over longer periods. To exemplify this concretely: while getting money to buy the family's next meal may be an indeterminate situation in which some genuine inquiry may go on, the same kind of situation is constituted by the present division of the world between East and West, a situation involving the whole human race and extending over a longer period of time, the length of which is itself indeterminate.

D. THE AXIOLOGY OF PRAGMATISM

This systematic overview of pragmatism may be rendered somewhat complete if we look now at the pragmatist at work in the value realm, an area which he has in no way slighted. First of all two general matters will be discussed: the foundation of value according to pragmatism, and the criterion of value; then, as heretofore, the ethical, aesthetic, religious, and social realms of value will be discussed more specifically.

1. First of all, from whence do values come, and in what is their existence rooted? In answer it may be said that pragmatism does not define values as though they existed in any ultimate or final manner. Values have their existence rather by virtue of their relation with individual-social activ-

[29] *Ibid.*, p. 42.

ities. They have existence to the extent that they function in, or accompany effective functioning in, the individual-social flow of events.

There are therefore several conditions which are presupposed by the experiencing of values or the realization of values. There must be language in order for meanings to be communicated; there must be the achievement of selfhood on the part of the individuals participating in value realization, in order for there to be any values; and there must be the counterpart of selfhood, with which it communicates and to which it responds, in society, facts, relations, and events. These are the prerequisites which help to define the level of activities at which value experience goes on; for it is only when these phenomena are present that the phenomenon of value occurs.

To some it might seem that the necessity of selfhood should be stated as a requirement before language; but for pragmatism this order does not follow. Selves do not first exist and then afterward create symbols of speech by which to communicate with each other. Instead, the means of communication, particularly words and speech, help provide the conditions in which selfhood comes into existence. For the tendency of the individual to interact with other individuals and things is prior to his tendency to collect his own thoughts and meanings privately. As a consequence, words come first and thoughts come later. First the self interacts with its counterpart in society and things, then, with this interactivity as a base, the self interacts within itself in the kind of talking-to-one's-self which we call thought.

It is within the context of this communication between the individual and its counterpart in society and things that selfhood arises in man. And it is because of the experience which the individual has first in this kind of communication that he is able to communicate between meanings within himself in the peculiar way which results in a consciousness of self. As a result of this communication, he comes to distinguish himself as unique and to refer to himself by a variety of personal and possessive pronouns which language has provided him. He comes to see himself as an agent in the flow of events who can change the direction of events and thereby produce consequences which otherwise would not take place. He comes to have a sense of a continuing past, present, and future, of past experiences and present situations; and in relation to this sense of time he sees himself as having continuity with the flow of events. And, particularly in connection with his recognition of himself as an agent, he comes to recognize that as an individual he is both responsible for and accountable for what he does.

Within the context of experience which possesses these conditions—language, selfhood in individuals, and the objective and social counterpart of selfhood—values can arise. It is experiences having these conditions which provide the basis of existence for values. This basis, it will be recognized, is not an ultimate or final ground; it is the same kind of flux and change already described as characterizing reality, according to the metaphysics of pragmatism.

2. The other general consideration has to do with the guiding principle by which values are appropriately determined in each situation. By what means can a person know that a particular course of action will yield the kind of value which is desired? This is one way of stating the question with which we are now concerned.

The word "desired" is not a completely acceptable word to be used in the attempt just made at stating the question regarding the criterion of value because it may suggest that desire is the guiding principle of value. This would be close to a theory of value already stated, which is to the effect that whatever is the object of a person's interest has value for him.[30] But pragmatic axiology is not based upon desire alone; it does not define value as that which fulfills desire in a purely subjective or selfish way. Its treatment of value is at the same time more critical, more objective, and less personal than this.

If a person were to adopt such a theory of value in its most crude and immediate intent, it might be said that he would not need to give critical attention to value considerations. For in each situation he could simply do what he most wanted to do, and thereby get the value which would satisfy his desire. But such blind passion as this is far removed from the critical examination of values, and even more removed from the critical adoption of some consistent approach to value selection which includes a larger perspective than the immediate present. Pragmatic axiology, in antithesis to this, insists that there must be a critical examination of values in order for wise selections to be made, and also that wisdom involves ascending to the level of value criticism at which a consistent principle of selection is operative.

It might be said that there are two perspectives which are involved in the guiding principle of value adopted by pragmatism: these are the perspective of the present situation in which a value selection is to be made, and the perspective of possible future situations to which the outworking of the present may lead. In the first of these perspectives, there is a kind of desire fulfillment which is involved; but it is not limited, nor selfish, nor strictly present-centered. The pragmatic logic has already evidenced the extent to which indeterminate situations provide the frame of reference for our thinking and acting, at least as pragmatists view life. Since there is necessarily tension in these situations, because of their problematic character and as a result of the suspended judgment and suspended action entailed, the desires naturally focus about the kind of resolutions of these situations which will bring relief and release. Therefore the values called for will

[30] Cf. p. 285.

necessarily satisfy some desire. But the situation, not the isolated self, will be the focus of the value; and consequently, the satisfaction will not be a limited selfish satisfaction. Value is better described as being satisfactory to the situation than as being satisfying to the person or persons involved in the situation.

But this is not all that there is to be said about the pragmatic guiding principle of value, because so far only the perspective of the present situation has been employed. So, in addition to finding a resolution of the present indeterminate situation which satisfies all of its demands, one must also find in one and the same resolution a course of action which does not mortgage future situations. That is to say that the resolution of the present situation is not completely satisfactory unless it promises, in addition to solving the present problem, to allow experience to flow freely into future situations, so favoring a satisfactory control and direction of them as well.[31]

1. ETHICAL VALUE

The two general aspects of pragmatic value theory which have just been outlined apply, of course, in the moral realm as in every other field of value. The basis for the existence of ethical values is constituted by the individual-social life process in which selves are in communication with other selves and with groups by means of language. Also, the guiding principle which leads to ethical value is that in the moral aspects of indeterminate situations value is to be realized by acting in such ways as satisfactorily resolve the indeterminate elements and at the same time open the way to the most satisfactory control of succeeding situations.

This value theory applied to the ethical side of life is regarded by pragmatism as resolving the common conflict in ethics between the subjective demand that one's motives be right, on the one hand, and the objective demand that one's conduct conform to acceptable standards, on the other. It is argued that this conflict of demands is resolved by the approach which is primarily concerned with satisfying the requirements of each indeterminate situation, because in this approach inner motives and outer behavior are fused in the kind of purposeful action which resolves the situation. This conflict in ethics and the synthesis which is proposed by pragmatism should be explored a bit more fully.

Dewey has observed that there are these two common approaches to ethical matters; some people stress one approach more than the other, but it is not uncommon for the two to get mixed up in a kind of confused simultaneous emphasizing of both. On the one hand, it is said that the

---

[31] Cf. John S. Brubacher (editor), *The Public Schools and Spiritual Values.* New York: Harper & Row, Publishers, 1944. Chapter III. Also, John Dewey, *Democracy and Education,* Chapter XXVI.

important thing in ethical affairs is that a person's intentions are good—as in Kant, for example, that the will be a good will. But if this emphasis on the inner aspect of morals becomes too exclusive, moral behavior may actually be very shoddy; i.e., conduct may actually suffer because judgment is focused on motives and intentions rather than on actions.

The antithesis to this is to base judgment completely upon behavior, on the conduct in which a person actually engages; in the manner of the adage, "Pretty is as pretty does." While this approach has the advantage of being more exacting than a morality which pays heed to intentions at the expense of that which issues in conduct, it easily becomes too rigid in requiring conformity or obedience, and in doing so reduces morality until it is purely an affair of doing what is expected without asking questions. In such cases morality is not yoked with intelligence, for the desired conduct is elicited without engaging the understanding of the persons involved.

When both of these approaches to morality are followed simultaneously by the same sponsorship, as in the classroom for example, the conflict may become quite acute. For, on the one hand a high degree of approbation is attached to a child's possession of right feelings or good intentions; but at the same time, he is expected to produce the goods in actual achievement, so that it would seem that good intentions do not count for as much as surface impressions might tend to suggest.

A real union of these external and internal aspects which is free from contradiction is nevertheless desirable. Intentions should be appropriate to the situation, and should not peter out before they are projected into appropriate actions. At the same time, there needs to be action appropriate to the situation, but it should not be divorced from feelings and attitudes by which the subject enters into the spirit of the appropriate acts. This genuine union of the inner and outer, Dewey argues, is achieved when each situation which confronts us is approached freshly as a new situation; when within this approach intentions are regarded not as ends in themselves but as operational instruments which may emerge in fruitful acts; and when such acts, fruitful because they are perfectly matched to the situation, are seen for what they are, the consequences which have emerged out of intentions given birth in the situation.[32]

2. AESTHETIC VALUE

There is also an aesthetic side to value experiences, as well as experiences of value which are more especially aesthetic in character than ethical, religious, social, utilitarian, etc. That is to say that the particular value which these experiences have, or that many, if not all, experiences have when viewed from the aesthetic side, is that they possess beauty or yield

[32] Cf. John Dewey, *Democracy and Education*, Chapter XXVI, "Theories of Morals."

meanings which we want to preserve. As is the case with all other values, these values exist because they take place in individual or social experiences in which selves are in communication with one another or with objects. But somewhat unlike other values, aesthetic values are often communicated by other media than words. While they may be conveyed by language, as in poetry and narrative, the medium of expression and appreciation as often takes the form of painting, sculpture, architecture, the acting and posturing of drama, the dance, or music.

In his lectures on the philosophy of art, published in book form as *Art as Experience*,[33] Dewey has outlined an aesthetic theory from which we may glean something of the nature of aesthetic values as viewed within the context of pragmatism. Understanding the nature of these values, as defined by pragmatism, is closely coupled with the kind of understanding of the nature of experience which has been outlined in this chapter. The element of beauty or the enjoyableness of life is intimately related to the cycles by which life processes go on. Life is not a steady, smooth-flowing stream, much less an inert mass ever remaining the same; it is a flowing stream, but it flows intermittently, in cycles, in units, in fields, in rhythms, the outlines of which are marked out by their own substance, like the waves of the sea. Some of these units or fields of experience are smooth in their direction and are therefore enjoyable. But as many of them as disturbing and tense, because they are indeterminate experiences which call for a resolution of some kind before the disturbing elements pass away and the enjoyable take their place. Although no artificial or uniform regularity is implied, it might be said that experience alternates between indeterminate and determinate situations, and therefore between tension and enjoyment, like the alternating flyings and perchings of the bird.

Dewey tells us that this is the only kind of world in which there can be aesthetic value. In a world in which everything is finished and complete, there would be no opportunity for the kind of living-through of indeterminacies which is the necessary basis for appreciating the finished and complete. And in a world in which everything is indeterminate, there would be no "perchings" to provide the occasion for the enjoyment of what has been completed; for it is the time of resolution which is the point of emergence of aesthetic values. The time when the indeterminate situation fades out and equilibrium is restored is the occasion for the release of tension and the coming of an enjoyment which is wholeheartedly embraced. Dewey describes this occasion concisely as follows:

That which distinguishes an experience as esthetic is conversion of resistance and tensions, of excitations that in themselves are temptations to diversion, into a movement toward an inclusive and fulfilling close.[34]

[33] New York: Minton, Balch & Co., 1934.
[34] *Ibid.*, p. 56.

But we must hasten to add that these recurrent occasions for enjoyment must not be stretched out in the attempt to prolong them longer than the rhythm of experience allows. To do this is to turn one's back upon the objective character of experience, and therefore to escape psychologically. We must courageously face life when it is unpleasant, as well as when it is pleasant; it will not do to stop the clock in an attempt to prolong some subjective state just because it is enjoyable. Experiences keep coming, in continual succession, and we must diligently attend in order to keep up with the flow responsively. Aesthetic meanings, as well as all others, are operational, and therefore cannot be divorced from objects and events. One of the primary prerequisites, therefore, of aesthetic sensitivity is this close continuity of the self with the objects and events of experience.

All of us can understand, however, this desire to prolong the seasons of enjoyment in which tension and indecision give way to release and enjoyment. For this enjoyment is attached to values which we want to preserve. It is primarily because of this desire to preserve them that art in its various forms has arisen. The artist, as he creates a work of art, gives expression to such values; and the rest of us, as we behold his creation, renew in our appreciation the value which we desire to preserve. But the difference should be noted between this kind of preservation of aesthetic value and the prolonging of the subjective enjoyment already excluded as psychological escape. The preservation of aesthetic value which works of art constitute is an objective preservation; there it is in an object which may become a medium for communicating value for all who behold it.

Of course, active and discerning perception is an essential qualification of all who would enjoy these values. Perception which experiences afresh is necessary to every subject who would drink deeply of the aesthetic worth native to his own experiences. And in the artist there must be all of this, plus an accumulation of experiences of expression in some medium, so that he can reproduce the glimpse of beauty when it comes. One evidence that these values have been communicated is the commonness of the experience that poet, or novelist, or playwright, or actor, or painter, or sculptor, or composer, or musician has given expression to values we have experienced but could not express for ourselves. So that those of us who come to appreciate aesthetic value cannot fall too far short of the artist in perceptual insight, though we may have little of his power of expression. Such a power of appreciaiton is not a special talent found only in exceptional people, and far removed from the intellectual or practical activities which are more commonly shared. There are aesthetic phases in every experience which constitutes a unity; therefore the same discernments which enable us to catch the patterns of experience have some connection with the beholding of aesthetic values. Blind adoption of conventional patterns at the one extreme, and excessive indulgence in particular pleasures at the other, are the habits militating against the freshness of insight which leads to aesthetic value. "Rigid abstinence, coerced submission, tightness on the one side and dissipation, incoherence and aimless indulgence on the other"[35] are the real enemies to be overcome if one is to possess aesthetic value.

It appears that Dewey's aesthetics centers quite completely in beauty, or pleasurable aesthetic values. But a secondary place is given to values which are the antithesis of beauty or pleasure. This place is that when ugliness, or anguish, or tragedy are preserved in some art form, it is within a large enough time perspective, the experience being sufficiently in the past, that it has lost its acutely self-involving grasp. In the art form it is reëxperienced in a more objective manner because of the larger perspective. For this reason, even though in essence it is still ugliness or tragedy, or some other negative value, it is yet beauty; and in response to it there is an acceptance which is resolution and quietude.

3. RELIGIOUS VALUE

Only a summary statement will be made within this particular context regarding the pragmatic treatment of religious value. Except for a few general remarks which will anticipate later discussion, enlargement of the pragmatic approach to religion is held in reserve for Chapter XXI, which deals solely with this subject. Religious value, particularly in the pragmatism of Dewey, if not of James, is closely identified with value realization as such; it might be defined as the value of realizing values. Like all other values, it is naturalistic, in the sense that it does not have a supernatural basis. The value of devotedly attending to every opportunity for realizing value, and all the qualities of life which stem from it, exist because of their occurrence within experience—experience in which selves are in communication with one another, society, and objects. Such experience has a genius which may call out of us a way of living, characterized by seriousness, purposefulness, and diligent application of our energies, which is well-nigh religious. This genius of experience is that it fuses meanings and objects, ideals and consequences, into an operational unity. Ideas and ideals are born in experience, in intimate relation with objects and events, not separate from them. Correspondingly, the consequences which follow from the direction of events, which our responses occasionally give to experience, are intimately related to ideas and ideals, by following directly from them as consequences. Because of this continuity of ideas and events, experience is the meeting ground of the actual and the possible, of present fact and possible value. It is also the living matrix in which alone selfhood thrives, because in experience the self finds its meaning and significance functionally, i.e., in and through action. In the flow of experiences then is the place where we must invest our lives, if we are to possess life's mean-

[35] *Ibid.*, p. 40.

ings and significances; for meanings are operational and emerge only as consequences in the flow of events. Experience then is the focus for our powers of devotion if we are to live significantly. Diligence and watchfulness at the points of transaction in experience at which fact and value meet should constitute for everyone life's primary devotion.

4. SOCIAL VALUE

The theme that values according to pragmatism, are rooted in the individual-social life process has been reiterated so often already that it is scarcely necessary to say that social values are fundamental in the philosophy of pragmatism. Almost every other kind of achievable value is achieved because of the social process in which each individual valuer is when he is normally fitted to his sphere. It may be that this is just another way of saying that for pragmatism society is not just a conglomeration of individuals but an organic process upon which individuals depend and by which they live. As the soil is to plants and trees, so society is to the individual, a matrix which nurtures human life in its individual forms and makes possible all of the flowerings of personality. People make two grave mistakes in one, therefore, when they withdraw into their ivory tower to concentrate upon aesthetic, ethical, or religious values. The first and more evident mistake is that they neglect social values and shirk their responsibilities as individuals to society. But the second mistake of which they are guilty is even a greater injustice to themselves than the first is to society; for they cut themselves off, by their withdrawal, from the very wellspring of value itself by their attempt to make life flourish in the artificial climate of isolation.

Generally speaking, then, the dependence of the individual upon society is a fundamental social value, for because of it most other values, if not all other values, have their origin. Possibly this can be made more explicit by being more specific about society as the normal soil in which individuals flourish and grow. It is somewhat incorrect to use the singular term *society* to describe the social matrix, for this may well be an abstraction as compared to the concrete social relations which each of us has as an individual. The social process confronts each one of us in a specific society or community, in fact in a multiplicity of them. That social counterpart of selfhood with which each individual communicates is a plurality of societies or communities: the home, the school, the church, the peer group, the neighborhood, the industrial community, one's clientele, the club, the labor union, the business or professional institution where a man works, the learned society, the racial or nationality group, and the political structure at the local, state, national, and international levels. These are some of the communities in relation to some combination of which each individual lives. Now, though at times it may seem irksome to have to maintain these relations, they are nevertheless essential, and an individual lives by his dependence upon these communities. It is a primary value to him to be enmeshed in these communities, for by them he has the warmth and companionship of the family, the means of earning his livelihood, the opportunity to participate in the decisions of the body politic, to mention only a few which represent the great variety of benefits these communities pay out to each individual.

While we will not dwell longer on such concrete values as these, some other social values are to be mentioned which are more specific than the general social value of dependence, but not so particular as the shelter of the home and one's daily bread. These more specific values can be seen from two sides: first from the standpoint of the links which weld the individual to communities, and then from the standpoint of the values that communities must foster in individuals. If an individual is to remain as a member of any community, there are a number of values he must prize. He will have a high regard for cooperation; he will both covet it in others and at the same time be ready to cooperate himself. He must know what self-denial and temperance mean, probably more as actions than as abstractions; for every individual cannot have the desires of his heart always fulfilled if there is to be an equitable sharing among all of the members of the group. He will value bravery and courage, if he does not know their meanings in action; for there are times when the well-being of the community necessitates that it be protected against intrusion from the outside. He will know the worth of kindness and love, for these savor of the warmth of interpersonal relations and prompt the kind of understanding which welds individuals together. He will also prize generosity and loyalty, for in sharing the common purposes of the group there is a basis for wider sharing; and in tenacious fulfillment of one's duty to the group the community is strengthened, whereas failure to be loyal would mean disintegration.

The dependence of the individual upon the group is by no means an inferior relation, however, from the standpoint of the individual, according to which the community is paramount and the individual is unimportant. For while the individual must be in relation to society in order to live, society must allow living space for the individuality of its members in order to thrive as a society. Consequently, there is another class of social values which are aspects of the freedom of individuals to live and grow. If the individual is to have this freedom within his relation to the community, then the community must respect him as an individual and regard him more in the light of what he may become rather than judge him on the basis of what he actually is at present. Accordingly, the community must afford him certain civil, religious, academic, and other freedoms, by means of which his various potentialities may be made actual. In addition it must allow him sufficient freedom for play and recreation that he may come into a possession of a sense of self-fulfillment which arises only in a free play of activities. But this must be balanced by the opportunity to work, by which an individual fulfills his place in society productively and gains thereby the self-realization which comes only as an accompaniment of meaningful work.

None of the various communities should be exalted to a place of superiority so that it is identified with the whole of society. Although the various values which have been menioned as social values are values to some degree in any kind of social organization, they are probably more in balance in a democratic society. For when the state is exalted to such a superior place, as in fascism, for example, the functioning of other communities is hampered, and the individual suffers proportionately. The political structure is rightfully only one of the communities in relation with which individuals live, and functions normally only when it is one among many and not the one of which the many are subordinate parts. This is the superiority of democracy as a scheme of political organization; it leaves room for the kind of sharing within communities and between communities upon which individuals thrive. It is within this kind of living space that individuals can best come to have a sense of community, and both to feel and enjoy their places as participating members in the individual-social life process.[36]

As heretofore, attention will now be directed to two important areas of practice in which the philosophy of pragmatism may be seen at work. The other three philosophies have each been presented according to the plan which has involved approaching them historically, systematically, and in practice. So far, also, pragmatism has been presented in the context of its history and as a systematically formulated point of view. It remains now, in the two following chapters, to see pragmatism at work in education and religion before going on to estimate its worth as a philosophy.

[36] Cf. John Dewey, *Democracy and Education*, Chapter VII, "The Democratic Conception in Education."

XX

Pragmatism in Education

A. Education as a Social Institution

B. The Pupil

C. The Objectives of Education

D. The Educative Process

    1. A REFORM IN EDUCATION
    2. THE EDUCATIVE USE OF EXPERIENCE
    3. THE TEACHER
    4. METHOD

Pragmatism has become a leading educational philosophy in America. Without embarrassment of any kind, it has given education a primary and central place among social institutions. Whereas it has not been uncommon for other philosophers to give educational considerations a menial place, this has never been the case with pragmatists. Most notable of course has been the influence of John Dewey in this regard. Years before his major writing was done he established his Laboratory School in Chicago (1896). In addition to marking the emergence of progressive education in this country, it was a notable event in another regard. For in founding this school, a man who was to become one of America's leading philosophers was engaging in the actual task of educating children, to the end that certain educational experiments might be carried forward which could open the way to a better education than had been known to that time. Of course, much philosophizing on Dewey's part had preceded this venture; but even so, much thought also followed it. And by 1916 some of this thought and experimentation became crystallized in a rather audacious work, now his famous *Democracy and Education*. This work was audacious because it dared to team philosophy and education together, but even more because it presumed to define philosophy as *"the general theory of education."*[1] It is not at all surprising, therefore, that there is an abundance of literature dealing with education from the pragmatist point of view. For at the same time that Dewey gained a wide following generally, his disciples became considerable among educators. While this chapter cannot do any degree of justice to the large accumulation of literature which is available on the subject, it can sketch the general outline of the pragmatist conception of education.

A. EDUCATION AS A SOCIAL INSTITUTION

It may be that pragmatism more than any other philosophy requires that there be concern with education as a social function. The necessity of having a discourse in each of the four education chapters in this book on education as a social establishment may be a tacit tribute to the impact of the pragmatic philosophy on educational thought. For pragmatists continually reiterate and John Dewey has made the case very pointed that education is scarcely anything at all unless it is a social institution. Earlier naturalism, even as recently applied to education as in Herbert Spencer, may treat education largely in individualistic terms. Idealists may fail to comprehend the essential social strain in their tradition and conceive education also largely in terms of the individual. So also realists, because of their tendency to regard the individual person as the most readily observable human unit, may make social concerns secondary in education and regard for the individual primary. But pragmatism must approach education as first and foremost a social phenomenon. It is a means by which society renews itself; and it is a process which in its inner essence is social, embracing individuals who, while they are separate and distinct physical and psychical entities, are at the same time society cast into individual forms.

Were the modern society of man simple and free from complication, it might be that education could all be informal, going on outside of institution. But since this is not the case, society must have an institution whose singular reason for existence is to carry learning activities forward. Yet within formal institutions education must remain informal in character and

[1] John Dewey, *Democracy and Education*. New York: The Macmillan Company, 1916. P. 383.

in touch with society, constituting throughout a process of social renewal. There are at least three necessities which justify the existence of the school as a distinct institution of society. (1) Were there no other circumstances requiring it, the school would be necessary to supply the volume of learning each new generation needs. Children simply have to know more than they can learn from informal and unintended learning experiences which daily life in society provides. (2) But there are two other circumstances which reinforce this demand. The complexity of modern life is such that we can not depend upon that alone which is near at hand for the extent of our resources. We must draw upon experience which is remote—remote both in time and in place. In order to meet the complexities of his life, modern man must have the help of other men of his own day and generation, some of whom are distant from him in space and separated from him in many cases by national and cultural barriers. More than this, he needs as much help as he can get from men who have lived in times past, from generations even which are centuries removed from him. (3) This second necessity for the school refers to the fact that the heritage of the past may function fruitfully in the present. But this also relates to another circumstance which makes the school necessary: the fact that language symbols are the means by which the heritage is communicated. It has become so complex and extensive that many centuries have passed since oral tradition was adequate for any except primitive societies. The large part of the heritage of the past which is available has been preserved in writing, and children must therefore achieve a command of language in order to make use of it. And this could not be accomplished with any great effect apart from a distinctive institution which addresses itself to the task.

Society can not therefore fulfill the educational task without an institution designed for this purpose. But the school must maintain intimate relation with society if its true role is to be played well. In fact its main functions stem from this relationship. (1) Being a specialized institution designed for a particular purpose it can be simple, whereas society is unavoidably complex. It can represent society to the child in a simplified form which makes learning possible, whereas the child might never get beyond confusion if confronted only by the complexity of society as it is. (2) The school can also be selective in a qualitative, if not ethical, manner as it represents society to the young. There are aspects of society as it actually is which are unworthy, which mislead and provide a wrong kind of education when impressionable youth are exposed to them. The school however is in a position to exercise value judgments in representing society. It can choose those kinds of social experience which are conducive to wholesome nuture and exclude those which are not. (3) A third element in the relation of the school to society is that it has the responsibility of giving the child a balanced and genuinely representative acquaintance with society at the same time that it simplifies and purifies this acquaintance. It must not become the agent of some segment of society as over against another. It can not be narrow or parochial in showing favor toward sectionalism, nationalism, a limited cultural perspective; it must not encourage class distinctions. This is to hint strongly at the place democracy has as an essential internal spirit in education. Children are not likely to get a balanced representative acquaintance with society unless the spirit and approach of their schools are democratic.[2]

B. THE PUPIL

In presenting the pragmatist conception of the pupil it may be well to reiterate some aspects of the process which is the context of all living, according to pragmatism, and in which and of which the pupil is.

To begin with the most general first, it may be said that biological, psychological, and sociological forces constitute a mammoth river, an ever-flowing stream, as the closest approximation of existence. In this river are surging currents, swirlings about, eddies, waves, and ripples, all the variety of movements displayed by a great river. Individual people are best typified, in the figure of the river, by the whitecaps which surge to the top on the crests of the waves. They are of the river of flux and change, not separate from it. They rise out of it for a brief transitory distinctness as a self, then merge back into the indistinctness of the flowing stream. Or, like the eddy, there is a whirling about of the life process, yielding for the time being a focus and a pattern of unity, such as the whirlpool; but the whirling pattern and the focus, after a while, merge back into the surging stream, lost again in its fluid indistinctness.

Most generally understood, students in any classroom are like this. For the present momentary days and years they are distinct and concrete centers of experience who must be guided so that they will be reasonably at home in the all-embracing flow of which they are a part. But we should not be misled by their present concreteness and distinctness, so that we think of them as self-substantial minds and souls, privately possessing an inner subjective realm of their own which is cut off from the public flow of events. They consist completely of this same life process, they are individuated aspects of it, whereas its most evident public form is its social aspect. Like whitecaps and whirlpools, they are given an individuated distinctness for a time; but that distinctness in no way separates them from the life process which constitutes them.

If this approach to an understanding of the nature of the pupil gives the impression that pragmatists do not make much of individuality, an injustice is done to the pragmatist conception. For individuality is a primary consid-

[2] Cf. *ibid.*, pp. 22–26.

eration with them, as witness, for example, the doctrine of individual differences which has gotten such wide currency in educational thought today. Pragmatists are not alone in making much of this doctrine; but they do make much of it. Individuation is a significant characteristic of life and experience in general. In the flow of experience there is a virtual infinity of individuals. There are individual things, individual events, individual relations, individual selves, and individual situations. So much are all of these individuals that there are no general rules that can be applied wholesale to any of them. Now individual selves and individual pupils are actually individuals. They are not divorced from the life process, which is an organic union of the individual and the social; but they are concrete individuals who must be dealt with as unique.

Of course there is the biological aspect of the pupil. Pragmatist educational philosophers are the last ones to regret that when little Johnny comes to school he must bring his body with him. For individual people are primarily organisms; and the wriggling and squirming and assorted misbehaving which have cast the shadow of unpleasantness into so much of our conventional schoolkeeping are, more than anything else, stubborn evidence that individual people are active organisms, partaking of the same kind of movement as constitutes the dynamic world of which they are a part. No passive receivers, waiting for impressions to be made upon them, they are ever and always reaching out to engage in the flow of experience. What was interpreted in yesterday's classroom as intrusion of the body into the things of the mind, or as deliberate and rebellious misbehavior, was in reality the consequence which should have been expected to follow from foisting a static and formalized education upon active organisms which really was designed for passive waxen tablets waiting to be written upon.

Then there are also the psychological and sociological aspects of the pupil. For he is not just an organism in a rigidly physiological sense; he is an organism who participates in meanings and therefore has value experiences which animals do not have. We already attempted some explanation of the way in which man rises to the level of value experience.[3] The first step, as pragmatists view this achievement, was the emergence of language. As experience went on, age after age, symbols gradually became identified with things experienced. Because of this identification, one syllable could have become the shorthand for a whole cluster of experiences. A single sound, such as *fire,* could represent the finding and gathering of dry wood, preparing of tinder, locating of rocks with which to strike sparks, catching the sparks and fanning them into a flame, and adding on larger and larger pieces of wood until the fire is made. In terms of what the fire could do, the single sound, *fire,* could also convey the idea of being warm, or maybe even the primitive roasting of food; it could also convey

[3] Cf. pp. 394–396.

the warning of imminent danger in the path of an uncontrolled fire. With one single symbol a device for communicating so much meaning, see how much past experience could be preserved for future experiencing, and see how much could be transferred from one individual's experience to the experience of another. And when one symbol is multiplied many thousand-fold to be a whole repertoire eventually of vocabulary, subjects, predicates, and sentences, something remarkably new emerged in the life process.

But remarkable as this achievement was, it prepared the way for an even more remarkable advance. When individuals became practiced in communicating with one another by means of language, so that they could telescope a whole cluster of experiences into the shorthand of speech, there emerged an experience of selfhood which before, it is assumed by pragmatists, was not there. No longer were primitive people living in an environment of actions to be engaged in within the limits of the proficiency for action which one's own experience or one's limited group had been able to achieve. Now there could be retention of experience within the limited group and between members of the group which formerly had not been possible. In addition there could be the gaining of meanings from the experiences of other groups, in this way enlarging the volume of resourcefulness. And still additional, there could be a carrying over of the learnings from the past experiences of generations which had gone before. Language, in this way, widened the horizon of resourcefulness not only in the present, by enlarging the circle from which learnings would come, but it reached backward into a longer time span by which this resourcefulness could also be increased. This was an important development in itself; but it provided the kind of opportunity for contrast between the individual and those with whom he communicated which could bring the individual into focus in his own consciousness as never before. And because of the contrast provided by this communication, the most important development took place; the experience of selfhood came to be added to what before had been a kind of impersonal experiencing. And this experience of selfhood became in turn the foundation stone for a cluster of important ideas which are necessarily rooted in it. Examples of these related ideas are the notion of agency, i.e., "by acting in such a way I can bring a certain end to pass"; and the conception of responsibility, i.e., "because I was the agent who brought to pass a given condition, a certain responsibility rests upon me for having acted the way I did."

This is a sketch, however inadequate, of the evolution of selfhood in the human species, according to pragmatism; and as such it is the very general context in which we must view the pupil. In addition, however, it also suggests the pattern followed by the genesis of selfhood in the individual pupil. First his biological birth and his growth and development at the physiological level; then the acquisition of language and his initiation thereby into the communication of meanings between individuals and groups; and last of all the emergence of selfhood and the cluster of meanings which hinge about this focus of conscious experience. This is the pattern by which the individual pupil has evolved into a distinct and concrete entity in the individual-social life process; and an understanding of this pattern is quite essential if there is to be an understanding of the pupils who mingle in the educational institutions of society.

C. THE OBJECTIVES OF EDUCATION

While the attempt to state the objectives of education has engaged educational thought in all ages, the task is especially perplexing to pragmatists. What is meant by the objectives of education? Some general all-inclusive objective? Or specific objectives for each learning situation? If the former is meant, then they say the formulation is so difficult as to be almost impossible. Whereas if specific objectives are sought, they are particular to each situation and will be as many in number as the many different learning situations through which the many different individuals must pass in their learning careers. Admittedly, specific objectives are so greatly multiplied that there is little chance of their being dealt with meaningfully in any general discussion. And at the same time there is no all-inclusive objective to be defined that can be completely adequate as a general aim. These difficulties will be explored a little more fully and, in spite of the obstacles they present, one approximation of a general objective will be stated.

Enough acquaintance with pragmatism has been afforded so far to disclose how completely the pragmatist sees life as being altogether fluid in character, and as being lived in the midst of a world setting which is literally fluid as well. Learning situations, both informal and within the schools, always are episodes in this continuing movement. Their objectives are always specific to the resolutions which are the outworkings of these episodes. So how can any meaningful generalization be made concerning the essence of them? Again, once they are achieved they always give way to a new objective because of the new episode which takes the place of the one just past which called for its particular learning, different from the particular learning now required. In relation to this episodic character of experience, and therefore of learning experience, it is often said by pragmatists that the general objective of education is more education. By this it is meant that every consummation of a learning episode is a means to new learnings which find their consummation in succeeding experiences.

Another generalization about the function of education which refers to this observation that every experience leads on to another is that the purpose of education is to give the learner experience in effective experiencing. For it is felt that it is effectiveness in coping with an ever-changing experience which is actually the only residue a person carries with him from one experience to another. He does not carry with him learnings already learned because, valuable as these learnings are as a resource from which to draw hypotheses for each present experience, they scarcely ever apply to another experience without some adaptation called for by the particularity of the experience to which they are adapted. Nor does the learner carry with him a conditioned response which has a guaranteed effectiveness giving it value for the type of experiences for which it is designed. Experiences cannot be so typed that any conditioned response can be effective in every experience within a given class of experiences. What the learner must carry away from his learning is something much less solidfied than either of these; neither a content learned nor a response in which he is conditioned, it is practice in coping with the indeterminacies of experience.

Nevertheless some approximate justice can be done to the pragmatic approach to objectives by elaborating one general objective upheld by Dewey with moderate enthusiasm. Before doing this, however, some related concerns will be mentioned which will go somewhat farther in giving an understanding of the problem posed by objectives for the pragmatist.

Of all the professions which require a "long look ahead," that of the educator makes it most imperative. One of his perennial concerns must be "connectedness in growth." This quality or concern implicit in his profession bears upon his approach to objectives. Wherever growth may lead, there must be continuity in the means by which objectives are reached.[4]

In trying to give form to the education of the new generation it is exceedingly important that full attention be given to the internal factors of experience. By internal factors is meant those ways in which the individual or group is involved in interaction with the situations through which they live. It is both inadequate and superficial to take seriously external factors only. This is to assume that human beings are within situations only in the spatial sense, as it were, of being inside them. Their withinness is much more subtle than this. And this insight reveals how external and lacking in psychological penetration the older education has been. It also has important bearing upon the kind of experiences which it is assumed will move toward the desired objectives; namely, these experiences cannot be judged externally alone but must be viewed primarily in the light of their internal connections.[5]

While it may have been well intentioned for the older education to emphasize preparation for the future, this also brought a narrowing of perspective which was detrimental to its best intention. The way to prepare

[4] Cf. John Dewey, *Experience and Education*. New York: The Macmillan Company, 1938. P. 90.
[5] Cf. *ibid.*, pp. 38–39.

for the future is to draw out fully from the present experience all there is in it of value for the learning subject at the time that he has it.[6]

It is accordingly not to be assumed that objectives, certainly for each concrete learning situation, can be determined by the teacher without any reference to what it is that the learners desire for themselves. Students have objectives as well as teachers. More than this, if they are to participate wholeheartedly in the purposes which direct their learning activities, they must be given the privilege of participating in the formation of these purposes.[7]

Freedom of activities in learning is not to be misinterpreted as freedom to act upon impulse or immediate desires which the learner may happen to have. Freedom involves the selection of activities which have a longer-term value than the expression of impulse. What is desired, in one sense, for each learning experience is that the learner will postpone impulsive action upon immediate desire until his action can be modified and given direction by the interposition of observation and judgment.[8]

Education, of course, must always start from a social and human center. But when it gives effective guidance, it moves toward a more objective and intellectual scheme of organization than is explicit in the human situation which is its point of departure. The social objective of education may be conceived as a "better organized environing world." Science is of course an important resource for reaching this end. While it may not be the only means to it, it provides an excellent example of the way in which experience can be given direction which is educational, when the methods of science are applied to the improvement of the social order. This brings our discussion back again to the unitedly scientific and social concern which approximates most closely the general objective of education.[9]

When it is remembered that life is primarily social for pragmatists, at the same time that it is individual, and when it is also recalled that values have such existence as they possess because of the social life process of which individuals are an integral part, it will not be a surprise to recognize that social efficiency is the closest approach to a definition of the general objective of education, according to pragmatic thought. For the values of life which are in and of the social life process are possessed quite in proportion to the effectiveness of an individual's relation to society. And societies achieve these values in proportion to their effectiveness in sharing their group life and in communicating with other groups. Social efficiency as the general aim of education cannot be defined as being set over against a

[6] Cf. *ibid.*, p. 50.
[7] Cf. *ibid.*, p. 77.
[8] Cf. *ibid.*, p. 81.
[9] Cf. *ibid.*, pp. 99–103.

liberal education and cultural values. For the pragmatists are not thinking of vocational effectiveness alone, as might be possessed by the learning of a trade or profession; by social efficiency they mean a many-sided effectiveness in maintaining social relations of all kinds. And furthermore, it should be remembered that pragmatists regard withdrawal from the main stream of society as the negation of value. In upholding social efficiency as the general aim of education, Dewey has made quite clear that it will be a more broadly defined social efficiency in which there will be much that has commonly passed as cultural value. And he has further contended that if culture were more liberally defined, as it ought to be, it would coincide closely with what he has intended in the term "social efficiency."[10]

D. THE EDUCATIVE PROCESS

There is valuable background for understanding the pragmatic conception of learning in the pragmatic epistemology and logic;[11] for the general method by which a person learns is considered, in pragmatism, to follow the same pattern as effective thinking. Since, generally speaking, experimental method is the method of thought, experimental method is also the method of learning.

Learning, like thinking, never begins from a static lag line; it always begins in the midst of movement and activity. At whatever point an outside observer might enter a situation in which learning is going on, whether it be a classroom or an informal play group, he will find motion and activity. This is something the effective teacher will remember; and whenever he wishes to give direction to an experience so that it will culminate in truly educative happenings, he will realize that he must always begin with experiences which are already going on.

The point at which a really effective beginning can be made is marked out by indeterminacies. It may be that this first stage of the educative cycle will have more form than this; the indeterminacies may be sufficiently focused to constitute a problem or maybe a set of problems which are felt by the pupils. If not, the earliest task of the teacher will be to help the members of the learning group to examine the indeterminate elements intently enough to come to see the problem or problems which they constitute. This early stage of the learning movement is the point at which the headwaters of interest spring up. For interests are not elements which are brought to learning either by teacher or pupil; they are not a froth or foam which is churned up by clever teaching devices. They are rooted in the relation of the student to the tensions of his experience, and are therefore

[10] Cf. John Dewey, *Democracy and Education*, Chapter IX, "Natural Development and Social Efficiency as Aims."
[11] Cf. pp. 377–380 and 388–394.

more to be discovered by the teacher than made by him. When a person has a problem, he is already interested because he is in a state of tension which needs to be resolved, and his interest is attached to possible resolutions.

After the problem takes form and is quite clearly understood to be the problem which is faced, learning then moves on to a still more effective examination of the indeterminacies which constitute the problem. This is a more advanced stage of observation than the one which may have preceded the definition of the problem, because the form which the definition of the problem has now given to the learning situation becomes a guide to the further study and observation of the situation. The turning over of the indeterminate elements, the recognition of relations which they may have to other elements in the situation, and the discovery of similarities and differences which they possess as compared to other experiences through which the learners have already lived fruitfully, all are pointed in the direction of finding possible solutions to the problem which is presently experenced.

This stage of the learning cycle challenges the student's powers of insight more than any other. For it is at this point that new patterns are born. The problem is felt; related data are brought together from within the situation and from other comparable situations which have a close bearing upon the problem and its possible solution. This is the springboard for ventures into the unformed future. The comparable situations which may become resources for learning are in the past as well as in the present. Pragmatism has of course been criticized for its preoccupation with the present. But its concern for continuity between past events and present experiences should not be overlooked. In any effective handling of the present, past experience is credited with great relevance in the guidance of experience so that it will lead purposefully into a future of value and worth. Dewey has made quite explicit his conviction regarding this bond within experience between "the achievements of the past and the issues of the present." Acquaintance with the past is therefore an important part of learning because it may become "a potent instrumentality for dealing effectively with the future."[12] While the objectives of learning are in the future and the immediate materials of learning are in the present, it is nevertheless recognized by Dewey that these materials can move toward the objectives "only in the degree that present experience is stretched, as it were, backward. It can expand into the future only as it is also enlarged to take in the past."[13]

What is the pattern into which the related factors can be cast so that the problem will be solved and the way will be opened freely to succeeding experiences? This is the question facing the learner which introduces the

[12] John Dewey, *Experience and Education*, p. 11.
[13] *Ibid.*, p. 93.

formulation of hypotheses. Tentative solutions are worked out, not by fanciful imagination, but by a kind of imagery which is born right in the situation itself. Such imagination is a consummate achievement in which insight has its most fruitful use. It is not a mere reproductive imagination, in which some thing is reproduced, the pattern of which has already been experienced; it is a productive imagination in which familiar facts and objects are put to a use unprecedented in the experience of the learner, and new patterns of action are born.

The final stage of the learning experience, if these different developments in the learning movement can be considered definite stages, is the stage of resolution in which the new hypothetical patterns are put to the test of action. Those not proving to be effective resolutions are discarded; and those by which the problem is found to unfold satisfactorily without jeopardizing later experiences are allowed to stand.

1. A REFORM IN EDUCATION

This conception of general method implies a reform in education in the realm of discerning the cycles of learning. Traditionally, education has been too formal; while it has been necessary for it to be formalized as a social institution, it has been not only unnecessary but also artificial for it to formalize learning activity as much as it has. It is no wonder that progressive education arose indigenously, both in Europe and America, not as the outgrowth of a concerted formulation of new educational theory, but as a practical and experimental revolt against coldly formalized teaching procedures. The pragmatic refinements in theory came later; and one of the insights which will probably continue to have a wide and enduring acceptance is that the cycle of learning is not so mechanical as to be segmented into departments, courses, and time schedules with a frozn rigidity.

Pragmatism as an educational theory is far from being the same as progressive education so called. The revolt which produced the progressive education movement antedated Dewey's accession to a place of leadership in educational thought in which he turned to educational ends the generic pragmatic principle of Peirce and James that the significance of things is in their consequences. Pragmatism is an educational philosophy, a theory of education; progressive education was predominantly a practice, started by a revolt against formalism and feeling its way, in some instances more, in others less, toward a responsible educational philosophy. While there has been close affinity between progressive education and the educational philosophy of John Dewey, there have been many who have embraced progressive practices without accepting a pragmatic philosophy, in some instances not even discerning the affinity between the two.

There is therefore no assumption here that pragmatism as an educational philosophy and the new education as a movement of reform in practice are to be identified. The affinity of the two is recognized however. Dewey recognized it as well and was frank to criticize the old education and point out wherein the new corrected it. He was also cautious, in making these criticisms, to modulate the extremes of the new which were out of harmony with responsible theory as he conceived it. In the light of pragmatism it may now be asked, in what ways did the new education correct the old, with clear justification?

Well, the old education was wrongly an education of imposition: imposition from above and outside the learner's experience; imposition of adult standards; imposition of a set subject matter; and imposition of methods. Consequently, it not only created a big gap between learning and experience but often seemed to operate on the assumption that this gap was a necessity.[14] The old education was also a practice in which subject matter was *the* centrality. It was contained in books, assumedly. It was in the heads of elders. It was essentially static. It was regarded as adequate for the future because of a companion assumption that the future will be very much the same as the past.[15]

The new education was a clear improvement over the old at a number of points. It substituted expression and cultivation of individuality for imposition from above. It supplemented discipline with greater freedom of activity. It paralleled learning from texts and teachers with learning through experience. It gave meaning to the acquisition of skills by making skills a means of realizing ends. It corrected the general objective of preparing for a remote future by full exploitation of its concern to make the most of present opportunities. It modified static aims by introduction of direct acquaintance with the world—an acquaintance which disclosed the world as changing and not static.[16]

2. THE EDUCATIVE USE OF EXPERIENCE

The cycles of learning have the same freedom, flow, variety, and newness of the cycles of experience. And if the educative process is to be discerned sufficiently for effective teaching to synchronize with it, these wider, more inclusive, and more plastic cycles must be recognized as basic. This means, more practically, that the unit of study is not necessarily a given class period or given course; it is an area which is marked out by the unitary or cyclical character of experience. Effective teaching will flow therefore by such cycles; and the effective teacher will guide learning by helping give form to units of study which transcend the artificiality of class

[14] Cf. *ibid.*, p. 4.
[15] Cf. *ibid.*, p. 5.
[16] Cf. *ibid.*, pp. 5–6.

periods. This is one way in which the learning of the school, as a formal institution of society, will go beyond the walls of the school to be fused and interrelated with the informal experiences which constitute life.

This means of course that for pragmatism all learning begins in experience, a dictum fully practiced by the new education, sometimes radically and with a distorted perspective. A corollary, which Dewey has taken pains to make clear but which has not been as generally observed in practice, is that while learning must begin in experience, it must so be guided as to give "a fuller and richer and also more organized form" to experience. The more developed experience accruing from the wise educative use of it will approximate the form in which "subject-matter is presented by the skilled, mature person."[17] But it should be remembered that this form is the achieved end of learning and is not present when learning begins. It is educationally important to recognize this second phase in learning. While learning must begin in experience, it is equally imperative that there be the kind of guidance which brings learning to this more mature achievement of form. These two necessities are set forward quite fully by Dewey in the following brief passage:

> . . . . It is part of the educator's responsibility to see equally two things: First, that the problem grows out of the conditions of the experience being had in the present, and that it is within the range of the capacity of the students; and, secondly, that it is such that it arouses in the learner an active quest for information and for production of new ideas.[18]

It has been stated earlier that one of the reasons for existence of the school, according to pragmatism, is that it is able to be more selective of the experiences by which people shall be educated than society or informal learnings can be. A further progression of this function of the school must be faced at this point: By what norms shall experiences be selected as having educational value? Dewey's answer is that the two major norms of educational value in experiences are interaction and continuity.

Interaction alludes to the complexity of the withinness by which people are inside of their experiences. They are within them by virtue of living through them as the settings, contexts, or fields of their activities. But they are also involved within them in a more intimate way than enduring or undergoing them. They are caught by their experiences in a way which requires that they respond to or interact with objects, events, and persons. Continuity of experiences refers to the connectedness of experience at the same time that it moves by episodes of fields. It requires that if experiences are to be of worth there must be recognition of this relatedness and accord-

[17] *Ibid.*, p. 87.
[18] *Ibid.*, pp. 96–97.

ingly the kind of behavior which will not bring jeopardy from one episode of experience to another.[19]

We will consider the continuity norm further at this point and then return to the interaction norm. Because of the importance of the continuity of experience, these experiences promise to have educational values which arouse curiosity, strengthen initiative, and set up "desires and purposes that are sufficiently intense to carry a person over dead places in the future."[20] The hope may be warranted that certain possible experiences will be educative if they lead to growth and will help build other experiences which are worth while.[21]

To the extent that the interaction norm is important, experiences are capable of being put to educative use if they can be formed in such a way that individual and group participate in an orderliness stemming from social control, and if the individual at the same time enjoys freedom both of intelligence and of movement. This norm of course calls for further explanation. It has already been stated that there must be an ordering of experiences to the end that they will be educative. But the norm of interaction requires that the ordering of experience be supplied by social control rather than by the solitary decision-making of teacher, parent, or some dominant member of the group. If the order stems from social control then the individual learner participates in setting it up. While he of course must abide by it, he has also helped make it. And this means that there is room in it for individual freedom, not just freedom of movement, action without parallel determination of purposes. The presence of freedom of purpose means freedom of the mind in thinking and learning; and this is essential if learning is to be intelligent. Apparently, all would agree that learning is an affair of intelligence. But if there is intelligence in it, there must be freedom to formulate purposes; and if there is to be this kind of freedom there must be social control. A tyranny of teacher or leader would seem to exclude learning so conceived. Learners as well as teachers must make decisions; and in some instances their decisions may be more determinative of the effectiveness of the learning than those of the teacher.[22]

3. THE TEACHER

To judge the educational value of learning experiences by such requirements as social control and freedom is not at the same time to say that the teacher is unimportant. The teacher is not the only decision-maker, true enough; but the new education involves a total change in the context of

[19] Cf. *ibid.*, pp. 31–32 and 42–43.
[20] *Ibid.*, p. 31.
[21] Cf. *ibid.*, p. 35.
[22] Cf. *ibid.*, pp. 53–54; 57; 69; 70; 73; and 74.

education, in which the responsibility of the teacher is more complex and more difficult than in the old education. A balanced view of the role to be played by the teacher may be approached from the analogy of the parent's place in the home. Families have probably always been more informal in their structure than school classes. There are occasions in the home when a parent must take things in hand and exercise authority. But in the well-ordered home these occasions are few in comparison to the many in which the family acts quite freely but with orderliness. Even so, parents are exceedingly important members of the family group in such a well-ordered home. It is because they give the guidance they do that the home is well ordered and the occasions consequently few which require that they take things in hand.[23]

In fact we cannot divorce the role of the teacher as disciplinarian and taskmaster from the setting in which conventional education has been cast. The class was for the most part a formal structure, not a group in which social controls were expected to operate. Consequently the teacher had to be the one to keep order, if there was to be any order at all.[24]

In the new kind of learning situation envisioned by the new education the teacher's responsibility is as great as before but of a different order. If guidance is to be given in an education which makes full use of the experience of the learner, the teacher cannot abdicate from being the kind of member of the group which he actually is. He must plan for learning activities just as much as in the older education but in a different way which makes higher demands upon the use of intelligence. He is the member of the learning group who must assess the capacities and needs of students; and he must also arrange the conditions which provide the subject matter and content for experiences that satisfy these needs and develop these capacities."[25] The teacher must of course respect the freedom of his students; in fact he will not get to know them as individuals unless he does. But this does not mean that the teacher thereby becomes so enslaved that he has no freedom of his own. In learning which fully employs experience, "the teacher loses the position of external boss or dictator but takes on that of leader of group activities."[26]

 Although it should not require special mention, the planning function of the responsible teacher calls of course for careful deliberation and intention. So much is this the case that it excludes reliance upon improvisation on the spur of the moment. It is a mistake to assume, as is sometimes done, that experimentalism in education means turning to as good account as possible the happenings of the classroom as they occur. Occasionally

[23] Cf. *ibid.*, pp. 58–59.
[24] Cf. *ibid.*, pp. 60–61.
[25] *Ibid.*, p. 65.
[26] *Ibid.*, p. 66.

improvisation will be a normal part of the free play of intelligence, on the part of both teacher and pupil; but the main line of learning activities, as well as the majority of them, will follow from careful planning on the part of the teacher.[27]

4. METHOD

Building and executing units of study patterned after and matching the cycles of experience will therefore be the most inclusive method of the effective teacher. But within this allover methodology a number of other methods will be embraced, some of them at times not appearing at all different from traditional methods to the casual observer; however, their effect is different because they have a functional context in the unit of study, from the standpoint of the student.

Creative and constructive projects also are heavily employed in this practice of education. Many of them go on within the school, many of them beyond it, some of them individually pursued, others common social efforts of the whole class, frequently reaching out into the community.

Discussion will also have its place, for it constitutes a means by which group thinking can go on, not only in the classroom but also in the life of the community. Its validity in the community is evidence of its validity in formal learning. In the early stages when indeterminacies are being identified and problems are being defined, by which a unit of study is starting to take shape, what more natural means is there for this activity than discussion? Of course it will be supplemented by research and discovery of certain facts, probably outside the classroom, but much of the struggle into form will be accomplished by means of discussion.

Although facts and subject matter are incidental to the unit or cycle of experience in which they have a relevance, they do have their place in this conception of learning. There will be much more factual knowledge and much more subject matter in these units of learning than might at first be assumed. How are indeterminacies understood as forming problems? How are factors discovered which relate to the problem and how is their relationship recognized? How and of what material are hypotheses formed that may contribute to the real learning which is the resolution of the unit? And how are hypotheses put to the test? These are all points in the flow of learning at which facts and certain items of content have their function. Consequently, the searching out of relevant facts will constitute an important proportion of the learning movement. Excursions beyond the classroom in a number of directions may bring in the needed facts. Conventional laboratory work may be necessary, reference study in the library will yield its share, and frequently actual visits to points away from the school will be made in order to observe certain phenomena directly. This concep-

27 Cf. *ibid.*, p. 96.

tion of education, truly enough, is not a content-centered education; but often it involves far more subject-matter mastery than is commonly assumed. Occasionally observations are made by library personnel that in schools in which more progressive practices are followed there is a greater and more effectove use of books than in conventional schools.

XXI

Pragmatism in Religion

A. The Status of Religion

B. The Nature of God

C. The Nature of Man

With regard to their attitudes toward religion, the four philosophies divide almost evenly, with the idealists and some realists paired together on the one side, and naturalists, some realists, and pragmatists on the other. While this grouping has little significance for the more detailed treatment of religion which each philosophy offers, it does bear significantly on the question as to whether there may be an affinity between philosophy and religion as conceived traditionally, or whether the concepts of religion must be redefined in order to have philosophical validity. For, as has been shown, idealism and realism, if the latter is not purely naturalistic, may become, as philosophies of religion, the intellectual schemes by which religion, as a means of effectively relating man and the supernatural, is given rational expression. It is acknowledged, of course, that realists who are naturalistic in their metaphysics do not subscribe to this kind of philosophy of religion. But naturalism and pragmatism, with the exception of William James in the case of the latter philosophy, stand quite unitedly in opposition to traditional religious beliefs. They insist that religion must be redefined so that it is understood as an attitude toward life as we know it in the human sphere and not a means of contact with the supernatural.

The last of the five chapters on philosophy of religion in this book, therefore, has much the same status as the first of the five, "Naturalism in Religion." For like naturalism, pragmatism can be a philosophy of religion only to the extent that religion can be redefined in harmony with its own pragmatic terms. There is more than a theoretical relevancy in giving some attention to such a redefinition of religion as attempted by pragmatism. For the pragmatists in religion are not straw men. There are both leaders in religion and adherents who have taken the pragmatism of Dewey seriously; and when they speak for religion, though the terms they use may be conventional, their meanings are closer to Dewey's meanings than they are to traditional religion.

It has already become clear that there is a James pragmatism and a Dewey pragmatism, and that although they do share a common spirit, there are marked differences between them. The attitude toward religion is one of the points of difference, William James being much closer to realism in his philosophy of religion than to Dewey's redefinition. Rather than omit any reference to the religion of William James, brief allusions will be made to him, although the major part of the discussion will center upon the approach to religion of the Dewey pragmatism.

A. THE STATUS OF RELIGION

James took experience of the reality of the unseen as the beginning point in philosophy of religion. His book, *The Varieties of Religious Experience*,[1] a classic both in psychology and philosophy of religion, is a study of the different ways in which people have experienced the unseen as being so real that they could not but respond as directly to it as we all respond to other stimuli when objects of sensation evoke the response. Religion consists, he said "of the belief that there is an unseen order, and that our supreme good lies in harmoniously adjusting ourselves thereto."[2] Although there is equivocation in the writings of William James, resulting possibly from his revolt against rationalism and its tendency toward unity, he was forthright in acknowledging his belief in the supernatural. At least, that is the case in this famous work. This unseen order, while eluding our senses, yet intrudes upon us in a manner which is more immediate than and prior to our thoughts about it. This approach to religion, comparison will reveal, is the same as that of realism.

As has been evident heretofore, one predominant tendency in the pragmatism of Dewey is to deal only with individual cases, making generalizations only in the form of hypotheses to be put to work in ensuing experi-

[1] New York: Longmans, Green & Co., 1902.
[2] *Ibid.*, p. 53.

ence. Dewey, in his book, *A Common Faith*,[3] tries to hew this line. Accordingly, he finds he cannot deal with religion as such, but must make specific religions his object. And in a review of the gamut of religions he finds such a complex of the bad and the good, together with such a variety of constituent elements, that he considers it impossible to extract any common element as characteristic of religion.

One of the sources of difficulty, he has contended, is preoccupation with the supernatural. As over against this complexity he finds religious attitudes, or possibly we should say religious values, to be desirable. And so he lends his weight to a modernized treatment of religion in which the focus is the realizing of religious values rather than adjustment to the supernatural.

This intention is followed by most of the writers representing the John Dewey Society in preparing the seventh yearbook of that body.[4] Considering seriously the responsibility of education to bring the young into possession of spiritual values, these authors, with one exception,[5] hold that spiritual values should be redefined so that the connotation of the word *spiritual* will refer to the quality or level of refinement of a particular value instead of implying, as is commonly the case, that such a value has metaphysical rooting in the supernatural.

In short, the status of religion is this: allied with it are experimental values which are worthwhile and should be preserved, but there is no supernatural base for religious experience.

B. THE NATURE OF GOD

We pass on to the conception of the nature of God held by pragmatists without taking the intermediary step of considering arguments for the existence of God. As William James was virtually a realist in religion, finding God in immediate experiences of the presence of the unseen, he was not at all attracted by rationalistic arguments for theistic belief. And as John Dewey relinquishes at the outset all conceptions of God as supernatural, he stands opposed to any apologetic for belief in the supernatural.

Corresponding to comparisons already made between James and Dewey, their conceptions of God are far removed from one another. James was really a polytheist. His love for the openness of pluralism in philosophy emerged in his religion as a leaning toward belief in several gods who are higher and more powerful than man, but yet finite and limited. In the Postscript of his book, *The Varieties of Religious Experience*, while he

[3] New Haven: Yale University Press, 1934.

[4] John S. Brubacher (editor), *The Public School and Spiritual Values*. New York: Harper & Row, Publishers, 1944.

[5] William J. Sanders is a Roman Catholic and makes a distinction between natural and supernatural spiritual values.

takes his stand for supernaturalism, he makes clear that he is a supernaturalist of the "crasser" sort who sees reality "piecemeal" rather than regarding it as one universally consistent unity. Unlike the scholars whom James termed "refined supernaturalists," he had much in common with popular religion in which God and angels, devils and demons, are dramatically opposed to one another in a precariously decisive world where man's actions have some cosmic weight in determining what the final results shall be. James says that all the facts of religious experience require is that there be a larger power which is friendly to man and his ideals, and which is capable of his trust for the next step.

It need not be infinite, it need not be solitary. It might conceivably even be only a larger and more godlike self, of which the present self would then be but the mutilated expression, and the universe might conceivably be a collection of such selves, of different degrees of inclusiveness, with no absolute unity realized in it at all.[6]

In turning to Dewey's conception of God, we must recall again the naturalistic conception held by Wieman.[7] For while Dewey's definition is not purely naturalistic in spirit, it is naturalistic in content. Attempting further clarification, we may review the comparison of naturalism, realism, and pragmatism in their attitudes toward the nature of God. A pure naturalism defines God completely within and of the natural order. Wieman exemplifies this in characterizing God as that factor in the natural order which makes possible the realizing of value. Realism, by comparison, is so open in its metaphysical alternatives that God may be defined as either natural or supernatural, as long as He is regarded as existing independently of, if not external to, the mind of man. This latter requirement is the only necessary one; and it holds because it follows from the theory of knowledge in which realists find their only rallying point, which is to the effect that objects of knowledge are completely independent of and unaffected by any mind which beholds them. Wieman's conception also fulfills this requirement, while at the same time being naturalistic; but far different conceptions fit in with realism just as well. Realism's one requirement is met by the conception held by Macintosh, which leans more toward the personal and spiritual; and it is also fulfilled by the conception of God held by the new theology, which is positively supernaturalistic.

Now we are ready to ask how it is that pragmatism comes along with a pattern of theistic conception which is distinct from either the naturalistic or the realistic. As has been acknowledged, the James variety of theism is distinct from naturalism but not from realism. The Dewey theism, if it can be called that, is positively not supernaturalistic, but it is more closely

6 William James, *op. cit.*, p. 525.
7 Cf. pp. 98–100.

allied with personal and social forces than is the naturalistic theism of Wieman. This difference is rooted in the difference in emphasis of naturalism and Dewey pragmatism. Naturalism, traditionally at least, like realism, has made the physical universe the primary context of human life; Dewey has shifted this emphasis to the biological and social arenas. The context of human life is man, his evolution, the biological forces of which he is a part, his psychology, his social relations, his institutions, and his ongoing common life with its thrust into the unknown future. This dynamic world of man is the predominant frame of reference in Dewey's thinking; and this context lends quite a different spirit and outlook than does the physical-universe reference frame of Wieman. With this overview as an immediate background, we can now catch the distinctive overtones of Dewey's definition of God.

It is at the point of man's thrust into the unknown future that Dewey finds what he calls God. For this is the point at which the ideal, which in the present is not, comes into existence and becomes an actual part of the life of man in the future, when that future becomes present. But this ideal is not something which exists before it is realized in human experience; for there is nothing existing apart from human experience. The ideal is the legitimate imagery of man. As in our ongoing experience we stand on the threshold of the future, ideals or possible values take shape in our imagery. They are not fancies removed from the actualities of experience; instead they grow out of present experience and provide the pattern for future experience. As the flow of events moves onward, ideal values become actual in experience, provided there is the kind of effective relation between the present and future possibilities by means of which experience is made to flow in their direction. Now this kind of relation between the ideal and the actual is what Dewey calls God, that uniting of the ideal and the actual in the experience of man. Dewey recognizes that this is far different from traditional conceptions of God, and he is therefore not insistent that the divine name be used to denote the object of his religious devotion. But since he feels that in order to thrive the religious attitude needs a sense of connection between man and his surrounding world, "in the way of both dependence and support," he holds that the "use of the words 'God' or 'divine' to convey the union of actual with ideal may protect man from a sense of isolation and from consequent despair of defiance."[8]

It may be made explicit in passing that God is good but He is neither ultimate goodness nor omnipotence. Of course, since God is defined as that relation of the ideal and the actual by which new values emerge in experience, it would not follow that such a relation is the unlimited whole of all reality, and therefore all powerful; for a relation relates things besides itself and by its very character is limited. In terms of its ethical value, this

[8] John Dewey, *A Common Faith*. New Haven: Yale University Press, 1934. P. 53.

relation between the ideal and the actual is good, because greater good comes out of it; but such goodness as it possesses is not ultimate and final goodness. For it is not a terminal in experience, but always a means to further good yet to be realized. The goodness of this relation of ideal and actual, which Dewey calls God, is a utilitarian or instrumental goodness, good not in itself but because it is the bridge to experience of other values.

Of course, William James was more theological than this; but even so, God was also finite, though good, in his conception. James did not conceive of God as Absolute Being, but as a being (or beings) who among other beings is definitely finite and limited, even able to profit by the help of man. While so limited, God was nevertheless regarded as good, struggling in the affairs of earth to emerge into higher levels of achievement. The part of man in this conception is one of joining sides with God in this cosmic struggle upward, lending his weight to the side of goodness.

C. THE NATURE OF MAN

Pragmatism has the same confidence in man that it has in Nature, for it regards man as an integral part of Nature and perfectly continuous with it. Of course, it must be remembered that pragmatism defines Nature as an open and dynamic order of change, not a closed mechanical system, as in the older naturalism. It is quite commonly understood that the current pragmatism, influenced more by Dewey than by James, is not pessimistic about man. There is a forthright break with any total-depravity treatment of man. Pragmatists hold that such pessimism is unwarranted by the more accurate and analytical understanding of man which science has given us. And furthermore, it is felt, its original motivation was to put man in such a bad light that it would be recognized at once that supernatural means could be his only salvation.

While pragmatism's rejection of pessimism about man is commonly recognized, it is not nearly such common knowledge that pragmatism does not swing to the opposite extreme of romantic optimism. Man is by no means a creature of pure sweetness and light whose future is guaranteed. He is a part of the natural order and he must be kept in continuous relation with natural and social processes. The trouble with traditional morality, Dewey says, is that it has frozen conduct into a system of conventional avoidances. It is negative; goodness is the avoidance of evils; in many cases even it is the escape from occasions for evil. Social disapproval in this system has been directed against singularly good acts as well as against the commission of positive evil. The great weakness of conventional morality has been that it has cut man off from the medium in which he can function morally. If men are to realize values progressively, they cannot escape the contingencies of experience; they must be in face-to-face relation with Nature and society and must act purposefully in meeting the problems and tensions which such direct relations yield.

This of course guarantees nothing beyond what the dependableness of natural processes guarantees. Man has a certain dignity in standing up to his experience and he has certain possibilities for action. But beyond this there is no halo of hope. Man's prospect as he faces the future is melioristic, not optimistic nor pessimistic. He has a certain possibility for making the best of his circumstances and achieving a purposeful control; beyond this there is unpredictable contingency, not secure guarantee.

Evil for pragmatism is the failure to stand up to life in this way and face the situations which our experiences present. Any inhibitions or conventional structures which prevent society from honestly facing its onward-moving demands are also evil. Most social evils are rooted in some outworn social scheme which still persists with us by sheer weight of inertia, to superimpose artificial barriers which prevent free and purposeful action. Notable, as an example, is the scheme of separation between leisure and labor classes. This separation reaches away back into the dim past when it was first discovered that the few could free themselves to achieve the refinements of life if the many were put to work as slaves and servants who made the wheels go round which maintain the equilibrium of society. The distinction between the inner and outer in morals is genetically rooted in this social distinction. Because of disdain for the slaving masses, the refined values of life came incorrectly to be regarded as purely inner, whereas the outer tasks of artisans and tradesmen have been falsely considered grosser pursuits of an unworthy lower level. Modern society no longer needs human slaves, because the machine is our new slave which maintains our existence and frees us for the meaningful pursuits of life. Why, then, should we perpetuate a social distinction based on human slavery, the death of which has been long overdue? Such accretions from the past only act as blocks to genuine morality, which, both individual and social, is actual engagement in the outward processes of life and society by which living moves on purposefully and is not fenced in by some static dead end.

XXII

Strengths and Weaknesses in the Philosophy of Pragmatism

A. The Strengths of Pragmatism

B. The Weaknesses of Pragmatism

The study of the philosophy of pragmatism has now been completed within the limits of the range and purpose of this book. After setting down in this chapter an estimate of the strengths and weaknesses of pragmatism, our examination of the four philosophies will be finished. As heretofore, the strengths of pragmatism will be mentioned first, and this will be followed by a statement of characteristics which, it is considered, constitute its weaknesses.

A. THE STRENGTHS OF PRAGMATISM

1. The philosophy of pragmatism may offer some wise counsel for day-by-day living which may help maintain mental health. This counsel is that we live through one experience at a time. Whatever experiences are in the past, are in the past; and they relate to the present experience only to the extent that they provide resource for effectiveness in the present experience. Future experiences are yet unformed; they grow out of the present experience and their character is determined to some extent by the success with which we cope with the experience which immediately confronts us.

Therefore, the only wise practical "realism" is to give ourselves fully to each present experience and make the most of it. For those who dwell so much in the past or are subject to such constant apprehension about what the future may bring that they are confused about and inadequate for the demands of present experience, the counsel of pragmatism to take one step at a time may help bring clarity. This is also the counsel, it so happens, of religious faith.

2. While there is something quite radical in the pragmatic correction of rationalism and empiricism, and the corresponding reform proposed for logic, there are some penetrating insights in this correction which may prove to be helpful. Conventional induction and deduction are inadequate tools of knowledge and need to be supplemented, at least, by methods more closely matching the vitality of experience. Possibly they need to be supplemented by entirely new methods. Experimentation offers some promise as providing a part of the supplement needed and indicating the character of the reform; but it will not be adequate in itself.

3. There is much value in the power of pragmatism to keep us close to experience and to shatter for us the artificiality of the cloistered and formally academic. It carries the student along rather convincingly, once he has begun to catch some of the insights offered. But this adequacy to experience is almost completely descriptive, in the last analysis. Pragmatism helps to discern the ways of experience and offers some resource in the control of experience. It offers also some measure of possession of the essence of life. But it does not give us possession of any enduring essence, nor does it tell us how to be established in an abiding existence.

4. Pragmatism's contribution to education is notable. While a purely pragmatic education has its limitations, pragmatic thought has lent insights because of which education will never be able to retreat to what it was formerly, short of the resurgence of some tyranny which takes away all freedoms. Truly educative happenings cannot be equated with what the teacher does, with class sessions, courses of study, schedules, nor any of the other formal accouterments of educational institutions; and pragmatism has helped us to see this. In helping us to discern the cycles of experience, it has also given us a sensitivity to the cycles of learning.

B. THE WEAKNESSES OF PRAGMATISM

1. Although, as has just been said, pragmatism may be somewhat acceptable as a description of life, it is not satisfactory as a way of representing essence and existence to us. It has the peculiar genius of following the ways of Spirit without believing in the existence of Spirit and possessing its essence.

2. There is a sense in which experimental method is arbitrarily applied,

at least to some situations, by the philosophy of pragmatism. Although experimental method is supposed to be applied individually to each new situation, the application seems sometimes to be forced, arbitrary, and formal. May there not be situations to which some other method might be more particularly applicable? And do we not, on occasion, initiate some action which directs events over a long time range, quite apart from a pressing problem which forces us to act?

3. Can we find a way out of all indeterminate situations? Of course, pragmatism does not say that we can, we may and we may not, however the only thing we can do is to try. But is there sufficient basis of hope for effective action, in the power of control or direction that we ourselves have, either as individuals or as societies? Is the way out not opened to us on occasion by contingencies in the pattern of events which we have done nothing to produce? That is to say that the unexpected in experience sometimes delivers us, not always posing difficulties for us, thereby evidencing a watchful providence.

4. Again, are meanings strictly operational in character? Are they not, however, closely identified with objects and events, grounded more basically in mind? It may be granted that individual minds need the counterpart in raw stuff with which to operate, in order for there to be any meanings. But how can these meanings come to be unless there is some mind to conceive them?

5. There is an overemphasis on individuation in pragmatism. While this lends concreteness and particularity to its dealings, it does not do justice to the elements common to many experiences, and especially to the universality of mind in all experience. The result is radical pluralism and discontinuity in its metaphysics and ontology. While there is continuity in its epistemology and social theory, there is multiplicity and discontinuity in almost every other realm of its thought.

6. This leads on to the further objection that there is a philosophical incompleteness in the lack of an overarching unity in pragmatism. As a point of view it does have a good bit more unity than the naïve opportunism which regards life as just one thing after another; but it does not go far enough in attaining the true genius of a philosophy, offering ultimate unity, interrelatedness, and meaning.

7. Pragmatism is too radically agnostic. It unnecessarily reduces the continuity of man and Nature to the level of Nature; for this continuity actually suggests just as much that Nature is the product of the same kind of spirit as is found in man. The result is a representation of man in which he is scarcely to be recognized; he is a piece of society, one who thinks because he first learned the use of words from society, one who has selfhood because he first learned notself, agency, and responsibility from society.

8. Pragmatism is also too radically negative in its ontology. It actually gives us no meaning at all for the word *is*. Everything is described as operational; everything is in motion. When anything is, it is in operation. But there must be more meaning than this in the word *is*. True enough, the meaning cannot be supplied by a static, inert, impersonal existence, as in naturalism and some realism. Pragmatism quite effectively opposes this kind of description of existence. But ultimate meaning is provided by the category of Spirit. For in Spirit is motion, change, freedom, life, vitality, all of these things; but in addition, existence. Pragmatism is unsuccessful in trying to divorce the ways of Spirit from the existence and essence of Spirit.

9. The question may be asked at this point, Just how much merit is there in the original pragmatic idea? Do the consequences following from an idea or object, when put in operation in the flow of events, constitute its essence? Is it not rather true that these consequences are the representations or evidences of essence, instead of the essence itself?

10. Further, the individual-social life process is not a sufficient existence base for values, as proposed in the philosophy of pragmatism. Now some values do have their basis of existence in this process. This is the basis of existence for evil, and ultimately unwonted values; it is also the foundation for many adulterated values, mixed good and evil, and approximate goods. But it is not the existence base for the ultimate good, of which the values which emerge in the life process are only approximations. The tares will not grow forever, and the bad wheat will not thrive forever either; but some day there will be a harvest in which there will be nothing but the good wheat, good because it partakes only of Him who is ultimate good.

11. While it must be recognized that the pragmatic ethics is not a low-level pleasure-seeking ethics, its adequacy must still be questioned. Many people who profess themselves to be holier than the devotees of this philosophy would experience some improvement if they humbled themselves to learn from the pragmatists. But the question still remains as to whether a situational standard of satisfactoriness does justice to the personal-spiritual elements in every moral situation. Need not moral value be satisfactory to the ultimate requirements of selfhood, both individually and collectively in a society of selves, in addition to being satisfactory to the situation in which it is relevant?

12. To turn to another value realm, it does not seem to me that Dewey gives enough place in his aesthetics to negative values. Aesthetic value is not all beauty but involves other qualities as well, even positive contradictions of beauty. True enough, we may prefer the positive aesthetic values, yet we do have appreciation for art which is able to preserve for us the qualities of suffering, anguish, despair, ugliness, deceit, cowardice, ambition, haughtiness, etc.

13. In education, the conception of the pupil, like the conception of the self in a more general context, is not satisfactory. Pupils are more than social-vocal phenomena, selves who have their selfhood only because of their give-and-take with society. There is a distinction which may be helpful at this point. While we come into our consciousness of selfhood only by our communication with objects, other selves, and society, *the existence and essence of selfhood are not constituted by this relation*. How could there be words without thoughts to be expressed in them? And how could there be thoughts to be communicated apart from thinking selves? Individual selves are not entities which can thrive in isolation; but their potentiality, made actual in social relations, is prior to and more than the social relations in which it is expressed and realized.

14. In education, again, the general objective should include more than social efficiency. It is well to redefine social efficiency so that it includes all that culture or the liberal arts now connote. There may be a gain in redefining culture so that it includes all that social efficiency now connotes. Certainly everything that can be done in the direction of resolving this dualism is desirable. But social efficiency only does justice to the social aspects of selfhood. And the objective of education, while it certainly must be social, should also do justice to the ultimate ends of selfhood. It should therefore include in its perspective the fullest realization of the self and the ultimate society of ends in which the self finds its true home.

15. Still further in education, it may be said that, just as experimental method is applied a bit more universally and arbitrarily by pragmatists than is warranted, so also it is applied too universally and arbitrarily as educational method. Its value should not be overlooked, indeed cannot be gainsaid; a great contribution has been made to educational method by pragmatism. But there are other general methods which are both relevant and effective in education; two will be mentioned. There is method in providing the occasion and inspiration for a self to launch out on its own because it is creatively interested, apart from a pressing indeterminacy which needs to be solved. And there is also a place for the use of the inner pressure of dialectical tension, in which it is not an experimental situation which needs resolution, but rather alternative principles, or ways, or life commitments which challenge initiative by their demand for decision.

16. The last comment concerning weaknesses in the philosophy of pragmatism has to do with its redefinition of religion. In fact, much the same criticism applies to the pragmatic treatment of religion as to the naturalistic treatment. Pragmatists show wisdom in pointing to certain attitudes in religious devotion which are needed for effective living. Many of us who are more conventionally religious would benefit much if we were to get the insight into the fact-value distinction which pragmatism stresses so much. If that were to happen, more religious living would be devoted to the

realization of value, and therefore would be a thrust into the future, instead of being devoted to preserving the status quo, as is more often the case than it should be.

But all of this would better be dealt with forthrightly, as Dewey is almost completely inclined to do, under other names than "religion" or "spiritual" or "God." The need for the use of such accepted words as these on the part of some people, which Dewey recognizes, is an evidence of the need of people for true religion, religion having a supernatural base. While supplying the words may restore a sense of relatedness for some, it may be said, without intending any unkindness, that this would probably be the effect only for the less penetrating minds; yet a greater evil results in the confusion and breakdown of communication which is necessarily involved. Our meanings should be made as clear as possible, and this cause is not helped by using hallowed words with meanings which are antithetical to their hallowed meanings. What needs to be supplied in the case of religion is not words, however hallowed, but a supernatural dwelling place in which the soul can find itself truly at home.

PART SIX

EXISTENTIALISM
AND LANGUAGE
ANALYSIS

Existentialism and Education

So far in this book we have dealt quite definitively with four philosophies each of which has made its impact felt in education and has become explicit as a philosophy of education. The contemporaneousness of the influence of these philosophies varies considerably. Realism and pragmatism are doubtless the more current by comparison with the other two. Although, at the same time, idealism is still very influential in a general way among many in education who do not follow philosophy of education as a technical discipline.

More recent than realism and pragmatism and at least making their influence felt in education are existentialism and language analysis. Neither has dealt fully with education, although language analysis has participated more in recent educational thought than has existentialism. Both have received attention from educational philosophers, existentialism more especially as a philosophy accompanied by speculations as to what effect it would have upon education were its specific meanings in this field to be made explicit.

Because of the influence—at least emerging influence—of these two philosophies, a chapter is now devoted to each as additions to the four older philosophies which have been explicit in education. Existentialism will be taken up first and then language analysis.

In this chapter we will try to understand existentialism by looking first at the origins from which it arose as a philosophy. We will then deal with what is now commonly observed regarding the two major traditions in existentialsm. Some call these traditions theistic and atheistic. My preference, borne out I believe by existentialist thinkers themselves, is to regard them rather as Christian and atheistic, respectively. Following these two discussions a number of different leading themes in existentialism will be considered one after the other. And the chapter will be brought to a close by the attempt to say something about what education would be were it guided by existentialist thought.

A. THE SOURCES OF EXISTENTIALISM

Except for Søren Kierkegaard's earlier place in history (1813–1855), which of course antedates the rise of existentialism to its place of prominence and influence in the twentieth century, the emergence of existentialism can be traced somewhat clearly. Put over-simply in terms of personalities, its ancestry is Edmund Husserl, Martin Heidegger, and Jean-Paul Sartre.

Edmund Husserl (1859–1938) was not an existentialist, of course. But Martin Heidegger (1889–   ), his most famous student and a singular exponent of the philosophy, came upon the important point of reference for his existentialism in a portion of his great mentor's thought. Husserl was a phenomenologist, actually in two parts, as it were. One of his concerns was phenomenological psychology. It was an exacting approach to the phenomena of existence as they can be discovered and described by sense perception or the many extensions of the senses which the various sciences may provide. Phenomenological psychology focuses solely upon the world as it is with no room whatsoever for flights of interpretation or alleged meanings which veer away from what is observed to be actual existence. Whether that which turns out to be actual existence is to the liking of man is quite irrelevant and unimportant.

The other concern of Husserl he called transcendental phenomenology. In this other approach to phenomena, which he also took, there was no more place for flights of interpretation or meaning than there was in his phenomenological psychology. But at the same time it was free from unyielding ties to existence as it actually is as verified by exploration, however refined and exacting. Transcendental phenomenology for Husserl was a consideration of the possible forms or ways of being which observable existence could conceivably have taken other than that which it actually has. It viewed the human mind as it is and within the patterns of human thought speculated, however with much realism, as to other ways of existing or other kinds of worlds which conceivably could have taken the place of the existence which actually is. In this other half of his thought Husserl was similar to Leibniz.[1] The latter was led by his interest in mathematics to recognize that there were conceivably many other combinations of entities and forces which could have comprised our cosmos than the particular and peculiar combination of them which actually constitutes it. But unlike Husserl, and evidently a born optimist, he went on to make the value judgment that the cosmos which we actually have is "the best of all possible worlds." That is, it is the best possible one of these conceivable combinations, at least from the standpoint of man's preferred interests and welfare[2]

While the transcendental phenomenology may open vistas of interesting speculation to many, it was rather from the phenomenological psychology of Husserl that Martin Heidegger chose to move and because of which, in part at least, he came to emphasize *existence* as it is "given," as it were, as the base of man's affairs. From it nothing can be subtracted; there is little enough there already. But certainly it is sheer fantasy to add any frills to existence, trying to make it something more than it is.

A brief sketch of some leading concepts in Heidegger will be in order before proceeding further, although some of these will require elaboration later. *Existence* in Heidegger is time-space being, empirically verifiable at least to the extent that it *is*, its quality is secondary and at best derived. Existence is not *being-as-such* which may transcend time-space, as in St. Thomas Aquinas or in terms of the meaning of existence which we ordinarily imply when we say we believe in the existence of God.

The kind of being which man has is inextricably tied to existence as understood by Heidegger. Man is not a peculiar species which has the

[1] Cf. pp. 121–122.
[2] Cf., Edmund Husserl, "Phenomenology," *Encyclopedia Britannica,* 1955. Vol. 17, pp. 699–702.

luxury of aloofness and separateness from existence. He is "there" in and of existence; "thrown," as it were, into existence so that he is inseparable from it. "Thrown-ness" is a favorite figure of Heidegger. Man cannot be an isolated and separate "subject" who can look at existence as a spectator and in his own subjective way. Nor is man an "object" which is so completely integral to existence that he has no subjective view of his own. He is both "subject" and "object" at the same time, and also at the same time tied to existence. So distinctly prior is existence in the nature of man as the base of his being, that the distinction between subject and object is artificial and arbitrary. Man as coexistent with existence in actuality transcends the subject-object distinction, as we will try to show later.

Being so inseparably bound to existence, man necessarily is given to certain moods; at least he cannot avoid this necessity if he forthrightly faces up to the given realities of his existence. For one thing, he is *anxious*; for another, he is also burdened with *care*. Not having any power to break the bonds which tie me to existence and the events which transpire in it, how can I avoid *anxiety* about life? Could I break this bond and flee into irreality, I would escape anxiety for the time being at least. But I cannot do it, and even if I could, my enjoyment of a holiday away from anxiety would have no effect whatsoever upon existence nor my eventual fate in relation to existence from which anxiety arises. Every individual man must recognize, however unwelcome, that his present being moves toward his own death, the termination of his own existence. I may try to ignore this inevitable end in various ways. I may lose myself activistically in the moving affairs and ritualistic observances of mass man, trying to forget that I am an individual who must die. With so much life and movement around me and all the unthinking actors going through the rituals of living before me, where is the sting of death? Or, even within the most devout religious observances (at least intended to be such), I may pay my tribute to a friend who has "passed away," as we say, virtually drowning myself in the illusion that my own death will be no more solitary than the dying of one who is not myself. Also, convincing myself by these ritualistic observances that death is not so bad after all; it is a part of life, I try to tell myself along with myriads of other men, and not the tragedy which marks the *end* of *my* existence.

Jean-Paul Sartre (1905–   ), the one man above all others who has put the word existentialism into the vocabulary of the intellectuals of the world following World War II, has made his own impact on this philosophy quite as much as popularizing it by his widely read literary productions. Indebted to Heidegger as well as to others, he has gone on to give shades of meaning to existentialism not in his predecessors. One of the chief of these is an emphasis on the negative side of existence, or its vacuum, as it were, at least as far as individual man is concerned. Yes, as man I exist now *in myself*. I am what I am at this time, commonly called the *facticity* of myself. But beyond this there is the possibility of what the self may become—by its own action. This is existence *for myself,* the generation by my own entirely free action of a self and its world quite beyond what the present self *in itself* is. In some small part this gives some meaning to a commonly reiterated existentialist principle that "existence precedes essence." Here in this theme of Sartre, the self as it now exists is the point of freely determined movement into the future by which the self *for itself* and its world are realized with many qualities, possessions, enjoyments and such, compared to which the self *in itself* now is a sheer existence devoid of essence.

Other philosophers of great importance are associated with existentialism, the ramified complexities of which defy literally—and by the nature of the case—any approximation of systematic treatment. H. J. Blackham in his important little book, *Six Existentialist Thinkers,*[3] devotes a chapter each to four men in addition to Heidegger and Sartre. They are Søren Kierkegaard (1813–1855), in point of time at least, the father of them all; Friedrich Nietzsche (1844–1900), the great philosopher and poet, of superman fame among the more vulgar; Karl Jaspers (1883–   ) whose thought was greatly influenced by both Kierkegaard and Nietzsche; and Gabriel Marcel (1889–   ), a distinguished Roman Catholic existentialist. Reference may also be made to still others in this all too brief chapter. But mention of these alone suggests the interlaced complexity of this philosophy and may betray that the description of the sources of existentialism here attempted is stated too simply to represent this movement fairly.

B. THEISTIC OR ATHEISTIC?

One of the common observations made about existentialism is that it has two different traditions which actually result in two kinds of existentialism. The point made by this interpretation is that there are atheistic existentialists and there are theistic existentialists. Some believe in God and some do not. Søren Kierkegaard is most commonly cited as a theistic existentialist, and also the father of this particular tradition. Jean-Paul Sartre is as commonly designated the atheistic adversary of Kierkegaard, most pointedly representing atheistic existentialism.

The argument to be advanced here is that while this observation about atheism and theism in this particular philosophy can be made at a more superficial level, actually it is a very minor and incidental distinction as compared to the kind of thrust made by existentialist philosophy and the spirit or motif in which all existentialists share very fully.

Let us look at notable examples of so-called theistic existentialists. Al-

[3] New York: Harper & Row, Publishers, 1959. Torchbook No. 1002.

most certainly Kierkegaard is actually the first to come to mind. Yes, Kierkegaard was a *theist* in the sense that he believed in God and, as we would commonly say, was a devoutly religious man. Actually this characterization is very tame; for Kierkegaard was religious with a malice, crying out against conventional Christianity and writing such unpopular books as *Attack Upon Christendom*.[4] Kierkegaard was first of all a Christian, one who earnestly believed in Jesus Christ, however maliciously or grumpily. It is because of this that he was a theist. We might say, "First a Christian, therefore religious; first a believer in Christ and because of this, a believer in the God of Jesus Christ." It is, therefore, too simple and superficial to assert blandly that Kierkegaard was a theistic existentialist. If such a statement is intended to take the edge off of existentialism by reminding the uninitiated that a person can be an existentialist without also being an atheist, it is both mistaken and misguided at the same time that this may be possible. Because Kierkegaard's faith in God was particularly rooted in the Christian faith, it was not a theism without historic roots simply wedded to existentialism.

We may also reiterate this same thesis by turning to others who were existentialists, and very sympathetic fellow travellers, who at the same time were or are theists because their religious conviction is somehow prior to their existentialism, however fused and of one piece. The great Jewish philosopher or theologian, Martin Buber (1878–1965), became largely what he was both in profession and thought because of his rootage in Hasidism, a warm, human, and earthy segment of European Judaism. Buber does not like designations, so it does not square with his preferences to be called philosopher, theologian, existentialist, or what not. But to the extent that there are strong existential elements in his thought, it must be recognized that these have also been paralleled by his profound commitment within Judaism. If he is called a theist, therefore, it should be remembered that he is also a member of the Jewish religious community and his theism derives from this.

Blaise Pascal (1625–1662) anticipated Kierkegaard in several existential motifs although he may not easily be given this name in our twentieth-century context. He was a Roman Catholic, at least by conviction and convention. A scientist of importance, he was converted to Christianity, the turning point being a striking visionary experience, if his own reports are reliable. In Roman Catholicism he was a Jansenist and thereby united with many followers of Cornelius Jansen who led an evangelical movement within Roman Catholicism. Now in general terms, of course, it could be said that Pascal was a theist. But again, he was a theist because of and in the Roman Catholic Christian sense. He was not just a theist and then a

---

[4] Translated by Walter Lowrie; Boston: The Beacon Press, 1944. Paperback, BP 28.

Roman Catholic, in that order. Consequently, however much we may identify Pascal as an existentialist, it is more proper to call him a Roman Catholic existentialist than a theistic existentialist.

Miguel de Unamuno (1864–1936) was one of the great intellectuals of Spain, distinguished in poetry, drama, fiction, and essays on a variety of subjects, as well as philosophy and religion. In his *Tragic Sense of Life*[5] he not only evidences the great influence of Kierkegaard, but also his existentialist tendencies. Although in and out of the rectorship of the University of Salamanca, according to the changes in fortune in his relation with the government, here again is a devout Roman Catholic who at the least was an existentialist fellow traveller. Again we must say Unamuno was a Roman Catholic existentialist. If he was a theistic existentialist, it was because first of all he was Roman Catholic and his theism was derived from that tradition of the Christian Faith.

The point can be made similarly with Etienne Gilson (1884–) and Gabriel Marcel (1889–). Gilson emphasizes the separation between philosophy and theology. Strongly influenced by Kierkegaard before turning to serious study of Aquinas, he discovered, at least so he believed, that Aquinas was a theologian rather than a philosopher. Also, he came to the conviction that those Thomists who find a deep indebtedness in Aquinas to Aristotle do not properly understand him. It is not difficult to understand one of his catch phrases to the effect that "all existential roads lead to Rome."[6] It seems fair to say that if Gilson is an existentialist, he is one who holds in high esteem the theology of St. Thomas Aquinas and whose theism derives from this theology and Roman Catholic Christianity.

Gabriel Marcel has been an obedient Roman Catholic churchman but never an orthodox theologian in any strict sense.[7] Existentialist though he may be, he insists that "Christianity begins with the recognition of Christ on the road to Emmaus,"[8] referring by his meaning to one account in the Gospel of Luke allegedly reporting one of the resurrection appearances of Christ.[9] Here again in Marcel we find an existentialist who is a Christian, rooting his faith in the resurrection faith of the primitive Christian Church. If he is a theist, he is such because of his Christian faith from which it is derived. It is possibly because of this that William Barrett considers Marcel the adversary of Jean-Paul Sartre. Of him he says he is "Sartre's extreme opposite and trenchant critic, a devout Catholic. . . ."[10]

---

[5] Translated by J. E. C. Flitch; London: Macmillan & Co., 1921.

[6] As paraphrased by William Barrett in *Irrational Man*. New York: Doubleday & Company, 1958. P. 93.

[7] Cf. H. J. Blackham, *Six Existentialist Thinkers*. New York: Harper & Row, Publishers, 1959. Torchbook 1002, p. 78.

[8] *Ibid.*, p. 79.

[9] Luke 24:13–35.

[10] William Barrett, *op. cit.*, p. 13.

The argument can be carried forward as well, although possibly not as clearly, using non-Roman Catholic Christians as examples. It is sometimes held, not without foundation, that the twentieth-century revival in the theology of Protestantism could never have taken place had these twentieth-century theologians not discovered Kierkegaard. Karl Barth (1886–   ) made his beginning as a great theologian in part because of the influence of Kierkegaard. But he also spurned it rather early in his career in order to free his passionate concern to formulate theology from the Word of God from all extrabiblical influences. To cite only one other example, and very tersely, the influence of Kierkegaard can easily be seen in Reinhold Niebuhr (1892–   ), especially in his conception of anxiety as the precondition of sin.

But the non-Roman Catholic theologians who show strongest and most consistent existentialist influence, if they themselves are not existentialists, are Rudolf Bultmann (1884–   ) and Paul Tillich (1886–1965). And it is Martin Heidegger who has singularly influenced both of these men. Rudolf Bultmann, who has contributed so much to modern New Testament studies, however we may criticize him, contends that a very broad strain of existentialism can be found in both Old and New Testaments. He may be guilty at times of importing existentialism into his New Testament studies and superimposing it upon some meanings in the New Testament which are not notably existentialist. However that may be, his contention has strong support in the literature of the Bible itself in that some of it is mightily tinged with existentialism, and of course it should also be noted that, by the distance of centuries alone, this was without benefit of the very earliest thinkers who were classified as existentialists.

Paul Tillich's use of Heidegger is not so clear as Bultmann's, although none the less evident. Like a many-sided Renaissance man, Tillich blends his own heritage in German idealism, his interest in depth psychology, his heavy preoccupation with culture, and a pertinent interest in the language of myth—to mention several components but not all—together with the existentialism of his friend Heidegger to make up a kind of theological whole. How well integrated or biblically rooted a theology this comprises requires a complicated evaluation far beyond and irrelevant to the discussion at hand. But what has been said is enough to indicate the extent to which Bultmann and Tillich both stand out as Protestant Christian existentialists.

Again, it can be argued as before that if these men are also theistic existentialists, this is so because they are first Christian theologians and their theism is derived therefrom. Generally, and probably also fundamentally, this is true when all is said and done. But the argument cannot be quite as clear and direct as it is for the others mentioned before, because of certain particularities in the theology of each. Bultmann, to be somewhat more specific, believes in the Christian kerygma or proclamation of the

New Testament and the primitive Christian Church. He holds this proclamation to be true whether or not the Jesus of empirically verifiable history was the Christ of God. Tillich's belief as a Christian follows a similar motif but it is not as much determined by New Testament theology as is Bultmann's. This would be expected, of course, since Tillich is a theologian rather than a New Testament scholar. Like Bultmann, Tillich also believes in the proclamation of the New Testament and primitive church but regards it as being suprahistorical, to the extent at least of transcending empirical history. There is no historic event the actuality of which, or lack of such actuality, could affect his faith, so Tillich commonly contends. It would seem fair to infer, therefore, that for Tillich the truth of the Christian faith does not hinge either upon the faith of the primitive church in the resurrection of Jesus, nor upon the historicity of Jesus as one who appeared at some time in empirically verifiable history.

In the cases of both Bultmann and Tillich the argument would still seem to hold that if they are theistic existentialists, this is so because they are first of all Christian existentialists. However it is in their cases the easiest to acknowledge that if there is such a phenomenon as a theistic existentialist, qua *theist* without also being Christian, they come closest to being examples of such a phenomenon. Their insistence on the Christian kerygma or proclamation, however sophisticated and full of difficult nuances, makes it very difficult nevertheless to denote them simply as theistic existentialists.

To turn quickly to the other end of the gamut, it, of course, must be acknowledged that Jean-Paul Sartre and Albert Camus (1913–1960) have made their atheism very clear. For them man has no hope but in this life. And that hope is in the action of each individual man by which he takes his own existence by the forelock, as it were, and fills it as full of as much essence as possible. But when an individual human life comes to an end, as it did for Camus in the suddenness of an automobile accident, death becomes the *final* and *irrevocable end* for both existence and essence.

In some others such a militant atheism is not present. More cautiously considered, blunt atheism may not even be intended. At the same time, however, it would be unwise in the case of these existentialists to rationalize that in some way they are theists. These less militant existentialists may best be exemplified by turning again to Martin Heidegger because he has shown great interest in *being as such,* as well as in human existence and the existing world of man. Because of this Heidegger is occasionally considered to be an *ontologist* as well as an existentialist. It must be acknowledged that this ontological interest if fully exploited is likely to bring one close to St. Thomas Acquinas' belief in a changeless category of being which can be intuited but not pinpointed in all of the evolution and disintegration in ourselves and the world around us.[11] From this point in his belief St.

[11] Cf. pp. 250–252.

Thomas made his departure in formulating his famous cosmological argument for the existence of God. But Heidegger does not go beyond an interest in being as such which admittedly is the possibility of something more than the atheistic existentialism of the twentieth century. This is hardly sufficient ground for inferring that Heidegger's ontologism is equal to or strongly suggestive of theism.

The point we have been laboring to make throughout this somewhat extended discussion is that we will better understand existentialism by laying emphasis upon the motifs which existentialists commonly emphasize whether they are atheistic or Christian. The too common concern to depict theistic and atheistic strains in existentialism has tended more to confuse our understanding of this philosophy than to clarify it. Furthermore the distinction of the two traditions has not really squared with the facts. Atheistic existentialists are quite easy to find, that is true. But it is very difficult to name an allegedly theistic existentialist who is not also a Christian; and what is more, a Christian prior to his theism and, therefore, a theist in a derived sense—derived from the Christian faith.

C. ANXIETY

Central among the various "moods" existentialists insist are occasioned in man by his feelings and understandings is the very painful state most commonly denoted in English by the word "anxiety." Because of problems of translation from Danish, German, or French, the fully intended meaning of this mood is not easily conveyed by any single English word. *Anxiety* comes close; *dread* may be a good equivalent; also, *despair* will convey the meaning quite well as long as it is not understood as the kind of despair in which there is no tension; the subject simply gives up. How do existentialists understand such a painful mood, and why do they emphasize it as they do? We will try to answer this double question. Of course, the answer will not be as complete as one given by any particular existentialist.

1. Anxiety is not just being anxious concerning the outcome of some uncertainty in the circumstances of life. This is a rather common psychological anxiety and not really existential at all. In fact, existential anxiety has no object in concrete human experience, nor can it have. It is a word which is much more inclusive in its reference; and at the same time what it denotes is easily missed by people whose attention is fully consumed by day-to-day activities.

Rather existential anxiety "discloses man in his being."[12] Macquarrie also further characterizes Heidegger's understanding of this word by saying

---

[12] John Macquarrie, *An Existentialist Theology.* London: S.C.M. Press, 1955. P. 68. A paraphrase of Heidegger.

that anxiety reveals to the self the possibility of its own "facticity."[13] That is that the state of anxiety, when unattached to any particular object or event, may show me that it is possible for me to exist, *merely exist,* without any quality, value, or meaning in my existence or selfhood. Kierkegaard makes this possibility even more pointed and threatening when he says of despair that it separates the self, forcing it into isolation, withdrawing it from preoccupation with objects, events, and people. In personal terms, anxiety thereby demands of me the decision by which I will choose whether or not I will be myself.[14]

2. Another aspect of existential anxiety is that it is the self being ill at ease in the world, an alien who cannot be "naturalized." It is the self as possibility and freedom "thrown" into the world where its freedom is bound up with the world.[15] It is the world as a whole, insofar as it can be seen as such, which evokes *dread,* and by no means any particular thing in the world. Accordingly, this particular existential "mood" invests everything alike with a common worthlessness.[16] In his discussion of Sartre on this aspect of anxiety, Blackham says that it is as though the individual human consciousness "comes into the world as a 'No,' as pure possibility separated from everything existent."[17] For Kierkegaard it is disrelationship egocentrically related to itself. He seems to imply by this what Heidegger made very explicit later, namely, that the self is tied to a "place" in existence. Yet the self in its despair tries to break this tie to place, increasing its despair all the more. For he says "Despair is the disrelationship in a relation which relates to itself."[18]

3. Existential anxiety, not having any particular object in the world of man, is a kind of *ontological* anxiety. This is so even though the majority of existentialists are not concerned with ontology and do not believe in any kind of being other than the time-space existence man experiences and of which he can give a description.

Most existentialists say that anxiety is ontological precisely because as an existential mood it has no relation whatever to anything in particular. It is experienced in the face of *nothingness* in antithesis to being anxious about something which exists.[19] Further on ontological anxiety in Hei-

[13] Cf. *ibid.,* p. 69.
[14] Cf. Søren Kierkegaard, *The Sickness Unto Death.* New York: Doubleday & Company, 1941. Anchor Paperback No. 30, combining *Fear and Trembling* and *The Sickness Unto Death* into one volume. Pp. 94–95. For this discussion "despair" as used in *Sickness Unto Death* has been chosen as the point of reference rather than "dread" in *The Concept of Dread.*
[15] Cf. John Macquarrie, *op. cit.,* p. 70. A paraphrase of Heidegger.
[16] Cf. H. J. Blackham, *op. cit.,* p. 94. A paraphrase of Heidegger.
[17] *Ibid.,* p. 111.
[18] Søren Kierkegaard, *op. cit.,* p. 148.
[19] Cf. John Macquarrie, *op. cit.,* p. 7; also H. J. Blackham, *op. cit.,* p. 94.

degger, it may be said that it is possibility bound up with the existing world in two ways. (a) It is the self being "thrown" as it were into an ocean of alien and hostile being. It is, therefore, the impossibility of the self having an existence of which it can be the master. (b) The second further explanation involves Heidegger's somewhat unique approximation of a conception of an enduring being which is beyond and more than the transient existences of man's world. Anxiety, he says, ontologically, is the self seeking a "ground of being" to take the place of being "thrown" into an existence which has no "ground of being."[20]

Kierkegaard views ontological despair in the setting of his Christian theism and thereby goes somewhat beyond Heidegger's approximation of a concept of a ground of being. For him the root of ontological despair is consciousness of being a self in which in some sense there is something eternal. One despairs because he is not willing to be just a self in a temporal world and no more. But he sees the termination of selfhood by way of suicide, for example, as no elimination of despair because there is the possibility of the eternal. But if a person does not believe in an eternal existence, his despair is not relieved because while rejecting selfhood limited to a transient existence, if not being tied down to a "place" in this existence, he has no assurance of an eternal existence although he may recognize the possibility of it, still not positively believing in it. Viewing such a predicament in the light of his Christian faith, the only solution to ontological despair for Kierkegaard is belief in God as revealed in Christ.[21]

4. Another theme in existentialism not as yet discussed, namely *authenticity,* is necessarily involved in a further look at anxiety. Existentialists are greatly attracted to anything, be it an experience, for example, or a work of art depicting some aspect of experience which has about it a "moment of truth," the unmistakable mark of reality, or the ring of authenticity. This may more commonly be expressed negatively than affirmatively, in the rejection of the allegedly phony or bogus. But on the positive side, let it be said to the credit of the existentialist that he is impatient with anything but the authentic.

Now one of the reasons for existentialism's preoccupation with *anxiety, dread,* and *despair* is that this mood," by whatever name it is called, is inescapably authentic. There is no playacting about anxiety; it just is and we cannot escape it. This reveals to us another aspect of anxiety in addition to those we have tried to depict so far. Anxiety is too authentic to be eradicated, glossed over or escaped, no matter what means we may use in the attempt to banish it. Not only is anxiety itself authentic but it makes each man fear for the authenticity of his own selfhood. It makes him afraid

[20] Cf. John Macquarrie, *op. cit.,* pp. 74–75.
[21] Cf. Søren Kierkegaard, *op. cit.,* pp. 180–182.

that he will be a phony rather than his true self. And, difficult though it may be and fraught with the continual pain of anxiety though it may be, a man cannot live with a bogus self.[22]

5. This brings us finally to consider fear in relation to *anxiety*. On just looking at the relation many might take the two words for close synonyms, denoting very much the same "mood." But to this assumption the existentialists are virtually unanimous in retorting with a resounding "No!" Rather than a near synonym, fear is the antithesis of anxiety. It is anxiety that we fear more than anything else. Because of this, fear is a flight, a running away from what we properly recognize in some rare moment of wide-eyed perception, as our terrible plight.

This is the chief motivation for individual man trying to lose himself in the rituals and activistic engagements of mass man—*fear*! Individual man is deeply anxious; he is inescapably anxious when he does his best to be himself; he is anxious over his own existence, and he is anxious about losing himself in a sea of nothingness. So joining in the dumb but concerted reassurance of man-in-the-mass he runs away from anxiety in mortal fear of it, hoping against hope, at least unconsciously, that the rituals and palliatives of mass society will separate him from anxiety—and at the same time, unfortunately, from his own individual selfhood.[23]

D. DEATH AND NOTHINGNESS

Two themes in existentialism which may very well be discussed together are *death* and *nothingness*. These would seem to be very gloomy subjects, as they are, of course, the objects of brooding "moods" at the very least. Nevertheless, existentialism is concerned with both death and nothingness in a hard-nosed intellectual facing of them, however weighted emotionally in moody gloom these subjects and their consideration may be.

1. One of the easiest things to say about death from the existentialist's point of view, dealing with it first and then moving on to nothingness, is that each man must personalize death for himself. When I receive the news of the death of a friend, am present at a funeral at which good taste requires my attendance, or get caught behind a slow moving funeral cortege on the street when I am in a lather to get to my next appointment, I do not face death as a reality but only as a socially objective phenomenon. Death does not begin to take on its due meaning for me, however much I may want to resist it, until I come to recognize that *death* taken seriously is *my death,* something which will happen to *me*. This is the least understanding of its meaning containing any degree of psychological realism.[24] In

---

[22] Cf. H. J. Blackham, *op. cit.*, pp. 94–95. A paraphrase of Heidegger.
[23] Cf. John Macquarrie, *op. cit.*, pp. 67–69. A paraphrase of Heidegger.
[24] Cf. H. J. Blackham, *op. cit.*, pp. 200–201. A paraphrase of Heidegger.

other words, death is a part of the "facticity" of my own selfhood. It is not something to be positively realized as one of the future possibilities of the self. It will happen to me regardless of what I do and is given to me, as it were, at the same time that by birth I am given existence as a self.[25]

2. Such a direct taking of death to myself as a forthrightly faced part of the facticity of my own being also is necessary in order for me to have an authentic existence. As long as I keep death at a distance as something which happens to men in general, or even as long as I put the thought of it off until some tomorrow far away when it will happen to me, I am refusing to open the door to full recognition of the nature of my existence. I must openly embrace death as a central element in my being in order to be myself. Short of this I am trying to pretend that I am a kind of being to which death is not possible.

3. It is probably not too uncommon for a person somberly to recognize that some day he will die. But to do this is to give death no more importance than constituting one of the boundaries of life. But for existentialism this is by no means enough. While death may be a boundary of life in that at some point it brings life coldly to an end, death is far more central to life than this. Death is better understood as the obverse of life—even just as much so as life is the obverse of death. In one of our common clichés we talk about "the other side of the coin," to suggest the necessary bound-togetherness of what may appear to be an antithesis. We may use this cliché quite literally about death and life to illustrate the centrality of death as viewed by existentialism. With a coin it is "heads" on one side and "tails" on the other. The life-and-death relation is life on one side and death on the other; death on one side and life on the other.   √

Now why be at such pains to make the point that death is not only the act of dying which marks the boundary of life? That instead death is at the center of life as the obverse of it? For existentialism it is important to do this because in order to give death its full due, we must realize that all the time we are in the process of dying, all the days of our lives while we are also in the process of living. In a sense, death and dying must be seen as one of the aspects of my being as a self. Death must be seen at least as a present possibility of my life at any time, if not also as a continuing process of decay and disintegration which is going on all the time I am living.[26]

4. Yet it is not quite sensible to talk about death as an ever present possibility which may happen to my life. As imprecise language, this suggests what the centrality of death is for the existentialist. But more precisely, while in the same vein, death is not a possibility. It is the negation of

[25] Cf. John Macquarrie, op. cit., p. 119. A paraphrase of Heidegger.
[26] H. J. Blackham, op. cit., p. 201; and John Macquarrie, op. cit., p. 118. Both paraphrases of Heidegger.

possibility, the end of all possibilities. Possibility is the open avenue by which the self as facticity may become something which it not now is. But death closes the door on all such open vistas. Death stops the clock of life at whatever time it is when it happens, and then that time is a part of the facticity of self which can never be changed. Death is no possibility for something beyond, e.g., immortality or eternal life, except for the Christian existentialists. For them death may be the end of *existential* existence but at the same time a transition to another kind of existence, namely, ontological existence, in which the atheistic existentialists do not believe.[27]

Such musings about death, if they can be denoted by such a light term, raise the broader question as to the *obverse* of *existence*. If for the existentialist *existence* is precisely time-space existence observable by man, then what is it that is on the other side of that particular coin? Is it the negation of existence, or *nothingness*? It would be reasonable to expect that this is the case. But let us see.

1. Heidegger would seem to bear out this supposition. For he holds that nothingness is a haunting presence in all of our being which is both fascinating and dreadful. Even when we are having a good time, lost in the social rituals of mass man and his merrymaking, it all really turns out to be whistling in the dark. For nothingness is the dark against the fear of which we whistle to reassure ourselves. It is the quaking underneath the apparent calm of our preoccupations, the negation hidden beneath all the reassurance of our merrymaking.[28]

2. Jean-Paul Sartre throws *nothingness* before us as a black night we must face, like it or not, by showing us some holes in the doubting routine of Descartes.[29] Sartre observes that there was a point in Descartes' sequence of doubting everything which was an opening to nothingness. This point was prior in the sequence to Descartes' recognition of the fact of his own act of doubting. At this point, before the affirmation "I am doubting," Descartes was a nothingness; he was a negation, a cipher. Such existence as he had just before his affirmation was outside of nature and history. This was so according to Sartre because Descartes by his doubting had rejected all belief in a world of bodies and recollections of happenings that had gone before. This reveals to Sartre a negating possibility in man. Because he is free to say "No," man can transcend nature and bring *nothingness*

[27] Cf. John Macquarrie, *op. cit.*, p. 118; and H. J. Blackham, *op. cit.*, pp. 52–53. Both are paraphrases of Jaspers. What is said above concerning an ontological existence for the self after death, of which he is not at all sure, may also be true for Martin Buber, the Jewish philosopher. Such existence as we may have after death is a pantheistic existence in which the individuality is lost in the totality of being as such.

[28] Cf. William Barrett, *Irrational Man*. New York: Doubleday & Company, 1953. P. 202. A paraphrase of Heidegger.

[29] Cf. 115–116.

into being. Contradictory as the words "nothingness" and "being" may be, they still refer to a real possibility that the words would seem insufficient to describe: man's no-saying brings nothingness into being.[30]

3. Sartre is more radical in his emphasis on *nothingness* than Heidegger, existence beyond the present existence which man now knows. For Heidegger, nothingness may be symbolized less forbiddingly as a *"not-yet"* or a *"no-longer."* But Sartre is more blunt and final about human existence and the existence man now sees about him. Barrett says of him that he noses "out all the worded and seedy strands of nothingness that haunt our human condition." Also, he says of this radical theme of Sartre, "never in the thought of the West has the self been so pervaded by negation."[31]

4. Another way of seeing how radical is Sartre's emphasis on nothingness is to view it in relation to the existence-essence distinction which will yet have to be discussed.[32] This is the final look we will take at nothingness in this particular discussion. As will yet have to be made clear, existence somehow precedes essence for all existentialists. One aspect of this important and inclusive connection, for Sartre at least, is his insistence that there is no structure of essences or values which has any being prior to man's existence, prior to the existence of all men who have ever existed, as well as prior to the existence of each individual man. Existence takes on meaning, and therefore some essence or quality, only as man by his freedom to say "No" says it and in this act brings into existence for himself at least some world of value and quality. Prior to this, there is nothing but dry sapless existence, sheer facticity.[33]

E. FACTICITY

So far incidental to the discussion of other subjects,[34] a favorite existentialist word, namely, *facticity* has been used. There may be some enlightening help in directing attention now to *facticity* itself as a primary rather than incidental subject. It may be unnecessary to comment in the very beginning that *facticity* has little similarity to the meaning of factuality, which denotes little more than the mere whether or not that something in question actually happened.

1. While the *facticity* theme is far broader in existentialism, it may be easier first of all to examine it partially as it refers only to the self. And this can be done quite readily by way of Sartre's thought about the self. Sartre speaks of the self in two ways: the self-in-itself and the self-for-itself. It is

[30] Cf. H. J. Blackham, *op. cit.*, p. 216. A paraphrase of Sartre.
[31] William Barrett, *op. cit.*, p. 220.
[32] Cf. pp. 458–460.
[33] Cf. William Barrett, *op. cit.*, p. 217. A paraphrase of Sartre.
[34] Cf. pp. 441–442, 442–443, 448–449, and 453–454.

the self-in-itself, or as it is at a given moment, which is its *facticity*. It may be, as a crude example, that I would like to have been born the son of a wealthy man. But actually I was born into a family of very modest means. The wish concerning my station of birth may be one for which I can give good reasons but it has nothing to do with the fact of the case for my particular self. A somewhat superficial and unimportant part of my own *facticity*, nevertheless an irrevocable part of it, is that I was given birth by parents who were by no means affluent.

To pursue this same rather gauche example, we may see the meaning of the *facticity* of the self by projecting possible antitheses to it. Suppose that I determine insofar as I have any power to do so that my own children will live a more comfortable life than I did as a child, as far as money can provide this comfort. This is to choose to be a person of some affluence, distinctly contrasted with the small degree my own parents had. Now to make this choice or set my sails in that direction is an aspect, however superficial, of the self-for-itself. Contrasted with this is my self-in-itself as it was at birth, a child of comparative poverty, a part of my own *facticity*.

Or, to look at the opposite pole of this *facticity* of myself in another way, let me ask what value judgment I make concerning my own birth in comparative poverty? Suppose I say, "I would not have had it otherwise. My parents were my parents; I love them, and could I ever have made the choice I would accept their economic circumstances, inadequate as they were." Suppose also that I go still further and say that the *facticity* of self, as determined by the economic condition of my parents, was a good thing and that by my own free choice I now embrace it gladly as part of my life history. This again is the contradiction of *facticity*, although it chooses a particular facticity as of worth. It is to make the station of my birth a part of my self-for-myself; something which, much more than having to face it as a fact which cannot be changed, but which I also freely accept and happily take to myself as part of myself.[35]

In Heidegger's dealings with *facticity*, the figure of "thrown-ness" is commonly inserted in some way. Any person in his living, and this means more deeply in coming to terms with himself, never really starts from scratch. He has to start from where he actually is; this is necessitated by his facticity. To speak personally about this, I am always already "thrown" into some situation or place which is the locus of my being. It is from this point that I must always make any beginnings I make. "Thrown-ness" is always outside of my control as a self. It is in the structure of existence into which I am "thrown" and, consequently, it marks out the boundaries of the possibilities within which I can become myself-for-myself. I can still, of

[35] Cf. Jean-Paul Sartre, *Being and Nothingness*. Translated by Hazel E. Barnes; New York: Philosophical Library, 1956. Pp. 79–95.

course, choose between possibilities in many cases, but even so the possibilities are limited by the facticity of the place or situation into which my self-in-itself has been thrown.[36] A man's possibilities are for this reason determined to a considerable degree by his facticity, the self-for-itself is determined to some degree by the self-in-itself. And in some instances possibility may even be frustrated by facticity, so constricting are its limits.[37]

2. Having begun with selfhood as a way of understanding facticity, we may now be able to move toward seeing facticity in existence itself quite apart from selfhood. We will attempt this first by looking at the perceptual relation between an alleged knower and its object as described by Sartre. Previously we have discussed this relation from several other vantage points in this book,[38] all of which may provide a fuller context for understanding Sartre on cognition, as well as helping us to see by contrast how radical is Sartre's position in the history of philosophy.

Sartre has some liking for Bishop Berkeley's dictum, "To be is to be perceived,"[39] but he changes its meaning so radically in his adaptation of it that Berkeley could scarcely do other than reject completely Sartre's adaptation. For Sartre, an object in perception is just what it appears to be and no more; the manner of its *appearing* is precisely what the object is. Any object perceived is *outside* of consciousness; it is a part of the process of existing and in no sense is in the consciousness of the perceiver. It is not even *represented* in consciousness.[40] It not only exists prior to the perceiver's consciousness of it; it exists independently of consciousness at the time perceived as well. This again is an aspect of *facticity*. Objects in existing simply exist as they are in themselves.

Turn now to the perceiver's side of this cognitive relation. The perceiver has some kind of consciousness, but of what is he conscious? Is he conscious of the object? The answer would have to be "Yes." Is he conscious of his own consciousness? Sartre's answer is "No," and he would probably go on from this answer to take Descartes to task for assuming that there was any validity in his consciousness of his own doubting.[41] The consciousness of the perceiver discloses, at least indirectly, that there is a self on the other end of the cognitive relation opposite to that of the object. This self, so disclosed, is a self which exists just as the object is existing. And in the cognitive relation the self is quite simply engaged as an existing self in a relation with an independently existing object. Both are existing entities. And in this way of treating cognition, we see another aspect of

[36] Cf. John Macquarrie, *op. cit.*, p. 83. A paraphrase of Heidegger.
[37] Cf. *ibid.*, p. 84. A paraphrase of Heidegger.
[38] Cf. pp. 73–77, 165–169, 270–273, and 379–382.
[39] Cf. pp. 125–127.
[40] Cf. pp. 270–273.
[41] Cf. pp. 115–116.

facticity; we see the facticity of the self but we also see the facticity of objects.[42]

We may now be in a position to understand Heidegger's somewhat famous insistence that the common subject-object distinction is transcended in existentialism. In more than one discussion in this book we have dealt with the subject-object distinction;[43] now we must listen to Heidegger's argument that it has no validity. We do have to recall enough at this point to be explicit that the subject aspect of selfhood is its living and active creative thrust if not its very center. We also need to restate that the object-aspect of the self is that which the subject creates as it is at any given moment. The object-self is not entirely different from the facticity element of the self-in-itself of Sartre. The argument of Heidegger is that no separation of the self into subject and object can be made, even for the sake of discussion. This is because the self is in existence and not outside of it. It is also because the self is tied down to a *place* in existence. The existing self tied down to a particular place is one existing entity; it is not a subject and an object. It is a self which because of its existence and place can have no such duality of aspects. And this one existence of the self once recognized is again another aspect of its *facticity*.[44]

3. No longer can we now delay the consideration of facticity as it pertains to existing as such, quite in contradistinction to the facticity of the self. We have approached this difficult concept in listening to Sartre on cognition where both an existing self and an existing object are implicated. But now we are forced to look at mere existing and the *facticity* of it.

The world of existing, alongside which man must live and of which he is also a part because of his own existing, is an "alien" world. There is no place in existing where man can really be at home. One condition which makes this so is that existence has no meaning implicit in it. The only meaning which the world of existing can have is what man superimposes upon it or projects into it by his various attempts to build his own world.[45]

Consequently, apart from his own creating activity, which after all can only reach so far, man is virtually at sea in an ocean in which the two parts of the water, as it were, are "possibility" and *facticity*. Adrift in such a foreign sea, the only alternatives open to man are despair (in the sense of giving up) or heroism, and at best a rather limited heroism. If man succumbs to the facticity of the world, there is nothing but despair and what is more, the kind of despair which completely lets go and says "We might as well jump over the abyss into nothingness." But if man scorns "facticity" and grasps "possibility," in the determination to make the best of things,

---

[42] Cf. Jean-Paul Sartre, *op. cit.*, pp. 1–1x.
[43] Cf. pp. 149–150, and 208–209.
[44] Cf. John Macquarrie, *op. cit.*, p. 83. A paraphrase of Heidegger.
[45] Cf. *ibid.*, p. 84. A paraphrase of Heidegger.

then he can be a hero for a day or so, as the short span of life may be symbolized; but also his heroism is necessarily limited by the boundaries of "facticity."[46] If this is the case, it is not difficult to understand John Macquarrie's characterization of Heidegger relevant to this predicament when he says facticity is "man's imprisonment within his destiny with the alien being of the world."[47]

But even so, as Heidegger would evidently say, it is both important and psychologically realistic for man to know that his environment threatens his own existence. Unwelcome as such grim knowledge may be, it is yet to be preferred to abstract theories about the alleged structure of the so-called cosmic environment of man.[48]

Possibly there is another alternative a man has in life in addition to heroism and despair, although it is difficult to see how individual man could persist in this alternative for a significant length of time without having more assurance than Heidegger holds out to us. This possible third alternative is the resolve by a person to be his true authentic self within the narrow limits *facticity* sets upon *possibility*, for man can have no mastery beyond the boundaries set by facticity. This would appear to be another way of saying that if we are not going to give up in despair or romantically aspire to be noble little heroes of pygmy proportions, then the only thing left for us to do is to live with our own anxiety, both psychological and existential.[49]

F   EXISTENCE AND ESSENCE

Reluctant as we may be to approach it, we must now come to a very central and patently abstract principle in existentialism. It is that *existence precedes essence*. There have been one or two incidental references to this principle heretofore in this chapter.[50] But the need for an attempted explication of it is broader than this because it is rooted in the history of philosophy and a number of cross-references can be found for it there.

One important reference and an early one is Plato's doctrine of ideas.[51] According to this doctrine there are universal ideas which *really* have existence in an order transcending the world of man. A very gross example is that allegedly there is a universal idea "tree," the idea of the perfect tree of which every existing tree in this world is an imperfect expression. Now what the Platonic doctrine of ideas says, therefore, with regard to the relation of existence and essence is that *essence* precedes *existence*, the

---

[46] Cf. *loc. cit.* A paraphrase of Heidegger.
[47] John Macquarrie, *op. cit.*, p. 86.
[48] Cf. *ibid.*, p. 84. A paraphrase of Heidegger.
[49] Cf. *ibid.*, p. 89. A paraphrase of Heidegger.
[50] Cf. pp. 440–442, and 455–457.
[51] Cf. pp. 113–114.

precise contradiction of the existentialist principle. Since there are universal ideas of trees, rocks, the various alleged virtues, etc., such universal ideas are prior to any concretions of them in time-space existence. But to this all existentialists, apparently without exception, would object with a loud Sartrian "No!" There are no ideas preceding the existence of objects or entities. They may be conceived by ideas after the fact of their existence, but they are not preceded by ideas.[52]

Another point of reference is the equally abstract principle of idealism that existence and essence are inseparably united as one.[53] According to this principle, there is no dualism between existence and essence, between being-as-such and quality or value. Rather, existence has quality as well as sheer existence, and quality or value have existence in being.

With reference to this idealist principle concerning the unity of existence and essence, the existentialists are not clear in advancing an anti-thesis or substitute. While they are emphatic that existence precedes essence, they are not so insistent that existence and essence are separate and mutually distinct. George Santayana's eternal dualism of existence and essence is clear, insistent, and radical as compared to most existentialists.[54]

Of course, we must remember just here especially that the atheistic existentialists make no commitments, intellectual or otherwise, concerning an eternal and, therefore, nontransient existence. The existence about which they are concerned, and with some feeling, is the time-space existence observable by man or potentially so, if not actually observable in any given moment. The possible exception is Heidegger who at times seems to bend his concern also to existence-as-such or to a kind of being that has led some to call him an "ontologist," as well as an existentialist.[55]

So our problem is compounded. We are primarily concerned here to ask whether existentialists believe existence and essence to be separate. But as soon as we ask the question we must specify what kind of existence we are talking about, temporal existence or allegedly eternal existence. And we must further consider whether specifically denoting the kind of existence to which our inquiry is directed makes any difference in the point of the question. It is at least possible that there is a tendency rather common to all existentialists to unite existence and essence in the characteristic existentialist way. This is quite common whether they are speaking of "existential" existence as among those atheistically inclined, or whether they are Christian existentialists who believe both in "existential" existence and the God revealed in Jesus Christ. In this bifurcation Heidegger is left

[52] Cf. William Barrett, *op. cit.*, pp. 264–265; and H. J. Blackham, *op. cit.*, p. 69. The former, a paraphrase of Kierkegaard; the latter, a paraphrase of Marcel.

[53] Cf. p. 165.

[54] Cf. pp. 272–273.

[55] Cf. John Macquarrie, *op. cit.*, pp. 31–32; also, cf. H. J. Blackham, *op. cit.*, p. 107.

somewhat to himself in a vague no-man's-land in between, but having the same tendency nevertheless.

If this noble but presumptuous attempt at a somewhat descriptive and accurate generalization has any validity, we can use it as a base for moving on to characterize the existentialist's apparent refusal to divorce existence and essence completely. In the common-law union of the two, it is clear that existence is the dominant pants-wearing partner. Essence is necessarily the receding, dominated, if not also the occasionally hidden spouse. Pick out any particular quality or essence and it always already has existence. In fact, it could not be an essence unless it was a quality of an existing thing. Furthermore, it is only one of the qualities of the existing object and, therefore, rather abstracted when singled out from the totality of the existing thing with all of its qualities.

And this, of course, does not take into consideration at all the essence which an existing thing may take on in the future. The essence of an existing object in the present is a part of the *facticity* of that object. This is comparable to the distinction already made between the self-in-itself and the self-for-itself upon which Sartre is so insistent. An existing thing, other than a self, has its essence as it now exists. But in the future it may acquire other qualities, adding to the totality of its then existing essence. Furthermore, it should be noted for the existentialists that this existing thing could not acquire additional essence without already existing. So back again we are taken to the principle, *existence precedes essence*, almost as if to say, "I told you so!"

All of this is quite abstract for many existentialists. The relation of existence and essence for them is primarily focused in the self and is related primarily to the self-in-itself, the self-for-itself, and the possibility of choices which makes the transformation from the first to the second.[56] Nevertheless, it seemed necessary to push this existentialist theme as far as possible, as we have attempted to do. And accordingly, if we have been at all accurate, we see that for at least some existentialists the relation of *existence* and *essence* characterizes the orbit of the not-self just as much as it does that of the self.

G. INDIVIDUALISM

It may be surprising to some to observe that existentialism is highly individualistic. In this regard this philosophical movement does not constitute a radical change of emphasis at all comparable to other things it has to say, some of which are ominously threatening to conventional assumptions.

In existentialism it is true that the individual is completely continuous

[56] This is very much the case with Sartre. Cf. *Being and Nothingness*; also, cf. William Barrett, *op. cit.*, p. 90.

with the observable existence of the time-space world. So much is this a characteristic of the self that it is impossible and fantastic to assume that any self could so withdraw from time-space existence as to be an impartial and disengaged spectator. The individual can never be isolated in his own subjectivism because he can never be divorced from his *place* in the world, as it were, which *place* is actually part of his selfhood.

But for existentialism it does not follow from *place in existence* as integral to the self that there is some common social ground which transcends individual selfhood. Each one of us individually may be in the same boat as far as the nature of our existence is concerned. But being in the same boat has no more significance than just that. There is no community of selves which derives therefrom, except possibly at such most superficial levels of communication as are without significance. We are still individuals, unrelieved in our isolation from alleged community, even though we are each inseparably tied to existence and more precisely to a place in existence at a given time.

This means that in existentialism there are no categories of community or social process, as in pragmatism, from relation with which the self derives its selfhood.[57] It also means that there is no category of the organismic, as in idealism, by relation with which the self grows into self-realization and in which the self has a kind of mother-matrix which is its home.[58]

Rather, the individual is an individual in a very strict sense. As with the monads of Leibniz, he has no windows. As far as society is concerned, it is a collection of such windowless individuals and there is no community, however ephemeral, giving the self even an occasional vista beyond itself to some ground of being in which all selves may be at home.

Inseparable from time-space existence as an essential part of its nature, the self is an individualistic entity. However free it may be, and however dependent on its own action any self may be in the determination of what it will become, the self is nevertheless by itself. However dynamic its impact on the world may eventually prove to be, it is the self as an isolated individualistic self which determines this.

The strictures and dilemmas of this extreme individualism can be depicted very pointedly, and without any sensationalism, by referring to sex which in relation to the authenticity of self is a real problem for existentialists. Does the sex relation transcend individualism, or does it fail to do this? For Sartre at least, the answer is that it does not transcend individualism; and because of this any party to the sex act, as to almost all other human relations, emerges as either the master of a conquest or the subject of exploitation. If I submit to another's sex desire, marriage or other legal

[57] Cf. pp. 394–396.
[58] Cf. pp. 148–154.

sanction notwithstanding, just to that extent I have ceased for the time being to be an authentic self. Instead I have been the object of exploitation. If on the other hand I am the aggressor in the relation, my will to power has made the other party to the relation less than a self in order that I may be my self-for-myself in some fuller way which by my own initiative I have chosen.

Now, were there some kind of community in the sex act of which both parties are members, and of which a child if so reproduced were also an issue—not of the father alone nor of the mother alone, but rather of the community between them—then there would be no problem of exploiting and being exploited. But for most existentialists at least there is no such community. The individual self has no windows; and an individual is an individual.[59]

H. EXISTENTIALISM AND EDUCATION

The philosophy of existentialism has not displayed any particular interest in education. It may be that explicitness concerning education is an addition which could come as existentialism develops its implications more fully. It may also be that because of its primary interest in the individual, existentialism will not take the pains to develop a philosophy having to do with education. Education may be for existentialists an institution which meddles with the lives of individuals in a manner not welcomed. In any case, as we attempt to infer what existentialism might be in part as a philosophy of education, we need to infer from what is implied and on this we must depend alone. We have no direct and explicit pronouncements from which we can draw.

We will attempt to make these inferences, however, and at one point in the end comment rather critically. Several of these inferences appear to pertain to the self and in education, therefore, have to do especially with the pupil. Concerned with selfhood, they also make implications about the teacher.

a. What do we make first of all of facticity? Students are born from particular parents, live in particular circumstances, and their selfhood is given consequently by such actualities as these. Those who have to do with their education must view them in terms of these actualities, and not as though in some way they are other than what the actual circumstances and conditions of their lives have made them. Even whatever potential they may have for becoming something other than they are must not be considered to the extent that it would discount in any way the facticity of their being.

b. Over against facticity there is, however, the *possibility* of the self.

[59] Cf. H. J. Blackham, *op. cit.*, pp. 123–124.

While the self of a student has a certain facticity, what it actually is in-itself, it also has certain possibilities relating to what it may become for-itself. Conceivably, a teacher of existentialist leanings would see the educative task as precisely that of helping the student to become for-himself what it is he wants to become. This, of course, is intended essentially and inwardly, and this is important to note. The vocational question is quite another matter and not involved here. It is of significance to note cautiously the nature of the help the teacher should give the student. It should not be a directed or superimposed helping. It should rather be general and permissive in character. It should be the kind of help which makes full leeway for the student to make choices that *he* wants to make and which in turn determine what it is that *he* wants to become.

c. For facticity and possibility also apply, of course, to the selfhood of the teacher. The teacher, as well as the student, is a self-in-itself and also a self-for-itself. Much like inanimate objects, the student in his being-in-himself may be an object to the teacher. Without careful discipline guided by existential thought the teacher may also too easily imagine the student's world as more friendly to him than it is. In the same way he may too easily posit a being-for-himself for the student which does not match his facticity, the alienness of his world, or his possibilities. Possibly, existentialism would warn educators that they have been too prone to set up objectives for the pupil, envisioning the kind of person, at least generally, that we would like him to become as a result of his education.

Is the common category of educational objectives a valid one? In the light of existentialism may it not be artificial and too facile? Do we really have the right to say or intend as much about what students should become as our many statements of objectives imply? Are we taking very much for granted the educational institution as a social agency through which students must move? And do we assume too easily that students shall emerge from this institution as beings-for-themselves which are quite artificially constructed as compared with real people who have their own peculiar facticities and possibilities? In part, this may be one reason we have so little evidence that existentialism is interested in education. It may be one of those institutions, for existentialists, which interferes with the being of individuals. It may defeat authenticity of being-for-itself by its very artificiality. It may do this by trying to conform the student to false objectives instead of leaving the way open for him to find his own authentic being.

d. It may appear that all of this would leave the door fully open to chaos and anarchy in what it is that education should permit students to become. Existentialists lay emphasis upon what it is the student *wants* to become. They imply fear that the institution of learning will conform the student to some preconceived end or absorb him so that he gets lost in society and never finds himself. Truly enough this is all quite individual-

istic, but it need not be chaotic. Because the existentialist is concerned for
·authenticity, and authenticity, among other things, must mean in education
authenticity in the student. Somewhere between the facticity of the student
and his possibility there is that self-for-itself which he may become. That
self is authentic because it is related to facticity and possibility. It is not
something schematic or "pulled out of the air," as it were. In a way of
saying it which existentialists would not like, there are guidelines, as it
were, in facticity and possibility which point the way to authenticity in
being-for-itself. So there are some real roots in the individual for his being-
for-himself. His becoming what he *wants* to become need not be mere
caprice; indeed, it should not be. Anything of this sort would be inauthentic
and, therefore, far removed from what those with existentialist leanings
would want for the student.

e. If existentialism is true or if it is to be taken seriously by a teacher,
then it says something further about selfhood which applies to both student
and teacher, and may even imply something about the climate of the school.
This is that it points out that each one of us is inescapably and incurably
anxious. *Anxiety* is a persisting and perennial characteristic of life as a
person. If this is so, education needs to take it fully into account. Should
this be done, school and its activities cannot be taken lightly as a day-by-
day affair in which many things happen, some pleasant and some not.
Schooling must rather be seen as a bringing together of people, some in the
position of guides and others in the position of supposed followers, but all
having deeply serious concern always with them and not easily allayed, if
at all. If existentialism is to be taken seriously, each person in the school
setting is caught in a deep anxiety not in any way dependent upon the
outcome of circumstances about which he may have real worry. This anxiety may be tied in part to the facticity of one's life. It may also make the
world seem to be alien and unfriendly. The seeming activism of other
people appears to be so carefree and to transcend so easily all such unre-
solved anxiety.

It may indeed be for most of us that schools do not appear to be filled
with people who are so deeply anxious and living in dread of life. Nevertheless this does not mean that this view need not be taken seriously by us as a
real possibility. Possibly it is because we are often so active and preoccupied at a superficial level that anxiety seems to be so foreign and even also
for this same reason be submerged beneath the level of consciousness.
Were we to be less active and to live and think more deeply, possibly this
somber view would not appear so out of line or distorted. Possibly we
would have more occasion to face an anxiety which is real, and by facing it
have new dimensions of life open to us, however unwelcome they first may
appear.

f. For the Christian existentialist, as distinguished from the atheistic, what the student may become and the authenticity of his self-for-itself are not removed from the relation of the self to God. Authenticity in selfhood has connection with God who may be thought of, at the least, as Ultimate Being. If facticity and possibility of selfhood mark out the borders of authenticity, so too in a more fundamental way does Ultimate Being mark out these borders. For facticity and possibility, having their roots eventually in Ultimate Being, when the self-in-itself becomes authentically the self-for-itself, it is moving in harmony with Ultimate Being. It may also be that it is moving into a "new being" or a new kind of being, because it is finding its ground in Ultimate Being as over against the transitoriness of the "accident" of its own facticity. It goes without saying, of course, that relation to God as an additional component of the authenticity of the self-for-itself is not granted by atheistic existentialists.

Another strain in existentialism which must not be overlooked in relation to education is the tragic element. This does have to do with the outlook of the student, but it also bears upon a more inclusive view of the school as an institution. This tragic element we infer from the attention existentialists give to death and nothingness.

Quite antithetical to it, most commonly, school is regarded as a happy place, at least not a completely unhappy one, where *life* is going on constantly. When something untoward or even tragic occurs, we pass it over as quickly as possible as "just one of those things." Unlike the existentialist, we do not commonly think of the tragic as just as much a part of life as the enoyable or inviting. It is foreign to us to think of schooling as containing the tragic element as well as a life which is inviting and fulfilling.

But as has been seen, the existentialist holds that death is part and parcel of life. We are constantly faced by the possibility of death as a part of the facticity of our own beings. And for existentialists who are atheists this is also the constant threat of nothingness. All the time we are living, we are also dying a little. In the more austere view of some existentialists such being as we have is all the time at the brink at which it may fall away into nothingness.

At the least, if true, this means for education that we should face this tragic element more openly and directly. In our teaching and learning we should recognize that there is tragedy in life, in the lives of all of us at least at some time. Are we really educating for all the living people have to do unless we do educate for tragedy? Since long before the existentialists appeared on the scene, some of our great literature has held this side of life up to us to be fully digested. And an education which takes existentialism at all seriously must do the same.

One further theme must be taken up, and this one somewhat more critically. It is existentialism's insistence upon individualism. Just before drawing these inferences concerning education, we called attention to this

individualism. In almost everything we have said in these inferences, implying an existentialist education, we have been talking primarily about the
individual people involved in the educational institution. Facticity is a
characteristic of individual selfhood. So also is possibility. The individual is
a self-in-itself, as an individual. While authenticity is by no means limited
to selfhood, there is this emphasis: the individual must live a life which is
authentic. Also, the individual self is deeply involved in anxiety. And to the
extent that he is facing life authentically, the individual is under the constant threat of tragedy and death.

It should not take too much imaginative effort to understand that the
existentialist is suspicious of any kind of "groupiness" or activism which
will shield the individual from these elements. He understands them as
essentials of life really lived and not to be escaped. Life must be faced at its
deepest and possibly starkest levels or it is superficial and we are just going
through the motions of living.

But without arguing against any of this rough facing of the "realities" of
living, we can still question "Is individualism as completely defensible as
the existentialists make it?" Is the individual this completely shut off to
himself with "no windows"? We can ask these questions seriously and still
be on the side of the existentialist in not wanting the individual to be
absorbed in a group of some kind which will make his life superficial.

As individuals we are all conceived and born in a social matrix in which
we also learn and grow, at least for a time. When we set ourselves over
against a social group in a rejecting spirit, we still have some relation
beyond ourselves as individuals, even to the society we reject. Is it not at
least conceivable, to go further, that a group life is possible in which there
is freedom and reciprocity which does not thwart the individual? Without
the individual being absorbed and shielded at a superficial level, can there
not be a reciprocity even within the school on which the individual may
thrive? And may he not thrive in this setting without in any way being
separated from the deep meaning of his existence as an individual?

XXIV

Language Analysis
and Education

A. *Sources of Language Analysis*

B. *Language Analysis and How We Think*

C. *Metaphysics is Out*

D. *Is Philosophy of Education Possible?*

E. *Values of Language Analysis*

It may be that the term *language analysis* is the most narrowly specific
name which can be used for the philosophy with which this chapter is
concerned. Two other names which could be used are *philosophical analysis* and *logical analysis*. The more specific name has been chosen because
language analysis as a term makes very clear the focus of this philosophy.

In the attempt to say enough to help the student understand what this
kind of analytic philosophy may have to say about education, several
subjects will be discussed, usually with some brevity. First of all, the
sources of language analysis will be discussed and some of its chief exponents named. This will be followed by a kind of inductive engagement of
the reader in the kind of thinking which language analysis does. Then the

very central subject of this philosophy will be taken up, namely, that it finds, in the nature of the case, that metaphysics has no legitimate place in philosophy. We turn then, in the fourth place, to consider the question, "Is philosophy of education possible for language analysis?" Also, the related question is included here as to what kind of an education it is if language analysis can have a philosophy of education. The last and closing part of the chapter is an attempt to evaluate language analysis as a philosophy.

A. SOURCES OF LANGUAGE ANALYSIS

The name most commonly associated with language analysis when it is considered as a definite movement in philosophy is that of Ludwig Wittgenstein (1889–1951). However, there are others who have had influence on analysis, the respective members of this group viewing the functions of analysis in differing ways. They by no means, therefore, constitute a harmony of opinion as to what the chief functions of analysis are.

Wittgenstein exerted the influence that he did chiefly because of his *Tractatus Logico-Philosophicus*,[1] first published in 1921 and translated into English the following year. Wittgenstein's academic appointment in England no doubt had much to do with the growth of analysis there. In 1929 he was appointed to the faculty at Cambridge University and served with distinction over a period of about two decades. His primary concern with language in his earlier years was to determine those requirements it must meet in order accurately to describe elements and structures of nature. His later concern was more with language itself than with its function of mirroring the world. It was with the limits of language and the kinds of questions that language can sensibly pose and answer.

Bertrand Russell, the great British philosopher and mathematician,[2] was one of Wittgenstein's teachers. In this way and others, Russell has been involved in language analysis. But since Russell's most trusted language is mathematics, his willingness to deal with verbal symbols is no doubt tinged with some condescension as well as necessity. Condescension, because mathematics is for him a language par excellence in which precision of meaning can really be expressed; verbal languages can do this only with great difficulty, if at all. Necessity, because the vast majority of people are not mathematicians who can begin to understand what Russell's preferred language is all about. Most people are creatures of words, and if there is to be some degree of precision in the use of words as well as some sense as to the limits of any kind of language, then verbal language must receive attention however tempting the luxury and exclusiveness of mathematical language.

[1] Edited by A. J. Ayre; New York: The Humanities Press, 1961.
[2] Cf. pp. 284–285.

G. E. Moore (1873–1958) was at least generally influential in contributing to the rise of language analysis by his vigorous opposition to idealism. The philosophy of idealism[3] was one of the temptations to the side in England away from what the analysts have considered the true task of philosophy. In contrast to the romanticized metaphysics of idealism, Moore was a man of "common sense" who dealt with "real" objects. Moore was a neo-realist[4] and, therefore, oversimplified our way of knowing objects in nature, as the critical realists[5] were at pains to point out. But it was this very assiduous insistence upon objects as real things which indirectly at least called philosophy in England back to a use of language which was more within its allegedly proper limits. Moore felt that he knew what an individual man with a body is and could talk about people in the particular. But when the idealist discoursed about the self or a soul, this was outside his ken and probably nothing but nonsense. When some idealists would propose to say that time is unreal, he was very quick to retort with some impatience, "Then what is to keep me from arguing that I had lunch before breakfast and breakfast after lunch?" The "outside" world of nature was very real and for Moore it was absurd to use language to speculate about things which were not manifestly existent in this world. It was the proper function of philosophy and, therefore, the proper function of language to deal with things which exist in the here and now, subject to our observation.

To speak of A. J. Ayre (1910–   ) is to mention one of the leading language analysts of today who is regarded by his peers both with criticism and appreciation. His *Language, Truth and Logic*[6], first published in 1936 and since 1952 in paperback in the United States, is a kind of classic of the field of language analysis. Other present leaders are Gilbert Ryle (1900–   ) of Oxford and W. V. Quine (1908–   ) of Harvard.

As this chapter progresses it should become evident that language analysis constitutes a real revolution both in philosophy and philosophy of education. It is just as much a revolution as is existentialism when viewed in the wide scope of the history of philosophy. Both existentialism and language analysis by their character defy being systematized as other older philosophies were. They have not only refused to build systems, but have found it impossible to follow the schema of philosophy traditionally conceived. At the same time there are elements in language analysis which are old as well as apparently new. For example, Immanuel Kant[7] was very analytical in his writing, and for the most part very cautious about what he affirmed. In the history of the discipline such philosophers—but few of his

[3] Cf. pp. 139–141.
[4] Cf. p. 266.
[5] Cf. pp. 266–267.
[6] New York: Dover Publications, 1952.
[7] Cf. pp. 128–132.

magnitude—anticipated the spirit of language analysis if they did not also put forward specifically some of its concerns. There is a sense, therefore, in which philosophic analysis may be said to be something old and something new.

B. LANGUAGE ANALYSIS AND HOW WE THINK

That men very commonly misunderstand one another because of ambiguity or confusion in discourse is well known. Mr. X may intend one particular meaning of a word but when I hear him I may understand the same word in an entirely different way. The same may also be said about sentences or statements comprised, of course, of several words. One meaning is often intended but an entirely different meaning is heard.

These observations are not only overly simple in relation to the task to which philosophical analysis is directed, they are also very innocent. For the philosophical analysis of language is not only directed to precision in communication. Also, and what is more important, it considers precision as exceedingly important in determining the kinds of statements for which meaning is possible. It is not primarily devoted to making meanings clear. In fact, language analysis is philosophical because it is concerned to sort out those concepts which can have meaning from those which cannot.

We might say that there are "picture" words, to start with one example. The word "cat" is supposed to refer to a kind of animal that exists in nature. It may refer to a particular cat or to the entire species of cats. If a particular cat is at hand while you and I are talking together and I point to it, also saying "that cat," there would be little likelihood of your not understanding that I mean that particular cat. But if we are talking about cats and I say, what would appear unnecessary, "All cats have four legs," there can be a problem of accuracy, strange as it may seem. Both of us have observed enough cats to know, we assume for practical purposes, that they all have four legs. But neither of us knows all cats that exist. Neither of us knows all cats that have been nor all that will be. So if we push such a "picture" statement to its limits, we have to admit that no one is in a position to assert that all cats have four legs. We have to be content with some modified general statement something like this: "All normal cats which have been known to exist to this time have had four legs."

It would appear fairly plain that such "picture" or descriptive statements should be quite easy to make and also to make accurately. But the philosophical analysis of language discloses that such precision in matching our conceptions with what exists in nature is by no means simple. Especially is this so when the conception is a general one making an assertion about some alleged class of objects in nature.

If we do attempt to make assertions about the existence of objects or some characteristic which we allege they have, the task of precision in conceptions becomes much clearer, if not easier. Suppose that instead of saying "All animals have four legs," I introduce an "if" which leaves the question of their existence open. Then my assertion becomes "If all animals have four legs." By itself this doesn't say very much. It is not even a complete sentence, but it does provide me a basis for other statements having precision because they do not raise the question of existence and existing characteristics. *If* all animals have four legs, I can assert that a given object or species has four legs because it is an animal. Because the "if" lays down as a condition a characteristic of animals, namely, that they have four legs, I can state that since a cat is an animal, it has four legs. The statement is true regardless of its correspondence to fact because of the "if."

As far as it goes, this is very similar, actually the same but approached in a different manner, as deductive logic already discussed in considering idealism and realism.[8] The somewhat new element here is that philosophical analysis is very sure about logical statements as compared to descriptive statements. Of course, the logical statements must conform to the demands of logic. But so long as they do this they do not need to be verified, for example as to their existence. The fact of the case does not make any difference in the truth of the statement "Since cats are animals, they have four legs," because it is preceded by the conditional clause, "If all animals have four legs."

This may begin to point the way to the kinds of uses of words or the formation of concepts which are acceptable to language analysis. Of course, permitted and excluded examples are almost without limit, so it is useless to attempt a survey of the field as it were. But even so it may well be in order to look at some others.

Statements which express very strong feelings may be made to be understood, but can they be held to be "true" according to this way of thinking? I may say with some emotion that modern art is ugly. But what is this statement more than an expression of conviction or prejudice? First of all, in speaking of modern art, I am taking in a very large area to say nothing of the differentiations in different kinds of modern art, so that the subject of the sentence is most vague and does not describe anything with any degree of accuracy. Similar questions are involved in the meaning of the word "ugly." But what is more important is that it attributes a quality or condition to something which originates only in my own feelings. Can it, therefore, say anything which has precise meaning for anyone else but myself? At least it cannot become a descriptive statement which can carry the weight of truth for all people.

The example just used is both an emotive statement and a value judg-

[8] Cf. pp. 170–175 and 283–285.

ment and, therefore, it may serve to indicate how language analysis looks at other somewhat similar statements about which great controversy may wage. There are some people who have very strong feelings in opposition to modern art. But it is doubtful that they are nearly as numerous as those who feel deeply about some other value judgments, particularly those commonly made regarding morals or ethics. "Modern art is ugly," excluded as it is by language analysis as a meaningful statement, is mild as compared to "It is wrong to steal." Is it to be understood that such a time-honored convention as respect for the property of others cannot be put into the form of a statement which can be given a clean bill of health by language analysis? First of all, it cannot be made very precise. What is the meaning of "wrong"? And what is meant by "stealing"? Is it "just borrowing" something which may never be returned? Is it petty larceny? Is it grand larceny? Is it all of these? But what is more important and difficult, how can it be established that this is a principle that everyone must follow? Is there in it any concept that can be said to be meaningful in a precise way? Is it not another value judgment which has its origin in the preferences of some person or group? And being such it is also likely to be a statement to which a great burden of strong feeling is attached.

It might be said for language analysis then without too great hazard of strong contradiction that there are only two kinds of statements which can be said to be "true." (1) There are logical statements which are always set within the "if" or "if-and-only-if" condition. These can be true if flawlessly constructed because they deal only with relations when certain conditions prevail and do not say anything about matters of fact. If they do speak of matters of fact to which they correspond, it is quite incidental and not at all primary to the statements.

(2) There are also some statements about matters of fact which may be confirmed by reference to the facts with which these statements deal. The more direct and immediate the confirmation can be, as in pointing to "that cat," for example, the more acceptable the confirmation. If in remote terms the confirmation is dependent upon reports by "all" scientists who have dealt with a certain fact, the confirmation is less satisfactory but because of it the statement about the matter of fact may be accepted as a "protocol" statement. Still more remote, confirmation based on what historians may say about a matter of fact in the past is still less acceptable, although it may be the only confirmation available to us.

It may be said, therefore, for most language analysts that *logical statements* may be *verified* by checking that they proceed flawlessly from the if-and-only-if condition. It may also be said that statements about *matters of fact* may be *confirmed* to a degree. But the more immediate or direct the observation of the matter of fact and the more free it is from generality, then the more acceptable the statement.

C. METAPHYSICS IS OUT

According to language analysis, metaphysical statements do not constitute a proper use of language. This is an important and significant negation because a good portion of philosophy has concerned itself with alleged metaphysical truth. We will not quibble as to whether this is a majority or minority concern in the sweep of the history of philosophy. It almost goes without saying that metaphysics has been the major concern of many philsophers. But language analysis rules it out as not a legitimate subject about which to use language. And, therefore, it is not a legitimate concern of philosophy.

Why is this the case? The assumption, or somewhat more strongly, the established conclusion of language analysis is that language can only be used legitimately to deal with that which can be confirmed or is verifiable. This is almost the same as saying language can only be used properly to formulate statements about objects which can be observed, or as will be shown later, *conceivably* may be observed. It is also to say that language can be used to formulate statements which can be logically verified. In other words, language only makes sense when it deals with that which can be confirmed or verified. When it presumes to deal with that which cannot be so checked for precision, it makes *nonsense* rather than sense, so it is alleged.

The statement may be made that there are mountains in the area of the South Pole. In connection with such a statement, the necessary observations can be made to verify the statement and confirm that the language used is serving a proper purpose. It is making a statement, which refers to a fact in nature, and as nearly as language can be made to correspond to fact, the language of this statement does do this.

Before we had space vehicles and the necessary photographic equipment, a similar statement could be made about mountains on the "backside" of the moon. This is somewhat different from the example just given because although then not capable of confirmation actually, it could conceivably be confirmed at such later time when man had developed the necessary equipment.

The exclusion of metaphysical statements by language analysis is made because such statements can neither be confirmed nor are they conceivably capable of confirmation.

It will be recalled that idealism and spiritual realism[9] have both been committed to what their exponents have believed to be metaphysically true. By metaphysics as used here is meant reference to a reality which transcends the natural order. Language analysts do not consider alleged truths

---

[9] Cf. pp. 147–162 and 280–283.

about nature to be metaphysical because they deal with some reality, but rather they are considered descriptive statements based on observation and confirmed thereby.

If we take a simpler example, harking back to idealism,[10] we can show quite concretely how language analysis excludes alleged metaphysical truth. Many idealists find a peculiar mystery in the fact that our perceptions are able to yield us qualities in consciousness, such as red or green, the direct equivalents of which are rather difficult to locate in nature. True enough there are light waves emanating from nature which yield these colors but where are the actual qualities other than being in our minds? The idealists have answered this mystery metaphysically by saying that there is a Mind behind nature which writes into nature, as it were, the qualities which our perceptions "read out." We have qualities of red and green in our consciousness because, to use more common terminology, God writes such things as reds and greens into nature. This is one of the ways that some metaphysicians have gone about saying that there is a God.

But all of this is beyond the region of legitimate philosophy, chiefly because it is not a proper use of language, according to language analysis. There is no way, analysts contend, that we can confirm such statements as are either explicit or implicit in such an argument. "There is a God," and, "God creates such qualities as red and green." These are statements for which there is no confirmation. What is more, it is not conceivable that there can be any way in which such statements can be confirmed.

Therefore, granting that these examples are representative, metaphysics has no legitimate place in philosophy. And the use of language to make metaphysical statements results in nonsense rather than truth.

Possibly a word should be added about poetry, metaphor, or myth as ways of using language which are not descriptive but nevertheless may tell us something about reality beyond nature. It could be contended, in fact frequently has been, that such poetic statements may convey insights or revelations which tell man something about reality beyond nature. But such statements also are excluded by language analysis and, of course, the metaphysical reality to which they allegedly point. If a particular metaphor or myth contains in it descriptive statements about matters of natural fact, these may be true if they can be confirmed. If according to the biblical record, for example, Moses saw a burning bush, a statement that "This is a burning bush," if his witness is accurate, can be a proper use of language. But it is an improper use of language to assume that there is a "deeper" level in the language about the burning bush which points to some reality beyond the actual burning of the bush. All proper use of language is for the making of statements which are formulas or descriptions and not poetry. Indeed, language can be used for poetic expression but such use can in no

10 Cf. pp. 164–165.

way be alleged to tell us something about a supposed reality beyond nature. The function of language is to make statements which are true because they can be confirmed or verified as true.

It would seem fair to say that language analysis greatly limits the range of philosophy. Philosophy can yet deal with history of philosophy because there is a history of certain men and what they thought, a good bit of which can be confirmed, within reason. However, a good bit of it is foolishness because it has been devoted to subjects with which philosophy cannot deal. As has just been said somewhat fully, philosophy cannot include metaphysics. Philosophy cannot deal with value because value statements are emotive, coming from the subjective judgments or prejudices of those who make them. The great exception seems to be that philosophy can deal with epistemology to the extent that it devotes itself to statements of knowledge to determine their *verifiability* as accurate and precise. This would seem virtually to limit the legitimate range of epistemology to logic. This is, possibly the reason that the terms "logical analysis," "philosophical analysis," and "language analysis" seem to be used almost interchangeably.

D. IS PHILOSOPHY OF EDUCATION POSSIBLE?

Language analysis for the most part questions the legitimacy of philosophy of education as a discipline. Of what is it comprised if there is such a field? Can there be general philosophical matter applicable to education, or from which educational practice can be legitimately deduced?

Metaphysics being rejected as having no legitimate place in philosophy, there cannot very well be a metaphysics of education. And even if metaphysics were legitimate, there is no reason to assume that any particular kind of educational practice can be deduced from some particular metaphysics. Value considerations are very shaky when under the scrutiny of the principle of confirmation. So how can value theory have a legitimate place in philosophy of education? And accordingly, how can the objectives of education be a component of philosophy of education? These are actually value statements couched in educational terms. They, therefore, can neither be confirmed nor proposed as broadly applicable in a way which could govern the direction in which education should move. Epistemology, as a general theory of knowledge not tied down to specific logical considerations, can scarcely claim a place in philosophy of education. If it is alleged that there is a connection between theory of knowledge and theory of learning, this will not be granted by analysis. General theory of learning has no more legitimacy than general theory of knowledge. It is only as particular confirmable statements about learning are possible that anything at all similar to philosophy can be conceived as having a place in philosophy of education.

This almost sweeps clean the area which has usually been claimed by philosophy of education. It is cluttered by nothing but generalities, mostly all without confirmation. And if there were any truth in these generalities, there is nothing to guarantee that guidance for educational practice can be deduced from them. The effect of language analysis upon philosophy of education as it has commonly been conceived is, therefore, largely one of deflation, if not demolition.

Another approach which may be explored is whether there can be a philosophy of education comprised of principles derived from various sources. If so, philosophy of education could be equated with a general theory of education. In addition to the history of educational thought and practice, there are a few sciences focusing on man which conceivably could be the source of ideas if not principles which as a composite could conceivably comprise a general theory of education. Among these sciences of man are physiology, psychology, and sociology.

From Plato to the present, there have been those who have put forward both in writing and practice their thoughts as to what education should be. Although there are, of course, conflicting views which would have to be resolved or from which preferential selections would need to be made, it is conceivable that this history of thought and practice could provide a fund of theory about education which might constitute philosophy of education as a general theory of education.

Also, the science of psychology has allegedly learned many things about man and, having acquired at least some of the discipline of a science, can be fairly precise about these findings. Those of these findings which are relevant could also be poured into the blend of general principles which would comprise a general theory of education. There is even a branch of this science, known as child psychology, which supposedly has sufficiently documented a certain knowledge about children which would be especially applicable to the lower reaches of education.

The older science of physiology is supposedly able to tell us those relevant facts about the bodily life of people which would be a helpful part of a general theory of education. In the same way the newer science of sociology can tell us in disciplined terms considerably more precise than common sense how individuals act in groups as well as the nature of groups and how they function. Since a very large portion of education is an institutional affair in which groups, if not masses of individual people are involved, sociology, it could be assumed, has a fund of relevant knowledge which would help comprise a general theory of education.

Two observations are clearly in order at this point. The first is that as a matter of fact schools and colleges of education have for years offered courses in educational psychology and educational sociology. This is not to mention courses in special methods of teaching particular subjects as well as courses in the administration of education. All of these would apparently constitute a general theory of education.

The other observation is that such a general theory of education is not at all what philosophers of education have conceived the discipline of philosophy of education to be. So a disparity, if not a direct conflict, results from this exploration. Philosophy of education and such a general theory of education are two different things, according to philosophers of education. But according to language analysis, there can be no philosophy of education as educational philosophers have commonly conceived it. There is question enough as to the validity of a general theory of education. Is it sufficiently confirmed and applicable with the kind of unusual inclusiveness that can make it a guide of any significance for educational practice?[11]

One thing wrong with philosophy of education, which is far less exacting a criticism than those bearing on its verifiability, is that it always envisions the stereotype of a school, a teacher, classes of students, different subject matter areas, etc. Is this necessarily so for all education? If there can be a philosophy of education, must it not be much broader and much more flexible about what education is and its institutional forms, if any?

This opens the door to another possibility for philosophy of education which is much less inclusive than the common conception of it, also than a general theory of education, and is, therefore, capable of an exactitude which is valid within a limited range of application. This is the consideration of models—models, not because they are ideals, but because they are constituted by modes which can have some application. The application would not be general and inclusive but rather limited to those circumstances in which the same conditions prevail as in the model.

An attempt will be made to exemplify a model as a legitimate form of philosophizing in education for language analysis. In doing this, we will lean heavily upon Kenneth B. Henderson's article, "A Logical Model for Conceptualizing and Other Related Activities."[12] This is a model for teaching concepts and possibly also the processes of conceptualizing, generalizing, and abstracting.

First of all in the teaching of a concept, the context must be taken fully into account because it may otherwise change the meaning of the name given the concept. If the context is a gasoline filling station, for example, the term *gas* is most likely to mean gasoline. But if the context is a chemistry laboratory, the term *gas* will very likely mean a substance distinguished from a solid or a liquid in its form.

The teacher will be at great pains in teaching a concept to make sure that the students associate the same meaning with the term used for the

[11] Cf. D. J. O'Connor, *An Introduction to the Philosophy of Education*. New York: Philosophical Library, 1957.
[12] *Educational Theory, XIII*, no. 4 (October, 1963), 277–284.

concept that the teacher has in mind.[13] There are *denotative* concepts, that is, those the terms for which point to a particular object or a particular class of objects. A *singular* denotative concept could be exemplified by the term "Washington, D.C." There is only one of these and there can be little confusion as to what is denoted as long as the student has other needed information about this particular city.

However, there are also denotative concepts which point to a class or "set." An example is "President of the United States." As we all know, there have been thirty-six presidents, as of Lyndon B. Johnson's period in office. This term, "President of the United States," refers to a class including thirty-six individual cases. Consequently, the term can be used to refer to all members of the class or to one of the members. Therefore, the point of reference in using the term for the concept needs to be made very clear and precise.

In addition to denotative concepts, there are also *connotative* concepts. Connotative concepts are those the terms for which point to a characteristic or condition of a thing which itself is pointed to by a denotative term. "Lives in the White House" would be a connotative term which could validly accompany the denotative term, "President of the United States." To keep the model more simple, we will refer only to connotative terms which we know or can confirm. For, as Henderson points out, there are also many connotative concepts such as "ugly," the meaning for which cannot be made very precise.

Denotative concepts can be taught by pointing to the object to which the term for the concept points. Connotative concepts, the meaning of which can be readily known, can be taught in the same way. Now conceptualizing can be taught by relating these two kinds of terms precisely so that they refer to the actuality denoted which can be confirmed as actually the case. For example, "A president of the United States lives in the White House."

Henderson's model for teaching concepts is more complex than it is represented here. In addition to including connotative terms, the meanings of which are not precisely known, he also deals with generalizing and abstracting as uses of concepts which can be taught according to the model he proposes.

What is important for our purposes is that he proposes a model for the teaching of concepts which he is convinced will function successfully for all concepts when followed with care. And this is a kind of philosophizing about education, or more precisely about teaching, to which language analysis is more likely to give a degree of consent than any other we have considered.

We are inclined to surmise even so that language analysts will rest easier

[13] Cf. *ibid.*, 279.

with one example of teaching which accomplishes its end with precision and clarity without generalizing upon it. The trouble with a model is that it purports to be itself inclusive of a class or set, in this case the teaching of concepts, all members of which can be dealt with effectively if this model is followed. It is probably even more precise, at least more cautious, to consider this one instance of the teaching of concepts as good or reasonably so and to be hesitant about generalizing upon it as having significance generally for one kind of teaching however particular and small in relation to the whole of education.

E. VALUES OF LANGUAGE ANALYSIS

Strictly speaking, is it possible to be consistent with language analysis and at the same time talk about its values as a philosophy? Even though it may result only in "emotive" statements, we will proceed now to speak of the values of this philosophy, both those which appear to be of worth and those which make it a limited system which would seem to comprise less than a philosophy or philosophy of education.

The single-mindedness of language analysis in striving for statements which are accurately confirmed as describing matters of fact is most commendable and much to be desired. In the same single-minded way language analysis demands statements which are logically verifiable. In both of these single-minded efforts *precision* can be seen as a prime value which is of great worth.

The more one becomes bored with run-of-the-mill conversation and also public address, occasionally being almost painfully excluded from it because of the way in which words are thrown together so as to say virtually nothing, the more he must come to appreciate the enterprise of the language analyst in striving for *precision*. Maybe it is a visionary norm, but it would seem that the human phenomenon of using words should rise to a level somewhere above the chatter of monkeys. Words should constitute more than a communication which is predominantly emotional or activistic and unconsciously designed to effect "togetherness," antagonism, persuasion by the impact of propaganda, covert grasping of power, the enclosing of the in-group more securely, the excluding of the out-group more disdainfully, or some other similar desiderata of questionable value. At least language analysis respects words as signs and tries to make these signs signify without ambiguity.

The problem, however, is whether it is possible to achieve such exacting precision in making language really significant as this philosophy tries to do. Rightly or wrongly, man is concerned about many more matters than can be *factually confirmed* or *logically verified* as language analysis wants them to be. This is one of the reasons why philosophy has on many occasions been devoted to subjects which language analysis cannot and does not consider to be a legitimate part of philosophy.

Is it not true that language analysis has become so narrowly concerned about language and other similar symbols that it has excluded the life of man from philosophy, or better still, reduced philosophy to a level at which it deals with symbols that have little to do with living people? Of course, by the nature of the case language analysis cannot answer this question. For such answers as would be possible can neither be adequately confirmed nor verified.

Even so some men do want to know *how they know*. They are not just satisfied to know how to confirm some matter of fact or verify some matter of logical relation. They want to know how an apparently nonmental world can somehow get into the mind of man, for example, in a pictorial form, to mention one among many other forms. And how can this picture in the mind be so interpreted as it may be in a work of art, to use a further example, so that it conveys meaning not at all to be found in the picture itself nor in the portion of the world the picture reflects? It is a meaning which could not be touched by the factual confirmation of language analysis at all, yet for many it is still a legitimate meaning.

In a similar way some men want to know what kind of world man is living in. And by this they do not mean only a *confirmation* of language symbols depicting a certain aggregation of facts in the world. Also, some men want to know about values even though statements about them may be little more than subjective and emotive judgments. They want to know how and why we have values. And they want to know if there are some general theories about value by which we may *evaluate* values and also sets of values. But the door of inquisitiveness about such things would seem to be closed by language analysis. Man may want to look into such things, but since it is not possible for precise language to represent this, they are meaningless subjects and, therefore, foolish as judged by language analysis.

To turn from defensive criticism and become slightly aggressive in criticizing language analysis, something of further significance can be said about the use of language. This argument could be extended to other forms of expression but we will restrict our remarks only to language. This is to criticize language analysis by saying that there are poetic uses of language in which the truth is in the *poetry* and not in the *literal language* which comprises it. This being the case, it is a truth which cannot be *confirmed* by pointing to matters of fact nor *verified* by being checked for its logical accuracy. This kind of poetic expression is, of course, in poetic writing itself. But it is also in metaphor as used in writing which does not have a strict poetic form. It is in myth. It is in drama, and in much of drama there may be no factual or logical truth at all. Yet in all these forms of expression which may generally be denoted as poetic, many persons find *meaning* expressed which is *meaning* because it conveys something about the world or life as it is lived which they have experienced just as much as factual confirmation or logical verification is experienced.

It is granted that within the framework of language analysis to affirm such poetry as meaningful is to open the door to *meaninglessness* and, therefore, to foolishness. Yet it is contended here that the narrow confines of language analysis exclude a whole world of meaning which this philosophy has not yet dreamed of.

PART SEVEN

CONCLUSION

XXV

Building a Philosophy of Education

A. *The Aims of Education*

B. *The Function of the School Among Social Institutions*

C. *Theory of Value*

D. *Theory of Reality*

E. *Theory of Knowledge*

I have chosen to bring this book to its conclusion by trying to analyze the structure of a philosophy of education without begging questions concerning the substance of it, i.e., any more than problems of form and the integrity of the author make it necessary. Unlike the two previous editions, I will not attempt a forthright presentation of the substance of the writer's philosophy. Explanation of this deletion will be made later.[1]

The task, therefore, of this chapter is to outline what seems to me to be

---

The material in this chapter was first delivered at the University of Pennsylvania as one of the Brumbough Lectures in the summer of 1956 and appears in Frederick C. Bruber, *Foundations of Education*. Philadelphia: University of Pennsylvania Press, 1957.

[1] See pp. 495–496.

the necessary form which a philosophy of education should take. While this involves some limiting presuppositions, I believe it will leave the student free to determine the substance of his own philosophy.

In trying to advise how to build a philosophy of education, I will not be able, of course, to hide my own philosophy, nor would I want to do this. My primary concern will be to engage the reader in philosophizing about education, in the hope that in so doing I may be of some help to him in building or refining his own educational philosophy.

I shall deal with five subjects in the following order: the aims of education, the function of the school among social institutions, theory of value, theory of reality, and theory of knowledge.

A. THE AIMS OF EDUCATION

It is common when teachers, administrators, boards of education, parents' groups, or groups of citizens start to think about education, that they begin with objectives. In trying to be responsible about the work of the school, it makes sense for them to ask, "Just what is it that education is trying to do, or should be trying to do? What do we wish to accomplish in the elementary grades, or in the secondary school?" And now in this day of the burgeoning of the college there are many voices heard in periodicals and books asking similar questions about the college.

In 1938 there was released a document intended to be of national significance which attempted this sort of thing. It was the statement of the Educational Policies Commission entitled *The Purposes of Education in American Democracy*.[2] It set forward four major objectives for American education: self-realization, human relationship, economic efficiency, and civic responsibility. The attempt was made to elaborate each of these in terms of respective sets of specific objectives which alleged to constitute each of the four broader objectives. Unfortunately, this publication was conceived only at the level of aims and was guided by the intention to build a statement of objectives which would be acceptable to all segments of the body politic. These conditions made it necessarily superficial and resulted unwittingly in the simultaneous attempt to say too much and too little.

Aims are often stated in terms of the skills it is expected that the pupil should have mastered at a given grade level and also the knowledges which he should possess. At this stage of theorizing about education—to my chagrin those who engage in it are quite free in calling it a philosophy—we can have heated discussions among ourselves and controversies in the press as to whether Johnny can do what he should be able to do and why not—not, because usually by our judgments he cannot. Nevertheless, there are two justifications for the level of educational thinking which is con-

[2] Washington, D.C.: Educational Policies Commission.

cerned to pinpoint aims. The first is that, if it is carefully done and fully grounded in more fundamental thinking, it can give helpful guidance to classroom teaching. The second justification is that, if it is undertaken with responsibility and intellectual penetration, it will disclose the need for philosophizing of another sort. By this I mean to say that to think responsibly about the aims of education may lead to the recognition that aims cannot just be pulled out of a hat, but must be derived from more fundamental and general thinking about value, reality, and knowledge.

I want to go on to say something about these more fundamental subjects, from which I believe light can be gained for the formulation of educational aims. But before I do, I would like to discuss another way of philosophizing about the school which is somewhat parallel to the formulation of objectives.

B. THE FUNCTION OF THE SCHOOL AMONG SOCIAL INSTITUTIONS

What is education all about? What should education try to do? These are questions which can and should be asked collectively as well as individually. To philosophize concerning aims in a social sense, and not just in terms of what the school should do for the individual, is to ask for a rationale and reason for being of the school as an institution. This is not an uncommon theme in the literature of educational philosophy. Plato in *The Republic* considered, at least speculatively, the possibility of taking chilen away from the corrupt society which had given them birth, and in some separate place, by means of an expurgated literature giving mankind a fresh start through a "proper" education, and also thereby building an ideal State.

John Amos Comenius, in the seventeenth century, regarded education as equal to physical procreation as a necessity in making man. He had come across reports of instances in which human infants had been reared by animals and as a result followed a pattern of life closer to that of the animals with which they had lived than to human patterns. He argued, therefore, that the culture of man has to lend form to the human potentialities with which we are born, in order for us to be men. And this is the task of education. This is why he charcterized education as "a true forging place of men."[3]

John Dewey, in our century, argued that the school exists to provide a special environment for the formative years of human life. Such a special environment is needed in part because civilization is too complex to provide an economical setting for learning. A special environment such as the school

[3] John Amos Comenius, *The Great Didactic*. Translated and edited by M. W. Keatinge; London: Adam and Charles Black, 1907. Part II, p. 228.

can also eliminate the unworthy features of human society as it is. And further, the school as a special environment can provide a balance of influence which society itself will not give, providing greater breadth from other cultures and avoiding parochialism.[4]

Theodore M. Greene, writing in the Fifty-Fourth Yearbook of The National Society for the Study of Education, tried to work out a division of labor among the institutions of society according to which the school is the "mind" of the body politic, the State being the "sword and shield," the family the "heart," the Church the "soul," and business the "hands."[5] Most readers would readily agree with Dr. Greene that these are risky metaphors. Do not other institutions than the school serve at least on occasion thinking or guiding functions such as the "mind" of society, if not very frequently? Is it possible to assign divisions of labor to the different institutions as neatly as Dr. Greene does?

The big question is, of course, On what grounds can functions or tasks be assigned to the school or any other institution? Can we say that we should think of the school in this or that particular way, and just leave it there? Or, must we not have some validation for assigning functions?

It seems to me that we come up against the same necessity here as in the attempt to formulate aims. We cannot say that aims should be thus and so, or that the function of education as an institution is such and such, except quite superficially, until our thinking has gone more deeply and taken on a larger perspective in which to state aims and assign institutional functions. This more profound thinking and larger perspective, it should be reiterated, will come from responsible thought concerning value, reality, and knowledge. It is to the first of these three that we will now turn.

C. THEORY OF VALUE

My argument is that responsible thinking about the aims of education necessarily involves more than casual consideration of the value aspect of life and existence. Such consideration may proceed to state a catalogue of values or even a hierarchy of values. But to be of much worth, it must begin with considerations prior to these. Some rather general questions concerning value must be asked. This is a necessary priority to the conceiving and listing of those values which are desired. The attempt will now be made to state some of these general questions and indicate their significance.

One important question, possibly the most important, is this: What is

[4] John Dewey, *Democracy and Education*. New York: The Macmillan Company, 1916. Cf. pp. 22–26.

[5] Theodore M. Greene, "A Liberal Christian Idealist Philosophy of Education," in Nelson B. Henry (editor), *Modern Philosophies of Education*. Chicago: University of Chicago Press, 1955. P. 116.

the status of values in existence? Are all values purely transient, as some say, and exist only because there is some human sentient subject who enjoys them? And will all values cease to be when mankind has passed from the scene? Or are there some values which are permanent and abiding? Are there values which exist independently of man and are good and to be desired whether man desires and possesses them or not? If there are such abiding values, how do they exist? Do they exist, as it were, under their own power, as Platonic ideas are supposed to exist, or as the law of gravity is alleged to exist? Or instead, and quite far differently, do these abiding values have permanence because they are in and of ultimate existence? Do they have permanence because they are attributes or qualities of character of a single ultimate existence and are dependent upon this One Being which alone has existence which is ultimate?

A second value question has to do with the manner in which human subjects come into the possession and enjoyment of values. Are values ready-made and do they simply pass into the experience of their possessors, who are assumed thereby to be perfectly passive recipients? Or must the human subject somehow put himself out, as we say, exert effort, or participate in some way in order to embrace value in his experience? In different ways, idealism, pragmatism and existentialism would all seem to hold that this is the case. If value experiences come to us without any reference to our actions in relation to them, then it would appear that there is no significance for education in value theory. It might even be that education itself has no significance, and value experience of a good order will be ours whether we are educated or not. On the other hand, if effort is involved in value experience, as I happen to believe, then it becomes clear that the growth and development of the human individual, together with the teaching thrust of human cultures in their institutions of education, reflect a profound aspect of value, namely, that implicit in the nature of value is the necessity for education.

I will select one other major value question for mention in addition to the two I have just discussed; it is the whether or not of a root value from which all other values stem, and what it may be. Now, if all values are transitory and contingent solely upon the sentient life of man, individual and collective, then human society and the individual man's relation to it become of prime importance. If I want to enter into the fullest possible value that I can have in my short span of living, it is imperative that I maintain unbroken relation with the social process. There is nothing but nothingness to be gained by withdrawing into an ivory tower, or escaping into my own private world. Education in such a value context must necessarily be social—education in society and for social relationships. This is the imperative stressed by John Dewey and those who have followed him; an imperative which has stemmed from the value assumptions just stated, that all value has its existence in the human social process, and all value for the individual arises from relation to this social source of value.

However, if some values exist independently of man and if they have their existence as qualities of One who alone has Being, then the source of value for man is quite different. The importance of human society is not made less, but it is no longer the exclusive source of value; it is rather a source derived from the Ultimate. Individual man is still a unit of mankind, still a *socius,* an individuation of society. But Ultimate Existence is the source of value both for individual and social man. And, accordingly, some kind of effectual relation to Ultimate Being becomes the gateway to value and value experience—at least to ultimate value. Education in such a value context should be no less social, but it will face the difficult fact that man's value experience is contingent upon theological concerns as well as social concerns. It will recognize that the full impact of man's value experience is not understood unless it is viewed as having a horizon beyond which there is an abiding value experience with which it has some connection.

D. THEORY OF REALITY

To raise such value questions as these clearly discloses that their answers involve beliefs about existence. To assume that values have no existence other than in human subjects who enjoy them, or to assume that some values have existence which is permanent, is to venture in either case a belief concerning the nature of reality. Similarly, to assume either that it is imperative for individual man to be related to the social process, because it is the soil in which all values grow, or that both individual and social man must be related to God, permanent values being permanent by virtue of their rootage in His nature, is again to venture belief about the nature of reality. Of course, we should no more load our value considerations with implied beliefs such as these than we should load our consideration of educational aims with implicit assumptions concerning the nature of value. We need to consider such beliefs openly and on their own merits. This means that to build a philosophy of education will not only involve a formulation of educational objectives, or even a theory of value, but also lay upon us the responsibility of making explicit a theory of reality.

There have been, of course, many views of the nature of reality. There is a simple or naive naturalism, not so common today among people of learning but still very prevalent, according to which reality and nature are identical and fondly thought of in the likeness of a perfect perpetual motion machine, operating with perfect efficiency and obeying implicitly such laws as gravitation and cause-and-effect. In this simple order of things, values as we enjoy them in our human experience just grow; they can be as rich and refined as anyone's taste would prefer, but they are still just a garden variety which grows in the soil of nature. Education has a place in this kind of order as guide and augmentation of natural maturation. Its function, of course, is to harmonize the life of the individual with nature and reduce to a minimum the artificialities by which human society so easily complicates things and pulls man's roots out of the soil of nature.

In the twentieth century there has arisen a more refined naturalism which does far more justice to the complexities of our experience and expresses more confidence in the social process. This kind of naturalism is found in the thought of John Dewey and many of those who have been influenced by him. It has been variously called by such names as pragmatism, experimentalism, instrumentalism, and more recently, in a slight variation, reconstructionism. According to it, nature is no simple machine nor does it operate according to fixed laws. Nature is rather a process in which all things are flowing and changing. Its process is a kind of mother-like matrix in which normal life as we know it is the usual occurrence and abnormality is at a minimum. In this fluid order of natural events, man, and society, the values which we enjoy arise and have their normal habitat. Here is the range for all the enrichment and refinement possible to human experience; but again, the values are a garden variety which just grow in the soil of the natural-human order. Education in this metaphysical context has the task of representing the social process to children and youth in the manner depicted earlier in the first reference to Dewey in this chapter. The task of the school is to provide a special environment for the young which will simplify, purify, and balance the environment of man as it grows naturally. The purpose to which the school is directed is that of equipping children to cope with the emergencies of a changing order and to keep them in relationship throughout with the human-social process.

Another view of reality, quite different from either of these but which may be just as naturalistic, is that whatever reality is, *it is real*. By this it is meant that reality is what it is in spite of man's knowledge of it, his relation with it, or any manipulations of it which he may attempt. Reality, according to this view, is completely objective and independent of man. According to some who hold this realist metaphysics, reality is just as naturalistic and devoid of any fundamentally spiritual quality as in either of the two views just described. According to other realists, however, reality is spiritual at the same time that it is physical, or it is fundamentally spiritual in a sense prior to the physical, or even it is positively supernatural. But being spiritual in essence, in any of these ways, it is still independent and objective as far as man is concerned, if not completely external to man and wholly other as compared to him. In such a world view, knowledge is of consummate importance. If we are to adjust our living as men in ways determined by the nature of reality as it is independently of us, we must have accurate, precise, and impersonal science. We must know all that we can know about the history of the world of man's past, his cultures and civilizations. The school in such a context is primarily the medium of transmission of dependable knowledge, and of the conforming of individuals and new generations to reality as it is.

In the mid-twentieth century two other views have become very popular although they are by no means new. I refer to existentialism and language analysis. The language analysis view of reality is much like that of naturalism or naturalistic realism. Metaphysics as referring to some possible existence beyond the world confirmable by observation shows itself up as nonsense whenever the attempt is made to reduce it to meaningful language. Reality is only that which can be observed or confirmed by some creditable source, as for example with alleged facts of history. Of the two traditions of existentialism, the atheistic tradition is also very much like naturalism in its view of reality. Christian existentialism, the other tradition in existentialism as we have contended, has a view of reality very unlike naturalism and very close to the view to be considered next.

The remaining world view which I will mention has been implied by some of the questions I have raised earlier. It is the view that reality, when all of its temporary wrappings are torn away, is One Being who is, and who is implied in all the various orders of being we observe in the cosmos, as well as in the stages of being to be seen in the processes of generation and decay. According to this view, to be, in the last analysis, is to be One Being. This, of course, is a theological view of reality. According to it, also, man reflects, however imperfectly, this One Being. Man as a person is made in the image of this One Being, however imperfect the reflection. In this view, the work of education can never be complete, however well it accomplishes its task in terms of human relationships, until it opens itself to the possibility that man may become related to this One Being in dependence and loyalty, becoming oriented toward a life which is external as well as to a life of human relationships.

I will stop now this scanning of world views, trusting that I have done two things in this survey. First, I believe the philosophies for which I have sketched views of reality, fairly well represent the range of metaphysical possibilities. But what is more important, I trust that as I have gone over these views it has become evident that we cannot pick and choose among them just as we wish. For I believe we cannot be guided by caprice or even genuine desire in determining which is true among them. At this point we face a further but final responsibility in the task of building a philosophy of education. This is the task of considering knowledge questions forthrightly and trying to determine how truth is validated to us.

E. THEORY OF KNOWLEDGE

In turning to knowledge theory now, the first question we confront is, Where shall we begin? Do we begin with reality? Do we begin with the self that wants knowledge? Or, is there a false antithesis between these two questions? John Dewey argued that because the theory of evolution has shown that man and nature are one, there is fundamentally no knowledge problem.

The question with which we began actually needs to be rephrased. Instead of asking, Where *do* we begin?; we should ask, Where *must* we begin? How can we begin with reality, when it is we ourselves who are making the beginning and asking for knowledge of *reality*? And how can we begin with the continuity of man and nature, when this is a point of beginning at least once removed from selfhood, namely, an assumption about a relationship which is at least partly other than ourselves? My questions show quite clearly where I stand, so I will acknowledge that there is a point of view implicit in them. The explicit position is that the self is the most immediate *Descartes* fact in the experience of each of us and this, therefore, is the necessary point of departure in the knowledge process.

The second question has to do with the kind of relation we find ourselves to have with the world which is beyond us. Does the world make no sense to us whatsoever? That is, is it so completely disparate with selfhood that there is no harmony, no communication, no trace of synchronization between the patterns of the world and the patterns of the self? Is this what we find in our experience of the world? Or, do we instead find that there is some degree of correspondence between the experience of the self and its environment, that there is some communication, that man has some native psychological sense of being at home in the world? Our recognition of what we observe concerning the relation of the self to the world is of utmost significance. For if there is complete disparity and disjointedness, then there is no effective relation at all. In this case, we have the conditions of insanity and no way of knowing anything beyond our own subjective enclosure. But if the latter set of questions more closely suggest our relation with the world, then we can rather certainly say that man is an interpreter who lives in a world that lends itself to interpretation. And if man is an interpreter in an interpretable world, the implication is that in essence reality partakes of the nature of selfhood or person and not of an essence which is entirely foreign to it, such as a cause-and-effect machine, or an impersonal process of events and relations.

In this connection something may be said as to the meaning of proof. We apparently have a propensity as humans for demonstration such as was possible in the old formalized structures of the geometric theorem. At the end of it we could write Q.E.D. and confidently rest assured that the matter at hand was settled. The syllogism of Aristotle captured the confidence of the human race for centuries. The induction of Francis Bacon took hold centuries later as a welcome supplement to deductive logic. In our century John Dewey questioned the adequacy of both of these and attempted to give us in their place a logic which is a generalization on scientific method. More recently symbolic logic and language analysis have attempted to deal with logical relations and their possible validation in a more precise manner than any of their predecessors. But it may be asked if any of these are proof even so. May there not be as legitimate a pattern of logic found in the relation between the human self and its world? May not proven truth be that which is tested by *selfhood being in the fullest living and working relation with the world of notself*? Such a logic has not been attempted as yet, but it might turn out to be very enlightening.[6] It might go beyond the classic arguments for the existence of God in countering the almost equally classic arguments for the nonexistence of God. And it might more closely approximate the patterns of revelation than the patterns of proof common to science.

I would, therefore, say one final word in this section on knowledge theory, and it concerns openness to the possibility of revelation as having a place in building a philsoophy of education. Education has been hindered in the past, and it is not infrequently assailed today, by religious bigotry which cannot avoid operating as a vested interest as it confronts the organized educational institution of society. At the same time, today we are as frequently bound in the thralldom of loyalty to a secularism which is just as much an impediment to truth-seeking as is domination by religion. True religion, I believe, is opposed to both of these tyrannies. It opposes totalitarianism in ideas regardless of whether the controlling authority is religious or secular. And it favors the kind of openness to investigation of which secularism at its best has been a champion. How can the truth be known unless we are *willing* to know it? Openness to the truth and willingness to know it means, among other things, openness to the possibility of revelation.

In final summation, let me sketch in retrospect what I have tried to do in this chapter. I made a beginning, in suggesting a pattern for building a philosophy of education, by considering the questions of educational aims and the function of the school in human society. I began at this point because I believe in common experience these are the subjects with which most people begin to think seriously about education. I have then argued that it is impossible even so to deal responsibly with the aims of education and the function of the school unless theory of value is taken very seriously

---

[6] Cf. the author's "Preface to a Logic," *Educational Theory*, *XIV*, no. 4 (October, 1964).

as the necessary rootage of educational aims and functions. In dealing with value theory, I have made the observation that value thinking necessarily involves conceptions of reality; and so I have led on to a brief discussion of representative world views. In addition to this succession of steps, I have proposed that an added and final step must be taken by anyone who will be responsible in building a philosophy of education. This added step is to address oneself to theory of knowledge and thereby determine how a world view is known to be true, and also what world view can have a value theory solidly based on it and educational aims or functions soundly formulated within its context. What this has amounted to, in my judgment, is a psychological approach to the task of building an educational philosophy.

This sequence of layers can now be rephrased in logical form in the following way. Epistemology, or knowledge theory, is the decisive crux of philosophical thought because it examines the means by which we come to have our alleged truths and thereby helps us to test them. Metaphysics, or theory of reality, is the broad inclusive context within which we consciously or unconsciously do our work as educators. We are not being responsible educators if we hold unexamined world views and are not self-consciously critical of the views we hold. Furthermore, we can scarcely have a value theory which is of any merit unless we forthrightly recognize the metaphysical assumptions implicit in it and hold these beliefs critically. But we must have a value theory if in turn we are to embrace aims or functions for education which will stand up against the ravages of time and the challenge of the uneducated of all levels and ages.

Postscript. The first and second editions of this book had as a concluding chapter my own confession of faith as it bears upon education. I have elected to close this edition of *Four Philosophies* with this present chapter. I will try to offer briefly some explanation for this.

My point of view has changed rather radically in the time intervening between the first two editions and this present one. Consequently, serious problems are raised for me in reworking that chapter. The task would likely be similar to writing a small book.

The change that has taken place in my thought is reflected somewhat in the critical section on idealism in this book and also in my Presidential Address, "Preface to a Logic."[7] It is reflected also in my article "Idealism in Education Today," Chapter 48 in the book, *Readings in the Foundations of Education: Commitment to Teaching*, Volume II, edited by James C. Stone and Frederick W. Schneider.[8] This chapter was first published in a special philosophy of education issue of *School and Society* in 1959.[9] In

[7] *Educational Theory, XIV*, no. 4 (October, 1964, 229–254.
[8] New York: Thomas Y. Crowell Company, 1965.
[9] Volume *LXXXVII*, no. 2145 (January 17, 1959), 8–10.

brief, I may say that the final chapter of the two previous editions is a fusion of the philosophy of idealism and the Christian Faith, several aspects of which I no longer hold as part of my personal belief. Similarly, in the decade or so intervening, other aspects have been added.

BIBLIOGRAPHY

GENERAL

Adams, George P., and William P. Montague (eds.), *Contemporary American Philosophy*. 2 vols. New York: The Macmillan Company, 1930.

Anderson, Paul Russell, and Max Harold Fisch, *Philosophy in America*. New York: Appleton-Century-Crofts, 1939.

Bakewell, Charles M., *Source Book in Ancient Philosophy*. Rev. ed. New York: Charles Scribner's Sons, 1939.

Baldwin, James Mark, *Dictionary of Philosophy and Psychology*. 3 vols. New York: The Macmillan Company, 1901–1905.

Bantock, G. H., *Education and Values*. New York: Humanities Press, 1966.

Bantock, G. H., *Education in an Industrial Society*. New York: Humanities Press, 1964.

Barrett, Clifford, *Philosophy*. New York: The Macmillan Company, 1935.

Bible, The

Blanshard, Brand, *et al.*, *Philosophy in American Education*. New York: Harper & Row, Publishers, Inc., 1945.

Brauner, C. J., and H. W. Burns, *Problems in Education and Philosophy*. Englewood Cliffs, N.J.: Prentice-Hall, Inc., 1966.

Brightman, Edgar S., *An Introduction to Philosophy*. New York: Holt, Rinehart and Winston, Inc., 1925.

Brubacher, John S., *History of the Problems of Education*. New York: McGraw-Hill Book Company, Inc., 1947.

Brubacher, John S., *Modern Philosophies of Education*. New York: McGraw-Hill Book Company, Inc., 1939.

Brubacher, John S. (ed.), *Philosophies of Education*. The Forty-First Yearbook of the National Society for the Study of Education, Part I. Bloomington, Ill.: Public School Publishing Company, 1942.

Brumbaugh, R. S., and N. M. Lawrence, *Philosophers on Education: Six Essays on the Foundations of Western Thought*. Boston: Houghton Mifflin Company, 1963.

Burtt, Edwin A., *Types of Religious Philosophy*. New York: Harper & Row, Publishers, Inc., 1946.

Byrne, H. W., *A Christian Approach to Education*. Grand Rapids, Mich.: Zondervan Publishing House, 1961.

Calkins, Mary Whiton, *The Persistent Problems of Philosophy*. 4th rev. ed. New York: The Macmillan Company, 1917.

Carren, M., and A. D. Cavanaugh (eds.), *Readings in the Philosophy of Education*. Detroit: University of Detroit Press, 1960.

Carter, H. J. (ed.), *Intellectual Foundations of American Education*. New York: Pitman Publishing Corporation, 1965.

Cunningham, G. Watts, *Problems of Philosophy*. New York: Holt, Rinehart and Winston, Inc., 1924.

Durant, Will, *Mansions of Philosophy*. New York: Simon and Schuster, Inc., 1929.

Durant, Will, *The Story of Philosophy*. New rev. ed. New York: Garden City Books, 1938.

Eby, Frederick, and Arrowood, Charles Flinn, *The History and Philosophy of Education Ancient and Medieval*. New York: Prentice-Hall, Inc., 1940.

Edman, Irwin, and Herbert W. Schneider, *Landmarks for Beginners in Philosophy*. New York: Harcourt, Brace & World, Inc., 1941.

Educational Policies Commission, *The Unique Function of Education in American Democracy*. Washington, D.C.: National Education Association, 1937.

Educational Policies Commission, *The Structure and Administration of Education in American Democracy*. Washington, D.C.: National Education Association, 1938.

Educational Policies Commission, *The Purposes of Education in American Democracy*. Washington, D.C.: National Education Association, 1938.

Educational Policies Commission, *Education for All American Youth*. Washington, D.C.: National Education Association, 1944.

Fletcher, B. A., *A Philosophy for the Teacher*. New York: Oxford University Press, 1961.

Fuller, E. (ed.), *The Christian Idea of Education*. New Haven: Yale University Press, 1962.

Gamertsfelder, W. S., and L. D. Evans, *Fundamentals of Philosophy*. New York: Prentice-Hall, Inc., 1936.

Garnett, Christopher Browne, Jr., *The Quest for Wisdom*. New York: Appleton-Century-Crofts, 1942.

Greene, Theodore M., *The Arts and the Art of Criticism*. Princeton: Princeton University Press, 1940.

Gruber, F. C., *Foundations for a Philosophy of Education*. New York: The Crowell-Collier Publishing Company, 1961.

Harvard Committee, *General Education in a Free Society*. Cambridge: Harvard University Press, 1945.

Haan, A. E., *Education for the Open Society*. Englewood Cliffs, N.J.: Allyn and Bacon, Inc., 1962.

Hansen, K. H., *Philosophy for American Education*. Englewood Cliffs, N.J.: Prentice-Hall, Inc., 1960.

Henderson, Stella Van Petten, *Introduction to Philosophy of Education*. Chicago: University of Chicago Press, 1947.

Henry, Nelson B. (ed.), *Modern Philosophies and Education*. The Fifty-Fourth Yearbook of the National Society for the Study of Education, Part I. Chicago: University of Chicago Press, 1955.

Hocking, William E., *Types of Philosophy*. New York: Charles Scribner's Sons, 1929.

Horne, Herman Harrell, *The Democratic Philosophy of Education*. New York: The Macmillan Company, 1932.

Hughes, A. G., and E. H., *Education, Some Fundamental Problems*. London: Longmans, Green & Co., Ltd., 1960.

Joad, C. E. M., *Guide to Philosophy*. New York: Dover Publications, Inc., 1946.

Johnston, H. L., *A Philosophy of Education*. New York: McGraw-Hill Book Company, Inc., 1963.

Judges, A. V. (ed.), *Education and the Philosophic Mind*. London: George G. Harrap & Co., Ltd., 1957.

Kilpatrick, William H., *Source Book in the Philosophy of Education*. New York: The Macmillan Company, 1937.

Kneller, G. F., *Foundations of Education*. New York: John Wiley & Sons, Inc., 1963.

Knode, Jay C., et al., *Foundations of an American Philosophy of Education*. D. Van Nostrand Company, Inc., 1942.

Kuehner, Quincy A., *A Philosophy of Education Based on Sources*. Englewood Cliffs, N.J.: Prentice-Hall, Inc., 1936.

Larrabee, Harold A., *What Philosophy Is*. New York: The Vanguard Press, Inc., 1928.

Lerner, M., *Education and A Radical Humanism*. Columbus: Ohio State University Press, 1962.

Lodge, Rupert C., *Philosophy of Education*. Rev. ed. New York: Harper & Row, Publishers, Inc., 1947.

Maritain, J., *The Education of Man*. New York: Doubleday & Company, Inc., 1962.

Martin, S. G., G. H. Clark, F. P. Clarke, and C. T. Ruddick, *A History of Philosophy*. New York: Appleton-Century-Crofts, 1941.

Mayer, F., *Man, Morals, and Education*. New Haven: College & University Press, 1962.

Meiklejohn, A., *Education Between Two Worlds*. New York: Atherton Press, 1966.

Metz, Rudolf, *A Hundred Years of British Philosophy*, J. H. Muirhead (ed.). Translated by J. W. Harvey, T. E. Jessop, and Henry Stuart. New York: The Macmillan Company, 1938.

Meyer, A. E. E., *Education for a New Morality*. New York: The Macmillan Company, 1957.

Morris, V. C., *Philosophy and The American School*. Boston: Houghton Mifflin Company, 1961.

Muelder, Walter G., and Laurence Sears, *The Development of American Philosophy*. Boston: Houghton Mifflin Company, 1940.

Muirhead, J. H. (ed.), *Contemporary British Philosophy*. 2 vols. New York: The Macmillan Company, 1924 and 1925.

Norton, J. K., *Critical Issues in American Education*. Pittsburgh: University of Pittsburgh Press, 1965.

Ortman, E. J., *Philosophy of Teaching*. New York: Philosophical Library, Inc., 1962.

Park, J. (ed.), *Selected Readings in The Philosophy of Education*. 2nd ed. New York: The Macmillan Company, 1963.

Parkhurst, H. H., *Beauty: An Interpretation of Art and The Imaginative Life*. New York: Harcourt, Brace & World, Inc., 1930.

Patrick, G. T. W., *Introduction to Philosophy*. Revised with the assistance of Frank Miller Chapman. Boston: Houghton Mifflin Company, 1935.

Paulsen, Friedrich, *Introduction to Philosophy*. Translated by Frank Thilly. New York: Holt, Rinehart and Winston, Inc., 1895.

Perry, R. B., *The Approach to Philosophy*. New York: Charles Scribner's Sons, 1905.

Perry, R. B., *Present Philosophical Tendencies*. New York: Longmans, Green & Co., Inc., 1912.

Perry, R. B., *A Defense of Philosophy*. Cambridge: Harvard University Press, 1931.

Peters, R. S., *Authority, Responsibility and Education*. New York: Atherton Press, 1966.

Phenix, P. H. (ed.), *Philosophies of Education*. New York: John Wiley & Sons, Inc., 1961.

Plato, *The Dialogues*. Translated into English with analyses and introductions by B. Jowett. 4 vols. New York: Charles Scribner's Sons, 1872.

Price, K., *Education and Philosophical Thought*. Englewood Cliffs, N.J.: Allyn and Bacon, Inc., 1962.

Reid, L. A., *Philosophy and Education*. New York: James H. Heinemann and Co., 1962.

Robinson, Daniel S., *An Anthology of Recent Philosophy*. New York: Thomas Y. Crowell Company, 1929.

Robinson, Daniel S., *An Anthology of Modern Philosophy*. New York: Thomas Y. Crowell Company, 1931.

Robinson, Daniel S., *An Introduction to Living Philosophy*. New York: Thomas Y. Crowell Company, 1932.

Royce, Josiah, *The Spirit of Modern Philosophy*. Boston: Houghton Mifflin Company, 1892.

Rugg, Harold (general ed.), *Readings in the Foundation of Education*. 2 vols. New York: Bureau of Publications, Teachers College, Columbia University, 1941.

Runes, Dagobert D., *The Dictionary of Philosophy*. New York: Philosophical Library, Inc., 1942.

Runes, Dagobert D. (ed.), *Twentieth Century Philosophy*. New York: Philosophical Library, Inc., 1943.

Rusk, Robert R., *The Philosophical Bases of Education*. Boston: Houghton Mifflin Company, 1929.

Russell, Bertrand, *A History of Western Philosophy*. New York: Simon and Schuster, Inc., 1945.

Saiyidain, K. G., *Education, Culture and The Social Order*, 2nd ed. New York: Asia Publishing House, 1959.

Scheffler, I. (ed.), *Philosophy and Education*. Englewood Cliffs, N.J.: Prentice-Hall, Inc., 1959.

Smith, P. G., *Philosophic-Mindedness in Educational Administration*, Columbus: Ohio State University Press, 1956.

Soderquist, H. O., *The Person and Education*. Columbus: Charles E. Merrill Books, Inc., 1964.

Thomas, Henry, and Dana Lee Thomas, *Living Biographies of Great Philosophers*. New York: Garden City Books, 1941.

Townsend, Harvey Gates, *Philosophical Ideas in the United States*. New York: American Book Company, 1934.

Ulich, Robert, *History of Educational Thought*. New York: American Book Company, 1945.

Ulich, Robert, *Three Thousand Years of Educational Wisdom*. Cambridge: Harvard University Press, 1947.

Valentine, P. F. (ed.), *Twentieth Century Education*. New York: Philosophical Library, Inc., 1946.

Wahlquist, John T., *Philosophy of American Education*. New York: The Ronald Press Company, 1943.

Walker, W., *Philosophy of Education*. New York: Philosophical Library, Inc., 1964.

Ward, L. R., *Philosophy of Education*. Chicago: Henry Regnery Company, 1963.

Weber, C. O., *Basic Philosophies of Education*. New York: Holt, Rinehart and Winston, Inc., 1960.

Wegener, F. C., *Organic Philosophy of Education*. Dubuque, Iowa: William C. Brown Company, 1957.

Weiss, T. M., and K. H. Hoover, *Scientific Foundations of Education,* 2nd ed. Dubuque, Iowa: William C. Brown Company, 1964.

Windelband, Wilhelm, *A History of Philosophy*. 2nd rev. ed. Translated by James H. Tufts. New York: The Macmillan Company, 1901.

Woelfel, Norman, *Molders of the American Mind*. New York: Columbia University Press, 1933.

Wright, William Kelley, *A History of Modern Philosophy*. New York: The Macmillan Company, 1941.

Wynn, J. P., *Theories of Education,* College ed. New York: Harper & Row, Publishers, Inc., 1963.

NATURALISM

Herbst, Jurgen, "Herbert Spencer and the Genteel Tradition in American Education," *Educational Theory*, *XI*, no. 2 (April, 1961), 99–110, 118.

Hobbes, Thomas, *The English Works of Thomas Hobbes*. 10 vols. Collected and edited by Sir William Molesworth, Bart. London: John Bohn, 1889.

Huxley, Thomas Henry, *Science and Education*. New York: Appleton-Century-Crofts, 1896.

Krikorian, Yervant H. (ed.), *Naturalism and the Human Spirit*. New York: Columbia University Press, 1944.

Lange, Frederick Albert, *History of Materialism*. 3 vols. Translated by Ernest Chester Thomas. Boston: James R. Osgood and Co., 1877.

Lucretius, *Of the Nature of Things*. Translated by William Ellery Leonard. London: J. M. Dent & Sons, Ltd., 1921.

Rousseau, Jean Jacques, *Emile*. London: J. M. Dent & Sons, Ltd., 1943.

Rousseau, Jean Jacques, *Social Contract*. In Sir Ernest Barker, *Social Contract: Essays by Locke, Hume, and Rousseau*. New York: Oxford University Press, 1948.

Spencer, Herbert, *First Principles of a New System of Philosophy*. 2nd ed. New York: Appleton-Century-Crofts, 1896.

Spencer, Herbert, *The Synthetic Philosophy*. 13 vols. New York: Appleton-Century-Crofts, 1900.

Spencer, Herbert, *Education: Intellectual, Moral, and Physical*. New York: Appleton-Century-Crofts, 1889.

Wieman, H. N., "God and Value," D. C. Macintosh (ed.), *Religious Realism*. New York: The Macmillan Company, 1931.

Wieman, H. N., and B. E. Meland, *American Philosophies of Religion*. New York: Willett, Clark and Co., 1936.

IDEALISM

Augustine, St. Aurelius, *Treatise on the City of God*. 2 vols. Edited by Marcus Dods. Edinburgh: T. & T. Clark, 1871.

Augustine, St. Aurelius, *Treatise on the City of God*. Translated by F. R. M. Hitchcock. New York: The Macmillan Company, 1922.

Barrett, Clifford, *Contemporary Idealism in America*. New York: The Macmillan Company, 1932.

Berkeley, George, *The Works of George Berkeley*. 3 vols. Edited by George Sampson. London: George Bell & Sons, Ltd., 1897–1898.

Bogoslovsky, B. B., *The Ideal School*. New York: The Macmillan Company, 1936.

Bowne, Borden Parker, *Personalism*. Boston: Houghton Mifflin Company, 1908.

Bradley, F. H., *Appearance and Reality*. 2nd ed. Oxford: Clarendon Press, 1930.

Brightman, Edgar S., *An Introduction to Philosophy*. New York: Holt, Rinehart and Winston, Inc., 1925.

Brightman, Edgar S., *The Problem of God*. Nashville: Abingdon Press, 1930.

Brightman, Edgar S., *Personality and Religion*. Nashville: Abingdon Press, 1934.

Brightman, Edgar S. (ed.), *Personalism in Theology*. Boston: Boston University Press, 1943.

Brightman, Edgar S., *Nature and Values*. Nashville: Abingdon Press, 1945.

Calkins, Mary Whiton, *The Persistant Problems of Philosophy*. 4th rev. ed. New York: The Macmillan Company, 1917.

Creighton, J. E., *An Introductory Logic*. New York: The Macmillan Company, 1919.

Demiashkevitch, Michael, *An Introduction to the Philosophy of Education*. New York: American Book Company, 1935.

Descartes, René, *Discourse on Method*. Translated by John Veitch. La Salle, Ill.: The Open Court Publishing Company, 1945.

Doughton, Isaac, *Modern Education, Its Philosophy and Background*. New York: Appleton-Century-Crofts, 1935.

Fairbairn, A. M., *The Place of Christ in Modern Theology*. New York: Charles Scribner's Sons, 1893.

Fairbairn, A. M., *The Philosophy of the Christian Religion*. New York: The Macmillan Company, 1902.

Froebel, F. W. A., *The Education of Man*. Translated and annotated by W. N. Hailman. New York: Appleton-Century-Crofts, 1899.

Gentile, Giovanni, *The Reform of Education*. Authorized translation by Dion Bigongiari. New York: Harcourt, Brace & World, Inc., 1922.

Harris, William T., *Psychologic Foundations of Education*. New York: Appleton-Century-Crofts, 1898.

Hegel, G. W. F., *The Logic of Hegel*. Translated by William Wallace. Oxford: Clarendon Press, 1874.

Hegel, G. W. F., *Lectures on the Philosophy of Religion*. Translated by E. B. Speirs and J. B. Sanderson. London: Routledge & Kegan Paul, Ltd., 1895.

Hegel, G. W. F., *The Philosophy of History*. Translated by J. Sibrie. New York: Willey Book Co., 1900.

Hegel, G. W. F., *Selections*. Edited by J. Loowenberg. New York: Charles Scribner's Sons, 1929.

Hocking, William E., *Human Nature and Its Remaking*. New Haven: Yale University Press, 1918.

Hocking, William E., *The Meaning of God in Human Experience*. New Haven: Yale University Press, 1928.

Hocking, William E., *Living Religions and a World Faith*. London: George Allen & Unwin, Ltd., 1940.

Hocking, William E., *The Self, Its Body and Freedom*. New Haven: Yale University Press, 1928.

Hocking, William E., *Types of Philosophy*. New York: Charles Scribner's Sons, 1929.

Hoernle, R. F. A., *Idealism as a Philosophy*. New York: Doubleday & Company, Inc., 1927.

Horne, Herman Harrell, *The Psychological Principles of Education*. New York: The Macmillan Company, 1908.

Horne, Herman Harrell, *Idealism in Education*. New York: The Macmillan Company, 1910.

Horne, Herman Harrell, *Free Will and Human Responsibility*. New York: The Macmillan Company, 1912.

Horne, Herman Harrell, *Jesus, The Master Teacher*. New York: Association Press, 1920.

Horne, Herman Harrell, *Christ in Man-Making*. Nashville: Abingdon Press, 1926.

Horne, Herman Harrell, *Philosophy of Education*. Rev. ed. New York: The Macmillan Company, 1927.

Horne, Herman Harrell, *This New Education*. Nashville: Abingdon Press, 1931.

Horne, Herman Harrell, *The Democratic Philosophy of Education*. New York: The Macmillan Company, 1932.

Horne, Herman Harrell, *The Philosophy of Christian Education*. New York: Fleming H. Revell Company, Publishers, 1937.

Horne, Herman Harrell, "An Idealistic Philosophy of Education," in *Philosophies of Education*. Bloomington, Ill.: Public School Publishing Company, 1942.

Humayun, K., *Indian Philosophy of Education*. New York: Asia Publishing House, 1961.

Kant, Immanuel, *The Critique of Pure Reason*. Translated by J. M. D. Meiklejohn. Rev. ed. London and New York: The Colonial Press, 1900.

Kant, Immanuel, *Fundamental Principles of the Metaphysics of Ethics*. Translated by Otto Manthey-Zorn. New York: Appleton-Century-Crofts, 1938.

Kant, Immanuel, *The Critique of Practical Reason*. Translated by L. W. Beck. Chicago: University of Chicago Press, 1949.

Leibniz, G. W. von, *The Philosophical Works of Leibniz*. Edited by G. M. Duncan. New Haven: Tuttle, Morehouse & Taylor, 1890.

Leighton, J. A., *Individuality and Education*. New York: Appleton-Century-Crofts, 1928.

Lodge, Rupert C., *The Questioning Mind*. New York: E. P. Dutton & Co., Inc., 1937.

Lodge, Rupert C., *Philosophy of Education*. Rev. ed. New York: Harper & Row, Publishers, Inc., 1947.

Lodge, Rupert C., *Plato's Theory of Education*. New York: Harcourt, Brace & World, Inc., 1947.

Minio-Paluello, *Education in Fascist Italy*. London: Oxford University Press, 1946.

Plato, *The Dialogues*. 4 vols. Translated by B. Jowett. New York: Charles Scribner's Sons, 1872.

Rosenkranz, J. K. F., *The Philosophy of Education*. Translated by Anna C. Brackett. New York: Appleton-Century-Crofts, 1898.

Royce, Josiah, *The Spirit of Modern Philosophy*. Boston: Houghton Mifflin Company, 1892.

Royce, Josiah, *The Philosophy of Loyalty*. New York: The Macmillan Company, 1908.

Royce, Josiah, *Lectures on Modern Idealism*. New Haven: Yale University Press, 1919.

Rutenber, C. G., *The Doctrine of the Imitation of God in Plato*. New York: King's Crown Press, 1947.

Schopenhauer, Arthur, *The World as Will and Idea*. 3 vols. Translated by R. B. Haldane and J. Kemp. London: Routledge & Kegan Paul, Ltd., 1896.

Spinoza, Benedicte de, *The Chief Works of Spinoza*. Translated by R. H. M. Elwes. London: G. Bell & Sons, 1883–1884.

Thompson, Merrit Moore, *The Educational Philosophy of Giovanni Gentile*. Los Angeles: University of Southern California Press, 1934.

Ulich, Robert, *Fundamentals of Democratic Education*. New York: American Book Company, 1940.

Ulich, Robert, *Conditions of Civilized Living*. New York: E. P. Dutton & Co., Inc., 1946.

Ulich, Robert, *Philosophy of Education*. New York: American Book Company, 1961.

Urban, W. M., *Valuation: Its Nature and Laws*. New York: The Macmillan Company, 1909.

Urban, W. M., *The Intelligible World*. New York: The Macmillan Company, 1929.

REALISM

Adler, Mortimer J., "In Defense of the Philosophy of Education," in *Philosophies of Education*. Bloomington, Ill.: Public School Publishing Company, 1942.

Alexander, Samuel, *Space, Time, and Deity*. 2 vols. London: Macmillan & Co., Ltd., 1920.

Aquinas, St. Thomas, *The Summa Contra Gentiles*. 4 vols. Translated by the English Dominican Fathers. London: Burns, Oates & Washbourne, Ltd., 1923–1929.

Aquinas, St. Thomas, *Summa Theologica*. 3 vols. Translated by Fathers of the English Dominican Province. New York: Benziger Bros., Inc., 1947.

Aristotle, *The Works of Aristotle*. 11 vols. Translated into English under the editorship of W. D. Ross. Oxford: Clarendon Press, 1908–1931.

Breed, F. S., *Education and the New Realism*. New York: The Macmillan Company, 1939.

Breed, F. S., "Education and the Realistic Outlook," in *Philosophies of Education*. Bloomington, Ill.: Public School Publishing Company, 1942.

Brettschneider, Bertram D., "Sketch for an Organismic Philosophy of Education," *Educational Theory*, X, no. 2 (April, 1960), 133–141.

Broudy, Harry S., *Building a Philosophy of Education*. 2nd ed. Englewood Cliffs, N.J.: Prentice-Hall, Inc., 1961.

Brunner, Emil, *The Philosophy of Religion*. Translated by A. J. D. Farrer and Bertram Lee Wolf. London: Ivor Nicholson and Watson, Ltd., 1937.

Brunner, Emil, *Revelation and Reason*. Philadelphia: The Westminster Press, 1946.

Burtt, E. A., *The Principles and Problems of Right Thinking*. New York: Harper & Row, Publishers, Inc., 1928.

Chambliss, J. J., "Thomas Tate's Forgotten Philosophy of Education," *Educational Theory, XIII*, no. 4 (October, 1963), 309–313.

Comenius, John Amos, *The Great Didactic*. Translated and edited by M. W. Keatinge. London: A. & C. Black, Ltd., 1907.

Cunningham, W. F., *Pivotal Problems in Education*. New York: The Macmillan Company, 1940.

Descartes, René, *Discourse on Method*. Translated by John Veitch. LaSalle, Ill.: The Open Court Publishing Company, 1945.

Donohue, John W., S.J. "From a Philosophy of Man: Reflections on Intelligence as a Dyadic Function," *Educational Theory, IX*, no. 3 (July, 1959), 140–151, 155.

Drake, Durant (ed.), *Essays in Critical Realism*. New York: The Macmillan Company, 1920.

Dupuis, A. M., and R. B. Nordberg, *Philosophy and Education: A Total View*. Milwaukee: The Bruce Publishing Company, 1964.

Fiebleman, J. K., *The Revival of Realism*. Chapel Hill: University of North Carolina Press, 1946.

Finney, Ross L., *A Sociological Philosophy of Education*. New York: The Macmillan Company, 1928.

Gallagher, D. A. (ed.), *Some Philosophers on Education*. Milwaukee: Marquette University Press, 1956.

Garnett, A. C., *A Realistic Philosophy of Religion*. Chicago and New York: Willett, Clark and Co., 1942.

Garnett, Christopher Browne, Jr., *The Quest for Wisdom*. New York: Appleton-Century-Crofts, 1942.

Garrigou-LaGrange, Reginald, *God: His Existence and His Nature*. 2 vols. St. Louis: B. Herder Book Co., 1941.

Gilson, E. H., *Reason and Revelation*. New York: Charles Scribner's Sons, 1938.

Gilson, E. H., *Christianity and Philosophy*. New York: Sheed & Ward, Inc., 1940.

Gilson, E. H., *History of Philosophy and Philosophical Education*. Milwaukee: Marquette University Press, 1948.

Gosen, Sister Mary De Sales, *The Status of Education as a Science*. New York: Pageant Press, 1963.

Gulley, A. D., *The Educational Philosophy of Saint Thomas Aquinas*. New York: Pageant Press, 1965.

Hampsch, John H., C.M.F., "Integrative Determinants in the Philosophy of Education of Saint Thomas Aquinas," *Educational Theory, IX*, no. 1 (January, 1959), 31–40.

Heath, Dwight B., "Liberal Education: John Henry Newman's Conception," *Educational Theory, IX*, no. 3 (July, 1959), 152–155.

Herbert, J. F., *The Science of Education*. Translated by Henry M. and Emmie Felkin. Boston: D. C. Heath and Company, 1893.

Herbert, J. F., *Textbook in Psychology*. Translated by Margaret K. Smith. New York: Appleton-Century-Crofts, 1897.

Holt, E. B. (ed.), *The New Realism*. New York: The Macmillan Company, 1912.

Houve, Franz de, *Philosophy and Education*. Translated by Edward B. Jordan. New York: Benziger Bros., Inc., 1931.

James, William, *The Varieties of Religious Experience*. New York: Longmans, Green & Co., Inc., 1916.

Justman, J. J., *Theories of Secondary Education*. New York: Bureau of Publications, Teachers College, Columbia University, 1940.

Kant, Immanuel, *The Critique of Pure Reason*. Rev. ed. Translated by J. M. D. Meiklejohn. London and New York: The Colonial Press, 1900.

Kant, Immanuel, *Fundamental Principles of the Metaphysics of Ethics*. Translated by Otto Manthey-Zorn. New York: Appleton-Century-Crofts, 1938.

Kant, Immanuel, *The Critique of Practical Reason*. Translated by L. W. Beck. Chicago: University of Chicago Press, 1949.

King, Beatrice, *Changing Man: The Education System of the U.S.S.R.* London: Victor Gollancz, Ltd., 1936.

King, Beatrice, *Russia Goes to School*. London: Published for The New Education Book Club by William Heinemann, Ltd., 1948.

Lange, Frederick Albert, *History of Materialism*. 3 vols. Translated by Ernest Chester Thomas. Boston: James R. Osgood and Co., 1877.

Locke, John, *Essay Concerning Human Understanding*. Philadelphia: Troutman and Hayes, 1853.

Locke, John, *Essay Concerning Human Understanding*. Selections edited by Mary Whiton Calkins. La Salle, Ill.: The Open Court Publishing Company, 1917.

Locke, John, *Some Thoughts Concerning Education*. With Introduction and Notes by R. H. Quick. Cambridge, England: At the University Press, 1934.

Macintosh, D. C. (ed.), *Religious Realism*. New York: The Macmillan Company, 1931.

Macintosh, D. C., *The Problem of Religious Knowledge*. New York: Harper & Row, Publishers, Inc., 1940.

McGucken, William J., *The Catholic Way in Education*. Milwaukee: The Bruce Publishing Company, 1934.

McGucken, William J., "The Philosophy of Catholic Education," in *Philosophies of Education*. Bloomington, Ill.: Public School Publishing Company, 1942.

Marique, Pierre J., *Philosophy of Christian Education*. Englewood Cliffs, N.J.: Prentice-Hall, Inc., 1939.

Maritain, Jacques, *Introduction to Philosophy*. New York: Sheed & Ward, Inc., 1934.

Maritain, Jacques, *Education at the Crossroads*. New Haven: Yale University Press, 1943.

Mercier, Cardinal D. F. F. J., *A Manual of Modern Scholastic Philosophy*. 2 vols. Authorized translation and eighth edition by T. L. Parker and S. A. Parker. London: Routledge & Kegan Paul, Ltd., 1916–1917.

Montague, William P., *The Ways of Knowing*. New York: The Macmillan Company, 1925.

Montague, William P., *The Ways of Things*. Englewood Cliffs, N.J.: Prentice-Hall, Inc., 1940.

Montague, William P., "The Story of American Realism," as reprinted in Walter G. Muelder and Laurence Sears, *The Development of American Philosophy*. Boston: Houghton Mifflin Company, 1940.

Park, J., *Bertrand Russell On Education*. Columbus: Ohio State University Press, 1963.

Perry, R. B., *Present Philosophical Tendencies*. New York: Longmans, Green & Co., Inc., 1912.

Perry, R. B., *General Theory of Value*. New York: Longmans, Green & Co., Inc., 1926.

Pratt, J. B., *Personal Realism*. New York: The Macmillan Company, 1937.

Redden, J. D., and F. A. Ryan, *A Catholic Philosophy of Education*. Milwaukee: The Bruce Publishing Company, 1942.

Reinhardt, K. F., *A Realistic Philosophy*. Milwaukee: The Bruce Publishing Company, 1944.

Russell, Bertrand, *Education and the Good Life*. New York: Boni & Liveright, 1926.

Santayana, George, *Skepticism and Animal Faith*. London: Constable & Co., Ltd., 1923.

Santayana, George, *Realms of Being*. 4 vols. New York: Charles Scribner's Sons, 1927–1940.

Schilpp, P. A., *The Philosophy of Bertrand Russell*. Evanston and Chicago: Northwestern University, 1944.

Sellars, R. W., *The Essentials of Logic*. Boston: Houghton Mifflin Company, 1925.

Sellars, R. W., *The Philosophy of Physical Realism*. New York: The Macmillan Company, 1932.

Shields, T. E., *Philosophy of Education*. Washington, D.C.: The Catholic Education Press, 1921.

Somerville, John, *Soviet Philosophy*. New York: Philosophical Library, Inc., 1946.

Tate, Thomas, *The Philosophy of Education; or, The Principles and Practice of Teaching*. New York: E. L. Kellogg and Co., 1885.

Wegener, Frank C., *Guide for Students in History and Philosophy of Education*. Dubuque, Iowa: William C. Brown Co., 1953.

Wegener, Frank C., *Problems and Principles of School and Society*. Dubuque, Iowa: William C. Brown Co., 1953.

Whitehead, A. N., *The Aims of Education*. New York: The Macmillan Company, 1929.

Yesipov, B. P., and N. K. Goncharov, *I Want to Be Like Stalin*. New York: The John Day Company, Inc., 1947. Title supplied by George S. Counts and Nucia P. Lodge, who made the selections from the Russian text on pedagogy by the authors and translated them into English.

PRAGMATISM

Bacon, Francis, *The Works of Francis Bacon*. 15 vols. Collected and edited by R. L. Ellis and D. D. Heath. Boston: Brown and Taggard, 1860–1871.

Baker, M. C., *Foundations of John Dewey's Educational Theory*. New York: Atherton Press, 1966.

Bayles, E. E., *Democratic Educational Theory*. New York: Harper & Row, Publishers, Inc., 1960.

Bayles, E. E., *Pragmatism in Education*. New York: Harper & Row, Publishers, Inc., 1966.

Berkson, I. B., *Preface to an Educational Philosophy*. New York: Columbia University Press, 1940.

Berkson, I. B., *Education Faces the Future*. New York: Harper & Row, Publishers, Inc., 1943.

Bode, Boyd H., *Modern Educational Theories*. New York: The Macmillan Company, 1927.

Bode, Boyd H., *Conflicting Psychologies of Learning*. Boston: D. C. Heath and Company, 1929.

Brameld, Theodore, *Ends and Means in Education: A Midcentury Appraisal*. New York: Harper & Row, Publishers, Inc., 1949.

Brameld, Theodore, *Patterns of Educational Philosophy: A Democratic Interpretation*. New York: Harcourt, Brace & World, 1950.

Brameld, Theodore, *Philosophies of Education*. New York: Holt, Rinehart and Winston, Inc., 1955.

Brameld, Theodore, *Toward a Reconstructed Philosophy of Education*. New York: Holt, Rinehart and Winston, Inc., 1956.

Brameld, Theodore, *Cultural Foundation of Education*. New York: Harper & Row, Publishers, Inc., 1957.

Brameld, Theodore, *Education for the Emerging Age*. New York: Harper & Row, Publishers, Inc., 1961.

Brameld, Theodore, *Education as Power*. New York: Holt, Rinehart and Winston, Inc., 1965.

Brubacher, John S., et al., *The Public School and Spiritual Values*. New York: Harper & Row, Publishers, Inc., 1944.

Brubacher, John S., *Modern Philosophies of Education*. 3rd ed. New York: McGraw-Hill Book Company, Inc., 1962.

Brubacher, John S. (ed.), *Eclectic Philosophy of Education*. Englewood Cliffs, N.J.: Prentice-Hall, Inc., 1951.

Childs, John L., *Education and the Philosophy of Experimentalism*. New York: Appleton-Century-Crofts, 1931.

Childs, John L., *Education and Morals: An Experimentalist Philosophy of Education*. New York: Appleton-Century-Crofts, 1950.

Childs, John L., *American Pragmatism and Education*. New York: Holt, Rinehart and Winston, Inc., 1956.

Comte, Auguste, *Positive Philosophy*. Translated by Harriet Martineau. New York: Calvin Blanchard, 1855.

Dewey, John, *Democracy and Education*. New York: The Macmillan Company, 1916.

Dewey, John, *Reconstruction in Philosophy*. London: University of London Press, Ltd., 1921.

Dewey, John, *Human Nature and Conduct*. New York: Holt, Rinehart and Winston, Inc., 1922.

Dewey, John, *Experience and Nature*. La Salle, Ill.: The Open Court Publishing Company, 1925.

Dewey, John, *The Quest for Certainty*. New York: Minton, Balch & Co., 1929.

Dewey, John, *How We Think*. New ed. Boston: D. C. Heath and Company, 1933.

Dewey, John, *Art as Experience*. New York: Minton, Balch & Co., 1934.

Dewey, John, *A Common Faith*. New Haven: Yale University Press, 1934.

Dewey, John, *Experience and Education*. New York: The Macmillan Company, 1938.

Dewey, John, *Logic, The Theory of Inquiry*. New York: Holt, Rinehart and Winston, Inc., 1938.

Dewey, John, *Intelligence in the Modern World*. Edited by Joseph Ratner. New York: Modern Library, 1939.

Dewey, John, *Education Today*. Edited by Joseph Ratner. New York: G. P. Putnam's Sons, 1940.

Dewey, John, *Problems of Men*. New York: Philosophical Library, Inc., 1946.

Dewey, John, and James H. Tufts, *Ethics*. New York: Holt, Rinehart and Winston, Inc., 1908.

Dewey, John, *et al.*, *Creative Intelligence*. New York: Holt, Rinehart and Winston, Inc., 1917.

Edman, Irwin, *John Dewey: His Contribution to the American Tradition*. Indianapolis: The Bobbs-Merrill Company, Inc., 1955.

Fiebleman, James, *An Introduction to Peirce's Philosophy*. New York: Harper & Row, Publishers, Inc., 1946.

Hartshorne, Charles, and Paul Weiss, *Papers of Charles Sanders Peirce*. 6 vols. Cambridge: Harvard University Press, 1931–1935.

Hook, Sidney, *The Metaphysics of Pragmatism*. La Salle, Ill. The Open Court Publishing Company, 1927.

Hook, S., *Education for Modern Man*. New York: Alfred A. Knopf, Inc., 1963.

Horne, Heman Harrell, *The Democratic Philosophy of Education*. New York: The Macmillan Company, 1932.

James, William, *Pragmatism*. New York: Longmans, Green & Co., Inc., 1907.

James, William, *A Pluralistic Universe*. New York: Longmans, Green & Co., Inc., 1909.

James, William, *Essays in Radical Empiricism*. New York: Longmans, Green & Co., Inc., 1912.

James, William, *The Will to Believe*. New York: Longmans, Green & Co., Inc., 1912.

James, William, *The Varieties of Religious Experience*. New York: Longmans, Green & Co., Inc., 1916.

James, William, *Talks to Teachers*. New ed. New York: Holt, Rinehart and Winston, Inc., 1946.

Johnson, Glen, *Some Ethical Implications of a Naturalistic Philosophy of Education*. New York: Bureau of Publications, Teachers College, Columbia University, 1947.

Kallen, Horace M., *The Philosophy of William James Drawn from His Own Works*. New York: Modern Library, n.d.

Kilpatrick, William H., *Education for a Changing Civilization*. New York: Appleton-Century-Crofts, 1926.

Kilpatrick, William H., *Philosophy of Education*. New York: The Macmillan Company, 1951.

Kilpatrick, William H. (ed.), *The Educational Frontier*. New York: Appleton-Century-Crofts, 1933.

Kilpatrick, W. H., *Philosophy of Education*. New York: The Macmillan Company, 1963.

Mason, R. E., *Educational Ideals in American Society*. Englewood Cliffs, N.J.: Allyn and Bacon, Inc., 1960.

Mayhew, K. C., and A. C. Edwards, *The Dewey School*. New York: Appleton-Century-Crofts, 1936.

Peirce, Charles Sanders, "The Fixation of Belief," *Popular Science Monthly* (November, 1877).

Peirce, Charles Sanders, "How To Make Our Ideas Clear," *Popular Science Monthly* (January, 1878).

Ratner, Joseph, *The Philosophy of John Dewey*. New York: Holt, Rinehart and Winston, Inc., 1929.

Raup, R. Bruce, *et al.*, *The Improvement of Practical Intelligence: The Central Task of Education*. New York: Harper & Row, Publishers, Inc., 1950.

Sayers, E. V., and W. E. Madden, *Education and The Democratic Faith*. New York: Appleton-Century-Crofts, 1959.

Schilpp, P. A., *The Philosophy of John Dewey*. Evanston and Chicago: Northwestern University, 1939.

Thomas, M. H., *A Bibliography of John Dewey, 1882–1939*. New York: Columbia University Press, 1939.

White, Morton G., *The Origins of Dewey's Instrumentalism*. New York: Columbia University Press, 1943.

Wynne, John P., *Philosophies of Education*. Englewood Cliffs, N.J.: Prentice-Hall, Inc., 1947.

Wynne, J. P., *Theories of Education*. New York: Harper & Row, Publishers, Inc., 1966.

EXISTENTIALISM

Barrett, William, *Irrational Man*. New York: Doubleday & Company, Inc. Doubleday Anchor Books, 1953.

Blackham, H. J. *Six Existentialist Thinkers*. New York: Harper & Row, Publishers, Inc. Harper Torchbooks, 1952.

Buber, Martin, *Eclipse of God*. New York: Harper & Row, Publishers, Inc., 1957.

Buber, Martin, *Good and Evil*. New York: Charles Scribner's Sons, 1953.

Buber, Martin, *I and Thou*. Translated by Ronald Gregor Smith. New York: Charles Scribner's Sons, 1958.

Friedman, Maurice S., "Martin Buber's Psychology of Education," *Educational Theory*, *VI*, no. 2 (April, 1956), 95–104.

Gilson, Etienne, *The Philosopher and Theology*. Translated by Cécile Gilson. New York: Random House, Inc., 1962.

Gotesky, Rubin, "Means, Ends-in-View, Anticipations and Outcomes," *Educational Theory, XIII*, no. 2 (April, 1963), 84–94.

Heidegger, Martin, *Being and Time*. New York: Harper & Row, Publishers, Inc., 1962.

Heidegger, Martin, *The Question of Being*. Translated by William Kluback and Jean T. Wilds. New York: Twayne Publishers Incorporated, 1956.

Husserl, Edmund, *Ideas*. Translated by W. R. Boyce Gibson. New York: The Macmillan Company, 1958.

Jaspers, Karl, *Reason and Existence*. New York: Farrar, Straus & Cudahy, 1955.

Kierkegaard, Søren, *Attack Upon "Christendom."* Translated by Walter Lowrie. Boston: Beacon Press, 1960.

Kierkegaard, Søren, *Christian Discourses*. Translated by Walter Lowrie. New York: Oxford University Press. A Galaxy Book, 1961.

Kierkegaard, Søren, *Fear and Trembling* and *The Sickness Unto Death*. Garden City, N.Y.: Doubleday & Company, Inc. Doubleday Anchor Books, 1953.

Kierkegaard, Søren, *Purity of Heart Is to Will One Thing*. New York: Harper & Row, Publishers, Inc. Harper Torchbooks, 1948.

Macquarrie, John, *An Existentialist Theology*. London: S.C.M. Press Limited, 1955.

Morris, Van Cleve, "Existentialism and the Education of Twentieth Century Man," *Educational Theory*, *XI*, no. 1 (January, 1961), 52–60.

Morris, Van Cleve, "Movable Furniture and A Theory of Man: . . . .," *Educational Theory*, *VII*, no. 3 (July, 1957), 187–192, 224.

Morris, Van Cleve, *Existentialism in Education*. New York: Harper & Row, Publishers, Inc., 1966.

Mortimer, Ernest, *Blaise Pascal: The Life and Work of a Realist*. New York: Harper & Row, Publishers, Inc., 1959.

Muuss, Rolf, "Existentialism and Psychology," *Educational Theory*, *VI*, no. 3 (July, 1956), 135–153.

Sartre, Jean-Paul, *Being and Nothingness*. Translated by Hazel E. Barnes. New York: Philosophical Library, Inc., 1956.

Unamuno de, Miguel, *The Agony of Christianity*. Translated by Kurt F. Reinhardt. New York: Frederick Ungar Publishing Co., 1960.

Winthrop, Henry, "Culture and Individuality," *Educational Theory*, *XIII*, no. 2 (April, 1963), 65–73.

LANGUAGE ANALYSIS

Archambault, Reginald D. (ed.), *Philosophical Analysis and Education*. New York: The Humanities Press, 1965.

Arnstine, Donald G., "Assumed Goals for Problem-Solving and Education: Chinks in the Defense of Verbal Learning," *Educational Theory*, *XII*, no. 4 (October, 1962), 226–229.

Ausubel, David P., "In Defense of Verbal Learning," *Educational Theory*, *XI*, no. 1 (January, 1961), 15–24.

Ausubel, David P., "In Defense of Verbal Learning: Beams in the Eyes of a Critic," *Educational Theory*, *XII*, no. 4 (October, 1962), 230–233.

Ayer, A. J., *Language, Truth and Logic*. New York: Dover Publications, Inc., 1952.

Ayer, A. J. (ed.), *Logical Positivism*. New York: The Free Press of Glencoe, 1959.

Burnett, Joe R., "Observations on the Logical Implications of Philosophic Theory for Educational Theory and Practice," *Educational Theory*, *XI*, no. 2 (April, 1961), 65–70.

Burns, Hobart W., "Cunningham's Analysis of Theological Concepts: A Reply," *Educational Theory*, *VIII*, no. 3 (July, 1958), 150–156.

Clements, Millard, "Three Observations about Language," *Educational Theory*, *XIII*, no. 2 (April, 1963), 149–154.

Cunningham, Earl C., "The Logico-Scientific Status of Selected Theological Concepts," *Educational Theory*, *VII*, no. 2 (April, 1957), 81–92.

Dettering, Richard W., "Philosophical Semantics and Education," *Educational Theory*, *VIII*, (July, 1958), 143–149, 168.

Dodd, Stuart C., "An Alphabet of Meanings for the Oncoming Revolution in Man's Thinking," *Educational Theory*, *IX*, no. 3 (July, 1959), 182–186.

Ferré, Frederick, *Language, Logic and God*. New York: Harper & Row, Publishers, Inc., 1961.

Halley, Frank C., "Context and the Analytic," *Educational Theory*, *IX*, no. 3 (July, 1959), 165–168, 192.

Henderson, Kenneth B., "A Logical Model for Conceptualizing and Other Related Activities," *Educational Theory*, *XIII*, no. 4 (October, 1963), 227–284.

Hospers, John, *An Introduction to Philosophical Analysis*. Englewood Cliffs, N.J.: Prentice-Hall, Inc., 1953.

Maccia, Elizabeth Steiner, "Epistemological Considerations in Relation to the Use of Teaching Machines," *Educational Theory*, *XII*, no. 4 (October, 1962), 234–240, 246.

Maccia, George S., "Hypothetical Thinking in Education," *Educational Theory*, *X*, no. 3 (July, 1960), 182–186.

Nielson, Kai, "Reason and the Language of Politics," *Educational Theory*, *X*, no. 4 (October, 1960), 248–254, 261.

O'Conner, D. J., *An Introduction to the Philosophy of Education*. New York: Philosophical Library, Inc., 1957.

Perkinson, H. J., "The Methodological Determination of the Aims of Education," *Educational Theory*, XI, no. 1 (January, 1961), 61–64.

Scheffler, Israel (ed.), *Modern Readings: Philosophy and Education*. Englewood Cliffs, N.J.: Allyn and Bacon, Inc., 1958.

Scheffler, I., *Language of Education*. Springfield, Ill.: Charles C Thomas, Publishers, 1960.

Smith, B. O., and R. H. Ennis (eds.), *Language and Concepts in Education*. Chicago: Rand McNally & Company, 1961.

Warnock, G. J., *English Philosophy Since 1900*. London: Oxford University Press, 1958.

Wilson, John, *Language and Christian Belief*. London: Macmillan & Co., Ltd., 1958.

Wittgenstein, Ludwig, *Philosophical Investigations*. Translated by G. E. M. Anscombe. New York: The Macmillan Company, 1953.

Wittgenstein, Ludwig, *Tractatus Logico-Philosophicus*. Translated by D. F. Pears and B. F. McGuinness. New York: The Humanities Press, 1961.

Index

74 75 10 9 8 7 6 5